***ASSEMBLY LANGUAGE PROGRAMMING
AND ORGANIZATION OF THE IBM PC***

Assembly Language Programming and Organization of the IBM PC

Ytha Yu
Department of Mathematics and Computer Science
California State University, Hayward, California

Charles Marut
Department of Mathematics and Computer Science
California State University, Hayward, California

Mitchell McGraw-Hill
New York St. Louis San Francisco Auckland Bogotá Caracas
Lisbon London Madrid Mexico Milan Montreal New Delhi
Paris San Juan Singapore Sydney Tokyo Toronto Watsonville

Mitchell **McGraw-Hill**

Assembly Language Programming and Organization of the IBM PC

Copyright © 1992 by McGraw-Hill, Inc. All rights reserved.
Printed in the United States of America. Except as permitted
under the United States Copyright Act of 1976, no part of this
publication may be reproduced or distributed in any form or by
any means, or stored in a database or retrieval system, without
the prior written permission of the publisher.

                    8 9 QPD QPD 9 0 9 8

ISBN   0-07-072692-2

Sponsoring editor: Stephen Mitchell
Editorial assistant: Denise Nickeson
Director of Production: Jane Somers
Production assistant: Richard De Vitto
Project management: BMR

Quebecor Printing/Dubuque was printer and binder.

Library of Congress Catalog Card Number 91-66269

IBM is a registered trademark of International Business Machines, Inc.
Intel is a registered trademark of Microsoft Corporation.

Dedication

In memory of my father, Ping Chau
To my mother, Monica
To my wife, Joanne and our children
  Alan, Yolanda, and Brian

For my parents, George and Ruth Marut
For Beth

Contents

Preface *xiii*

Chapter 1
Microcomputer Systems
3

1.1 The Components of a Microcomputer System *3*
    1.1.1 Memory 4
    1.1.2 The CPU 7
    1.1.3 I/O Ports 9
1.2 Instruction Execution *9*
1.3 I/O Devices *11*
1.4 Programming Languages *12*
1.5 An Assembly Language Program *14*
Glossary *15*
Exercises *17*

Chapter 2
Representation of Numbers and Characters
19

2.1 Number Systems *19*
2.2 Conversion Between Number Systems *22*
2.3 Addition and Subtraction *24*
2.4 How Integers Are Represented in the Computer *26*
    2.4.1 Unsigned Integers 26
    2.4.2 Signed Integers 26
    2.4.3 Decimal Interpretation 28
2.5 Character Representation *30*
Summary *33*
Glossary *34*
Exercises *34*

Chapter 3
Organization of the IBM Personal Computers
37

3.1 The Intel 8086 Family of Microprocessors *37*
3.2 Organization of the 8086/8088 Microprocessors *39*
    3.2.1 Registers 39
    3.2.2 Data Registers: AX, BX, CX, DX 39
    3.2.3 Segment Registers: CS, DS, SS, ES 41
    3.2.4 Pointer and Index Registers: SP, BP, SI, DI 44
    3.2.5 Instruction Pointer: IP 45
    3.2.6 FLAGS Register 45
3.3 Organization of the PC *45*
    3.3.1 The Operating System 46
    3.3.2 Memory Organization of the PC 47
    3.3.3 I/O Port Addresses 49
    3.3.4 Start-up Operation 49
Summary *49*
Glossary *50*
Exercises *51*

viii   Contents

Chapter 4
Introduction to IBM PC Assembly Language
53

4.1 Assembly Language Syntax *54*
    4.1.1 Name Field 54
    4.1.2 Operation Field 55
    4.1.3 Operand Field 55
    4.1.4 Comment Field 55
4.2 Program Data *56*
4.3 Variables *57*
    4.3.1 Byte Variables 57
    4.3.2 Word Variables 57
    4.3.3 Arrays 58
4.4 Named Constants *59*
4.5 A Few Basic Instructions *60*
    4.5.1 MOV and XCHG 60
    4.5.2 ADD, SUB, INC, and DEC 62
    4.5.3 NEG 64
4.6 Translation of High-Level Language to Assembly Language *64*
4.7 Program Structure *65*
    4.7.1 Memory Models 65
    4.7.2 Data Segment 66
    4.7.3 Stack Segment 66
    4.7.4 Code Segment 66
    4.7.5 Putting It Together 67
4.8 Input and Output Instructions *67*
    4.8.1 INT 21h 67
4.9 A First Program *69*
4.10 Creating and Running a Program *70*
4.11 Displaying a String *73*
4.12 A Case Conversion Program *75*
Summary *76*
Glossary *77*
Exercises *78*
Programming Exercises *80*

Chapter 5
The Processor Status and the FLAGS Register
81

5.1 The FLAGS Register *81*
5.2 Overflow *83*
5.3 How Instructions Affect the Flags *85*
5.4 The DEBUG Program *87*
Summary *90*
Glossary *91*
Exercises *91*

Chapter 6
Flow Control Instructions
93

6.1 An Example of a Jump *93*
6.2 Conditional Jumps *94*
6.3 The JMP Instruction *98*
6.4 High-Level Language Structures *98*
    6.4.1 Branching Structures 98
    6.4.2 Looping Structures 104
6.5 Programming with High-Level Structures *108*
Summary *112*
Glossary *113*
Exercises *113*
Programming Exercises *115*

Chapter 7
Logic, Shift, and Rotate Instructions
117

7.1 Logic Instructions *118*
    7.1.1 AND, OR, and XOR Instructions 119
    7.1.2 NOT Instruction 121
    7.1.3 TEST Instruction 122
7.2 Shift Instructions *122*

7.2.1 Left Shift Instructions **123**
7.2.2 Right Shift Instructions **125**
7.3 Rotate Instructions **127**
7.4 Binary and Hex I/O **130**
Summary **134**
Glossary **135**
Exercises **135**
Programming Exercises **136**

Chapter 8
The Stack and Introduction to Procedures
139

8.1 The Stack **139**
8.2 A Stack Application **144**
8.3 Terminology of Procedures **146**
8.4 CALL and RET **147**
8.5 An Example of a Procedure **150**
Summary **157**
Glossary **158**
Exercises **158**
Programming Exercises **159**

Chapter 9
Multiplication and Division Instructions
161

9.1 MUL and IMUL **161**
9.2 Simple Applications of MUL and IMUL **164**
9.3 DIV and IDIV **165**
9.4 Sign Extension of the Dividend **166**
9.5 Decimal Input and Output Procedures **167**
Summary **175**
Exercises **176**
Programming Exercises **177**

Chapter 10
Arrays and Addressing Modes
179

10.1 One-Dimensional Arrays **179**
10.2 Addressing Modes **181**
10.2.1 Register Indirect Mode **182**
10.2.2 Based and Indexed Addressing Modes **184**
10.2.3 The PTR Operator and the LABEL Pseudo-op **186**
10.2.4 Segment Override **188**
10.2.5 Accessing the Stack **189**
10.3 An Application: Sorting an Array **189**
10.4 Two-Dimensional Arrays **192**
10.5 Based Indexed Addressing Mode **194**
10.6 An Application: Averaging Test Scores **195**
10.7 The XLAT Instruction **197**
Summary **200**
Glossary **201**
Exercises **201**
Programming Exercises **203**

Chapter 11
The String Instructions
205

11.1 The Direction Flag **205**
11.2 Moving a String **206**
11.3 Store String **209**
11.4 Load String **211**
11.5 Scan String **214**
11.6 Compare String **217**
11.6.1 Finding a Substring of a String **219**
11.7 General Form of the String Instructions **223**
Summary **224**
Glossary **225**
Exercises **225**
Programming Exercises **226**

Chapter 12
Text Display and Keyboard Programming
231

12.1 The Monitor **231**
12.2 Video Adapters and Display Modes **232**
12.3 Text Mode Programming **234**
    12.3.1 The Attribute Byte **235**
    12.3.2 A Display Page Demonstration **237**
    12.3.3 INT 10H **238**
    12.3.4 A Comprehensive Example **243**
12.4 The Keyboard **244**
12.5 A Screen Editor **247**
Summary **252**
Glossary **253**
Exercises **254**
Programming Exercises **254**

Chapter 13
Macros
257

13.1 Macro Definition and Invocation **257**
13.2 Local Labels **262**
13.3 Macros That Invoke Other Macros **263**
13.4 A Macro Library **264**
13.5 Repetition Macros **268**
13.6 An Output Macro **270**
13.7 Conditionals **272**
13.8 Macros and Procedures **276**
Summary **276**
Glossary **277**
Exercises **278**

Chapter 14
Memory Management
281

14.1 .COM Programs **281**
14.2 Program Modules **285**
14.3 Full Segment Definitions **291**
    14.3.1 Form of an .EXE Program with Full Segment Definitions **295**
    14.3.2 Using the Full Segment Definitions **295**
14.4 More About the Simplified Segment Definitions **299**
14.5 Passing Data Between Procedures **300**
    14.5.1 Global Variables **300**
    14.5.2 Passing the Addresses of the Data **302**
    14.5.3 Using the Stack **303**
Summary **306**
Glossary **306**
Exercises **307**
Programming Exercises **307**

Chapter 15
BIOS and DOS Interrupts
309

15.1 Interrupt Service **309**
    15.1.1 Interrupt Vector **310**
    15.1.2 Interrupt Routines **312**
15.2 BIOS Interrupts **312**
15.3 DOS Interrupts **316**
15.4 A Time Display Program **316**
15.5 User Interrupt Procedures **318**
15.6 Memory Resident Program **322**
Summary **329**
Glossary **329**
Exercises **330**
Programming Exercises **330**

Chapter 16
Color Graphics
331

16.1 Graphics Modes *331*
16.2 CGA Graphics *333*
16.3 EGA Graphics *339*
16.4 VGA Graphics *340*
16.5 Animation *341*
16.6 An Interactive Video Game *347*
    16.6.1 Adding Sound 347
    16.6.2 Adding a Paddle 350
Summary *355*
Glossary *356*
Exercises *356*
Programming Exercises *356*

Chapter 17
Recursion
357

17.1 The Idea of Recursion *357*
17.2 Recursive Procedures *358*
17.3 Passing Parameters on the Stack *360*
17.4 The Activation Record *361*
17.5 Implementation of Recursive Procedures *363*
17.6 More Complex Recursion *367*
Summary *369*
Glossary *369*
Exercises *370*
Programming Exercises *370*

Chapter 18
Advanced Arithmetic
371

18.1 Double-Precision Numbers *371*
    18.1.1 Double-Precision Addition, Subtraction, and Negation 372
    18.1.2 Double-Precision Multiplication and Division 374
18.2 Binary-Coded Decimal Numbers *374*
    18.2.1 Packed and Unpacked BCD 375
    18.2.2 BCD Addition and the AAA Instruction 375
    18.2.3 BCD Subtraction and the AAS Instruction 377
    18.2.4 BCD Multiplication and the AAM Instruction 378
    18.2.5 BCD Division and the AAD Instruction 378
18.3 Floating-Point Numbers *379*
    18.3.1 Converting Decimal Fractions into Binary 379
    18.3.2 Floating-Point Representation 380
    18.3.3 Floating-Point Operations 380
18.4 The 8087 Numeric Processor *381*
    18.4.1 Data Types 381
    18.4.2 8087 Registers 382
    18.4.3 Instructions 382
    18.4.4 Multiple-Precision Integer I/O 384
    18.4.5 Real-Number I/O 389
Summary *391*
Glossary *392*
Exercises *393*
Programming Exercises *394*

Chapter 19
Disk and File Operations
395

19.1 Kinds of Disks *395*
19.2 Disk Structure *397*
    19.2.1 Disk Capacity 398
    19.2.2 Disk Access 399
    19.2.3 File Allocation 399
19.3 File Processing *402*
    19.3.1 File Handle 402
    19.3.2 File Errors 403
    19.3.3 Opening and Closing a File 403
    19.3.4 Reading a File 405

19.3.5 *Writing a File* **406**
19.3.6 *A Program to Read and Display a File* **406**
19.3.7 *The File Pointer* **410**
19.3.8 *Changing a File's Attribute* **414**
19.4 Direct Disk Operations **415**
19.4.1 *INT 25h and INT 26h* **415**
Summary **418**
Glossary **419**
Exercises **420**
Programming Exercises **420**

Chapter 20
Intel's Advanced
Microprocessors
421

20.1 The 80286 Microprocessor **421**
20.1.1 *Extended Instruction Set* **422**
20.1.2 *Real Address Mode* **423**
20.1.3 *Protected Mode* **424**
20.1.4 *Extended Memory* **426**
20.2 Protected-Mode Systems **429**
20.2.1 *Windows and OS/2* **430**
20.2.2 *Programming* **431**
20.3 80386 and 80486 Microprocessors **433**
20.3.1 *Real Address Mode* **433**
20.3.2 *Protected Mode* **433**
20.3.3 *Programming the 80386* **434**
Summary **437**
Glossary **437**
Exercises **438**
Programming Exercises **438**

Appendicies
439

Appendix A IBM Display Codes **441**
Appendix B DOS Commands **445**
Appendix C BIOS and DOS Interrupts **449**
Appendix D MASM and LINK Options **461**
Appendix E DEBUG and CODEVIEW **471**
Appendix F Assembly Instruction Set **489**
Appendix G Assembler Directives **517**
Appendix H Keyboard Scan Codes **527**

Index
531

Preface

This book is the outgrowth of our experience in teaching assembly language at California State University, Hayward. Our goal is to write a textbook that is easy to read, yet covers the topics fully. We present the material in a logical order and explore the organization of the IBM PC with practical and interesting examples.

Assembly language is really just a symbolic form of machine language, the language of the computer, and because of this, assembly language instructions deal with computer hardware in a very intimate way. As you learn to program in assembly language you also learn about computer organization. Also because of their close connection with the hardware, assembly language programs can run faster and take up less space in memory than high-level language programs—a vital consideration when writing computer game programs, for instance.

While this book is intended to be used in an assembly language programming class taught in a university or community college, it is written in a tutorial style and can be read by anyone who wants to learn about the IBM PC and how to get the most out of it. Instructors will find the topics covered in a pedagogical fashion with numerous examples and exercises.

It is not necessary to have prior knowledge of computer hardware or programming to read this book, although it helps if you have written programs in some high-level language like Basic, Fortran, or Pascal.

Hardware and Software Requirements

To do the programming assignments and demonstrations, you need to own or have access to the following:

1. An IBM PC or compatible.
2. The MS-DOS or PC-DOS operating system.
3. Access to assembler and linker software, such as Microsoft's MASM and LINK, or Borland's TASM and TLINK.
4. An editor or word processing program.

Balanced Presentation

The world of IBM PCs and compatibles consists of many different computer models with different processors and structures. Similarly, there are different versions of assemblers and debuggers. We have taken the following approach to balance our presentation:

1. Emphasis is on the architecture and instruction set for the 8086/8088 processors, with a separate chapter on the advanced processors. The reason is that the methods learned in programming the 8086/8088 are common to all the Intel 8086 family because the instruction set for the advanced processors is largely just an extension of the 8086/8088 instruction set. Programs written for the 8086/8088 will execute without modification on the advanced processors.
2. Simplified segment definitions, introduced with MASM 5.0, are used whenever possible.
3. The DOS environment is used, because it is still the most popular operating system on PCs.
4. DEBUG is used for debugging demonstrations because it is part of DOS and its general features are common to all assembly debuggers. Microsoft's CODEVIEW is covered in Appendix E.

Features of the Book

All the materials have been classroom tested. Some of the features that we believe make this book special are:

Writing programs early

You are naturally eager to start writing programs as soon as possible. However, because assembly language instructions refer to the hardware, you first need to know the essentials of the machine architecture and the basics of the binary and hexadecimal number systems. The first program appears in Chapter 1, and by the end of Chapter 4 you will have the necessary tools to write simple but interesting programs.

Handling input and output

Input and output in assembly language are difficult because the instruction set is so basic. Our approach is to program input and output by using DOS function calls. This enables us to present completely functioning programs early in the book.

Structured code

The advantages of structured programming in high-level languages carry over to assembly language. In Chapter 6, we show how the standard high-level branching and looping structures can be implemented in assembly language; subsequent programs are developed from a high-level pseudocode in a top-down manner.

Definitions

To have a clear understanding of the ideas of assembly language programming, it's important to have a firm grasp of the terminology. To facilitate this, new terms appear in boldface the first time they are used, and are included in a glossary at the end of the chapter.

Advanced applications

One of the fun things that can easily be done in assembly language is manipulating the keyboard and screen. Two chapters are devoted to this topic; the high point is the development of a video game similar to Pong. Another interesting application is the development of a memory resident program that displays and updates the time.

Numeric processor

The operations and instructions of the numeric processor are given detailed treatment.

Advanced processors

The structure and operations of the advanced processors are covered in a separate chapter. Because DOS is still the dominant operating system for the PC, most examples are DOS applications.

Note to Instructors

The book is divided into two parts. Part One covers the topics that are basic to all applications of assembly language; Part Two is a collection of advanced topics. The following table shows how chapters in Part Two depend on material from earlier chapters:

Chapter	Uses material from chapters
12	1–10
13	1–11, 12 (some exercises)
14	1–10
15	1–12, 14
16	1–15
17	1–10
18	1–10, 13
19	1–10
20	1–11, 13, 14

The chapters in Part One should be covered in sequence. If the students have strong backgrounds in computer science, Chapter 1 can be covered lightly or be assigned as independent reading. In a ten-week course that meets four hours a week, we are usually able to cover the first four chapters in two weeks, and make the first programming assignment at the end of the second week or the beginning of the third week. In ten weeks we are usually able to cover chapters 1–12, and then go on to choose topics from chapters 13–16 as time and interest allow.

Exercises

Every chapter ends with numerous exercises to reinforce the concepts and principles covered. The exercises are grouped into practice exercises and programming exercises.

Instructor's Manual

A comprehensive instructor's manual is available. It includes general comments, programming hints, and solutions to the practice exercises. It also includes a set of transparency masters for figures and program listings.

Student Data Disk

A student data disk containing the source code for the programs in the text is available with the accompanying instructor's manual.

Acknowledgments

We would like to thank our editor, Raleigh Wilson, and the staff at Mitchell McGraw-Hill, including Stephen Mitchell, Denise Nickeson, Jane Somers, and Richard de Vitto, for their support in this project. We would like to thank the staff at BMR, especially Matt Lusher, Jim Love, and Alex Leason for their outstanding work in producing this book.

We would also like to thank our students for their patience, support, and criticism as the manuscript developed. Finally, our thanks go to the following reviewers, whose insights helped to make this a much better book:

David Hayes, San Jose State University, San Jose, California
Jim Ingram, Amarillo College, Amarillo, Texas
Linda Kieffer, Cheney, Washington
Paul LeCoq, Spokane Falls Community College, Washington
Thom Luce, Ohio University, Ohio
Eric Lundstrom, Diablo Valley College, Pleasant Hill, California
Mike Michaelson, Palomar College, San Marcos, California
Don Myers, Vincennes University, Vincennes, Indiana
Loren Radford, Baptist College, Charleston, South Carolina
Francis Rice, Oklahoma State University, Oklahoma
David Rosenlof, Sacramento City College, California
Paul W. Ross, Millersville State University, Pennsylvania
R.G. Shurtleff, Colorado Technical College, Colorado
Mel Stone, St. Petersburg Jr. College, Clearwater Campus, Florida
James VanSpeyboeck, St. Ambrose College, Davenport, Iowa
Richard Weisgerber, Mankato State University, Mankato, Minnesota

We would appreciate any comments that you, the reader, may offer. Correspondence should be addressed to Ytha Yu or Charles Marut, Department of Mathematics and Computer Science, California State University, Hayward, Hayward California 94542. Internet electronic mail should be addressed to yyu@seq.csuhayward.edu or cmarut@seq.csuhayward.edu.

Part One

Elements of Assembly Language Programming

1
Microcomputer Systems

Overview

This chapter provides an introduction to the architecture of microcomputers in general and to the IBM PC in particular. You will learn about the main hardware components: the central processor, memory, and the peripherals, and their relation to the software, or programs. We'll see exactly what the computer does when it executes an instruction, and discuss the main advantages (and disadvantages) of assembly language programming. If you are an experienced microcomputer user, you are already familiar with most of the ideas discussed here; if you are a novice, this chapter introduces many of the important terms used in the rest of the book.

1.1 The Components of a Microcomputer System

Figure 1.1 shows a typical microcomputer system, consisting of a system unit, a keyboard, a display screen, and disk drives. The system unit is often referred to as "the computer," because it houses the circuit boards of the computer. The keyboard, display screen, and disk drives are called **I/O devices** because they perform input/output operations for the computer. They are also called **peripheral devices** or **peripherals**.

Integrated-circuit (IC) chips are used in the construction of computer circuits. Each IC chip may contain hundreds or even thousands of transistors. These IC circuits are known as **digital circuits** because they operate on discrete voltage signal levels, typically, a high voltage and a low voltage. We use the symbols 0 and 1 to represent the low- and high-voltage signals, respectively. These symbols are called **binary digits**, or **bits**. All information processed by the computer is represented by strings of 0's and 1's; that is, by bit strings.

Figure 1.1 A Microcomputer System

Functionally, the computer circuits consist of three parts: the **central processing unit (CPU)**, the memory circuits, and the I/O circuits. In a microcomputer, the CPU is a single-chip processor called a **microprocessor**. The CPU is the brain of the computer, and it controls all operations. It uses the memory circuits to store information, and the I/O circuits to communicate with I/O devices.

The System Board

Inside the system unit is a main circuit board called the **system board**, which contains the microprocessor and memory circuits. The system board is also called a **motherboard** because it contains **expansion slots**, which are connectors for additional circuit boards called **add-in boards** or **add-in cards**. I/O circuits are usually located on add-in cards. Figure 1.2 shows the picture of a motherboard.

1.1.1 Memory

Bytes and Words

Information processed by the computer is stored in its memory. A memory circuit element can store one bit of data. However, the memory circuits are usually organized into groups that can store eight bits of data, and a string of eight bits is called a **byte**. Each **memory byte circuit**—or **memory byte**, for short—is identified by a number that is called its **address**, like the street address of a house. The first memory byte has address

Figure 1.2 A Motherboard

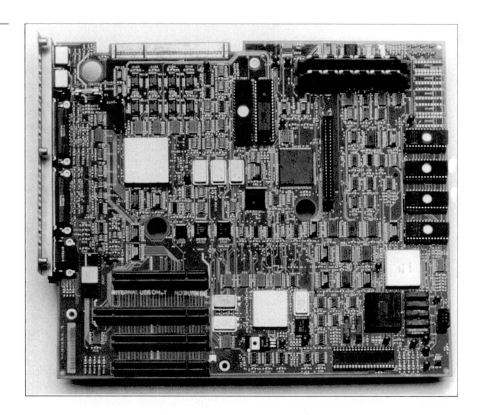

0. The data stored in a memory byte are called its **contents**. When the contents of a memory byte are treated as a single number, we often use the term *value* to denote them.

It is important to understand the difference between address and contents. The address of a memory byte is fixed and is different from the address of any other memory byte in the computer. Yet the contents of a memory byte are not unique and are subject to change, because they denote the data *currently* being stored. Figure 1.3 shows the organization of memory bytes; the contents are arbitrary.

Another distinction between address and contents is that while the contents of a memory byte are always eight bits, the number of bits in an

Figure 1.3 Memory Represented as Bytes

Address	Contents
.	
.	
.	
.	. . . .
7	0 0 1 0 1 1 0 1
6	1 1 0 0 1 1 1 0
5	0 0 0 0 1 1 0 1
4	1 1 1 0 1 1 0 1
3	0 0 0 0 0 0 0 0
2	1 1 1 1 1 1 1 1
1	0 1 0 1 1 1 1 0
0	0 1 1 0 0 0 0 1

address depends on the processor. For example, the Intel 8086 microprocessor assigns a 20-bit address, and the Intel 80286 microprocessor uses a 24-bit address. The number of bits used in the address determines the number of bytes that can be accessed by the processor.

Example 1.1 Suppose a processor uses 20 bits for an address. How many memory bytes can be accessed?

Solution: A bit can have two possible values, so in a 20-bit address there can be $2^{20} = 1,048,576$ different values, with each value being the potential address of a memory byte. In computer terminology, the number 2^{20} is called *1* **mega**. Thus, a 20-bit address can be used to address 1 **megabyte** or 1 **MB**.

In a typical microcomputer, two bytes form a **word**. To accommodate word data, the IBM PC allows any pair of successive memory bytes to be treated as a single unit, called a **memory word**. The lower address of the two memory bytes is used as the address of the memory word. Thus the memory word with the address 2 is made up of the memory bytes with the addresses 2 and 3. The microprocessor can always tell, by other information contained in each instruction, whether an address refers to a byte or a word.

In this book, we use the term **memory location** to denote either a memory byte or a memory word.

Bit Position

Figure 1.4 shows the bit positions in a microcomputer word and a byte. The positions are numbered from right to left, starting with 0. In a word, the bits 0 to 7 form the *low byte* and the bits 8 to 15 form the *high byte*. For a word stored in memory, its low byte comes from the memory byte with the lower address and its high byte is from the memory byte with the higher address.

Memory Operations

The processor can perform two operations on memory: *read* (fetch) the contents of a location and *write* (store) data at a location. In a read operation, the processor only gets a copy of the data; the original contents

Figure 1.4 Bit Positions in a Byte and a Word

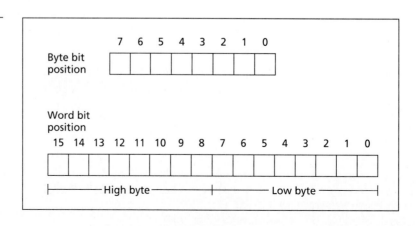

Figure 1.5 Bus Connections of a Microcomputer

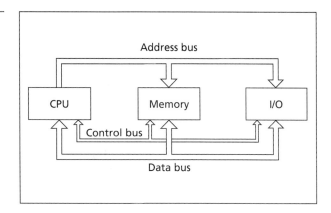

of the location are unchanged. In a write operation, the data written become the new contents of the location; the original contents are thus lost.

RAM and ROM

There are two kinds of memory circuits: **random access memory (RAM)** and **read-only memory (ROM)**. The difference is that RAM locations can be read and written, while, as the name implies, ROM locations can only be read. This is because the contents of ROM memory, once initialized, cannot be changed.

Program instructions and data are normally loaded into RAM memory. However, the contents of RAM memory are lost when the machine is turned off, so anything valuable in RAM must be saved on a disk or printed out beforehand. ROM circuits retain their values even when the power is off. Consequently, ROM is used by computer manufacturers to store system programs. These ROM-based programs are known as **firmware**. They are responsible for loading start-up programs from disk as well as for self-testing the computer when it is turned on.

Buses

A processor communicates with memory and I/O circuits by using signals that travel along a set of wires or connections called **buses** that connect the different components. There are three kinds of signals: address, data, and control. And there are three buses: **address bus, data bus**, and **control bus**. For example, to read the contents of a memory location, the CPU places the address of the memory location on the address bus, and it receives the data, sent by the memory circuits, on the data bus. A control signal is required to inform the memory to perform a read operation. The CPU sends the control signal on the control bus. Figure 1.5 is a diagram of the bus connections for a microcomputer.

1.1.2 The CPU

As stated, the CPU is the brain of the computer. It controls the computer by executing programs stored in memory. A program might be a system program or an application program written by a user. In any case, each instruction that the CPU executes is a bit string (for the Intel 8086, instructions are from one to six bytes long). This language of 0's and 1's is called **machine language**.

Figure 1.6 Intel 8086 Microprocessor Organization

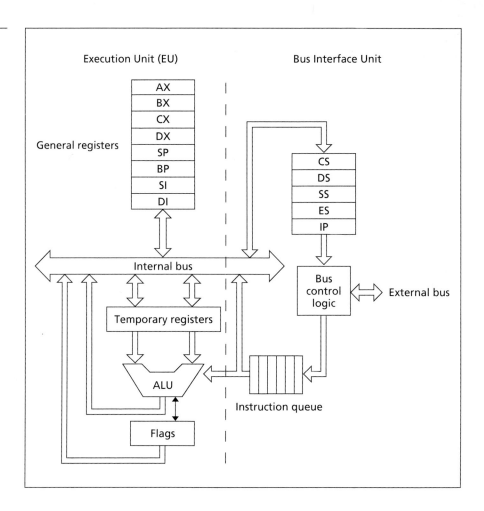

The instructions performed by a CPU are called its **instruction set**, and the instruction set for each CPU is unique. To keep the cost of computers down, machine language instructions are designed to be simple; for example, adding two numbers or moving a number from one location to another. The amazing thing about computers is that the incredibly complex tasks they perform are, in the end, just a sequence of very basic operations.

In the following, we will use the Intel 8086 microprocessor as an example of a CPU. Figure 1.6 shows its organization. There are two main components: the **execution unit** and the **bus interface unit**.

Execution Unit (EU)

As the name implies, the purpose of the execution unit (EU) is to execute instructions. It contains a circuit called the **arithmetic and logic unit (ALU)**. The ALU can perform arithmetic ($+$, $-$, $\times$, $/$) and logic (AND, OR, NOT) operations. The data for the operations are stored in circuits called **registers**. A register is like a memory location except that we normally refer to it by a name rather than a number. The EU has eight registers for storing data; their names are AX, BX, CX, DX, SI, DI, BP, and SP. We'll become acquainted with them in Chapter 3. In addition, the EU contains temporary registers for holding operands for the ALU, and the FLAGS register whose individual bits reflect the result of a computation.

Bus Interface Unit (BIU)

The bus interface unit (BIU) facilitates communication between the EU and the memory or I/O circuits. It is responsible for transmitting addresses, data, and control signals on the buses. Its registers are named CS, DS, ES, SS, and IP; they hold addresses of memory locations. The **IP (instruction pointer)** contains the address of the next instruction to be executed by the EU.

The EU and the BIU are connected by an internal bus, and they work together. While the EU is executing an instruction, the BIU fetches up to six bytes of the next instruction and places them in the instruction queue. This operation is called *instruction prefetch*. The purpose is to speed up the processor. If the EU needs to communicate with memory or the peripherals, the BIU suspends instruction prefetch and performs the needed operations.

1.1.3 I/O Ports

I/O devices are connected to the computer through I/O circuits. Each of these circuits contains several registers called **I/O ports**. Some are used for data while others are used for control commands. Like memory locations, the I/O ports have addresses and are connected to the bus system. However, these addresses are known as *I/O addresses* and can only be used in input or output instructions. This allows the CPU to distinguish between an I/O port and a memory location.

I/O ports function as transfer points between the CPU and I/O devices. Data to be input from an I/O device are sent to a port where they can be read by the CPU. On output, the CPU writes data to an I/O port. The I/O circuit then transmits the data to the I/O device.

Serial and Parallel Ports

The data transfer between an I/O port and an I/O device can be 1 bit at a time (serial), or 8 or 16 bits at a time (parallel). A parallel port requires more wiring connections, while a serial port tends to be slower. Slow devices, like the keyboard, always connect to a serial port, and fast devices, like the disk drive, always connect to a parallel port. But some devices, like the printer, can connect to either a serial or a parallel port.

1.2 Instruction Execution

To understand how the CPU operates, let's look at how an instruction is executed. First of all, a machine instruction has two parts: an **opcode** and **operands**. The opcode specifies the type of operation, and the operands are often given as memory addresses to the data to be operated on. The CPU goes through the following steps to execute a machine instruction (the **fetch–execute cycle**):

Fetch

1. Fetch an instruction from memory.
2. Decode the instruction to determine the operation.
3. Fetch data from memory if necessary.

Execute

4. Perform the operation on the data.
5. Store the result in memory if needed.

To see what this entails, let's trace through the execution of a typical machine language instruction for the 8086. Suppose we look at the instruction that adds the contents of register AX to the contents of the memory word at address 0. The CPU actually adds the two numbers in the ALU and then stores the result back to memory word 0. The machine code is

```
00000001  00000110  00000000  00000000
```

Before execution, we assume that the first byte of the instruction is stored at the location indicated by the IP.

1. Fetch the instruction. To start the cycle, the BIU places a memory read request on the control bus and the address of the instruction on the address bus. Memory responds by sending the contents of the location specified—namely, the instruction code just given—over the data bus. Because the instruction code is four bytes and the 8086 can only read a word at a time, this involves two read operations. The CPU accepts the data and adds four to the IP so that the IP will contain the address of the next instruction.
2. Decode the instruction. On receiving the instruction, a decoder circuit in the EU decodes the instruction and determines that it is an ADD operation involving the word at address 0.
3. Fetch data from memory. The EU informs the BIU to get the contents of memory word 0. The BIU sends address 0 over the address bus and a memory read request is again sent over the control bus. The contents of memory word 0 are sent back over the data bus to the EU and are placed in a holding register.
4. Perform the operation. The contents of the holding register and the AX register are sent to the ALU circuit, which performs the required addition and holds the sum.
5. Store the result. The EU directs the BIU to store the sum at address 0. To do so, the BIU sends out a memory write request over the control bus, the address 0 over the address bus, and the sum to be stored over the data bus. The previous contents of memory word 0 are overwritten by the sum.

The cycle is now repeated for the instruction whose address is contained in the IP.

Timing

The preceding example shows that even though machine instructions are very simple, their execution is actually quite complex. To ensure that the steps are carried out in an orderly fashion, a clock circuit controls the processor

Figure 1.7 Train of Clock Pulses

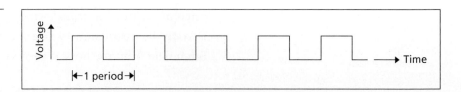

by generating a train of **clock pulses** as shown in Figure 1.7. The time interval between two pulses is known as a **clock period**, and the number of pulses per second is called the **clock rate** or **clock speed**, measured in **megahertz (MHz)**. One megahertz is 1 million cycles (pulses) per second. The original IBM PC had a clock rate of 4.77 MHz, but the latest PS/2 model has a clock rate of 33 MHz.

The computer circuits are activated by the clock pulses; that is, the circuits perform an operation only when a clock pulse is present. Each step in the instruction fetch and execution cycle requires one or more clock periods. For example, the 8086 takes four clock periods to do a memory read and a multiplication operation may take more than seventy clock periods. If we speed up the clock circuit, a processor can be made to operate faster. However, each processor has a rated maximum clock speed beyond which it may not function properly.

1.3 I/O Devices

I/O devices are needed to get information into and out of the computer. The primary I/O devices are magnetic disks, the keyboard, the display monitor, and the printer.

Magnetic Disks

We've seen that the contents of RAM are lost when the computer is turned off, so magnetic disks are used for permanent storage of programs and data. There are two kinds of disks: **floppy disks** (also called diskettes) and **hard disks**. The device that reads and writes data on a disk is called a **disk drive**.

Floppy disks come in 5¼-inch or 3½-inch diameter sizes. They are lightweight and portable; it is easy to put a diskette away for safekeeping or use it on different computers. The amount of data a floppy disk can hold depends on the type; it ranges from 360 kilobytes to 1.44 megabytes. A **kilobyte (KB)** is 2^{10} bytes.

A hard disk and its disk drive are enclosed in a hermetically sealed container that is not removable from the computer; thus, it is also called a **fixed disk**. It can hold a lot more data than a floppy disk—typically 20, 40, to over 100 megabytes. A program can also access information on a hard disk much faster than a floppy disk.

Disk operations are covered in Chapter 19.

Keyboard

The keyboard allows the user to enter information into the computer. It has the keys usually found on a typewriter, plus a number of control and function keys. It has its own microprocessor that sends a coded signal to the computer whenever a key is pressed or released.

When a key is pressed, the corresponding key character normally appears on the screen. But interestingly enough, there is no direct connection between the keyboard and the screen. The data from the keyboard are received by the current running program. The program must send the data to the screen before a character is displayed. In Chapter 12 you will learn how to control the keyboard.

Display Monitor

The display monitor is the standard output device of the computer. The information displayed on the screen is generated by a circuit in the computer called a **video adapter**. Most adapters can generate both text characters and graphics images. Some monitors are capable of displaying in color.

We discuss text mode operations in Chapter 12, and cover graphics mode in Chapter 16.

Printers

Although monitors give fast visual feedback, the information is not permanent. Printers, however, are slow but provide more permanent output. Printer outputs are known as **hardcopies**.

The three common kinds of printers are *daisy wheel, dot matrix,* and *laser* printers. The output of a daisy wheel printer is similar to that of a typewriter. A dot matrix printer prints characters composed of dots; depending on the number of dots used per character, some dot matrix printers can generate near-letter-quality printing. The advantage of dot matrix printers is that they can print characters with different fonts as well as graphics.

The laser printer also prints characters composed of dots; however, the resolution is so high (300 dots per inch) that it has typewriter quality. The laser printer is expensive, but in the field of desktop publishing it is indispensable. It is also quiet compared to the other printers.

1.4 Programming Languages

The operations of the computer's hardware are controlled by its software. When the computer is on, it is always in the process of executing instructions. To fully understand the computer's operations, we must also study its instructions.

Machine Language

A CPU can only execute machine language instructions. As we've seen, they are bit strings. The following is a short machine language program for the IBM PC:

Machine instruction	Operation
`10100001 00000000 00000000`	Fetch the contents of memory word 0 and put it in register AX.
`00000101 00000100 00000000`	Add 4 to AX.
`10100011 00000000 00000000`	Store the contents of AX in memory word 0.

As you can well imagine, writing programs in machine language is tedious and subject to error!

Assembly Language

A more convenient language to use is **assembly language**. In assembly language, we use symbolic names to represent operations, registers, and memory locations. If location 0 is symbolized by A, the preceding program expressed in IBM PC assembly language would look like this:

Assembly language instruction	Comment
`MOV AX,A`	;fetch the contents of ;location A and ;put it in register AX
`ADD AX,4`	;add 4 to AX
`MOV A,AX`	;move the contents of AX ;into location A

A program written in assembly language must be converted to machine language before the CPU can execute it. A program called the **assembler** translates each assembly language statement into a single machine language instruction.

High-Level Languages

Even though it's easier to write programs in assembly language than machine language, it's still difficult because the instruction set is so primitive. That is why high-level languages such as FORTRAN, Pascal, C, and others were developed. Different high-level languages are designed for different applications, but they generally allow programmers to write programs that look more like natural language text than is possible in assembly language.

A program called a **compiler** is needed to translate a high-level language program into machine code. Compilation is more involved than assembling because it entails the translation of complex mathematical expressions and natural language commands into simple machine operations. A high-level language statement typically translates into many machine language instructions.

Advantages of High-Level Languages

There are many reasons why a programmer might choose to write a program in a high-level language rather than in assembly language.

First, because high-level languages are closer to natural languages, it's easier to convert a natural language algorithm to a high-level language program than to an assembly language program. For the same reason, it's easier to read and understand a high-level language program than an assembly language program.

Second, an assembly language program generally contains more statements than an equivalent high-level language program, so more time is needed to code the assembly language program.

Third, because each computer has its own unique assembly language, assembly language programs are limited to one machine, but a high-level language program can be executed on any machine that has a compiler for that language.

Advantages of Assembly Languages

The main reason for writing assembly language programs is efficiency: because assembly language is so close to machine language, a well-written assembly language program produces a faster, shorter machine language program. Also, some operations, such as reading or writing to specific memory locations and I/O ports, can be done easily in assembly language but may be impossible at a higher level.

Actually, it is not always necessary for a programmer to choose between assembly language and high-level languages, because many high-level languages accept subprograms written in assembly language. This means that crucial parts of a program can be written in assembly language, with the rest written in a high-level language.

In addition to these considerations, there is another reason for learning assembly language. Only by studying assembly language is it possible to gain a feeling for the way the computer "thinks" and why certain things happen the way they do inside the computer. High-level languages tend to obscure the details of the compiled machine language program that the computer actually executes. Sometimes a slight change in a program produces a major increase in the run time of that program, or arithmetic overflow unexpectedly occurs. Such things can be understood on the assembly language level.

Even though here you will study assembly language specifically for the IBM PC, the techniques you will learn are typical of those used in any assembly language. Learning other assembly languages should be relatively easy after you have read this book.

1.5 An Assembly Language Program

To give an idea of what an assembly language program looks like, here is a simple example. The following program adds the contents of two memory locations, symbolized by A and B. The sum is stored in location SUM.

Program Listing PGM1_1.ASM
```
TITLE PGM1_1: SAMPLE PROGRAM
.MODEL   SMALL
.STACK   100H
.DATA
A    DW   2
B    DW   5
SUM  DW   ?
.CODE
MAIN   PROC
;initialize DS
       MOV AX,@DATA
       MOV DS,AX
;add the numbers
       MOV AX,A            ;AX has A
       ADD AX,B            ;AX has A+B
       MOV SUM,AX          ;SUM = A+B
;exit to DOS
       MOV AX,4C00H
       INT 21H
MAIN   ENDP
       END MAIN
```

Assembly language programs consist of statements. A statement is either an instruction to be executed when the program is run, or a directive for the assembler. For example, .MODEL SMALL is an assembler directive that specifies the size of the program. MOV AX,A is an instruction. Anything that follows a semicolon is a comment, and is ignored by the assembler.

The preceding program consists of three parts, or segments: the *stack segment*, the *data segment*, and the *code segment*. They begin with the directives .STACK, .DATA, and .CODE, respectively.

The stack segment is used for temporary storage of addresses and data. If no stack segment is declared, an error message is generated, so there must be a stack segment even if the program doesn't utilize a stack.

Variables are declared in the data segment. Each variable is assigned space in memory and may be initialized. For example, A DW 2 sets aside a memory word for a variable called A and initializes it to 2 (DW stands for "Define Word"). Similarly, B DW 5 sets aside a word for variable B and initializes it to 5 (these initial values were chosen arbitrarily). SUM DW ? sets aside an uninitialized word for SUM.

A program's instructions are placed in the code segment. Instructions are usually organized into units called *procedures*. The preceding program has only one procedure, called MAIN, which begins with the line MAIN PROC and ends with line MAIN ENDP.

The main procedure begins and ends with instructions that are needed to initialize the DS register and to return to the DOS operating system. Their purpose is explained in Chapter 4. The instructions for adding A and B and putting the answer in SUM are as follows:

```
MOV AX,A         ;AX has A
ADD AX,B         ;AX has A+B
MOV SUM,AX       ;SUM = A+B
```

MOV AX,A copies the contents of word A into register AX. ADD AX,B adds the contents of B to it, so that AX now holds the total, 7. MOV SUM,AX stores the answer in variable SUM.

Before this program could be run on the computer, it would have to be assembled into a machine language program. The steps are explained in Chapter 4. Because there were no output instructions, we could not see the answer on the screen, but we could trace the program's execution in a debugger such as the DEBUG program.

Glossary

add-in board or card	Circuit board that connects to the motherboard, usually contains I/O circuits or additional memory
address	A number that identifies a memory location
address bus	The set of electrical pathways for address signals
arithmetic and logic unit, ALU	CPU circuit where arithmetic and logic operations are done
assembler	A program that translates an assembly language program into machine language
assembly language	Symbolic representation of machine language
binary digit	A symbol that can have value 0 or 1
bit	Binary digit
bus	A set of wires or connections connecting the CPU, memory, and I/O ports

bus interface unit, BIU	Part of the CPU that facilitates communication between the CPU, memory, and I/O ports
byte	8 bits
central processing unit, CPU	The main processor circuit of a computer
clock period	The time interval between two clock pulses
clock pulse	An electrical signal that rises from a low voltage to a high voltage and down again to a low voltage, used to synchronize computer circuit operations
clock rate	The number of clock pulses per second, measured in megahertz (MHz)
clock speed	Clock rate
compiler	A program that translates a high-level language to machine language
contents	The data stored in a register or memory location
control bus	The set of electrical paths for control signals
data bus	The set of electrical paths for data signals
digital circuits	Circuits that operate on discrete voltage levels
disk drive	The device that reads and writes data on a disk
execution unit, EU	Part of the CPU that executes instructions
expansion slots	Connectors in the motherboard where other circuit boards can be attached
fetch–execute cycle	Cycle the CPU goes through to execute an instruction
firmware	Software supplied by the computer manufacturer, usually stored in ROM
fixed disk	Nonremovable disk, made of metal
floppy disk	Removable, flexible disk
hardcopy	Printer output
hard disk	Fixed disk
I/O devices	Devices that handle input and output data of the computer; typical I/O devices are display monitor, disk drive, and printer
I/O ports	Circuits that function as transfer points between the CPU and I/O devices
instruction pointer, IP	A CPU register that contains the address of the next instruction
instruction set	The instructions the CPU is capable of performing
kilobyte, KB	2^{10} or 1024 bytes
machine language	Instructions coded as bit strings: the language of the computer

mega	A unit that usually denotes 1 million, but in computer terminology 1 mega is 2^{20} (or 1,048,576)
megabyte, MB	2^{20} or 1,048,576 bytes
megahertz, MHz	1,000,000 cycles per second
memory byte (circuit)	A memory circuit that can store one byte
memory location	A memory byte or memory word
memory word	Two memory bytes
microprocessor	A processing unit fabricated on a single circuit chip
motherboard	The main circuit board of the computer
opcode	Numeric or symbolic code denoting the type of operation for an instruction
operand	The data specified in an instruction
peripheral (device)	I/O device
random access memory, RAM	Memory circuits that can be read or written
read-only memory, ROM	Memory circuits that can only be read
register	A CPU circuit for storing information
system board	Motherboard
video adapter	Computer circuit that converts computer data into video signals for the display monitor
word	16 bits

Exercises

1. Suppose memory bytes 0–4 have the following contents:

Address	Contents
0	01101010
1	11011101
2	00010001
3	11111111
4	01010101

    a. Assuming that a word is 2 bytes, what are the contents of
       - the memory word at address 2?
       - the memory word at address 3?
       - the memory word whose high byte is the byte at address 2?

    b. What is
       - bit 7 of byte 2?
       - bit 0 of word 3?
       - bit 4 of byte 2?
       - bit 11 of word 2?

2. A **nibble** is four bits. Each byte is composed of a high nibble and a low nibble, similar to the high and low bytes of a word. Using the data in exercise 1, give the contents of
   a. the low nibble of byte 1.
   b. the high nibble of byte 4.

3. The two kinds of memory are RAM and ROM. Which kind of memory
   a. holds a user's program?
   b. holds the program used to start the machine?
   c. can be changed by the user?
   d. retains its contents, even when the power is turned off?

4. What is the function of
   a. the microprocessor?
   b. the buses?

5. The two parts of the microprocessor are the EU and the BIU.
   a. What is the function of the EU?
   b. What is the function of the BIU?

6. In the microprocessor, what is the function of
   a. the IP?
   b. the ALU?

7. a. What are the I/O ports used for?
   b. How are they different from memory locations?

8. What is the maximum length (in bytes) of an instruction for the 8086-based IBM PC?

9. Consider a machine language instruction that moves a copy of the contents of register AX in the CPU to a memory word. What happens during
   a. the fetch cycle?
   b. the execute cycle?

10. Give
    a. three advantages of high-level language programming.
    b. the primary advantage of assembly language programming.

2

Representation of Numbers and Characters

Overview

You saw in Chapter 1 that computer circuits are capable of processing only binary information. In this chapter, we show how numbers can be expressed in binary; this is called the **binary number system**. We also introduce a very compact way of representing binary information called the **hexadecimal number system**.

Conversions between binary, decimal, and hexadecimal numbers are covered in section 2.2. Section 2.3 treats addition and subtraction in these number systems.

Section 2.4 shows how negative numbers are represented and what effects the fixed physical size of a byte or word has on number representation.

We conclude the chapter by exploring how characters are encoded and used by the computer.

2.1 Number Systems

Before we look at how numbers are represented in binary, it is instructive to look at the familiar decimal system. It is an example of a *positional number system*; that is, each digit in the number is associated with a power of 10, according to its position in the number. For example, the decimal number 3932 represents 3 thousands, 9 hundreds, 3 tens, and 2 ones. In other words,

$$3,932 = 3 \times 10^3 + 9 \times 10^2 + 3 \times 10^1 + 2 \times 10^0$$

In a positional system, some number b is selected as the base and symbols are assigned to numbers between 0 and b − 1. For example, in the decimal system there are ten basic symbols (digits): 0, 1, 2, 3, 4, 5, 6, 7, 8, and 9. The base ten is represented as 10.

Binary Number System

In the binary number system, the base is two and there are only two digits, 0 and 1. For example, the binary string 11010 represents the number

$$1 \times 2^4 + 1 \times 2^3 + 0 \times 2^2 + 1 \times 2^1 + 0 \times 2^0 = 26$$

The base two is represented in binary as 10.

Hexadecimal Number System

Numbers written in binary tend to be long and difficult to express. For example, 16 bits are needed to represent the contents of a memory word in an 8086-based computer. But decimal numbers are difficult to convert into binary. When we write assembly language programs we tend to use both binary, decimal, and a third number system called *hexadecimal*, or *hex* for short. The advantage of using hex numbers is that the conversion between binary and hex is easy.

The hexadecimal (hex) system is a base sixteen system. The hex digits are 0, 1, 2, 3, 4, 5, 6, 7, 8, 9, A, B, C, D, E, and F. The hex letters A through F denote numbers ten to fifteen, respectively. After F comes the base sixteen, represented in hex by 10.

Because sixteen is 2 to the power of 4, each hex digit corresponds to a unique four-bit number, as shown in Table 2.1. This means that the contents of a byte—eight bits—may be expressed neatly as two hex digits, which makes hex numbers useful with byte-oriented computers.

Table 2.2 shows the relations among binary, decimal, and hexadecimal numbers. It is a good idea to take a few minutes and memorize the first

Table 2.1 Hex Digits and Binary Equivalent

Hex Digits	*Binary*
0	0000
1	0001
2	0010
3	0011
4	0100
5	0101
6	0110
7	0111
8	1000
9	1001
A	1010
B	1011
C	1100
D	1101
E	1110
F	1111

Table 2.2 Decimal, Binary, and Hexadecimal Numbers

Decimal	Binary	Hexadecimal
0	0	0
1	1	1
2	10	2
3	11	3
4	100	4
5	101	5
6	110	6
7	111	7
8	1000	8
9	1001	9
10	1010	A
11	1011	B
12	1100	C
13	1101	D
14	1110	E
15	1111	F
16	10000	10
17	10001	11
18	10010	12
19	10011	13
20	10100	14
21	10101	15
22	10110	16
23	10111	17
24	11000	18
25	11001	19
26	11010	1A
27	11011	1B
28	11100	1C
29	11101	1D
30	11110	1E
31	11111	1F
32	100000	20
.	.	.
.	.	.
.	.	.
256	100000000	100
.	.	.
.	.	.
.	.	.
1024	.	400
.	.	.
.	.	.
.	.	.
32767	.	7FFF
32768	.	8000
.	.	.
.	.	.
.	.	.
65535	.	FFFF

1 Kilobyte   (1 KB) = 1024 = 400h
64 Kilobytes (64 KB) = 65536 = 10000h
1 Megabyte (1 MB) = 1,048,576 = 100000h

16 or so lines of the table, because you will often need to express small numbers in all three systems.

A problem in working with different number systems is the meaning of the symbols used. For example, as you have seen, 10 means ten in the decimal system, sixteen in hex, and two in binary. In this book, the following convention is used whenever confusion may arise: hex numbers are followed by the letter h; for example, 1A34h. Binary numbers are followed by the letter b; for example, 101b. Decimal numbers are followed by the letter d; for example, 79d.

2.2 Conversion Between Number Systems

In working with assembly language, it is often necessary to take a number expressed in one system and write it in a different system.

Converting Binary and Hex to Decimal

Consider the hex number 82AD. It can be written as

$$8A2Dh = 8 \times 16^3 + A \times 16^2 + 2 \times 16^1 + D \times 16^0$$
$$= 8 \times 16^3 + 10 \times 16^2 + 2 \times 16^1 + 13 \times 16^0 = 35373d$$

Similarly, the binary number 11101 may be written as

$$11101b = 1 \times 2^4 + 1 \times 2^3 + 1 \times 2^2 + 0 \times 2^1 + 1 \times 2^0 = 29d$$

This gives one way to convert a binary or hex number to decimal, but an easier way is to use nested multiplication. For example,

$$8A2D = 8 \times 16^3 + A \times 16^2 + 2 \times 16^1 + D \times 16^0$$
$$= ((8 \times 16 + A) \times 16 + 2) \times 16 + D$$
$$= ((8 \times 16 + 10) \times 16 + 2) \times 16 + 13$$
$$= 35373d$$

This can be easily implemented with a calculator: Multiply the first hex digit by 16, and add the second hex digit. Multiply that result by 16, and add the third hex digit. Multiply the result by 16, add the next hex digit, and so on.

The same procedure converts binary to decimal. Just multiply each result by 2 instead of 16.

Example 2.1 Convert 11101 to decimal.

Solution:
$$\quad 1 \quad\quad 1 \quad\quad 1 \quad\quad 0 \quad\quad 1$$
$$= 1 \times 2 + 1 \rightarrow 3 \times 2 + 1 \rightarrow 7 \times 2 + 0 \rightarrow 14 \times 2 + 1 = 29d$$

Example 2.2 Convert 2BD4h to decimal.

Solution:
$$\quad 2 \quad\quad B \quad\quad D \quad\quad 4$$
$$= 2 \times 16 + 11 \rightarrow 43 \times 16 + 13 \rightarrow 701 \times 16 + 4 = 11220$$

where we have used the fact that Bh = 11 and Dh = 13.

Converting Decimal to Binary and Hex

Suppose we want to convert 11172 to hex. The answer 2BA4h may be obtained as follows. First, divide 11172 by 16. We get a quotient of 698 and a remainder of 4. Thus

$$11172 = 698 \times 16 + 4$$

The remainder 4 is the unit's digit in hex representation of 11172. Now divide 698 by 16. The quotient is 43, and the remainder is 10 = Ah. Thus

$$698 = 43 \times 16 + Ah$$

The remainder Ah is the sixteen's digit in the hex representation of 11172. We just continue this process, each time dividing the most recent quotient by 16, until we get a 0 quotient. The remainder each time is a digit in the hex representation of 11172. Here are the calculations:

$$\begin{aligned} 11172 &= 698 \times 16 + 4 \\ 698 &= 43 \times 16 + 10(Ah) \\ 43 &= 2 \times 16 + 11(Bh) \\ 2 &= 0 \times 16 + 2 \end{aligned}$$

Now just convert the remainders to hex and put them together in reverse order to get 2BA4h.

This same process may be used to convert decimal to binary. The only difference is that we repeatedly divide by 2.

Example 2.3 Convert 95 to binary.

Solution:
$$\begin{aligned} 95 &= 47 \times 2 + 1 \\ 47 &= 23 \times 2 + 1 \\ 23 &= 11 \times 2 + 1 \\ 11 &= 5 \times 2 + 1 \\ 5 &= 2 \times 2 + 1 \\ 2 &= 1 \times 2 + 0 \\ 1 &= 0 \times 2 + 1 \end{aligned}$$

Taking the remainders in reverse order, we get 95 = 1011111b.

Conversions Between Hex and Binary

To convert a hex number to binary, we need only express each hex digit in binary.

Example 2.4 Convert 2B3Ch to binary.

Solution:
$$\begin{aligned} &\quad 2 \quad B \quad 3 \quad C \\ &= 0010\ 1011\ 0011\ 1100 \\ &= 0010101100111100 \end{aligned}$$

To go from binary to hex, just reverse this process; that is, group the binary digits in fours starting from the right. Then convert each group to a hex digit.

Example 2.5 Convert 1110101010 to hex.

Solution: 1110101010 = 11 1010 1010 = 3AAh

2.3 Addition and Subtraction

Sometimes you will want to do binary or hex addition and subtraction. Because these operations are done by rote in decimal, let's review the process to see what is involved.

Addition

Consider the following decimal addition

$$\begin{array}{r} 2546 \\ + 1872 \\ \hline 4418 \end{array}$$

To get the unit's digit in the sum, we just compute 6 + 2 = 8. To get the ten's digit, compute 4 + 7 = 11. We write down 1 and carry 1 to the hundred's column. In that column we compute 5 + 8 + 1 = 14. We write down 4 and carry 1 to the last column. In that column we compute 2 + 1 + 1 = 4 and write it down, and the sum is complete.

A reason that decimal addition is easy for us is that we memorized the addition table for small numbers a long time ago. Table 2.3A is an addition table for small hex numbers. To compute Bh + 9h, for example, just intersect the row containing B and the column containing 9, and read 14h.

By using the addition table, hex addition may be done in exactly the same way as decimal addition. Suppose we want to compute the following hex sum:

Table 2.3A Hexadecimal Addition Table

	0	1	2	3	4	5	6	7	8	9	A	B	C	D	E	F
0	0	1	2	3	4	5	6	7	8	9	A	B	C	D	E	F
1	1	2	3	4	5	6	7	8	9	A	B	C	D	E	F	10
2	2	3	4	5	6	7	8	9	A	B	C	D	E	F	10	11
3	3	4	5	6	7	8	9	A	B	C	D	E	F	10	11	12
4	4	5	6	7	8	9	A	B	C	D	E	F	10	11	12	13
5	5	6	7	8	9	A	B	C	D	E	F	10	11	12	13	14
6	6	7	8	9	A	B	C	D	E	F	10	11	12	13	14	15
7	7	8	9	A	B	C	D	E	F	10	11	12	13	14	15	16
8	8	9	A	B	C	D	E	F	10	11	12	13	14	15	16	17
9	9	A	B	C	D	E	F	10	11	12	13	14	15	16	17	18
A	A	B	C	D	E	F	10	11	12	13	14	15	16	17	18	19
B	B	C	D	E	F	10	11	12	13	14	15	16	17	18	19	1A
C	C	D	E	F	10	11	12	13	14	15	16	17	18	19	1A	1B
D	D	E	F	10	11	12	13	14	15	16	17	18	19	1A	1B	1C
E	E	F	10	11	12	13	14	15	16	17	18	19	1A	1B	1C	1D
F	F	10	11	12	13	14	15	16	17	18	19	1A	1B	1C	1D	1E

Table 2.3B Binary Addition Table

	0	1
0	0	1
1	1	10

$$\begin{array}{r} 5B39h \\ + 7AF4h \\ \hline D62Dh \end{array}$$

In the unit's column, we compute 9h + 4h = 13d = Dh. In the next column, we get 3h + Fh = 12h. Write down 2 and carry 1 to the next column. In that column, compute Bh + Ah + 1 = 16h. Write 6, and carry 1 to the last column. There we compute 5h + 7h + 1 = Dh, and we are done.

Binary addition is done the same way as decimal and hex addition, but is a good deal easier because the binary addition table is so small (Table 2.3B). To do the sum

$$\begin{array}{r} 100101111 \\ + 110110 \\ \hline 101100101 \end{array}$$

Compute 1 + 0 = 1 in the unit's column. In the next column, add 1 + 1 = 10b. Write down 0 and carry 1 to the next column, where we get 1 + 1 + 1 = 11b. Write down 1, carry 1 to the next column, and so on.

Subtraction

Let's begin with the decimal subtraction

$$\begin{array}{r} bb \\ 9145 \\ - 7283 \\ \hline 1862 \end{array}$$

In the unit's column, we compute 5 − 3 = 2. To do the ten's, we first borrow 1 from the hundred's column (to remember that we have done this, we may place a "b" above the hundred's column), and compute 14 − 8 = 6. In the hundred's column, we must again borrow 1 from the next column, and compute 11 − 2 − 1 (the previous borrow) = 8. In the last column, we get 9 − 7 − 1 = 1.

Hex subtraction may be done the same way as decimal subtraction. To compute the hex difference

$$\begin{array}{r} bb \\ D26F \\ - BA94 \\ \hline 17DB \end{array}$$

we start with Fh − 4h = Bh. To do the next (sixteen's) column, we must borrow 1 from the third column, and compute

$$16h - 9h = ?$$

The easy way to figure this is to go to row 9 in Table 2.3A, and notice that 16 appears in column D. This means that 9h + Dh = 16h, so 16h − 9h = Dh. In the third column, after borrowing, we must compute 12h − Ah − 1 = 11h − Ah. In row A, 11 appears in column 7 so 11h − Ah = 7h. Finally in the last column, we have Ch − Bh = 1.

Now let us look at binary subtraction, for example,

$$\begin{array}{r} bb \\ 1001 \\ - 0111 \\ \hline 0010 \end{array}$$

The unit's column is easy, 1 − 1 = 0. We must borrow to do the two's column, getting 10 − 1 = 1. To do the four's column, we must again borrow, computing 10 − 1 − 1 (since we borrowed from this column) = 0. Finally in the last column, we have 0 − 0 = 0.

2.4 How Integers Are Represented in the Computer

The hardware of a computer necessarily restricts the size of numbers that can be stored in a register or memory location. In this section, we will see how integers can be stored in an 8-bit byte or a 16-bit word. In Chapter 18 we talk about how real numbers can be stored.

In the following, we'll need to refer to two particular bits in a byte or word: the **most significant bit**, or **msb**, is the leftmost bit. In a word, the msb is bit 15; in a byte, it is bit 7. Similarly, the **least significant bit**, or **lsb**, is the rightmost bit; that is, bit 0.

2.4.1 Unsigned Integers

An **unsigned integer** is an integer that represents a magnitude, so it is never negative. Unsigned integers are appropriate for representing quantities that can never be negative, such as addresses of memory locations, counters, and ASCII character codes (see later). Because unsigned integers are by definition nonnegative, none of the bits are needed to represent the sign, and so all 8 bits in a byte, or 16 bits in a word, are available to represent the number.

The largest unsigned integer that can be stored in a byte is 11111111 = FFh = 255. This is not a very big number, so we usually store integers in words. The biggest unsigned integer a 16-bit word can hold is 1111111111111111 = FFFFh = 65535. This is big enough for most purposes. If not, two or more words may be used.

Note that if the least significant bit of an integer is 1, the number is odd, and it's even if the lsb is 0.

2.4.2 Signed Integers

A **signed integer** can be positive or negative. The most significant bit is reserved for the sign: 1 means negative and 0 means positive. Negative integers are stored in the computer in a special way known as **two's complement**. To explain it, we first define **one's complement**, as follows.

One's Complement

The one's complement of an integer is obtained by complementing each bit; that is, replace each 0 by a 1 and each 1 by a 0. In the following, we assume numbers are 16 bits.

Example 2.6 Find the one's complement of 5 = 0000000000000101.

Solution: 5 = 0000000000000101
One's complement of 5 = 1111111111111010

Note that if we add 5 and its one's complement, we get 1111111111111111.

Two's Complement

To get the two's complement of an integer, just add 1 to its one's complement.

Example 2.7 Find the two's complement of 5.

Solution: From above,

$$\begin{aligned}\text{one's complement of 5} &= 1111111111111010 \\ &+ 1 \\ \hline \text{two's complement of 5} &= 1111111111111011 = \text{FFFBh}\end{aligned}$$

Now look what happens when we add 5 and its two's complement:

$$\begin{aligned}5 &= 0000000000000101 \\ + \text{two's complement of } 5 &= 1111111111111011 \\ \hline &10000000000000000\end{aligned}$$

We end up with a 17-bit number. Because a computer word circuit can only hold 16 bits, the 1 carried out from the most significant bit is lost, and the 16-bit result is 0. As 5 and its two's complement add up to 0, the two's complement of 5 must be a correct representation of –5.

It is easy to see why the two's complement of any integer N must represent $-N$: Adding N and its one's complement gives 16 ones; adding 1 to this produces 16 zeros with a 1 carried out and lost. The result stored is always 0000000000000000.

The following example shows what happens when a number is complemented two times.

Example 2.8 Find the two's complement of the two's complement of 5.

Solution: We would guess that after complementing 5 two times, the result should be 5. To verify this, from above,

$$\begin{aligned}\text{two's complement of 5} &= 1111111111111011 \\ \text{one's complement of } 1111111111111011 &= 0000000000000100 \\ &+ 1 \\ \hline \text{two's complement of } 1111111111111011 &= 0000000000000101 = 5\end{aligned}$$

Example 2.9 Show how the decimal integer –97 would be represented (a) in 8 bits, and (b) in 16 bits. Express the answers in hex.

Solution: A decimal-to-hex conversion using repeated division by 16 yields

$$\begin{aligned}97 &= 6 \times 16 + 1 \\ 6 &= 0 \times 16 + 6\end{aligned}$$

Thus 97 = 61h. To represent –97, we need to express 61h in binary and take the two's complement.

a. In 8 bits, we get

$$61h = 0110\ 0001$$
$$\text{one's complement} = 1001\ 1110$$
$$+\ 1$$
$$\text{two's complement} = 1001\ 1111 = 9Fh$$

b. In 16 bits, we get

$$61h = 0000\ 0000\ 0110\ 0001$$
$$\text{one's complement} = 1111\ 1111\ 1001\ 1110$$
$$+\ 1$$
$$1111\ 1111\ 1001\ 1111 = FF9Fh$$

Subtraction as Two's Complement Addition

The advantage of two's complement representation of negative integers in the computer is that subtraction can be done by bit complementation and addition, and circuits that add and complement bits are easy to design.

Example 2.10 Suppose AX contains 5ABCh and BX contains 21FCh. Find the difference of AX minus BX by using complementation and addition.

Solution:

$$\text{AX contains } 5ABCh = 0101\ 1010\ 1011\ 1100$$
$$\text{BX contains } 21FCh = 0010\ 0001\ 1111\ 1100$$
$$5ABCh = 0101\ 1010\ 1011\ 1100$$
$$+ \text{ one's complement of } 21FCh = 1101\ 1110\ 0000\ 0011$$
$$+\ 1$$
$$\text{Difference} = 1\ 0011\ 1000\ 1100\ 0000 = 38C0h$$

A one is carried out of the most significant bit and is lost. The answer stored, 38C0h, is correct, as may be verified by hex subtraction.

2.4.3 Decimal Interpretation

In the last section, we saw how signed and unsigned decimal integers may be represented in the computer. The reverse problem is to interpret the contents of a byte or word as a signed or unsigned decimal integer.

- *Unsigned decimal interpretation:* Just do a binary-to-decimal conversion. It's usually easier to convert binary to hex first, and then convert hex to decimal.

- *Signed decimal interpretation:* If the most significant bit is 0, the number is positive, and the signed decimal is the same as the unsigned decimal. If the msb is 1, the number is negative, so call it $-N$. To find N, just take the twos' complement and then convert to decimal as before.

Example 2.11 Suppose AX contains FE0Ch. Give the unsigned and signed decimal interpretations.

Table 2.4A Signed and Unsigned Decimal Interpretations of 16-Bit Register/Memory Contents

Hex	Unsigned decimal	Signed decimal
0000	0	0
0001	1	1
0002	2	2
.	.	.
.	.	.
.	.	.
0009	9	9
000A	10	10
.	.	.
.	.	.
.	.	.
7FFE	32766	32766
7FFF	32767	32767
8000	32768	-32768
8001	32769	-32767
.	.	.
.	.	.
.	.	.
FFFE	65534	-2
FFFF	65535	-1

Solution: Conversion of FE0Ch to decimal yields 65036, which is the unsigned decimal interpretation.

For the signed interpretation, FE0Ch = 1111111000001100. Since the sign bit is 1, this is a negative number, call it $-N$. To find N, get the two's complement.

$$\begin{aligned} \text{FE0Ch} &= 1111\ 1110\ 0000\ 1100 \\ \text{one's complement} &= 0000\ 0001\ 1111\ 0011 \\ &\quad + 1 \\ \hline N &= 0000\ 0001\ 1111\ 0100 = \text{01F4h} = 500 \end{aligned}$$

Thus, AX contains –500.

Tables 2.4A and 2.4B give 16-bit word and 8-bit byte hex values and their signed and unsigned decimal interpretations. Note the following:

1. Because the most significant bit of a positive signed integer is 0, the leading hex digit of a positive signed integer is 0 – 7; integers beginning with 8–Fh have 1 in the sign bit, so they are negative.

2. The largest 16-bit positive signed integer is 7FFFh = 32767; the smallest negative integer is 8000h = –32768. For a byte, the largest positive integer is 7Fh = 127 and the smallest is 80h = –128.

3. The following relationship holds between the unsigned and signed decimal interpretations of the contents of a 16-bit word:

Table 2.4B Signed and Unsigned Decimal Interpretations of a Byte

Hex	Unsigned decimal	Signed decimal
00	0	0
01	1	1
02	2	2
.	.	.
.	.	.
.	.	.
09	9	9
0A	10	10
.	.	.
.	.	.
.	.	.
7E	126	126
7F	127	127
80	128	-128
81	129	-127
.	.	.
.	.	.
.	.	.
FE	254	-2
FF	255	-1

For 0000h–7FFFh, signed decimal = unsigned decimal.
For 8000h–FFFFh, signed decimal = unsigned decimal – 65536.

There are similar relations for the contents of an eight-bit byte:

For 00h–7Fh, signed decimal = unsigned decimal.
For 80h–FFh, signed decimal = unsigned decimal – 256.

Example 2.12 Use observation 3, from the above, to rework example 2.11.

Solution: We saw that the unsigned decimal interpretation of FE0Ch is 65036. Because the leading hex digit is Fh, the content is negative in a signed sense. To interpret it, just subtract 65536 from the unsigned decimal. Thus

signed decimal interpretation = 65036 – 65536 = –500

2.5 Character Representation

ASCII Code

Not all data processed by the computer are treated as numbers. I/O devices such as the video monitor and printer are character oriented, and programs such as word processors deal with characters exclusively. Like all data, characters must be coded in binary in order to be processed by the computer. The most popular encoding scheme for characters is **ASCII (American Standard Code for Information Interchange) code**. Originally used in communications by teletype, ASCII code is used by all personal computers today.

The ASCII code system uses seven bits to code each character, so there are a total of $2^7 = 128$ ASCII codes. Table 2.5 gives the ASCII codes and the characters associated with them.

Notice that only 95 ASCII codes, from 32 to 126, are considered to be printable. The codes 0 to 31 and also 127 were used for communication control purposes and do not produce printable characters. Most microcomputers use only the printable characters and a few control characters such as LF, CR, BS, and Bell.

Because each ASCII character is coded by only seven bits, the code of a single character fits into a byte, with the most significant bit set to zero. The printable characters can be displayed on the video monitor or printed by the printer, while the control characters are used to control the operations of these devices. For example, to display the character A on the screen, a program sends the ASCII code 41h to the screen; and to move the cursor back to the beginning of the line, a program sends the ASCII code 0Dh, which is the CR character, to the screen.

A computer may assign special display characters to some of the non-printed ASCII codes. As you will see later, the screen controller for the IBM PC can actually display an extended set of 256 characters. Appendix A shows the 256 display characters of the IBM PC.

Example 2.13 Show how the character string "RG 2z" is stored in memory, starting at address 0.

Solution: From Table 2.5, we have

Character	ASCII Code (hex)	ASCII Code (binary)
R	52	0101 0010
G	47	0100 0111
space	20	0010 0000
2	32	0011 0010
z	7A	0111 1010

So memory would look like this:

Address	Contents
0	01010010
1	01000111
2	00100000
3	00110010
4	01111010

The Keyboard

It's reasonable to guess that the keyboard identifies a key by generating an ASCII code when the key is pressed. This was true for a class of keyboards known as *ASCII keyboards* used by some early microcomputers.

Table 2.5 ASCII Code

Dec	Hex	Char	Dec	Hex	Char	Dec	Hex	Char	Dec	Hex	Char
0	00	<CC>	32	20	SP	64	40	@	96	60	'
1	01	<CC>	33	21	!	65	41	A	97	61	a
2	02	<CC>	34	22	"	66	42	B	98	62	b
3	03	<CC>	35	23	#	67	43	C	99	63	c
4	04	<CC>	36	24	$	68	44	D	100	64	d
5	05	<CC>	37	25	%	69	45	E	101	65	e
6	06	<CC>	38	26	&	70	46	F	102	66	f
7	07	<CC>	39	27	'	71	47	G	103	67	g
8	08	<CC>	40	28	(	72	48	H	104	68	h
9	09	<CC>	41	29	)	73	49	I	105	69	i
10	0A	<CC>	42	2A	*	74	4A	J	106	6A	j
11	0B	<CC>	43	2B	+	75	4B	K	107	6B	k
12	0C	<CC>	44	2C	,	76	4C	L	108	6C	l
13	0D	<CC>	45	2D	-	77	4D	M	109	6D	m
14	0E	<CC>	46	2E	.	78	4E	N	110	6E	n
15	0F	<CC>	47	2F	/	79	4F	O	111	6F	o
16	10	<CC>	48	30	0	80	50	P	112	70	p
17	11	<CC>	49	31	1	81	51	Q	113	71	q
18	12	<CC>	50	32	2	82	52	R	114	72	r
19	13	<CC>	51	33	3	83	53	S	115	73	s
20	14	<CC>	52	34	4	84	54	T	116	74	t
21	15	<CC>	53	35	5	85	55	U	117	75	u
22	16	<CC>	54	36	6	86	56	V	118	76	v
23	17	<CC>	55	37	7	87	57	W	119	77	w
24	18	<CC>	56	38	8	88	58	X	120	78	x
25	19	<CC>	57	39	9	89	59	Y	121	79	y
26	1A	<CC>	58	3A	:	90	5A	Z	122	7A	z
27	1B	<CC>	59	3B	;	91	5B	[	123	7B	{
28	1C	<CC>	60	3C	<	92	5C	\	124	7C		
29	1D	<CC>	61	3D	=	93	5D	]	125	7D	}
30	1E	<CC>	62	3E	>	94	5E	^	126	7E	~
31	1F	<CC>	63	3F	?	95	5F	_	127	7F	<CC>

<CC> denotes a control character
SP = blank space

Special Control Characters

Dec	Hex	Char	Meaning
7	07	BEL	bell
8	08	BS	backspace
9	09	HT	horizontal tab
10	0A	LF	line feed
12	0C	FF	form feed
13	0D	CR	carriage return

However, modern keyboards have many control and function keys in addition to ASCII character keys, so other encoding schemes are used. For the IBM PC, each key is assigned a unique number called a **scan code**; when a key is pressed, the keyboard sends the key's scan code to the computer. Scan codes are discussed in Chapter 12.

SUMMARY

- Numbers are represented in different ways, according to the basic symbols used. The binary system uses two symbols, 0 and 1. The decimal system uses 0–9. The hexadecimal system uses 0–9, A–F.

- Binary and hex numbers can be converted to decimal by a process of nested multiplication.

- A hex number can be converted to decimal by a process of repeated division by 16; similarly, a binary number can be converted to decimal by a process of repeated division by 2.

- Hex numbers can be converted to binary by converting each hex digit to binary; binary numbers are converted to hex by grouping the bits in fours, starting from the right, and converting each group to a hex digit.

- The process of adding and subtracting hex and binary numbers is the same as for decimal numbers, and can be done with the help of the appropriate addition table.

- Negative numbers are stored in two's complement form. To get the two's complement of a number, complement each bit and add 1 to the result.

- If A and B are stored integers, the processor computes A – B by adding the two's complement of B to A.

- The range of unsigned integers that can be stored in a byte is 0–255; in a 16-bit word, it is 0–65535.

- For signed numbers, the most significant bit is the sign bit; 0 means positive and 1 means negative. The range of signed numbers that can be stored in a byte is –128 to 127; in a word, it is –32768 to 32767.

- The unsigned decimal interpretation of a word is obtained by converting the binary value to decimal. If the sign bit is 0, this is also the signed decimal interpretation. If the sign bit is 1, the signed decimal interpretation may be obtained by subtracting 65536 from the unsigned decimal interpretation.

- The standard encoding scheme for characters is the ASCII code.

- A character requires seven bits to code, so it can be stored in a byte.

- The IBM screen controller can generate a character for each of the 256 possible numbers that can be stored in a byte.

Glossary

ASCII (American Standard Code for Information Interchange) codes   The encoding scheme for characters used on all personal computers

binary number system   Base two system in which the digits are 0 and 1

hexadecimal number system   Base sixteen system in which the digits are 0, 1, 2, 3, 4, 5, 6, 7, 8, 9, A, B, C, D, E, and F

least significant bit, lsb   The rightmost bit in a word or byte; that is, bit 0

most significant bit, msb   The leftmost bit in a word or byte; that is, bit 15 in a word or bit 7 in a byte

one's complement of a binary number   Obtained by replacing each 0 bit by 1 and each 1 bit by 0

scan code   A number used to identify a key on the keyboard

signed integer   An integer that can be positive or negative

two's complement of a binary number   Obtained by adding 1 to the one's complement

unsigned integer   An integer representing a magnitude; that is, always positive

Exercises

1. In many applications, it saves time to memorize the conversions among small binary, decimal, and hex numbers. Without referring to Table 2.2, fill in the blanks in the following table:

Binary	Decimal	Hex
____	9	____
1010	____	____
____	____	D
____	12	____
1110	____	____
____	____	B

2. Convert the following binary and hex numbers to decimal:
   a. 1110
   b. 100101011101
   c. 46Ah
   d. FAE2Ch

3. Convert the following decimal numbers:
   a. 97 to binary
   b. 627 to binary
   c. 921 to hex
   d. 6120 to hex

4. Convert the following numbers:

a. 1001011 to hex
b. 1001010110101110 to hex
c. A2Ch to binary
d. B34Dh to binary

5. Perform the following additions:
    a. 100101b + 10111b
    b. 100111101b + 10001111001b
    c. B23CDh + 17912h
    d. FEFFEh + FBCADh

6. Perform the following subtractions:
    a. 11011b − 10110b
    b. 10000101b − 111011b
    c. 5FC12h − 3ABD1h
    d. F001Eh − 1FF3Fh

7. Give the 16-bit representation of each of the following decimal integers. Write the answer in hex.
    a. 234
    b. −16
    c. 31634
    d. −32216

8. Do the following binary and hex subtractions by two's complement addition.
    a. 10110100 − 10010111
    b. 10001011 − 11110111
    c. FE0Fh − 12ABh
    d. 1ABCh − B3EAh

9. Give the unsigned and signed decimal interpretations of each of the following 16-bit or 8-bit numbers.
    a. 7FFEh
    b. 8543h
    c. FEh
    d. 7Fh

10. Show how the decimal integer −120 would be represented
    a. in 16 bits.
    b. in 8 bits.

11. For each of the following decimal numbers, tell whether it could be stored (a) as a 16-bit number (b) as an 8-bit number.
    a. 32767
    b. −40000
    c. 65536
    d. 257
    e. −128

12. For each of the following 16-bit signed numbers, tell whether it is positive or negative.
    a. 1010010010010100b
    b. 78E3h

c. CB33h
d. 807Fh
e. 9AC4h

13. If the character string "$12.75" is being stored in memory starting at address 0, give the hex contents of bytes 0–5.

14. Translate the following secret message, which has been encoded in ASCII as 41 74 74 61 63 6B 20 61 74 20 44 61 77 6E.

15. Suppose that a byte contains the ASCII code of an uppercase letter. What hex number should be added to it to convert it to lower case?

16. Suppose that a byte contains the ASCII code of a decimal digit; that is, "0"..."9." What hex number should be subtracted from the byte to convert it to the numerical form of the characters?

17. It is not really necessary to refer to the hex addition table to do addition and subtraction of hex digits. To compute Eh + Ah, for example, first copy the hex digits:

    0 1 2 3 4 5 6 7 8 9 A B C D E F

    Now starting at Eh, move to the right Ah = 10 places. When you go off the right end of the line, continue on from the left end and attach a 1 to each number you pass:

    10 11 12 13 14 15 16 17 18 9 A B C D E F
                      STOP ^   START ^

    You get Eh + Ah = 18h. Subtraction can be done similarly. For example, to compute 15h – Ch, start at 15h and move left Ch = 12 places. When you go off the left end, continue on at the right:

    10 11 12 13 14 15 6 7 8 9 A B C D E F
                ^ START   ^ STOP

    You get 15h – Ch = 9h.
    Rework exercises 5(c) and 6(c) by this method.

3

Organization of the IBM Personal Computers

Overview

Chapter 1 described the organization of a typical microcomputer system. This chapter takes a closer look at the IBM personal computers. These machines are based on the Intel 8086 family of microprocessors.

After a brief survey of the 8086 family in section 3.1, section 3.2 concentrates on the architecture of the 8086. We introduce the registers and mention some of their special functions. In section 3.2.3, the important idea of segmented memory is discussed.

In section 3.3, we look at the overall structure of the IBM PC; the memory organization, I/O ports, and the DOS and BIOS routines.

3.1 The Intel 8086 Family of Microprocessors

The IBM personal computer family consists of the IBM PC, PC XT, PC AT, PS/1, and PS/2 models. They are all based on the Intel 8086 family of microprocessors, which includes the 8086, 8088, 80186, 80188, 80286, 80386, 80386SX, 80486, and 80486SX. The 8088 is used in the PC and PC XT; the 80286 is used in the PC AT and PS/1. The 80186 is used in some PC-compatible lap-top models. The PS/2 models use either the 8086, 80286, 80386, or 80486.

The 8086 and 8088 Microprocessors

Intel introduced the 8086 in 1978 as its first 16-bit microprocessor (a 16-bit processor can operate on 16 bits of data at a time). The 8088 was introduced in 1979. Internally, the 8088 is essentially the same as the 8086. Externally, the 8086 has a 16-bit data bus, while the 8088 has an 8-bit data bus. The 8086 also has a faster clock rate, and thus has better performance. IBM chose the 8088 over the 8086 for the original PC because it was less expensive to build a computer around the 8088.

The 8086 and 8088 have the same instruction set, and it forms the basic set of instructions for the other microprocessors in the family.

The 80186 and 80188 Microprocessors

The 80186 and 80188 are enhanced versions of the 8086 and 8088, respectively. Their advantage is that they incorporate all the functions of the 8086 and 8088 microprocessors plus those of some support chips. They can also execute some new instructions called the *extended instruction set*. However, these processors offered no significant advantage over the 8086 and 8088 and were soon overshadowed by the development of the 80286.

The 80286 Microprocessor

The 80286, introduced in 1982, is also a 16-bit microprocessor. However, it can operate faster than the 8086 (12.5 MHz versus 10 MHz) and offers the following important advances over its predecessors:

1. *Two modes of operation.* The 80286 can operate in either **real address mode** or **protected virtual address mode**. In real address mode, the 80286 behaves like the 8086, and programs for the 8086 can be executed in this mode without modification. In protected virtual address mode, also called **protected mode**, the 80286 supports **multitasking**, which is the ability to execute several programs (tasks) at the same time, and **memory protection**, which is the ability to protect the memory used by one program from the actions of another program.

2. *More addressable memory.* The 80286 in protected mode can address 16 megabytes of physical memory (as opposed to 1 megabyte for the 8086 and 8088).

3. *Virtual memory in protected mode.* This means that the 80286 can treat external storage (that is, a disk) as if it were physical memory, and therefore execute programs that are too large to be contained in physical memory; such programs can be up to 1 gigabyte (2^{30} bytes).

The 80386 and 80386SX Microprocessors

Intel introduced its first 32-bit microprocessor, the 80386 (or 386), in 1985. It is much faster than the 80286 because it has a 32-bit data path, high clock rate (up to 33 MHz), and the ability to execute instructions in fewer clock cycles than the 80286.

Like the 80286, the 386 can operate in either real or protected mode. In real mode, it behaves like an 8086. In protected mode, it can emulate the 80286. It also has a *virtual 8086 mode* designed to run multiple 8086 applications under memory protection. The 386, in protected mode, can address 4 gigabytes of physical memory, and 64 terabytes (2^{46} bytes) of virtual memory.

The 386SX has essentially the same internal structure as the 386, but it has only a 16-bit data bus.

The 80486 and 80486SX Microprocessors

Introduced in 1989, the 80486 (or 486), is another 32-bit microprocessor. It is the fastest and most powerful processor in the family. It incorporates the functions of the 386 together with those of other support chips, including the 80387 numeric processor, which performs floating-point number operations, and an 8-KB cache memory that serves as a fast memory area to buffer data coming from the slower memory unit. With its numeric processor, cache memory, and more advanced design, the 486 is three times faster than a 386 running at the same clock speed. The 486SX is similar to the 486 but without the floating-point processor.

3.2 Organization of the 8086/8088 Microprocessors

In the rest of this chapter we'll concentrate on the organization of the 8086 and 8088. These processors have the simplest structure, and most of the instructions we will study are 8086/8088 instructions. They also provide insight to the organization of the more advanced processors, discussed in Chapter 20.

Because the 8086 and 8088 have essentially the same internal structure, in the following, the name "8086" applies to both 8086 and 8088.

3.2.1 Registers

As noted in Chapter 1, information inside the microprocessor is stored in registers. The registers are classified according to the functions they perform. In general, *data registers* hold data for an operation, *address registers* hold the address of an instruction or data, and a *status register* keeps the current status of the processor.

The 8086 has four general data registers; the address registers are divided into *segment*, *pointer*, and *index registers*; and the status register is called the *FLAGS register*. In total, there are fourteen 16-bit registers, which we now briefly describe. See Figure 3.1. *Note:* You don't need to memorize the special functions of these registers at this time. They will become familiar with use.

3.2.2 Data Registers: AX, BX, CX, DX

These four registers are available to the programmer for general data manipulation. Even though the processor can operate on data stored in memory, the same instruction is faster (requires fewer clock cycles) if the data are stored in registers. This is why modern processors tend to have a lot of registers.

The high and low bytes of the data registers can be accessed separately. The high byte of AX is called AH, and the low byte is AL. Similarly, the high and low bytes of BX, CX, and DX are BH and BL, CH and CL, DH and DL, respectively. This arrangement gives us more registers to use when dealing with byte-size data.

These four registers, in addition to being general-purpose registers, also perform special functions such as the following.

Figure 3.1 8086 Registers

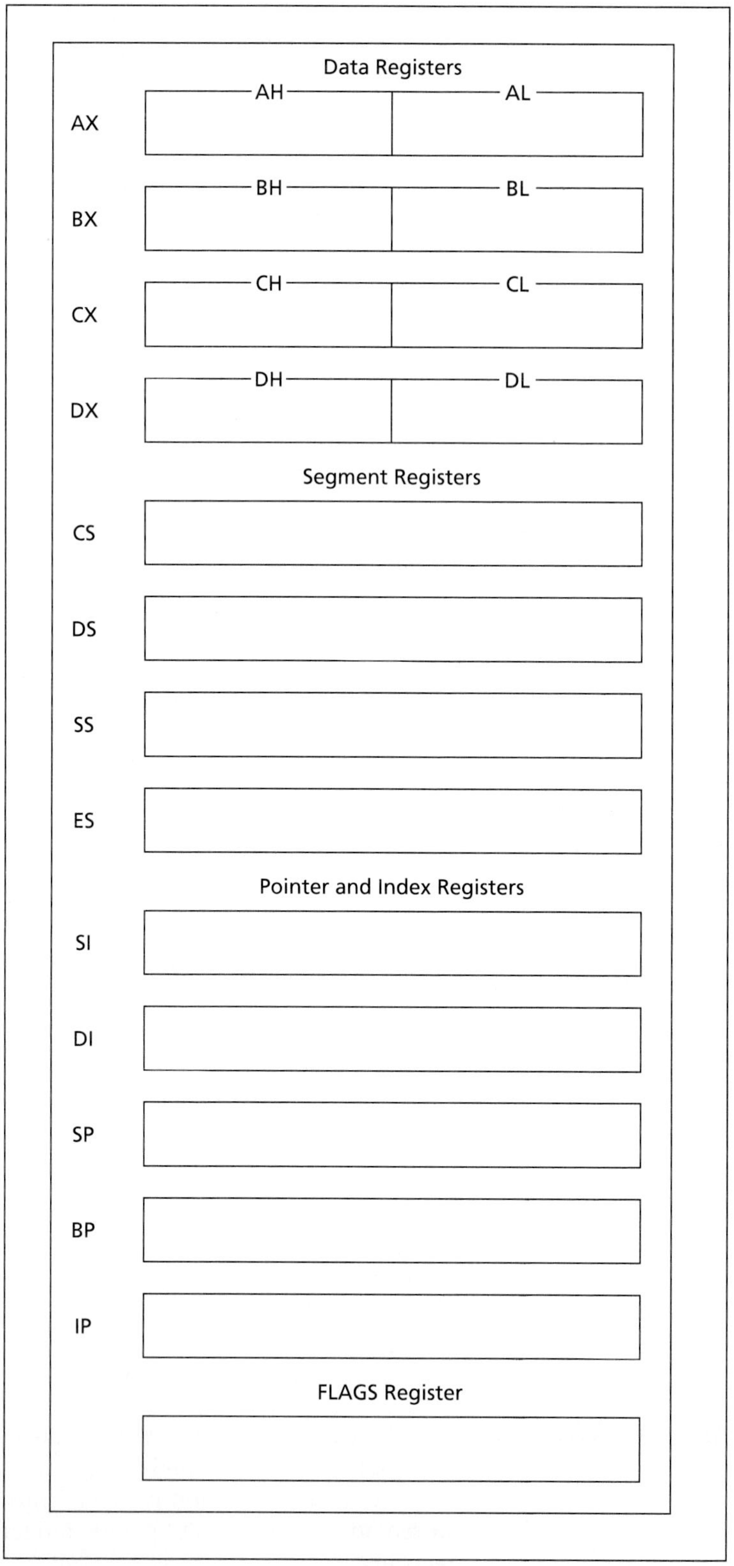

Data Registers

AX : AH | AL
BX : BH | BL
CX : CH | CL
DX : DH | DL

Segment Registers

CS
DS
SS
ES

Pointer and Index Registers

SI
DI
SP
BP
IP

FLAGS Register

AX (Accumulator Register)

AX is the preferred register to use in arithmetic, logic, and data transfer instructions because its use generates the shortest machine code.

In multiplication and division operations, one of the numbers involved must be in AX or AL. Input and output operations also require the use of AL and AX.

BX (Base Register)

BX also serves as an address register; an example is a table look-up instruction called XLAT (translate).

CX (Count Register)

Program loop constructions are facilitated by the use of CX, which serves as a loop counter. Another example of using CX as counter is REP (repeat), which controls a special class of instructions called *string operations*. CL is used as a count in instructions that shift and rotate bits.

DX (Data Register)

DX is used in multiplication and division. It is also used in I/O operations.

3.2.3
Segment Registers: CS, DS, SS, ES

Address registers store addresses of instructions and data in memory. These values are used by the processor to access memory locations. We begin with the memory organization.

Chapter 1 explained that memory is a collection of bytes. Each memory byte has an address, starting with 0. The 8086 processor assigns a 20-bit **physical address** to its memory locations. Thus it is possible to address 2^{20} = 1,048,576 bytes (one megabyte) of memory. The first five bytes in memory have the following addresses:

$$00000000000000000000$$
$$00000000000000000001$$
$$00000000000000000010$$
$$00000000000000000011$$
$$00000000000000000100$$

Because addresses are so cumbersome to write in binary, we usually express them as five hex digits, thus

$$00000$$
$$00001$$
$$00002$$
$$\cdot$$
$$\cdot$$
$$\cdot$$
$$00009$$
$$0000A$$
$$0000B$$
$$\cdot$$
$$\cdot$$
$$\cdot$$

and so on. The highest address is FFFFFh.

In order to explain the function of the segment registers, we first need to introduce the idea of memory segments, which is a direct consequence of using a 20-bit address in a 16-bit processor. The addresses are too big to fit in a 16-bit register or memory word. The 8086 gets around this problem by partitioning its memory into segments.

Memory Segment

A **memory segment** is a block of 2^{16} (or 64 K) consecutive memory bytes. Each segment is identified by a **segment number**, starting with 0. A segment number is 16 bits, so the highest segment number is FFFFh.

Within a segment, a memory location is specified by giving an **offset**. This is the number of bytes from the beginning of the segment. With a 64-KB segment, the offset can be given as a 16-bit number. The first byte in a segment has offset 0. The last offset in a segment is FFFFh.

Segment:Offset Address

A memory location may be specified by providing a segment number and an offset, written in the form *segment:offset*; this is known as a **logical address**. For example, A4FB:4872h means offset 4872h within segment A4FBh. To obtain a 20-bit physical address, the 8086 microprocessor first shifts the segment address 4 bits to the left (this is equivalent to multiplying by 10h), and then adds the offset. Thus the physical address for A4FB:4872 is

$$\begin{array}{r} \text{A4FB0h} \\ + \text{4872h} \\ \hline \text{A9822h} \quad \text{(20–bit physical address)} \end{array}$$

Location of Segments

It is instructive to see the layout of the segments in memory. Segment 0 starts at address 0000:0000 = 00000h and ends at 0000:FFFF = 0FFFFh. Segment 1 starts at address 0001:0000 = 00010h and ends at 0001:FFFF = 1000Fh. As we can see, there is a lot of overlapping between segments. Figure 3.2 shows the locations of the first three memory segments. The segments start every 10h = 16 bytes and the starting address of a segment always ends with a hex digit 0. We call 16 bytes a **paragraph**. We call an address that is divisible by 16 (ends with a hex digit 0) a **paragraph boundary**.

Because segments may overlap, the segment:offset form of an address is not unique, as the following example shows.

Example 3.1 For the memory location whose physical address is specified by 1256Ah, give the address in segment:offset form for segments 1256h and 1240h.

Solution: Let X be the offset in segment 1256h and Y the offset in segment 1240h. We have

$$1256\text{Ah} = 12560\text{h} + X \text{ and } 1256\text{Ah} = 12400\text{h} + Y$$

and so

$$X = 1256\text{Ah} - 12560\text{h} = \text{Ah and } Y = 1256\text{Ah} - 12400\text{h} = 16\text{Ah}$$

thus

$$1256\text{Ah} = 1256\text{:}000\text{A} = 1240\text{:}016\text{A}$$

Figure 3.2 Location of Memory Segments

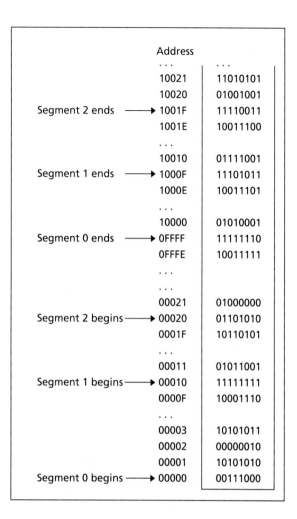

It is also possible to calculate the segment number when the physical address and the offset are given.

Example 3.2 A memory location has physical address 80FD2h. In what segment does it have offset BFD2h?

Solution: We know that

$$\text{physical address} = \text{segment} \times 10h + \text{offset}$$

Thus

$$\text{segment} \times 10h = \text{physical address} - \text{offset}$$

in this example

$$\begin{aligned}\text{physical address} &= 80FD2h \\ -\text{offset} &= BFD2h \\ \hline \text{segment} \times 10h &= 75000h\end{aligned}$$

So the segment must be 7500h.

Figure 3.3 Segment Registers

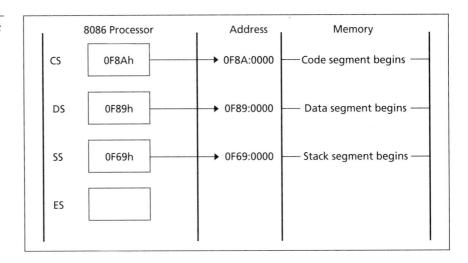

Program Segments

Now let us talk about the registers CS, DS, SS, and ES. A typical machine language program consists of instructions (code) and data. There is also a data structure called the **stack** used by the processor to implement procedure calls. The program's code, data, and stack are loaded into different memory segments, we call them the **code segment**, **data segment**, and **stack segment**.

To keep track of the various program segments, the 8086 is equipped with four segment registers to hold segment numbers. The CS, DS, and SS registers contain the code, data, and stack segment numbers, respectively. If a program needs to access a second data segment, it can use the ES (extra segment) register.

A program segment need not occupy the entire 64 kilobytes in a memory segment. The overlapping nature of the memory segments permits program segments that are less than 64 KB to be placed close together. Figure 3.3 shows a typical layout of the program segments in memory (the segment numbers and the relative placement of the program segments shown are arbitrary).

At any given time, only those memory locations addressed by the four segment registers are accessible; that is, only four memory segments are *active*. However, the contents of a segment register can be modified by a program to address different segments.

3.2.4 Pointer and Index Registers: SP, BP, SI, DI

The registers SP, BP, SI, and DI normally point to (contain the offset addresses of) memory locations. Unlike segment registers, the pointer and index registers can be used in arithmetic and other operations.

SP (Stack Pointer)

The SP (stack pointer) register is used in conjunction with SS for accessing the stack segment. Operations of the stack are covered in Chapter 8.

BP (Base Pointer)

The BP (base pointer) register is used primarily to access data on the stack. However, unlike SP, we can also use BP to access data in the other segments.

SI (Source Index)

The SI (source index) register is used to point to memory locations in the data segment addressed by DS. By incrementing the contents of SI, we can easily access consecutive memory locations.

DI (Destination Index)

The DI (destination index) register performs the same functions as SI. There is a class of instructions, called *string operations,* that use DI to access memory locations addressed by ES.

3.2.5 Instruction Pointer: IP

The memory registers covered so far are for data access. To access instructions, the 8086 uses the registers CS and IP. The CS register contains the segment number of the next instruction, and the IP contains the offset. IP is updated each time an instruction is executed so that it will point to the next instruction. Unlike the other registers, the IP cannot be directly manipulated by an instruction; that is, an instruction may not contain IP as its operand.

3.2.6 FLAGS Register

The purpose of the FLAGS register is to indicate the status of the microprocessor. It does this by the setting of individual bits called **flags**. There are two kinds of flags: **status flags** and **control flags**. The status flags reflect the result of an instruction executed by the processor. For example, when a subtraction operation results in a 0, the ZF (zero flag) is set to 1 (true). A subsequent instruction can examine the ZF and branch to some code that handles a zero result.

The control flags enable or disable certain operations of the processor; for example, if the IF (interrupt flag) is cleared (set to 0), inputs from the keyboard are ignored by the processor. The status flags are covered in Chapter 5, and the control flags are discussed in Chapters 11 and 15.

3.3 Organization of the PC

A computer system is made up of both hardware and software. It is the software that controls the hardware operations. So, to fully understand the operations of the computer, you also study the software that controls the computer.

3.3.1
The Operating System

The most important piece of software for a computer is the **operating system**. The purpose of the operating system is to coordinate the operations of all the devices that make up the computer system. Some of the operating system functions are

1. reading and executing the commands typed by the user
2. performing I/O operations
3. generating error messages
4. managing memory and other resources

At present, the most popular operating system for the IBM PC is the **disk operating system (DOS)**, also referred to as PC DOS or MS DOS. DOS was designed for the 8086/8088-based computers. Because of this, it can manage only 1 megabyte of memory and it does not support multitasking. However, it can be used on 80286, 80386, and 80486-based machines when they run in real address mode.

One of the many functions performed by DOS is reading and writing information on a disk. Programs and other information stored on a disk are organized into **files**. Each file has a **file name**, which is made up of one to eight characters followed by an optional **file extension** of a period followed by one to three characters. The extension is commonly used to identify the type of file. For example, COMMAND.COM has a file name COMMAND and an extension .COM.

There are several versions of DOS, with each new version having more capabilities. Most commercial programs require the use of version 2.1 or later. DOS is not just one program; it consists of a number of service routines. The user requests a service by typing a command. The latest version, DOS 5.0, also supports a **graphical user interface (gui)**, allowing the use of a mouse.

The DOS routine that services user commands is called **COMMAND.COM**. It is responsible for generating the DOS prompt—that is, C>— and reading user commands. There are two types of user commands, **internal** and **external**.

Internal commands are performed by DOS routines that have been loaded into memory, external commands may refer to DOS routines that have not been loaded or to application programs. In normal operations, many DOS routines are not loaded into memory so as to save memory space.

Because DOS routines reside on disk, a program must be operating when the computer is powered up to read the disk. In Chapter 1 we mentioned that there are system routines stored in ROM that are not destroyed when the power is off. In the PC, they are called **BIOS (Basic Input/Output System)** routines.

BIOS

The BIOS routines perform I/O operations for the PC. Unlike the DOS routines, which operate over the entire PC family, the BIOS routines are machine specific. Each PC model has its own hardware configuration and its own BIOS routines, which invoke the machine's I/O port registers for input and output. The DOS I/O operations are ultimately carried out by the BIOS routines.

Other important functions performed by BIOS are circuit checking and loading of the DOS routines. In section 3.3.4, we discuss the loading of DOS routines.

Figure 3.4 Memory Partitioned into Disjoint Segments

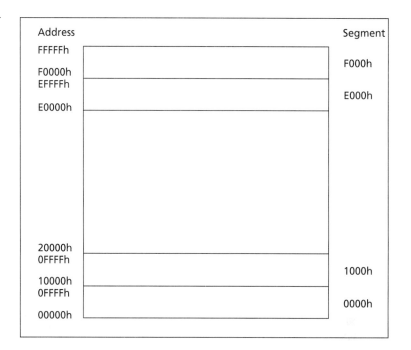

To let DOS and other programs use the BIOS routines, the addresses of the BIOS routines, called **interrupt vectors**, are placed in memory, starting at 00000h. Some DOS routines also have their addresses stored there.

Because IBM has copyrighted its BIOS routines, IBM compatibles use their own BIOS routines. The degree of compatibility has to do with how well their BIOS routines match the IBM BIOS.

3.3.2
Memory Organization of the PC

As indicated in section 3.2.3, the 8086/8088 processor is capable of addressing 1 megabyte of memory. However, not all the memory can be used by an application program. Some memory locations have special meaning for the processor. For example, the first kilobyte (00000 to 003FFh) is used for interrupt vectors.

Other memory locations are reserved by IBM for special purposes, such as for BIOS routines and **video display memory**. The display memory holds the data that are being displayed on the monitor.

To show the memory map of the IBM PC, it is useful to partition the memory into disjoint segments. We start with segment 0, which ends at location 0FFFFh, so the next disjoint segment would begin at 10000h = 1000:0000. Similarly, segment 1000h ends at 1FFFFh and the next disjoint segment begins at 20000h = 2000:0000. Therefore the disjoint segments are 0000h, 1000h, 2000h, ... F000h, and so memory may be partitioned into 16 disjoint segments. See Figure 3.4.

Only the first 10 disjoint memory segments are used by DOS for loading and running application programs. These ten segments, 0000h to 9000h, give us 640 KB of memory. The memory sizes of 8086/8088-based PCs are given in terms of these memory segments. For example, a PC with a 512-KB memory has only eight of these memory segments.

Figure 3.5 Memory Map of the PC

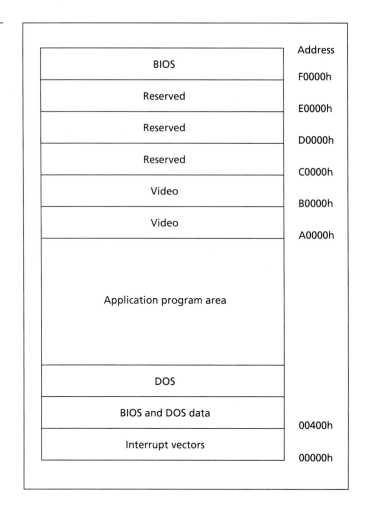

Segments A000h and B000h are used for video display memory. Segments C000h to E000h are reserved. Segment F000h is a special segment because its circuits are ROM instead of RAM, and it contains the BIOS routines and ROM BASIC. Figure 3.5 shows the memory layout.

Table 3.1 Some Common I/O Ports for the PC

Port Address	Description
20h–21h	interrupt controller
60h–63h	keyboard controller
200h–20Fh	game controller
2F8h–2FFh	serial port (COM 2)
320h–32Fh	hard disk
378h–37Fh	parallel printer port 1
3C0h–3CFh	EGA
3D0h–3DFh	CGA
3F8h–3FFh	serial port (COM1)

3.3.3
I/O Port Addresses

The 8086/8088 supports 64 KB of I/O ports. Some common port addresses are given in Table 3.1. In general, direct programming of I/O ports is not recommended because I/O port address usage may vary among computer models.

3.3.4
Start-up Operation

When the PC is powered up, the 8086/8088 processor is put in a reset state, the CS register is set to FFFFh, and IP is set to 0000h. So the first instruction it executes is located at FFFF0h. This memory location is in ROM, and it contains an instruction that transfers control to the starting point of the BIOS routines.

The BIOS routines first check for system and memory errors, and then initialize the interrupt vectors and BIOS data area. Finally, BIOS loads the operating system from the system disk. This is done in two steps; first, the BIOS loads a small program, called the **boot program**, then the boot program loads the actual operating system routines. The boot program is so named because it is part of the operating system; having it load the operating system is like the computer pulling itself up by the bootstraps. Using the boot program isolates the BIOS from any changes made to the operating system and lets it be smaller in size. After the operating system is loaded into memory, COMMAND.COM is then given control.

Summary

- The IBM personal computer family consists of the PC, PC XT, PC AT, PS/1, and the PS/2 models. They use the Intel 8086 family of microprocessors.

- The 8086 family of microprocessors consists of the 8086, 8088, 80186, 80188, 80286, 80386, 80386SX, 80486, and 80486SX.

- The 8086 and 8088 have the same instruction set, and this forms the basic set of instructions for the other microprocessors.

- The 8086 microprocessor contains 14 registers. They may be classified as data registers, segment registers, pointer and index registers, and the FLAGS register.

- The data registers are AX, BX, CX, and DX. These registers may be used for general purposes, and they also perform special functions. The high and low bytes can be addressed separately.

- Each byte in memory has a 20-bit = 5 hex-digit address, starting with 00000h.

- A segment is a 64-KB block of memory. Addresses in memory may be given in segment:offset form. The physical address is obtained by multiplying the segment number by 10h, and adding the offset.

- The segment registers are CS, DS, SS, and ES. When a machine language program is executing, these registers contain the segment numbers of the code, data, stack, and extra data segments.

- The pointer and index registers are SP, BP, SI, DI, and IP. SP is used exclusively for the stack segment. BP can be used to access the stack segment. SI and DI may be used to access data in arrays.
- The IP contains the offset address of the next instruction to be executed.
- The FLAGS register contains the status and control flags. The status flags are set according to the result of an operation. The control flags may be used to enable or disable certain operations of the microprocessor.
- DOS is a collection of routines that coordinates the operations of the computer. The routine that executes user commands is COMMAND.COM.
- Information stored on disk is organized into files. A file has a name and an optional extension.
- The BIOS routines are used to perform I/O operations. The compatibility of PC clones with the IBM PC depends on how well their BIOS routines match those of the IBM PC.
- The BIOS routines are responsible for system testing and loading the operating system when the machine is turned on.

Glossary

basic input/output system, BIOS	Routines that handle input and output operations
boot program	The routine that loads the operating system during start-up
code segment	Memory segment containing a machine language program's instructions
COMMAND.COM	The command processor for DOS
control flags	Flags that enable or disable certain actions of the processor
data segment	Memory segment containing a machine language program's data
disk operating system, DOS	The operating system for the IBM PC
external commands	Commands that correspond to routines residing on disk
file	An organized, named collection of data items treated as a single unit for storage on devices such as disks
file extension	A period followed by one to three characters; used to identify the kind of file
file name	A one- to eight-character name of a file
flags	Bits of the FLAGS register
graphical user interface, gui	A user interface with pointers and graphical symbols

internal commands	DOS commands that are executed by routines that are present in memory
interrupt vectors	Addresses of the BIOS and DOS routines
logical address	An address given in the form segment:offset
memory protection	The ability of a processor to protect the memory used by one program from being used by another running program
memory segment	A 64-KB block of memory
multitasking	The ability of a computer to execute several programs at the same time
offset (of a memory location)	The number of bytes of the location from the beginning of a segment
operating system	A collection of programs that coordinate the operations of the devices that make up a computer system
paragraph	16 bytes
paragraph boundary	A hex address ending in 0
physical address	Address of a memory location; 8086-based machines have 20-bit addresses
protected (virtual address) mode	A processor mode in which the memory used by one program is protected from the actions of another program
real address mode	A processor mode in which the addresses used in a program correspond to a physical memory address
segment number	Number that identifies a memory segment
stack	A data structure used by the processor to implement procedure calls
stack segment	Memory segment containing a machine language program's stack
status flags	Flags that reflect the actions of the processor
video display memory	Memory used for storing data for display on the monitor
virtual memory	The ability of the advanced processors to treat external storage as if it were real internal memory, and therefore execute programs that are too large to be contained in internal memory

Exercises

1. What are the main differences between the 80286 and the 8086 processors?
2. What are the differences between a register and a memory location?
3. List one special function for each of the data registers AX, BX, CX, and DX.

4. Determine the physical address of a memory location given by 0A51:CD90h.
5. A memory location has a physical address 4A37Bh. Compute
   a. the offset address if the segment number is 40FFh.
   b. the segment number if the offset address is 123Bh.
6. What is a paragraph boundary?
7. What determines how compatible an IBM PC clone is with an authentic IBM PC?
8. What is the maximum amount of memory that DOS allocates for loading run files? Assume that DOS occupies up to the byte 0FFFFh.

For the following exercises, refer to Appendix B.

9. Give DOS commands to do the following. Suppose that A is the logged drive.
   a. Copy FILE1 in the current directory to FILE1A on the disk in drive B.
   b. Copy all files with an .ASM extension to the disk in drive B.
   c. Erase all files with a .BAK extension
   d. List all file names in the current directory that begin with A.
   e. Set the date to September 21, 1991.
   f. Print the file FILE5.ASM on the printer.
10. Suppose that (a) the root directory has subdirectories A, B, and C; (b) A has subdirectories A1 and A2; (c) A1 has a subdirectory A1A. Give DOS commands to
    a. Create the preceding directory tree.
    b. Make A1A the current directory.
    c. Have DOS display the current directory.
    d. Remove the preceding directory tree.

4
Introduction to IBM PC Assembly Language

Overview

This chapter covers the essential steps in creating, assembling, and executing an assembly language program. By the chapter's end you will be able to write simple but interesting programs that carry out useful tasks, and run them on the computer.

As with any programming language, the first step is to learn the syntax, which for assembly language is relatively simple. Next we show how variables are declared, and introduce basic data movement and arithmetic instructions. Finally, we cover program organization; you'll see that assembly language programs are comprised of code, data, and the stack, just like a machine language program.

Because assembly language instructions are so basic, input/output is much harder in assembly language than in high-level languages. We use DOS functions for I/O; they are easy to invoke and are fast enough for all but the most demanding applications.

An assembly language program must be converted to a machine language program before it can be executed. Section 4.10 explains the steps. To demonstrate, we'll create sample programs. They illustrate some standard assembly language programming techniques and serve as models for the exercises.

4.1 Assembly Language Syntax

Assembly language programs are translated into machine language instructions by an assembler, so they must be written to conform to the assembler's specifications. In this book we use the Microsoft Macro Assembler (MASM). Assembly language code is generally not case sensitive, but we use upper case to differentiate code from the rest of the text.

Statements

Programs consist of statements, one per line. Each statement is either an **instruction**, which the assembler translates into machine code, or an **assembler directive**, which instructs the assembler to perform some specific task, such as allocating memory space for a variable or creating a procedure. Both instructions and directives have up to four fields:

name   operation   operand(s)   comment

At least one blank or tab character must separate the fields. The fields do not have to be aligned in a particular column, but they must appear in the above order.

An example of an instruction is

```
START:        MOV CX,5       ;initialize counter
```

Here, the name field consists of the label START:. The operation is MOV, the operands are CX and 5, and the comment is ;initialize counter.

An example of an assembler directive is

```
MAIN            PROC
```

MAIN is the name, and the operation field contains PROC. This particular directive creates a procedure called MAIN.

4.1.1 Name Field

The name field is used for instruction labels, procedure names, and variable names. The assembler translates names into memory addresses.

Names can be from 1 to 31 characters long, and may consist of letters, digits, and the special characters ? . @ _ $ %. Embedded blanks are not allowed. If a period is used, it must be the first character. Names may not begin with a digit. The assembler does not differentiate between upper and lower case in a name.

Examples of legal names

```
COUNTER1
@character
SUM_OF_DIGITS
$1000
DONE?
.TEST
```

Examples of illegal names

`TWO WORDS`	contains a blank
`2abc`	begins with a digit
`A45.28`	. not first character
`YOU&ME`	contains an illegal character

4.1.2
Operation Field

For an instruction, the operation field contains a symbolic operation code (opcode). The assembler translates a symbolic opcode into a machine language opcode. Opcode symbols often describe the operation's function; for example, MOV, ADD, SUB.

In an assembler directive, the operation field contains a pseudo-operation code (**pseudo-op**). Pseudo-ops are not translated into machine code; rather, they simply tell the assembler to do something. For example, the PROC pseudo-op is used to create a procedure.

4.1.3
Operand Field

For an instruction, the operand field specifies the data that are to be acted on by the operation. An instruction may have zero, one, or two operands. For example,

`NOP`	no operands; does nothing
`INC  AX`	one operand; adds 1 to the contents of AX
`ADD  WORD1,2`	two operands; adds 2 to the contents of memory word WORD1

In a two-operand instruction, the first operand is the **destination operand**. It is the register or memory location where the result is stored (*note:* some instructions don't store the result). The second operand is the **source operand**. The source is usually not modified by the instruction.

For an assembler directive, the operand field usually contains more information about the directive.

4.1.4
Comment Field

The comment field of a statement is used by the programmer to say something about what the statement does. A semicolon marks the beginning of this field, and the assembler ignores anything typed after the semicolon. Comments are optional, but because assembly language is so low-level, it is almost impossible to understand an assembly language program without comments. In fact, good programming practice dictates a comment on almost every line. The art of good commentary is developed through practice. Don't say something obvious, like this:

`MOV CX,0            ;move 0 to CX`

Instead, use comments to put the instruction into the context of the program:

`MOV CX,0            ;CX counts terms, initially 0`

It is also permissible to make an entire line a comment, and to use them to create space in a program:

```
;
;initialize registers
;
MOV AX,0
MOV BX,0
```

4.2 Program Data

The processor operates only on binary data. Thus, the assembler must translate all data representation into binary numbers. However, in an assembly language program we may express data as binary, decimal, or hex numbers, and even as characters.

Numbers

A binary number is written as a bit string followed by the letter "B" or "b"; for example, 1010B.

A decimal number is a string of decimal digits, ending with an optional "D" or "d".

A hex number must begin with a decimal digit and end with the letter "H" or "h"; for example, 0ABCH (the reason for this is that the assembler would be unable to tell whether a symbol such as "ABCH" represents the variable name "ABCH" or the hex number ABC).

Any of the preceding numbers may have an optional sign.

Here are examples of legal and illegal numbers for MASM:

Number	Type
11011	decimal
11011B	binary
64223	decimal
-21843D	decimal
1,234	illegal—contains a nondigit character
1B4DH	hex
1B4D	illegal hex number—doesn't end in "H"
FFFFH	illegal hex number—doesn't begin with a decimal digit
0FFFFH	hex

Characters

Characters and character strings must be enclosed in single or double quotes; for example, "A" or 'hello'. Characters are translated into their ASCII codes by the assembler, so there is no difference between using "A" and 41h (the ASCII code for "A") in a program.

Table 4.1 Data-Defining Pseudo-ops

Pseudo-op	Stands for
DB	define byte
DW	define word
DD	define doubleword (two consecutive words)
DQ	define quadword (four consecutive words)
DT	define tenbytes (ten consecutive bytes)

4.3 Variables

Variables play the same role in assembly language that they do in high-level languages. Each variable has a data type and is assigned a memory address by the program. The data-defining pseudo-ops and their meanings are listed in Table 4.1. Each pseudo-op can be used to set aside one or more data items of the given type.

In this section we use DB and DW to define byte variables, word variables, and arrays of bytes and words. The other data-defining pseudo-ops are used in Chapter 18 in connection with multiple-precision and noninteger operations.

4.3.1 Byte Variables

The assembler directive that defines a byte variable takes the following form:

```
name    DB              initial_value
```

where the pseudo-op DB stands for "Define Byte".

For example,

```
ALPHA   DB              4
```

This directive causes the assembler to associate a memory byte with the name ALPHA, and initialize it to 4. A question mark ("?") used in place of an initial value sets aside an uninitialized byte; for example,

```
BYT     DB              ?
```

The decimal range of initial values that can be specified is –128 to 127 if a signed interpretation is being given, or 0 to 255 for an unsigned interpretation. These are the ranges of values that fit in a byte.

4.3.2 Word Variables

The assembler directive for defining a word variable has the following form:

```
name    DW              initial_value
```

The pseudo-op DW means "Define Word." For example,

```
WRD          DW                      -2
```

as with byte variables, a question mark in place of an initial value means an uninitialized word. The decimal range of initial values that can be specified is –32768 to 32767 for a signed interpretation, or 0 to 65535 for an unsigned interpretation.

4.3.3 Arrays

In assembly language, an **array** is just a sequence of memory bytes or words. For example, to define a three-byte array called B_ARRAY, whose initial values are 10h, 20h, and 30h, we can write,

```
B_ARRAY      DB                      10H,20H,30H
```

The name B_ARRAY is associated with the first of these bytes, B_ARRAY+1 with the second, and B_ARRAY+2 with the third. If the assembler assigns the offset address 0200h to B_ARRAY, then memory would look like this:

Symbol	Address	Contents
B_ARRAY	200h	10h
B_ARRAY+1	201h	20h
B_ARRAY+2	202h	30h

In the same way, an array of words may be defined. For example,

```
W_ARRAY      DW                      1000,40,29887,329
```

sets up an array of four words, with initial values 1000, 40, 29887, and 329. The initial word is associated with the name W_ARRAY, the next one with W_ARRAY + 2, the next with W_ARRAY + 4, and so on. If the array starts at 0300h, it will look like this:

Symbol	Address	Contents
W_ARRAY	0300h	1000d
W_ARRAY+2	0302h	40d
W_ARRAY+4	0304	29887d
W_ARRAY+6	0306h	329d

High and Low Bytes of a Word

Sometimes we need to refer to the high and low bytes of a word variable. Suppose we define

```
WORD1        DW                      1234H
```

The low byte of WORD1 contains 34h, and the high byte contains 12h. The low byte has symbolic address WORD1, and the high byte has symbolic address WORD1+1.

Character Strings

An array of ASCII codes can be initialized with a string of characters. For example,

```
LETTERS            DB                   'ABC'
```
is equivalent to
```
LETTERS            DB                   41H,42H,43H
```

Inside a string, the assembler differentiates between upper and lower case. Thus, the string "abc" is translated into three bytes with values 61h, 62h, and 63h.

It is possible to combine characters and numbers in one definition; for example,

```
MSG DB                     'HELLO',0AH,0DH,'$'
```
is equivalent to
```
MSG DB                     48H,45H,4CH,4CH,4FH,0AH,0DH,24H
```

4.4 Named Constants

To make assembly language code easier to understand, it is often desirable to use a symbolic name for a constant quantity.

EQU *(Equates)*

To assign a name to a constant, we can use the **EQU** (equates) pseudo-op. The syntax is

```
name               EQU                        constant
```

For example, the statement

```
LF                 EQU                        0AH
```

assigns the name LF to 0Ah, the ASCII code of the line feed character. The name LF may now be used in place of 0Ah anywhere in the program. Thus, the assembler translates the instructions

```
MOV DL,0AH
```
and
```
MOV DL,LF
```
into the same machine instruction.

The symbol on the right of an EQU can also be a string. For example,
```
PROMPT EQU 'TYPE YOUR NAME'
```
Then instead of
```
MSG DB       'TYPE YOUR NAME'
```
we could say
```
MSG DB             PROMPT
```

Note: no memory is allocated for EQU names.

Figure 4.1 MOV AX,WORD1

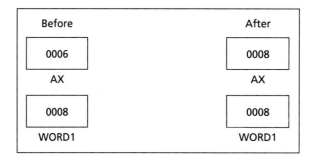

4.5
A Few Basic Instructions

There are over a hundred instructions in the instruction set for the 8086 CPU; there are also instructions designed especially for the more advanced processors (see Chapter 20). In this section we discuss six of the most useful instructions for transferring data and doing arithmetic. The instructions we present can be used with either byte or word operands.

In the following, WORD1 and WORD2 are word variables, and BYTE1 and BYTE2 are byte variables. Recall from Chapter 3 that AH is the high byte of register AX, and BL is the low byte of BX.

4.5.1
MOV and XCHG

The **MOV** instruction is used to transfer data between registers, between a register and a memory location, or to move a number directly into a register or memory location. The syntax is

```
MOV   destination,source
```

Here are some examples:

```
MOV   AX,WORD1
```

This reads "Move WORD1 to AX". The contents of register AX are replaced by the contents of memory location WORD1. The contents of WORD1 are unchanged. In other words, a copy of WORD1 is sent to AX (Figure 4.1).

```
MOV   AX,BX
```

AX gets what was previously in BX. BX is unchanged.

```
MOV   AH,'A'
```

Figure 4.2 XCHG AH,BL

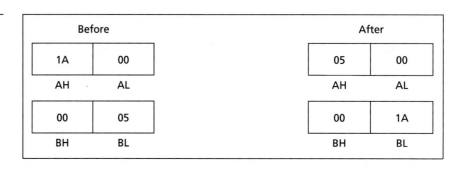

Table 4.2 Legal Combinations of Operands for MOV and XCHG

MOV

Source Operand	Destination Operand			
	General register	Segment register	Memory location	Constant
General register	yes	yes	yes	no
Segment register	yes	no	yes	no
Memory location	yes	yes	no	no
Constant	yes	no	yes	no

XCHG

Source Operand	Destination Operand	
	General register	Memory location
General register	yes	yes
Memory location	yes	no

This is a move of the number 041h (the ASCII code of "A") into register AH. The previous value of AH is overwritten (replaced by new value).

The **XCHG** (exchange) operation is used to exchange the contents of two registers, or a register and a memory location. The syntax is

```
XCHG   destination,source
```

An example is

```
XCHG   AH,BL
```

This instruction swaps the contents of AH and BL, so that AH contains what was previously in BL and BL contains what was originally in AH (Figure 4.2). Another example is

```
XCHG   AX,WORD1
```

which swaps the contents of AX and memory location WORD1.

Restrictions on MOV and XCHG

For technical reasons, there are a few restrictions on the use of MOV and XCHG. Table 4.2 shows the allowable combinations. Note in particular that a MOV or XCHG between memory locations is not allowed. For example,

```
ILLEGAL: MOV WORD1,WORD2
```

but we can get around this restriction by using a register:

```
MOV   AX,WORD2
MOV   WORD1,AX
```

Figure 4.3 ADD WORD1,AX

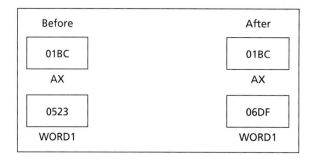

4.5.2
ADD, SUB, INC, and DEC

The **ADD** and **SUB** instructions are used to add or subtract the contents of two registers, a register and a memory location, or to add (subtract) a number to (from) a register or memory location. The syntax is

```
ADD   destination,source
SUB   destination,source
```

For example,

```
ADD   WORD1,AX
```

This instruction, "Add AX to WORD1," causes the contents of AX and memory word WORD1 to be added, and the sum is stored in WORD1. AX is unchanged (Figure 4.3).

```
SUB   AX,DX
```

In this example, "Subtract DX from AX," the value of DX is subtracted from the value of AX, with the difference being stored in AX. DX is unchanged (Figure 4.4).

Table 4.3 Legal Combinations of Operands for ADD and SUB

Source Operand	Destination Operand	
	General register	Memory location
General register	yes	yes
Memory location	yes	no
Constant	yes	yes

Figure 4.4 SUB AX,DX

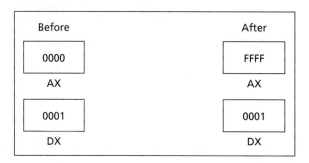

Figure 4.5 INC WORD1

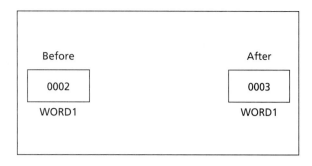

```
ADD  BL,5
```

This is an addition of the number 5 to the contents of register BL.

As was the case with MOV and XCHG, there are some restrictions on the combinations of operands allowable with ADD and SUB. The legal ones are summarized in Table 4.3. Direct addition or subtraction between memory locations is illegal; for example,

```
ILLEGAL: ADD BYTE1,BYTE2
```

A solution is to move BYTE2 to a register before adding, thus

```
MOV AL,BYTE2           ;AX gets BYTE2
ADD BYTE1,AL           ;add it to BYTE1
```

INC (increment) is used to add 1 to the contents of a register or memory location and **DEC** (decrement) subtracts 1 from a register or memory location. The syntax is

```
INC destination
DEC destination
```

For example,

```
INC WORD1
```

adds 1 to the contents of WORD1 (Figure 4.5).

```
DEC BYTE1
```

subtracts 1 from variable BYTE1 (Figure 4.6).

Figure 4.6 DEC BYTE1

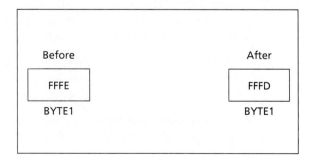

Figure 4.7 NEG BX

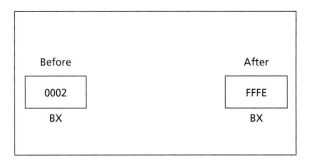

4.5.3
NEG

NEG is used to negate the contents of the destination. NEG does this by replacing the contents by its two's complement. The syntax is

```
NEG  destination
```

The destination may be a register or memory location. For example,

```
NEG BX
```

negates the contents of BX (Figure 4.7).

Type Agreement of Operands

The operands of the preceding two-operand instruction must be of the same type; that is, both bytes or words. Thus an instruction such as

```
MOV AX,BYTE1      ;illegal
```

is not allowed. However, the assembler will accept both of the following instructions:

```
MOV AH, 'A'
```

and

```
MOV AX, 'A'
```

In the former case, the assembler reasons that since the destination AH is a byte, the source must be a byte, and it moves 41h into AH. In the latter case, it assumes that because the destination is a word, so is the source, and it moves 0041h into AX.

4.6
Translation of High-Level Language to Assembly Language

To give you a feeling for the preceding instructions, we'll translate some high-level language assignment statements into assembly language. Only MOV, ADD, SUB, INC, DEC, and NEG are used, although in some cases a better job could be done by using instructions that are covered later. In the discussion, A and B are word variables.

Statement	Translation	
B = A	MOV AX,A	;move A into AX
	MOV B,AX	;and then into B

As was pointed out earlier, a direct memory–memory move is illegal, so we must move the contents of A into a register before moving it to B.

```
                A = 5 - A               MOV  AX,5           ;put 5 in AX
                                        SUB  AX,A           ;AX contains 5 - A
                                        MOV  A,AX           ;put it in A
```

This example illustrates one approach to translating assignment statements: do the arithmetic in a register—for example, AX—then move the result into the destination variable. In this case, there is another, shorter way:

```
                                        NEG  A              ;A = -A
                                        ADD  A,5            ;A = 5 - A
```

The next example shows how to do multiplication by a constant.

```
                A = B - 2 x A           MOV  AX,B           ;AX has B
                                        SUB  AX,A           ;AX has B - A
                                        SUB  AX,A           ;AX has B - 2 x A
                                        MOV  A,AX           ;move result to A
```

4.7 Program Structure

Chapter 3 noted that machine language programs consist of code, data, and stack. Each part occupies a memory segment. The same organization is reflected in an assembly language program. This time, the code, data, and stack are structured as program segments. Each program segment is translated into a memory segment by the assembler.

We will use the simplified segment definitions that were introduced for the Microsoft Macro Assembler (MASM), version 5.0. They are discussed further in Chapter 14, along with the full segment definitions.

4.7.1 Memory Models

The size of code and data a program can have is determined by specifying a **memory model** using the .MODEL directive. The syntax is

```
                .MODEL          memory_model
```

The most frequently used memory models are SMALL, MEDIUM, COMPACT, and LARGE. They are described in Table 4.4. Unless there is a lot of code or data, the appropriate model is SMALL. The .MODEL directive should come before any segment definition.

Table 4.4 Memory Models

Model	Description
SMALL	code in one segment data in one segment
MEDIUM	code in more than one segment data in one segment
COMPACT	code in one segment data in more than one segment
LARGE	code in more than one segment data in more than one segment no array larger than 64k bytes
HUGE	code in more than one segment data in more than one segment arrays may be larger than 64k bytes

4.7.2 Data Segment

A program's **data segment** contains all the variable definitions. Constant definitions are often made here as well, but they may be placed elsewhere in the program since no memory allocation is involved. To declare a data segment, we use the directive .DATA, followed by variable and constant declarations. For example,

```
.DATA
WORD1           DW 2
WORD2           DW 5
MSG             DB 'THIS IS A MESSAGE'
MASK            EQU 10010010B
```

4.7.3. Stack Segment

The purpose of the **stack segment** declaration is to set aside a block of memory (the stack area) to store the stack. The stack area should be big enough to contain the stack at its maximum size. The declaration syntax is

```
.STACK          size
```

where size is an optional number that specifies the stack area size in bytes. For example,

```
.STACK          100H
```

sets aside 100h bytes for the stack area (a reasonable size for most applications). If size is omitted, 1 KB is set aside for the stack area.

4.7.4 Code Segment

The **code segment** contains a program's instructions. The declaration syntax is

```
.CODE name
```

where name is the optional name of the segment (there is no need for a name in a SMALL program, because the assembler will generate an error).

Inside a code segment, instructions are organized as procedures. The simplest procedure definition is

```
name    PROC
;body of the procedure
name    ENDP
```

where name is the name of the procedure; PROC and ENDP are pseudo-ops that delineate the procedure.

Here is an example of a code segment definition:

```
.CODE
MAIN PROC
;main procedure instructions
MAIN ENDP
;other procedures go here
```

4.7.5
Putting It Together

Now that you have seen all the program segments, we can construct the general form of a .SMALL model program. With minor variations, this form may be used in most applications:

```
.MODEL SMALL
.STACK 100H
.DATA
;data definitions go here
.CODE
MAIN    PROC
;instructions go here
MAIN    ENDP
;other procedures go here
END     MAIN
```

The last line in the program should be the END directive, followed by name of the main procedure.

4.8
Input and Output Instructions

In Chapter 1, you saw that the CPU communicates with the peripherals through I/O registers called *I/O ports*. There are two instructions, IN and OUT, that access the ports directly. These instructions are used when fast I/O is essential; for example, in a game program. However, most applications programs do not use IN and OUT because (1) port addresses vary among computer models, and (2) it's much easier to program I/O with the service routines provided by the manufacturer.

There are two categories of I/O service routines: (1) the Basic Input/Output System *(BIOS)* routines and (2) the DOS routines. The BIOS routines are stored in ROM and interact directly with the I/O ports. In Chapter 12, we use them to carry out basic screen operations such as moving the cursor and scrolling the screen. The DOS routines can carry out more complex tasks; for example, printing a character string; actually they use the BIOS routines to perform direct I/O operations.

The INT Instruction

To invoke a DOS or BIOS routine, the **INT** (interrupt) instruction is used. It has the format

```
INT interrupt_number
```

where interrupt_number is a number that specifies a routine. For example, INT 16h invokes a BIOS routine that performs keyboard input. Chapter 15 covers the INT instruction in more detail. In the following, we use a particular DOS routine, INT 21h.

4.8.1
INT 21h

INT 21h may be used to invoke a large number of DOS functions (see Appendix C); a particular function is requested by placing a function number in the AH register and invoking INT 21h. Here we are interested in the following functions:

Function number	Routine
1	single-key input
2	single-character output
9	character string output

INT 21h functions expect input values to be in certain registers and return output values in other registers. These are listed as we describe each function.

Function 1:
Single-Key Input

Input: AH = 1
Output: AL = ASCII code if character key is pressed
              = 0 if non-character key is pressed

To invoke the routine, execute these instructions:

```
MOV AH,1            ;input key function
INT 21h             ;ASCII code in AL
```

The processor will wait for the user to hit a key if necessary. If a character key is pressed, AL gets its ASCII code; the character is also displayed on the screen. If any other key is pressed, such as an arrow key, F1–F10, and so on, AL will contain 0. The instructions following the INT 21h can examine AL and take appropriate action.

Because INT 21h, function 1, doesn't prompt the user for input, he or she might not know whether the computer is waiting for input or is occupied by some computation. The next function can be used to generate an input prompt.

Function 2:
Display a character or execute a control function

Input: AH = 2
          DL = ASCII code of the display character or
                control character
Output: AL = ASCII code of the display character or
                control character

To display a character with this function, we put its ASCII code in DL. For example, the following instructions cause a question mark to appear on the screen:

```
MOV AH,2            ;display character function
MOV DL,'?'          ;character is '?'
INT 21h             ;display character
```

After the character is displayed, the cursor advances to the next position on the line (if at the end of the line, the cursor moves to the beginning of the next line).

Function 2 may also be used to perform control functions. If DL contains the ASCII code of a control character, INT 21h causes the control function to be performed. The principal control characters are as follows:

ASCII code (Hex)	Symbol	Function
7	BEL	beep (sounds a tone)
8	BS	backspace
9	HT	tab
A	LF	line feed (new line)
D	CR	carriage return (start of current line)

On execution, AL gets the ASCII code of the control character.

4.9 A First Program

Our first program will read a character from the keyboard and display it at the beginning of the next line.

We start by displaying a question mark:

```
MOV AH,2             ;display character function
MOV DL,'?'           ;character is '?'
INT 21h              ;display character
```

The second instruction moves 3Fh, the ASCII code for "?", into DL.

Next we read a character:

```
MOV AH,1             ;read character function
INT 21h              ;character in AL
```

Now we would like to display the character on the next line. Before doing so, the character must be saved in another register. (We'll see why in a moment.)

```
MOV BL,AL            ;save it in BL
```

To move the cursor to the beginning of the next line, we must execute a carriage return and line feed. We can perform these functions by putting the ASCII codes for them in DL and executing INT 21h.

```
MOV AH,2             ;display character function
MOV DL,0DH           ;carriage return
INT 21h              ;execute carriage return
MOV DL,0AH           ;line feed
INT 21h              ;execute line feed
```

The reason why we had to move the input character from AL to BL is that the INT 21h, function 2, changes AL.

Finally we are ready to display the character:

```
MOV DL,BL            ;get character
INT 21h              ;and display it
```

Here is the complete program:

Program Listing PGM4_1.ASM

```
TITLE PGM4_1: ECHO PROGRAM
.MODEL SMALL
.STACK 100H
.CODE
MAIN PROC
;display prompt
     MOV AH,2             ;display character function
```

```
                MOV DL,'?'           ;character is '?'
                INT 21H              ;display it
        ;input a character
                MOV AH,1             ;read character function
                INT 21H              ;character in AL
                MOV BL,AL            ;save it in BL
        ;go to a new line
                MOV AH,2             ;display character function
                MOV DL,0DH           ;carriage return
                INT 21H              ;execute carriage return
                MOV DL,0AH           ;line feed
                INT 21H              ;execute line feed
        ;display character
                MOV DL,BL            ;retrieve character
                INT 21H              ;and display it
        ;return to DOS
                MOV AH,4CH           ;DOS exit function
                INT 21H              ;exit to DOS
        MAIN    ENDP
                END     MAIN
```

Because no variables were used, the data segment was omitted.

Terminating a Program

The last two lines in the MAIN procedure require some explanation. When a program terminates, it should return control to DOS. This can be accomplished by executing INT 21h, function 4Ch.

4.10 Creating and Running a Program

We are now ready to look at the steps involved in creating and running a program. The preceding program is used to demonstrate the process. The four steps are (Figure 4.8):

1. Use a text editor or word processor to create a **source program file**.
2. Use an assembler to create a machine language **object file**.
3. Use the LINK program (see description later) to link one or more object files to create a **run file**.
4. Execute the run file.

In this demonstration, the system files we need (assembler and linker) are in drive C and the programmer's disk is in drive A. We make A the default drive so that the files created will be stored on the programmer's disk.

Step 1. Create the Source Program File

We used an editor to create the preceding program, with file name PGM4_1.ASM. The .ASM extension is the conventional extension used to identify an assembly language source file.

Figure 4.8 Programming Steps

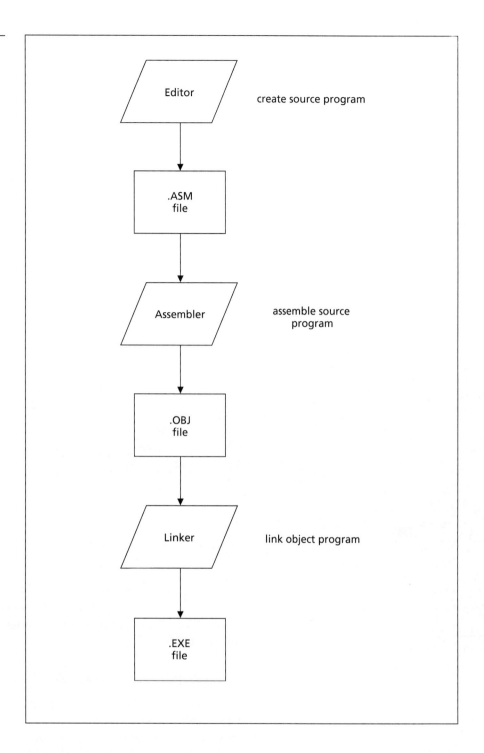

Step 2. Assemble the Program

We use the Microsoft Macro Assembler (MASM) to translate the source file PGM4_1.ASM into a machine language object file called PGM 4_1.OBJ. The simplest command is (user's response appears in boldface):

```
A>C:MASM PGM4_1;
Microsoft (R) Macro Assembler Version 5.10
Copyright (C) Microsoft Corp 1981, 1988. All rights reserved.
 50060 + 418673 Bytes symbol space free
     0 Warning Errors
     0 Severe Errors
```

After printing copyright information, MASM checks the source file for syntax errors. If it finds any, it will display the line number of each error and a short description. Because there are no errors here, it translates the assembly language code into a machine language object file named PGM4_1.OBJ.

The semicolon after the preceding command means that we *don't* want certain optional files generated. Let's omit it and see what happens:

```
A>C:MASM PGM4_1
Microsoft (R) Macro Assembler Version 5.10
Copyright (C) Microsoft Corp 1981, 1988. All rights reserved.
Object filename [PGM4_1.OBJ]:
Source listing [NUL.LST]: PGM4_1
Cross-reference [NUL.CRF]: PGM4_1
 50060 + 418673 Bytes symbol space free
     0 Warning Errors
     0 Severe Errors
```

This time MASM prints the names of the files it can create, then waits for us to supply names for the files. The default names are enclosed in square brackets. To accept a name, just press return. The default name NUL means that no file will be created unless the user does specify a name, so we reply with the name PGM4_1.

The Source Listing File

The source listing file (**.LST file**) is a line-numbered text file that displays assembly language code and the corresponding machine code side by side, and gives other information about the program. It is especially helpful for debugging purposes, because MASM's error messages refer to line numbers.

The Cross-Reference File

The cross-reference file (**.CRF file**) is a listing of names that appear in the program and the line numbers on which they occur. It is useful in locating variables and labels in a large program.

Examples of .LST and .CRF files are shown in Appendix D, along with other MASM options.

Step 3. Link the Program

The .OBJ file created in step 2 is a machine language file, but it cannot be executed because it doesn't have the proper run file format. In particular,

1. because it is not known where a program will be loaded in memory for execution, some machine code addresses may not have been filled in.
2. some names used in the program may not have been defined in the program. For example, it may be necessary to create several files for a large program and a procedure in one file may refer to a name defined in another file.

The LINK program takes one or more object files, fills in any missing addresses, and combines the object files into a single executable file (**.EXE file**). This file can be loaded into memory and run.
To link the program, type

`A>C:LINK PGM4_1;`

As before, if the semicolon is omitted, the linker will prompt you for names of the output files generated. See Appendix D.

Step 4. Run the Program

To run it, just type the run file name, with or without the .EXE extension.

```
A>PGM4_1
?A
A
```

The program prints a "?" and waits for us to enter a character. We enter "A" and the program echoes it on the next line.

4.11 Displaying a String

In our first program, we used INT 21h, functions 1 and 2, to read and display a single character. Here is another INT 21h function that can be used to display a character string:

INT 21h, Function 9:
Display a String

Input: DX = offset address of string.
        The string must end with a '$' character.

The "$" marks the end of the string and is not displayed. If the string contains the ASCII code of a control character, the control function is performed.
To demonstrate this function, we will write a program that prints "HELLO!" on the screen. This message is defined in the data segment as

`MSG DB    'HELLO!$'`

The LEA Instruction

INT 21h, function 9, expects the offset address of the character string to be in DX. To get it there, we use a new instruction:

```
LEA destination, source
```

where destination is a general register and source is a memory location. **LEA** stands for "Load Effective Address." It puts a copy of the source offset address into the destination. For example,

```
LEA DX, MSG
```

puts the offset address of the variable MSG into DX.

Because our second program contains a data segment, it will begin with instructions that initialize DS. The following paragraph explains why these instructions are needed.

Program Segment Prefix

When a program is loaded in memory, DOS prefaces it with a 256-byte **program segment prefix (PSP)**. The PSP contains information about the program. So that programs may access this area, DOS places its segment number in both DS and ES before executing the program. The result is that DS does not contain the segment number of the data segment. To correct this, a program containing a data segment begins with these two instructions:

```
MOV AX,@DATA
MOV DS,AX
```

@Data is the name of the data segment defined by .DATA. The assembler translates the name @DATA into a segment number. Two instructions are needed because a number (the data segment number) may not be moved directly into a segment register.

With DS initialized, we may print the "HELLO!" message by placing its address in DX and executing INT 21h:

```
LEA   DX,MSG          ;get message
MOV   AH,9            ;display string function
INT   21h             ;display string
```

Here is the complete program:

Program Listing PGM4_2.ASM

```
TITLE PGM4_2: PRINT STRING PROGRAM
.MODEL   SMALL
.STACK   100H
.DATA
MSG   DB    'HELLO!$'
.CODE
MAIN  PROC
;initialize DS
      MOV AX,@DATA
      MOV DS,AX          ;initialize DS
;display message
      LEA DX,MSG         ;get message
      MOV AH,9           ;display string function
      INT 21h            ;display message
;return to DOS
      MOV AH,4CH
```

```
            INT 21h               ;DOS exit
MAIN    ENDP
        END MAIN
```

And here is a sample execution:

A> **PGM4_2**
HELLO!

4.12 A Case Conversion Program

We will now combine most of the material covered in this chapter into a single program. This program begins by prompting the user to enter a lowercase letter, and on the next line displays another message with the letter in uppercase. For example,

ENTER A LOWERCASE LETTER: **a**
IN UPPER CASE IT IS: A

We use EQU to define CR and LF as names for the constants 0DH and 0AH.

```
CR  EQU 0DH
LF  EQU 0AH
```

The messages and the input character can be stored in the data segment like this:

```
MSG1 DB 'ENTER A LOWERCASE LETTER: $'
MSG2 DB CR,LF,'IN UPPER CASE IT IS: '
CHAR DB ?,'$'
```

In defining MSG2 and CHAR, we have used a helpful trick: because the program is supposed to display the second message and the letter (after conversion to upper case) on the next line, MSG2 starts with the ASCII codes for carriage return and line feed; when MSG2 is displayed with INT 21h, function 9, these control functions are executed and the output is displayed on the next line. Because MSG2 does not end with '$', INT 21h goes on and displays the character stored in CHAR.

Our program begins by displaying the first message and reading the character:

```
LEA DX,MSG1         ;get first message
MOV AH,9            ;display string function
INT 21h             ;display first message
MOV AH,1            ;read character function
INT 21h             ;read a small letter into AL
```

Having read a lowercase letter, the program must convert it to upper case. In the ASCII character sequence, the lowercase letters begin at 61h and the uppercase letters start at 41h, so subtraction of 20h from the contents of AL does the conversion:

```
SUB AL,20H          ;convert it to upper case
MOV CHAR,AL         ;and store it
```

Now the program displays the second message and the uppercase letter:

```
        LEA DX,MSG2            ;get second message
        MOV AH,9               ;display string function
        INT 21h                ;display message and uppercase letter
```

Here is the complete program:

Program Listing PGM4_3.ASM

```
TITLE PGM4_3: CASE CONVERSION PROGRAM
.MODEL   SMALL
.STACK   100H
.DATA
MSG1    DB      'ENTER A LOWER CASE LETTER: $'
MSG2    DB      0DH,0AH,'IN UPPER CASE IT IS: '
CHAR    DB      ?,'$'
.CODE
MAIN    PROC
;initialize DS
        MOV     AX,@DATA       ;get data segment
        MOV     DS,AX          ;initialize DS
;print user prompt
        LEA     DX,MSG1        ;get first message
        MOV     AH,9           ;display string function
        INT     21H            ;display first message
;input a character and convert to upper case
        MOV     AH,1           ;read character function
        INT     21H            ;read a small letter into AL
        SUB     AL, 20H        ;convert it to upper case
        MOV     CHAR,AL        ;and store it
;display on the next line
        LEA     DX, MSG2       ;get second message
        MOV     AH,9           ;display string function
        INT     21H            ;display message and upper case
;DOS exit                      ;letter in front
        MOV     AH,4CH
        INT     21H            ;DOS exit
MAIN    ENDP
        END MAIN
```

Summary

- Assembly language programs are made up of statements. A statement is either an instruction to be executed by the computer, or a directive for the assembler.

- Statements have name, operation, operand(s), and comment fields.

- A symbolic name can contain up to 31 characters. The characters can be letters, digits, and certain special symbols.

- Numbers may be written in binary, decimal, or hex.

- Characters and character strings must be enclosed in single or double quotes.

- Directives DB and DW are used to define byte and word variables, respectively. EQU can be used to give names to constants.
- A program generally contains a code segment, a data segment, and a stack segment.
- MOV and XCHG are used to transfer data. There are some restrictions for the use of these instructions; for example, they may not operate directly between memory locations.
- ADD, SUB, INC, DEC, and NEG are some of the basic arithmetic instructions.
- There are two ways to do input and output on the IBM PC: (1) by direct communication with I/O devices, (2) by using BIOS or DOS interrupt routines.
- The direct method is fastest, but is tedious to program and depends on specific hardware circuits.
- Input and output of characters and strings may be done by the DOS routine INT 21h.
- INT 21h, function 1, causes a keyboard character to be read into AL.
- INT 21h, function 2, causes the character whose ASCII code is in DL to be displayed. If DL contains the code of a control character, the control function is performed.
- INT 21h, function 9, causes the string whose offset address is in DX to be displayed. The string must end with a "$" character.

Glossary

array	A sequence of memory bytes or words
assembler directive	Directs the assembler to perform some specific task
code segment	Part of the program that holds the instructions
.CRF file	A file created by the assembler that lists names that appear in a program and line numbers where they occur
data segment	Part of the program that holds variables
destination operand	First operand in an instruction—receives the result
.EXE file	Same as run file
instruction	A statement that the assembler translates to machine code
.LST file	A line-numbered file created by the assembler that displays assembly language code, machine code, and other information about a program
memory model	Organization of a program that indicates the amount of code and data

object file	The machine language file created by the assembler from the source program file
Program segment prefix, PSP	The 256-byte area that precedes the program in memory—contains information about the program
pseudo-op	Assembler directive
run file	The executable machine language file created by the LINK program
source operand	Second operand in an instruction—usually not changed by the instruction
source program file	A program text file created with a word processor or text editor
stack segment	Part of the program that holds the run-time stack
variable	Symbolic name for a memory location that stores data

New Instructions

ADD	INT	NEG
DEC	LEA	SUB
INC	MOV	XCHG

New Pseudo-Ops

.CODE	.MODEL	EQU
.DATA	.STACK	

Exercises

1. Which of the following names are legal in IBM PC assembly language?
    a. TWO_WORDS
    b. ?1
    c. Two words
    d. .@?
    e. $145
    f. LET'S_GO
    g. @DATA

2. Which of the following are legal numbers? If they are legal, tell whether they are binary, decimal, or hex numbers.
    a. 246
    b. 246h
    c. 1001
    d. 1,101
    e. 2A3h
    f. FFFEh

g. 0Ah

h. Bh

i. 1110b

3. If it is legal, give data definition pseudo-ops to define each of the following.

   a. A word variable A initialized to 52
   b. A word variable WORD1, uninitialized
   c. A byte variable B, initialized to 25h
   d. A byte variable C1, uninitialized
   e. A word variable WORD2, initialized to 65536
   f. A word array ARRAY1, initialized to the first five positive integers (i.e. 1–5)
   g. A constant BELL equal to 07h
   h. A constant MSG equal to 'THIS IS A MESSAGE$'

4. Suppose that the following data are loaded starting at offset 0000h:

   ```
   A       DB          7
   B       DW          1ABCh
   C       DB          'HELLO'
   ```

   a. Give the offset address assigned to variables A, B, and C.
   b. Give the contents of the byte at offset 0002h in hex.
   c. Give the contents of the byte at offset 0004h in hex.
   d. Give the offset address of the character "O" in "HELLO."

5. Tell whether each of the following instructions is legal or illegal. W1 and W2 are word variables, and B1 and B2 are byte variables.

   a. `MOV   DS,AX`
   b. `MOV   DS,1000h`
   c. `MOV   CS,ES`
   d. `MOV   W1,DS`
   e. `XCHG  W1,W2`
   f. `SUB   5,B1`
   g. `ADD   B1,B2`
   h. `ADD   AL,256`
   i. `MOV   W1,B1`

6. Using only MOV, ADD, SUB, INC, DEC, and NEG, translate the following high-level language assignment statements into assembly language. A, B, and C are word variables.

   a. A = B − A
   b. A = −(A + 1)
   c. C = A + B
   d. B = 3 × B + 7
   e. A = B − A − 1

7. Write instructions (not a complete program) to do the following.

   a. Read a character, and display it at the next position on the same line.
   b. Read an uppercase letter (omit error checking), and display it at the next position on the same line in lower case.

Programming Exercises

8. Write a program to (a) display a "?", (b) read two decimal digits whose sum is less than 10, (c) display them and their sum on the next line, with an appropriate message.

   Sample execution:

   ```
   ?27
   THE SUM OF 2 AND 7 IS 9
   ```

9. Write a program to (a) prompt the user, (b) read first, middle, and last initials of a person's name, and (c) display them down the left margin.

   Sample execution:

   ```
   ENTER THREE INITIALS: JFK
   J
   F
   K
   ```

10. Write a program to read one of the hex digits A–F, and display it on the next line in decimal.

    Sample execution:

    ```
    ENTER A HEX DIGIT: C
    IN DECIMAL IT IS 12
    ```

11. Write a program to display a 10 × 10 solid box of asterisks.
    Hint: declare a string in the data segment that specifies the box, and display it with INT 21h, function 9h.

12. Write a program to (a) display "?", (b) read three initials, (c) display them in the middle of an 11 × 11 box of asterisks, and (d) beep the computer.

5

The Processor Status and the FLAGS Register

Overview

One important feature that distinguishes a computer from other machines is the computer's ability to make decisions. The circuits in the CPU can perform simple decision making based on the current state of the processor. For the 8086 processor, the processor state is implemented as nine individual bits called **flags**. Each decision made by the 8086 is based on the values of these flags.

The flags are placed in the FLAGS register and they are classified as either status flags or control flags. The status flags reflect the result of a computation. In this chapter, you will see how they are affected by the machine instructions. In Chapter 6, you will see how they are used to implement jump instructions that allow programs to have multiple branches and loops. The control flags are used to enable or disable certain operations of the processor; they are covered in later chapters.

In section 5.4 we introduce the DOS program DEBUG. We'll show how to use DEBUG to trace through a user program and to display registers, flags, and memory locations.

5.1 The FLAGS Register

Figure 5.1 shows the **FLAGS register**. The **status flags** are located in bits 0, 2, 4, 6, 7, and 11 and the **control flags** are located in bits 8, 9, and 10. The other bits have no significance. *Note:* it's not important to remember

Figure 5.1 The FLAGS Register

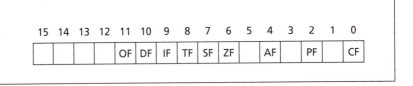

which bit is which flag—Table 5.1 gives the names of the flags and their symbols. In this chapter, we concentrate on the status flags.

The Status Flags

As stated earlier, the processor uses the status flags to reflect the result of an operation. For example, if SUB AX,AX is executed, the zero flag becomes 1, thereby indicating that a zero result was produced. Now let's get to know the status flags.

Carry Flag (CF)

CF = 1 if there is a carry out from the most significant bit (msb) on addition, or there is a borrow into the msb on subtraction; otherwise, it is 0. CF is also affected by shift and rotate instructions (Chapter 7).

Parity Flag (PF)

PF = 1 if the low byte of a result has an even number of one bits (even parity). It is 0 if the low byte has odd parity. For example, if the result of a word addition is FFFEh, then the low byte contains 7 one bits, so PF = 0.

Table 5.1 Flag Names and Symbols

Status Flags

Bit	Name	Symbol
0	Carry flag	CF
2	Parity flag	PF
4	Auxiliary carry flag	AF
6	Zero flag	ZF
7	Sign flag	SF
11	Overflow flag	OF

Control Flags

Bit	Name	Symbol
8	Trap flag	TF
9	Interrupt flag	IF
10	Direction flag	DF

Auxiliary Carry Flag (AF)

AF = 1 if there is a carry out from bit 3 on addition, or a borrow into bit 3 on subtraction. AF is used in binary-coded decimal (BCD) operations (Chapter 18).

Zero Flag (ZF)

ZF = 1 for a zero result, and ZF = 0 for a nonzero result.

Sign Flag (SF)

SF = 1 if the msb of a result is 1; it means the result is negative if you are giving a signed interpretation. SF = 0 if the msb is 0.

Overflow Flag (OF)

OF = 1 if signed overflow occurred, otherwise it is 0. The meaning of overflow is discussed next.

5.2 Overflow

The phenomenon of overflow is associated with the fact that the range of numbers that can be represented in a computer is limited.

Chapter 2 explained that the (decimal) range of signed numbers that can be represented by a 16-bit word is –32768 to 32767; for an 8-bit byte the range is –128 to 127. For unsigned numbers, the range for a word is 0 to 65535; for a byte, it is 0 to 255. If the result of an operation falls outside these ranges, overflow occurs and the truncated result that is saved will be incorrect.

Examples of Overflow

Signed and unsigned overflows are independent phenomena. When we perform an arithmetic operation such as addition, there are four possible outcomes: (1) no overflow, (2) signed overflow only, (3) unsigned overflow only, and (4) both signed and unsigned overflows.

As an example of unsigned overflow but not signed overflow, suppose AX contains FFFFh, BX contains 0001h, and ADD AX,BX is executed. The binary result is

```
    1111 1111 1111 1111
  + 0000 0000 0000 0001
  ---------------------
  1 0000 0000 0000 0000
```

If we are giving an unsigned interpretation, the correct answer is 10000h = 65536, but this is out of range for a word operation. A 1 is carried out of the msb and the answer stored in AX, 0000h, is wrong, so unsigned overflow occurred. But the stored answer is correct as a signed number, for FFFFh = –1, 0001h = 1, and FFFFh + 0001h = –1 + 1 = 0, so signed overflow did not occur.

As an example of signed but not unsigned overflow, suppose AX and BX both contain 7FFFh, and we execute ADD AX,BX. The binary result is

```
    0111 1111 1111 1111
+   0111 1111 1111 1111
    ───────────────────
    1111 1111 1111 1110  = FFFEh
```

The signed and unsigned decimal interpretation of 7FFFh is 32767. Thus for both signed and unsigned addition, 7FFFh + 7FFFh = 32767 + 32767 = 65534. This is out of range for signed numbers; the signed interpretation of the stored answer FFFEh is –2, so signed overflow occurred. However, the unsigned interpretation of FFFEh is 65534, which is the right answer, so there is no unsigned overflow.

There are two questions to be answered in connection with overflow: (1) how does the CPU indicate overflow, and (2) how does it know that overflow occurred?

How the Processor Indicates Overflow

The processor sets OF = 1 for signed overflow and CF = 1 for unsigned overflow. It is then up to the program to take appropriate action, and if nothing is done immediately the result of a subsequent instruction may cause the overflow flag to be turned off.

In determining overflow, the processor does not interpret the result as either signed or unsigned. The action it takes is to use both interpretations for each operation and to turn on CF or OF for unsigned overflow or signed overflow, respectively.

It is the programmer who is interpreting the results. If a signed interpretation is being given, then only OF is of interest and CF can be ignored; conversely, for an unsigned interpretation CF is important but not OF.

How the Processor Determines that Overflow Occurred

Many instructions can cause overflow; for simplicity, we'll limit the discussion to addition and subtraction.

Unsigned Overflow

On addition, unsigned overflow occurs when there is a carry out of the msb. This means that the correct answer is larger than the biggest unsigned number; that is, FFFFh for a word and FFh for a byte. On subtraction, unsigned overflow occurs when there is a borrow into the msb. This means that the correct answer is smaller than 0.

Signed Overflow

On addition of numbers with the same sign, signed overflow occurs when the sum has a different sign. This happened in the preceding example when we were adding 7FFFh and 7FFFh (two positive numbers), but got FFFEh (a negative result).

Subtraction of numbers with different signs is like adding numbers of the same sign. For example, A – (–B) = A + B and –A –(+B) = –A + –B. Signed overflow occurs if the result has a different sign than expected. See example 5.3, in the next section.

In addition of numbers with different signs, overflow is impossible, because a sum like A + (–B) is really A – B, and because A and B are small enough to fit in the destination, so is A – B. For exactly the same reason, subtraction of numbers with the same sign cannot give overflow.

Actually, the processor uses the following method to set the OF: If the carries into and out of the msb don't match—that is, there is a carry into the msb but no carry out, or if there is a carry out but no carry in—then signed overflow has occurred, and OF is set to 1. See example 5.2, in the next section.

5.3 How Instructions Affect the Flags

In general, each time the processor executes an instruction, the flags are altered to reflect the result. However, some instructions don't affect any of the flags, affect only some of them, or may leave them undefined. Because the jump instructions studied in Chapter 6 depend on the flag settings, it's important to know what each instruction does to the flags. Let's return to the seven basic instructions introduced in Chapter 4. They affect the flags as follows:

Instruction	Affects flags
MOV/XCHG	none
ADD/SUB	all
INC/DEC	all except CF
NEG	all (CF = 1 unless result is 0, OF = 1 if word operand is 8000h, or byte operand is 80h)

To get you used to seeing how these instructions affect the flags, we will do several examples. In each example, we give an instruction, the contents of the operands, and predict the result and the settings of CF, PF, ZF, SF, and OF (we ignore AF because it is used only for BCD arithmetic).

Example 5.1 ADD AX,BX, where AX contains FFFFh, BX contains FFFFh.

Solution:
```
   FFFFh
 + FFFFh
 ───────
 1 FFFEh
```

The result stored in AX is FFFEh = 1111 1111 1111 1110.

- SF = 1 because the msb is 1.
- PF = 0 because there are 7 (odd number) of 1 bits in the low byte of the result.
- ZF = 0 because the result is nonzero.
- CF = 1 because there is a carry out of the msb on addition.
- OF = 0 because the sign of the stored result is the same as that of the numbers being added (as a binary addition, there is a carry into the msb and also a carry out).

Example 5.2 ADD AL,BL, where AL contains 80h, BL contains 80h.

Solution:
```
   80h
 + 80h
 ─────
 1 00h
```

The result stored in AL is 00h.

- SF = 0 because the msb is 0.
- PF = 1 because all the bits in the result are 0.
- ZF = 1 because the result is 0.
- CF = 1 because there is a carry out of the msb on addition.
- OF = 1 because the numbers being added are both negative, but the result is 0 (as a binary addition, there is no carry into the msb but there is a carry out).

Example 5.3 SUB AX,BX, where AX contains 8000h and BX contains 0001h.

Solution:
```
    8000h
  - 0001h
  -------
    7FFFh = 0111 1111 1111 1111
```

The result stored in AX is 7FFFh.

- SF = 0 because the msb is 0.
- PF = 1 because there are 8 (even number) one bits in the low byte of the result.
- ZF = 0 because the result is nonzero.
- CF = 0 because a smaller unsigned number is being subtracted from a larger one.

Now for OF. In a signed sense, we are subtracting a positive number from a negative one, which is like adding two negatives. Because the result is positive (the wrong sign), OF = 1.

Example 5.4 INC AL, where AL contains FFh.

Solution:
```
     FFh
   + 1h
   -----
   1 00h
```

The result stored in AL is 00h. SF = 0, PF = 1, ZF = 1. Even though there is a carry out, CF is unaffected by INC. This means that if CF = 0 before the execution of the instruction, CF will still be 0 afterward.

OF = 0 because numbers of unlike sign are being added (there is a carry into the msb and also a carry out).

Example 5.5 MOV AX, −5

Solution: The result stored in AX is −5 = FFFBh.

None of the flags are affected by MOV.

Example 5.6 NEG AX, where AX contains 8000h.

Solution:
$$8000h = 1000\ 0000\ 0000\ 0000$$
$$\text{one's complement} = 0111\ 1111\ 1111\ 1111$$
$$+\ 1$$
$$\overline{1000\ 0000\ 0000\ 0000} = 8000h$$

The result stored in AX is 8000h.

- SF = 1, PF = 1, ZF = 0.
- CF = 1, because for NEG CF is always 1 unless the result is 0.
- OF = 1, because the result is 8000h; when a number is negated, we would expect a sign change, but because 8000h is its own two's complement, there is no sign change.

In the next section, we introduce a program that lets us see the actual setting of the flags.

5.4 The DEBUG Program

The DEBUG program provides an environment in which a program may be tested. The user can step through a program, and display and change the registers and memory. It is also possible to enter assembly code directly, which DEBUG converts to machine code and stores in memory. A tutorial for DEBUG and CODEVIEW, a more sophisticated debugger, may be found in Appendix E.

We use DEBUG to demonstrate the way instructions affect the flags. To that end, the following program has been created.

Program Listing PGM5_1.ASM
```
TITLE PGM5_1:CHECK FLAGS
;used in DEBUG to check flag settings
.MODEL   SMALL
.STACK   100H
.CODE
MAIN     PROC
         MOV   AX,4000H      ;AX = 4000h
         ADD   AX,AX         ;AX = 8000h
         SUB   AX,0FFFFH     ;AX = 8001h
         NEG   AX            ;AX = 7FFFh
         INC   AX            ;AX = 8000h
         MOV   AH,4CH
         INT   21H           ;DOS exit
MAIN     ENDP
         END   MAIN
```

We assemble and link the program, producing the run file PGM5_1.EXE, which is on a disk in drive A. In the following, the user's responses are in boldface.

The DEBUG program is on the DOS disk, which is in drive C. To enter DEBUG with our demonstration program, we type

C>**DEBUG A:PGM5_1.EXE**

DEBUG responds by its prompt, " –", and waits for a command to be entered. First, we can view the registers by typing "R".

```
-R
AX=0000  BX=0000  CX=001F  DX=0000  SP=000A  BP=0000  SI=0000  DI=0000
DS=0ED5  ES=0ED5  SS=0EE5  CS=0EE6  IP=0000   NV UP DI PL NZ NA PO NC
0EE6:0000 B80040      MOV     AX,4000
```

The display shows the contents of the registers in hex. On the third line of the display, we see

```
0EE6:0000 B80040      MOV     AX,4000
```

0EE6:0000 is the address of the next instruction to be executed, in segment:offset form. B80040h is the machine code of that instruction. Segment 0EE6h is where DOS decided to load the program; if you try this demonstration, you will probably see a different segment number.

The eight pairs of letters appearing on the second line at the right are the current flag settings. The flags appear in this order: OF, DF, IF, SF, ZF, AF, PF, and CF. Table 5.2 gives the symbols DEBUG uses for the flags. You can see that they have been cleared by DEBUG. The meaning of the control flag symbols are explained in Chapters 11 and 15.

To step through our program, we use the "T" (trace) command. Before doing so, let's display the registers again.

```
-R
AX=0000  BX=0000  CX=001F  DX=0000  SP=000A  BP=0000  SI=0000  DI=0000
DS=0ED5  ES=0ED5  SS=0EE5  CS=0EE6  IP=0000   NV UP DI PL NZ NA PO NC
0EE6:0000 B80040      MOV     AX,4000
```

The first instruction is MOV AX,4000h.

```
-T
AX=4000  BX=0000  CX=001F  DX=0000  SP=000A  BP=0000  SI=0000  DI=0000
DS=0ED5  ES=0ED5  SS=0EE5  CS=0EE6  IP=0003   NV UP DI PL NZ NA PO NC
0EE6:0003 03C0        ADD     AX,AX
```

Execution of MOV AX,4000h puts 4000h in AX. The flags are unchanged since a MOV doesn't affect them. Now let's execute ADD AX,AX:

```
-T
AX=8000  BX=0000  CX=001F  DX=0000  SP=000A  BP=0000  SI=0000  DI=0000
DS=0ED5  ES=0ED5  SS=0EE5  CS=0EE6  IP=0005   OV UP DI NG NZ NA PE NC
0EE6:0005 2DFFFF      SUB     AX,FFFF
```

Table 5.2 DEBUG Flag Symbols

Status Flag	Set (1) Symbol	Clear (0) Symbol
CF	CY (carry)	NC (no carry)
PF	PE (even parity)	PO (odd parity)
AF	AC (auxiliary carry)	NA (no auxiliary carry)
ZF	ZR (zero)	NZ (nonzero)
SF	NG (negative)	PL (plus)
OF	OV (overflow)	NV (no overflow)
Control Flag		
DF	DN (down)	UP (up)
IF	EI (enable interrupts)	DI (disable interrupts)

AX now contains 4000h + 4000h = 8000h. SF becomes 1 (NG) to indicate a negative result. Signed overflow is indicated by OF = 1 (OV) because we added two positive numbers and got a negative result. PF = 1 (PE) because the low byte of AX contains no 1's.

Next we trace SUB AX,0FFFFh:

```
-T
AX=8001  BX=0000  CX=001F  DX=0000  SP=000A  BP=0000  SI=0000  DI=0000
DS=0ED5  ES=0ED5  SS=0EE5  CS=0EE6  IP=0008  NV UP DI NG NZ AC PO CY
0EE6:0008 F7D8         NEG     AX
```

AX gets 8000h − FFFFh = 8001h. OF changes back to 0 (NV), because we are subtracting numbers of like sign, so signed overflow is impossible. However, CF = 1 (CY) indicates that we got unsigned overflow, because we have subtracted a bigger unsigned number from a smaller one, which requires a borrow into the msb. PF = 0 (PO) because the low byte of AX has a single 1.

Now let's trace NEG AX:

```
-T
AX=7FFF  BX=0000  CX=001F  DX=0000  SP=000A  BP=0000  SI=0000  DI=0000
DS=0ED5  ES=0ED5  SS=0EE5  CS=0EE6  IP=000A  NV UP DI PL NZ AC PE CY
0EE6:000A 40           INC     AX
```

AX gets the two's complement of 8001h = 7FFFh. For NEG, CF = 1 (CY) unless the result is 0, which is not the case here. OF = 0 (NV) because the result is not 8000h.

Finally, we execute INC AX:

```
-T
AX=8000  BX=0000  CX=001F  DX=0000  SP=000A  BP=0000  SI=0000  DI=0000
DS=0ED5  ES=0ED5  SS=0EE5  CS=0EE6  IP=000B   OV UP DI NG NZ AC PE CY
0EE6:000B B44C          MOV     AH,4C
```

OF changes back to 1 (OV) because we added two positives (7FFFh and 1), and got a negative result. Even though there was no carry out of the msb, CF stays 1 because INC doesn't affect this flag.

To complete execution of the program, we can type "G" (go):

```
-G
Program terminated normally
```

and to exit DEBUG, type "Q" (quit)

```
-Q
C>
```

Summary

- The FLAGS register is one of the registers in the 8086 microprocessor. Six of the bits are called status flags, and three are control flags.

- The status flags reflect the result of an operation. They are the carry flag (CF), parity flag (PF), auxiliary carry flag (AF), zero flag (ZF), sign flag (SF), and overflow flag (OF).

- CF is 1 if an add or subtract operation generates a carry out or borrow into the most significant bit position; otherwise, it is 0.

- PF is 1 if there is an even number of 1 bits in the result; otherwise, it is 0.

- AF is 1 if there is a carry out or borrow into bit 3 in the result; otherwise, it is 0.

- ZF is 1 if the result is 0; otherwise, it is 0.

- SF is 1 if the most significant bit of the result is 1; otherwise, it is 0.

- OF is 1 if the correct signed result is too big to fit in the destination; otherwise, it is 0.

- Overflow occurs when the correct result is outside the range of values represented by the computer. Unsigned overflow occurs if an unsigned interpretation is being given to the result, and signed overflow happens if a signed interpretation is being given.
- The processor uses CF and OF to indicate overflow: CF = 1 means that unsigned overflow occurred, and OF = 1 indicates signed overflow.
- The processor sets CF if there is a carry out of the msb on addition, or a borrow into the msb on subtraction. In the latter case, this means that a larger unsigned number is being subtracted from a smaller one.
- The processor sets OF if there is a carry into the msb but no carry out, or if there is a carry out of the msb but no carry in.
- There is another way to tell whether signed overflow occurred on addition and subtraction. On addition of numbers of like sign, signed overflow occurs if the result has a different sign; subtraction of numbers of different sign is like adding numbers of the same sign, and signed overflow occurs if the result has a different sign.
- On addition of numbers of different sign, or subtraction of numbers of the same sign, signed overflow is impossible.
- Generally the execution of each instruction affects the flags, but some instructions don't affect any of the flags, and some affect only some of the flags.
- The settings of the flags is part of the DEBUG display.
- The DEBUG program may be used to trace a program. Some of its commands are "R", to display registers; "T", to trace an instruction; and "G", to execute a program.

Glossary

control flags	Flags that are used to enable or disable certain operations of the CPU
flags	Bits of the FLAGS register that represent a condition of the CPU
FLAGS register	Register in the CPU whose bits are flags
status flags	Flags that reflect the result of an instruction executed by the CPU

Exercises

1. For each of the following instructions, give the new destination contents and the new settings of CF, SF, ZF, PF, and OF. Suppose that the flags are initially 0 in each part of this question.

    a. `ADD AX,BX`   where AX contains 7FFFh and BX contains 0001h
    b. `SUB AL,BL`   where AL contains 01h and BL contains FFh
    c. `DEC AL`   where AL contains 00h

d. NEG AL   where AL contains 7Fh
e. XCHG AX,BX   where AX contains 1ABCh and BX contains 712Ah
f. ADD AL,BL   where AL contains 80h and BL contains FFh
g. SUB AX,BX   where AX contains 0000h and BX contains 8000h
h. NEG AX   where AX contains 0001h

2. a. Suppose that AX and BX both contain positive numbers, and ADD AX,BX is executed. Show that there is a carry into the msb but no carry out of the msb if, and only if, signed overflow occurs.

    b. Suppose AX and BX both contain negative numbers, and ADD AX,BX is executed. Show that there is a carry out of the msb but no carry into the msb if, and only if, signed overflow occurs.

3. Suppose ADD AX,BX is executed. In each of the following parts, the first number being added is the contents of AX, and the second number is the contents of BX. Give the resulting value of AX and tell whether signed or unsigned overflow occurred.

    a.   512Ch
       + 4185h

    b.   FE12h
       + 1ACBh

    c.   E1E4h
       + DAB3h

    d.   7132h
       + 7000h

    e.   6389h
       + 1176h

4. Suppose SUB AX,BX is executed. In each of the following parts, the first number is the initial contents of AX and the second number is the contents of BX. Give the resulting value of AX and tell whether signed or unsigned overflow occurred.

    a.   2143h
       − 1986h

    b.   81FEh
       − 1986h

    c.   19BCh
       − 81FEh

    d.   0002h
       − FE0Fh

    e.   8BCDh
       − 71ABh

6

Flow Control Instructions

Overview

For assembly language programs to carry out useful tasks, there must be a way to make decisions and repeat sections of code. In this chapter we show how these things can be accomplished with the jump and loop instructions.

The jump and loop instructions transfer control to another part of the program. This transfer can be unconditional or can depend on a particular combination of status flag settings.

After introducing the jump instructions, we'll use them to implement high-level language decision and looping structures. This application will make it much easier to convert a pseudocode algorithm to assembly code.

6.1 An Example of a Jump

To get an idea of how the jump instructions work, we will write a program to display the entire IBM character set.

Program Listing PGM6_1.ASM
```
1:      TITLE       PGM6_1: IBM CHARACTER DISPLAY
2:      .MODEL      SMALL
3:      .STACK      100H
4:      .CODE
5:      MAIN        PROC
6:                  MOV     AH,2        ;display char function
7:                  MOV     CX,256      ;no. of chars to display
8:                  MOV     DL,0        ;DL has ASCII code of null char
9:      PRINT_LOOP:
```

```
10:             INT     21h             ;display a char
11:             INC     DL              ;increment ASCII code
12:             DEC     CX              ;decrement counter
13:             JNZ     PRINT_LOOP      ;keep going if CX not 0
14: ;DOS exit
15:             MOV     AH,4CH
16:             INT     21h
17: MAIN        ENDP
18:             END     MAIN
```

There are 256 characters in the IBM character set. Those with codes 32 to 127 are the standard ASCII display characters introduced in Chapter 2. IBM also provides a set of graphics characters with codes 0 to 31 and 128 to 255.

To display the characters, we use a loop (lines 9 to 13). Before entering the loop, AH is initialized to 2 (single-character display) and DL is set to 0, the initial ASCII code. CX is the loop counter; it is set to 256 before entering the loop and is decremented after each character is displayed.

The instruction that controls the loop is JNZ (Jump if Not Zero). If the result of the preceding instruction (DEC CX) is not zero, then the JNZ instruction transfers control to the instruction at label PRINT_LOOP. When CX finally contains 0, the program goes on to execute the DOS return instructions. Figure 6.1 shows the output of the program. Of course, the ASCII codes of backspace, carriage return, and so on cause a control function to be performed, rather than displaying a symbol.

Note: PRINT_LOOP is the first statement label we've used in a program. Labels are needed in situations where one instruction refers to another, as is the case here. Labels end with a colon, and to make labels stand out they are usually placed on a line by themselves. If so, they refer to the instruction that follows.

6.2 Conditional Jumps

JNZ is an example of a **conditional jump instruction**. The syntax is

```
Jxxx                    destination_label
```

Figure 6.1 Output of PGM6_1

If the condition for the jump is true, the next instruction to be executed is the one at destination_label, which may precede or follow the jump instruction itself. If the condition is false, the instruction immediately following the jump is done next. For JNZ, the condition is that the result of the previous operation is not zero.

Range of a Conditional Jump

The structure of the machine code of a conditional jump requires that destination_label must precede the jump instruction by no more than 126 bytes, or follow it by no more than 127 bytes (we'll show how to get around this restriction later).

How the CPU Implements a Conditional Jump

To implement a conditional jump, the CPU looks at the FLAGS register. You already know it reflects the result of the last thing the processor did. If the conditions for the jump (expressed as a combination of status flag settings) are true, the CPU adjusts the IP to point to the destination label, so that the instruction at this label will be done next. If the jump condition is false, then IP is not altered; this means that the next instruction in line will be done.

In the preceding program, the CPU executes JNZ PRINT_LOOP by inspecting ZF. If ZF = 0, control transfers to PRINT_LOOP; if ZF = 1, the program goes on to execute MOV AH,4CH.

Table 6.1 shows the conditional jumps. There are three categories: (1) the **signed jumps** are used when a signed interpretation is being given to results, (2) the **unsigned jumps** are used for an unsigned interpretation, and (3) the **single-flag jumps**, which operate on settings of individual flags. *Note:* the jump instructions themselves do not affect the flags.

The first column of Table 6.1 gives the opcodes for the jumps. Many of the jumps have two opcodes; for example, JG and JNLE. Both opcodes produce the same machine code. Use of one opcode or its alternate is usually determined by the context in which the jump appears.

The CMP Instruction

The jump condition is often provided by the **CMP** *(compare)* instruction. It has the form

```
CMP    destination, source
```

This instruction compares destination and source by computing destination contents minus source contents. The result is not stored, but the flags are affected. The operands of CMP may not both be memory locations. Destination may not be a constant. *Note:* CMP is just like SUB, except that destination is not changed.

For example, suppose a program contains these lines:

```
CMP    AX,BX
JG     BELOW
```

where AX = 7FFFh, and BX = 0001. The result of CMP AX,BX is 7FFFh − 0001h = 7FFEh. Table 6.1 shows that the jump condition for JG is satisfied, because ZF = SF = OF = 0, so control transfers to label BELOW.

Table 6.1 Conditional Jumps

Signed Jumps

Symbol	Description	Condition for Jumps
JG/JNLE	jump if greater than / jump if not less than or equal to	ZF = 0 and SF = OF
JGE/JNL	jump if greater than or equal to / jump if not less than	SF = OF
JL/JNGE	jump if less than / jump if not greater than or equal to	SF <> OF
JLE/JNG	jump if less than or equal / jump if not greater than	ZF = 1 or SF <> OF

Unsigned Conditional Jumps

Symbol	Description	Condition for Jumps
JA/JNBE	jump if above / jump if not below or equal	CF = 0 and ZF = 0
JAE/JNB	jump if above or equal / jump if not below	CF = 0
JB/JNAE	jump if below / jump if not above or equal	CF = 1
JBE/JNA	jump if equal / jump if not above	CF = 1 or ZF = 1

Single-Flag Jumps

Symbol	Description	Condition for Jumps
JE/JZ	jump if equal / jump if equal to zero	ZF = 1
JNE/JNZ	jump if not equal / jump if not zero	ZF = 0
JC	jump if carry	CF = 1
JNC	jump if no carry	CF = 0
JO	jump if overflow	OF = 1
JNO	jump if no overflow	OF = 0
JS	jump if sign negative	SF = 1
JNS	jump if nonnegative sign	SF = 0
JP/JPE	jump if parity even	PF = 1
JNP/JPO	jump if parity odd	PF = 0

Interpreting the Conditional Jumps

In the example just given, we determined by looking at the flags after CMP was executed that control transfers to label BELOW. This is how the CPU implements a conditional jump. But it's not necessary for a programmer to think about the flags; you can just use the name of the jump to decide if control transfers to the destination label. In the following,

```
CMP   AX,BX
JG    BELOW
```

if AX is greater than BX (in a signed sense), then JG (jump if greater than) transfers to BELOW.

Even though CMP is specifically designed to be used with the conditional jumps, they may be preceded by other instructions, as in PGM6_1. Another example is

```
DEC   AX
JL    THERE
```

Here, if the contents of AX, in a signed sense, is less than 0, control transfers to THERE.

Signed Versus Unsigned Jumps

Each of the signed jumps corresponds to an analogous unsigned jump; for example, the signed jump JG and the unsigned jump JA. Whether to use a signed or unsigned jump depends on the interpretation being given. In fact, Table 6.1 shows that these jumps operate on different flags: the signed jumps operate on ZF, SF, and OF, while the unsigned jumps operate on ZF and CF. Using the wrong kind of jump can lead to incorrect results.

For example, suppose we're giving a signed interpretation. If AX = 7FFFh, BX = 8000h, and we execute

```
CMP   AX,BX
JA    BELOW
```

then even though 7FFFh > 8000h in a signed sense, the program does not jump to BELOW. The reason is that 7FFFh < 8000h in an unsigned sense, and we are using the unsigned jump JA.

Working with Characters

In working with the standard ASCII character set, either signed or unsigned jumps may be used, because the sign bit of a byte containing a character code is always zero. However, unsigned jumps should be used when comparing extended ASCII characters (codes 80h to FFh).

Example 6.1 Suppose AX and BX contain signed numbers. Write some code to put the biggest one in CX.

Solution:

```
      MOV   CX,AX        ;put AX in CX
      CMP   BX,CX        ;is BX bigger?
      JLE   NEXT         ;no, go on
      MOV   CX,BX        ;yes, put BX in CX
NEXT:
```

6.3 The JMP Instruction

The **JMP** *(jump)* instruction causes an unconditional transfer of control **(unconditional jump)**. The syntax is

```
JMP   destination
```

where destination is usually a label in the same segment as the JMP itself (see Appendix F for a more general description).

JMP can be used to get around the range restriction of a conditional jump. For example, suppose we want to implement the following loop:

```
TOP:

;body of the loop
DEC   CX                ;decrement counter
JNZ   TOP               ;keep looping if CX > 0
MOV   AX,BX
```

and the loop body contains so many instructions that label TOP is out of range for JNZ (more than 126 bytes before JMP TOP). We can do this:

```
TOP:

;body of the loop
              DEC   CX          ;decrement counter
              JNZ   BOTTOM      ;keep looping if CX > 0
              JMP   EXIT
BOTTOM:
              JMP   TOP
EXIT:
              MOV   AX,BX
```

6.4 High-Level Language Structures

We've shown that the jump instructions can be used to implement branches and loops. However, because the jumps are so primitive, it is difficult, especially for beginning programmers, to code an algorithm with them without some guidelines.

Because you have probably had some experience with high-level language constructs—such as the IF-THEN-ELSE decision structure or WHILE loops—we'll show how these structures can be simulated in assembly language. In each case, we will first express the structure in a high-level pseudocode.

6.4.1 Branching Structures

In high-level languages, branching structures enable a program to take different paths, depending on conditions. In this section, we'll look at three structures.

IF-THEN

The IF-THEN structure may be expressed in pseudocode as follows:

```
IF condition is true
 THEN
   execute true-branch statements
END_IF
```

See Figure 6.2.

The *condition* is an expression that is true or false. If it is true, the true-branch statements are executed. If it is false, nothing is done, and the program goes on to whatever follows.

Example 6.2 Replace the number in AX by its absolute value.

Solution: A pseudocode algorithm is

```
IF AX < 0
 THEN
   replace AX by -AX
END_IF
```

It can be coded as follows:

```
;if AX < 0
            CMP    AX,0         ;AX < 0 ?
            JNL    END_IF       ;no, exit
;then
            NEG    AX           ;yes, change sign
END_IF:
```

The condition AX < 0 is expressed by CMP AX,0. If AX is not less than 0, there is nothing to do, so we use a JNL (jump if not less) to jump around the NEG AX. If condition AX < 0 is true, the program goes on to execute NEG AX.

Figure 6.2 IF-THEN

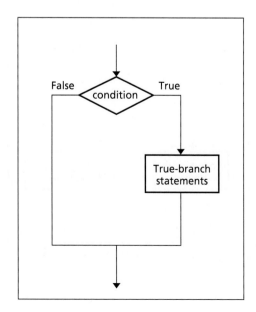

IF-THEN-ELSE

```
IF condition is true
 THEN
   execute true-branch statements
 ELSE
   execute false-branch statements
END_IF
```

See Figure 6.3.

In this structure, if *condition* is true, the true-branch statements are executed. If *condition* is false, the false-branch statements are done.

Example 6.3 Suppose AL and BL contain extended ASCII characters. Display the one that comes first in the character sequence.

Solution:

```
IF AL <= BL
 THEN
   display the character in AL
 ELSE
   display the character in BL
END_IF
```

It can be coded like this:

```
              MOV  AH,2        ;prepare to display
;if AL <= BL
              CMP  AL,BL       ;AL <= BL?
              JNBE ELSE_       ;no, display char in BL
;then                          ;AL <= BL
              MOV  DL,AL       ;move char to be displayed
              JMP  DISPLAY     ;go to display
ELSE_:                         ;BL < AL
              MOV  DL,BL
```

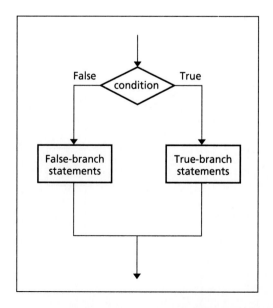

Figure 6.3 IF-THEN-ELSE

```
DISPLAY:
                INT 21h         ;display it
END_IF
```

Note: the label ELSE_ is used because ELSE is a reserved word.

The condition AL <= BL is expressed by CMP AL,BL. If it's false, the program jumps around the true-branch statements to ELSE_. We use the unsigned jump JNBE (jump if not below or equal), because we're comparing extended characters.

If AL <= BL is true, the true-branch statements are done. Note that JMP DISPLAY is needed to skip the false branch. This is different from the high-level language IF-THEN-ELSE, in which the false-branch statements are automatically skipped if the true-branch statements are done.

CASE

A CASE is a multiway branch structure that tests a register, variable, or expression for particular values or a range of values. The general form is as follows:

```
CASE expression
    values_1: statements_1
    values_2: statements_2
       .
       .
       .
    values_n: statements_n
END_CASE
```

See Figure 6.4.

In this structure, expression is tested; if its value is a member of the set values_i, then statements_i are executed. We assume that sets values_1,..,values_n are disjoint.

Example 6.4 If AX contains a negative number, put –1 in BX; if AX contains 0, put 0 in BX; if AX contains a positive number, put 1 in BX.

Figure 6.4 CASE

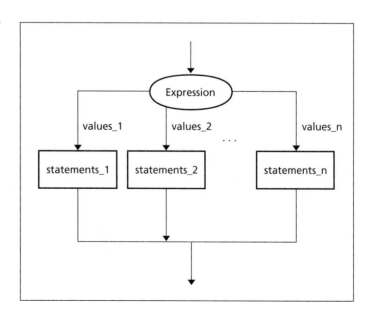

Solution:

```
CASE AX
   <0: put -1 in BX
   =0: put  0 in BX
   >0: put  1 in BX
END_CASE
```

It can be coded as follows:

```
;case AX
            CMP   AX,0         ;test ax
            JL    NEGATIVE     ;AX < 0
            JE    ZERO         ;AX = 0
            JG    POSITIVE     ;AX > 0
NEGATIVE:
            MOV   BX,-1        ;put -1 in BX
            JMP   END_CASE     ;and exit
ZERO:
            MOV   BX,0         ;put 0 in BX
            JMP   END_CASE     ;and exit
POSITIVE:
            MOV   BX,1         ;put 1 in BX
END_CASE:
```

Note: only one CMP is needed, because jump instructions do not affect the flags.

Example 6.5 If AL contains 1 or 3, display "o"; if AL contains 2 or 4, display "e".

Solution:

```
CASE AL
   1,3: display 'o'
   2,4: display 'e'
END_CASE
```

The code is

```
;case AL
; 1,3:
            CMP   AL,1         ;AL = 1?
            JE    ODD          ;yes, display 'o'
            CMP   AL,3         ;AL = '3'
            JE    ODD          ;yes, display 'o'
; 2,4:
            CMP   AL,2         ;AL = 2?
            JE    EVEN         ;yes, display 'e'
            CMP   AL,4         ;AL = 4?
            JE    EVEN         ;yes, display 'e'
            JMP   END_CASE     ;not 1..4
ODD:                           ;display 'o'
            MOV   DL,'o'       ;get 'o'
            JMP   DISPLAY      ;go to display
EVEN:                          ;display 'e'
            MOV   DL,'e'       ;get 'e'
DISPLAY:
```

```
                MOV     AH,2
                INT     21H         ;display char
END_CASE:
```

Branches with Compound Conditions

Sometimes the branching condition in an IF or CASE takes the form

```
condition_1 AND condition_2
```

or

```
condition_1 OR condition_2
```

where condition_1 and condition_2 are either true or false. We will refer to the first of these as an **AND condition** and to the second as an **OR condition**.

AND Conditions

An AND condition is true if and only if condition_1 and condition_2 are both true. Likewise, if either condition is false, then the whole thing is false.

Example 6.6 Read a character, and if it's an uppercase letter, display it.

Solution:

```
Read a character (into AL)
IF ('A' <= character) and (character <= 'Z')
 THEN
   display character
END_IF
```

To code this, we first see if the character in AL follows "A" (or is "A") in the character sequence. If not, we can exit. If so, we still must see if the character precedes "Z" (or is "Z") before displaying it. Here is the code:

```
;read a character
            MOV     AH,1        ;prepare to read
            INT     21H         ;char in AL
;if ('A' <= char) and (char <= 'Z')
            CMP     AL,'A'      ;char >= 'A'?
            JNGE    END_IF      ;no, exit
            CMP     AL,'Z'      ;char <= 'Z'?
            JNLE    END_IF      ;no, exit
;then display char
            MOV     DL,AL       ;get char
            MOV     AH,2        ;prepare to display
            INT     21H         ;display char
END_IF:
```

OR Conditions

Condition_1 OR condition_2 is true if at least one of the conditions is true; it is only false when both conditions are false.

Example 6.7 Read a character. If it's "y" or "Y", display it; otherwise, terminate the program.

Solution:

```
Read a character (into AL)
IF (character = 'y') OR (character = 'Y')
 THEN
   display it
 ELSE
   terminate the program
END_IF
```

To code this, we first see if character = "y". If so, the OR condition is true and we can execute the THEN statements. If not, there is still a chance the OR condition will be true. If character = "Y", it will be true, and we execute the THEN statements; if not, the OR condition is false and we do the ELSE statements. Here is the code:

```
;read a character
            MOV   AH,1       ;prepare to read
            INT   21H        ;char in AL
;if (character = 'y') or (character = 'Y')
            CMP   AL,'y'     ;char = 'y'?
            JE    THEN       ;yes, go to display it
            CMP   AL,'Y'     ;char = 'Y'?
            JE    THEN       ;yes, go to display it
            JMP   ELSE_      ;no, terminate
THEN:
            MOV   AH,2       ;prepare to display
            MOV   DL,AL      ;get char
            INT   21H        ;display it
            JMP   END_IF     ;and exit
ELSE_:
            MOV   AH,4CH
            INT   21H        ;DOS exit
END_IF:
```

6.4.2 Looping Structures

A **loop** is a sequence of instructions that is repeated. The number of times to repeat may be known in advance, or it may depend on conditions.

FOR LOOP

This is a loop structure in which the loop statements are repeated a known number of times (a count-controlled loop). In pseudocode,

```
FOR  loop_count times DO
  statements
END_FOR
```

See Figure 6.5.

The **LOOP** instruction can be used to implement a FOR loop. It has the form

```
LOOP  destination_label
```

The counter for the loop is the register CX which is initialized to loop_count. Execution of the LOOP instruction causes CX to be decremented automatically,

Figure 6.5 FOR LOOP

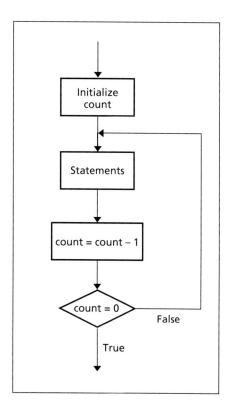

and if CX is not 0, control transfers to destination_label. If CX = 0, the next instruction after LOOP is done. Destination_label must precede the LOOP instruction by no more than 126 bytes.

Using the instruction LOOP, a FOR loop can be implemented as follows:

```
            ;initialize CX to loop_count
TOP:
            ;body of the loop
            LOOP TOP
```

Example 6.8 Write a count-controlled loop to display a row of 80 stars.

Solution:

```
FOR 80 times DO
            display '*'
END_FOR
```

The code is

```
            MOV  CX,80      ;number of stars to display
            MOV  AH,2       ;display character function
            MOV  DL,'*'     ;character to display
TOP:
            INT  21h        ;display a star
            LOOP TOP        ;repeat 80 times
```

You may have noticed that a FOR loop, as implemented with a LOOP instruction, is executed at least once. Actually, if CX contains 0 when the loop is entered, the LOOP instruction causes CX to be decremented to FFFFh, and the loop is then executed FFFFh = 65535 more times! To prevent this, the instruction **JCXZ** *(jump if CX is zero)* may be used before the loop. Its syntax is

```
JCXZ          destination_label
```

If CX contains 0, control transfers to the destination label. So a loop implemented as follows is bypassed if CX is 0:

```
              JCXZ SKIP
TOP:
              ;body of the loop
              LOOP TOP
SKIP:
```

WHILE LOOP

This loop depends on a condition. In pseudocode,

```
WHILE condition DO
   statements
END_WHILE
```

See Figure 6.6.
The *condition* is checked at the top of the loop. If true, the statements are executed; if false, the program goes on to whatever follows. It is possible that the *condition* will be false initially, in which case the loop body is not executed at all. The loop executes as long as the *condition* is true.

Example 6.9 Write some code to count the number of characters in an input line.

Solution:

```
initialize count to 0
read a character
WHILE character <> carriage_return DO
 count = count + 1
 read a character
END_WHILE
```

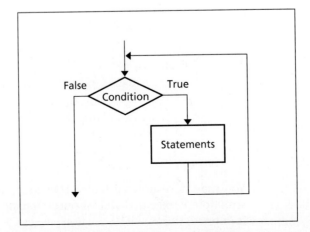

Figure 6.6 WHILE LOOP

The code is

```
                MOV   DX,0        ;DX counts characters
                MOV   AH,1        ;prepare to read
                INT   21H         ;character in AL
WHILE_:
                CMP   AL,0DH      ;CR?
                JE    END_WHILE   ;yes, exit
                INC   DX          ;not CR, increment count
                INT   21H         ;read a character
                JMP   WHILE_      ;loop back
END_WHILE:
```

Note that because a WHILE loop checks the terminating condition at the top of the loop, you must make sure that any variables involved in the condition are initialized before the loop is entered. So you read a character before entering the loop, and read another one at the bottom. The label WHILE_: is used because WHILE is a reserved word.

REPEAT LOOP

Another conditional loop is the REPEAT LOOP. In pseudocode,

```
REPEAT
statements
UNTIL condition
```

See Figure 6.7.

In a REPEAT . . . UNTIL loop, the statements are executed, and then the *condition* is checked. If true, the loop terminates; if false, control branches to the top of the loop.

Example 6.10 Write some code to read characters until a blank is read.

Solution:

```
REPEAT
 read a character
UNTIL character is a blank
```

Figure 6.7 REPEAT LOOP

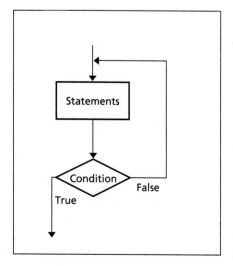

The code is

```
                MOV   AH,1      ;prepare to read
REPEAT:
                INT   21H       ;char in AL
;until
                CMP   AL,' '    ;a blank?
                JNE   REPEAT    ;no, keep reading
```

WHILE Versus REPEAT

In many situations where a conditional loop is needed, use of a WHILE loop or a REPEAT loop is a matter of personal preference. The advantage of a WHILE is that the loop can be bypassed if the terminating condition is initially false, whereas the statements in a REPEAT must be done at least once. However, the code for a REPEAT loop is likely to be a little shorter because there is only a conditional jump at the end, but a WHILE loop has two jumps: a conditional jump at the top and a JMP at the bottom.

6.5 Programming with High-Level Structures

To show how a program may be developed from high-level pseudo-code to assembly code, let's solve the following problem.

Problem

Prompt the user to enter a line of text. On the next line, display the capital letter entered that comes first alphabetically and the one that comes last. If no capital letters are entered, display "No capital letters". The execution should look like this:

```
Type a line of text:
THE QUICK BROWN FOX JUMPED.
First capital = B  Last capital = X
```

To solve this problem, we will use the method of **top-down program design** that you may have encountered in high-level language programming. In this method, the original problem is solved by solving a series of subproblems, each of which is easier to solve than the original problem. Each subproblem is in turn broken down further until we reach a level of subproblems that can be coded directly. The use of procedures (Chapter 8) may enhance this method.

First refinement

1. Display the opening message.
2. Read and process a line of text.
3. Display the results.

Step 1. Display the opening message.

This step can be coded immediately

```
MOV  AH,9           ;display string function
LEA  DX,PROMPT      ;get opening message
INT  21H            ;display it
```

The message will be stored in the data segment as

```
PROMPT  DB      'Type a line of text:',0DH,0AH,'$'
```

We include a carriage return and line feed to move the cursor to the next line so the user can type a full line of text.

Step 2. Read and process a line of text.

This step does most of the work in the program. It takes input from the keyboard, and returns the first and last capital letters read (it should also indicate if no capitals were read). Here is a breakdown:

```
Read a character
WHILE character is not a carriage return DO
IF character is a capital letter (*)
 THEN
   IF character precedes first capital
    THEN
     first capital = character
    END_IF
   IF character follows last capital
    THEN
     last capital = character
    END_IF
END_IF
Read a character
END_WHILE
```

Line (*) is actually an AND condition:

```
IF ('A' <= character) AND (character <= 'Z')
```

Step 2 can be coded as follows:

```
                MOV  AH,1       ;read char function
                INT  21H        ;char in AL
WHILE_:
;while character is not a carriage return do
                CMP  AL,0DH     ;CR?
                JE   END_WHILE  ;yes, exit
;if character is a capital letter
                CMP  AL,'A'     ;char >= 'A'?
                JNGE END_IF     ;not a capital letter
                CMP  AL,'Z'     ;char <= 'Z'?
                JNLE END_IF     ;not a capital letter
;then
; if character precedes first capital
                CMP  AL,FIRST   ;char < FIRST?
                JNL  CHECK_LAST ;no, >=
;then first capital = character
                MOV  FIRST,AL   ;FIRST = char
; end_if
CHECK_LAST:
```

```
                ; if character follows last capital
                        CMP     AL,LAST     ;char > LAST?
                        JNG     END_IF      ;no, <=
                ;then last capital = character
                        MOV     LAST,AL     ;LAST = char
                ; end_if
                END_IF:
                ;read a character
                        INT     21H         ;char in AL
                        JMP     WHILE_      ;repeat loop
                END_WHILE:
```

Variables FIRST and LAST must have values before the WHILE loop is executed the first time. They can be initialized in the data segment as follows:

```
FIRST           DB                  ']'
LAST            DB                  '@'
```

The initial values "]" and "@" were chosen because "]" follows "Z" in the ASCII sequence, and "@" precedes "A". Thus the first capital entered will replace both of these values.

With step 2 coded, we can proceed to the final step.

Step 3. Display the results.

```
IF no capitals were typed,
 THEN
   display "No capitals"
 ELSE
   display first capital and last capital
END_IF
```

This step will display one of two possible messages; NOCAP_MSG if no capitals are entered, and CAP_MSG if there are capitals. We can declare them in the data segment as follows:

```
NOCAP_MSG       DB              'No capitals $'
CAP_MSG         DB              'First capital = '
FIRST           DB              ']'
                DB              ' Last capital = '
LAST            DB              '@ $'
```

When CAP_MSG is displayed, it will display "First capital =", then the value of FIRST, then "Last capital =", then the value of LAST. We used this same technique in the last program of Chapter 4.

The program decides, by inspecting FIRST, whether any capitals were read. If FIRST contains its initial value "]", then no capitals were read.

Step 3 may be coded as follows:

```
                        MOV     AH,9        ;display string function
                ;if no capitals were typed
                        CMP     FIRST,']'   ;FIRST = ']'?
                        JNE     CAPS        ;no, display results
                ;then
                        LEA     DX,NOCAP_MSG
                        JMP     DISPLAY
                CAPS:
                        LEA     DX,CAP_MSG
                DISPLAY:
                        INT     21H         ;display message
                ;end_if
```

Here is the complete program:

Program Listing PGM6_2.ASM

```
TITLE PGM6_2: FIRST AND LAST CAPITALS
.MODEL SMALL
.STACK 100H
.DATA
PROMPT  DB      'Type a line of text',0DH,0AH,'$'
NOCAP_MSG DB 0DH,0AH,'No capitals $'
CAP_MSG     DB              0DH,0AH,'First capital = '
FIRST DB    ']'
      DB    ' Last capital = '
LAST  DB    '@ $'

.CODE
MAIN  PROC
;initialize DS
      MOV   AX,@DATA
      MOV   DS,AX
;display opening message
      MOV   AH,9           ;display string function
      LEA   DX,PROMPT      ;get opening message
      INT   21H            ;display it
;read and process a line of text
      MOV   AH,1            ;read char function
      INT   21H             ;char in AL
WHILE_:
;while character is not a carriage return do
      CMP   AL,0DH          ;CR?
      JE    END_WHILE       ;yes, exit
;if character is a capital letter
      CMP   AL,'A'          ;char >= 'A'?
      JNGE  END_IF          ;not a capital letter
      CMP   AL,'Z'          ;char <= 'Z'?
      JNLE  END_IF          ;not a capital letter
;then
;if character precedes first capital
      CMP   AL,FIRST        ;char < first capital?
      JNL   CHECK_LAST      ;no, >=
;    then first capital = character
      MOV   FIRST,AL        ;FIRST = char
;end_if
CHECK_LAST:
;  if character follows last capital
      CMP   AL,LAST         ;char > last capital?
      JNG   END_IF          ;no, <=
;  then last capital = character
      MOV   LAST,AL         ;LAST = char
;  end_if
END_IF:
;read a character
      INT   21H             ;char in AL
      JMP   WHILE_          ;repeat loop
END_WHILE:
;display results
```

```
                MOV     AH,9            ;display string function
;if no capitals were typed
        CMP     FIRST,']'       ;first = ']'
        JNE     CAPS            ;no, display results
;then
        LEA     DX,NOCAP_MSG    ;no capitals
        JMP     DISPLAY
CAPS:
        LEA     DX,CAP_MSG      ;capitals
DISPLAY:
        INT     21H             ;display message
;end_if
;dos exit
        MOV     AH,4CH
        INT     21H
MAIN    ENDP
        END     MAIN
```

Summary

- The jump instructions may be divided into unconditional and conditional jumps. The conditional jumps may be classified as signed, unsigned, and single-flag jumps.

- The conditional jumps operate on the settings of the status flags. The CMP (compare) instruction is often used to set the flags just before a jump instruction.

- The destination label of a conditional jump must be less than 126 bytes before or 127 bytes after the jump. A JMP can often be used to get around this restriction.

- In an IF-THEN decision structure, if the test condition is true, then the true-branch statements are done; otherwise, the next statement in line is done.

- In an IF-THEN-ELSE decision structure, if the test condition is true, then the true-branch statements are done; otherwise the false-branch statements are done. A JMP must follow the true-branch statements so that the false-branch will be bypassed.

- In a CASE structure, branching is controlled by an expression; the branches correspond to the possible values of the expression.

- A FOR loop is executed a known number of times. It may be implemented by the LOOP instruction. Before entering the loop, CX is initialized to the number of times to repeat the loop statements.

- In a WHILE loop, the loop condition is checked at the top of the loop. The loop statements are repeated as long as the condition is true. If the condition is initially false, the loop statements are not done at all.

- In a REPEAT loop, the loop condition is checked at the bottom of the loop. The statements are repeated until the condition is true. Because the condition is checked at the bottom of the loop, the statements are done at least once.

Glossary

AND condition — A logical AND of two conditions

conditional jump instruction — A jump instruction whose execution depends on status flag settings

loop — A sequence of instructions that is repeated

OR condition — A logical OR of two conditions

signed jump — A conditional jump instruction used with signed numbers

single-flag jump — A conditional jump that operates on the setting of an individual status flag

top-down program design — Program development by breaking a large problem into a series of smaller problems

unconditional jump — An unconditional transfer of control

unsigned jump — A conditional jump instruction used with unsigned numbers

New Instructions

```
CMP          JCXZ         JLE/JNG
JA/JNBE      JE/JZ        JMP
JAE/JNB      JG/JNLE      JNC
JB/JNAE      JGE/JNL      JNE/JNZ
JBE/JNA      JL/JNLE      LOOP
JC
```

Exercises

1. Write assembly code for each of the following decision structures.

   a. ```
      IF AX < 0
         THEN
            PUT -1 IN BX
      END_IF
      ```

   b. ```
      IF AL < 0
         THEN
            put FFh in AH
         ELSE
            put 0 in AH
      END_IF
      ```

   c. Suppose DL contains the ASCII code of a character.
      ```
      (IF DL >= "A") AND (DL <= 'Z')
         THEN
            display DL
      END_IF
      ```

   d. ```
      IF AX < BX
         THEN
            IF BX < CX
               THEN
      ```
      ```

```
            put 0 in AX
      ELSE
            put 0 in BX
      END_IF
END_IF
```

e.
```
IF (AX < BX) OR (BX < CX)
   THEN
      put 0 in DX
   ELSE
      put 1 in DX
END_IF
```

f.
```
IF AX < BX
   THEN
      put 0 in AX
   ELSE
      IF BX < CX
         THEN
            put 0 in BX
         ELSE
            put 0 in CX
      END_IF
END_IF
```

2. Use a CASE structure to code the following:

   Read a character.

   If it's "A", then execute carriage return.

   If it's "B", then execute line feed.

   If it's any other character, then return to DOS.

3. Write a sequence of instructions to do each of the following:
   a. Put the sum $1 + 4 + 7 + \ldots + 148$ in AX.
   b. Put the sum $100 + 95 + 90 + \ldots + 5$ in AX.

4. Employ LOOP instructions to do the following:
   a. put the sum of the first 50 terms of the arithmetic sequence $1, 5, 9, 13, \ldots$ in DX.
   b. Read a character and display it 80 times on the next line.
   c. Read a five-character password and overprint it by executing a carriage return and displaying five X's. You need not store the input characters anywhere.

5. The following algorithm may be used to carry out division of two nonnegative numbers by repeated subtraction:

```
initialize quotient to 0
WHILE dividend >= divisor DO
increment quotient
subtract divisor from dividend
END_WHILE
```

Write a sequence of instructions to divide AX by BX, and put the quotient in CX.

6. The following algorithm may be used to carry out multiplication of two positive numbers M and N by repeated addition:

   ```
   initialize product to 0
   REPEAT
    add M to product
    decrement N
   UNTIL N = 0
   ```

   Write a sequence of instructions to multiply AX by BX, and put the product in CX. You may ignore the possibility of overflow.

7. It is possible to set up a count-controlled loop that will continue to execute as long as some condition is satisfied. The instructions

   ```
   LOOPE label         ;loop while equal
   ```

   and

   ```
   LOOPZ label         ;loop while zero
   ```

   cause CX to be decremented, then if CX <> 0 and ZF = 1, control transfers to the instruction at the destination label; if either CX = 0 or ZF = 0, the instruction following the loop is done. Similarly, the instructions

   ```
   LOOPNE label        ;loop while not equal
   ```

   and

   ```
   LOOPNZ label        ;loop while not zero
   ```

   cause CX to be decremented, then if CX <> 0 and ZF = 0, control transfers to the instruction at the destination label; if either CX = 0 or ZF = 1, the instruction following the loop is done.

   a. Write instructions to read characters until either a nonblank character is typed, or 80 characters have been typed. Use LOOPE.

   b. Write instructions to read characters until either a carriage return is typed or 80 characters have been typed. Use LOOPNE.

Programming Exercises

8. Write a program to display a "?", read two capital letters, and display them on the next line in alphabetical order.

9. Write a program to display the extended ASCII characters (ASCII codes 80h to FFh). Display 10 characters per line, separated by blanks. Stop after the extended characters have been displayed once.

10. Write a program that will prompt the user to enter a hex digit character ("0" ... "9" or "A" ... "F"), display it on the next line in decimal, and ask the user if he or she wants to do it again. If the user types "y" or "Y", the program repeats; if the user types anything else, the program terminates. If the user enters an illegal character, prompt the user to try again.

Sample execution:

```
ENTER A HEX DIGIT: 9
IN DECIMAL IS IT 9
DO YOU WANT TO DO IT AGAIN? y
ENTER A HEX DIGIT: c
ILLEGAL CHARACTER - ENTER 0..9 OR A..F: C
IN DECIMAL IT IS 12
DO YOU WANT TO DO IT AGAIN? N
```

11. Do programming exercise 10, except that if the user fails to enter a hex-digit character in three tries, display a message and terminate the program.

12. (hard) Write a program that reads a string of capital letters, ending with a carriage return, and displays the longest sequence of consecutive alphabetically increasing capital letters read.

    Sample execution:

    ```
    ENTER A STRING OF CAPITAL LETTERS:
    FGHADEFGHC
    THE LONGEST CONSECUTIVELY INCREASING STRING IS:
    DEFGH
    ```

7

Logic, Shift, and Rotate Instructions

Overview

In this chapter we discuss instructions that can be used to change the bit pattern in a byte or word. The ability to manipulate bits is generally absent in high-level languages (except C), and is an important reason for programming in assembly language.

In section 7.1, we introduce the logic instructions AND, OR, XOR, and NOT. They can be used to clear, set, and examine bits in a register or variable. We use these instructions to do some familiar tasks, such as converting a lowercase letter to upper case, and some new tasks, such as determining if a register contains an even or odd number.

Section 7.2 covers the shift instructions. Bits can be shifted left or right in a register or memory location; when a bit is shifted out, it goes into CF. Because a left shift doubles a number and a right shift halves it, these instructions give us a way to multiply and divide by powers of 2. In Chapter 9, we'll use the MUL and DIV instructions for doing more general multiplication and division; however, these latter instructions are much slower than the shift instructions.

In section 7.3, the rotate instructions are covered. They work like the shifts, except that when a bit is shifted out one end of an operand it is put back in the other end. These instructions can be used in situations where we want to examine and/or change bits or groups of bits.

In section 7.4, we use the logic, shift, and rotate instructions to do binary and hexadecimal I/O. The ability to read and write numbers lets us solve a great variety of problems.

7.1 Logic Instructions

As noted earlier, the ability to manipulate individual bits is one of the advantages of assembly language. We can change individual bits in the computer by using logic operations. The binary values of 0 and 1 are treated as *false* and *true*, respectively. Figure 7.1 shows the truth tables for the logic operators AND, OR, XOR (exclusive OR), and NOT.

When a logic operation is applied to 8- or 16-bit operands, the result is obtained by applying the logic operation at each bit position.

Example 7.1 Perform the following logic operations:

1. `10101010 AND 11110000`
2. `10101010 OR  11110000`
3. `10101010 XOR 11110000`
4. `NOT 10101010`

Solutions:

1.  ```
        10101010
    AND 11110000
      = 10100000
    ```

2.  ```
        10101010
    OR  11110000
      = 11111010
    ```

3.  ```
        10101010
    XOR 11110000
      = 01011010
    ```

4.  ```
    NOT 10101010
      = 01010101
    ```

Figure 7.1 Truth Tables for AND, OR, XOR, and NOT (0 = false, 1 = true)

a	b	a AND b	a OR b	a XOR b
0	0	0	0	0
0	1	0	1	1
1	0	0	1	1
1	1	1	1	0

a	NOT a
0	1
1	0

7.1.1 AND, OR, and XOR Instructions

The **AND**, **OR**, and **XOR** instructions perform the named logic operations. The formats are

```
AND    destination,source
OR     destination,source
XOR    destination,source
```

The result of the operation is stored in the destination, which must be a register or memory location. The source may be a constant, register, or memory location. However, memory-to-memory operations are not allowed.

Effect on flags:

SF, ZF, PF reflect the result

AF is undefined

CF, OF = 0

One use of AND, OR, and XOR is to selectively modify the bits in the destination. To do this, we construct a source bit pattern known as a **mask**. The mask bits are chosen so that the corresponding destination bits are modified in the desired manner when the instruction is executed.

To choose the mask bits, we make use of the following properties of AND, OR, and XOR. From Figure 7.1, if b represents a bit (0 or 1)

b AND 1 = b   b OR 0 = b   b XOR 0 = b
b AND 0 = 0   b OR 1 = 1   b XOR 1 = ~b (complement of b)

From these, we may conclude that

1. The AND instruction can be used to **clear** specific destination bits while preserving the others. A 0 mask bit clears the corresponding destination bit; a 1 mask bit preserves the corresponding destination bit.

2. The OR instruction can be used to **set** specific destination bits while preserving the others. A 1 mask bit sets the corresponding destination bit; a 0 mask bit preserves the corresponding destination bit.

3. The XOR instruction can be used to **complement** specific destination bits while preserving the others. A 1 mask bit complements the corresponding destination bit; a 0 mask bit preserves the corresponding destination bit.

Example 7.2 Clear the sign bit of AL while leaving the other bits unchanged.

Solution: Use the AND instruction with 01111111b = 7Fh as the mask. Thus,

```
AND    AL,7Fh
```

Example 7.3 Set the most significant and least significant bits of AL while preserving the other bits.

Solution: Use the OR instruction with 10000001b = 81h as the mask. Thus,

```
OR    AL,81h
```

Example 7.4 Change the sign bit of DX.

Solution: Use the XOR instruction with a mask of 8000h. Thus,

```
XOR   DX,8000h
```

Note: to avoid typing errors, it's best to express the mask in hex rather than binary, especially if the mask would be 16 bits long.

The logic instructions are especially useful in the following frequently occurring tasks.

Converting an ASCII Digit to a Number

We've seen that when a program reads a character from the keyboard, AL gets the ASCII code of the character. This is also true of digit characters. For example, if the "5" key is pressed, AL gets 35h instead of 5. To get 5 in AL, we could do this:

```
SUB   AL,30h
```

Another method is to use the AND instruction to clear the high nibble (high four bits) of AL:

```
AND   AL,0Fh
```

Because the codes of "0" to "9" are 30h to 39h, this method will convert any ASCII digit to a decimal value.

By using the logic instruction AND instead of SUB, we emphasize that we're modifying the bit pattern of AL. This is helpful in making the program more readable.

The reverse problem of converting a stored decimal digit to its ASCII code is left as an exercise.

Converting a Lowercase Letter to Upper Case

The ASCII codes of "a" to "z" range from 61h to 7Ah; the codes of "A" to "Z" go from 41h to 5Ah. Thus for example, if DL contains the code of a lowercase letter, we could convert to upper case by executing

```
SUB   DL,20h
```

This method was used in Chapter 4. However, if we compare the binary codes of corresponding lowercase and uppercase letters

Character	*Code*	*Character*	*Code*
a	01100001	A	01000001
b	01100010	B	01000010
.	.	.	.
.	.	.	.
.	.	.	.
z	01111010	Z	01011010

it is apparent that to convert lower to upper case we need only clear bit 5. This can be done by using an AND instruction with the mask 11011111b, or 0DFh. So if the lowercase character to be converted is in DL, execute

```
AND    DL,0DFh
```

The reverse problem of conversion from upper to lower case is left as an exercise.

Clearing a Register

We already know two ways to clear a register. For example, to clear AX we could execute

```
MOV    AX,0
```

or

```
SUB    AX,AX
```

Using the fact that 1 XOR 1 = 0 and 0 XOR 0 = 0, a third way is

```
XOR    AX,AX
```

The machine code of the first method is three bytes, versus two bytes for the latter two methods, so the latter are more efficient. However, because of the prohibition on memory-to-memory operations, the first method must be used to clear a memory location.

Testing a Register for Zero

Because 1 OR 1 = 1, 0 OR 0 = 0, it might seem like a waste of time to execute an instruction like

```
OR     CX,CX
```

because it leaves the contents of CX unchanged. However, it affects ZF and SF, and in particular if CX contains 0 then ZF = 1. So it can be used as an alternative to

```
CMP    CX,0
```

to test the contents of a register for zero, or to check the sign of the contents.

7.1.2 NOT Instruction

The **NOT** instruction performs the one's complement operation on the destination. The format is

```
NOT    destination
```

There is no effect on the status flags.

Example 7.5 Complement the bits in AX.

Solution:

```
NOT    AX
```

7.1.3
TEST Instruction

The **TEST** instruction performs an AND operation of the destination with the source but does not change the destination contents. The purpose of the TEST instruction is to set the status flags. The format is

```
TEST destination,source
```

Effect on flags

SF, ZF, PF reflect the result
AF is undefined
CF, OF = 0

Examining Bits

The TEST instruction can be used to examine individual bits in an operand. The mask should contain 1's in the bit positions to be tested and 0's elsewhere. Because 1 AND b = b, 0 AND b = 0, the result of

```
TEST destination,mask
```

will have 1's in the tested bit positions if and only if the destination has 1's in these positions; it will have 0's elsewhere. If destination has 0's in all the tested positions, the result will be 0 and so ZF = 1.

Example 7.6 Jump to label BELOW if AL contains an even number.

Solution: Even numbers have a 0 in bit 0. Thus, the mask is 00000001b = 1.

```
TEST  AL,1         ;is AL even?
JZ    BELOW        ;yes, go to BELOW
```

7.2
Shift Instructions

The shift and rotate instructions shift the bits in the destination operand by one or more positions either to the left or right. For a shift instruction, the bits shifted out are lost; for a rotate instruction, bits shifted out from one end of the operand are put back into the other end. The instructions have two possible formats. For a single shift or rotate, the form is

```
Opcode    destination,1
```

For a shift or rotate of *N* positions, the form is

```
Opcode    destination,CL
```

where CL contains *N*. In both cases, destination is an 8- or 16-bit register or memory location. Note that for Intel's more advanced processors, a shift or rotate instruction also allows the use of an 8-bit constant.

As we'll see presently, these instructions can be used to multiply and divide by powers of 2, and we will use them in programs for binary and hex I/O.

7.2.1 Left Shift Instructions

The SHL Instruction

The **SHL** (shift left) instruction shifts the bits in the destination to the left. The format for a single shift is

```
SHL    destination,1
```

A 0 is shifted into the rightmost bit position and the msb is shifted into CF (Figure 7.2). If the shift count N is different from 1, the instruction takes the form

```
SHL    destination,CL
```

where CL contains N. In this case, N single left shifts are made. The value of CL remains the same after the shift operation.

Effect on flags

SF, PF, ZF reflect the result

AF is undefined

CF = last bit shifted out

OF = 1 if result changes sign on last shift

Example 7.7 Suppose DH contains 8Ah and CL contains 3. What are the values of DH and of CF after the instruction SHL DH,CL is executed?

Solution: The binary value of DH is 10001010. After 3 left shifts, CF will contain 0. The new contents of DH may be obtained by erasing the leftmost three bits and adding three zero bits to the right end, thus 01010000b = 50h.

Multiplication by Left Shift

Consider the decimal number 235. If each digit is shifted left one position and a 0 attached to the right end, we get 2350; this is the same as multiplying 235 by ten.

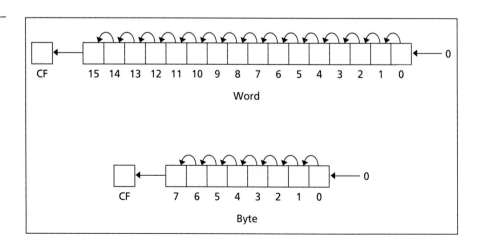

Figure 7.2 SHL and SAL

In the same way, a left shift on a binary number multiplies it by 2. For example, suppose that AL contains 5 = 00000101b. A left shift gives 00001010b = 10d, thus doubling its value. Another left shift yields 00010100 = 20d, so it is doubled again.

The SAL instruction

Thus, the SHL instruction can be used to multiply an operand by multiples of 2. However, to emphasize the arithmetic nature of the operation, the opcode **SAL** (shift arithmetic left) is often used in instances where numeric multiplication is intended. Both instructions generate the same machine code.

Negative numbers can also be multiplied by powers of 2 by left shifts. For example, if AX is FFFFh (–1), then shifting three times will yield AX = FFF8h (–8).

Overflow

When we treat left shifts as multiplication, overflow may occur. For a single left shift, CF and OF accurately indicate unsigned and signed overflow, respectively. However, the overflow flags are not reliable indicators for a multiple left shift. This is because a multiple shift is really a series of single shifts, and CF, OF only reflect the result of the last shift. For example, if BL contains 80h, CL contains 2 and we execute SHL BL,CL, then CF = OF = 0 even though both signed and unsigned overflow occur.

Example 7.8 Write some code to multiply the value of AX by 8. Assume that overflow will not occur.

Solution: To multiply by 8, we need to do three left shifts.

```
MOV   CL,3              ;number of shifts to do
SAL   AX,CL             ;multiply by 8
```

Figure 7.3 SHR

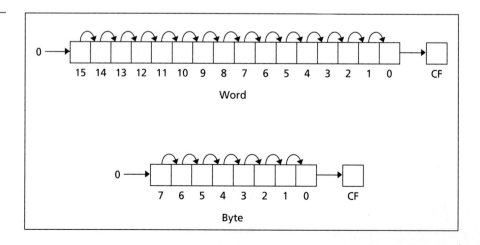

7.2.2 Right Shift Instructions

The SHR Instruction

The instruction **SHR** (shift right) performs right shifts on the destination operand. The format for a single shift is

```
SHR    destination,1
```

A 0 is shifted into the msb position, and the rightmost bit is shifted into CF. See Figure 7.3. If the shift count N is different from 1, the instruction takes the form

```
SHR    destination,CL
```

where CL contains N. In this case N single right shifts are made.

The effect on the flags is the same as for SHL.

Example 7.9 Suppose DH contains 8Ah and CL contains 2. What are the values of DH and CF after the instruction SHR DH,CL is executed?

Solution: The value of DH in binary is 10001010. After two right shifts, CF = 1. The new value of DH is obtained by erasing the rightmost two bits and adding two 0 bits to the left end, thus DH = 00100010b = 22h.

The SAR Instruction

The **SAR** instruction (shift arithmetic right) operates like SHR, with one difference: the msb retains its original value. See Figure 7.4. The syntax is

```
SAR    destination,1
```

and

```
SAR    destination,CL
```

The effect on flags is the same as for SHR.

Division by Right Shift

Because a left shift doubles the destination's value, it's reasonable to guess that a right shift might divide it by 2. This is correct for even numbers.

Figure 7.4 SAR

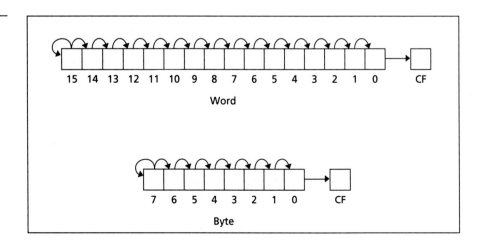

For odd numbers, a right shift halves it and rounds down to the nearest integer. For example, if BL contains 00000101b = 5, then after a right shift BL will contain 00000010 = 2.

Signed and Unsigned Division

In doing division by right shifts, we need to make a distinction between signed and unsigned numbers. If an unsigned interpretation is being given, SHR should be used. For a signed interpretation, SAR must be used, because it preserves the sign.

Example 7.10 Use right shifts to divide the unsigned number 65143 by 4. Put the quotient in AX.

Solution: To divide by 4, two right shifts are needed. Since the dividend is unsigned, we use SHR. The code is

```
MOV    AX,65143      ;AX has number
MOV    CL,2          ;CL has number of right shifts
SHR    AX,CL         ;divide by 4
```

Example 7.11 If AL contains –15, give the decimal value of AL after SAR AL,1 is performed.

Solution: Execution of SAR AL,1 divides the number by 2 and rounds down. Dividing –15 by 2 yields –7.5, and after rounding down we get –8. In terms of the binary contents, we have –15 = 11110001b. After shifting, we have 11111000b = –8.

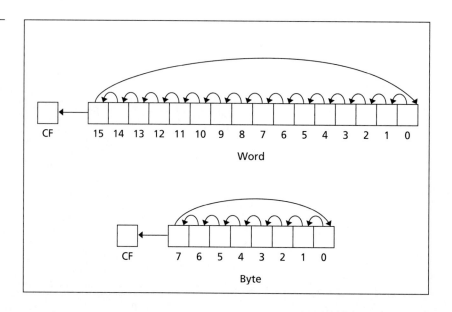

Figure 7.5 ROL

More General Multiplication and Division

We've seen that multiplication and division by powers of 2 can be accomplished by left and right shifts. Multiplication by other numbers, such as 10d, can be done by a combination of shifting and addition (see Chapter 8).

In Chapter 9, we cover the MUL and IMUL, DIV and IDIV instructions. They are not limited to multiplication and division by powers of 2, but are much slower than the shift instructions.

7.3 Rotate Instructions

Rotate Left

The instruction **ROL** (rotate left) shifts bits to the left. The msb is shifted into the rightmost bit. The CF also gets the bit shifted out of the msb. You can think of the destination bits forming a circle, with the least significant bit following the msb in the circle. See Figure 7.5. The syntax is

```
ROL    destination,1
```

and

```
ROL    destination,CL
```

Rotate Right

The instruction **ROR** (rotate right) works just like ROL, except that the bits are rotated to the right. The rightmost bit is shifted into the msb, and also into the CF. See Figure 7.6. The syntax is

```
ROR    destination,1
```

and

```
ROR    destination,CL
```

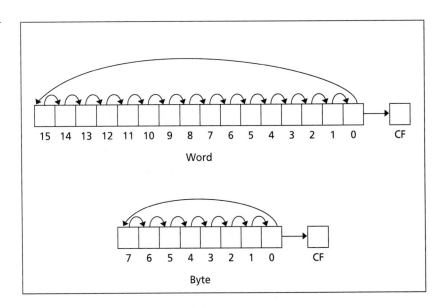

Figure 7.6 ROR

Figure 7.7 RCL

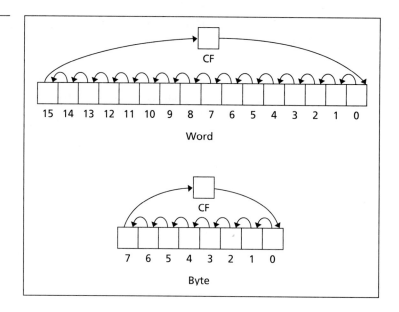

In ROL and ROR, CF reflects the bit that is rotated out. The next example shows how this can be used to inspect the bits in a byte or word, without changing the contents.

Example 7.12 Use ROL to count the number of 1 bits in BX, without changing BX. Put the answer in AX.

Solution:

```
        XOR   AX,AX      ;AX counts bits
        MOV   CX,16      ;loop counter
TOP:
        ROL   BX,1       ;C F = bit rotated out
        JNC   NEXT       ;0 bit
        INC   AX         ;1 bit, increment total
NEXT:
        LOOP  TOP        ;loop until done
```

In this example, we used JNC (Jump if No Carry), which causes a jump if CF = 0. In section 7.4, we use ROL to output the contents of a register in binary.

Rotate Carry Left

The instruction **RCL** (Rotate through Carry Left) shifts the bits of the destination to the left. The msb is shifted into the CF, and the previous value of CF is shifted into the rightmost bit. In other words, RCL works like just like ROL, except that CF is part of the circle of bits being rotated. See Figure 7.7. The syntax is

```
RCL   destination,1
```

and

```
RCL   destination,CL
```

Figure 7.8 RCR

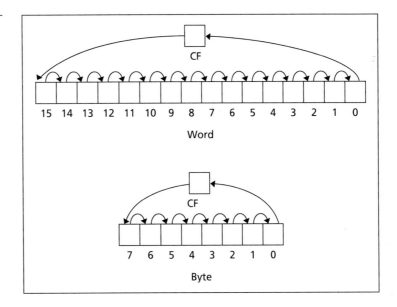

Rotate Carry Right

The instruction **RCR** (Rotate through Carry Right) works just like RCL, except that the bits are rotated to the right. See Figure 7.8. The syntax is

```
RCR   destination,1
```

and

```
RCR   destination,CL
```

Example 7.13 Suppose DH contains 8Ah, CF = 1, and CL contains 3. What are the values of DH and CF after the instruction RCR DH,CL is executed?

Solution:

	CF	DH
initial values	1	10001010
after 1 right rotation	0	11000101
after 2 right rotations	1	01100010
after 3 right rotations	0	10110001 = B1h

Effect of the rotate instructions on the flags

    SF, PF, ZF reflect the result

    AF is undefined

    CF = last bit shifted out

    OF = 1 if result changes sign on the last rotation

An Application: Reversing a Bit Pattern

As an application of the shift and rotate instructions, let's consider the problem of reversing the bit pattern in a byte or word. For example, if AL contains 11011100, we want to make it 00111011.

An easy way to do this is to use SHL to shift the bits out the left end of AL into CF, and then use RCR to move them into the left end of another register; for example, BL. If this is done eight times, BL will contain the reversed bit pattern and it can be copied back into AL. The code is

```
          MOV   CX,8      ;number of operations to do
REVERSE:
          SHL   AL,1      ;get a bit into CF
          RCR   BL,1      ;rotate it into BL
          LOOP  REVERSE   ;loop until done
          MOV   AL,BL     ;AL gets reversed pattern
```

7.4 Binary and Hex I/O

One useful application of the shift and rotate instructions is in binary and hex I/O.

Binary Input

For binary input, we assume a program reads in a binary number from the keyboard, followed by a carriage return. The number actually is a character string of 0's and 1's. As each character is entered, we need to convert it to a bit value, and collect the bits in a register. The following algorithm reads a binary number from the keyboard and stores its value in BX.

Algorithm for Binary Input

```
Clear BX      /* BX will hold binary value */
Input a character /* '0' or '1' */
WHILE character <> CR DO
  Convert character to binary value
  Left shift BX
  Insert value into lsb of BX
  Input a character
END_WHILE
```

Demonstration (for input 110)

```
Clear BX
  BX = 0000 0000 0000 0000
Input character '1', convert to 1
Left shift BX
  BX = 0000 0000 0000 0000
Insert value into lsb
  BX = 0000 0000 0000 0001
Input character '1', convert to 1
Left shift BX
  BX = 0000 0000 0000 0010
Insert value into lsb
  BX = 0000 0000 0000 0011
```

```
Input character '0', convert to 0
Left shift BX
  BX = 0000 0000 0000 0110
Insert value into lsb
  BX = 0000 0000 0000 0110
BX contains 110b.
```

The algorithm assumes (1) input characters are either "0", "1", or CR, and (2) at most 16 binary digits are input. As a new digit is input, the previous bits in BX must be shifted to the left to make room; then an OR operation can be used to insert the new bit into BX. The assembly instructions are

```
          XOR  BX,BX      ;clear BX
          MOV  AH,1       ;input char function
          INT  21H        ;read a character
WHILE_:
          CMP  AL,0DH     ;CR?
          JE   END_WHILE  ;yes, done
          AND  AL,0FH     ;no, convert to binary value
          SHL  BX,1       ;make room for new value
          OR   BL,AL      ;put value into BX
          INT  21H        ;read a character
          JMP  WHILE_     ;loop back
END_WHILE:
```

Binary Output

Outputting the contents of BX in binary also involves the shift operation. Here we only give an algorithm; the assembly code is left to be done as an exercise.

Algorithm for Binary Output

```
FOR 16 times DO
  Rotate left BX /* BX holds output value,
      put msb into CF */
  IF CF = 1
   THEN
    output '1'
   ELSE
    output '0'
  END_IF
END_FOR
```

Hex Input

Hex input consists of digits ("0" to "9") and letters ("A" to "F") followed by a carriage return. For simplicity, we assume that (1) only uppercase letters are used, and (2) the user inputs no more than four hex characters. The process of converting characters to binary values is more involved than it was for binary input, and BX must be shifted four times to make room for a hex value.

Algorithm for Hex Input

```
Clear BX    /* BX will hold input value */
input hex character
WHILE character <> CR DO
  convert character to binary value
  left shift BX 4 times
  insert value into lower 4 bits of BX
  input a character
END_WHILE
```

Demonstration (for input 6AB)

```
Clear BX
  BX = 0000 0000 0000 0000
Input '6', convert to 0110
Left shift BX 4 times
  BX = 0000 0000 0000 0000
Insert value into lower 4 bits of BX
  BX = 0000 0000 0000 0110
Input 'A', convert to Ah = 1010
Left shift BX 4 times
  BX = 0000 0000 0110 0000
Insert value into lower 4 bits of BX
  BX = 0000 0000 0110 1010
Input 'B', convert to 1011
Left shift BX 4 times
  BX = 0000 0110 1010 0000
Insert value into lower 4 bits of BX
  BX = 0000 0110 1010 1011
BX contains 06ABh.
```

Here is the code:

```
                XOR   BX,BX      ;clear BX
                MOV   CL,4       ;counter for 4 shifts
                MOV   AH,1       ;input character function
                INT   21H        ;input a character
WHILE_:
                CMP   AL,0DH     ;CR?
                JE    END_WHILE  ;yes, exit
;convert character to binary value
                CMP   AL,39H     ;a digit?
                JG    LETTER     ;no, a letter
;input is a digit
                AND   AL,0FH     ;convert digit to binary value
                JMP   SHIFT      ;go to insert in BX
LETTER:
                SUB   AL,37H     ;convert letter to binary value
SHIFT:
                SHL   BX,CL      ;make room for new value
;insert value into BX
                OR    BL,AL      ;put value into low 4 bits
                                 ;of BX
                INT   21H        ;input a character
                JMP   WHILE_     ;loop until CR
END_WHILE:
```

Note that the program does not check for valid input characters.

Hex Output

BX contains 16 bits, which equal four hex digit values. To output the contents of BX, we start from the left and get hold of each digit, convert it to a hex character, and output it. The algorithm which follows is similar to that for binary output.

Algorithm for Hex Output

```
FOR 4 times DO
  Move BH to DL    /* BX holds output value */
  shift DL 4 times to the right
  IF DL < 10
   THEN
    convert to character in '0'..'9'
   ELSE
    convert to character in 'A'..'F'
  END_IF
  output character
  Rotate BX left 4 times
END_FOR
```

Demonstration (BX Contains 4CA9h)

```
  BX = 4CA9h = 0100 1100 1010 1001
Move BH to DL
  DL = 0100 1100
Shift DL 4 times to the right
  DL = 0000 0100
Convert to character and output
  DL = 0011 0100 = 34h = '4'
Rotate BX left 4 times
  BX = 1100 1010 1001 0100
Move BH to DL
  DL = 1100 1010
Shift DL 4 times to the right
  DL = 0000 1100
Convert to character and output
  DL = 0100 0011 = 43h = 'C'
Rotate BX left 4 times
  BX = 1010 1001 0100 1100
Move BH to DL
  DL = 1010 1001
Shift DL 4 times to the right
  DL = 0000 1010
Convert to character and output
  DL = 0100 0010 = 42h = 'B'
Rotate BX left 4 times
  BX = 1001 0100 1100 1010
Move BH to DL
  DL = 1001 0100
Shift DL 4 times to the right
```

```
  DL = 0000 1001
Convert to character and output
  DL = 0011 1001 = 39h = '9'
Rotate BX 4 times to the left
  BX = 0100 1100 1010 1001 = original contents
```

Coding the algorithm is left to be done as an exercise.

Summary

- The five logic instructions are AND, OR, NOT, XOR, and TEST.

- The AND instruction can be used to clear individual bits in the destination.

- The OR instruction is useful in setting individual bits in the destination. It can also be used to test the destination for zero.

- The XOR instruction can be used to complement individual bits in the destination. It can also be used to zero out the destination.

- The NOT instruction performs the one's complement operation on the destination.

- The TEST instruction can be used to examine individual bits of the destination. For example, it can determine if the destination contains an even or odd number.

- SAL and SHL shift each destination bit left one place. The most significant bit goes into CF, and a 0 is shifted into the least significant bit.

- SHR shifts each destination bit right one place. The least significant bit goes into CF, and a 0 is shifted into the most significant bit.

- SAR operates like SHR, except that the value of the most significant bit is preserved.

- The shift instructions can be used to do multiplication and division by 2. SHL and SAL double the destination's value unless overflow occurs. SHR and SAR halve the destination's value if it is even; if odd, they halve the destination's value and round down to the nearest integer. SHR should be used for unsigned arithmetic, and SAR for signed arithmetic.

- ROL shifts each destination bit left one position; the most significant bit is rotated into the least significant bit. For ROR, each bit goes right one position, and the least significant bit rotates into the most significant bit. For both instructions, CF gets the last bit rotated out.

- RCL and RCR operate like ROL and ROR, except that a bit rotated out goes into CF, and the value of CF rotates into the destination.

- Multiple shifts and rotates can be performed. CL must contain the number of times the shift or rotate is to be executed.

- The shift and rotate instructions are useful in doing binary and hex I/O.

Glossary

clear — Change a value to 0

complement — Change from a 0 to a 1 or from a 1 to a 0

mask — A bit pattern used in logical operations to clear, set, or test specific bits in an operand

set — Change a bit value to a 1

New Instructions

AND	RCR	SAR
NOT	ROL	SHR
OR	ROR	TEST
RCL	SAL/SHL	XOR

Exercises

1. Perform the following logic operations
   a. 10101111 AND 10001011
   b. 10110001 OR 01001001
   c. 01111100 XOR 11011010
   d. NOT 01011110

2. Give a logic instruction to do each of the following.
   a. Clear the even-numbered bits of AX, leaving the other bits unchanged.
   b. Set the most and least significant bits of BL, leaving the other bits unchanged.
   c. Complement the msb of DX, leaving the other bits unchanged.
   d. Replace the value of the word variable WORD1 by its one's complement.

3. Use the TEST instruction to do each of the following.
   a. Set ZF if the contents of AX is zero.
   b. Clear ZF if BX contains an odd number.
   c. Set SF if DX contains a negative number.
   d. Set ZF if DX contains a zero or positive number.
   e. Set PF if BL contains an even number of 1 bits.

4. Suppose AL contains 11001011b and CF = 1. Give the new contents of AL after each of the following instructions is executed. Assume the preceding initial conditions for each part of this question.
   a. SHL AL,1
   b. SHR AL,1
   c. ROL AL,CL if CL contains 2
   d. ROR AL,CL if CL contains 3
   e. SAR AL,CL if CL contains 2
   f. RCL AL,1
   g. RCR AL,CL if CL contains 3

5. Write one or more instructions to do each of the following. Assume overflow does not occur.
   a. Double the value of byte variable B5.
   b. Multiply the value of AL by 8.
   c. Divide 32142 by 4 and put the quotient in AX.
   d. Divide –2145 by 16 and put the quotient in BX.
6. Write instructions to do each of the following:
   a. Assuming AL has a value less than 10, convert it to a decimal character.
   b. Assuming DL contains the ASCII code of an uppercase letter, convert it to lower case.
7. Write instructions to do each of the following.
   a. Multiply the value of BL by 10d. Assume overflow does not occur.
   b. Suppose AL contains a positive number. Divide AL by 8, and put the remainder in AH. (*Hint:* use ROR.)

Programming Exercises

8. Write a program that prompts the user to enter a character, and on subsequent lines prints its ASCII code in binary, and the number of 1 bits in its ASCII code.

   Sample execution:

   ```
   TYPE A CHARACTER: A
   THE ASCII CODE OF A IN BINARY IS 01000001
   THE NUMBER OF 1 BITS IS 2
   ```

9. Write a program that prompts the user to enter a character and prints the ASCII code of the character in hex on the next line. Repeat this process until the user types a carriage return.

   Sample execution:

   ```
   TYPE A CHARACTER: Z
   THE ASCII CODE OF Z IN HEX IS 5A
   TYPE A CHARACTER:
   ```

10. Write a program that prompts the user to type a hex number of four hex digits or less, and outputs it in binary on the next line. If the user enters an illegal character, he or she should be prompted to begin again. Accept only uppercase letters.

    Sample execution:

    ```
    TYPE A HEX NUMBER (0 TO FFFF): 1a
    ILLEGAL HEX DIGIT, TRY AGAIN: 1ABC
    IN BINARY IT IS 0001101010111100
    ```

    Your program may ignore any input beyond four characters.

11. Write a program that prompts the user to type a binary number of 16 digits or less, and outputs it in hex on the next line. If the user enters an illegal character, he or she should be prompted to begin again.

    Sample execution:

    ```
    TYPE A BINARY NUMBER, UP TO 16 DIGITS: 11100001
    IN HEX IT IS E1
    ```

Your program may ignore any input beyond 16 characters.

12. Write a program that prompts the user to enter two binary numbers of up to 8 digits each, and prints their sum on the next line in binary. If the user enters an illegal character, he or she should be prompted to begin again. Each input ends with a carriage return.

    Sample execution:

    ```
    TYPE A BINARY NUMBER, UP TO 8 DIGITS:11001010
    TYPE A BINARY NUMBER, UP TO 8 DIGITS:10011100
    THE BINARY SUM IS 101100110
    ```

13. Write a program that prompts the user to enter two unsigned hex numbers, 0 to FFFFh, and prints their sum in hex on the next line. If the user enters an illegal character, he or she should be prompted to begin again. Your program should be able to handle the possibility of unsigned overflow. Each input ends with a carriage return.

    Sample execution:

    ```
    TYPE A HEX NUMBER, 0 - FFFF: 21AB
    TYPE A HEX NUMBER, 0 - FFFF: FE03
    THE SUM IS 11FAE
    ```

14. Write a program that prompts the user to enter a string of decimal digits, ending with a carriage return, and prints their sum in hex on the next line. If the user enters an illegal character, he or she should be prompted to begin again.

    Sample execution:

    ```
    ENTER A DECIMAL DIGIT STRING: 1299843
    THE SUM OF THE DIGITS IN HEX IS 0024
    ```

8

The Stack and Introduction to Procedures

Overview

The stack segment of a program is used for temporary storage of data and addresses. In this chapter we show how the stack can be manipulated, and how it is used to implement procedures.

In section 8.1, we introduce the PUSH and POP instructions that add and remove words from the stack. Because the last word to be added to the stack is the first to be removed, a stack can be used to reverse a list of data; this property is exploited in section 8.2.

Procedures are extremely important in high-level language programming, and the same is true in assembly language. Sections 8.3 and 8.4 discuss the essentials of assembly language procedures. At the machine level, we can see exactly how a procedure is called and how it returns to the calling program. In section 8.5, we present an example of a procedure that performs binary multiplication by bit shifting and addition. This example also gives us an excuse to learn a little more about the DEBUG program.

8.1 The Stack

A *stack* is one-dimensional data structure. Items are added and removed from one end of the structure; that is, it is processed in a "last-in, first-out" manner. The most recent addition to the stack is called the **top of the stack**. A familiar example is a stack of dishes; the last dish to go on the stack is the top one, and it's the only one that can be removed easily.

A program must set aside a block of memory to hold the stack. We have been doing this by declaring a stack segment; for example,

```
.STACK    100H
```

When the program is assembled and loaded in memory, SS will contain the segment number of the stack segment. For the preceding stack declaration, SP, the stack pointer, is initialized to 100h. This represents the empty stack position. When the stack is not empty, SP contains the offset address of the top of the stack.

PUSH and PUSHF

To add a new word to the stack we **PUSH** it on. The syntax is

```
PUSH    source
```

where source is a 16-bit register or memory word. For example,

```
PUSH    AX
```

Execution of PUSH causes the following to happen:

1. SP is decreased by 2.
2. A copy of the source content is moved to the address specified by SS:SP. The source is unchanged.

The instruction **PUSHF**, which has no operands, pushes the contents of the FLAGS register onto the stack.

Initially, SP contains the offset address of the memory location immediately following the stack segment; the first PUSH decreases SP by 2, making it point to the last word in the stack segment. Because each PUSH

Figure 8.1A Empty Stack

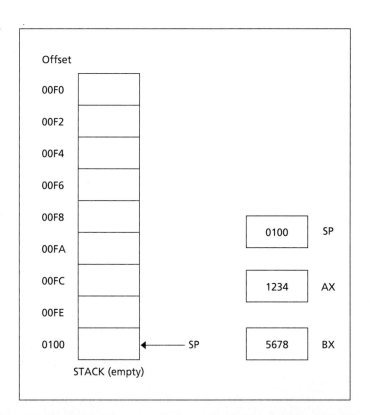

Figure 8.1B After PUSH AX

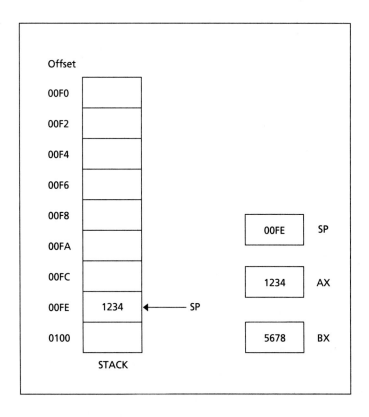

decreases SP, the stack grows toward the beginning of memory. Figure 8.1 shows how PUSH works.

8.1C After PUSH BX

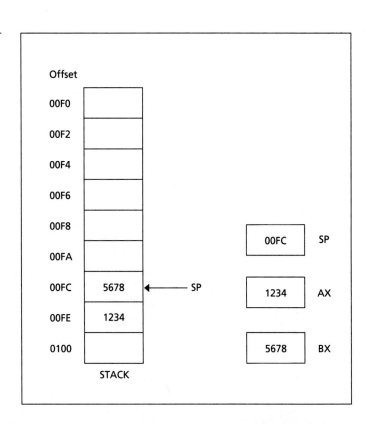

POP and POPF

To remove the top item from the stack, we **POP** it. The syntax is

```
POP    destination
```

where destination is a 16-bit register (except IP) or memory word. For example,

```
POP    BX
```

Executing POP causes this to happen:

1. The content of SS:SP (the top of the stack) is moved to the destination.
2. SP is increased by 2.

Figure 8.2 shows how POP works.

The instruction **POPF** pops the top of the stack into the FLAGS register. There is no effect of PUSH, PUSHF, POP, POPF on the flags.

Note that PUSH and POP are word operations, so a byte instruction such as

Illegal: PUSH DL

is illegal. So is a push of immediate data, such as

Illegal: PUSH 2

Note: an immediate data push is legal for the 80186/80486 processors. These processors are discussed in Chapter 20.

In addition to the user's program, the operating system uses the stack for its own purposes. For example, to implement the INT 21h functions, DOS saves any registers it uses on the stack and restores them when the interrupt routine is completed. This does not cause a problem for the user

8.2A Before POP

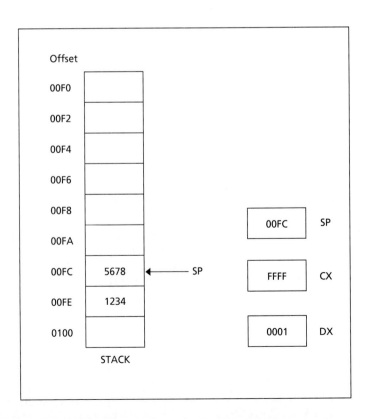

8.2B After POP CX

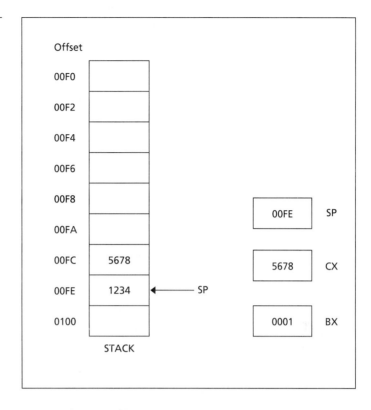

because any values DOS pushes onto the stack are popped off by DOS before it returns control to the user's program.

8.2C After POP DX

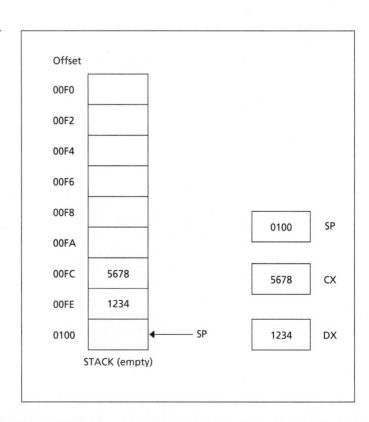

8.2 A Stack Application

Because the stack behaves in a last-in, first-out manner, the order that items come off the stack is the reverse of the order they enter it. The following program uses this property to read a sequence of characters and display them in reverse order on the next line.

Algorithm to Reverse Input

```
Display a '?'
Initialize count to 0
Read a character
WHILE character is not a carriage return DO
   push character onto the stack
   increment count
   read a character
END_WHILE;
Go to a new line
FOR count times DO
   pop a character from the stack;
   display it;
END_FOR
```

Here is the program:

Program Listing PGM8_1.ASM

```
1:      TITLE PGM8_1:REVERSE INPUT
2:      .MODEL    SMALL
3:      .STACK    100H
4:      .CODE
5:      MAIN      PROC
6:      ;display user prompt
7:              MOV     AH,2        ;prepare to display
8:              MOV     DL,'?'      ;char to display
9:              INT     21H         ;display '?'
10:     ;initialize character count
11:             XOR     CX,CX       ;count = 0
12:     ;read a character
13:             MOV     AH,1        ;prepare to read
14:             INT     21H         ;read a char
15:     ;while character is not a carriage return do
16:     WHILE_:
17:             CMP     AL,0DH      ;CR?
18:             JE      END_WHILE   ;yes, exit loop
19:             ;save character on the stack and increment count
20:             PUSH    AX          ;push it on stack
21:             INC     CX          ;count = count + 1
22:     ;read a character
23:             INT     21H         ;read a char
24:             JMP     WHILE_      ;loop back
25:     END_WHILE:
26:     ;go to a new line
27:             MOV     AH,2        ;display char fcn
28:             MOV     DL,0DH      ;CR
29:             INT     21H         ;execute
30:             MOV     DL,0AH      ;LF
```

```
31:             INT     21H             ;execute
32:             JCXZ    EXIT            ;exit if no characters read
33: ;for count times do
34: TOP:
35: ;pop a character from the stack
36:             POP     DX              ;get a char from stack
37: ;display it
38:             INT     21H             ;display it
39:             LOOP    TOP
40: ;end_for
41: EXIT:
42:             MOV     AH,4CH
43:             INT     21H
44: MAIN        ENDP
45:             END     MAIN
```

Because the number of characters to be entered is unknown, the program uses CX to count them. CX controls the FOR loop that displays the characters in reverse order.

In lines 16–24, the program executes a WHILE loop that pushes characters on the stack and reads new ones, until a carriage return is entered. Even though the input characters are in AL, it's necessary to save all of AX on the stack, because the operand of PUSH must be a word.

When the program exits the WHILE loop (line 25), all the characters are on the stack, with the low byte of the top of the stack containing the last character to be entered. AL contains the ASCII code of the carriage return.

At line 32, the program checks to see if any characters were read. If not, CX contains 0 and the program jumps to the DOS exit. If any characters *were* read, the program enters a FOR loop that repeatedly pops the stack into DX (so that DL will get a character code), and displays a character.

Sample executions:

```
C>PGM8_1
?THIS IS A TEST
TSET A SI SIHT

C>PGM8_1
?A
A

C>PGM8_1
?       (only carriage return typed)
        (no output)
C>
```

8.3 Terminology of Procedures

In Chapter 6, we mentioned the idea of top-down program design. The idea is to take the original problem and decompose it into a series of subproblems that are easier to solve than the original problem. High-level languages usually employ procedures to solve these subproblems, and we can do the same thing in assembly language. Thus an assembly language program can be structured as a collection of procedures.

One of the procedures is the main procedure, and it contains the entry point to the program. To carry out a task, the main procedure **calls** one of the other procedures. It is also possible for these procedures to call each other, or for a procedure to call itself.

When one procedure calls another, control transfers to the called procedure and its instructions are executed; the called procedure usually returns control to the caller at the next instruction after the call statement (Figure 8.3). For high-level languages, the mechanism by which call and return are implemented is hidden from the programmer, but in assembly language we can see how it works (see section 8.4).

Procedure Declaration

The syntax of procedure declaration is the following:

```
name      PROC    type
;body of the procedure
          RET
name      ENDP
```

Name is the user-defined name of the procedure. The optional operand type is **NEAR** or **FAR** (if type is omitted, NEAR is assumed). NEAR means that the statement that calls the procedure is in the same segment as the procedure itself; FAR means that the calling statement is in a different segment. In the following, we assume all procedures are NEAR; FAR procedures are discussed in Chapter 14.

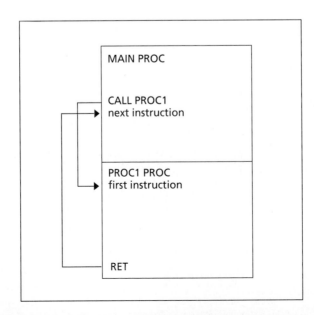

Figure 8.3 *Procedure Call and Return*

RET

The **RET** (return) instruction causes control to transfer back to the calling procedure. Every procedure (except the main procedure) should have a RET someplace; usually it's the last statement in the procedure.

Communication Between Procedures

A procedure must have a way to receive values from the procedure that calls it, and a way to return results. Unlike high-level language procedures, assembly language procedures do not have parameter lists, so it's up to the programmer to devise a way for procedures to communicate. For example, if there are only a few input and output values, they can be placed in registers. The general issue of procedure communication is discussed in Chapter 14.

Procedure Documentation

In addition to the required procedure syntax, it's a good idea to document a procedure so that anyone reading the program listing will know what the procedure does, where it gets its input, and where it delivers its output. In this book, we generally document procedures with a comment block like this:

```
; (describe what the procedure does)
; input:   (where it receives information from
            the calling program)
; output:  (where it delivers results to
            the calling program)
; uses:    (a list of procedures that it calls)
```

8.4 CALL and RET

To invoke a procedure, the **CALL** instruction is used. There are two kinds of procedure calls, **direct** and **indirect**. The syntax of a direct procedure call is

```
CALL    name
```

where name is the name of a procedure. The syntax of an indirect procedure call is

```
CALL    address_expression
```

where address_expression specifies a register or memory location containing the address of a procedure.

Executing a CALL instruction causes the following to happen:

1. The return address to the calling program is saved on the stack. This is the offset of the next instruction after the CALL statement. The segment:offset of this instruction is in CS:IP at the time the call is executed.

8.4 CALL and RET

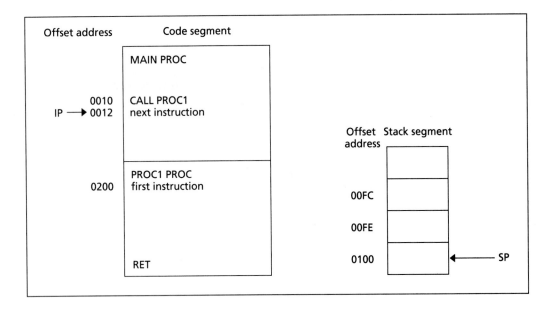

Figure 8.4A Before CALL

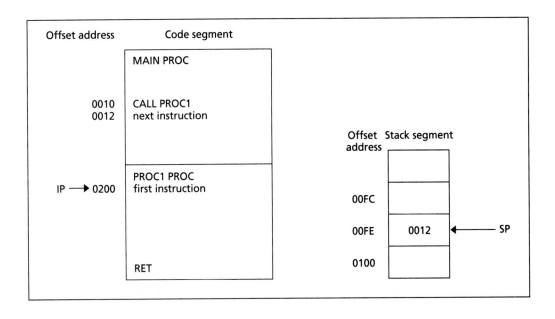

Figure 8.4B After CALL

2. IP gets the offset address of the first instruction of the procedure. This transfers control to the procedure. See Figures 8.4A and 8.4B.

To return from a procedure, the instruction

```
RET    pop_value
```

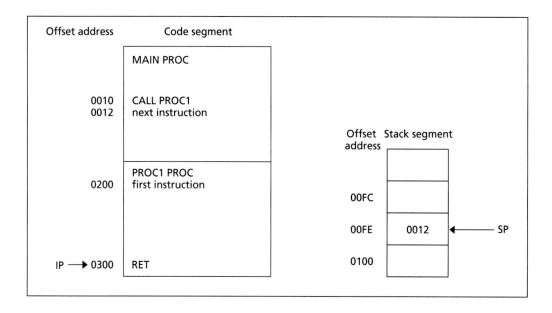

Figure 8.5A Before RET

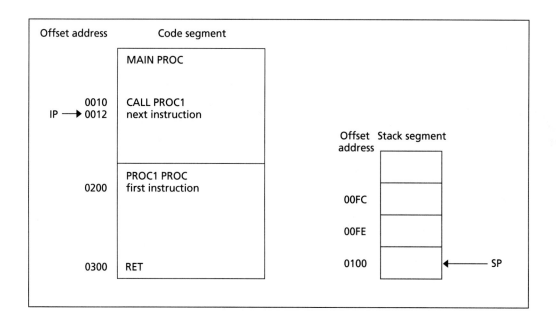

Figure 8.5B After RET

is executed. The integer argument pop_value is optional. For a NEAR procedure, execution of RET causes the stack to be popped into IP. If a pop_value N is specified, it is added to SP, and thus has the effect of removing N additional bytes from the stack. CS:IP now contains the segment:offset of the return address, and control returns to the calling program. See Figures 8.5A and 8.5B.

8.5 An Example of a Procedure

As an example, we will write a procedure for finding the product of two positive integers A and B by addition and bit shifting. This is one way unsigned multiplication may be implemented on the computer (in Chapter 9 we introduce the multiplication instructions).

Multiplication algorithm:

```
Product = 0
REPEAT
   IF lsb of B is 1     (Recall lsb = least
            significant bit)
   THEN
      Product = Product + A
   END_IF
   Shift left A
   Shift right B
UNTIL B = 0
```

For example, if A = 111b = 7 and B = 1101b = 13

```
Product = 0
Since lsb of B is 1, Product = 0 + 111b = 111b
Shift left A: A = 1110b
Shift right B: B = 110b

Since lsb of B is 0,
Shift left A: A = 11100b
Shift right B: B = 11b

Since lsb of B is 1
Product = 111b + 11100b = 100011b
Shift left A: A = 111000b
Shift right B: B = 1

Since lsb of B is 1
Product = 100011b + 111000b = 1011011b
Shift left A: A = 1110000b
Shift right B: B = 0

Since lsb of B = 0
Return Product = 1011011b = 91d
```

Note that we get the same answer by performing the usual decimal multiplication process on the binary numbers:

$$
\begin{array}{r}
111b \\
\times\, 1101b \\
\hline
111 \\
000 \\
111 \\
111 \\
\hline
1011011b
\end{array}
$$

In the following program, the algorithm is coded as a procedure MULTIPLY. The main program has no input or output; we will use DEBUG for the I/O.

Program Listing PGM8_2.ASM

```
1:  TITLE     PGM8_2: MULTIPLICATION BY ADD AND SHIFT
2:  .MODEL    SMALL
3:  .STACK    100H
4:  .CODE
5:  MAIN      PROC
6:  ;execute in DEBUG. Place A in AX and B in BX
7:            CALL    MULTIPLY
8:  ;DX will contain the product
9:            MOV     AH,4CH
10:           INT     21H
11: MAIN      ENDP
12: MULTIPLY PROC
13: ;multiplies two nos. A and B by shifting and addition
14: ;input:   AX = A, BX = B. Nos. in range 0 - FFh
15: ;output:  DX = product
16:           PUSH    AX
17:           PUSH    BX
18:           XOR     DX,DX           ;product = 0
19: REPEAT:
20: ;if B is odd
21:           TEST    BX,1            ;is B odd?
22:           JZ      END_IF          ;no, even
23: ;then
24:           ADD     DX,AX           ;prod = prod + A
25: END_IF:
26:           SHL     AX,1            ;shift left A
27:           SHR     BX,1            ;Shift right B
28: ;until
29:           JNZ     REPEAT
30:           POP     BX
31:           POP     AX
32:           RET
33: MULTIPLY ENDP
34:           END     MAIN
```

Procedure MULTIPLY receives its input A and B through registers AX and BX, respectively. Values are placed in these registers by the user inside the DEBUG program; the product is returned in DX. In order to avoid overflow, A and B are restricted to range from 0 to FFh.

A procedure usually begins by saving all the registers it uses on the stack and ends by restoring these registers. This is done because the calling program may have data stored in registers, and the actions of the procedure could cause unwanted side effects if the registers are not preserved. Even though it's not really necessary in this program, we illustrate this practice by pushing AX and BX on the stack in lines 16 and 17, and restoring them in lines 30 and 31. The registers are popped off the stack in the reverse order that they were pushed on.

After clearing DX, which will hold the product, the procedure enters a REPEAT loop (lines 19–29). At line 22, the procedure checks BX's least significant bit. If the lsb of BX is 1, then AX is added to the product in DX; if the lsb of BX is 0, the procedure skips to line 26. Here AX is shifted left, and BX is shifted right; the loop continues until BX = 0. The procedure exits with the product in DX.

8.5 An Example of a Procedure

After assembling and linking the program, we take it into DEBUG (in the following, the user's response appears in boldface):

C> **DEBUG PGM8_2.EXE**

DEBUG responds with its command prompt "-". To get a listing of the program, we use the U (unassemble) command.

```
-U
177F:0000 E80400         CALL    0007
177F:0003 B44C           MOV     AH,4C
177F:0005 CD21           INT     21
177F:0007 50             PUSH    AX
177F:0008 53             PUSH    BX
177F:0009 33D2           XOR     DX,DX
177F:000B F7C30100       TEST    BX,0001
177F:000F 7402           JZ      0013
177F:0011 03D0           ADD     DX,AX
177F:0013 D1E0           SHL     AX,1
177F:0015 D1EB           SHR     BX,1
177F:0017 75F2           JNZ     000B
177F:0019 5B             POP     BX
177F:001A 58             POP     AX
177F:001B C3             RET
177F:001C E3D1           JCXZ    FFEF
177F:001E E38B           JCXZ    FFAB
```

The U command causes DEBUG to interpret the contents of memory as machine language instructions. The display gives the segment:offset of each instruction, the machine code, and the assembly code. All numbers are expressed in hex. From the first statement, CALL 0007, we can see that procedure MAIN extends from 0000 to 0005; procedure MULTIPLY begins at 0007 and ends at 001B with RET. The instructions after this are garbage.

Before entering the data, let's look at the registers.

```
-R
AX=0000  BX=0000  CX=001C  DX=0000  SP=0100  BP=0000  SI=0000  DI=0000
DS=176F  ES=176F  SS=1781  CS=177F  IP=0000  NV UP EI PL NZ NA PO NC
177F:0000 E80400     CALL    0007
```

The initial value of SP = 100h reflects that fact that we allocated 100h bytes for the stack. To have a look at the empty stack, we can dump memory with the D command.

```
DSS:F0 FF
1781:00F0  00 00 00 00 00 00 6F 17-A4 13 07 00 6F 17 00 00
```

The command DSS:F0 FF means to display the memory bytes from SS:F0 to SS:FF. This is the last 16 bytes in the stack segment. The contents of each byte is displayed as two hex digits. Because the stack is empty, everything in this display is garbage.

Before executing the program, we need to place the numbers A and B in AX and BX, respectively. We will use A = 7 and B = 13 = Dh. To enter A, we use the R command:

```
-RAX
AX 0000:7
```

The command RAX means that we want to change the content of AX. DEBUG displays the current value (0000), followed by a colon, and waits for us to enter the new value. Similarly we can change the initial value of B in BX:

```
-RBX
BX 0000:D
```

Now let's look at the registers again.

```
-R
AX=0007  BX=000D  CX=001C  DX=0000  SP=0100  BP=0000  SI=0000  DI=0000
DS=176F  ES=176F  SS=1781  CS=177F  IP=0000  NV UP EI PL NZ NA PO NC
177F:0000 E80400     CALL    0007
```

We see that AX and BX now contain the initial values.

To see the effect of the first instruction, CALL 0007, we use the T (trace) command. It will execute a single instruction and display the registers.

154   8.5 An Example of a Procedure

```
-T
AX=0007  BX=000D  CX=001C  DX=0000  SP=00FE  BP=0000  SI=0000  DI=0000
DS=176F  ES=176F  SS=1781  CS=177F  IP=0007  NV UP EI PL NZ NA PO NC
177F:0007 50         PUSH    AX
```

We notice two changes in the registers: (1) IP now contains 0007, the starting offset of procedure MULTIPLY; and (2) because the CALL instruction pushes the return address to procedure MAIN on the stack, SP has decreased from 0100h to 00FEh. Here are the last 16 bytes of the stack segment again:

```
-D SS:F0 FF
1781:00F0   00 00 00 00 07 00 00 00-07 00 7F 17 A4 13 03 00
```

The return address is 0003, but is displayed as 03 00. This is because DEBUG displays the low byte of a word before the high byte.

The first three instructions of procedure MULTIPLY push AX and BX onto the stack, and clear DX. To see the effect, we use the **G** (go) command. The syntax is

```
G offset
```

It causes the program to execute instructions and stop at the specified offset. From the unassembled listing given earlier, we can see that the next instruction after XOR DX,DX is at offset 000Bh.

```
-G B
AX=0007  BX=000D  CX=001C  DX=0000  SP=00FA  BP=0000  SI=0000  DI=0000
DS=176F  ES=176F  SS=1781  CS=177F  IP=000B  NV UP EI PL ZR NA PE NC
177F:000B F7C30100   TEST    BX,0001
```

We see that the two PUSHes have caused SP to decrease by 4, from 00FEh to 00FAh. Now the stack looks like this:

```
-D SS:F0 FF
1781:00F0   00 00 00 00 07 00 00 17-A4 13 0D 00 07 00 03 00
```

The stack now contains three words; the values of BX (000D), AX (0007), and the return address (0003). These are shown as 0D 00 07 00 03 00.

Now let's watch the procedure in action. To do so, we will execute to the end of the REPEAT loop at offset 0017h:

```
-G17
AX=000E  BX=0006  CX=001C  DX=0007  SP=00FA  BP=0000  SI=0000  DI=0000
DS=176F  ES=176F  SS=1781  CS=177F  IP=0017  NV UP EI PL NZ AC PE CY
177F:0017 75F2        JNZ  000B
```

Because the initial value of B in BX was 0Dh = 1101b, the lsb of BX is 1, so AX is added to the product in DX, giving 111b = 0007h. AX is shifted left, which doubles A to 14d = 000Eh, and BX is shifted right, which halves BX (and rounds down) to 0006h = 110b.

To get to the top of the loop, we'll use the T command again:

```
-T
AX=000E  BX=0006  CX=001C  DX=0007  SP=00FA  BP=0000  SI=0000  DI=0000
DS=176F  ES=176F  SS=1781  CS=177F  IP=000B  NV UP EI PL NZ AC PE CY
177F:000B F7C30100    TEST BX,0001
```

and execute again to the bottom:

```
-G17
AX=001C  BX=0003  CX=001C  DX=0007  SP=00FA  BP=0000  SI=0000  DI=0000
DS=176F  ES=176F  SS=1781  CS=177F  IP=0017  NV UP EI PL NZ AC PE NC
177F:0017 75F2        JNZ  000B
```

Because BX = 0006h = 110b, the lsb of BX is 0, so the product in DX stays the same. AX is shifted left to 11100b = 1Ch and BX is shifted right to 11b = 3h.

After two more trips through the loop, the product is in DX. Watch AX, BX, and DX change:

```
-T
AX=001C  BX=0003  CX=001C  DX=0007  SP=00FA  BP=0000  SI=0000  DI=0000
DS=176F  ES=176F  SS=1781  CS=177F  IP=000B  NV UP EI PL NZ AC PE NC
177F:000B F7C30100    TEST BX,0001

-G17
AX=0038  BX=0001  CX=001C  DX=0023  SP=00FA  BP=0000  SI=0000  DI=0000
DS=176F  ES=176F  SS=1781  CS=177F  IP=0017  NV UP EI PL NZ AC PO CY
177F:0017 75F2        JNZ  000B
```

8.5 An Example of a Procedure

```
-T
AX=0038  BX=0001  CX=001C  DX=0023  SP=00FA  BP=0000  SI=0000  DI=0000
DS=176F  ES=176F  SS=1781  CS=177F  IP=000B  NV UP EI PL NZ AC PO CY
177F:000B F7C30100      TEST BX,0001

-G17
AX=0070  BX=0000  CX=001C  DX=005B  SP=00FA  BP=0000  SI=0000  DI=0000
DS=176F  ES=176F  SS=1781  CS=177F  IP=0017  NV UP EI PL ZR AC PE CY
177F:0017 75F2          JNZ 000B
```

The last right shift made BX = 0, ZF = 1, so the loop ends. The product = 91 = 5Bh is in DX.

To terminate the procedure, we trace through the JNZ and the two POP instructions:

```
-T
AX=0070  BX=0000  CX=001C  DX=005B  SP=00FA  BP=0000  SI=0000  DI=0000
DS=176F  ES=176F  SS=1781  CS=177F  IP=0019  NV UP EI PL ZR AC PE CY
177F:0019 5B            POP BX

-T
AX=0070  BX=000D  CX=001C  DX=005B  SP=00FC  BP=0000  SI=0000  DI=0000
DS=176F  ES=176F  SS=1781  CS=177F  IP=001A  NV UP EI PL ZR AC PE CY
177F:001A 58            POP AX

-T
AX=0007  BX=000D  CX=001C  DX=005B  SP=00FE  BP=0000  SI=0000  DI=0000
DS=176F  ES=176F  SS=1781  CS=177F  IP=001B  NV UP EI PL ZR AC PE CY
177F:001B C3            RET
```

The two POPs have restored AX and BX to their original values. Let's look at the stack:

```
-DSS:F0 FF
1781:00F0  70 00 70 00 07 00 00 00-1B 00 7F 17 A4 13 03 00
```

The values 000D and 0007 are no longer in the display. This is not a result of the POP instruction; it's because DEBUG is also using the stack.

Finally, we trace the RET.

```
-T
AX=0007  BX=000D  CX=001C  DX=005B  SP=0100  BP=0000  SI=0000  DI=0000
DS=176F  ES=176F  SS=1781  CS=177F  IP=0003  NV UP EI PL ZR AC PE CY
177F:0003 B44C      MOV  AH,4C
```

RET causes IP to get 0003, the return address to MAIN. SP goes back to 100h, its original value. To finish executing the program, we just type G:

```
-G
Program terminated normally
```

and we exit DEBUG by typing Q (quit).

```
-Q
>C
```

Summary

- The stack is a temporary storage area used by both application programs and the operating system.

- The stack is a last-in, first-out data structure. SS:SP points to the top of the stack.

- The stack-altering instructions are PUSH, PUSHF, POP, and POPF. PUSH adds a new top word to the stack, and POP removes the top word. PUSHF saves the FLAGS register on the stack and POPF puts the stack top into the FLAGS register.

- SP decreases by 2 when PUSH or PUSHF is executed, and it increases by 2 when POP or POPF is executed. SP is initialized to the first word after stack segment when the program is loaded.

- A procedure is a subprogram. Assembly language programs are typically broken into two procedures. One of the procedures is the main procedure, which contains the entry point to the program. Procedures may call other procedures, or themselves.

- There are two kinds of procedures, NEAR and FAR. A NEAR procedure is in the same code segment as the calling program, and a FAR procedure is in a different segment.

- The CALL instruction is used to invoke a procedure. For a NEAR procedure, execution of CALL causes the offset address of the next instruction in line after the CALL to be saved on the stack, and the IP gets the offset of the first instruction in the procedure.

- Procedures end with a RET instruction. Its execution causes the stack to be popped into IP, and control returns to the calling program. In order for the return address to be accessible, the procedure must ensure that it is at the top of the stack when RET is executed.
- In assembly language, procedures often pass data through registers.

Glossary

direct procedure call	A procedure call of form CALL name
FAR procedure	A procedure that can be called by procedures residing in any segment
indirect procedure call	A procedure call of form CALL addr_exp
NEAR procedure	A procedure that can only be called by another procedure residing in the same segment
top of the stack	The last word of data added to the stack

New Instructions

```
CALL         POPF         PUSHF
POP          PUSH         RET
```

Exercises

1. Suppose the stack segment is declared as follows:

   ```
   .STACK   100h
   ```

   a. What is the hex contents of SP when the program begins?
   b. What is the maximum hex number of words that the stack may contain?

2. Suppose that AX = 1234h, BX = 5678h, CX = 9ABCh, and SP = 100h. Give the contents of AX, BX, CX, and SP after executing the following instructions:

   ```
   PUSH   AX
   PUSH   BX
   XCHG   AX,CX
   POP    CX
   PUSH   AX
   POP    BX
   ```

3. When the stack has completely filled the stack area, SP = 0. If another word is pushed onto the stack, what would happen to SP? What might happen to the program?

4. Suppose a program contains the lines

   ```
   CALL   PROC1
   MOV    AX,BX
   ```

   and (a) instruction MOV AX,BX is stored at 08FD:0203h, (b) PROC1 is a NEAR procedure that begins at 08FD:300h, (c) SP = 010Ah. What are the contents of IP and SP just after CALL PROC1 is executed? What word is on top of the stack?

5. Suppose SP = 0200h, top of stack = 012Ah. What are the contents of IP and SP
   a. after RET is executed, where RET appears in a NEAR procedure?
   b. after RET 4 is executed, where RET appears in a NEAR procedure?
6. Write some code to
   a. place the top of the stack into AX, without changing the stack contents.
   b. place the word that is below the stack top into CX, without changing the stack contents. You may use AX.
   c. exchange the top two words on the stack. You may use AX and BX.
7. Procedures are supposed to return the stack to the calling program in the same condition that they received it. However, it may be useful to have procedures that alter the stack. For example, suppose we would like to write a NEAR procedure SAVE_REGS that saves BX,CX,DX,SI,DI,BP,DS, and ES on the stack. After pushing these registers, the stack would look like this:

   ```
   ES content
   .
   .
   .
   DX content
   CX content
   BX content
   return_address (offset)
   ```

   Now, unfortunately, SAVE_REGS can't return to the calling program, because the return address is not at the top of the stack.
   a. Devise a way to implement a procedure SAVE_REGS that gets around this problem (you may use AX to do this).
   b. Write a procedure RESTORE_REGS that restores the registers that SAVE_REGS has saved.

Programming Exercises

8. Write a program that lets the user type some text, consisting of words separated by blanks, ending with a carriage return, and displays the text in the same word order as entered, but with the letters in each word reversed. For example, "this is a test" becomes "siht si a tset". *Hint:* modify program PGM8_2.ASM in section 8.3.

9. A problem in elementary algebra is to decide if an expression containing several kinds of brackets, such as, [,],{,},(,), is correctly bracketed. This is the case if (a) there are the same number of left and right brackets of each kind, and (b) when a right bracket appears, the most recent preceding unmatched left bracket should be of the same type. For example,

   (a + [b − {c × (d − e)}] + f) is correctly bracketed, but

   (a + [b − {c × (d − e)] } + f) is not

   Correct bracketing can be decided by using a stack. The expression is scanned left to right. When a left bracket is encountered, it is pushed onto the stack. When a right bracket is encountered, the stack is popped (if the stack is empty, there are too many right brackets) and the brackets are compared. If they are of the same type, the scanning continues. If there is a mismatch, the expression is incorrectly bracketed. At the end of the expression, if the stack is empty the expression is correctly bracketed. If the stack is not empty, there are too many left brackets.

Write a program that lets the user type in an algebraic expression, ending with a carriage return, that contains round (parentheses), square, and curly brackets. As the expression is being typed in, the program evaluates each character. If at any point the expression is incorrectly bracketed (too many right brackets or a mismatch between left and right brackets), the program tells the user to start over. After the carriage return is typed, if the expression is correct, the program displays "expression is correct." If not, the program displays "too many left brackets". In both cases, the program asks the user if he or she wants to continue. If the user types 'Y', the program runs again.

Your program does not need to store the input string, only check it for correctness.

Sample execution:

```
ENTER AN ALGEBRAIC EXPRESSION:
(a + b)]TOO MANY RIGHT BRACKETS. BEGIN AGAIN!
ENTER AN ALGEBRAIC EXPRESSION
(a + [b - c] x d)
EXPRESSION IS CORRECT
TYPE Y IF YOU WANT TO CONTINUE:Y
ENTER AN ALGEBRAIC EXPRESSION:
[a + b x (c - d) - e}BRACKET MISMATCH. BEGIN AGAIN!
ENTER AN ALGEBRAIC EXPRESSION:
((a + [b - {c x (d - e) } ] + f)
TOO MANY LEFT BRACKETS. BEGIN AGAIN!
ENTER AN ALGEBRAIC EXPRESSION:
I'VE HAD ENOUGH
EXPRESSION IS CORRECT
TYPE Y IF YOU WANT TO CONTINUE:N
```

10. The following method can be used to generate random numbers in the range 1 to 32767.

Start with any number in this range.
Shift left once.
Replace bit 0 by the XOR of bits 14 and 15.
Clear bit 15.

Write the following procedures:

a. A procedure READ that lets the user enter a binary number and stores it in AX. You may use the code for binary input given in section 7.4.

b. A procedure RANDOM that receives a number in AX and returns a random number in AX.

c. A procedure WRITE that displays AX in binary. You may use the algorithm given in section 7.4.

Write a program that displays a '?', calls READ to read a binary number, and calls RANDOM and WRITE to compute and display 100 random numbers. The numbers should be displayed four per line, with four blanks separating the numbers.

9

Multiplication and Division Instructions

Overview

In Chapter 7, we saw how to do multiplication and division by shifting the bits in a byte or word. Left and right shifts can be used for multiplying and dividing by powers of 2. In this chapter, we introduce instructions for multiplying and dividing any numbers.

The process of multiplication and division is different for signed and unsigned numbers, so there are different instructions for signed and unsigned multiplication and division. Also, these instructions have byte and word forms. Sections 9.1 through 9.4 cover the details.

One of the most useful applications of multiplication and division is to implement decimal input and output. In section 9.5, we write procedures to carry out these operations. This application greatly extends our program's I/O capability.

9.1 MUL and IMUL

Signed Versus Unsigned Multiplication

In binary multiplication, signed and unsigned numbers must be treated differently. For example, suppose we want to multiply the eight-bit numbers 10000000 and 11111111. Interpreted as unsigned numbers, they represent 128 and 255, respectively. The product is 32,640 = 0111111110000000b. However, taken as signed numbers, they represent –128 and –1, respectively, and the product is 128 = 0000000010000000b.

Because signed and unsigned multiplication lead to different results, there are two multiplication instructions: **MUL** (multiply) for unsigned multiplication and **IMUL** (integer multiply) for signed multiplication. These instructions multiply bytes or words. If two bytes are multiplied, the product is a word (16 bits). If two words are multiplied, the product is a doubleword (32 bits). The syntax of these instructions is

```
MUL    source
```

and

```
IMUL   source
```

Byte Form

For byte multiplication, one number is contained in the source and the other is assumed to be in AL. The 16-bit product will be in AX. The source may be a byte register or memory byte, but not a constant.

Word Form

For word multiplication, one number is contained in the source and the other is assumed to be in AX. The most significant 16 bits of the doubleword product will be in DX, and the least significant 16 bits will be in AX (we sometimes write this as DX:AX). The source may be a 16-bit register or memory word, but not a constant.

For multiplication of positive numbers (0 in the most significant bit), MUL and IMUL give the same result.

Effect of MUL/IMUL on the status flags

`SF,ZF,AF,PF:`	undefined.
`CF/OF:`	
After `MUL, CF/OF`	= 0 if the upper half of the result is zero.
	= 1 otherwise.
After `IMUL, CF/OF`	= 0 if the upper half of the result is the sign extension of the lower half (this means that the bits of the upper half are the same as the sign bit of the lower half).
	= 1 otherwise.

For both MUL and IMUL, CF/OF = 1 means that the product is too big to fit in the lower half of the destination (AL for byte multiplication, AX for word multiplication).

Examples

To illustrate MUL and IMUL, we will do several examples. Because hex multiplication is usually difficult to do, we'll predict the product by converting the hex values of multiplier and multiplicand to decimal, doing decimal multiplication, and converting the product back to hex.

Example 9.1 Suppose AX contains 1 and BX contains FFFFh:

Instruction	Decimal product	Hex product	DX	AX	CF/OF
MUL BX	65535	0000FFFF	0000	FFFF	0
IMUL BX	−1	FFFFFFFF	FFFF	FFFF	0

For MUL, DX = 0, so CF/OF = 0.

For IMUL, the signed interpretation of BX is −1, and the product is also −1. In 32 bits, this is FFFFFFFFh. CF/OF = 0 because DX is the sign extension of AX.

Example 9.2 Suppose AX contains FFFFh and BX contains FFFFh:

Instruction	Decimal product	Hex product	DX	AX	CF/OF
MUL BX	4294836225	FFFE0001	FFFE	0001	1
IMUL BX	1	00000001	0000	0001	0

For MUL, CF/OF = 1 because DX is not 0. This reflects the fact that the product FFFE0001h is too big to fit in AX.

For IMUL, AX and BX both contain −1, so the product is 1. DX has the sign extension of AX, so CF/OF = 0.

Example 9.3 Suppose AX contains 0FFFh:

Instruction	Decimal product	Hex product	DX	AX	CF/OF
MUL AX	16769025	00FFE001	00FF	E001	1
IMUL AX	16769025	00FFE001	00FF	E001	1

Because the msb of AX is 0, both MUL and IMUL give the same product. Because the product is too big to fit in AX, CF/OF = 1.

Example 9.4 Suppose AX contains 0100h and CX contains FFFFh:

Instruction	Decimal product	Hex product	DX	AX	CF/OF
MUL CX	16776960	00FFFF00	00FF	FF00	1
IMUL CX	−256	FFFFFF00	FFFF	FF00	0

For MUL, the product FFFF00 is obtained by attaching two zeros to the source value FFFFh. Because the product is too big to fit in AX, CF/OF = 1.

For IMUL, AX contains 256 and CX contains −1, so the product is −256, which may be expressed as FF00h in 16 bits. DX has the sign extension of AX, so CF/OF = 0.

Example 9.5 Suppose AL contains 80h and BL contains FFh:

Instruction	Decimal product	Hex product	AH	AL	CF/OF
MUL BL	128	7F80	7F	80	1
IMUL BL	128	0080	00	80	1

For byte multiplication, the 16-bit product is contained in AX.

For MUL, the product is 7F80. Because the high eight bits are not 0, CF/OF = 1.

For IMUL, we have a curious situation. 80h = −128, FFh = −1, so the product is 128 = 0080h. AH does not have the sign extension of AL, so CF/OF = 1. This reflects the fact that AL does not contain the correct answer in a signed sense, because the signed decimal interpretation of 80h is −128.

9.2 Simple Applications of MUL and IMUL

To get used to programming with MUL and IMUL, we'll show how some simple operations can be carried out with these instructions.

Example 9.6 Translate the high-level language assignment statement A = 5 × A − 12 × B into assembly code. Let A and B be word variables, and suppose there is no overflow. Use IMUL for multiplication.

Solution:

```
MOV  AX,5          ;AX = 5
IMUL A             ;AX = 5 x A
MOV  A,AX          ;A  = 5 x A
MOV  AX,12         ;AX = 12
IMUL B             ;AX = 12 x B
SUB  A,AX          ;A  = 5 x A - 12 x B
```

Example 9.7 Write a procedure FACTORIAL that will compute N! for a positive integer N. The procedure should receive N in CX and return N! in AX. Suppose that overflow does not occur.

Solution: The definition of N! is

$$N! = 1 \text{ if } N = 1$$
$$= N \times (N-1) \times (N-2) \times .. \times 1 \text{ if } N > 1$$

Here is an algorithm:

```
product = 1
term = N
FOR N times DO
 product = product x term
 term = term - 1
ENDFOR
```

It can be coded as follows:

```
FACTORIAL   PROC
;computes N!
;input: CX = N
;output: AX = N!
            MOV  AX,1       ;AX holds product
TOP:
            MUL  CX         ;product = product x term
            LOOP TOP
            RET
FACTORIAL   ENDP
```

Here CX is both loop counter and term; the LOOP instruction automatically decrements it on each iteration through the loop. We assume the product does not overflow 16 bits.

9.3 DIV and IDIV

When division is performed, we obtain two results, the quotient and the remainder. As with multiplication, there are separate instructions for unsigned and signed division; **DIV** (divide) is used for unsigned division and **IDIV** (integer divide) for signed division. The syntax is

```
DIV divisor
```

and

```
IDIV divisor
```

These instructions divide 8 (or 16) bits into 16 (or 32) bits. The quotient and remainder have the same size as the divisor.

Byte Form

In this form, the divisor is an 8-bit register or memory byte. The 16-bit dividend is assumed to be in AX. After division, the 8-bit quotient is in AL and the 8-bit remainder is in AH. The divisor may not be a constant.

Word Form

Here the divisor is a 16-bit register or memory word. The 32-bit dividend is assumed to be in DX:AX. After division, the 16-bit quotient is in AX and the 16-bit remainder is in DX. The divisor may not be a constant.

For signed division, the remainder has the same sign as the dividend. If both dividend and divisor are positive, DIV and IDIV give the same result.

The effect of DIV/IDIV on the flags is that all status flags are undefined.

Divide Overflow

It is possible that the quotient will be too big to fit in the specified destination (AL or AX). This can happen if the divisor is much smaller than the dividend. When this happens, the program terminates (as shown later) and the system displays the message "*Divide Overflow*".

Example 9.8 Suppose DX contains 0000h, AX contains 0005h, and BX contains 0002h.

Instruction	Decimal quotient	Decimal remainder	AX	DX
DIV BX	2	1	0002	0001
IDIV BX	2	1	0002	0001

Dividing 5 by 2 yields a quotient of 2 and a remainder of 1. Because both dividend and divisor are positive, DIV and IDIV give the same results.

Example 9.9 Suppose DX contains 0000h, AX contains 0005h, and BX contains FFFEh.

Instruction	Decimal quotient	Decimal remainder	AX	DX
DIV BX	0	5	0000	0005
IDIV BX	−2	1	FFFE	0001

For DIV, the dividend is 5 and the divisor is FFFEh = 65534; 5 divided by 65534 yields a quotient of 0 and a remainder of 5.

For IDIV, the dividend is 5 and the divisor is FFFEh = −2; 5 divided by −2 gives a quotient of −2 and a remainder of 1.

Example 9.10 Suppose DX contains FFFFh, AX contains FFFBh, and BX contains 0002.

Instruction	Decimal quotient	Decimal remainder	AX	DX
IDIV BX	−2	−1	FFFE	FFFF
DIV BX	DIVIDE OVERFLOW			

For IDIV, DX:AX = FFFFFFFBh = −5, BX = 2. −5 divided by 2 gives a quotient of −2 = FFFEh and a remainder of −1 = FFFFh.

For DIV, the dividend DX:AX = FFFFFFFBh = 4294967291 and the divisor = 2. The actual quotient is 2147483646 = 7FFFFFFEh. This is too big to fit in AX, so the computer prints DIVIDE OVERFLOW and the program terminates. This shows what can happen if the divisor is a lot smaller than the dividend.

Example 9.11 Suppose AX contains 00FBh and BL contains FFh.

Instruction	Decimal quotient	Decimal remainder	AX	AL
DIV BL	0	251	FB	00
IDIV BL	DIVIDE OVERFLOW			

For byte division, the dividend is in AX; the quotient is in AL and the remainder in AH.

For DIV, the dividend is 00FBh = 251 and the divisor is FFh = 256. Dividing 251 by 256 yields a quotient of 0 and a remainder of 251 = FBh.

For IDIV, the dividend is 00FBh = 251 and the divisor is FFh = −1. Dividing 251 by −1 yields a quotient of −251, which is too big to fit in AL, so the message DIVIDE OVERFLOW is printed.

9.4 Sign Extension of the Dividend

Word Division

In word division, the dividend is in DX:AX even if the actual dividend will fit in AX. In this case DX should be prepared as follows:

1. For DIV, DX should be cleared.
2. For IDIV, DX should be made the sign extension of AX. The instruction **CWD** (convert word to doubleword) will do the extension.

Example 9.12 Divide −1250 by 7.

Solution:

```
MOV   AX,-1250        ;AX gets dividend
CWD                   ;Extend sign to DX
MOV   BX,7            ;BX has divisor
IDIV  BX              ;AX gets quotient, DX has remainder
```

Byte Division

In byte division, the dividend is in AX. If the actual dividend is a byte, then AH should be prepared as follows:

1. For DIV, AH should be cleared.
2. For IDIV, AH should the sign extension of AL. The instruction **CBW** (convert byte to word) will do the extension.

Example 9.13 Divide the signed value of the byte variable XBYTE by −7.

Solution:

```
MOV   AL,XBYTE        ;AL has dividend
CBW                   ;Extend sign to AH
MOV   BL,-7           ;BL has divisor
IDIV  BL              ;AL has quotient, AH has remainder
```

There is no effect of CBW and CWD on the flags.

9.5 Decimal Input and Output Procedures

Even though the computer represents everything in binary, it's more convenient for the user to see input and output expressed in decimal. In this section, we write procedures for handling decimal I/O.

On input, if we type 21543, for example, then we are actually typing a character string, which must be converted internally to the binary equivalent of the decimal integer 21543. Conversely on output, the binary contents of a register or memory location must be converted to a character string representing a decimal integer before being printed.

Decimal Output

We will write a procedure OUTDEC to print the contents of AX as a signed decimal integer. If AX >= 0, OUTDEC will print the contents in decimal; if AX < 0, OUTDEC will print a minus sign, replace AX by −AX (so that AX now contains a positive number), and print the contents in decimal. Thus in either case, the problem comes down to printing the decimal equivalent of a positive binary number. Here is the algorithm:

Algorithm for Decimal Output

```
1.  IF AX < 0    /* AX holds output value */
2.  THEN
```

3. print a minus sign
4. replace AX by its two's complement
5. END_IF
6. Get the digits in AX's decimal representation
7. Convert these digits to characters and print them

To see what line 6 entails, suppose the content of AX, expressed in decimal, is 24168. To get the digits in the decimal representation, we can proceed as follows:

Divide 24618 by 10. Quotient = 2461, remainder = 8

Divide 2461 by 10. Quotient = 246, remainder = 1

Divide 246 by 10. Quotient = 24, remainder = 6

Divide 24 by 10. Quotient = 2, remainder = 4

Divide 2 by 10. Quotient = 0, remainder = 2

Thus, the digits we want appear as remainders after repeated division by 10. However, they appear in reverse order; to turn them around, we can save them on the stack. Here's how line 6 breaks down:

Line 6

```
count = 0  /* will count decimal digits */
REPEAT
   divide quotient by 10
   push remainder on the stack
   count = count + 1
UNTIL quotient = 0
```

where the initial value of quotient is the original contents of AX.

Once the digits are on the stack, all we have to do is pop them off, convert them to characters, and print them. Line 7 may be expressed as follows:

Line 7

```
FOR count times DO
   pop a digit from the stack
   convert it to a character
   output the character
END_FOR
```

Now we can code the procedure as follows:

Program Listing PGM9_1.ASM

```
1:  OUTDEC    PROC
2:  ;prints AX as a signed decimal integer
3:  ;input: AX
4:  ;output: none
5:            PUSH   AX              ;save registers
6:            PUSH   BX
7:            PUSH   CX
8:            PUSH   DX
9:  ;if AX < 0
10:           OR     AX,AX           ;AX < 0?
11:           JGE    @END_IF1        ;NO, > 0
12: ;then
```

```
13:         PUSH    AX              ;save number
14:         MOV     DL,'-'          ;get '-'
15:         MOV     AH,2            ;print char function
16:         INT     21H             ;print '-'
17:         POP     AX              ;get AX back
18:         NEG     AX              ;AX = -AX
19: @END_IF1:
20: ;get decimal digits
21:         XOR     CX,CX           ;CX counts digits
22:         MOV     BX,10D          ;BX has divisor
23: @REPEAT1:
24:         XOR     DX,DX           ;prepare high word of dividend
25:         DIV     BX              ;AX = quotient, DX = remainder
26:         PUSH    DX              ;save remainder on stack
27:         INC     CX              ;count = count + 1
28: ;until
29:         OR      AX,AX           ;quotient = 0?
30:         JNE     @REPEAT1        ;no, keep going
31: ;convert digits to characters and print
32:         MOV     AH,2            ;print char function
33: ;for count times do
34: @PRINT_LOOP:
35:         POP     DX              ;digit in DL
36:         OR      DL,30H          ;convert to character
37:         INT     21H             ;print digit
38:         LOOP    @PRINT_LOOP     ;loop until done
39: ;end_for
40:         POP     DX              ;restore registers
41:         POP     CX
42:         POP     BX
43:         POP     AX
44:         RET
45: OUTDEC  ENDP
```

After saving the registers, at line 10 the sign of AX is examined by ORing AX with itself. If AX >= 0, the program jumps to line 19; if AX < 0, a minus sign is printed and AX is replaced by its two's complement. In either case, at line 19, AX will contain a positive number.

At line 21, OUTDEC prepares for division. Because division by a constant is illegal, we must put the divisor 10 in a register.

The REPEAT loop in lines 23–30 will get the digits and put them on the stack. Because we'll be doing unsigned division, DX is cleared. After division, the quotient will be in AX and the remainder in DX (actually it is in DL, because the remainder is between 0 and 9). At line 29, AX is tested for 0 by ORing it with itself; repeated division by 10 guarantees a zero quotient eventually.

The FOR loop in lines 34–38 gets the digits from the stack and prints them. Before a digit is printed, it must first be converted to an ASCII character (line 36).

The INCLUDE Pseudo-op

We can verify OUTDEC by placing it inside a short program and running the program inside DEBUG. To insert OUTDEC into the program without having to type it in, we use the **INCLUDE** pseudo-op. It has the form

```
INCLUDE         filespec
```

9.5 Decimal Input and Output Procedures

where filespec identifies a file (with optional drive and path). For example, the file containing OUTDEC is PGM9_1.ASM. We could use

```
INCLUDE A:PGM9_1.ASM
```

When MASM encounters this line during assembly, it retrieves file PGM9_1.ASM from the disk in drive A and inserts it into the program at the position of the INCLUDE directive.

Here is the testing program:

Program Listing PGM9_2.ASM

```
TITLE PGM9_2: DECIMAL OUTPUT
.MODEL   SMALL
.STACK   100H
.CODE
MAIN   PROC
       CALL    OUTDEC
       MOV     AH,4CH
       INT     21H              ;DOS exit
MAIN   ENDP
INCLUDE A:PGM9_1.ASM
       END     MAIN
```

To test the program, we'll enter DEBUG and run the program twice, first for AX = –25487 = 9C71h and then for AX = 654 = 28Eh:

```
C>DEBUG PGM9_2.EXE
-RAX
AX 0000
:9C71
-G
-25487                    (first output)
Program terminated normally.
-RAX
AX 9C71
:28E
-G
654                       (second output)
```

Note that after the first run, DEBUG automatically resets IP to the beginning of the program.

Decimal Input

To do decimal input, we need to convert a string of ASCII digits to the binary representation of a decimal integer. We will write a procedure INDEC to do this.

In procedure OUTDEC, to output the contents of AX in decimal we repeatedly divided AX by 10. For INDEC we need repeated multiplication by 10. The basic idea is the following:

Decimal Input Algorithm (first version)

```
total = 0
read an ASCII digit
REPEAT
 convert character to a binary value
 total = 10 x total + value
 read a character
UNTIL character is a carriage return
```

For example, an input of 123 is processed as follows:

```
total = 0
read '1'
convert '1' to 1
total = 10 x 0 + 1 = 1
read '2'
convert '2' to 2
total = 10 x 1 + 2 = 12
read '3'
convert '3' to 3
total = 10 x 12 + 3 = 123
```

We will design INDEC so that it can handle signed decimal integers in the range –32768 to 32767. The program prints a question mark, and lets the user enter an optional sign, followed by a string of digits, followed by a carriage return. If the user enters a character outside the range "0" ... "9", the procedure goes to a new line and starts over. With these added requirements, the preceding algorithm becomes the following:

Decimal Input Algorithm (second version)

```
Print a question mark
total = 0
negative = false
Read a character
CASE character OF
 '-': negative = true
      read a character
 '+': read a character
END_CASE
REPEAT
 IF character is not between '0' and '9'
  THEN
   go to beginning*
  ELSE
   convert character to a binary value
   total = 10 x total + value
 END_IF
 read a character
UNTIL character is a carriage return
IF negative = true
 THEN
  total = -total
ENDIF
```

Note: A jump like this is not really "structured programming." Sometimes it's necessary to violate structure rules for the sake of efficiency; for example, when error conditions occur.

9.5 Decimal Input and Output Procedures

The algorithm can be coded as follows:

Program Listing PGM9_3.ASM

```
 1:  INDEC    PROC
 2:  ;reads a number in range -32768 to 32767
 3:  ;input: none
 4:  ;output: AX = binary equivalent of number
 5:           PUSH    BX              ;save registers used
 6:           PUSH    CX
 7:           PUSH    DX
 8:  ;print prompt
 9:  @BEGIN:
10:           MOV     AH,2
11:           MOV     DL,'?'
12:           INT     21H             ;print '?'
13:  ;total = 0
14:           XOR     BX,BX           ;BX holds total
15:  ;negative = false
16:           XOR     CX,CX           ;CX holds sign
17:  ;read a character
18:           MOV     AH,1
19:           INT     21H             ;character in AL
20:  ;case character of
21:           CMP     AL,'-'          ;minus sign?
22:           JE      @MINUS          ;yes, set sign
23:           CMP     AL,'+'          ;plus sign
24:           JE      @PLUS           ;yes, get another character
25:           JMP     @REPEAT2        ;start processing characters
26:  @MINUS:
27:           MOV     CX,1            ;negative = true
28:  @PLUS:
29:           INT     21H             ;read a character
30:  ;end_case
31:  @REPEAT2:
32:  ;if character is between '0' and '9'
33:           CMP     AL,'0'          ;character >= '0'?
34:           JNGE    @NOT_DIGIT      ;illegal character
35:           CMP     AL,'9'          ;character <= '9'?
36:           JNLE    @NOT_DIGIT      ;no, illegal character
37:  ;then convert character to a digit
38:           AND     AX,000FH        ;convert to digit
39:           PUSH    AX              ;save on stack
40:  ;total = total x 10 + digit
41:           MOV     AX,10           ;get 10
42:           MUL     BX              ;AX = total x 10
43:           POP     BX              ;retrieve digit
44:           ADD     BX,AX           ;total = total x 10 + digit
45:  ;read a character
46:           MOV     AH,1
47:           INT     21H
48:           CMP     AL,0DH          ;carriage return?
49:           JNE     @REPEAT2        ;no, keep going
50:  ;until CR
51:           MOV     AX,BX           ;store number in AX
52:  ;if negative
53:           OR      CX,CX           ;negative number
```

```
54:            JE      @EXIT           ;no, exit
55: ;then
56:            NEG     AX              ;yes, negate
57: ;end_if
58: @EXIT:
59:            POP     DX              ;restore registers
60:            POP     CX
61:            POP     BX
62:            RET                     ;and return
63: ;here if illegal character entered
64: @NOT_DIGIT:
65:            MOV     AH,2            ;move cursor to a new line
66:            MOV     DL,0DH
67:            INT     21H
68:            MOV     DL,0AH
69:            INT     21H
70:            JMP     @BEGIN          ;go to beginning
71: INDEC      ENDP
```

The procedure begins by saving the registers and printing a "?". BX holds the total; in line 14, it is cleared.

CX is used to keep track of the sign; 0 means a positive number and 1 means negative. We initially assume the number is positive, so CX is cleared at line 16.

The first character is read at lines 18 and 19. It could be "+", "–" or a digit. If it's a sign, CX is adjusted if necessary and another character is read (line 29). Presumably this next character will be a digit.

At line 31, INDEC enters the REPEAT loop, which processes the current character and reads another one, until a carriage return is typed.

At lines 33–36, INDEC checks to see if the current character is in fact a digit. If not, the procedure jumps to label @NOT_DIGIT (line 64), moves the cursor to a new line, and jumps to @BEGIN. This means that the user can't escape from the procedure without entering a legitimate number.

If the current character in AL is a decimal digit, it is converted to a binary value (line 38). Then the value is saved on the stack (line 39), because AX is used when the total is multiplied by 10.

In lines 41 and 42, the total in BX is multiplied by 10. The product will be in DX:AX; however, DX will contain 0 unless the number is out of range (more about this later). At line 43, the value saved is popped from the stack and 10 times total is added to it.

At line 51, INDEC exits the REPEAT loop with the number in BX. After moving it to AX, INDEC checks the sign in CX; if CX contains 1, AX is negated before the procedure exits.

Testing INDEC

We can test INDEC by creating a program that uses INDEC for input and OUTDEC for output.

Program Listing PGM9_4.ASM
```
TITLE PGM9_4: DECIMAL I/O
.MODEL SMALL
.STACK
.CODE
MAIN PROC
```

```
        ;input a number
                CALL    INDEC           ;number in AX
                PUSH    AX              ;save number
        ;move cursor to a new line
                MOV     AH,2
                MOV     DL,0DH
                INT     21H
                MOV     DL,0AH
                INT     21H
        ;output the number
                POP     AX              ;retrieve number
                CALL    OUTDEC
        ;dos exit
                MOV     AH,4CH
                INT     21H
        MAIN    ENDP
        INCLUDE A:PGM9_1.ASM            ;include OUTDEC
        INCLUDE A:PGM9_3.ASM            ;include INDEC
                END     MAIN
```

Sample execution:

```
C>PGM9_4
?21345
21345Overflow
```

Overflow

Procedure INDEC can handle input that contains illegal characters, but it cannot handle input that is outside the range −32768 to 32767. We call this *input overflow*.

Overflow can occur in two places in INDEC: (1) when total is multiplied by 10, and (2) when a value is added to total. As an example of the first overflow, the user could enter 99999; overflow occurs when the total = 9999 is multiplied by 10. As an example of the second overflow, if the user types 32769, then when the total = 32760, overflow occurs when 9 is added. The algorithm can be made to perform overflow checks as follows:

Decimal Input Algorithm (third version)

```
Print a question mark
total = 0
negative = false
Read a character
CASE character OF
  '-': negative = true
       read a character
  '+': read a character
END_CASE
REPEAT
  IF character is not between '0' and '9'
```

```
    THEN
      go to beginning
    ELSE
      convert character to a value
      total = 10 x total
      IF overflow
        THEN
          go to beginning
        ELSE
          total = total + value
          IF overflow
            THEN
              go to beginning
          END_IF
        END_IF
    END_IF
    read a character
UNTIL character is a carriage return
IF negative = true
  THEN
    total = -total
END_IF
```

The implementation of this algorithm is left to the student as an exercise.

Summary

- The multiplication instructions are MUL for unsigned multiplication and IMUL for signed multiplication.

- For byte multiplication, AL holds one number, and the other is in an 8-bit register or memory byte. For word multiplication, AX holds one number, and the other is in an 16-bit register or memory word.

- For byte multiplication, the 16-bit product is in AX. For word multiplication, the 32-bit product is in DX:AX.

- The division instructions are DIV for unsigned division and IDIV for signed division.

- The divisor may be a memory or register, byte or word. For division by a byte, the dividend is in AX; for division by a word, the dividend is in DX:AX.

- After byte division, AL has the quotient and AH the remainder. After word division, AX has the quotient and DX the remainder.

- For signed word division, if AX contains the dividend, then CWD can be used to extend the sign into DX. Similarly, for byte division, CBW extends the sign of AL into AH. For unsigned word division, if AX contains the dividend, then DX should be cleared. For unsigned byte division, if AL contains the dividend then AH should be cleared.

- Multiply and divide instructions are useful in doing decimal I/O.

- The INCLUDE pseudo-op provides a way to insert text from an external file into a program.

New Instructions

CBW	DIV	IMUL
CWD	IDIV	MUL

New Pseudo-Ops

INCLUDE

Exercises

1. If it is a legal instruction, give the values of DX, AX, and CF/OF after each of the following instructions is executed.
    a. MUL BX, if AX contains 0008h and BX contains 0003h
    b. MUL BX, if AX contains 00FFh and BX contains 1000h
    c. IMUL CX, if AX contains 0005h and CX contains FFFFh
    d. IMUL WORD1, if AX contains 8000h and WORD1 contains FFFFh
    e. MUL 10h, if AX contains FFE0h

2. Give the new values of AX and CF/OF for each of the following instructions.
    a. MUL BL, if AL contains ABh and BL contains 10h
    b. IMUL BL, if AL contains ABh and BL contains 10h
    c. MUL AH, if AX contains 01ABh
    d. IMUL BYTE1, if AL contains 02h and BYTE1 contains FBh

3. Give the new values of AX and DX for each of the following instructions, or tell if overflow occurs
    a. DIV BX, if DX contains 0000h, AX contains 0007h, and BX contains 0002h
    b. DIV BX, if DX contains 0000h, AX contains FFFEh, and BX contains 0010h
    c. IDIV BX, if DX contains FFFFh, AX contains FFFCh, and BX contains 0003h
    d. DIV BX, same values as part c.

4. Give the new values of AL and AH for each of the following instructions, or tell if overflow occurs
    a. DIV BL, if AX contains 000Dh and BL contains 03h
    b. IDIV BL, if AX contains FFFBh and BL contains FEh
    c. DIV BL, if AX contains 00FEh and BL contains 10h
    d. DIV BL, if AX contains FFE0h and BL contains 02h

5. Give the value of DX after executing CWD if AX contains
    a. 7E02h
    b. 8ABCh
    c. 1ABCh

6. Give the value of AX after executing CBW if AL contains
   a. F0h
   b. 5Fh
   c. 80h

7. Write assembly code for each of the following high-level language assignment statements. Suppose that A, B, and C are word variables and all products will fit in 16 bits. Use IMUL for multiplication. It's not necessary to preserve the contents of variables A, B, and C.
   a. `A = 5 x A - 7`
   b. `B = (A - B) x (B + 10)`
   c. `A = 6 - 9 x A`
   d.
   ```
   IF A^2 + B^2 = C^2   / * where ^ denotes
                                 exponentiation * /
   THEN
     set CF
   ELSE
     clear CF
   END_IF
   ```

Programming Exercises

Note: Some of the following exercises ask you to use INDEC and/or OUTDEC for I/O. These procedures are on the student disk and can be inserted into your program by using the INCLUDE pseudo-op (see section 9.5). Be sure not to use the same labels as these procedures, or you'll get a duplicate label assembly error (this should be easy, because all the labels in INDEC and OUTDEC begin with "@".

8. Modify procedure INDEC so that it will check for overflow.

9. Write a program that lets the user enter time in seconds, up to 65535, and outputs the time as hours, minutes, and seconds. Use INDEC and OUTDEC to do the I/O.

10. Write a program to take a number of cents C, $0 <= C <= 99$, and express C as half-dollars, quarters, dimes, nickels, and pennies. Use INDEC to enter C.

11. Write a program to let the user enter a fraction of the form *M/N* ($M < N$), and the program prints the expansion to *N* decimal places, according to the following algorithm:

    1. `Print "."`

    Execute the following steps *N* times:

    2. `Divide 10 x M by N, getting quotient Q and remainder R.`
    3. `Print Q.`
    4. `Replace M by R and go to step 2.`

    Use INDEC to read *M* and *N*.

12. Write a program to find the greatest common divisor (GCD) of two integers *M* and *N*, according to the following algorithm:
    1. `Divide M by N, getting quotient Q and remainder R.`
    2. `If R = 0, stop. N is the GCD of M and N.`
    3. `If R <> 0, replace M by N, N by R, and repeat step 1.`

    Use INDEC to enter M and N and OUTDEC to print the GCD.

10

Arrays and Addressing Modes

Overview

In some applications, it is necessary to treat a collection of values as a group. For example, we might need to read a set of test scores and print the median score. To do so, we would first have to store the scores in ascending order (this could be done as the scores are entered, or they could be sorted after they are all in memory). The advantage of using an array to store the data is that a single name can be given to the whole structure, and an element can be accessed by providing an index.

In section 10.1 we show how one-dimensional arrays are declared in assembly language. To access the elements, in section 10.2 we introduce new ways of expressing operands—the register indirect, based and indexed addressing modes. In section 10.3, we use these addressing modes to sort an array.

A two-dimensional array is a one-dimensional array whose elements are also one-dimensional arrays (an array of arrays). In section 10.4, we show how they are stored. These arrays have two indexes, and are most easily manipulated by the based indexed addressing mode of section 10.5. Section 10.6 provides a simple application.

Section 10.7 introduces the XLAT (translate) instruction. This instruction is useful when we want to do data conversion; we use it to encode and decode a secret message.

10.1 One-Dimensional Arrays

A **one-dimensional array** is an ordered list of elements, all of the same type. By "ordered," we mean that there is a first element, second element, third element, and so on. In mathematics, if A is an array, the elements

Figure 10.1 A One-Dimensional Array A

Index	
1	A[1]
2	A[2]
3	A[3]
4	A[4]
5	A[5]
6	A[6]

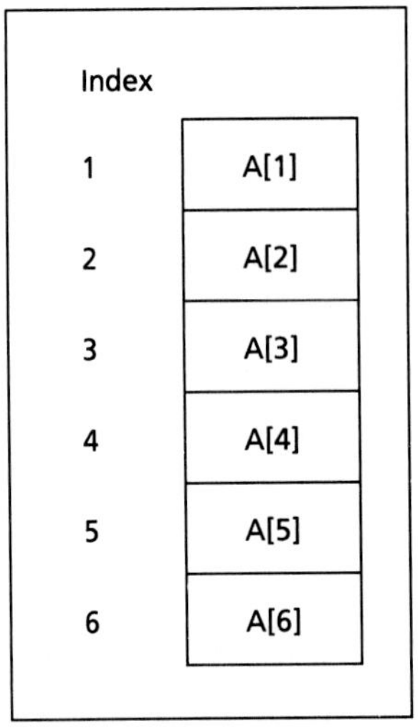

are usually denoted by A[1], A[2], A[3], and so on. Figure 10.1 shows a one-dimensional array A with six elements.

In Chapter 4, we used the DB and DW pseudo-ops to declare byte and word arrays; for example, a five-character string named MSG,

```
MSG   DB   'abcde'
```

or a word array W of six integers, initialized to 10,20,30,40,50,60.

```
W     DW   10,20,30,40,50,60
```

The address of the array variable is called the **base address of the array.** If the offset address assigned to W is 0200h, the array looks like this in memory:

Offset address	Symbolic address	Decimal content
0200h	W	10
0202h	W+2h	20
0204h	W+4h	30
0206h	W+6h	40
0208h	W+8h	50
020Ah	W+Ah	60

The DUP Operator

It is possible to define arrays whose elements share a common initial value by using the **DUP** (duplicate) operator. It has this form:

```
repeat_count        DUP (value)
```

This operator causes value to be repeated the number of times specified by repeat_count. For example,

```
GAMMA  DW 100 DUP (0)
```

sets up an array of 100 words, with each entry initialized to 0. Similarly,

```
DELTA  DB 212 DUP (?)
```

creates an array of 212 uninitialized bytes. DUPs may be nested. For example,

```
LINE    DB          5,4, 3 DUP (2, 3 DUP (0), 1)
```
which is equivalent to
```
LINE    DB          5,4,2,0,0,0,1,2,0,0,0,1,2,0,0,0,1
```

Location of Array Elements

The address of an array element may be specified by adding a constant to the base address. Suppose A is an array and S denotes the number of bytes in an element (S = 1 for a byte array, S = 2 for a word array). The position of the elements in array A can be determined as follows:

Position	Location
1	A
2	A = 1 × S
3	A = 2 × S
.	.
.	.
.	.
N	A = (N − 1) × S

Example 10.1 Exchange the 10th and 25th elements in a word array W.

Solution: W[10] is located at address W + 9 × 2 = W + 18 and W[25] is at W + 24 × 2 = W + 48, so we can do the exchange as follows:

```
MOV   AX,W+18         ;AX has W[10]
XCHG  W+48,AX         ;AX has W[25]
MOV   W+18,AX         ;complete exchange
```

In many applications, we need to perform some operation on each element of an array. For example, suppose array A is a 10-element array, and we want to add the elements. In a high-level language, we could do it like this:

```
sum = 0
N = 1
REPEAT
   sum = sum + A[N]
   N = N + 1
UNTIL N > 10
```

To code this in assembly language, we need a way to move from one array element to the next one. In the next section, we'll see how to accomplish this by indirect addressing.

10.2 Addressing Modes

The way an operand is specified is known as its **addressing mode**. The addressing modes we have used so far are (1) **register mode**, which means that an operand is a register; (2) **immediate mode**, when an operand is a constant; and (3) **direct mode**, when an operand is a variable. For example,

```
        MOV AX,0                    (Destination AX is register mode,
                                    source 0 is immediate mode.)
        ADD ALPHA,AX                (Destination ALPHA is direct mode,
                                    source AX is register mode.)
```

There are four additional addressing modes for the 8086: (1) Register Indirect, (2) Based, (3) Indexed, and (4) Based Indexed. These modes are used to address memory operands indirectly. In this section, we discuss the first three of these modes; they are useful in one-dimensional array processing. Based indexed mode can be used with two-dimensional arrays; it is covered in section 10.5.

10.2.1
Register Indirect Mode

In this mode, the offset address of the operand is contained in a register. We say that the register acts as a **pointer** to the memory location. The operand format is

```
[register]
```

The register is BX, SI, DI, or BP. For BX, SI, or DI, the operand's segment number is contained in DS. For BP, SS has the segment number.

For example, suppose that SI contains 0100h, and the word at 0100h contains 1234h. To execute

```
MOV     AX,[SI]
```

the CPU (1) examines SI and obtains the offset address 100h, (2) uses the address DS:0100h to obtain the value 1234h, and (3) moves 1234h to AX. This is not the same as

```
MOV     AX,SI
```

which simply moves the value of SI, namely 100h, into AX.

Example 10.2 Suppose that

BX contains 1000h   Offset 1000h contains 1BACh
SI contains 2000h   Offset 2000h contains 20FEh
DI contains 3000h   Offset 3000h contains 031Dh

where the above offsets are in the data segment addressed by DS.
Tell which of the following instructions are legal. If legal, give the source offset address and the result or number moved.

```
        a. MOV BX,[BX]
        b. MOV CX,[SI]
        c. MOV BX,[AX]
        d. ADD [SI],[DI]
        e. INC [DI]
```

Solution:

	Source offset	*Result*
a.	1000h	1BACh
b.	2000h	20FEh
c.	illegal source register	(must be BX, SI, or DI)
d.	illegal memory–memory addition	
e.	3000h	031Eh

Now let's return to the problem of adding the elements of an array.

Example 10.3 Write some code to sum in AX the elements of the 10-element array W defined by

```
W    DW     10,20,30,40,50,60,70,80,90,100
```

Solution: The idea is to set a pointer to the base of the array, and let it move up the array, summing elements as it goes.

```
        XOR     AX,AX           ;AX holds sum
        LEA     SI,W            ;SI points to array W
        MOV     CX,10           ;CX has number of elements
ADDNOS:
        ADD     AX,[SI]         ;sum = sum + element
        ADD     SI,2            ;move pointer to the next
                                ;element
        LOOP    ADDNOS          ;loop until done
```

Here we must add 2 to SI on each trip through the loop because W is a word array (recall from Chapter 4 that LEA moves the source offset address into the destination).

The next example shows how register indirect mode can be used in array processing.

Example 10.4 Write a procedure REVERSE that will reverse an array of N words. This means that the Nth word becomes the first, the $(N–1)$st word becomes the second, and so on, and the first word becomes the Nth word. The procedure is entered with SI pointing to the array, and BX has the number of words N.

Solution: The idea is to exchange the 1st and Nth words, the 2nd and $(N–1)$st words, and so on. The number of exchanges will be $N/2$ (rounded down to the nearest integer if N is odd). Recall from section 10.1 that the Nth element in a word array A has address $A + 2 \times (N - 1)$.

Program Listing PGM10_1.ASM
```
REVERSE PROC
;reverses a word array
;input:  SI = offset of array
;        BX = number of elements
;output: reversed array
```

```
            PUSH    AX              ;save registers
            PUSH    BX
            PUSH    CX
            PUSH    SI
            PUSH    DI
;make DI point to nth word
            MOV     DI,SI           ;DI pts to 1st word
            MOV     CX,BX           ;CX = n
            DEC     BX              ;BX = n-1
            SHL     BX,1            ;BX = 2 x (n-1)
            ADD     DI,BX           ;DX pts to nth word
            SHR     CX,1            ;CX = n/2 = no. of swaps to do
;swap elements
XCHG_LOOP:
            MOV     AX,[SI]         ;get an elt in lower half of array
            XCHG    AX,[DI]         ;insert in upper half
            MOV     [SI],AX         ;complete exchange
            ADD     SI,2            ;move ptr
            SUB     DI,2            ;move ptr
            LOOP    XCHG_LOOP       ;loop until done
            POP     DI              ;restore registers
            POP     SI
            POP     CX
            POP     BX
            POP     AX
            RET
REVERSE     ENDP
```

10.2.2 Based and Indexed Addressing Modes

In these modes, the operand's offset address is obtained by adding a number called a **displacement** to the contents of a register. Displacement may be any of the following:

the offset address of a variable

a constant (positive or negative)

the offset address of a variable plus or minus a constant

If A is a variable, examples of displacements are:

A   (offset address of a variable)

−2   (constant)

A + 4   (offset address of a variable plus a constant)

The syntax of an operand is any of the following equivalent expressions:

```
[register + displacement]
[displacement + register]
[register] + displacement
displacement + [register]
displacement[register]
```

The register must be BX, BP, SI, or DI. If BX, SI, or DI is used, DS contains the segment number of the operand's address. If BP is used, SS has the segment number. The addressing mode is called **based** if BX (base register) or

BP (base pointer) is used; it is called **indexed** if SI (source index) or DI (destination index) is used.

For example, suppose W is a word array, and BX contains 4. In the instruction

```
MOV AX,W[BX]
```

the displacement is the offset address of variable W. The instruction moves the element at address W + 4 to AX. This is the third element in the array. The instruction could also have been written in any of these forms:

```
MOV AX, [W+BX]
MOV AX, [BX+W]
MOV AX,W+[BX]
MOV AX, [BX]+W
```

As another example, suppose SI contains the address of a word array W. In the instruction

```
MOV AX, [SI+2]
```

the displacement is 2. The instruction moves the contents of W + 2 to AX. This is the second element in the array. The instruction could also have been written in any of these forms:

```
MOV AX, [2+SI]
MOV AX,2+[SI]
MOV AX, [SI]+2
MOV AX,2[SI]
```

Example 10.5 Rework example 10.3 by using based mode.

Solution: The idea is to clear base register BX, then add 2 to it on each trip through the summing loop.

```
        XOR    AX,AX        ;AX holds sum
        XOR    BX,BX        ;clear base register
        MOV    CX,10        ;CX has number of elements
ADDNOS:
        ADD    AX,W[BX]     ;sum = sum + element
        ADD    BX,2         ;index next element
        LOOP   ADDNOS       ;loop until done
```

Example 10.6 Suppose that ALPHA is declared as

```
ALPHA   DW   0123h,0456h,0789h,0ABCDh
```

in the segment addressed by DS. Suppose also that

BX contains 2   Offset 0002 contains 1084h
SI contains 4   Offset 0004 contains 2BACh
DI contains 1

Tell which of the following instructions are legal. If legal, give the source offset address and the number moved.

a. MOV AX,[ALPHA+BX]
b. MOV BX,[BX+2]
c. MOV CX,ALPHA[SI]
d. MOV AX,-2[SI]
e. MOV BX,[ALPHA+3+DI]
f. MOV AX,[BX]2
g. ADD BX,[ALPHA+AX]

Solution:

	Source offset	Number moved
a.	ALPHA+2	0456h
b.	2+2 = 4	2BACh
c.	ALPHA+4	0789h
d.	−2+4 = 2	1084h
e.	ALPHA+3+1 = ALPHA+4	0789h
f.	Illegal form of source operand	
g.	Illegal source register	

The next two examples illustrate array processing by based and indexed modes.

Example 10.7 Replace each lowercase letter in the following string by its upper case equivalent. Use index addressing mode.

```
MSG DB          'this is a message'
```

Solution:

```
        MOV  CX,17          ;no. of chars in string
        XOR  SI,SI          ;SI indexes a char
TOP:
        CMP  MSG[SI],' '    ;blank?
        JE   NEXT           ;yes, skip over
        AND  MSG[SI],0DFh   ;no, convert to upper case
NEXT:
        INC  SI             ;index next byte
        LOOP TOP            ;loop until done
```

10.2.3
The PTR Operator and the LABEL Pseudo-op

You saw in Chapter 4 that the operands of an instruction must be of the same type; for example, both bytes or both words. If one operand is a constant, the assembler attempts to infer the type from the other operand. For example, the assembler treats the instruction

```
MOV AX,1
```

as a word instruction, because AX is a 16-bit register. Similarly, it treats

```
MOV BH,5
```

as a byte instruction. However, it can't assemble

```
MOV [BX],1           ;illegal
```

because it can't tell whether the destination is the byte pointed to by BX or the word pointed to by BX. If you want the destination to be a byte, you can say,

```
MOV BYTE PTR [BX],1
```

and if you want the destination to be a word, you say,

```
MOV WORD PTR [BX],1
```

Example 10.8 In the string of example 10.7, replace the character "t" by "T".

Solution 1: Using register indirect mode,

```
LEA SI,MSG              ;SI points to MSG
MOV BYTE PTR [SI],'T'   ;replace 't' by 'T'
```

Solution 2: Using index mode

```
XOR SI,SI           ;clear SI
MOV MSG[SI],'T'     ;replace 't' by 'T'
```

Here it is not necessary to use the PTR operator, because MSG is a byte variable.

Using PTR to Override a Type

In general, the PTR operator can be used to override the declared type of an address expression. The syntax is

```
type PTR address_expression
```

where the type is BYTE, WORD, or DWORD (doubleword), and the address expression has been typed as DB, DW, or DD.

For example, suppose you have the following declaration:

```
DOLLARS   DB    1Ah
CENTS     DB    52h
```

and you'd like to move the contents of DOLLARS to AL and CENTS to AH with a single MOV instruction. Now

```
MOV AX,DOLLARS    ;illegal
```

is illegal because the destination is a word and the source has been typed as a byte variable. But you can override the type declaration with WORD PTR as

```
MOV AX, WORD PTR DOLLARS   ;AL = dollars, AH = cents
```

and the instruction will move 521Ah to AX.

The LABEL Pseudo-Op

Actually, there is another way to get around the problem of type conflict in the preceding example. Using the **LABEL** pseudo-op, we could declare

```
MONEY       LABEL       WORD
DOLLARS     DB          1Ah
CENTS       DB          52h
```

This declaration types MONEY as a word variable, and the components DOLLARS and CENTS as byte variables, with MONEY and DOLLARS being assigned the same address by the assembler. The instruction

```
MOV AX, MONEY          ;AL = dollars, AH = cents
```

is now legal. So are the following instructions, which have the same effect:

```
MOV AL, DOLLARS
MOV AH, CENTS
```

Example 10.9 Suppose the following data are declared:

```
.DATA
A  DW    1234h
B  LABEL BYTE
   DW    5678h
C  LABEL WORD
C1 DB    9Ah
C2 DB    0BCh
```

Tell whether the following instructions are legal, and if so, give the number moved.

Instruction

    a. `MOV AX,B`
    b. `MOV AH,B`
    c. `MOV CX,C`
    d. `MOV BX, WORD PTR B`
    e. `MOV DL, BYTE PTR C`
    f. `MOV AX, WORD PTR C1`

Solution:

    a. illegal—type conflict
    b. legal, 78h
    c. legal, 0BC9Ah
    d. legal, 5678h
    e. legal, 9Ah
    f. legal, 0BC9Ah

10.2.4 Segment Override

In register indirect mode, the pointer register BX, SI, or DI specifies an offset address relative to DS. It is also possible to specify an offset relative to one of the other segment registers. The form of an operand is

```
segment_register:[pointer_register]
```

For example,

```
MOV AX,ES:[SI]
```

If SI contains 0100h, the source address in this instruction is ES:0100h. You might want to do this in a program with two data segments, where ES contains the segment number of the second data segment.

Segment overrides can also be used with based and indexed modes.

10.2.5 Accessing the Stack

We mentioned earlier that when BP specifies an offset in register indirect mode, SS supplies the segment number. This means that BP may be used to access items on the stack.

Example 10.10 Move the top three words on the stack into AX, BX, and CX without changing the stack.

Solution:

```
MOV BP,SP          ;BP points to stacktop
MOV AX,[BP]        ;move stacktop to AX
MOV BX,[BP+2]      ;move second word to BX
MOV CX,[BP+4]      ;move third word to CX
```

A primary use of BP is to pass values to a procedure (see Chapter 14).

10.3 An Application: Sorting an Array

It is much easier to locate an item in an array if the array has been sorted. There are dozens of sorting methods; the method we will discuss here is called *selectsort*. It is one of the simplest sorting methods.

To sort an array A of *N* elements, we proceed as follows:

Pass 1. Find the largest element among A[1] . . . A[N]. Swap it and A[N]. Because this puts the largest element in position N, we need only sort A[1] . . . A[N–1] to finish.

Pass 2. Find the largest element among A[1] . . . A[N–1]. Swap it and A[N–1]. This places the next-to-largest element in its proper position.

.
.
.

Pass N–1. Find the largest element among A[1], A[2]. Swap it and A[2]. At this point A[2] . . . A[N] are in their proper positions, so A[1] is as well, and the array is sorted.

For example, suppose the array A consists of the following integers:

Position	1	2	3	4	5
initial data	21	5	16	40	7
pass 1	21	5	16	7	40
pass 2	7	5	16	21	40
pass 3	7	5	16	21	40
pass 4	5	7	16	21	40

Selectsort algorithm

```
i = N
FOR N-1 times DO
  Find the position k of the largest element
      among A[1]..A[i]
(*) Swap A[k] and A[i]
  i = i-1
END_FOR
```

Step (*) will be handled by a procedure SWAP. The code for the procedures is the following (we'll suppose the array to be sorted is a byte array):

Program Listing PGM10_2.ASM

```
 1:  SELECT  PROC
 2:  ;sorts a byte array by the selectsort method
 3:  ;input:  SI = array offset address
 4:  ;        BX = number of elements
 5:  ;output: SI = offset of sorted array
 6:  ;uses: SWAP
 7:          PUSH    BX
 8:          PUSH    CX
 9:          PUSH    DX
10:          PUSH    SI
11:          DEC     BX              ;N = N-1
12:          JE      END_SORT        ;exit if 1-elt array
13:          MOV     DX,SI           ;save array offset
14:  ;for N-1 times do
15:  SORT_LOOP:
16:          MOV     SI,DX           ;SI pts to array
17:          MOV     CX,BX           ;no. of comparisons to make
18:          MOV     DI,SI           ;DI pts to largest element
19:          MOV     AL,[DI]         ;AL has largest element
20:  ;locate biggest of remaining elts
21:  FIND_BIG:
22:          INC     SI              ;SI pts to next element
23:          CMP     [SI],AL         ;is new element > largest?
24:          JNG     NEXT            ;no, go on
25:          MOV     DI,SI           ;yes, move DI
26:          MOV     AL,[DI]         ;AL has largest element
27:  NEXT:
28:          LOOP    FIND_BIG        ;loop until done
29:  ;swap biggest elt with last elt
30:          CALL    SWAP            ;Swap with last elt
31:          DEC     BX              ;N = N-1
32:          JNE     SORT_LOOP       ;repeat if N <> 0
33:  END_SORT:
34:          POP     SI
35:          POP     DX
36:          POP     CX
37:          POP     BX
38:          RET
39:  SELECT  ENDP
40:  SWAP    PROC
41:  ;swaps two array elements
42:  ;input: SI = one element
43:  ;       DI = other element
```

```
44:     ;output: exchange elements
45:             PUSH    AX              ;save AX
46:             MOV     AL,[SI]         ;get A[i]
47:             XCHG    AL,[DI]         ;place in A[k]
48:             MOV     [SI],AL         ;put A[k] in A[i]
49:             POP     AX              ;restore AX
50:             RET
51: SWAP        ENDP
```

Procedure SELECT is entered with the array offset address in SI, and the number of elements N in BX. The algorithm sorts the array in $N - 1$ passes so BX is decremented; if it contains 0, then we have a one-element array and there is nothing to do, so the procedure exits.

In the general case, the procedure enters as the main processing loop (lines 15–32). Each pass through this loop places the largest of the remaining unsorted elements in its proper place.

In lines 21–28, a loop is entered to find the largest of the remaining unsorted elements; the loop is exited with DI pointing to the largest element and SI pointing to the last element in the array. At line 30, procedure SWAP is called to exchange the elements pointed to by SI and DI.

The procedure can be tested by inserting them in a testing program.

Program Listing PGM10_3.ASM

```
TITLE PGM10_3: TEST SELECT
.MODEL SMALL
.STACK 100H
.DATA
A       DB      5,2,1,3,4
.CODE
MAIN    PROC
        MOV     AX,@DATA
        MOV     DS,AX
        LEA     SI,A
        MOV     BX,5
        CALL    SELECT
        MOV     AH,4CH
        INT     21H
MAIN    ENDP
;select goes here
        END     MAIN
```

After assembling and linking, we enter DEBUG and execute down to the procedure call (the addresses in the following demonstration were determined in a previous DEBUG session):

```
-GC
AX=100D BX=0005 CX=0049 DX=0000 SP=0100 BP=0000 SI=0004 DI=0000
DS=100D ES=0FF9 SS=100E CS=1009 IP=000C NV UP EI PL NZ NA PO NC
1009:000C E80400       CALL    0013
```

Before calling the procedure, let's look at the unsorted array:

```
-D4 8
100D:0000     05 02 01 03-04
```

The data appear in the order 5, 2, 1, 3, 4. Now let's execute SELECT:

```
-GF
AX=1002 BX=0005 CX=0049 DX=0000 SP=0100 BP=0000 SI=0004 DI=0005
DS=100D ES=0FF9 SS=100E CS=1009 IP=000F  NV UP EI PL ZR NA PE NC
1009:000F B44C     MOV    AH,4C
```

and look at the array again:

```
-D4 8
100D:0000     01 02 03 04-05
```

It is now in ascending order.

10.4 Two-Dimensional Arrays

A **two-dimensional array** is an array of arrays; that is, a one-dimensional array whose elements are one-dimensional arrays. We can picture the elements as being arranged in rows and columns. Figure 10.2 shows a two-dimensional array B with three rows and four columns (a 3 × 4 array); B[i,j] is the element in row i and column j.

How Two-Dimensional Arrays Are Stored

Because memory is one-dimensional, the elements of a two-dimensional array must be stored sequentially. There are two commonly used ways: In **row-major order**, the row 1 elements are stored, followed by the row 2 elements, then the row 3 elements, and so on. In **column-major order**, the elements of the first column are stored, followed by the second column, third column, and so on. For example, suppose array B has 10, 20, 30, and 40 in the first row, 50, 60, 70, and 80 in the second row, and 90, 100, 110, and 120 in the third row. It could be stored in row-major order as follows:

Figure 10.2 A Two-Dimensional Array B

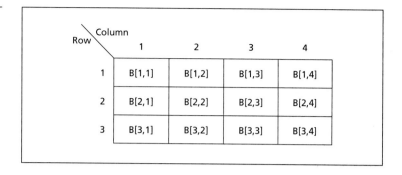

```
B   DW   10,20,30,40
    DW   50,60,70,80
    DW   90,100,110,120
```

or in column-major order as follows:

```
B   DW   10,50,90
    DW   20,60,100
    DW   30,70,110
    DW   40,80,120
```

Most high-level language compilers store two-dimensional arrays in row-major order. In assembly language, we can do it either way. If the elements of a row are to be processed together sequentially, then row-major order is better, because the next element in a row is the next memory location. Conversely, column-major order is better if the elements of a column are to be processed together.

Locating an Element in a Two-Dimensional Array

Suppose an $M \times N$ array A is stored in row-major order, where the size of the elements is S ($S = 1$ for a byte array, $S = 2$ for a word array). To find the location of A[i, j],

1. Find where row i begins.
2. Find the location of the *j*th element in that row.

Here is the first step. Row 1 begins at location A. Because there are N elements in each row, each of size S bytes, Row 2 begins at location $A + N \times S$, Row 3 begins at location $A + 2 \times N \times S$, and in general, Row i begins at location $A + (i - 1) \times N \times S$.

Now for the second step. We know from our discussion of one-dimensional arrays that the *j*th element in a row is stored $(j - 1) \times S$ bytes from the beginning of the row.

Adding the results of steps 1 and 2, we get the final result:

If A is an $M \times N$ array, with element size S bytes, stored in row-major order, then

(1)   A[i, j] has address $A + ((i - 1) \times N + (j - 1)) \times S$

There is a similar expression for column-major ordered arrays:

If A is an $M \times N$ array, with element size S, stored in column-major order, then

(2)   A[i,j] has address $A + ((i - 1) + (j - 1) \times M) \times S$

Example 10.12 Suppose A is an $M \times N$ word array stored in row-major order.

1. Where does row i begin?
2. Where does column j begin?
3. How many bytes are there between elements in a column?

Solution:

1. Row i begins at A[i, 1]; by formula (1) its address is $A + (i - 1) \times N \times 2$.
2. Column j begins at A[1, j]; by formula (1) the address is $A + (j - 1) \times 2$.
3. Because there are N columns, there are $2 \times N$ bytes between elements in any given column.

10.5 Based Indexed Addressing Mode

In this mode, the offset address of the operand is the sum of

1. the contents of a base register (BX or BP)
2. the contents of an index register (SI or DI)
3. optionally, a variable's offset address
4. optionally, a constant (positive or negative)

If BX is used, DS contains the segment number of the operand's address; if BP is used, SS has the segment number. The operand may be written several ways; four of them are

1. `variable[base_register][index_register]`
2. `[base_register + index_register + variable + constant]`
3. `variable[base_register + index_register + constant]`
4. `constant[base_register + index_register + variable]`

The order of terms within these brackets is arbitrary.

For example, suppose W is a word variable, BX contains 2, and SI contains 4. The instruction

`MOV AX,W[BX][SI]`

moves the contents of W+2+4 = W+6 to AX. This instruction could also have been written in either of these ways:

`MOV AX,[W+BX+SI]`

or

`MOV AX,W[BX+SI]`

Based indexed mode is especially useful for processing two-dimensional arrays, as the following example shows.

Example 10.13 Suppose A is a 5- × 7-word array stored in row-major order. Write some code to (1) clear row 3, (2) clear column 4. Use based indexed mode.

Solution:

1. From example 10.12, we know that in an *M*- × *N*-word array A, row i begins at A + (i – 1) × N × 2. Thus in a 5 × 7 array, row 3 begins at A + (3 – 1) × 7 × 2 = A + 28. So we can clear row 3 as follows:

    ```
               MOV   X,28;           BX indexes row 3
               XOR   SI,SI           ;SI will index columns
               MOV   CX,7            ;number of elements in a row
    CLEAR:
               MOV   A[BX][SI],0     ;clear A[3,j]
               ADD   SI,2            ;go to next column
               LOOP  CLEAR           ;loop until done
    ```

2. Again from example 10.12, column j begins at A + (j – 1) × 2 in an *M*- × *N*-word array. Thus column 4 begins at A + (4 – 1) × 2 = A + 6. Since A is a seven-column word array stored in row-major order, to get to the next element in column 4 we need to add 7 × 2 = 14. We can clear column 4 as follows:

    ```
               MOV   SI,6            ;SI will index column 4
               XOR   BX,BX           ;BX will index rows
               MOV   CX,5            ;number of elements in a column
    CLEAR:
               MOV   A[BX][SI],0     ;clear A[i,4]
               ADD   BX,1            ;go to next row
               LOOP  CLEAR           ;loop until done
    ```

10.6 An Application: Averaging Test Scores

Suppose a class of five students is given four exams. The results are recorded as follows:

	Test 1	Test 2	Test 3	Test 4
MARY ALLEN	67	45	98	33
SCOTT BAYLIS	70	56	87	44
GEORGE FRANK	82	72	89	40
BETH HARRIS	80	67	95	50
SAM WONG	78	76	92	60

We will write a program to find the class average on each exam. To do this, we sum the entries in each column and divide by 5.

Algorithm

1. j = 4
2. REPEAT
3.   sum the scores in column j
4.   divide sum by 5 to get the average in column j
4.   j = j-1
5. UNTIL j = 0

We choose to start summing in column 4 because it makes the code a little shorter. Step 3 may be broken down further as follows:

```
sum[j] = 0
i = 1
FOR 5 times DO
  sum[j] = sum[j] + score[i,j]
  i = 1+1
END_FOR
```

Program Listing PGM10_4.ASM

```
0:     TITLE   PGM10_4: CLASS AVERAGE
1:     .MODEL  SMALL
2:     .STACK  100H
3:     .DATA
4:     FIVE    DW      5
5:     SCORES  DW      67,45,98,33    ;Mary Allen
6:             DW      70,56,87,44    ;Scott Baylis
7:             DW      82,72,89,40    ;George Frank
8:             DW      80,67,95,50    ;Beth Harris
9:             DW      78,76,92,60    ;Sam Wong
10:    AVG     DW      5 DUP (0)
11:    .CODE
12:    MAIN    PROC
13:            MOV     AX,@DATA
14:            MOV     DS,AX          ;initialize DS
15:    ;j=4
16:            MOV     SI,6           ;col index, initially col 4
17:    REPEAT:
18:            MOV     CX,5           ;no. of rows
19:            XOR     BX,BX          ;row index, initially 1
20:            XOR     AX,AX          ;col_sum, initially 0
21:    ;sum scores in column j
22:    FOR:
23:            ADD     AX,SCORES[BX+SI];col_sum=col_sum + score
24:            ADD     BX,8           ;index next row
25:            LOOP    FOR            ;keep adding scores
26:    ;endfor
27:    ;compute average in column j
28:            XOR     DX,DX          ;clear high part of divnd
29:            DIV     FIVE           ;AX =   average
30:            MOV     AVG[SI],AX     ;store in array
31:            SUB     SI,2           ;go to next column
32:            ;until j=0
33:            JNL     REPEAT         ;unless SI < 0
34:    ;dos exit
35:            MOV     AH,4CH
36:            INT     21H
37:    MAIN    ENDP
38:            END     MAIN
```

The test scores are stored in a two-dimensional array (lines 5–9).
    In lines 22–25, a column is summed and the total placed in the array AVG. In lines 28–30, this total is divided by 5 to compute the column average.

Rows and columns of array SCORE are indexed by BX and SI, respectively. We choose to begin summing column 4; this column begins in SCORES+6, so SI is initialized to 6 (line 16). After a column is summed, SI is decreased by 2, until it is 0.

The execution of the program may be seen in DEBUG. We execute down to the DOS exit, then dump the array AVG (the addresses in this demonstration were determined in a previous DEBUG session).

```
-G29
AX=4C4B  BX=0028  CX=0000  DX=0002  SP=0100  BP=0000  SI=FFFE  DI=0000
DS=100B  ES=0FF9  SS=100F  CS=1009  IP=0029  NV UP EI NG NZ AC PO CY
1009:0029 CD21    INT     21

-D36 3D
100B:0030         4B 00-3F 00 5C 00 2D 00
```

The averages are 004Bh, 003Fh, 005Ch, and 002Dh, or—in decimal 75, 63, 92, and 45.

10.7 The XLAT Instruction

In some applications, it is necessary to translate data from one form to another. For example, the IBM PC uses ASCII codes for characters, but IBM mainframes use EBCDIC (Extended Binary Coded Decimal Interchange Code). To translate a character string encoded in ASCII to EBCDIC, a program must replace the ASCII code of each character in the string with the corresponding EBCDIC code.

The instruction **XLAT** (translate) is a no-operand instruction that can be used to convert a byte value into another value that comes from a table. The byte to be converted must be in AL, and BX has the offset address of the conversion table. The instruction (1) adds the contents of AL to the address in BX to produce an address within the table, and (2) replaces the contents of AL by the value found at that address.

For example, suppose the contents of AL are in the range 0 to Fh and we want to replace it by the ASCII code of its hex equivalent; for example, 6h by 036h = "6", Bh by 042h = "B". The conversion table is

```
TABLE   DB 030h,031h,032h,033h,034h,035,036h,037h,038h,039h
        DB 041h,042h,043h,044h,045h,046h
```

For instance, to convert 0Ch to "C", we do the following:

```
MOV AL,0Ch          ;number to convert
LEA BX,TABLE        ;BX has table offset
XLAT                ;AL has 'C'
```

Here XLAT computes address TABLE + Ch = TABLE + 12, and replaces the contents of AL by the number stored there, namely 043h = "C".

In this example, if AL contained a value *not* in the range 0 to 15, XLAT would translate it to some garbage value.

Example: Coding and Decoding a Secret Message

The following program prompts the user to type a message, encodes it in unrecognizable form, prints the coded message, translates it back, and prints the translation.
Sample output:

```
ENTER A MESSAGE:,
GATHER YOUR FORCES AND ATTACK AT DAWN, (input)
ZXKBGM WULM HUMPGN XJO XKKXPD XK OXSJ, (encoded)
GATHER YOUR FORCES AND ATTACK AT DAWN, (translated)
```

Algorithm for Coding and Decoding a Secret Message

```
Print prompt
Read and encode message
Go to a new line
Print encoded message
Go to a new line
Translate and print message
```

Program Listing PGM10_5.ASM

```
0:      TITLE PGM 10_5: SECRET MESSAGE
1:.     MODEL    SMALL
2:      .STACK   100H
3:      .DATA
4:      ;alphabet                            ABCDEFGHIJKLMNOPQRSTUVWXYZ
5:      CODE_KEY DB 65 DUP (' '),   'XQPOGHZBCADEIJUVFMNKLRSTWY'
6:               DB 37 DUP (' ')
7:      DECODE_KEY DB 65 DUP (' '), 'JHIKLQEFMNTURSDCBVWXOPYAZG'
8:               DB 37 DUP (' ')
9:      CODED    DB 80 DUP ('$')
10:     PROMPT   DB 'ENTER A MESSAGE:',0DH,0AH,'$'
11:     CRLF     DB    0DH,0AH,'$'
12:     .CODE
13:     MAIN     PROC
14:              MOV    AX,@DATA       ;initialize DS
15:              MOV    DS,AX
16:     ;print input prompt
17:              MOV    AH,9           ;print string fcn
18:              LEA    DX,PROMPT      ;DX pts to prompt
19:              INT    21H            ;print message
20:     ;read and encode message
21:              MOV    AH,1           ;read char fcn
22:              LEA    BX,CODE_KEY    ;BX pts to code key
23:              LEA    DI,CODED       ;DI pts to coded message
24:     WHILE_:
25:              INT    21H            ;read a char
26:              CMP    AL,0DH         ;carriage return?
27:              JE     ENDWHILE       ;yes, go to print coded message
28:              XLAT                  ;no, encode char
```

```
29:            MOV     [DI],AL         ;store in coded message
30:            INC     DI              ;move pointer
31:            JMP     WHILE_          ;process next char
32: ENDWHILE:
33: ;go to a new line
34:            MOV     AH,9
35:            LEA     DX,CRLF
36:            INT     21H             ;new line
37: ;print encoded message
38:            LEA     DX,CODED        ;DX pts to coded
39:            INT     21H             ;print coded message
40: ;go to a new line
41:            LEA     DX,CRLF
42:            INT     21H             ;new line
43: ;decode message and print it
44:            MOV     AH,2            ;print char fcn
45:            LEA     BX,DECODE_KEY   ;BX pts to decode key
46:            LEA     SI,CODED        ;SI pts to encoded message
47: WHILE1:
48:            MOV     AL,[SI]         ;get a character from message
49:            CMP     AL,'$'          ;end of message?
50:            JE      ENDWHILE1       ;yes, exit
51:            XLAT                    ;no, decode character
52:            MOV     DL,AL           ;put in DL
53:            INT     21H             ;print translated char
54:            INC     SI              ;move ptr
55:            JMP     WHILE1          ;process next char
56: ENDWHILE1:
57:            MOV     AH,4CH
58:            INT     21H             ;dos exit
59: MAIN       ENDP
60:            END     MAIN
```

Three arrays are declared in the data segment:

1. CODE_KEY is used to encode English text.
2. CODED holds the encoded message; it is initialized to a string of dollar signs so that it may be printed with INT 21h, function 9.
3. DECODE_KEY is used to translate the encoded text back to English.

Line 4 is a comment line containing the alphabet, which makes it easier to see how characters are encoded and decoded.

In lines 24–32, characters are read and encoded until a carriage return is typed. AL receives the ASCII code of each input character; XLAT adds it to address CODE_KEY in BX to produce an address within the CODE_KEY table.

CODE_KEY is set up as follows: 65 blanks, followed by the letters to which A to Z will be encoded, followed by 37 more blanks for a total of 128 bytes (128 bytes are needed, because the standard ASCII characters range from 0 to 127). Suppose, for example, an "A" is typed. The ASCII code of "A" is 65. XLAT computes address CODE_KEY+65, picks up the value of that byte, which is "X", and stores it in AL. At line 33, this value is moved into byte array CODED. Similarly, "B" is translated into 'Q', 'C' into 'P'...'Z' into "Y" (the encoding table was constructed arbitrarily). Characters other than capital letters (including the blank character) have ASCII code in the ranges 0 to 64 or 92 to 127, and are translated into blanks. In lines 38–39, the encoded message is printed.

DECODE_KEY also begins with 65 blanks and ends with 37 blanks. The positions of the letters in this array may be deduced as follows. First, lay down the alphabet (line 4). Now since "A" was coded into "X", the letter at position "X" in the decoding sequence should be "A". Similarly, because "B" was coded into "Q", there should be a "B" at position "Q", and so on.

In lines 47–56, the encoded message is translated. After placing the addresses of DECODE_KEY and CODED in BX and SI, respectively, the program moves a byte of the coded message into AL. If it's a dollar sign, the message has been translated and the program exits. If not, XLAT adds AL to address DECODE_KEY to produce an address within the decoding table, and puts the character found there into AL. At line 52, the character is moved to DL so that it can be printed with INT 21h, function 2.

Summary

- A one-dimensional array is an ordered list of elements of the same type. The DB and DW pseudo-ops are used to declare byte and word arrays.

- An array element can be located by adding a constant to the base address.

- The way that an operand is specified is its addressing mode. The addressing modes are register, immediate, direct, register indirect, based, indexed, and based indexed.

- In register indirect mode, an operand has the form [register], where register is BX, SI, DI, or BP. The operand's offset is contained in the register. For BP, the operand's segment number is in SS; for the other registers, the segment number is in DS.

- In based or indexed mode, an operand has the form [register + displacement]. Register is BX, BP, SI, or DI. The operand's offset is obtained by adding the displacement to the contents of the register. For BX, SI, or DI, the segment number is in DS; for BP, the segment number is in SS.

- The operators BYTE PTR and WORD PTR in front of an operand may be used to override the operand's declared type.

- The LABEL pseudo-op may be used to assign a type to a variable.

- A two-dimensional array is a one-dimensional array whose elements are one-dimensional arrays. Two-dimensional arrays may be stored row by row (row-major order), or column by column (column-major order).

- In based indexed mode, the offset address of the operand is the sum of (1) BX or BP; (2) SI or DI; (3) optionally, a memory offset address; (4) optionally, a constant. One (of several) possible forms is [base_register + index_register + memory_location + constant]. DS has the segment number if BX is used; if BP is used, SS has the segment number.

- Based indexed mode may be used to process two-dimensional arrays.

- The XLAT instruction can be used to convert a byte value into another value that comes from a table. AL contains the value to be converted and BX the address of the table. The instruction adds AL to the offset contained in BX to produce a table address. The contents of AL is replaced by the value found at that address.

Glossary

addressing mode	The way the operand is specified
base address of an array	The address of the array variable
based addressing mode	An indirect addressing mode in which the contents of BX or BP are added to a displacement to form an operand's offset address
column-major order	Column by column
direct mode	The operand is a variable
displacement	In based or indexed mode, a number added to the contents of a register to produce an operand's offset address
immediate mode	The operand is constant
indexed addressing mode	An indirect addressing mode in which the contents of SI or DI are added to a displacement to form an operand's offset address
one-dimensional array	An ordered list of element of the same type
pointer	A register that contains an offset address of an operand
register mode	The operand is a register
row-major order	Row by row
two-dimensional array	A one-dimensional array whose elements are one-dimensional arrays

New instructions

XLAT

New Pseudo-Ops

DUP   LABEL   PTR

Exercises

1. Suppose
   AX contains 0500h   offset 1000h contains 0100h
   BX contains 1000h   offset 1500h contains 0150h
   SI contains 1500h   offset 2000h contains 0200h
   DI contains 2000h   offset 3000h contains 0400h
                               offset 4000h contains 0300h
   and BETA is a word variable whose offset address is 1000h

For each of the following instructions, if it is legal, give the source offset address or register and the result stored in the destination.

  a. MOV DI,SI
  b. MOV DI,[DI]
  c. ADD AX,[SI]
  d. SUB BX,[DI]
  e. LEA BX,BETA[BX]
  f. ADD [SI],[DI]
  g. ADD BH,[BL]
  h. ADD AH,[SI]
  i. MOV AX,[BX + DI + BETA]

2. Given the following declarations

   A   DW   1,2,3
   B   DB   4,5,6
   C   LABEL WORD
   MSG DB   'ABC'

   and suppose that BX contains the offset address of C. Tell which of the following instructions are legal. If so, give the number moved.

   a. MOV   AH, BYTE PTR A
   b. MOV   AX, WORD PTR B
   c. MOV   AX, C
   d. MOV   AX, MSG
   e. MOV   AH, BYTE PTR C

3. Use BP and based mode to do the following stack operations. (You may use other registers as well, but don't use PUSH or POP.)

   a. Replace the contents of the top two words on the stack by zeros.
   b. Copy a stack of five words into a word array ST_ARR, so that ST_ARR contains the stack top, ST_ARR + 2 contains the next word on the stack, and so on.

4. Write instructions to carry out each of the following operations on a word array A of 10 elements or a byte array B of 15 elements.

   a. Move A[i+1] to position i, i = 1 . . . 9, and move A[1] to position 10.
   b. Count in DX the number of zero entries in array A.
   c. Suppose byte array B contains a character string. Search B for the first occurrence of the letter "E". If found, make SI point to its location; if not found, set CF.

5. Write a procedure FIND_IJ that returns the offset address of the element in row i and column j in a two-dimensional $M \times N$ word array A stored in row-major order. The procedure receives i in AX, j in BX, N in CX, and the offset of A in DX. It returns the offset address of the element in DX. *Note:* you may ignore the possibility of overflow.

Programming Exercises

6. To sort an array A of N elements by the bubblesort method, we proceed as follows:

   Pass 1. For $j = 2 \ldots N$, if $A[j] < A[j-1]$ then swap $A[j]$ and $A[j-1]$. This will place the largest element in position N.

   Pass 2. For $j = 2 \ldots N-1$, if $A[j] < A[j-1]$ then swap $A[j]$ and $A[j-1]$. This will place the second largest element in position $N-1$.

   .
   .
   .

   Pass N − 1. If $A[2] < A[1]$, then swap $A[2]$ and $A[1]$. At this point the array is sorted.

   ### Demonstration

initial data	7	5	3	9	1
pass 1	5	3	7	1	9
pass 2	3	5	1	7	9
pass 3	3	1	5	7	9
pass 4	1	3	5	7	9

   Write a procedure BUBBLE to sort a byte array by the bubblesort algorithm. The procedure receives the offset address of the array in SI and the number of elements in BX. Write a program that lets the user type a list of single-digit numbers, with one blank between numbers, calls BUBBLE to sort them, and prints the sorted list on the next line. For example,

   ```
   ?2 1 6 5 3 7
   1 2 3 5 6 7
   ```

   Your program should be able to handle an array with only one element.

7. Suppose the class records in the example of section 10.4.3 are stored as follows

   ```
   CLASS
   DB      'MARY ALLEN  ',67,45,9 8,33
   DB      'SCOTT BAYLIS',70,56,87,44
   DB      'GEORGE FRANK',82,72,89,40
   DB      'SAM WONG    ',78,76,92,60
   ```

   Each name occupies 12 bytes. Write a program to print the name of each student and his or her average (truncated to an integer) for the four exams.

8. Write a program that starts with an initially undefined byte array of maximum size 100, and lets the user insert single characters

into the array in such a way that the array is always sorted in ascending order. The program should print a question mark, let the user enter a character, and display the array with the new character inserted. Input ends when the user hits the ESC key. Duplicate characters should be ignored.

Sample execution:

```
?A
A
?D
AD
?B
ABD
?a
ABDa
?D
ABDa
?   <ESC>
```

9. Write a program that uses XLAT to (a) read a line of text, and (b) print it on the next line with all small letters converted to capitals. The input line may contain any characters—small letters, capital, letters, digit characters, punctuation, and so on.

10. Write a procedure PRINTHEX that uses XLAT to display the content of BX as four hex digits. Test it in a program that lets the user type a four-digit hex integer, stores it in BX using the hex input algorithm of section 7.4, and calls PRINTHEX to print it on the next line.

11

The String Instructions

Overview

In this chapter we consider a special group of instructions called the *string instructions*. In 8086 assembly language, a **memory string** or **string** is simply a byte or word array. Thus, string instructions are designed for array processing.

Here are examples of operations that can be performed with the string instructions:
- Copy a string into another string.
- Search a string for a particular byte or word.
- Store characters in a string.
- Compare strings of characters alphabetically.

The tasks carried out by the string instructions can be performed by using the register indirect addressing mode we studied in Chapter 10; however, the string instructions have some built-in advantages. For example, they provide automatic updating of pointer registers and allow memory–memory operations.

11.1 The Direction Flag

In Chapter 5, we saw that the FLAGS register contains six status flags and three control flags. We know that the status flags reflect the result of an operation that the processor has done. The control flags are used to control the processor's operations.

One of the control flags is the *direction flag (DF)*. Its purpose is to determine the direction in which string operations will proceed. These operations are implemented by the two index registers SI and DI. Suppose, for example, that the following string has been declared:

```
STRING1      DB              'ABCDE'
```

And this string is stored in memory starting at offset 0200h:

Offset address	Content	ASCII character
0200h	041h	A
0201h	042h	B
0202h	043h	C
0203h	044h	D
0204h	045h	E

If DF = 0, SI and DI proceed in the direction of increasing memory addresses: from left to right across the string. Conversely, if DF = 1, SI and DI proceed in the direction of decreasing memory addresses: from right to left.

In the DEBUG display, DF = 0 is symbolized by UP, and DF = 1 by DN.

CLD and STD

To make DF = 0, use the **CLD** instruction

```
CLD    ;clear directio flag
```

To make DF = 1, use the **STD** instruction:

```
STD    ;set direction flag
```

CLD and STD have no effect on the other flags.

11.2 Moving a String

Suppose we have defined two strings as follows:

```
.DATA
STRING1    DB    'HELLO'
STRING2    DB    5 DUP (?)
```

and we would like to move the contents of STRING1 (the source string) into STRING2 (the destination string). This operation is needed for many string operations, such as duplicating a string or concatenating strings (attaching one string to the end of another string).

The **MOVSB** instruction

```
MOVSB                  ;move string byte
```

copies the contents of the byte addressed by DS:SI, to the byte addressed by ES:DI. The contents of the source byte are unchanged. After the byte has been moved, both SI and DI are automatically incremented if DF = 0, or decremented if DF = 1. For example, to move the first two bytes of STRING1 to STRING2, we execute the following instructions:

```
MOV AX,@DATA
MOV DS,AX              ;initialize DS
MOV ES,AX              ;and ES
LEA SI,STRING1         ;SI points to source string
LEA DI,STRING2         ;DI points to destination string
CLD                    ;clear DF
MOVSB                  ;move first byte
MOVSB                  ;and second byte
```

See Figure 11.1.

Figure 11.1 MOVSB

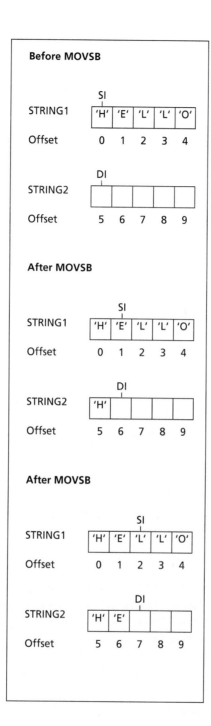

MOVSB is the first instruction we have seen that permits a memory–memory operation. It is also the first instruction that involves the ES register.

The REP Prefix

MOVSB moves only a single byte from the source string to the destination string. To move the entire string, first initialize CX to the number N of bytes in the source string and execute

```
REP MOVSB
```

The **REP** prefix causes MOVSB to be executed *N* times. After each MOVSB, CX is decremented until it becomes 0. For example, to copy STRING1 of the preceding section into STRING2, we execute

```
CLD
LEA SI,STRING1
LEA DI,STRING2
MOV CX,5                  ;no. of chars in STRING1
REP MOVSB
```

Example 11.1 Write instructions to copy STRING1 of the preceding section into STRING2 in reverse order.

Solution: The idea is to get SI pointing to the end of STRING1, DI to the beginning of STRING2, then move characters as SI travels to the left across STRING1.

```
        LEA   SI,STRING1+4    ;SI pts to end of STRING1
        LEA   DI,STRING2      ;DI pts to beginning of STRING2
        STD                   ;right to left processing
        MOV   CX,5
MOVE:
        MOVSB                 ;move a byte
        ADD   DI,2
        LOOP  MOVE
```

Here it is necessary to add 2 to DI after each MOVSB. Because we do this when DF = 1, MOVSB automatically decrements both SI and DI, and we want to increment DI.

MOVSW

There is a word form of MOVSB. It is

```
MOVSW     ;move string word
```

MOVSW moves a word from the source string to the destination string. Like MOVSB, it expects DS:SI to point to a source string word, and ES:DI to point to a destination string word. After a string word has been moved, both SI and DI are increased by 2 if DF = 0, or are decreased by 2 if DF = 1.

MOVSB and MOVSW have no effect on the flags.

Example 11.2 For the following array,

```
ARR DW   10,20,40,50,60,?
```

write instructions to insert 30 between 20 and 40. (Assume DS and ES have been initialized to the data segment.)

Solution: The idea is to move 40, 50, and 60 forward one position in the array, then insert 30.

```
          STD                        ;right to left processing
          LEA SI,ARR+8h              ;SI pts to 60
          LEA DI,ARR+Ah              ;DI pts to ?
          MOV CX,3                   ;3 elts to move
          REP MOVSW                  ;move 40,50,60
          MOV WORD PTR [DI],30       ;insert 30
```

Note: the PTR operator was introduced in section 10.2.3.

11.3 Store String

The STOSB Instruction

```
          STOSB              ;store string byte
```

moves the contents of the AL register to the byte addressed by ES:DI. DI is incremented if DF = 0 or decremented if DF = 1. Similarly, the **STOSW** instruction

```
          STOSW              ;store string word
```

moves the contents of AX to the word at address ES:DI and updates DI by 2, according to the direction flag setting.

STOSB and STOSW have no effect on the flags.

As an example of STOSB, the following instructions will store two "A"s in STRING1:

```
MOV AX,@DATA
MOV ES,AX              ;initialize ES
LEA DI,STRING1         ;DI points to STRING1
CLD                    ;process to the right
MOV AL,'A'             ;AL has character to store
STOSB                  ;store an 'A'
STOSB                  ;store another one
```

See Figure 11.2.

Reading and Storing a Character String

INT 21h, function 1 reads a character from the keyboard into AL. By repeatedly executing this interrupt with STOSB, we can read and store a character string. In addition, the characters may be processed before storing them.

The following procedure READ_STR reads and stores characters in a string, until a carriage return is typed. The procedure is entered with the string offset address in DI. It returns the string offset in DI, and number of characters entered in BX. If the user makes a typing mistake and hits the backspace key, the previous character is removed from the string.

This procedure is similar to DOS INT 21h, function 0Ah (see exercise 11.11).

Algorithm for READ_STR

```
chars_read = 0
read a char
WHILE char is not a carriage return DO
  IF char is a backspace
    THEN
      chars_read = chars_read - 1
```

11.3 Store String

Figure 11.2 STOSB

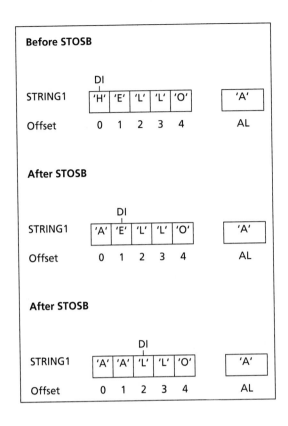

```
    remove previous char from string
  ELSE
    store char in string
    chars_read = chars_read + 1
  END_IF
  read a char
END_WHILE
```

Program Listing PGM11_1.ASM
```
 1: READ_STR PROC NEAR
 2: ; Reads and stores a string
 3: ; input: DI offset of string
 4: ;output: DI offset of string
 5: ;BX number of characters read
 6:         PUSH    AX
 7:         PUSH    DI
 8:         CLD                     ;process from left
 9:         XOR     BX,BX           ;no. of chars read
10:         MOV     AH,1            ;input char function
11:         INT     21H             ;read a char into AL
12: WHILE1:
13:         CMP     AL,0DH          ;CR?,
14:         JE      END_WHILE1      ;yes, exit
15: ;if char is backspace
16:         CMP     AL,8H           ;backspace?
17:         JNE     ELSE1           ;no,store in string
18: ;then
19:         DEC     DI              ;yes, move string ptr back
20:         DEC     BX              ;decrement char counter
```

```
21:             JMP     READ            ;and go to read another char
22: ELSE1:
23:             STOSB                   ;store char in string
24:             INC     BX              ;increment char count
25: READ:
26:             INT     21H             ;read a char into AL
27:             JMP     WHILE1          ;and continue loop
28: END_WHILE1:
29:             POP     DI
30:             POP     AX
31:             RET
32: READ_STR ENDP
```

At line 23, the procedure uses STOSB to store input characters in the string. STOSB automatically increments DI; at line 24, the character count in BX is incremented.

The procedure takes into account the possibility of typing errors. If the user hits the backspace key, then at line 19 the procedure decrements DI and BX. The backspace itself is not stored. When the next legitimate character is read, it replaces the wrong one in the string. *Note:* if the last characters typed before the carriage return are backspaces, the wrong characters will remain in the string, but the count of legitimate characters in BX will be correct.

We use READ_STR for string input in the following sections.

11.4 Load String

The **LODSB** instruction

```
LODSB                   ;load string byte
```

moves the byte addressed by DS:SI into AL. SI is then incremented if DF = 0 or decremented if DF = 1. The word form is

```
LODSW                   ;load string word
```

it moves the word addressed by DS:SI into AX; SI is increased by 2 if DF = 0 or decreased by 2 if DF = 1.

LODSB can be used to examine the characters of a string, as shown later.

LODSB and LODSW have no effect on the flags.

To illustrate LODSB, suppose STRING1 is defined as

```
STRING1   DB    'ABC'
```

The following code successively loads the first and second bytes of STRING1 into AL

```
MOV AX,@DATA
MOV DS,AX               ;initialize DS
LEA SI,STRING1          ;SI points to STRING1
CLD                     ;process left to right
LODSB                   ;load first byte into AL
LODSB                   ;load second byte into AL
```

See Figure 11.3.

Figure 11.3 LODSB

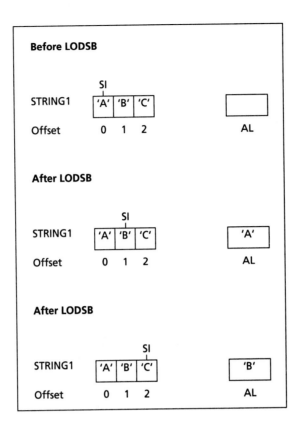

Displaying a Character String

The following procedure DISP_STR displays the string pointed to by SI, with the number of characters in BX. It can be used to display all or part of a string.

Algorithm for DISP_STR

```
FOR count times DO   /* count = no. of characters to display */
  load a string character into AL
  move it to DL
  output character
END_FOR
```

Program Listing PGM 11_2.ASM

```
DISP_STR    PROC
;displays a string
;input:  SI = offset of string
;        BX = no. of chars. to display
;output: none
        PUSH    AX
        PUSH    BX
        PUSH    CX
        PUSH    DX
        PUSH    SI
        MOV     CX,BX           ;no. of chars
        JCXZ    P_EXIT          ;exit if none
        CLD                     ;process left to right
```

```
              MOV     AH,2              ;prepare to print
TOP:
              LODSB                     ;char in AL
              MOV     DL,AL             ;move it to DL
              INT     21H               ;print char
              LOOP    TOP               ;loop until done
P_EXIT:
              POP     SI
              POP     DX
              POP     CX
              POP     BX
              POP     AX
              RET
DISP_STR      ENDP
```

To demonstrate READ_STR and DISP_STR, we'll write a program that reads a string (up to 80 characters) and displays the first 10 characters on the next line.

Program Listing PGM11_3.ASM

```
TITLE PGM11_3: TEST READ_STR and PRINT_STR
.MODEL    SMALL
.STACK
.DATA
STRING DB     80  DUP (0)
CRLF   DB     0DH,0AH,'$'
.CODE
MAIN   PROC
              MOV     AX,@DATA
              MOV     DS,AX
              MOV     ES,AX
;read a string
              LEA     DI,STRING         ;DI pts to string
              CALL    READ_STR          ;BX = no. of chars read
;go to a new line
              LEA     DX,CRLF
              MOV     AH,9
              INT     21H
;print string
              LEA     SI,STRING         ;SI pts to string
              MOV     BX,10             ;display 10 chars
              CALL    DISP_STR
;dos exit
              MOV     AH,4CH
              INT     21H
MAIN   ENDP
;READ_STR goes here
;DISP_STR goes here
              END     MAIN
```

Sample execution:

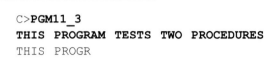
```
C>PGM11_3
THIS PROGRAM TESTS TWO PROCEDURES
THIS PROGR
```

11.5 Scan String

The instruction

```
SCASB        ;scan string byte
```

can be used to examine a string for a target byte. The target byte is contained in AL. SCASB subtracts the string byte pointed to by ES:DI from the contents of AL and uses the result to set the flags. The result is not stored. Afterward, DI is incremented if DF = 0 or decremented if DF = 1.

The word form is

```
SCASW        ;scan string word
```

in this case, the target word is in AX. SCASW subtracts the word addressed by ES:DI from AX and sets the flags. DI is increased by 2 if DF = 0 or decreased by 2 if DF = 1.

All the status flags are affected by SCASB and SCASW.

Figure 11.4 SCASB

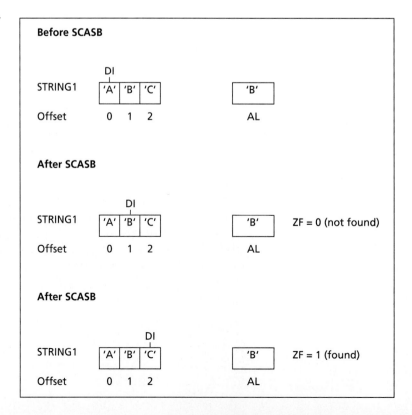

For example, if the string

```
STRING1    DB     'ABC'
```

is defined, then these instructions examine the first two bytes of STRING1, looking for "B"

```
MOV AX,@DATA
MOV AX,ES           ;initialize ES
CLD                 ;left to right processing
LEA DI,STRING1      ;DI pts to STRING1
MOV AL,'B'          ;target character
SCASB               ;scan first byte
SCASB               ;scan second byte
```

See Figure 11.4. Note that when the target "B" was found, ZF = 1 and because SCASB automatically increments DI, DI points to the byte after the target, not the target itself.

In looking for a target byte in a string, the string is traversed until the byte is found or the string ends. If CX is initialized to the number of bytes in the string,

```
REPNE    SCASB      ;repeat SCASB while not equal
                    (to target)
```

will repeatedly subtract each string byte from AL, update DI, and decrement CX until there is a zero result (the target is found) or CX = 0 (the string ends). *Note:* **REPNZ** (repeat while not zero) generates the same machine code as **REPNE**.

As an example, let's write a program to count the number of vowels and consonants in a string.

Algorithm for Counting Vowels and Consonants

```
Initialize vowel_count and consonant_count to 0;
Read and store a string
REPEAT
  Load a string character;
  IF it's a vowel
    THEN
      increment vowel_count
    ELSE IF it's a consonant
      THEN increment consonant_count
  END_IF
UNTIL end of string
display no. of vowels
display no. of consonants
```

We'll use procedure READ_STR (section 11.3) to read the string. It returns with DI pointing to the string and BX containing the number of characters read. To display the number of vowels and consonants in the string, we'll use procedure OUTDEC of Chapter 9. It displays the contents of AX as a signed decimal integer. For simplicity, we'll suppose the input is in upper case.

Program Listing PGM11_4.ASM

```
0:  TITLE PGM 11_4: COUNT VOWELS AND CONSONANTS
1:  .MODEL SMALL
2:  .STACK 100H
3:  .DATA
4:  STRING       DB  80 DUP (0)
```

```
 5:     VOWELS      DB      'AEIOU'
 6:     CONSONANTS  DB      'BCDFGHJKLMNPQRSTVWXYZ'
 7:     OUT1        DB      0DH,0AH,'vowels = $'
 8:     OUT2        DB      ', consonants = $'
 9:     VOWELCT DW  0
10:     CONSCT  DW  0
11:     .CODE
12:     MAIN    PROC
13:             MOV     AX,@DATA
14:             MOV     DS,AX           ;initialize DS
15:             MOV     ES,AX           ;and ES
16:             LEA     DI,STRING       ;DI pts to string
17:             CALL    READ_STR        ;BX = no. of chars read
18:             MOV     SI,DI           ;SI pts to string
19:             CLD                     ;left to right processing
20:     REPEAT:
21:     ;load a string character
22:             LODSB                   ;char in AL
23:     ;if it's a vowel
24:             LEA     DI,VOWELS       ;DI pts to vowels
25:             MOV     CX,5            ;5 vowels
26:             REPNE   SCASB           ;is char a vowel?
27:             JNE     CK_CONST        ;no other char
28:     ;then increment vowel count
29:             INC     VOWELCT
30:             JMP     UNTIL
31:     ;else if it's a consonant
32:     CK_CONST:
33:             LEA     DI,CONSONANTS   ;DI pts to consonants
34:             MOV     CX,21           ;21 consonants
35:             REPNE   SCASB           ;is char a consonant?
36:             JNE     UNTIL           ;no
37:     ;then increment consonant count
38:             INC     CONSCT
39:     UNTIL:
40:             DEC     BX              ;BX has no. chars left in string
41:             JNE     REPEAT          ;loop if chars left
42:     ;output no. of vowels
43:             MOV     AH,9            ;prepare to print
44:             LEA     DX,OUT1         ;get vowel message
45:             INT     21H             ;print it
46:             MOV     AX,VOWELCT      ;get vowel count
47:             CALL    OUTDEC          ;print it
48:     ;output no. of consonants
49:             MOV     AH,9            ;prepare to print
50:             LEA     DX,OUT2         ;get consonant message
51:             INT     21H             ;print it
52:             MOV     AX,CONSCT       ;get consonant count
53:             CALL    OUTDEC          ;print it
54:     ;dos exit
55:             MOV     AH,4CH
56:             INT     21H
57:     MAIN    ENDP
58:     ;READ_STR goes here
59:     ;OUTDEC goes here
60:             END     MAIN
```

Because the program uses both LODSB, which loads the byte in DS:SI, and SCASB, which scans the byte in ES:DI, both DS and ES must be initialized. BX is used as a loop counter and is set to the number of bytes in the string (CX is used elsewhere in the program).

Line 22. LODSB puts a string character in AL and advances SI to the next one.

Line 26. To see if the character in AL is a vowel, the program scans the string VOWELS by executing REPNE SCASB. This instruction subtracts each byte of VOWELS from AL and sets the flags. The instruction returns ZF = 1 if the character is a vowel and ZF = 0 if it isn't.

Line 35. If the target was not a vowel, the program scans the string CONSONANTS, in exactly the same way it scanned VOWELS.

Sample execution:

```
C>PGM11_4
A,E,I,O,U ARE VOWELS.
vowels = 9,   consonants = 5
```

11.6 Compare String

The CMPSB Instruction

```
CMPSB                   ;compare string byte
```

subtracts the byte with address ES:DI from the byte with address DS:SI, and sets the flags. The result is not stored. Afterward, both SI and DI are incremented if DF = 0, or decremented if DF = 1.

The word version of CMPSB is

```
CMPSW                   ;compare string word
```

It subtracts the word with address ES:DI from the word whose address is DS:SI, and sets the flags. If DF = 0, SI and DI are increased by 2; if DF = 1, they are decreased by 2. CMPSW is useful in comparing word arrays of numbers.

All the status flags are affected by CMPSB and CMPSW.

For example, suppose

```
.DATA
STRING1  DB           'ACD'
STRING2  DB           'ABC'
```

The following instructions compare the first two bytes of the preceding strings:

```
MOV AX,@DATA
MOV DS,AX             ;initialize DS
MOV ES,AX             ;and ES
CLD                   ;left to right processing
LEA SI,STRING1        ;SI pts to STRING1
```

11.6 Compare String

Figure 11.5 CMPSB

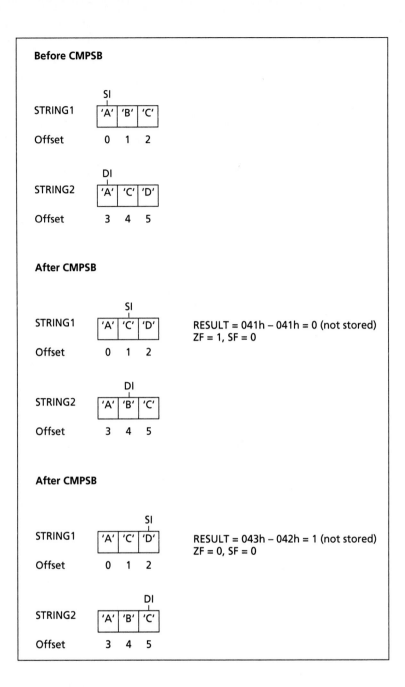

```
LEA DI,STRING2          ;DI pts to STRING2
CMPSB                   ;compare first bytes
CMPSB                   ;compare second bytes
```

See Figure 11.5.

REPE and REPZ

String comparison may be done by attaching the prefix **REPE** (repeat while equal) or **REPZ** (repeat while zero) to CMPSB or CMPSW. CX is initialized to the number of bytes in the shorter string, then

```
REPE CMPSB       ;compare string bytes while equal
```

or

```
REPE CMPSW       ;compare string words while equal
```

repeatedly executes CMPSB or CMPSW and decrements CX until (1) there is a mismatch between corresponding string bytes or words, or (2) CX = 0. The flags are set according to the result of the last comparison.

CMPSB may be used to compare two character strings to see which comes first alphabetically, or if they are identical, or if one string is a substring of the other (this means that one string is contained within the other as a sequence of consecutive characters).

As an example, suppose STR1 and STR2 are strings of length 10. The following instructions put 0 in AX if the strings are identical, put 1 in AX if STR1 comes first alphabetically, or put 2 in AX if STR2 comes first alphabetically (assume DS and ES are initialized).

```
            MOV   CX,10           ;length of strings
            LEA   SI,STR1          ;SI points to STR1
            LEA   DI,STR2          ;DI points to STR2
            CLD                    ;left to right processing
            REPE  CMPSB            ;compare string bytes
            JL    STR1_FIRST       ;STR1 precedes STR2
            JG    STR2_FIRST       ;STR2 precedes STR1
;here if strings are identical
            MOV   AX,0             ;put 0 in AX
            JMP   EXIT             ;and exit
;here if STR1 precedes STR2
STR1_FIRST:
            MOV   AX,1             ;put 1 in AX
            JMP   EXIT             ;and exit
;here if STR2 precedes STR1
STR2_FIRST:
            MOV   AX,2             ;PUT 2 in AX
EXIT:
```

11.6.1
Finding a Substring of a String

There are several ways to determine whether one string is a substring of another. The following way is probably the simplest. Suppose we declare

```
SUB1    DB          'ABC'
SUB2    DB          'CAB'
MAINST  DB          'ABABCA'
```

and we want to see whether SUB1 and SUB2 are substrings of MAINST.

Let's begin with SUB1. We can compare corresponding characters in the strings

```
SUB1            A B C
                | | +
MAINST          A B A B C A
```

Because there is a mismatch at the third comparison, we backtrack and try to match SUB1 with the part of MAINST from position MAINST+1 on:

```
SUB1            A B C
                +
MAINST          A B A B C A
```

There is a mismatch immediately, so we begin again, and at position MAINST+2

```
SUB1                    A B C
                        | | |
MAINST                  A B A B C A
```

This time we are successful; SUB1 is a substring of MAINST.

Now let's try with SUB2. The search proceeds as before until we reach

```
SUB2                    C A B
                          |
MAINST          A B A B C A
```

There is a mismatch, and there is no need to proceed further, for if we did we would be trying to match the three characters of SUB2 with the two remaining characters "CA" of MAINST. Thus SUB2 is not a substring of MAINST.

Actually, we could have predicted the last place to search. It is

STOP = MAINST + length of MAINST − length of SUB2

= MAINST + 6 − 3 = MAINST + 3

Here is an algorithm and a program that searches a main string MAINST for a substring SUBST.

Algorithm for Substring Search

```
Prompt user to enter SUBST
Read SUBST
Prompt user to enter MAINST
Read MAINST
IF (length of MAINST is 0) OR (length of SUBST is 0)
OR (SUBST is longer than MAINST)
   THEN
     SUBST is not a substring of MAINST
   ELSE
    compute STOP
    START = offset of MAINST
    REPEAT
    compare corresponding characters in MAINST
    (from START on) and SUBST
    IF all characters match
     THEN
       SUBST found in MAINST
     ELSE
       START = START + 1
    END_IF
    UNTIL (SUBST found in MAINST)
      OR (START > STOP)
Display results
```

After reading SUBST and MAINST, and verifying that neither string is null and SUBST is not longer than MAINST, in lines 44–50 the program computes STOP (the place in MAINST to stop searching), and initializes START (the place to start searching) to the beginning of MAINST.

Program Listing PGM11_5.ASM

```
 1:    TITLE    PGM11_5: SUBSTRING DEMONSTRATION
 2:    .MODEL SMALL
 3:    .STACK 100H
 4:    .DATA
 5:   MSG1     DB    'ENTER SUBST',0DH,0AH,'$'
 6:   MSG2     DB    0DH,0AH,'ENTER MAINST',0DH,0AH,'$'
 7:   MAINST   DB    80 DUP (0)
 8:   SUBST    DB    80 DUP (0)
 9:   STOP     DW    ?             ;last place to begin search
10:   START    DW    ?             ;place to resume search
11:   SUB_LEN  DW?   ;substring length
12:   YESMSG   DB    0DH,0AH,'SUBST IS A SUBSTRING OF MAINST$'
13:   NOMSG    DB    0DH,0AH,'SUBST IS NOT A SUBSTRING OF MAINST
14:    .CODE
15:   MAIN   PROC
16:          MOV    AX,@DATA
17:          MOV    DS,AX
18:          MOV    ES,AX
19:   ;prompt for SUBST
20:          MOV    AH,9          ;print string fcn
21:          LEA    DX,MSG1       ;substring prompt
22:          INT    21H           ;prompt for SUBST
23:   ;read SUBST
24:          LEA    DI,SUBST
25:          CALL   READ_STR      ;BX has SUBST length
26:          MOV    SUB_LEN,BX    ;save in SUB_LEN
27:   ;prompt for MAINST
28:          LEA    DX,MSG2       ;main string prompt
29:          INT    21H           ;prompt for MAINST
30:   ;read MAINST
31:          LEA    DI,MAINST
32:          CALL   READ_STR      ;BX has MAINST length
33:   ;see if string null or SUBST longer than MAINST
34:          OR     BX,BX         ;MAINST null?
35:          JE     NO            ;yes, SUBST not a substring
36:          CMP    SUB_LEN,0     ;SUBST null?
37:          JE     NO            ;yes, SUBST not a substring
38:          CMP    SUB_LEN,BX    ;substring > main string?
39:          JG     NO            ;yes, SUBST not a substring
40:   ;see if SUBST is a substring of MAINST
41:          LEA    SI,SUBST      ;SI pts to SUBST
42:          LEA    DI,MAINST     ;DI pts to MAINST
43:          CLD                  ;left to right processing
44:   ;compute STOP
45:          MOV    STOP,DI       ;STOP has MAINST address
46:          ADD    STOP,BX       ;add MAINST length
47:          MOV    CX,SUB_LEN
48:          SUB    STOP,CX       ;subtract SUBST length
49:   ;initialize start
50:          MOV    START,DI      ;place to start search
51:   REPEAT:
52:   ;compare characters
53:          MOV    CLEN          ;length of substring
54:          MOV    DI,START      ;reset DI
```

```
55:             LEA     SI,SUBST        ;reset SI
56:             REPE    CMPSB           ;compare characters
57:             JE      YES             ;SUBST found
58: ;substring not found yet
59:             INC     START           ;update START
60: ;see if start <= stop
61:             MOV     AX,START
62:             CMP     AX,STOP         ;START <= STOP?
63:             JNLE    NO              ;no,exit
64:             JMP     REPEAT          ;keep going
65: ;display results
66: YES:
67:             LEA     DX,YESMSG
68:             JMP     DISPLAY
69: NO:
70:             LEA     DX,NOMSG
71: DISPLAY:
72:             MOV     AH,9
73:             INT     21H             ;display results
74: ;DOS exit
75:             MOV     AH,4CH
76:             INT     21H
77: MAIN    ENDP
78: ;READ_STR goes here
79:             END     MAIN
```

At line 51, the program enters a REPEAT loop where the characters of SUBST are compared with the part of MAINST from START on. In lines 53–56, CX is set to the length of SUBST, SI is pointed to SUBST, DI is pointed to START, and corresponding characters are compared with REPE CMPSB. If ZF = 1, then the match is successful and the program jumps to line 66 where the message "SUBST is a substring of MAINST" is displayed. If ZF = 0, there was a mismatch between characters and START is incremented at line 59. The search continues until SUBST matches part of MAINST or START > STOP; in the latter case, the message "SUBST is not a substring of MAINST" is displayed.

Sample executions:

```
C>PGM11_5
ENTER SUBST
ABC
ENTER MAINST
XYZABABC
SUBST IS A SUBSTRING OF MAINST

C>PGM11_5
ENTER SUBST
ABD
ENTER MAINST
ABACADACD
SUBST IS NOT A SUBSTRING OF MAINST
```

11.7 General Form of the String Instructions

Let us summarize the byte and word forms of the string instructions:

Instruction	Destination	Source	Byte form	Word form
Move string	ES:DI	DS:SI	MOVSB	MOVSW
Compare string*	ES:DI	DS:SI	CMPSB	CMPSW
Store string	ES:DI	AL or AX	STOSB	STOSW
Load string	AL or AX	DS:SI	LODSB	LODSW
Scan string	ES:DI	AL or AX	SCASB	SCASW

* Result not stored.

The operands of these instructions are implicit; that is, they are not part of the instructions themselves. However, there are forms of the string instructions in which the operands appear explicitly. They are as follows:

Instruction		Example
MOVS	destination_string, source_string	MOVSB
CMPS	destination_string, source_string	CMPSB
STOS	destination_string	STOS STRING2
LODS	source_string	LODS STRING1
SCAS	destination_string	SCAS STRING2

When the assembler encounters one of these general forms, it checks to see if (1) the source string is in the segment addressed by DS and the destination string is in the segment addressed by ES, and (2) in the case of MOVS and CMPS, if the strings are of the same type; that is, both byte strings or word strings. If so, then the instruction is coded as either a byte form, such as MOVSB, or a word form, such as MOVSW, to match the data declaration of the string. For example, suppose that DS and ES address the following segment:

```
.DATA
STRING1    DB      'ABCDE'
STRING2    DB      'EFGH'
STRING3    DB      'IJKL'
STRING4    DB      'MNOP'
STRING5    DW      1,2,3,4,5
STRING6    DW      7,8,9
```

Then the following pairs of instructions are equivalent

```
MOVS STRING2,STRING1        MOVSB
MOVS STRING6,STRING5        MOVSW
LODS STRING4                LODSB
LODS STRING5                LODSW
SCAS STRING1                SCASB
STOS STRING6                STOSW
```

It is important to note that if the general forms are used, it is still necessary to make DS:SI and ES:DI point to the source and destination strings, respectively.

There are advantages and disadvantages in using the general forms of the string instructions. An advantage is that because the operands appear as part of the code, program documentation is improved. A disadvantage is that only by checking the data definitions is it possible to tell whether a general string instruction is a byte form or a word form. In fact, the operands specified in a general string instruction may not be the actual operands used when the instruction is executed! For example, consider the following code:

```
LEA  SI,STRING1        ;SI PTS TO STRING1
LEA  DI,STRING2        ;DI PTS TO STRING2
MOVS STRING4,STRING3
```

Even though the specified source and destination operands are STRING3 and STRING4, respectively, when MOVS is executed the first byte of STRING1 is moved to the first byte of STRING2. This is because the assembler translates MOVS STRING4, STRING3 into the machine code for MOVSB, and SI and DI are pointing to the first bytes of STRING1 and STRING2, respectively.

Summary

- The string instructions are a special group of array-processing instructions.

- The setting of the direction flag (DF) determines the direction that string operations will proceed. If DF = 0, they proceed left to right across a string; if DF = 1, they proceed right to left. CLD makes DF = 0 and STD makes it 1.

- MOVSB moves the string byte pointed to by DS:SI into the byte pointed to by ES:DI, and SI and DI to be updated according to DF. MOVSW is the word form. These instructions may be used with the prefix REP, which causes the instruction to be repeated CX times.

- REPE and REPNE are conditional prefixes that may be used with string instructions. REPE causes the string instruction that follows to be repeated CX times as long as ZF = 1. REPNE causes the following string instruction to be repeated CX times as long as ZF = 0. REPZ and REPNZ are alternate names for REPE and REPNE, respectively.

- STOSB moves AL to the byte addressed by ES:DI, and updates DI according to DF. STOSW is the word form. STOSB may be used to read a character string into an array.

- LODSB moves the byte addressed by DS:SI into AL, and updates SI according to DF. LODSW is the word form. LODSB may be used to examine the contents of a character string.

- SCASB subtracts the byte pointed to by ES:DI from AL and uses the result to set the flags. The result is not stored, and DI is updated according to DF. SCASW is the word form; it subtracts the word pointed to by ES:DI from AX, sets the flags, and updates DI. The result is not stored. These instructions may be used to scan a string for a target byte or word in AL or AX.

- CMPSB subtracts the byte pointed to by ES:DI from the byte pointed to by DS:SI, sets the flags, and updates both SI and DI according to DF. The result is not stored. The word form is CMPSW. These instructions may be used to compare character strings alphabetically, to see if two strings are identical, or if one string is a substring of another.

- The string instructions have general forms in which the operands are explicit. The assembler uses the operands only to decide whether to code the instructions in byte or word form.

Glossary

(memory) string　　　　A byte or word array

New Instructions

```
CLD         LODSW       SCASW
CMPS        MOVS        STD
CMPSB       MOVSB       STOS
CMPSW       MOVSW       STOSB
LODS        SCAS        STOSW
LODSB       SCASB
```

String Instruction Prefixes

```
REP         REPNE       REPZ
REPE        REPNZ
```

Exercises

1. Suppose

    SI contains 100h   Byte 100h contains 10h
    DI contains 200h   Byte 101h contains 15h
    AX contains 4142h Byte 200h contains 20h
    DF = 0   Byte 201h contains 25h

    Give the source, destination, and value moved for each of the following instructions. Also give the new contents of SI and DI.

    a. MOVSB
    b. MOVSW
    c. STOSB
    d. STOSW
    e. LODSB
    f. LODSW

2. Suppose the following declarations have been made:

    ```
    STRING1 DB 'FGHIJ'
    STRING2 DB 'ABCDE'
            DB 5 DUP (?)
    ```

    Write instructions to move STRING1 to the end of STRING2, producing the string "ABCDEFGHIJ".

3. Write instructions to exchange STRING1 and STRING2 in exercise 2. You may use the five bytes after STRING2 for temporary storage.

4. An ASCIIZ string is a string that ends with a 0 byte; for example,

   ```
   STR DB   'THIS IS AN ASCIIZ STRING',0
   ```

   Write a procedure LENGTH that receives the address of an ASCIIZ string in DX, and returns its length in CX.

5. Use the addressing modes of Chapter 10 to write instructions equivalent to each of the following string instructions. Assume where necessary that SI already has the offset address of the source string, DI has the offset address of the destination string, and DF = 0. You may use AL for temporary storage. For SCASB and CMPSB, the flags should reflect the result of the comparison.

   a. MOVSB
   b. STOSB
   c. LODSB
   d. SCASB
   e. CMPSB

6. Suppose the following string has been declared:

   ```
   STRING DB   'TH*S* G*S* AR* B*ASTS'
   ```

   Write instructions that will cause each "*" to be replaced by "E".

7. Suppose the following string has been declared:

   ```
   STRING1 DB   'T H I S I S A T E S T'
   STRING2 DB   11 DUP (?)
   ```

   Write some code that will cause STRING1 to be copied into STRING2 with the blank characters removed.

Programming Exercises

8. A palindrome is a character string that reads the same forward or backward. In deciding if a string is a palindrome, we ignore blanks, punctuation, and letter case. For example "Madam, I'm Adam" or "A man, a plan, a canal, Panama!"

   Write a program that (a) lets the user input a string, (b) prints it forward and backward without punctuation and blanks on successive lines, and (c) decides whether it is a palindrome and prints the conclusion.

9. In spreadsheet applications, it is useful to display numbers right-justified in fixed fields. For example, these numbers are right-justified in a field of 10 characters:

   ```
         1345
      2342545
           56
   ```

   Write a program to read ten numbers of up to 10 digits each, and display them as above.

10. A character string STRING1 precedes another string STRING2 alphabetically if (a) the first character of STRING1 comes before the first character of STRING2 alphabetically, or (b) the first $N - 1$ characters of the strings are identical, but the Nth character of STRING1 precedes the Nth character of STRING2, or (c) STRING1 matches the beginning of STRING2, but STRING2 is longer.

    Write a program that lets the user enter two character strings on separate lines, and decides which string comes first alphabetically, or if the strings are identical.

11. INT 21h, function 0Ah, can be used to read a character string. The first byte of the array to hold the string (the string buffer) must be initialized to the maximum number of characters expected. After execution of INT 21h, the second byte contains the actual number of characters read. Input ends with a carriage return, which is stored but not included in the character count. If the user enters more than the expected number of characters, the computer beeps.

    Write a program that prints a "?"; reads a character string of up to 20 characters using INT 21h, function 0Ah; and prints the string on the next line. Set up the string buffer like this:

    ```
    STRING    LABEL       BYTE
    MAX_LEN   DB   20          ;maximum no. of chars expected
    ACT_LEN   DB   ?           ;actual no. of chars read
    CHARS     DB 21 DUP (?)    ;20 bytes for string
                               ;extra byte for carriage
                               ;return
    ```

12. Write a procedure INSERT that will insert a string STRING1 into a string STRING2 at a specified point.

    ### Input
    SI offset address of STRING1
    DI offset address of STRING2
    BX length of STRING1
    CX length of STRING2
    AX offset address at which to insert STRING1

    ### Output
    DI offset address of new string
    BX length of new string

    The procedure may assume that neither string has 0 length, and that the address in AX is within STRING2.

    Write a program that inputs two strings STRING1 and STRING2, a nonnegative decimal integer N, $0 <= N <= 40$, inserts STRING1 into STRING2 at position N bytes after the beginning of STRING2, and displays the resulting string. You may assume that $N <=$ length of STRING2 and that the length of each string is less than 40.

13. Write a procedure DELETE that will remove N bytes from a string at a specified point and close the gap.

    Input

    DI offset address of string
    BX length of string
    CX number of bytes N to be removed
    SI offset address within string at which to remove bytes

    Output

    DI offset address of new string
    BX length of new string

    The procedure may assume that the string has nonzero length, the number of bytes to be removed is not greater than the length of the string, and that the address in SI is within the string.

    Write a program that reads a string STRING, a decimal integer S that represents a position in STRING, a decimal integer N that represents the number of bytes to be removed (both integers between 0 and 80), calls DELETE to remove N bytes at position S, and prints the resulting string. You may assume $0 \leq N \leq L - S$, where L = length of STRING.

Part Two

Advanced Topics

12

Text Display and Keyboard Programming

Overview

One of the most interesting and useful applications of assembly language is in controlling the monitor display. In this chapter, we program such operations as moving the cursor, scrolling windows on the screen, and displaying characters with various attributes. We also show how to program the keyboard, so that if the user presses a key, a screen control function is performed; for example, we'll show how to make the arrow keys operate.

The display on the screen is determined by data stored in memory. The chapter begins with a discussion of how the display is generated and how it can be controlled by altering the display memory directly. Next, we'll show how to do screen operations by using BIOS function calls. These functions can also be used to detect keys being pressed; as a demonstration, we'll write a simple screen editor.

12.1 The Monitor

A computer monitor operates on the same principle as a TV set. An electron gun is used to shoot a stream of electrons at a phosphor screen, creating a bright spot. Lines are generated by sweeping the stream across the screen; dots are created by turning the beam on and off as it moves.

A raster of lines is created by starting the beam at the top left corner, sweeping it to the right, then turning it off and repositioning it at the beginning of the next line. This process is repeated until the last line has been traced, at which point the beam is repositioned at the top left corner and the process is repeated.

There are two kinds of monitors: monochrome and color. A monochrome monitor uses a single electron beam and the screen shows only one color, typically amber or green. By varying the intensity of the electron beam, dots of different brightness can be created; this is called a **gray scale**.

For a color monitor, the screen is coated with three kinds of phosphors capable of displaying the three primary colors of red, green, and blue. Three electron beams are used in writing dots on the screen; each one is used to display a different color. Varying the intensity of the electron beams produces different intensities of red, green, and blue dots. Because the red, green, and blue dots are very close together, the human eye detects a single homogeneous color spot. This is what makes the monitor show different colors.

12.2 Video Adapters and Display Modes

Video Adapters

The display on the monitor is controlled by a circuit in the computer called a **video adapter**. This circuit, which is usually on an add-in card, has two basic units: a **display memory** (also called a **video buffer**) and a **video controller**.

The display memory stores the information to be displayed. It can be accessed by both the CPU and the video controller. The memory address starts at segment A000h and above, depending on the particular video adapter.

The video controller reads the display memory and generates appropriate video signals for the monitor. For color display, the adapter can either generate three separate signals for red, green, and blue, or can generate a composite output when the three signals are combined. A composite monitor uses the composite output, and an RGB monitor uses the separate signals. The composite output contains a color burst signal, and when this signal is turned off, the monitor displays in black and white.

Display Modes

We commonly see both text and picture images displayed on the monitor. The computer has different techniques and memory requirements for displaying text and picture graphics. So the adapters have two display modes: text and graphics. In **text mode**, the screen is divided into columns and rows, typically 80 columns by 25 rows, and a character is displayed at each screen position. In **graphics mode**, the screen is again divided into columns and

Table 12.1 Video Adapters

Mnemonic	Stands For
MDA	Monochrome Display Adapter
CGA	Color Graphics Adapter
EGA	Enhanced Graphics Adapter
MCGA	Multi-color Graphics Array
VGA	Video Graphics Array

rows, and each screen position is called a *pixel*. A picture can be displayed by specifying the color of each pixel on the screen. In this chapter we concentrate on text mode; graphics mode is covered in Chapter 16.

Let's take a closer look at character generation in text mode. A character on the screen is created from a dot array called a **character cell**. The adapter uses a character generator circuit to create the dot patterns. The number of dots in a cell depends on the **resolution** of the adapter, which refers to the number of dots it can generate on the screen. The monitor also has its own resolution, and it is important that the monitor be compatible with the video adapter.

Kinds of Video Adapters

Table 12.1 lists the video adapters for the IBM PC. They differ in resolution and the number of colors that can be displayed.

IBM introduced two adapters with the original PC, the **MDA** (Monochrome Display Adapter) and **CGA** (Color Graphics Adapter). The MDA can only display text and was intended for business software, such as word processors and spread sheets, which at that time did not use graphics. It has good resolution, with each character cell being 9×14 dots. The CGA can display in color both text and graphics, but it has a lower resolution. In text mode, each character cell is only 8×8 dots.

In 1984 IBM introduced the **EGA** (Enhanced Graphics Adapter), which has good resolution and color graphics. The character cell is 8×14 dots.

In 1988 IBM introduced the PS/2 models, which are equipped with the **VGA** (Video Graphics Array) and **MCGA** (Multi-color Graphics Array) adapters. These adapters have better resolution and can display more colors in graphics mode than EGA. The character cell is 8×19.

Mode Numbers

Depending on the kind of adapter present, a program can select text or graphics modes. Each mode is identified by a **mode number**; Table 12.2 lists the text modes for the different kinds of adapters.

Table 12.2 Video Adapter Text Modes

Mode Number	Description	Adapters
0	40 x 25 16-color text (color burst off)	CGA,EGA,MCGA,VGA
1	40 x 25 16-color text	CGA,EGA,MCGA,VGA
2	80 x 25 16-color text (color burst off)	CGA,EGA,MCGA,VGA
3	80 x 25 16-color text	CGA,EGA,MCGA,VGA
7	80 x 25 monochrome text	MDA,EGA,VGA

Note: For modes 0 and 2, the color burst signal is turned off for composite monitors; RGB monitors will display 16 colors.

12.3 Text Mode Programming

As discussed earlier, the screen in text mode is usually divided into 80 columns by 25 rows. However, a 40-column by 25-row display is also possible for the color graphics adapters.

A position on the screen may be located by giving its (column, row) coordinates. The upper left corner has coordinate (0,0); for a 80 × 25 display, rows are 0–24 and columns are 0–79. Table 12.3 gives the coordinates of some screen positions.

The character displayed at a screen position is specified by the contents of a word in the display memory. The low byte of the word contains the character's ASCII code; the high byte contains its **attribute**, which tells how the character will be displayed (its color, whether it is blinking, underlined, and so on). Actually, all 256 byte combinations have display characters (see Appendix A). Attributes are discussed later.

Display Pages

For the MDA, the display memory can hold one screenful of data. The graphics adapters, however, can store several screens of text data. This is because graphics display requires more memory, so the memory unit in a graphics adapter is bigger. To fully use the display memory, a graphics adapter divides its display memory into **display pages**. One page can hold the data for one screen. The pages are numbered, starting with 0; the number of pages available depends on the adapter and the mode selected. If more than one page is available, the program can display one page while updating another one.

Table 12.4 shows the number of display pages for the MDA, CGA, EGA, and VGA in text mode. In the 80 × 25 text mode, each display page is 4 KB. The MDA has only one page, page 0; it starts at location B000:0000h. The CGA has four pages, starting at address B800:0000h. In text mode, the EGA and VGA can emulate either the MDA or CGA.

Table 12.3 Some 80 x 25 Screen Positions

Position	Decimal		Hex	
	Column	Row	Column	Row
Upper left corner	0	0	0	0
Lower left corner	0	24	0	18
Upper right corner	79	0	4F	0
Lower right corner	79	24	4F	18
Center of the screen	39	12	27	C

Table 12.4 Number of Text Mode Display Pages

	Maximum Number of Pages		
Modes	CGA	EGA	VGA
0–1	8	8	8
2–3	4	8	8
7	NA	8	8

The Active Display Page

The **active display page** is the page currently being displayed. For 80 × 25 text mode, the memory requirement is 80 × 25 = 2000 words = 4000 bytes (thus the display does not use up all the 4 KB, or 4096 bytes, in the page). The video controller displays the first word in the active display page at the upper left corner of the screen (column 0, row 0). The next word is displayed in column 1, row 0. In general, the active display page is displayed on the screen row by row; this means that the screen may be considered as the image of a two-dimensional array stored in row-major order.

12.3.1 The Attribute Byte

In a display page, the high byte of the word that specifies a display character is called the **attribute byte**. It describes the color and intensity of the character, the background color, and whether the character is blinking and/or underlined.

16-Color Display

The attribute byte for 16-color text display (modes 0–3) has the format shown in Figure 12.1. A 1 in a bit position selects an attribute characteristic. Bits 0–2 specify the color of the character (foreground color) and bits 4–6 give the color of the background at the character's position. For example, to display a red character on a blue background, the attribute byte should be 0001 0100 = 14h.

By adding red, blue, and green, other colors can be created. On the additive color wheel (Figure 12.2), a complement color can be produced by adding adjacent primary colors; for example, magenta is the sum of red and blue. To display a magenta character on a cyan background, the attribute is 0011 0101 = 35h.

If the *intensity bit* (bit 3) is 1, the foreground color is lightened. If the *blinking bit* (bit 7) is 1, the character turns on and off. Table 12.5 shows the possible colors in 16-color display. All the colors can be used for the color of the character; the background can use only the basic colors.

Monochrome Display

For monochrome display, the possible colors are white and black. For white, the RGB bits are all 1; for black, they are all 0. **Normal video** is a white character on a black background; the attribute byte is 0000 0111 = 7h. **Reverse video** is a black character on a white background, so the attribute is 0111 0000 = 70h.

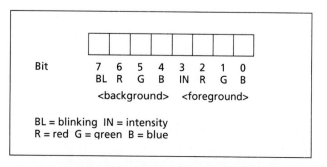

Figure 12.1 Attribute Byte

Figure 12.2 Additive Color Wheel

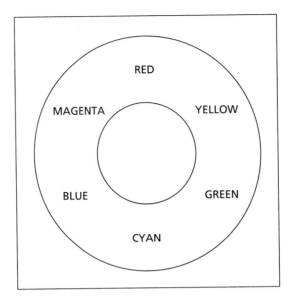

As with color display, the intensity bit can be used to brighten a white character and the blinking bit can turn it on and off. For the monochrome adapter only, two attributes give an underlined character. They are 01h for normal underline and 09h for bright underline. Table 12.6 lists the possible monochrome attributes.

Table 12.5 Sixteen-Color Text Display

Basic Colors	I R G B	Color
	0 0 0 0	black
	0 0 0 1	blue
	0 0 1 0	green
	0 0 1 1	cyan
	0 1 0 0	red
	0 1 0 1	magenta
	0 1 1 0	brown
	0 1 1 1	white
Bright Colors	1 0 0 0	gray
	1 0 0 1	light blue
	1 0 1 0	light green
	1 0 1 1	light cyan
	1 1 0 0	light red
	1 1 0 1	light magenta
	1 1 1 0	yellow
	1 1 1 1	intense white

I = intensity, R = red, G = green, B = blue.

Table 12.6 Monochrome Attributes

Attribute Byte

Binary	Hex	Result
0000 0000	00	black on black
0000 0111	07	normal (white on black)
0000 0001	01	normal underline
0000 1111	0F	bright (intense white on black)
0000 1001	09	bright underline
0111 0000	70	reverse video (black on white)
1000 0111	80	normal blinking
1000 1111	8F	bright blinking
1111 1111	FF	bright blinking
1111 0000	F0	reverse video blinking

12.3.2 A Display Page Demonstration

To display a character with attribute at any screen position, it is only necessary to store the character and attribute at the corresponding word in the active display page. The following program fills the color screen with red "A"s on a blue background.

Program Listing PGM12_1.ASM

```
 1:     TITLE  PGM12_1: SCREEN DISPLAY_1
 2:     .MODEL    SMALL
 3:     .STACK    100H
 4:     .CODE
 5: MAIN    PROC
 6: ;set DS to active display page
 7:         MOV    AX,0B800h     ;color active display page
 8:         MOV    DS,AX
 9:         MOV    CX,2000       ;80 x 25 = 2000 words
10:         MOV    DI,0          ;initialize DI
11: ;fill active display page
12: FILL_BUF:
13:         MOV    WORD PTR[DI],1441h   ;red A on blue
14:         ADD    DI,2          ;go to next word
15:         LOOP   FILL_BUF      ;loop until done
16: ;dos exit
17:         MOV    AH,4CH
18:         INT    21H
19: MAIN    ENDP
20:         END    MAIN
```

To display a red "A" on a blue background at a screen position, the corresponding active display page word should contain 14h in the high byte and 41h in the low byte.

The program begins by initializing DS to the video buffer segment, which is B800h for a color adapter. Loop counter CX is set to 2000—the number of words in the active display page—and DI is initialized to 0. At line 13, the program enters a loop that moves 1441h into each word of the video buffer.

After the program is run, the screen positions retain the same attributes unless another program changes it or the computer is reset.

12.3.3 INT 10H

Even though we can display data by moving them directly into the active display page, this is a very tedious way to control the screen.

Instead we use the BIOS video screen routine which is invoked by the INT 10h instruction; a video function is selected by putting a function number in the AH register.

In the following, we discuss the most important INT 10h functions used in text mode and give examples of their use. The INT 10h functions used in graphics mode are discussed in Chapter 16. Appendix C has a more complete list.

INT 10h, Function 0:
Select Display Mode

Input: AH = 0
             AL = mode number (see Table 12.2)
Output: none

Example 12.1 Set the CGA adapter for 80 × 25 color text display.

Solution:

```
XOR   AH,AH              ;select display mode function
MOV   AL,3               ;80x25 color text mode
INT   10H                ;select mode
```

when BIOS sets the display mode, it also clears the screen.

INT 10h, Function 1:
Change Cursor Size

Input: AH = 1
             CH = starting scan line
            CL = ending scan line
Output: none

In text mode, the cursor is displayed as a small dot array at a screen position (in graphics mode, there is no cursor). For the MDA and EGA, the dot array has 14 rows (0–13) and for the CGA, there are 8 rows (0–7). Normally only rows 6 and 7 are lit for the CGA cursor, and rows 11 and 12 for the MDA and EGA cursor. To change the cursor size, put the starting and ending numbers of the rows to be lit in CH and CL, respectively.

Example 12.2 Make the cursor as large as possible for the MDA.

Solution:

```
MOV   AH,1          ;cursor size function
MOV   CH,0          ;starting row
MOV   CL,13         ;ending row
INT   10H           ;change cursor size
```

INT 10h, Function 2:
Move Cursor

Input: AH = 2
         DH = new cursor row (0–24)
         DL = new cursor column. 0–79 for 80 × 25 display,
              0–39 for 40 × 25 display
         BH = page number
Output: none

This function lets the program move the cursor anywhere on the screen. The page doesn't have to be the one currently being displayed.

Example 12.3 Move the cursor to the center of the 80 × 25 screen on page 0.

Solution: The center of the 80 × 25 screen is column 39 = 27h, row 12 = 0Ch.

```
MOV   AH,2          ;move cursor function
XOR   BH,BH         ;page 0
MOV   DX,0C27h      ;row = 12, column = 39
INT   10H           ;move cursor
```

INT 10h, Function 3:
Get Cursor Position and Size

Input: AH = 3
         BH = page number
Output: DH = cursor row
         DL = cursor column
         CH = cursor starting scan line
         CL = cursor ending scan line

For some applications, such as moving the cursor up one row, we need to know its current location.

Example 12.4 Move the cursor up one row if not at the top of the screen on page 0.

Solution:
```
      MOV   AH,3       ;read cursor location function
      XOR   BH,BH      ;page 0
      INT   10H        ;DH = row, DL = column
      OR    DH,DH      ;cursor at top of screen?
      JZ    EXIT       ;yes, exit
      MOV   AH,2       ;move cursor function
      DEC   DH         ;row = row - 1
      INT   10H        ;move cursor
EXIT:
```

INT 10h, Function 5:
Select Active Display Page

Input: AH = 5
        AL = active display page
             0–7 for modes 0, 1
             0–3 for CGA modes 2, 3
             0–7 for EGA, MCGA, VGA modes 2, 3
             0–7 for EGA, VGA mode 7
Output: none

This function selects the page to be displayed.

Example 12.5 Select page 1 for the CGA.

Solution:
```
MOV   AH,5       ;select active display page function
MOV   AL,1       ;page 1
INT   10H        ;select page
```

INT 10h, Function 6:
Scroll the Screen or a Window Up

Input: AH = 6
        AL = number of lines to scroll (AL = 0 means
             scroll the whole screen or window)
        BH = attribute for blank lines
        CH,CL = row, column for upper left corner of window
        DH,DL = row, column for lower right corner of window
Output: none

Scrolling the screen up one line means moving each display line up one row, and bringing in a blank line at the bottom. The previous top row disappears from the screen.

The whole screen, or any rectangular area (window) may be scrolled. AL contains the number of lines to be scrolled. If AL = 0, all the lines are scrolled and this provides a way to clear the screen or a window. CH and CL get the row and column of the upper left corner of the window, and DH and DL get the row and column of the lower right corner. BH contains the attribute for the blank lines.

Example 12.6 Clear the screen to black for the 80 × 25 display.

Solution:

```
MOV   AH,6           ;scroll up function
XOR   AL,AL          ;clear whole screen
XOR   CX,CX          ;upper left corner is (0,0)
MOV   DX,184Fh       ;lower right corner is (4Fh,18h)
MOV   BH,7           ;normal video attribute
INT   10H            ;clear screen
```

INT 10h, Function 7:
Scroll the Screen or a Window Down

Input: AH = 7
           AL = number of lines to scroll (AL = 0 means
                 scroll the whole screen or window)
           BH = attribute for blank lines
           CH,CL = row, column for upper left corner of window
           DH,DL = row, column for lower right corner of window
Output: none

If the screen or window is scrolled down one line, each line moves down one row, a blank line is brought in at the top, and the bottom row disappears.

INT 10h, Function 8:
Read Character at the Cursor

Input: AH = 8
           BH = page number
Output: AH = attribute of character
           AL = ASCII code of character

In some applications, we need to know the character at the cursor position. BH contains a page number, which doesn't have to be the one being displayed. After execution, AL contains the ASCII code of the character, and AH contains its attribute. We'll see an example that uses this function in a moment. Let's first look at a function that writes a character.

> **INT 10h, Function 9:**
> **Display Character at the Cursor with Any Attribute**
>
> Input: AH = 9
>   BH = page number
>   AL = ASCII code of character
>   CX = number of times to write character
>   BL = attribute of character
> Output: none

With function 9, the programmer can specify an attribute for the character. CX contains the number of times to display the character, starting at the cursor position.

Unlike INT 21h, function 2, the cursor doesn't advance after the character is displayed. Also, if AL contains the ASCII code of a control character, a control function is not performed; instead, a display symbol is shown.

The following example shows how functions 8 and 9 can be used together to change the attribute of a character.

Example 12.7 Change the attribute of the character under the cursor to reverse video for monochrome display.

Solution:

```
MOV   AH,8          ;read character
XOR   BH,BH         ;on page 0
INT   10H           ;character in AL, attribute in AH
MOV   AH,9          ;display character with attribute
MOV   CX,1          ;display 1 character
MOV   BL,70H        ;reverse video attribute
INT   10H           ;display character
```

> **INT 10h, Function Ah:**
> **Display Character at the Cursor with Current Attribute**
>
> Input: AH = 0Ah
>   BH = page number
>   AL = ASCII code of character
>   CX = number of times to write character
> Output: none

This function is like function 9, except that the attribute byte is not changed, so the character is displayed with the current attribute.

> **INT 10h, Function Eh:**
> **Display Character and Advance Cursor**
>
> Input: AH = 0Eh
>   AL = ASCII code of character
>   BH = page number
>   BL = foreground color (graphics mode only)
> Output: none

This function displays the character in AL and advances the cursor to the next position in the row, or if at the end of a row, it sends it to the beginning of the next row. If the cursor is in the lower right corner, the screen is scrolled up and the cursor is set to the beginning of the last row. This is the BIOS function used by INT 21h, function 2, to display a character. The control characters bell (07h), backspace (08h), line feed (0Ah), and carriage return (0Dh) cause control functions to be performed.

> **INT 10h, Function Fh:**
> **Get Video Mode**
>
> Input: AH = 0Fh
> Output: AH = number of screen columns
>   AL = display mode (see Table 12.2)
>   BH = active display page

This function can be used with function 5 to switch between pages being displayed.

Example 12.8 Change the display page from page 0 to page 1, or from page 1 to page 0.

Solution:

```
MOV  AH,0FH        ;get video mode
INT  10H           ;BH = active page
MOV  AL,BH         ;move to AL
XOR  AL,1          ;complement bit 0
MOV  AH,5          ;select active page
INT  10H           ;select new page
```

12.3.4 A Comprehensive Example

To demonstrate several of the INT 10h functions, we write a program to do the following:

1. Set the display to mode 3 (80 × 25 16-color text).
2. Clear a window with upper left corner at column 26, row 8, and lower right corner at column 52, row 16, to red.

3. Move the cursor to column 39, row 12.
4. Print a blinking, cyan "A" at the cursor position.

If you have a color adapter and monitor, you can see the output by running the program in program listing PGM12_2.ASM.

Program Listing PGM12_2.ASM

```
TITLE PGM12_2: SCREEN DISPLAY_2
;red screen with blinking cyan 'A' in middle of screen
        .MODEL      SMALL
        .STACK      100H
        .CODE
MAIN    PROC
;set video mode
        MOV     AH,0            ;select mode function
        MOV     AL,3            ;80x25 color text
        INT     10H             ;select mode
;clear window to red
        MOV     AH,6            ;scroll up function
        MOV     CX,081Ah        ;upper left corner (1Ah,08h)
        MOV     DX,1034h        ;lower right corner (34h,10h)
        MOV     BH,43H          ;cyan chars on red background
        MOV     AL,0            ;scroll all lines
        INT     10H             ;clear window
;move cursor
        MOV     AH,2            ;move cursor function
        MOV     DX,0C27h        ;center of screen
        XOR     BH,BH           ;page 0
        INT     10H             ;move cursor
;display character with attribute
        MOV     AH,09           ;display character function
        MOV     BH,0            ;page 0
        MOV     BL,0C3H         ;blinking cyan char, red back
        MOV     CX,1            ;display one character
        MOV     AL,'A'          ;character is 'A'
        INT     10H             ;display character
;dos exit
        MOV     AH,4CH
        INT     21H
MAIN    ENDP
        END     MAIN
```

12.4 The Keyboard

There are several keyboards in use for the IBM PC. The original keyboard has 83 keys. Now, more computers use the enhanced keyboard with 101 keys. In general, we can group the keys into three categories:

1. ASCII keys; that is, keys that correspond to ASCII display and control characters. These include letters, digits, punctuation, arithmetic and other special symbols; and the control keys Esc (escape), Enter (carriage return), Backspace, and Tab.

2. Shift keys: left and right shifts, Caps Lock, Ctrl, Alt, Num Lock, and Scroll Lock. These keys are usually used in combination with other keys.
3. Function keys: F1–F10 (F1–F12 for the enhanced keyboard), the arrow keys, Home, PgUp, PgDn, End, Ins, and Del. We call them **function keys** because they are used in programs to perform special functions.

Scan Codes

Each key on the keyboard is assigned a unique number called a **scan code**; when a key is pressed, the keyboard circuit sends the corresponding scan code to the computer. Scan code values start with 1; Table 12.7 shows the scan codes of shift and function keys. A complete list of scan codes for the 101-key keyboard may be found in Appendix H.

You may wonder how the computer detects a combination of keys, such as the Ctrl-Alt-Del combination that resets the computer. There must be a way for the computer to know that a key has been pressed, but not yet released.

To indicate a key's release, the keyboard circuit sends another code called a **break code**; derived from the key's scan code by changing the msb to 1 (the scan code itself is also known as a **make code**). For example, the make code for the Esc key is 01h and its break code is 81h.

The computer does not store information on every key that is pressed and not yet released; it only does so for the function key Ins, and the shift keys. This information is saved as individual bits called *keyboard flags* stored

Table 12.7 Scan Codes for Shift and Function Keys

Hex	Decimal	Key
1D	29	Ctrl
2A	42	Left Shift
38	56	Alt
3A	58	Caps Lock
3B–44	59–68	F1–F10
45	69	Num Lock
46	70	Scroll Lock
47	71	Home
48	72	Up arrow
49	73	PgUp
4B	75	Left arrow
4C	76	Keypad 5
4D	77	Right arrow
4F	79	End
50	80	Down arrow
51	81	PgDn
52	82	Ins
53	83	Del

in the byte at 0040:0017. A program can call a BIOS routine to investigate these flags.

The Keyboard Buffer

To prevent the user from typing ahead of a program, the computer uses a 15-word block of memory called the **keyboard buffer** to store keys that have been typed but not yet read by the program. Each keystroke is stored as a word, with the high byte containing the key's scan code, and the low byte containing its ASCII code if it's an ASCII key, or 0 if it's a function key. A shift key is not stored in the buffer. When a left or right shift, Ctrl, or Alt key is down, some keys will cause a combination key scan code to be placed in the keyboard buffer (see Appendix H).

The contents of the buffer are released when a program requests key inputs. The key values are passed onto the program in the same order that they come in; that is, the keyboard buffer is a queue. If a key input is requested and the buffer is empty, the system waits until a key is pressed. If the buffer is full and the user presses a key, the computer sounds a tone.

Keyboard Operation

To summarize the preceding discussion, let's see what happens when you press a key that is read by the current executing program:

1. The keyboard sends a request (interrupt 9) to the computer.
2. The interrupt 9 service routine obtains the scan code from the keyboard I/O port and stores it in a word in the keyboard buffer (high byte = scan code, low byte = ASCII code for an ASCII key, 0 for a function key).
3. The current program may use INT 21h, function 1, to read the ASCII code. This also causes the ASCII code to be displayed (echoed) to the screen.

In the next section, we'll show how a program can process keyboard inputs using INT 16h. To get both the scan code and ASCII code, a program may access the keyboard buffer directly or use the BIOS routine INT 16h.

INT 16H

BIOS INT 16h provides keyboard services. As with INT 10h, a program can request a service by placing the function number in AH before calling INT 16h. In what follows, we use only function 0.

INT 16h, Function 0:
Read Keystroke

Input: AH = 0
Output: AL = ASCII code if an ASCII key is pressed
             = 0 for function keys
          AH = scan code of key

This function transfers the first available key value in the keyboard buffer into AX. If the buffer is empty, the computer waits for the user to press a key. ASCII keys are not echoed to the screen.

The function provides a way for the program to decide if a function key is pressed. If AL = 0, this must be the case, and the program can check the scan code in AH to see which key it is.

Example 12.9 Move the cursor to the upper left corner if the F1 key is pressed, to the lower right corner if any other function key is pressed. If a character key is pressed, do nothing.

Solution:

```
                MOV     AH,0        ;read keystroke function
                INT     16H         ;AL = ASCII code or 0,
                                    ;AH = scan code
                OR      AL,AL       ;AL = 0 (function key) ?
                JNE     EXIT        ;no, character key
                CMP     AH,3BH      ;scan code for F1 ?
                JE      F1          ;yes, go to move cursor
;other function key
                MOV     DX,184FH    ;lower right corner
                JMP     EXECUTE     ;go to move cursor
F1:
                XOR     DX,DX       ;upper left corner
EXECUTE:
                MOV     AH,2        ;move cursor function
                XOR     BH,BH       ;page 0
                INT     10H         ;move cursor
EXIT:
```

12.5 A Screen Editor

To show how the function keys may be programmed, here is a program that does some of the things that a basic word processor does. It first clears the screen and puts the cursor in the upper left corner, then lets the user type text on the screen, operate some of the function keys, and finally exits when the Esc key is pressed.

Screen Editor Algorithm

```
Clear the screen
Move the cursor to the upper left corner
Get a keystroke
WHILE key is not the Esc key DO
  IF function key
    THEN
      perform function
    ELSE /* key must be a character key */
      display character
  END_IF
  Get a keystroke
END_WHILE
```

The Esc key can be detected by checking for an ASCII code of 1Bh. To demonstrate how the function keys can be programmed, a procedure DO_FUNCTION is written to program the arrow keys. They operate as follows:

Up arrow. Causes the cursor to move up one row unless it's at the top of the screen. If so, the screen scrolls down one line.

Down arrow. Causes the cursor to move down one row unless it's at the bottom of the screen. If so, the screen scrolls up one line.

Right arrow. Causes the cursor to move right one column, unless it's at the right margin. If so, it moves to the beginning of the next row. But if it's in the lower right corner, the screen scrolls up one line.

Left arrow. Causes the cursor to move left one column, unless it's at the left margin. If so, it moves to the end of the previous row. But if it's in the upper right corner, the screen scrolls down one line.

DO_FUNCTION Algorithm

```
Get cursor position;
Examine scan code of last key pressed;
CASE scan code OF
  up arrow:
    IF cursor is at the top of the screen /* row 0 */
      THEN
        scroll screen down
      ELSE
        move cursor up one row
    END_IF
  down arrow:
    IF cursor is at the bottom of the screen /* row 24 */
      THEN
        scroll screen up
      ELSE
        move cursor down
    END_IF
  left arrow:
    IF cursor is not at beginning of a row /* column 0 */
      THEN
        move cursor to the left
      ELSE /* cursor is at beginning of a row */
        IF cursor is in row 0 /* position (0,0) */
          THEN
            scroll screen down
          ELSE
            move cursor to the end of previous row
        END_IF
    END_IF
  right arrow:
    IF cursor it not at end of a row
      THEN
        move cursor to the right
      ELSE /* cursor is at end of a row */
        IF cursor is in last row /* row 24 */
          THEN
            scroll screen up
          ELSE
            move cursor to the beginning of next row
        END_IF
    END_IF
END_CASE
```

Here is the program:

Program Listing PGM12_3.ASM

```
0:      TITLE PGM12_3: SCREEN EDITOR
1:      .MODEL  SMALL
2:      .STACK  100H
3:      .CODE
4:      MAIN    PROC
5:      ;set video mode and clear screen
6:              MOV     AH,0            ;set mode function
7:              MOV     AL,3            ;80 x 25 color text
8:              INT     10H             ;set mode
9:      ;move cursor to upper left corner
10:             MOV     AH,2            ;move cursor function
11:             XOR     DX,DX           ;position (0,0)
12:             MOV     BH,0            ;page 0
13:             INT     10H             ;move cursor
14:     ;get keystroke
15:             MOV     AH,0            ;keyboard input function
16:             INT     16H             ;AH=scan code,AL=ASCII code
17:     WHILE_:
18:             CMP     AL,1BH          ;ESC (exit character)?
19:             JE      END_WHILE       ;yes, exit
20:     ;if function key
21:             CMP     AL,0            ;AL = 0?
22:             JNE     ELSE_           ;no, character key
23:     ;then
24:             CALL    DO_FUNCTION     ;execute function
25:             JMP     NEXT_KEY        ;get next keystroke
26:     ELSE_:                          ;display character
27:             MOV     AH,2            ;display character func
28:             MOV     DL,AL           ;get character
29:             INT     21H             ;display character
30:     NEXT_KEY:
31:             MOV     AH,0            ;get keystroke function
32:             INT     16H             ;AH=scan code,AL=ASCII code
33:             JMP     WHILE_
34:     END_WHILE:
35:     ;dos exit
36:             MOV     AH,4CH
37:             INT     21H
38:     MAIN    ENDP
39:
40:     DO_FUNCTION     PROC
41:     ; operates the arrow keys
42:     ; input: AH = scan code
43:     ; output: none
44:             PUSH    BX
45:             PUSH    CX
46:             PUSH    DX
47:             PUSH    AX              ;save scan code
48:     ;locate cursor
49:             MOV     AH,3            ;get cursor position
50:             MOV     BH,0            ;on page 0
51:             INT     10H             ;DH = row, DL = col
```

```
52:            POP     AX              ;retrieve scan code
53: ;case scan code of
54:            CMP     AH,72           ;up arrow?
55:            JE      CURSOR_UP       ;yes, execute
56:            CMP     AH,75           ;left arrow?
57:            JE      CURSOR_LEFT     ;yes, execute
58:            CMP     AH,77           ;right arrow?
59:            JE      CURSOR_RIGHT    ;yes, execute
60:            CMP     AH,80           ;down arrow?
61:            JE      CURSOR_DOWN     ;yes, execute
62:            JMP     EXIT            ;other function key
63: CURSOR_UP:
64:            CMP     DH,0            ;row 0?
65:            JE      SCROLL_DOWN     ;yes, scroll down
66:            DEC     DH              ;no, row = row - 1
67:            JMP     EXECUTE         ;go to execute
68: CURSOR_DOWN:
69:            CMP     DH,24           ;last row?
70:            JE      SCROLL_UP       ;yes, scroll up
71:            INC     DH              ;no, row = row + 1
72:            JMP     EXECUTE         ;go to execute
73: CURSOR_LEFT:
74:            CMP     DL,0            ;column 0?
75:            JNE     GO_LEFT         ;no, move to left
76:            CMP     DH,0            ;row 0?
77:            JE      SCROLL_DOWN     ;yes, scroll down
78:            DEC     DH              ;row = row - 1
79:            MOV     DL,79           ;last column
80:            JMP     EXECUTE         ;go to execute
81: CURSOR_RIGHT:
82:            CMP     DL,79           ;last column?
83:            JNE     GO_RIGHT        ;no, move to right
84:            CMP     DH,24           ;last row?
85:            JE      SCROLL_UP       ;yes, scroll up
86:            INC     DH              ;row = row + 1
87:            MOV     DL,0            ;col = 0
88:            JMP     EXECUTE         ;go to execute
89: GO_LEFT:
90:            DEC     DL              ;col = col - 1
91:            JMP     EXECUTE         ;go to execute
92: GO_RIGHT:
93:            INC     DL              ;col = col + 1
94:            JMP     EXECUTE         ;go to execute
95: SCROLL_DOWN:
96:            MOV     AL,1            ;scroll 1 line
97:            XOR     CX,CX           ;upper left corner = (0,0)
98:            MOV     DH,24           ;last row
99:            MOV     DL,79           ;last column
100:           MOV     BH,07           ;normal video attribute
101:           MOV     AH,7            ;scroll down function
102:           INT     10H             ;scroll down 1 line
103:           JMP     EXIT            ;exit procedure
104: SCROLL_UP:
105:           MOV     AL,1            ;scroll up 1 line
106:           XOR     CX,CX           ;upper left corner = (0,0)
```

```
107:            MOV     DX,184FH        ;lower rt corner (4Fh,18h)
108:            MOV     BH,07           ;normal video attribute
109:            MOV     AH,6            ;scroll up function
110:            INT     10H             ;scroll up
111:            JMP     EXIT            ;exit procedure
112: EXECUTE:
113:            MOV     AH,2            ;cursor move function
114:            INT     10H             ;move cursor
115: EXIT:
116:            POP     DX
117:            POP     CX
118:            POP     BX
119:            RET
120: DO_FUNCTION        ENDP
121:            END     MAIN
```

The program begins by setting the video mode to 80 × 25 color text (mode 3). This also clears the screen. After moving the cursor to the upper left corner, the program accepts the first keystroke and enters a WHILE loop at line 17. AH has the scan code of the key, AL the ASCII code for a character key, and 0 for a function key. If the key is the Esc key (AL = 1BH), the program terminates. If not, the program checks for a function key (AL = 0). If so, the procedure DO_FUNCTION is called. If not, the key must have been a character key, and the character is displayed with INT 21h, function 2. This function automatically advances the cursor after displaying the character. At the bottom of the WHILE loop (line 30), another keystroke is accepted.

Procedure DO_FUNCTION is entered with the scan code of the last keystroke in AH. This is saved on the stack (line 47), while the procedure determines the cursor position (lines 49–51). After restoring the scan code to AH (line 52), the procedure checks to see if it is the scan code of one of the arrow keys (lines 54–61). If not, the procedure terminates.

If AH contains the scan code of an arrow key, the procedure jumps to a block of code where the appropriate cursor move is executed. DH and DL contain the row and column of the cursor location, respectively.

If the cursor is not at the edge of the screen (row 0 or 24, column 0 or 79), DH and DL are updated. To move up, the row number in DH is decremented; to move down, it is incremented. To move left, the column number in DL is decremented; to move right, it is incremented. After updating DH and DL, the procedure jumps to line 112, where INT 10h, function 2, does the actual cursor move.

For the up arrow key, if the cursor is in row 0 the procedure at line 64 jumps to code block SCROLL_DOWN, which scrolls the screen down one line. Similarly, for the down arrow key, if the cursor is in row 24 the procedure at line 72 jumps to code block SCROLL_UP where the screen is scrolled up one line.

For the left arrow key, if the cursor is in the upper left corner (0,0) the procedure jumps to SCROLL_DOWN (line 77). If it's at the left margin and not row 0, we want to move to the end of the previous row. To do this, the row number in DH is decremented, DL gets 79, and the procedure jumps to line 112 to do the cursor move.

Similarly for the right arrow key, if the cursor is in the lower right corner the procedure jumps to SCROLL_UP (line 85). If it's at the right margin and not row 24, we want to move to the beginning of the next row. To do this, the row number in DH is incremented, DL gets 0, and the procedure jumps to line 112 to do the cursor move.

The program can be run by assembling and linking file PGM12_3.ASM. As you play with it, its shortcomings become apparent. For example, text scrolled off the screen is lost. It is possible to type over text, but not to insert or delete text.

Summary

- A video adapter contains memory and a video controller, which translates data into an image on the screen. The adapters are the MDA, CGA, EGA, MCGA, and VGA. They differ in resolution and the number of colors they can display.

- There are two kinds of display modes: text mode and graphics mode. In text mode, a character is displayed at each screen position; in graphics mode, a pixel is displayed.

- In text mode, a screen position is specified by its (column, row) coordinates. A character and its attribute can be displayed at each position.

- In 80 × 25 text mode, the memory on the video adapter is divided into 4-KB blocks called *display pages*. The number of pages available depends on the kind of adapter. The screen can display one page at a time; the page being displayed is called the *active display page*.

- The display at each screen position is specified by a word in the active display page. The low byte of the word gives the ASCII code of the character and the high byte its attribute.

- The attribute byte specifies the foreground (color of the character) and background at each screen position. Other attributes are blinking and underline (MDA only).

- For monochrome display, the foreground and background colors are white (RGB bits all 1's) or black (RGB bits all 0's). Normal video attribute is 07h; reverse video is 70h.

- BIOS interrupt INT 10h routine performs screen processing. A number placed in AH identifies the screen function.

- INT 16h, function 0, is a BIOS function for reading keystrokes. AH gets the scan code, and AL the ASCII code for a character key. For a function key, AH gets the scan code and AL = 0.

- A program can use INT 16h and INT 10h to program the function keys for controlling the screen display.

Glossary

active display page	The display page currently being shown on the screen
attribute	A number that specifies how a character will be displayed
attribute byte	The high byte of the word that specifies a display character; it contains the character's attribute
break code	Number used to indicate when a key is released—obtained by putting 1 in the msb of a key's scan code
CGA	Color Graphics Adapter
character cell	Dot array used to form a character on the screen
display memory	Memory unit of a video adapter
display page	The portion of display memory that holds one screenful of data
EGA	Enhanced Graphics Adapter
function keys	Keys that don't correspond to ASCII characters or shifts
graphics mode	Display mode that can show pictures
gray scale	Different levels of brightness in monochrome display
keyboard buffer	A 15-word block of memory used to hold keystrokes
make code	Same as scan code
MCGA	Multi-color Graphics Array
MDA	Monochrome Display Adapter
mode number	A number used to select a text or graphics display mode
normal video	White character on a black background
resolution	The number of dots a video adapter can display
reverse video	Black character on a white background
scan codes	Numbers used to identify a key
text mode	Display mode in which only characters are shown
VGA	Video Graphics Array
video adapter	Circuit that controls monitor display
video buffer	The memory that stores data to be displayed on the monitor; same as display memory
video controller	Control unit of a video adapter

Exercises

1. To demonstrate the video buffer, enter DEBUG and do the following:
   a. If your machine has a monochrome adapter, use the R command to put B000h in DS; if it has a color adapter, put B800h in DS.
   b. We can now enter data directly into the video buffer, and see the results on the screen. To do so, use the E command to enter data, starting at offset 0. For example, to display a blinking reverse video A in the upper left corner of the screen, put 41h in byte 0 and F0h in byte 1. Now enter different character:attribute values in words 2, 4, and so on, and watch the changes on the top row of the screen.

2. Write some code to do the following (assume 80 × 25 monochrome display, page 0). Each part of this exercise is independent.
   a. Move the cursor to the lower right corner of the screen.
   b. Locate the cursor and move it to the end of the current row.
   c. Locate the cursor and move it to the top of the screen in the current column.
   d. Move the cursor to the left one position if not at the beginning of a row.
   e. Clear the row the cursor is in to white.
   f. Scroll the column the cursor is in down one line (normal video).
   g. Display five blinking reverse video "A"s, starting in the upper left corner of the screen.

3. Assuming 80 × 25 color display, write some code to turn the color of each capital letter character in row 0 to red and the local background to brown. Other characters should retain their previous foreground and background colors. Assume page 0.

Programming Exercises

4. Write a program to
   a. Clear the screen, make the cursor as large as possible, and move it to the upper left corner.
   b. Program the following function keys:

   Home key: Cursor moves to the upper left corner.
   End key: Cursor moves to the lower left corner.
   PgUp key: Cursor moves to the upper right corner.
   PgDn key: Cursor moves to the lower right corner.
   Esc key: Program terminates.
   Any other key: Nothing happens.

5. Write a program to
   a. Clear the screen to black, move the cursor to the upper left corner.
   b. Let the user type his or her name.

c. Clear the input line, and display the name vertically in column 40, starting at the top of the screen. Use 80 × 25 display. For MDA, display the name in reverse video. For color display, display it in green letters on a magenta background.

6. Write a program that does the following:
    a. Clear the screen, move the cursor to row 12, column 0.
    b. If the user types a character, the character is displayed at the cursor position. Cursor does *not* advance.
    c. Program the following function keys:

    Right Arrow: The program moves cursor and character to the right one position, unless it is at the right margin. A blank appears at the cursor's previous position.

    Left Arrow: The program moves cursor and character to the left one position, unless it is at the left margin. A blank appears at the cursor's previous position.

    Escape: The program terminates.

    Other function keys: Nothing happens.

7. Write a one-line screen editor that does the following:
    a. Clear screen, and position cursor at the beginning of row 12.
    b. Let the user type text. Cursor advances after each character is displayed unless cursor is at the right margin.
    c. Left arrow moves cursor left except at left margin; right arrow moves cursor right except at right margin. Other arrow keys do not operate.
    d. Ins key makes the cursor and each character to the right of the cursor (in the cursor's row) move right one position. A blank appears at the cursor's previous position. The last character in the cursor's row is pushed off the screen.
    e. Del key causes each character to the right of the cursor (in the cursor's row) to move left one position, and a blank is brought in at the right.
    f. Esc key terminates the program.

13

Macros

Overview

In previous chapters we have shown how programming may be simplified by using procedures. In this chapter, we discuss a program structure called a *macro*, which is similar to a procedure.

As with procedures, a macro name represents a group of instructions. Whenever the instructions are needed in the program, the name is used. However, the way procedures and macros operate is different. A procedure is called at execution time; control transfers to the procedure and returns after executing its statements. A macro is invoked at assembly time. The assembler copies the macro's statements into the program at the position of the invocation. When the program executes, there is no transfer of control.

Macros are especially useful for carrying out tasks that occur frequently. For example, we can write macros to initialize the DS and ES registers, print a character string, terminate a program, and so on. We can also write macros to eliminate restrictions in existing instructions; for example, the operand of MUL can't be a constant, but we can write a multiplication macro that doesn't have this restriction.

13.1 Macro Definition and Invocation

A **macro** is a block of text that has been given a name. When MASM encounters the name during assembly, it inserts the block into the program. The text may consist of instructions, pseudo-ops, comments, or references to other macros.

The syntax of macro definition is

```
macro_name     MACRO   d1,d2,...dn
               statements
               ENDM
```

Here macro_name is the user-supplied name for the macro. The pseudo-ops MACRO and ENDM indicate the beginning and end of the macro definition; d1, d2, . . . dn is an optional list of dummy arguments used by the macro.

One use of macros is to create new instructions. For example, we know that the operands of MOV can't both be word variables, but we can get around this restriction by defining a macro to move a word into a word.

Example 13.1 Define a macro to move a word into a word.

Solution:

```
MOVW     MACRO   WORD1,WORD2
         PUSH    WORD2
         POP     WORD1
         ENDM
```

Here the name of the macro is MOVW. WORD1 and WORD2 are the dummy arguments.

To use a macro in a program, we **invoke** it. The syntax is

```
macro_name    a1,a2, . . . an
```

where a1, a2, . . . an is a list of actual arguments. When MASM encounters the macro name, it **expands** the macro; that is, it copies the macro statements into the program at the position of the invocation, just as if the user had typed them in. As it copies the statements, MASM replaces each dummy argument di by the corresponding actual argument ai and creates the machine code for any instructions.

A macro definition must come before its invocation in a program listing. To ensure this sequence, macro definitions are usually placed at the beginning of a program. It is also possible to create a library of macros to be used by any program, and we do this later in the chapter.

Example 13.2 Invoke the macro MOVW to move B to A, where A and B are word variables.

Solution: `MOVW A,B`

To expand this macro, MASM would copy the macro statements into the program at the position of the call, replacing each occurrence of WORD1 by A, and WORD2 by B. The result is

```
PUSH B
POP  A
```

In expanding a macro, the assembler simply substitutes the character strings defining the actual arguments for the corresponding dummy ones. For example, the following calls to the MOVW macro

```
MOVW A,DX       and         MOVW A+2,B
```

cause the assembler to insert this code into the program:

```
PUSH DX          and         PUSH B
POP  A                       POP  A+2
```

Illegal Macro Invocations

There are often restrictions on the arguments for a macro. For example, the arguments in the MOVW macro must be memory words or 16-bit registers. The macro invocation

```
MOVW AX,1ABCh
```

generates the code

```
PUSH 1ABCh
POP  AX
```

and because an immediate data push is illegal (for the 8086/8088), this results in an assembly error. One way to guard against this situation is to put a comment in the macro; for example,

```
MOVW    MACRO   WORD1,WORD2
;arguments must be memory words or 16-bit registers
        PUSH    WORD2
        POP     WORD1
        ENDM
```

Restoring Registers

Good programming practice requires that a procedure should restore the registers it uses, unless they contain output values. The same is usually true for macros. As an example, the following macro exchanges two memory words. Because it uses AX to perform the exchange, this register is restored.

```
EXCH    MACRO   WORD1,WORD2
        PUSH    AX
        MOV     AX,WORD1
        XCHG    AX,WORD2
        MOV     WORD1,AX
        POP     AX
        ENDM
```

Macro Expansion in the .LST File

The .LST file is one of the files that can be generated when a program is assembled (see Appendix D). It shows assembly code and the corresponding machine code, addresses of variables, and other information about the program. The .LST file also shows how macros are expanded. To demonstrate this, the following program contains the MOVW macro and two invocations:

Program Listing PGM13_1.ASM

```
TITLE PGM13_1: MACRO DEMO
.MODEL SMALL
MOVW    MACRO WORD1,WORD2
        PUSH WORD2
        POP  WORD1
        ENDM
.STACK 100H
.DATA
A       DW      1,2
B       DW      3
.CODE
```

260 13.1 *Macro Definition and Invocation*

```
        MAIN    PROC
                MOV     AX,@DATA
                MOV     DS,AX
                MOVW    A,DX
                MOVW    A+2,B
        ;dos exit
                MOV     AH,4CH
                INT     21H
        MAIN    ENDP
                END     MAIN
```

Figure 13.1 shows file PGM13_1.LST. In this file, MASM prints the macro invocations, followed by their expansions (shown in boldface). The digit 1 that appears on each line of the expansions means these macros were invoked at the "top level"; that is, by the program itself. We will show later that a macro may invoke another macro.

Figure 13.1 PGM 13_1.LST

```
Microsoft (R) Macro Assembler Version 5.10
1/18/92 00:03:08
PGM13_1: MACRO DEMO                               Page    1-1
                                TITLE PGM13_1: MACRO DEMO
                                .MODEL SMALL
                                MOVW    MACRO   WORD1,WORD2
                                        PUSH WORD2
                                        POP  WORD1
                                        ENDM
                                .STACK  100H
                                .DATA
 0000  0001 0002 A              DW      1,2
 0004  0003                     B       DW      3
                                .CODE
 0000                           MAIN    PROC
 0000  B8 —— R                          MOV     AX,@DATA
 0003  8E D8                            MOV     DS,AX
                                        MOVW    A,DX
 0005  52                    1          PUSH    DX
 0006  8F 06 0000 R          1          POP     A
                                        MOVW    A+2,B
 000A  FF 36 0004 R          1          PUSH    B
 000E  8F 06 0002 R          1          POP     A+2
                                ;dos exit
 0012  B4 4C                            MOV     AH,4CH
 0014  CD 21                            INT     21H
 0016                           MAIN    ENDP
                                        END     MAIN

Microsoft (R) Macro Assembler Version 5.10
1/18/92 00:03:08
PGM13_1: MACRO DEMO                               Symbols-1
Macros:
```

Figure 13.1 PGM13_1.LST

(Continued)

```
    N  a  m  e                       Lines

MOVW . . . . . . . . . . . . .   2

Segments and Groups:

   N   a   m   e              Length  Align  Combine  Class

DGROUP . . . . . . . . . GROUP
_DATA  . . . . . . . . .  0006    WORD   PUBLIC   'DATA'
 STACK . . . . . . . . .  0100    PARA   STACK    'STACK'
_TEXT  . . . . . . . . .  0016    WORD   PUBLIC   'CODE'

Symbols:
   N   a   m   e              Type  Value  Attr

A  . . . . . . . . . .   L WORD  0000  _DATA

B  . . . . . . . . . .   L WORD  0004  _DATA

MAIN . . . . . . . .     N PROC  0000  _TEXT
Length = 0016

@CODE . . . . . . . .               TEXT   _TEXT
@CODESIZE . . . . . .               TEXT   0
@CPU . . . . . . . .                TEXT   0101h
@DATASIZE . . . . .                 TEXT   0
@FILENAME  . . . . .                TEXT   PGM13_1
@VERSION . . . . . .                TEXT   510

    21 Source  Lines
    25 Total   Lines
    21 Symbols

 47930 + 4220033 Bytes symbol space free

     0 Warning  Errors
     0 Severe   Errors
```

.LST File Options

Three assembler directives govern how macro expansions appear in the .LST file. These directives pertain to the macros that follow them in the program.

1. After **.SALL** (suppress all), the assembly code in a macro expansion is not listed. You might want to use this option for large macros, or if there are a lot of macro invocations.
2. After **.XALL**, only those source lines that generate code or data are listed. For example, comment lines are not listed. This is the default option.
3. After **.LALL** (list all), all source lines are listed, except those beginning with a double semicolon (;;).

These directives do not affect the machine code generated in the macro invocations, only the way the macro expansion appear in the .LST file.

Example 13.3 Suppose the MOVW macro is rewritten as follows:

```
MOVW    MACRO      WORD1,WORD2
;moves source to destination
;;uses the stack
        PUSH WORD2
        POP WORD1
        ENDM
```

Show how the following macro invocations would appear in a .LST file

```
.XALL
    MOVW DS,CS
.LALL
    MOVW P,Q
.SALL
    MOVW AX,[SI]
```

Solution:

```
.XALL
    MOVW DS,CS
        PUSH CS
        POP  DS
.LALL
    MOVW P,Q
        ;moves source to destination
        PUSH Q
        POP  P
.SALL
    MOVW AX,[SI]
```

Finding Assembly Errors

If MASM finds an error during macro expansion, it indicates an error at the point of the macro invocation; however, it's more likely that the problem is within the macro itself. To find where the mistake really is, you need to inspect the macro expansion in the .LST file. The .LST file is especially helpful if you have a macro that invokes other macros (see discussion later).

13.2 Local Labels

A macro with a loop or decision structure contains one or more labels. If such a macro is invoked more than once in a program, a duplicate label appears, resulting in an assembly error. This problem can be avoided by using **local labels** in the macro. To declare them, we use the **LOCAL** pseudo-op, whose syntax is

```
LOCAL     list_of_labels
```

where list_of_labels is a list of labels, separated by commas. Every time the macro is expanded, MASM assigns different symbols to the labels in the list. The LOCAL directive must appear on the next line after the MACRO statement; not even a comment can precede it.

Example 13.4 Write a macro to place the largest of two words in AX.

Solution:

```
GET_BIG   MACRO     WORD1,WORD2
          LOCAL     EXIT
          MOV       AX,WORD1
          CMP       AX,WORD2
          JG        EXIT
          MOV       AX,WORD2
    EXIT:
          ENDM
```

Now suppose that FIRST, SECOND, and THIRD are word variables. A macro invocation of the form

```
GET_BIG   FIRST,SECOND
```

expands as follows:

```
          MOV AX,FIRST
          CMP AX,SECOND
          JG  ??0000
          MOV AX,SECOND
??0000:
```

A later call of the form

```
GET_BIG   SECOND,THIRD
```

expands to this code:

```
          MOV AX,SECOND
          CMP AX,THIRD
          JG  ??0001
          MOV AX,THIRD
??0001:
```

Subsequent invocations of this macro or to other macros with local labels causes MASM to insert labels ??0002, ??0003, and so on into the program. These labels are unique and not likely to conflict with ones the user would choose.

13.3 Macros that Invoke Other Macros

A macro may invoke another macro. Suppose, for example, we have two macros that save and restore three registers:

```
SAVE_REGS   MACRO R1,R2,R3      RESTORE_REGS   MACRO S1,S2,S3
            PUSH  R1                            POP   S1
            PUSH  R2                            POP   S2
            PUSH  R3                            POP   S3
            ENDM                                ENDM
```

These macros are invoked by the macro in the following example.

Example 13.5 Write a macro to copy a string. Use the SAVE_REGS and RESTORE_REGS macros.

Solution:
```
COPY    MACRO           SOURCE,DESTINATION,LENGTH
        SAVE_REGS       CX,SI,DI
        LEA             SI,SOURCE
        LEA             DI,DESTINATION
        CLD
        MOV             CX,LENGTH
        REP             MOVSB
        RESTORE_REGS    DI,SI,CX
        ENDM
```

If MASM encounters the macro invocation

```
COPY    STRING1,STRING2,15
```

it will copy the following code into the program:

```
PUSH CX
PUSH SI
PUSH DI
LEA SI,STRING1
LEA DI,STRING2
CLD
MOV CX,15
REP MOVSB
POP DI
POP SI
POP CX
```

Note: A macro may invoke itself; such macros are called *recursive macros*. They are not discussed in this book.

13.4 A Macro Library

The macros that a program invokes may be contained in a separate file. This makes it possible to create a library file of useful macros. For example, suppose the file's name is MACROS, on a disk in drive A. When MASM encounters the pseudo-op

```
INCLUDE   A:MACROS
```

in a program, it copies all the macro definitions from the file MACROS into the program at the position of the INCLUDE statement (*note:* the INCLUDE directive was discussed in section 9.5). The INCLUDE statement may appear anywhere in the program, as long as it precedes the invocations of its macros.

The IF1 Conditional

If a macro library is included in a program, all its macro definitions will appear in the .LST file, even if they're not invoked in the program. To prevent this, we can insert the following:

```
        IF1
                INCLUDE   MACROS
ENDIF
```

Here, IF1 and ENDIF are pseudo-ops. The IF1 directive causes the assembler to access the MACROS file during the first assembly pass, when macros are expanded, but not during the second pass, when the .LST file is created. *Note:* Other conditional pseudo-ops are discused in section 13.6.

Examples of Useful Macros

The following are examples of macros that are useful to have in a macro library file.

Example 13.6 Write a macro to return to DOS.

Solution:

```
DOS_RTN   MACRO
          MOV AH,4CH
          INT 21H
          ENDM
```

The macro invocation is

```
DOS_RTN
```

Example 13.7 Write a macro to execute a carriage return and line feed.

Solution:

```
NEW_LINE  MACRO
          MOV  AH,2
          MOV  DL,0DH
          INT  21H
          MOV  DL,0AH
          INT  21H
          ENDM
```

The macro invocation is

```
NEW_LINE
```

The next example is one of the more interesting macros.

Example 13.8 Write a macro to display a character string. The string is the macro parameter.

Solution:

```
DISP_STR MACRO      STRING
         LOCAL      START,MSG
;save registers
         PUSH       AX
         PUSH       DX
         PUSH       DS
         JMP        START
```

```
            MSG     DB          STRING,'$'
START:
            MOV     AX,CS
            MOV     DS,AX   ;set DS to code segment
            MOV     AH,9
            LEA     DX, MSG
            INT     21H
;restore registers
            POP     DS
            POP     DX
            POP     AX
            ENDM
```

Sample invocation:

```
DISP_STR    'this is a string'
```

When this macro is invoked, the string parameter replaces the dummy parameter STRING. Because the string is being stored in the code segment, CS must be moved to DS; this takes two instructions, because a direct move between segment registers is forbidden.

Including a Macro Library

The preceding macros have been placed in file MACROS on the student disk. They are used in the following program, which displays a message, goes to a new line, and displays another message.

Program Listing PGM13_2.ASM
```
TITLE PGM13_2: MACRO DEMO
.MODEL SMALL
.STACK 100H
IF1
INCLUDE     MACROS
ENDIF
.CODE
MAIN    PROC
        DISP_STR    'this is the first line'
        NEW_LINE
        DISP_STR    'and this is the second line'
        DOS_RTN
MAIN    ENDP
        END  MAIN
```

Sample execution:

```
C>PGM13_2
this is the first line
and this is the second line
```

The macro expansions are shown in file PGM13_2.LST (Figure 13.2). To save space, the machine code has been edited out.

Figure 13.2 PGM13_2.LST

```
TITLE PGM13_2: MACRO DEMO
.MODEL          SMALL
.STACK          100H
.CODE
MAIN            PROC
DISP_STR            'this is the first line'
    1               PUSH    AX
    1               PUSH    DX
    1               PUSH    DS
    1               JMP     ??0000
    1   ??0001      DB      'this is the
                             first line',
            $'
    1   ??0000:
    1               MOV     AX,CS
    1               MOV     DS,AX   ;set DX to
code segment
    1               MOV     AH,9
    1               LEA     DX, ??0001
    1               INT     21H
    1               POP     DS
    1               POP     DX
    1               POP     AX
NEW_LINE
    1               MOV     AH,2
    1               MOV     DL,0DH
    1               INT     21H
    1               MOV     DL,0AH
    1               INT     21H
DISP_STR    'and this is the second line '
    1               PUSH    AX
    1               PUSH    DX
    1               PUSH    DS
    1               JMP     ??0002
    1   ??0003      DB      'and this is the
second line ','$'
    1   ??0002:
    1               MOV     AX,CS
    1               MOV     DS,AX   ;set DX to
code segment
    1               MOV     AH,9
    1               LEA     DX, ??0003
    1               INT     21H
    1               POP     DS
    1               POP     DX
    1               POP     AX
DOS_RTN
    1               MOV     AH,4CH
    1               INT     21H
MAIN    ENDP
END     MAIN
```

13.5 Repetition Macros

The **REPT** macro can be used to repeat a block of statements. Its syntax is

```
REPT expression
 statements
ENDM
```

When the assembler encounters this macro, the statements are repeated the number of times given by the value of the expression. A REPT macro may be invoked by placing it in the program at the point that the macro's statements are to be repeated. For example, to declare a word array A of five zeros the following can appear in the data segment:

```
A    LABEL     WORD
     REPT      5
     DW        0
     ENDM
```

Note: The LABEL pseudo-op was discussed in section 10.2.3. MASM expands this as follows:

```
A    DW        0
     DW        0
     DW        0
     DW        0
     DW        0
```

Of course, this example is trivial because we can just write

```
A    DW        5 DUP(0)
```

Another way to invoke a REPT macro is to place it an ordinary macro, and invoke that macro.

Example 13.9 Write a macro to initialize a block of memory to the first N integers. Then invoke it in a program to initialize an array to the first 100 integers.

Solution:

```
BLOCK    MACRO N
         K=1
         REPT   N
         DW     K
         K=K+1
         ENDM
         ENDM
```

Note: In this macro, we used the **= (equal)** pseudo-op. Like EQU, it can be used to give a name to a constant. The expression to the right of the equals sign must evaluate to a number. Unlike EQU, a constant defined with an = may be redefined; for example, $K = K + 1$. Remember, all this takes place at assembly time, rather than execution time.

To define a word array A and initialize it to the first 100 integers, we can place the following statements in the data segment:

```
A       LABEL       WORD
        BLOCK       100
```

Invocation of the BLOCK macro initializes K to 1 and the statements inside the REPT are assembled 100 times. The first time, DW 1 is generated and K is increased to 2; the second time, DW 2 is generated and K becomes 3, ... the 100th time, DW 100 is generated and $K = 101$. The final result is equivalent to

```
A       DW          1
        DW          2
        .
        .
        .
        DW          100
```

Example 13.10 Write a macro to initialize an n-word array to $1!, 2!, \ldots n!$ and show how to invoke it.

Solution:

```
FACTORIALS  MACRO  N
            M   = 1
            FAC = 1
            REPT    N
            DW      FAC
            M   = M+1
            FAC = M*FAC
            ENDM
            ENDM
```

To define a word array B of the first eight factorials, the data segment can contain

```
B       LABEL       WORD
        FACTORIALS  8
```

Because $8! = 40320$ is the largest factorial that will fit in a 16-bit word, it doesn't make sense to invoke this macro for larger values of N. The expansion is

```
B       DW          1
        DW          2
        DW          6
        DW          24
        DW          120
        DW          720
        DW          5040
        DW          40320
```

The IRP Macro

Another repetition macro is **IRP** (indefinite repeat). It has the form

```
IRP  d, <a1,a2,..an>
   statements
ENDM
```

Note: The angle brackets in the above definition are part of the syntax.

When it is expanded, this macro causes the statements to be assembled n times; on the ith expansion, each occurrence of parameter d is replaced by ai.

Example 13.11 Write macros to save and restore an arbitrary number of registers.

Solutions:

```
SAVE_REGS MACRO REGS           RESTORE_REGS MACRO REGS
        IRP    D,<REGS>                IRP    D,<REGS>
        PUSH   D                       POP    D
        ENDM                           ENDM
        ENDM                           ENDM
```

To save AX,BX,CX,DX, we can write

```
SAVE_REGS <AX,BX,CX,DX>
```

It has the following expansion:

```
PUSH AX
PUSH BX
PUSH CX
PUSH DX
```

To restore these registers, write,

```
RESTORE_REGS <DX,CX,BX,AX>
```

13.6 An Output Macro

To use the macro structures introduced so far, we write a macro HEX_OUT that displays the contents of a word as four hex digits. The hex output algorithm, discussed in Chapter 7, is the following:

Algorithm for Hex Output (of BX)

```
1:  FOR 4 times DO
2:    Move BH to DL
3:    shift DL 4 times to the right
4:    IF DL < 10
5:      THEN
6:        convert contents of DL to a character in '0'..'9'
7:      ELSE
8:        convert contents of DL to a character in 'A'..'F'
9:    END_IF
10:   output character
11:   Rotate BX left 4 times
12: END_FOR
```

The following listing contains the macro HEX_OUT and a program to test it. HEX_OUT invokes four other macros: (1) SAVE_REGISTERS and (2) RESTORE_REGISTERS from example 13.11; (3) CONVERT_TO_CHAR, which converts the contents of a byte to a hex digit character (lines 4–9 in the algorithm); and (4) DISP_CHAR, which displays a character (line 10 in the algorithm).

Program Listing PGM13_3.ASM

```
0:    TITLE PGM13_3: HEX OUTPUT MACRO DEMO
1:    .MODEL SMALL
2:
3:    SAVE_REGS MACRO REGS
4:            IRP    D,<REGS>
5:            PUSH   D
6:            ENDM
7:            ENDM
8:
9:    RESTORE_REGS MACRO REGS
10:           IRP    D,<REGS>
11:           POP    D
12:           ENDM
13:           ENDM
14:
15:   CONVERT_TO_CHAR MACRO  BYT
16:           LOCAL  ELSE_, EXIT
17:   ;converts contents of BYT to a hex digit char
18:   ;if
19:           CMP    BYT,9      ;contents <= 9?
20:           JNLE   ELSE_      ;no, >= 0Ah
21:   ;then
22:           OR     BYT,30H    ;convert to digit char
23:           JMP    EXIT
24:   ELSE_:
25:           ADD    BYT,37H    ;convert to digit char
26:   EXIT:
27:           ENDM
28:
29:   DISP_CHAR  MACRO  BYT
30:   ;displays contents of BYT
31:           PUSH   AX
32:           MOV    AH,2
33:           MOV    DL,BYT
34:           INT    21H
35:           POP    AX
36:           ENDM
37:
38:   HEX_OUT  MACRO  WRD
39:   ;displays contents of WRD as 4 hex digits
40:          SAVE_REGS <BX,CX,DX>
41:          MOV    BX,WRD
42:          MOV    CL,4              ;shift and rotate count
43:          REPT   4
44:          MOV    DL,BH
45:          SHR    DL,CL             ;shift right 4 times
46:          CONVERT_TO_CHAR DL       ;convert DL to digit char
47:          DISP_CHAR       DL       ;display D
48:          ROL    BX,CL             ;rotate left 4 times
49:          ENDM
50:          RESTORE_REGS <DX,CX,BX>
51:          ENDM
52:
53:   .STACK
```

```
54:         .CODE
55:     ;program to test above macros
56: MAIN    PROC
57:         MOV     AX,1AF4h        ;test data
58:         HEX_OUT AX              ;display in hex
59:         MOV     AH,4CH          ;dos exit
60:         INT     21H
61: MAIN    ENDP
62:         END     MAIN
```

Sample execution:

```
C>PGM13_3
1AF4
```

To code the FOR loop in the hex output algorithm, HEX_OUT uses a REPT ... ENDM (lines 43–49). This was done mostly for illustrative purposes; it makes the machine code of the expanded macro longer, but it has the advantage of freeing CL for use as a shift and rotate counter.

At line 46, macro CONVERT_TO_CHAR is invoked to transform the contents of DL to a hex digit character. This macro has two local labels, declared at line 16. At line 47, macro DISP_CHAR is invoked to display the contents of DL.

13.7 Conditionals

Conditional pseudo-ops may be used to assemble certain statements and exclude others. They may be used anywhere in an assembly language program, but are most often used inside macros. The basic forms are

```
Conditional          and      Conditional
statements                    statements1
ENDIF                         ELSE
                              statements2
                              ENDIF
```

In the first form, if Conditional evaluates to true, the statements are assembled; if not, nothing is assembled. In the second form, if Conditional is true, then statements1 are assembled; if not, statements2 are assembled (ELSE and ENDIF are pseudo-ops).

Table 13.1 gives the forms of the most useful conditional pseudo-ops and what is required for them to be evaluated as true.

In section 13.4, we used the conditional IF1 to include a macro library in a program. The next examples show how some of the other conditionals may be used.

Table 13.1 Conditional Pseudo-Ops

Form	TRUE IF
IF exp	Constant expression exp is nonzero.
IFE exp	Exp is zero.
IFB <arg>	Argument arg is missing (blank). Angle brackets are required.
IFNB <arg>	Arg is not missing (not blank).
IFDEF sym	Symbol sym is defined in the program (or declared as EXTRN).
	Note: The EXTRN directive is discussed in Chapter 14.
IFNDEF sym	Sym is not defined or EXTRN.
IFIDN <str1>,<str2>	Strings str1 and str2 are identical. Angle brackets are required.
IFDIF <str1>,<str2>	Strings str1 and str2 are not identical.
IF1	Assembler is making the first assembly pass.
IF2	Assembler is making the second assembly pass.

A Macro that Uses IF

Example 13.12 Write a macro to define a block of memory words with N entries, consisting of the first K integers, followed by $N - K$ zero words, and use it to initialize an array of 10 words to values 1, 2, 3, 4, 5, 0, 0, 0, 0, and 0.

Solution:

```
BLOCK    MACRO  N,K
         I = 1
         REPT   N
         IF  K+1-I
         DW      I
         I = I+1
         ELSE
         DW      0
         ENDIF
         ENDM
         ENDM
```

If this macro is invoked to define an array A as follows,

```
A            LABEL        WORD
BLOCK        10,5
```

the expansion initializes N to 10, K to 5, I to 1, and assemble the statements inside REPT 10 times. After five passes, DW 1 ... DW 5 are generated and $K = 6$. After that, since $K + 1 - I = 5 + 1 - 6 = 0$, the statement following ELSE—namely DW 0—is assembled. The result is equivalent to

```
A    DW    1,2,3,4,5,0,0,0,0,0
```

A Macro that Uses IFNB

Recall from Chapter 11, exercise 9, that INT 21h, function 0AH, stores a string that the user types in the byte array whose offset address is contained in DX. The first byte of the array must contain the maximum number of characters expected. DOS fills in the next byte with the actual number of characters read.

Example 13.13 Write a macro READ MACRO BUF,LEN that either uses INT 21h, function 0Ah, to read a string into the byte array BUF of length LEN (if both arguments are present), or uses INT 21h, function 1, to read a single character into AL (if both arguments are missing).

Solution:

```
READ MACRO BUF,MAXCHARS
; BUF = STRING BUFFER ADDRESS
; LEN = MAX NO. OF CHARS TO READ
    IFNB <BUF>
    IFNB <LEN>
        MOV     AH,0AH          ;read string FCN
        LEA     DX,BUF          ;DX has string ADDR
        MOV     BUF,LEN         ;1st byte has array size
        INT     21H             ;read string
    ENDIF
    ELSE
        MOV     AH,1            ;read char FCN
        INT     21H             ;read char
    ENDIF
ENDM
```

If the preceding macro is invoked by the statement

READ MSG,10

then since both arguments are present, the code

```
MOV     AH,0AH
LEA     DX,MSG
MOV     MSG,10
INT     21H
```

is assembled. String MSG must be a declared array of at least 13 bytes (1 byte for the maximum number of characters expected, 1 byte for the actual number of characters read, 10 bytes for the characters, and 1 byte for a carriage return). If the macro invocation is

READ

then since both arguments are blank, the code following ELSE, namely

```
MOV     AH,1
INT     21h
```

is assembled. If this macro is improperly invoked with only one argument—for example, READ MSG—then no code is assembled.

The .ERR Directive

Because macros may be called in a variety of situations, it's possible they may be invoked incorrectly. The **.ERR** directive provides a way for the assembler to tell the user about this. If MASM encounters this directive, it displays the message "forced error", which indicates a fatal assembly error.

Example 13.14 Write a program containing a macro to display a character. The macro should produce an assembly error if its parameter is omitted.

Solution:

Program Listing PGM13_4.ASM
```
TITLE PGM13_4:  .ERR DEMO
  .MODEL SMALL
  .STACK 100H
DISP_CHAR MACRO CHAR
          IFNB  <CHAR>
          MOV   AH,2
          MOV   DL,CHAR
          INT   21H
          ELSE
          .ERR
          ENDIF
          ENDM
  .CODE
MAIN      PROC
          DISP_CHAR 'A'          ;legal call
          DISP_CHAR              ;illegal call
          MOV   AH,4CH
          INT   21H
MAIN      ENDP
          END   MAIN
```

```
C>MASM PGM13_4;

Microsoft (R) Macro Assembler Version 5.10.
Copyright (C) Microsoft Corp 1981, 1988. All rights reserved.

PGM13_4.ASM(15): error A2089: Forced error

 50050 + 418683 Bytes symbol space free
  0 Warning Errors
  1 Severe Errors
```

13.8 Macros and Procedures

Macros and procedures are alike in the sense that both are written to carry out tasks for a program, but it can sometimes be difficult for a programmer to decide which structure is best in a given situation. Here are some considerations:

Assembly Time

A program containing macros usually takes longer to assemble than a similar program containing procedures, because it takes time to expand the macros. This is especially true if library macros are involved.

Execution Time

The code generated by a macro expansion generally executes faster than a procedure call, because the latter involves saving the return address, transferring control to the procedure, passing data into the procedure, and returning from the procedure.

Program Size

A program with macros is generally larger than a similar program with procedures, because each macro invocation causes a separate code block to be copied into the program. However, a procedure is coded only once.

Other Considerations

Macros are especially suitable for small, frequently occurring tasks. Liberal use of such macros can result in source code that resembles high-level language. However, big jobs are usually best handled by procedures, because big macros generate large amount of code if they are called very often.

Summary

- A macro is a named block of text. It may consist of instructions, pseudo-ops, or references to other macros.

- A macro is invoked at assembly time. To expand a macro, MASM copies the macro text into the program at the position of the invocation, just as if the user had typed it in. If the macro has a dummy parameter list, actual parameters replace the dummy ones. MASM replaces any instructions by machine language code.

- An important use of macros is to create new instructions.

- Macro expansions may be viewed in a program's .LST file. Three assembler directives govern how the expansion will appear. After .SALL, the macro expansion is not listed. After .XALL, only those lines that generate source code are listed. After .LALL, all source lines are listed, except comments that are preceded by ;;.

- Local labels may be used within a macro. Each time the macro is invoked, a different label is generated. This gets around the problem of having duplicate labels resulting from several macro invocations.

- A macro may invoke another macro, or itself.
- A library file of macros can be created. Its macros may be used in a program if the INCLUDE pseudo-op is used.
- The REPT macro may be used to repeat a block of statements. It has a single argument that specifies the number of times to repeat the statements. It can be placed in the program at the point the statements are to be repeated, or enclosed in another macro. The REPT macro has no name field.
- The IRP macro may be used to repeat statements an arbitrary number of times.
- By using conditional pseudo-ops within macros, MASM can be made to assemble certain statements and exclude others.
- The .ERR directive provides a way to inform the user that a macro is being incorrectly called.
- Macro and procedures each have advantages. Programs with macros usually take longer to assemble, and they generate more machine code, but execute faster. Small tasks are often best handled by macros, and procedures are better for large tasks.

Glossary

conditional pseudo-ops — Pseudo-ops used to assemble certain statements and exclude others

expand (a macro) — When MASM encounters a macro name in a program, it replaces the macro name by its body

invoke (a macro) — Use the macro name in a program

local label — A label defined with the LOCAL pseudo-op inside a macro. Each time the macro is invoked, MASM generates a different numerical label when the local label is encountered

New Pseudo-Ops

```
=
conditional macros*        ENDM         LOCAL
ELSE                       .ERR         MACRO
ENDIF                      IRP          REPT
```

(*see Table 13.1)

Exercises

1. Write the following macros. All registers used by the macros should be restored, except those that return results.
   a. MUL_N MACRO N, which puts the signed 32-bit product of AX and the number *N* in DX and AX.
   b. DIV_N MACRO, N which divides the number in AX by the number *N* and puts the signed 16-bit quotient in AX. You may assume that *N* is not 0.
   c. MOD MACRO M,N, which returns in AX the remainder after *M* is divided by *N*. Note that *M* and *N* may be 16-bit words, registers, or constants. You may assume that *N* is not 0.
   d. POWER MACRO N, which takes the number in AX and raises it to the power of *N*, where *N* is a positive number. The result should be stored in AX. If the result is too big to fit in 16 bits, the macro should set CF/OF.

2. Write a macro C_TO_F, which takes an argument C (which represents a centigrade temperature), and converts it to Fahrenheit temperature *F* according to the formula $F = (9/5 \times C) + 32$. To do the multiplication by 9 and division by 5, your macro should invoke the MUL_N and DIV_N macros of exercises 1(a) and 1(b). The result, truncated to an integer, is returned in AX. If overflow occurs on multiplication, CF/OF should be set.

3. Write a macro CGD MACRO M,N that computes the greatest common divisor of arguments *M* and *N*. Euclid's algorithm for computing the CGD of M and N is

   ```
   WHILE N ≠ 0 DO
     M = M MOD N
     Swap M and N
   END_WHILE
   RETURN M
   ```

   Your macro should invoke the MOD macro of exercise 1(c).

4. Macros are especially useful in graphics applications. Write the following macros:

   a. A macro MOV_CURSOR MACRO R,C that moves the cursor to row R and column C.
   b. A macro DISP_CHAR MACRO CHAR,ATTR that displays character CHAR with attribute ATTR once at the cursor position.
   c. A macro CLEAR_WINDOW MACRO R1,C1,R2,C2,COLOR that clears a window with upper left corner at (C1,R1), lower right corner at (C2,R2), and attribute COLOR.
   d. A macro DRAW_BOX MACRO R1,C1,R2,C2 that draws a box outline with upper left corner at (C1,R1), and lower right corner at (C2,R2). Use extended ASCII characters for the corners and sides.

5. Use a REPT to write the following macros:
   a. A macro ALT MACRO N, where N is a positive even integer, that initializes a block of N memory bytes to alternating 0's and 1's, beginning with 0. Show how the macro would be invoked to initialize a 100-byte array BYT.
   b. A macro ARITH MACRO B,I,N, where B, I, and N are positive integers, that initializes a block of memory words to the following arithmetic progression: $B, B + I, B + 2 \times I \ldots B + (N - 1) \times I$. Show how the macro would be invoked to initialize a 100-word array WRD whose first two elements are 10 and 12.
   c. A macro POWERS_OF_TWO MACRO N, where N is a nonnegative integer, that may be used to initialize a block of N memory words to 1, 2, 4, 8, 16, ..., 2^{N-1}. Show how the macro is invoked to initialize a 10-word array W.
   d. A macro BIN MACRO N, K, where N and K are nonnegative integers, that will move the binomial coefficient $B(N, K) = N \times (N - 1) \times \ldots (N - K + 1)$ into AX.

6. State what code, if any, would be assembled in the following macro:

```
MAC1    MACRO M
        IF M-1
        MOV AX,M
        M=M-1
        IFE M
        MOV BX,M
        ENDIF
        ENDIF
        ENDM
```

   a. For the macro invocation MAC1 1?
   b. For the macro invocation MAC1 2?

7. State what code, if any, would be assembled in the following macro:

```
MAC2    MACRO M,K
        REPT M
        MOV AX,M
        K=K+1
        IF K-3
        MOV BX,M
        ENDIF
        ENDM
        ENDM
```

   a. For the macro invocation MAC2 5,1?
   b. For the macro invocation MAC2 2,2?

8. The Fibonacci sequence is 1, 1, 2, 3, 5, 8, 13, 21, 34 . . . . Write a macro FIB MACRO N whose invocation will cause the instruction MOV AX,FN to be assembled, where FN is the Nth Fibonacci number. For example, the call FIB 8 would cause the instruction MOV AX,21 to be assembled.

Here is an iterative algorithm for producing the Nth Fibonacci number:

```
IF N = 1
 THEN FN = 1
  ELSE
   LO = 0
   HI = 1
   REPEAT N-1 TIMES
    X = LO
    LO = HI
    HI = X + LO
   FN = HI
```

14

Memory Management

Overview

Until now, all our programs have consisted of a code segment, a stack segment, and perhaps a data segment. If there were other procedures besides the main procedure, they were placed in the code segment after the main procedure. In this chapter, you will see that programs can be constructed in other ways.

In section 14.1, we discuss the .COM program format in which code, data, and stack fit into a single segment. .COM programs have a simple structure and don't take up as much disk space as .EXE programs, so system programs are often written in this format.

Section 14.2 shows how procedures can be placed in different modules, assembled separately, and linked into a single program. In this way they can be written and tested separately. The modules containing these procedures may have their own code and data segments; when the modules are linked, the code segments can be combined, as can the data segments.

Section 14.3 covers the full segment definitions. They provide complete control over the ordering, combination, and placement of program segments.

Section 14.4 provides more information about the simplified segment definitions that we have been using throughout the book.

The procedures we've written so far have generally passed data values through registers. Section 14.5 shows other ways for procedures to communicate.

14.1 .COM Programs

In this section we discuss a program format in which the code, data, and stack segments coincide. This type of program is also known as a **.COM program**, because that is the extension given the run file. As you will see, the primary advantages of .COM programs are their simple structure and the fact that they take up relatively little disk space. The disadvantages are inflexibility and limited size, because everything—code, data, and stack—must fit into the single segment.

A problem with .COM programs is where to place the data, if any, because they are in the same segment as the code. They can be put at the end of the program, but this requires use of the full segment declarations (section 14.3). We choose to place the data at the beginning of the program. Here is the form of a .COM program:

.COM Program Format

```
 0:  TITLE
 1:  .MODEL SMALL
 2:  .CODE
 3:     ORG  100H
 4:  START:
 5:     JMP  MAIN
 6:  ;data goes here
 7:  MAIN   PROC
 8:  ;instructions go here
 9:  ;dos exit
10:     MOV  AH,4CH
11:     INT  21H
12:  MAIN ENDP
13:  ;other procedures go here
14:     END  START
```

Let's look at the differences between this format and the format we've been using up till now (.EXE program format). First, there is only one segment, defined by .CODE. Because the first statement must be an instruction, the procedure begins with a JMP around the data. The label START indicates the entry point to the program; this label is also the operand of the END in line 14. The reason for the ORG 100h directive is explained as follows.

The ORG Directive

In Chapter 4 we mentioned that when an .EXE program is loaded in memory, it is preceded by a 100h-byte information area called the *program segment prefix (PSP)*. The same is true for .COM programs, and for them, the PSP occupies the first 100h bytes of the segment.

The **ORG** 100h directive assigns 100h to the *location counter*, which keeps track of the relative location of the statement currently being assembled. Ordinarily, the location counter is set to 0 at the beginning of a segment. ORG 100h makes it start at 100h instead.

Now suppose a .COM program has some data. Without the ORG 100h, the assembler would assign addresses to variables relative to the beginning of the segment; this would incorrectly place them in the PSP. With the ORG 100h, variables are correctly assigned addresses relative to the beginning of the program, which starts 100h bytes after the beginning of the segment.

.COM Program Stack

In a .COM program, the stack is in the same segment as the code and data. Unlike an .EXE program, the programmer does not have to define a stack area. When the program is loaded, SP is initialized to FFFEh, the last

Figure 14.1 A .COM Program in Memory

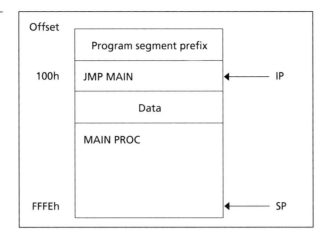

word in the segment. Because the stack grows toward the beginning of memory, there is little danger that the stack will interfere with the code, unless the stack gets very large or there is a lot of code. Figure 14.1 shows how a .COM program looks after it has been loaded in memory, if defined with the preceding format.

An Example of a .COM Program

As an example, let's rewrite PGM4_2.ASM in .COM format. The program just displays HELLO! on the screen. To aid in the comparison, PGM4_2.ASM is reproduced here and renumbered PGM14_1.ASM.

Program Listing PGM14_1.ASM (a repeat of PGM4_2.ASM)

```
TITLE PGM14_1: HELLO
.MODEL      SMALL
.STACK      100H
.DATA
 MSG   DB   'HELLO!$'
.CODE
MAIN   PROC
;initialize DS
       MOV   AX,@DATA
       MOV   DS,AX          ;initialize DS
;display message
       LEA   DX,MSG          ;get message
       MOV   AH,9            ;display string function
       INT   21h             ;display message
;return to DOS
       MOV   AH,4CH
       INT   21h
MAIN   ENDP
       END   MAIN
```

Now here is the program written in .COM format.

Program Listing PGM14_2.ASM

```
TITLE PGM14_2:.COM DEMO
.MODEL SMALL
.CODE
  ORG  100H
START:
       JMP    MAIN
MSG    DB     'HELLO$'
MAIN   PROC
       LEA    DX,MSG      ;get message
       MOV    AH,9        ;display string function
       INT    21H         ;display 'HELLO'
       MOV    AH,4CH      ;dos exit
       INT    21H
MAIN   ENDP
       END    START
```

Note that because there is only one segment, the instructions

```
MOV AX,@DATA
MOV DS,AX
```

which are required for an .EXE program that has data, are not needed in a .COM program.

The assemble and link steps are the same as before:

```
A>C:MASM PGM14_2;

Microsoft (R) Macro Assembler Version 5.10
Copyright (C) Microsoft Corp 1981, 1988. All rights reserved.

 50116 + 418713 Bytes symbol space free

    0 Warning Errors
    0 Severe Errors

A>C:LINK PGM14_2;

Microsoft (R) Overlay Linker Version 3.64
Copyright (C) Microsoft Corp 1983-1988. All rights reserved.
LINK : warning L4021: no stack segment
```

This warning may be ignored since a .COM program doesn't have a separate stack segment.

For a .COM program, the .EXE file that is produced by the LINK program is not the run file. It must be converted to .COM file format by running the DOS utility program EXE2BIN.

```
A>C:EXE2BIN PGM14_2 PGM14_2.COM
```

The first argument to EXE2BIN is PGM14_2. The default extension is .EXE. The second argument PGM14_2.COM is the output file name. The .EXE file that was created in the preceding steps is no longer needed and should be erased before running the program. To execute it, we type

```
A>PGM14_2
HELLO!
A>
```

As mentioned before, a primary advantage of .COM programs is their small size. The size of PGM14_1.EXE is 801 bytes vs. 22 bytes for PGM14_2.COM. The main reason for the size discrepancy is that an .EXE file has a 512-byte header block, which contains information about the size of the executable code, where it is to be located in memory, and other data. Another reason is that an .EXE program contains a separate stack segment.

14.2 Program Modules

For large programs with many procedures, it is convenient to put procedures in separate files. There are two primary reasons for doing this:

1. The procedures can be coded, assembled, and tested separately, possibly by different programmers.
2. When procedures are assembled separately, they can use the same names for variables and/or statement labels. This is because the assembler allows a name to be local to a file and it will not conflict with the same name in a different file.

Assembly and Object Modules

A separately-assembled procedure must be contained in an **assembly module**. This is an .ASM file consisting of at least one segment definition. The assembler takes an assembly module and produces an .OBJ file called an **object module**. The linker then combines object modules into an .EXE file that can be executed.

NEAR and FAR Procedures

In section 8.3, we noted that the syntax of procedure declaration is

```
procedure_name PROC type
```

where type is NEAR or FAR (the default is NEAR). A procedure is NEAR if the statement that calls it is in the same segment as the procedure itself; a procedure is FAR if it is called from a different segment.

Because a FAR procedure is in a different segment from its calling statement, the CALL instruction causes first CS and then IP to be saved on the stack, then CS:IP gets the segment:offset of the procedure. To return, RET pops the stack twice to restore the original CS:IP.

You'll see in a moment that a procedure can be NEAR, even if it's assembled separately. A procedure must be typed as FAR if it's impossible for the calling statement and the procedure to fit into a single memory segment, or if the procedure will be called from a high-level language.

EXTRN

When assembling a module, the assembler must be informed of names which are used in the module but are defined in other modules; otherwise these names will be flagged as undeclared. This is done by the **EXTRN** pseudo-op, whose syntax is

```
EXTRN     external_name_list
```

Here, external_name_list is a list of arguments of the form name:type where name is an external name, and type is one of the following: NEAR, FAR, WORD, BYTE, or DWORD. For externally declared procedures, type would be NEAR or FAR. The types WORD, BYTE, and DWORD are used for variables.

For example, to inform MASM of the existence of a NEAR procedure PROC1 and a FAR procedure PROC2 that are defined in separate modules, we would say,

```
EXTRN     PROC1:NEAR, PROC2:FAR
```

Now suppose MASM encounters the statement

```
CALL      PROC1
```

MASM knows from the EXTRN list that PROC1 is in another assembly module, and allocates an undefined address to PROC1. The address is filled in when the modules are linked.

The EXTRN pseudo-op may appear anywhere in the program, as long as it precedes the first reference to any of the names in the external name list. We will place it at the beginning of the program.

PUBLIC

A procedure or variable must be declared with the **PUBLIC** pseudo-op if it is to be used in a different module. The syntax is

```
PUBLIC    name_list
```

where name_list is a list of procedure and variable names that may be referred to in a different module. The PUBLIC pseudo-op can appear anywhere in a module but we will usually place it near the beginning of the module.

Linking Object Modules

The LINK program combines object modules into a single executable machine language program. It tries to match names that are declared in EXTRN directives with PUBLIC declarations in the other modules. It combines code and data segments in different modules according to the segment declarations of these segments (see section 14.3). With the relative positions of instructions and data known, it is able to fill in the addresses left undefined by MASM.

As an example, we will rewrite PGM4_3.ASM, which displays a prompt, reads a lowercase letter, and converts it to upper case.

There are two assembly modules. The first module contains the main procedure; it displays a message, lets the user enter the lowercase letter, and calls a procedure CONVERT, which converts the letter to uppercase and displays it with another message. CONVERT is defined in another module.

Program Listing 14_3.ASM: First Module

```
0:      TITLE PGM14_3: CASE CONVERSION
1:      EXTRN    CONVERT:NEAR
2:      .MODEL SMALL
3:      .STACK          100H
4:      .DATA
5:      MSG      DB     'ENTER A LOWERCASE LETTER:$'
6:      .CODE
7:      MAIN     PROC
8:               MOV    AX,@DATA
9:               MOV    DS,AX          ;initialize ds
10:              MOV    AH,9           ;display string fcn
11:              LEA    DX,MSG         ;get MSG
12:              INT    21H            ;display it
13:              MOV    AH,1           ;read char fcn
14:              INT    21H            ;input char
15:              CALL   CONVERT        ;convert to uppercase
16:              MOV    AH,4CH
17:              INT    21H            ;DOS exit
18:     MAIN     ENDP
19:              END    MAIN
```

The first module consists of stack, data, and code segments. After initializing DS at lines 8 and 9, the program prints the message "ENTER A LOWERCASE LETTER:" and calls procedure CONVERT. The existence of CONVERT as a procedure in another module is made known to the assembler by the EXTRN directive in line 1. The first module ends with an END directive in line 19, with the entry point MAIN to the program.

Program Listing 14_3A.ASM: Second Module

```
0:      TITLE PGM14_3A: CONVERT
1:      PUBLIC   CONVERT
2:      .MODEL SMALL
3:      .DATA
4:      MSG      DB     0DH,0AH,'IN UPPERCASE IT IS '
5:      CHAR     DB     -20H,'$'
6:      .CODE
7:      CONVERT  PROC   NEAR
8:      ;converts char in AL to uppercase
9:               PUSH   BX
10:              PUSH   DX
11:              ADD    CHAR,AL        ;convert to uppercase
12:              MOV    AH,9           ;display string fcn
13:              LEA    DX,MSG         ;get MSG
```

```
14:              INT     21H             ;display it
15:              POP     DX
16:              POP     BX
17:              RET
18: CONVERT      ENDP
19:              END
```

The module containing CONVERT has its own data and code segments. When the modules are linked, the code segments from the two modules are combined into a single code segment; similarly, the data segments are combined into a single segment (you'll see the reason for this in section 14.3).

At line 1, CONVERT is declared PUBLIC, enabling it to be called from the first module. At line 7, procedure CONVERT is declared as type NEAR because the code segments of the two modules are combined. Because the data segments are also combined, it's not necessary to initialize DS in the second module; this was done in the first module. The module ends with an END directive; unlike the first module, the END has no operand.

After saving the registers used, CONVERT begins at line 11 by adding the lowercase letter in AL to the -20h stored in byte variable CHAR. This converts the letter to upper case (assuming a lowercase letter was entered). At lines 12–14, the procedure outputs the final message. Note that the name MSG is used in both modules.

Now let's assemble and link the modules. MASM and LINK will be in drive C, and the source files in drive A. A is the logged drive.

```
A>C:MASM PGM14_3;

Microsoft (R) Macro Assembler Version 5.10
Copyright (C) Microsoft Corp 1981, 1988. All rights reserved.

 49984 + 390317 Bytes symbol space free

     0 Warning Errors
     0 Severe Errors
```

```
A>C:MASM PGM14_3A;

Microsoft (R) Macro Assembler Version 5.10
Copyright (C) Microsoft Corp 1981, 1988. All rights reserved.

 49976 + 390325 Bytes symbol space free

     0 Warning Errors
     0 Severe Errors
```

MASM has created object modules PGM14_3.OBJ and PGM14_3A.OBJ. To link them, we type

```
A>C:LINK PGM14_3 + PGM14_3A

Microsoft (R) Overlay Linker Version 3.64
Copyright (C) Microsoft Corp 1983-1988. All rights reserved.

Run File [PGM14_3.EXE]:
List File [NUL.MAP]:PGM14_3
Libraries [.LIB]:
```

The .EXE file has the same name as the first module linked. We asked for a .MAP file to be created, so we can see the size and arrangement of the code, data, and stack segments. The .MAP file is listed in Figure 14.2.

In the .MAP file, we see that the code segments of the two modules have been combined, as have the data segments. LINK has chosen the order: code, data, stack. We'll show later how to control the order of the segments, but in most stand-alone assembly language programs the order is not important.

Sample execution:

```
C>PGM14_3
ENTER A LOWERCASE LETTER:r
IN UPPERCASE IT IS R
```

Libraries

Instead of linking individual object modules to form an .EXE file, as just shown, we can create a *library file* of object modules containing procedures. When a library is specified during the linking step, LINK retrieves any procedures a program needs from the library, and creates an .EXE file.

Figure 14.2 PGM14_3.MAP

```
Start   Stop    Length  Name            Class
00000H  00028H  00029H  _TEXT           CODE
0002AH  0005DH  00034H  _DATA           DATA
00060H  0015FH  00100H  STACK           STACK

Origin  Group
0002:0  DGROUP

Program entry point at 0000:0000
```

The LIB program is used to maintain libraries. For example, to create a library called MYLIB, type

```
LIB MYLIB;
```

This creates a library file MYLIB.LIB. To add an object module to the library—for example, PGM14_3A.OBJ—type

```
LIB MYLIB + PGM14_3A;
```

If MYLIB.LIB didn't already exist, the above line would create it and attach PGM14_3A.OBJ.

If a program PROG.ASM needs a procedure from the library, we first assemble PROG.ASM into PROG.OBJ, and then type

```
LINK PROG + MYLIB.LIB;
```

For example, we can retrieve procedure CONVERT from the library and attach it to PGM14_3.OBJ by typing

```
LINK PGM14_3 + MYLIB.LIB;
```

This creates PGM14_3.EXE, which will run, as shown:

```
C>PGM14_3
ENTER A LOWERCASE LETTER:a
IN UPPERCASE IT IS A
```

You can get a list of the procedures in a library by asking LIB to create a list file. For example,

```
C>LIB MYLIB

Microsoft (R) Library Manager Version 3.10
Copyright (C) Microsoft Corp 1983-1988. All rights reserved.

Operations:
List file:MYLIB
```

When LIB asks for a list file, we reply MYLIB. This creates a listing file MYLIB, which looks like this:

```
C>Type MYLIB

CONVERT..........pgm14_3a

pgm14_3a   Offset: 00000010H  Code and data size: 29H
CONVERT
```

The listing shows the object module names and the procedures they contain. In this case, the only object module in the library is PGM14_3A.OBJ, and it contains only procedure CONVERT.

For more information about the LIB utility, consult the Microsoft *Codeview and Utilities* manual.

14.3 Full Segment Definitions

The simplified segment definitions that we have been using up till now are adequate for most purposes. In this section we consider the full segment definitions. The primary reasons for using them are as follows:

1. Full segment definitions must be used for versions of MASM earlier than version 5.0.
2. With the full segment definitions, the programmer can control how segments are ordered, combined with each other, and aligned relative to each other in memory.

The Segment Directive

The full form of the segment directive is

name   **SEGMENT**   align   combine   'class'

The operands align, combine, and class are optional types, and are discussed in the next section. To end a segment, we say

name   ENDS

For example, we could define a data segment called D_SEG as follows:

```
D_SEG   SEGMENT
;data goes here
D_SEG   ENDS
```

Now let's look at the segment operands.

Align Type

The *align type* of a segment declaration determines how the starting address of the segment is selected when the program is loaded in memory. Table 14.1 gives the options.

The significance of a segment's align type may be illustrated by the following example. Let SEG1 and SEG2 be segments declared like this:

```
SEG1            SEGMENT     PARA
    DB          11H DUP (1)
SEG1            ENDS
SEG2            SEGMENT     PARA
    DB          10H DUP (2)
SEG2            ENDS
```

Suppose these segments are loaded sequentially, with SEG1 being assigned segment number 1010h. The 11h bytes of SEG1 will extend from 1010:0000h to 1010:0010h. Now, because SEG2 has a PARA align type, it begins at the next available paragraph boundary, which is at 1012:0000 = 1010:0020. Here is a DEBUG display of memory:

```
1010:0000  01 01 01 01 01 01 01 01-01 01 01 01 01 01 01 01
1010:0010  01 00 00 00 00 00 00 00-00 00 00 00 00 00 00 00
1010:0020  02 02 02 02 02 02 02 02-02 02 02 02 02 02 02 02
```

We see there is a gap of Fh = 15 bytes (represented by 00 bytes) from the end of SEG1 to the start of SEG2. This gap represents wasted space, because it is not part of the data in either segment.

Table 14.1 Align Types

PARA	Segment begins at the next available paragraph (least significant hex digit of physical address is 0).
BYTE	Segment begins at the next available byte.
WORD	Segment begins at the next available word (least significant bit of physical address is 0).
PAGE	Segment begins at the next available page (two least significant hex digits of physical address are 0).

PARA is the default align type.

Now suppose the segments are declared as follows:

```
SEG1            SEGMENT         PARA
    DB              11H DUP (1)
SEG1            ENDS
SEG2            SEGMENT         BYTE
    DB              10H DUP (2)
SEG2            ENDS
```

where SEG2 is given a BYTE align type. If these segments are loaded sequentially, memory will look like this:

```
1010:0000  01 01 01 01 01 01 01 01-01 01 01 01 01 01 01 01
1010:0010  01 02 02 02 02 02 02 02-02 02 02 02 02 02 02 02
1010:0020  02 00 00 00 00 00 00 00-00 00 00 00 00 00 00 00
```

The segments have been combined into a single memory segment with no wasted space.

Combine Type

If a program contains segments of the same name, the *combine type* tells how they are to be combined when the program is loaded in memory. Table 14.2 gives the most frequently used choices.

The assembler indicates an error if a stack segment does not have a STACK combine type. For other segments, if the combine type is omitted the program segment is loaded into its own memory segment.

A frequent use of the *PUBLIC* combine type is to combine code segments with the same name from different modules into a single code segment. This means that all procedures can be typed as NEAR. Similarly, PUBLIC data segments can be combined into a single data segment. The advantage is that DS needs only to be initialized once, and does not need to be modified to access any of the data. This is what happened in PGM14_3 when data segments were combined.

Data segments in different modules can be given the same name and a *COMMON* combine type so that variables in one module can share

Table 14.2 Combine Types

PUBLIC	Segments with the same name are concatenated (placed one after the other) to form a single, continuous memory block.
COMMON	Segments with the same name begin at the same place in memory: that is, are overlaid.
STACK	Has the same effect as PUBLIC, except that all offset addresses of instructions and data in the segment are relative to the SS register. SP is initialized to the end of the segment.
AT paragraph	Indicates that the segment should begin at the specified paragraph.

the same memory locations as variables in the other module. To show how COMMON works, suppose we declare

```
D_SEG           SEGMENT         COMMON
A               DB              11H DUP (1)
D_SEG           ENDS
```

in FIRST.ASM, and

```
D_SEG           SEGMENT         COMMON
B               DB              10H DUP (2)
D_SEG           ENDS
```

in SECOND.ASM. If the modules are assembled and linked as follows:

```
C>LINK FIRST + SECOND;
```

then they will be overlaid in memory and variables A and B will be assigned the same address. The size of the common data segment will be that of the larger segment (11h bytes). However, the values of the bytes will be those that appear in SECOND, because it is the last module mentioned on the LINK command line. Memory will look like this:

```
1010:0000 02 02 02 02 02 02 02 02-02 02 02 02 02 02 02 02
1010:0010 01 00 00 00 00 00 00 00-00 00 00 00 00 00 00 00
```

Class Type

The *class* type of a segment declaration determines the order in which segments are loaded in memory. Class type declarations must be enclosed in single quotes.

If two or more segments have the same class, they are loaded in memory one after the other. If classes are not specified in segment declarations, segments are loaded in the order they appear in the source listing.

For example, suppose we declare

```
C_SEG           SEGMENT         'CODE'
;main procedure goes here
C_SEG           ENDS
```

in module FIRST.ASM, and

```
C1_SEG          SEGMENT         'CODE'
;another procedure goes here
C1_SEG          ENDS
```

in module SECOND.ASM and these are the only segments of class 'CODE'. When the modules are assembled and linked by

```
C>LINK FIRST + SECOND
```

then C1_SEG will follow C_SEG in memory. However, there may be a gap between the segments; to eliminate it, C1_SEG could be given a BYTE align type.

14.3.1
Form of an .EXE Program with Full Segment Definitions

The form of an .EXE program with the full segment definitions is a little different from the way it is with simplified segment definitions. Here is the standard format:

```
S_SEG    SEGMENT   STACK
         DB        100H DUP (?)
S_SEG    ENDS
D_SEG    SEGMENT
;data goes here
D_SEG    ENDS
C_SEG    SEGMENT
         ASSUME    CS:C_SEG, SS:S_SEG, DS:D_SEG
MAIN     PROC
;initialize DS
         MOV       AX,D_SEG
         MOV       DS,AX
;other instructions
;dos exit
         MOV       AH,4CH
         INT       21H
MAIN ENDP
;other procedures can go here
C_SEG    ENDS
         END       MAIN
```

The segment names in this form are arbitrary. The ASSUME directive is unfamiliar, so we need to explain its role here.

The ASSUME Directive

When a program is assembled, MASM needs to be told which segments are the code, data, and stack; the purpose of the **ASSUME** directive is to associate the CS, SS, DS, and possibly ES registers with the appropriate segment. With the simplified segment directives, the segment registers are automatically associated with the correct segments, so no ASSUME is needed. However, for programs with data we still need to move the data segment number into DS at run time because, as we noted in Chapter 4, DS initially contains the segment number of the PSP.

14.3.2
Using the Full Segment Definitions

To show how the full Segment definitions work, we'll use them to rewrite PGM14_3.ASM and PGM14_3A.ASM. We will do this two ways: in the first version, we'll use the default operands of the segment directives.

Program Listing 14_4.ASM: First Module

```
0:   TITLE PGM14_4: CASE CONVERSION
1:   EXTRN    CONVERT:FAR
2:   S_SEG    SEGMENT STACK
3:            DB 100 DUP (0)
```

```
 4:  S_SEG      ENDS
 5:  D_SEG      SEGMENT
 6:  MSG        DB      'ENTER A LOWERCASE LETTER:$'
 7:  D_SEG      ENDS
 8:  C_SEG      SEGMENT
 9:             ASSUME CS:C_SEG,DS:D_SEG,SS:S_SEG
10:  MAIN       PROC
11:             MOV     AX,D_SEG
12:             MOV     DS,AX           ;initialize DS
13:             MOV     AH,9            ;display string fcn
14:             LEA     DX,MSG          ;get MSG
15:             INT     21H             ;display it
16:             MOV     AH,1            ;read char fcn
17:             INT     21H             ;input char
18:             CALL    CONVERT         ;convert to uppercase
19:             MOV     AH,4CH
20:             INT     21H             ;dos exit
21:  MAIN       ENDP
22:  C_SEG      ENDS
23:             END     MAIN
```

Program Listing 14_4A.ASM: Second Module

```
24:  TITLE PGM14_4A: CONVERT
25:  PUBLIC     CONVERT
26:  D_SEG      SEGMENT
27:  MSG        DB      0DH,0AH,'IN UPPERCASE IT IS '
28:  CHAR       DB      -20H,'$'
29:  D_SEG      ENDS
30:  C_SEG      SEGMENT
31:             ASSUME  CS:C_SEG,DS:D_SEG
32:  CONVERT    PROC    FAR
33:  ;converts char in AL to uppercase
34:             PUSH    DS              ;save DS
35:             PUSH    DX              ;and DX
36:             MOV     DX,D_SEG        ;reset DS
37:             MOV     DS,DX           ;to local data segment
38:             ADD     CHAR,AL         ;convert to uppercase
39:             MOV     AH,9            ;display string fcn
40:             LEA     DX,MSG          ;get MSG
41:             INT     21H             ;display it
42:             POP     DX              ;restore DX
43:             POP     DS              ;and DS
44:             RET
45:  CONVERT    ENDP
46:  C_SEG      ENDS
47:             END
```

Note the following:

1. We chose the same name C_SEG for the code segments in both modules, but because they don't have combine type PUBLIC, they will occupy separate memory segments when the modules are assembled and linked. This means procedure CONVERT must be typed as FAR (lines 1, 32).

2. Because the data segments are also not PUBLIC, they occupy separate memory segments. This means procedure CONVERT needs to change DS in order to access the data in the second module (lines 36, 37). We use DX (instead of AX) to move the segment number into DS, because CONVERT receives its input in AL.

After assembling and linking the modules, let's look at the .MAP file (Figure 14.3). The segments appear in the order they appear in the source listings. Because the segments were defined with the default (PARA) align type, there are gaps between them.

Now let's rewrite the preceding modules to take full advantage of the SEGMENT directives. Here are the requirements:

1. The code segments from the two programs are combined into a single segment, as are the data segments.
2. Gaps between segments are eliminated.
3. The order of the segments in the final program is: stack, data, code.

Program Listing 14_5.ASM: First Module

```
 0:    TITLE   PGM14_5: CASE CONVERSION
 1:    EXTRN   CONVERT:NEAR
 2:    S_SEG   SEGMENT STACK
 3:            DB 100 DUP (0)
 4:    S_SEG   ENDS
 5:    D_SEG   SEGMENT BYTE    PUBLIC 'DATA'
 6:    MSG     DB      'ENTER A LOWERCASE LETTER:$'
 7:    D_SEG   ENDS
 8:    C_SEG   SEGMENT  BYTE PUBLIC 'CODE'
 9:            ASSUME  CS:C_SEG,DS:D_SEG,SS:S_SEG
10:    MAIN    PROC
11:            MOV     AX,D_SEG
12:            MOV     DS,AX           ;initialize DS
13:            MOV     AH,9            ;display string fcn
14:            LEA     DX,MSG          ;get MSG
15:            INT     21H             ;display it
16:            MOV     AH,1            ;read char fcn
17:            INT     21H             ;input char
18:            CALL    CONVERT         ;convert to uppercase
19:            MOV     AH,4CH
20:            INT     21H             ;dos exit
21:    MAIN    ENDP
22:    C_SEG   ENDS
23:            END     MAIN
```

Figure 14.3 PGM14_4.MAP

Start	Stop	Length	Name	Class
00000H	00063H	00064H	S_SEG	
00070H	0008AH	0001BH	D_SEG	
00090H	000A9H	0001AH	C_SEG	
000B0H	000C7H	00018H	D_SEG	
000D0H	000E5H	00016H	C_SEG	

Program entry point at 0009:0000

Program Listing 14_5A.ASM: Second Module

```
 0:    TITLE PGM14_5A: CONVERT
 1:    PUBLIC  CONVERT
 2:    D_SEG    SEGMENT   BYTE  PUBLIC  'DATA'
 3:    MSG      DB     0DH,0AH,'IN UPPERCASE IT IS '
 4:    CHAR     DB     -20H,'$'
 5:    D_SEG    ENDS
 6:    C_SEG    SEGMENT   BYTE PUBLIC 'CODE'
 7:             ASSUME    CS:C_SEG,DS:D_SEG
 8:    CONVERT PROC      NEAR
 9:    ;converts char in AL to uppercase
10:             PUSH    DX
11:             ADD     CHAR,AL       ;convert to uppercase
12:             MOV     AH,9          ;display string fcn
13:             LEA     DX,MSG        ;get MSG
14:             INT     21H           ;display it
15:             POP     DX
16:             RET
17:    CONVERT ENDP
18:    C_SEG    ENDS
19:             END
```

As before, we assemble and link the modules. Figure 14.4 shows the .MAP file. It shows that the data and code segments of the two modules have been combined into single segments with no gaps between them. Here's how the SEGMENT operands were used:

1. By using the same names for code and data segments in the two modules, and using a PUBLIC combine type, we formed a program consisting of only three segments. Also, gaps were eliminated by using a BYTE align type. Because the PUBLIC combine type causes segments with the same name to be concatenated, the use of class types 'CODE' and 'DATA' is actually redundant.

2. Because the data for both modules now form a single segment, it wasn't necessary to reset DS in procedure CONVERT, and CONVERT doesn't need to save and restore DS. This is the primary reason for combining data segments.

3. Because there is now only one code segment, we can give CONVERT a NEAR attribute.

Figure 14.4 PGM14_5.MAP

Start	Stop	Length	Name	Class
00000H	00063H	00064H	S_SEG	
00064H	00096H	00033H	D_SEG	DATA
00097H	000BDH	00027H	C_SEG	CODE

Program entry point at 0009:0007

14.4 More About the Simplified Segment Definitions

Now that we have seen the full segment definitions, we can say more about the features of the simplified segment directives that we have been using throughout the book.

First, as we saw in section 4.7.1, a memory model must be specified when the simplified segment definitions are used. The choice of memory model depends on how many code and data segments there are. The syntax is

```
.MODEL    memory_model
```

where memory_model is one of the choices listed in Table 14.3. Unless there is a lot of code or data, the .SMALL model is adequate for most assembly language programs.

Second, for the SMALL model, Table 14.4 gives the simplified segments, their default names and align, combine, and class types. In addition to the .CODE, .DATA, and .STACK segments we have been using, uninitialized data can be declared in a separate **.DATA?** segment, and data that won't be changed by the program may be placed in a **.CONST** segment. For example,

```
.MODEL      SMALL
.STACK      100H
.DATA
X           DW          5
.DATA?
Y           DW          ?
.CONST
MSG         DB          'HELLO$'
```

Table 14.3 Memory Models

Model	Description
SMALL	Code in one segment Data in one segment
MEDIUM	Code in more than one segment Data in one segment
COMPACT	Code in one segment Data in more than one segment
LARGE	Code in more than one segment Data in more than one segment No array larger than 64 KB
HUGE	Code in more than one segment Data in more than one segment Arrays may be larger than 64 KB

Table 14.4 SMALL Model Segments

Segment	Default Name	Align	Combine	Class
.CODE	_TEXT	WORD	PUBLIC	'CODE'
.DATA	_DATA	WORD	PUBLIC	'DATA'
.DATA?	_BSS	WORD	PUBLIC	'BSS'
.STACK	STACK	PARA	STACK	'STACK'
.CONST	CONST	WORD	PUBLIC	'CONST'

```
                .CODE
                MAIN        PROC
                ...
                MAIN        ENDP
                END         MAIN
```

Here the usual initializing statements

```
MOV AX,@DATA
MOV DS,AX
```

allow the program access to the .DATA, .DATA?, and .CONST segments. This is because LINK actually combines these program segments into a single memory segment.

Third, for the .SMALL model, when .CODE is used to define code segments in separately assembled modules, these segments have the same default name (_TEXT) and a PUBLIC combine type. Thus when the modules are linked, the code segments combine into a single code segment; likewise, segments defined with .DATA combine into a single data segment. We saw a demonstration of this in PGM14_3.

14.5 Passing Data Between Procedures

In section 8.3, we briefly discussed the problem of passing data between procedures. Because assembly language procedures do not have associated parameter lists, as do high-level language procedures, it is up to the programmer to devise strategies for passing data between them. So far, we have been passing data to procedures through registers.

14.5.1 Global Variables

We have used the EXTRN and PUBLIC directives to show how a procedure defined in one module can be called from another. We can also use these directives to have variables defined in one module and referred to in another. Following high-level language practice, these variables are called **global variables**. An advantage of using global variables is that procedures need not use additional instructions to move data between themselves.

As an example, the following program prints a user prompt, reads two decimal digits whose sum is less than 10, and prints them and their sum on the next line. This problem was exercise 4.7.

Program Listing 14_6.ASM: First Module

```
 0:     TITLE PGM14_6: ADD DIGITS
 1:     EXTRN     ADDNOS:              NEAR
 2:     PUBLIC    DIGIT1, DIGIT2, SUM
 3:     .MODEL    SMALL
 4:     .STACK    100H
 5:     .DATA
 6:     MSG       DB       'ENTER TWO DIGITS:$'
 7:     MSG1      DB       0DH,0AH,'THE SUM OF '
 8:     DIGIT1    DB       ?
 9:               DB       ' AND '
10:     DIGIT2    DB       ?
11:               DB       ' IS '
```

```
12:     SUM     DB      -30H,'$'
13:     .CODE
14:     MAIN    PROC
15:     ;initialize DS
16:             MOV     AX,@DATA
17:             MOV     DS,AX           ;initialize DS
18:     ;prompt user
19:             MOV     AH,9            ;display string fcn
20:             LEA     DX,MSG          ;get prompt
21:             INT     21H             ;display it
22:     ;read two digits
23:             MOV     AH,1            ;input char fcn
24:             INT     21H             ;char in AL
25:             MOV     DIGIT1,AL       ;store in DIGIT1
26:             INT     21H             ;char in AL
27:             MOV     DIGIT2,AL       ;store in DIGIT2
28:     ;add the digits
29:             CALL    ADDNOS          ;add nos
30:     ;display results
31:             LEA     DX,MSG1
32:             MOV     AH,9
33:             INT     21H             ;output result
34:             MOV     AH,4CH
35:             INT     21H             ;dos exit
36:     MAIN    ENDP
37:             END     MAIN
```

The digits and their sum are contained in variables DIGIT1, DIGIT2, and SUM, declared in the first module. In line 2, they are declared PUBLIC so that external procedure ADDNOS can have access to them.

Program Listing 14_6A.ASM: Second Module

```
0:      TITLE   PGM14_6A: ADDNOS
1:      EXTRN   DIGIT1:BYTE, DIGIT2:BYTE, SUM:BYTE
2:      PUBLIC  ADDNOS
3:      .MODEL  SMALL
4:      .CODE
5:      ADDNOS  PROC    NEAR
6:      ;adds two digits
7:      ;input: byte variables DIGIT1, DIGIT2 in PGM14_4
8:      ;output: byte variable SUM in PGM14_4
9:              PUSH    AX
10:             MOV     AL,DIGIT1
11:             ADD     AL,DIGIT2
12:             ADD     SUM,AL
13:             POP     AX
14:             RET
15:     ADDNOS  ENDP
16:             END
```

DIGIT1, DIGIT2, and SUM appear in the second module's EXTRN list, line 1. The procedure adds them (actually, it adds the ASCII codes of the digit characters), then adds the sum to the –30h that has been stored in variable SUM. This puts the ASCII code of the sum in SUM.

Sample execution:

```
C>PGM14_5
ENTER TWO DIGITS:26
THE SUM OF 2 AND 6 IS 8
```

14.5.2
Passing the Addresses of the Data

A second method for passing data to a procedure is to send the address of the data. This method is known as **call by reference**; it is particularly useful when dealing with arrays. Call by reference is different from **call by value** in which the actual data values are passed to the called procedure. Both methods can be used in the same procedure; for example, the selectsort procedure discussed in section 10.3 receives the address of the array to be sorted in SI (call by reference), and the number of elements in the array in BX (call by value).

Here is the program to add two digits using call by reference.

Program Listing 14_7.ASM: First Module

```
 0:    TITLE PGM14_7: ADD DIGITS
 1:    EXTRN    ADDNOS:    NEAR
 2:    .MODEL   SMALL
 3:    .STACK   100H
 4:    .DATA
 5:    MSG      DB      'ENTER TWO DIGITS:$'
 6:    MSG1     DB      0DH,0AH,'THE SUM OF '
 7:    DIGIT1   DB      ?
 8:             DB      ' AND '
 9:    DIGIT2   DB      ?
10:             DB      ' IS '
11:    SUM      DB      -30H,'$'
12:    .CODE
13:    MAIN     PROC
14:    ;initialize DS
15:             MOV     AX,@DATA
16:             MOV     DS,AX         ;initialize DS
17:    ;display prompt
18:             MOV     AH,9          ;display string function
19:             LEA     DX,MSG        ;get prompt
20:             INT     21H           ;display it
21:    ;read two digits
22:             MOV     AH,1          ;input char function
23:             INT     21H           ;char in AL
24:             MOV     DIGIT1,AL     ;store in DIGIT1
25:             INT     21H           ;char in AL
26:             MOV     DIGIT2,AL     ;store in DIGIT2
27:    ;add them
28:             LEA     SI,DIGIT1     ;SI has offset of DIGIT1
29:             LEA     DI,DIGIT2     ;DI has offset of DIGIT2
```

```
30:             LEA     BX,SUM          ;BX has offset of SUM
31:             CALL    ADDNOS          ;add nos
32: ;display results
33:             MOV     AH,9            ;display string fcn
34:             LEA     DX,MSG1         ;DX has message
35:             INT     21H             ;output result
36: ;dos exit
37:             MOV     AH,4CH
38:             INT     21H
39: MAIN        ENDP
40:             END     MAIN
```

At lines 28–30, the addresses of the DIGIT1, DIGIT2, and SUM are passed to procedure ADDNOS in pointer registers SI, DI, and BX.

Program Listing 14_7A.ASM: Second Module

```
0:  TITLE PGM14_7A: ADDNOS
1:  PUBLIC   ADDNOS
2:  .MODEL   SMALL
3:  .CODE
4:  ADDNOS   PROC    NEAR
5:  ;adds two digits
6:  ;input:  SI = address of DIGIT1
7:  ;        DI = offset of DIGIT2
8:  ;        BX = offset of SUM
9:  ;output: [BX] = sum
10:          PUSH    AX
11:          MOV     AL,[SI]         ;AL has DIGIT1
12:          ADD     AL,[DI]         ;AL has DIGIT1 + DIGIT2
13:          ADD     [BX],AL         ;add to SUM
14:          POP     AX
15:          RET
16: ADDNOS   ENDP
17:          END
```

In lines 11 and 12, ADDNOS uses indirect addressing to place the sum of digits in AL. In line 13, indirect addressing is used to add the sum to the –30h in variable SUM.

14.5.3
Using the Stack

Instead of using registers, a procedure can place data values and addresses on the stack before calling another procedure. The called procedure then uses BP and indirect addressing to access the data (recall from section 10.2.1 that if BP is used in register indirect mode, SS has the operand's segment number). This method is used by high-level languages to pass data to assembly language procedures; we use it in Chapter 17 to implement recursive procedures (procedures that call themselves).

Because the CALL instruction causes the return address to be placed on top of the stack, the called procedure begins by saving BP on the stack, then it moves SP to BP; this makes BP point to the top of the stack. The resulting stack looks like this:

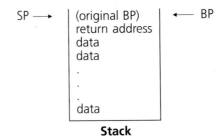

Stack

Now BP may be used with indirect addressing to access the data (we use BP because SP can't be used in indirect addressing). To return to the calling procedure, BP is popped off the stack and a RET N is executed, where N is the number of data bytes that the calling procedure pushed onto the stack. This restores CS:IP and removes N more bytes from the stack, leaving it in its original condition.

Here is the program to add two digits using this method:

Program Listing 14_8.ASM: First Module

```
 0:    TITLE PGM14_8: ADD DIGITS
 1:    EXTRN    ADDNOS:              NEAR
 2:    .MODEL   SMALL
 3:    .STACK   100H
 4:    .DATA
 5:    MSG      DB       'ENTER TWO DIGITS:$'
 6:    MSG1     DB       0DH,0AH,'THE SUM OF '
 7:    DIGIT1   DB       ?
 8:             DB       ' AND '
 9:    DIGIT2   DB       ?
10:             DB       ' IS '
11:    SUM      DB       -30H,'$'
12:    .CODE
13:    MAIN     PROC
14:    ;initialize DS
15:             MOV      AX,@DATA
16:             MOV      DS,AX        ;initialize DS
17:    ;display prompt
18:             MOV      AH,9         ;display string function
19:             LEA      DX,MSG       ;get prompt
20:             INT      21H          ;display it
21:    ;read two digits
22:             MOV      AH,1         ;input char function
23:             INT      21H          ;char in AL
24:             MOV      DIGIT1,AL    ;store in DIGIT1
25:             PUSH     AX           ;save on stack
26:             INT      21H          ;char in AL
27:             MOV      DIGIT2,AL    ;store in DIGIT2
28:             PUSH     AX           ;save on stack
29:    ;add the digits
30:             CALL     ADDNOS       ;AX has sum
31:             ADD      SUM,AL       ;store sum
32:    ;display results
```

```
33:             MOV     AH,9            ;display string fcn
34:             LEA     DX,MSG1         ;DX has message
35:             INT     21H             ;output result
36: ;dos exit
37:             MOV     AH,4CH
38:             INT     21H
39: MAIN        ENDP
40:             END     MAIN
```

At lines 24–28, the two digits are read, stored, and pushed onto the stack (because PUSH requires a word operand, we have to push AX). At line 30, ADDNOS is called to add the digits; it returns with the sum in AL, and this is added to the -30h in SUM.

Program Listing 14_8A.ASM: Second Module

```
0:  TITLE PGM14_8A: ADDNOS
1:  PUBLIC      ADDNOS
2:  .MODEL      SMALL
3:  .CODE
4:  ADDNOS      PROC    NEAR
5:  ;adds two digits
6:  ;stack on entry:  ret. addr (top), digit2, digit1
7:  ;output: AX = sum
8:              PUSH    BP              ;save BP
9:              MOV     BP,SP           ;BP pts to stack top
10:             MOV     AX,[BP+6]       ;AL has DIGIT1
11:             ADD     AX,[BP+4]       ;AL has SUM
12:             POP     BP              ;restore BP
13:             RET     4               ;restore stack, exit
14: ADDNOS      ENDP
15:             END
```

At line 9, the stack looks like this:

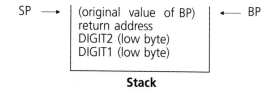

Stack

DIGIT1 and DIGIT2 are in the low bytes of the words on the stack. After adding them, BP is popped and the procedure executes a RET 4, which removes the two data words from the stack.

Summary

- In a .COM format program, stack, data, and code all fit into a single segment. A .COM program takes up much less disk space than a comparable .EXE program, but the fact that code, data, and stack must all fit into a single segment limits its versatility.

- There are two kinds of procedures, NEAR and FAR. A NEAR procedure is in the same code segment as the calling procedure, and a FAR procedure is in a different segment. When a FAR procedure is called, both CS and IP are saved on the stack.

- The EXTRN pseudo-op is used to inform the assembler of the existence of procedures and variables that are defined in another assembly module.

- A procedure must be contained in an assembly module, which consists of at least one segment definition. MASM translates an assembly module into a machine language object (.OBJ) module.

- The PUBLIC pseudo-op is used to inform the assembler that certain names in a module may be referred to in another module.

- The LINK program combines object modules into an executable machine language program. It matches EXTRN declarations in object modules with PUBLIC declarations in other object modules.

- The LIB program can be used to create and maintain a file of object modules.

- The SEGMENT directive may have align, combine, and class types.

- The align type determines how the segment's starting address will be selected when the program is loaded in memory.

- The combine type determines how segments of the same name are to be combined in memory.

- If two or more segments have the same class, they are loaded sequentially in memory.

- Procedures in different modules can communicate through global variables. Other methods are call by value or call by reference; the calling procedure can implement these methods by placing data values and addresses in registers, or pushing them onto the stack.

Glossary

assembly module   An .ASM file consisting of at least one segment definition

call by reference   Communication with a procedure by passing it the addresses of variables containing the data the procedure needs

call by value   Communication with a procedure by passing the procedure the actual data values it needs

.COM program	A program in which the code, data, and stack segments coincide
global variable	A variable that is declared as PUBLIC, so it can be accessed by statements in other program modules
object module	The .OBJ file that MASM creates by assembling an assembly module

New Pseudo-Ops

```
ASSUME          EXTRN           PUBLIC
.CONST          ORG             SEGMENT
.DATA?
```

Exercises

1. Suppose a program contains the lines

   ```
   CALL   PROC1
   MOV    AX,BX
   ```

   and (a) instruction MOV AX,BX is stored at 08FD:0200h, (b) PROC1 is a FAR procedure that begins at 1000:0200h, and (c) SP = 010Ah.

   What are the contents of CS, IP, and SP just after CALL PROC1 is executed? What word is on top of the stack?

2. Suppose SP = 00FAh, CS = 1000h, top of stack = 0200h, next word on the stack = 08FDh. What are the contents of CS, IP and SP after the following happens:

   a. After RET is executed, where RET appears in a NEAR procedure.
   b. After RET is executed, where RET appears in a FAR procedure.
   c. After RET 4 is executed, where RET appears in a NEAR procedure.

Programming Exercises

3. Consider a program that does the following:
   - The main procedure MAIN displays the message "INSIDE MAIN PROGRAM", calls procedure PROC1, and exits to DOS.
   - PROC1 displays the message "INSIDE PROC1" on a new line, calls procedure PROC2, and returns to MAIN.
   - PROC2 displays the message "INSIDE PROC2" on a new line and returns to PROC1.

   Write this program in the following ways:

   a. As a .COM program.
   b. As an .EXE program in which PROC1 and PROC2 are NEAR procedures contained in separately assembled modules. Each procedure's module contains the message that the procedure displays.

c. As an .EXE program in which the PROC1 and PROC2 are FAR procedures contained in separately assembly modules. Each procedure's module contains the message that the procedure displays.

d. As an .EXE program in which the three messages are contained in MAIN's module and declared PUBLIC there. The other procedures are NEAR procedures contained in separately assembled modules. These procedures refer to the appropriate messages via an EXTRN directive.

e. As an .EXE program in which the three messages are contained in MAIN's module. PROC1 and PROC2 are separately assembled NEAR procedures. Before calling PROC1, MAIN places the addresses of the messages "INSIDE PROC1" and "INSIDE PROC2" in SI and DI, respectively.

f. As an .EXE program in which the three messages are contained in MAIN's module. PROC1 and PROC2 are separately assembled NEAR procedures. Before calling PROC1, MAIN pushes the addresses of the messages "INSIDE PROC2" and "INSIDE PROC1" onto the stack.

4. The *position* of a substring within a string is the number of bytes from the beginning of the string to the start of the substring.

Write a separately assembled NEAR procedure FIND_SUBST that receives the offset addresses of the first string in SI and the second string in DI and determines whether the second string is a substring of the first; if so, FIND_SUBST returns its position in AX. If the second string is not a substring of the first string, the procedure returns a negative number in AX.

Write a program to test FIND_SUBST; the testing program reads the strings, calls FIND_SUBST, and displays the result. This problem is a variation of PGM11_5.ASM.

15

BIOS and DOS Interrupts

Overview

In previous chapters, we used the INT (interrupt) instruction to call system routines. In this chapter, we discuss different kinds of interrupts and take a closer look at the operation of the INT instruction. In sections 15.2 and 15.3, we discuss the services provided by various BIOS (basic input/output systems) and DOS interrupt routines.

To demonstrate the use of interrupts, we will write a program that displays the current time on the screen. There are three versions: the first version simply displays the time and then terminates, the second version shows the time updated every second, and the third version is a memory resident program that can be called up when other programs are running.

15.1 Interrupt Service

Hardware Interrupt

The notion of interrupt originally was conceived to allow hardware devices to interrupt the operation of the CPU. For example, whenever a key is pressed, the 8086 must be notified to read a key code into the keyboard buffer. The general **hardware interrupt** goes like this: (1) a hardware that needs service sends an **interrupt request signal** to the processor; (2) the 8086 suspends the current task it is executing and transfers control to an **interrupt routine**; (3) the interrupt routine services the hardware device by performing some I/O operation; and (4) control is transferred back to the original executing task at the point where it was suspended.

Some questions to be answered are how does the 8086 find out a device is signaling? How does it know which interrupt routine to execute? How does it resume the previous task?

Because an interrupt signal may come at any time, the 8086 checks for the signal after executing each instruction. On detecting the interrupt signal, the 8086 acknowledges it by sending an **interrupt acknowledge signal**. The interrupting device responds by sending an eight-bit number on the data bus, called an **interrupt number**. Each device uses a different interrupt number to identify its own service routine. The process of sending control signals back and forth is called **hand-shaking**; it is needed to identify the interrupt device. We say that a type N interrupt occurs when a device uses an interrupt number N to interrupt the 8086.

The transfer to an interrupt routine is similar to a procedure call. Before transferring control to the interrupt routine, the 8086 first saves the address of the next instruction on the stack; this is the return address. The 8086 also saves the FLAGS register on the stack; this ensures that the status of the suspended task will be restored. It is the responsibility of the interrupt routine to restore any registers it uses.

Before we talk about how the 8086 uses the interrupt number to locate the interrupt routine, let's look at the other kinds of interrupts.

Software Interrupt

Software interrupts are used by programs to request system services. A **software interrupt** occurs when a program calls an interrupt routine using the INT instruction. The format of the INT instruction is

```
INT interrupt-number
```

The 8086 treats this interrupt number in the same way as the interrupt number generated by a hardware device. We have already given a number of examples of doing I/O with INT 21h.

Processor Exception

There is a third kind of interrupt, called a **processor exception**. A processor exception occurs when a condition arises inside the processor, such as divide overflow, that requires special handling. Each condition corresponds to a unique interrupt type. For example, divide overflow is type 0, so when overflow occurs in a divide instruction the 8086 automatically executes interrupt 0 to handle the overflow condition.

Next we take on the address calculation for interrupt routines.

15.1.1 Interrupt Vector

The interrupt numbers for the 8086 processor are unsigned byte values. Thus, it is possible to specify a total of 256 types of interrupts. Not every interrupt number has a corresponding interrupt routine. The computer manufacturer provides some hardware device service routines in ROM; these are the BIOS interrupt routines. The high-level system interrupt routines, like INT 21h, are part of DOS and are loaded into memory when the machine is started. Some additional interrupt numbers are reserved by IBM for future use; the remaining numbers are available for the user. See Table 15.1.

The 8086 does not generate the interrupt routine's address directly from the interrupt number. Doing so would mean that a particular interrupt routine must be placed in exactly the same location in every computer—an impossible

Table 15.1 Interrupt Types

Interrupt Types 0–1Fh:	BIOS Interrupts
Interrupt Types 20h–3Fh:	DOS Interrupts
Interrupt Types 40h–7Fh:	reserved
Interrupt Types 80h–F0h:	ROM BASIC
Interrupt Types F1h–FFh:	not used

task, given the number of computer models and updated versions of the routines. Instead, the 8086 uses the interrupt number to calculate the address of a memory location that contains the actual address of the interrupt routine. This means that the routine may appear anywhere, so long as its address, called an **interrupt vector**, is stored in a predefined memory location.

All interrupt vectors are placed in an **interrupt vector table**, which occupies the first 1 KB of memory. Each interrupt vector is given as segment:offset and occupies four bytes; the first four bytes of memory contain interrupt vector 0. See Figure 15.1.

To find the vector for an interrupt routine, we simply multiply the interrupt number by 4. This gives the memory location containing the offset of the routine; the segment address of the routine is in the next word. For example, take interrupt 9, the keyboard interrupt routine: the offset address is stored in location $9 \times 4 = 36 = 00024h$, and the segment address is found in location $24h + 2 = 00026h$. BIOS initializes its interrupt vectors when the computer is turned on, and the DOS interrupt vectors are initialized when DOS is loaded.

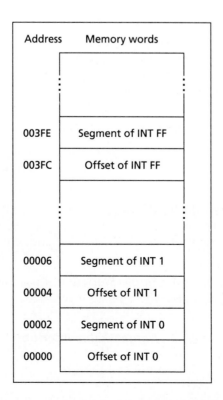

Figure 15.1 Interrupt Vector Table

15.1.2
Interrupt Routines

Let's see how the 8086 executes an INT instruction. First, it saves the flags by pushing the contents of the FLAGS register onto the stack. Then it clears the control flags IF (interrupt flag) and TF (trap flag); the reason for this action is explained later. Next it saves the current address by pushing CS and IP on the stack. Finally, it uses the interrupt number to get the interrupt vector from memory and transfers control to the interrupt routine by loading CS:IP with the interrupt vector. The 8086 transfers to a hardware interrupt routine or processor exception routine in a similar fashion.

On completion, an interrupt routine executes an **IRET** (interrupt return) instruction that restores the IP, CS, and FLAGS registers.

The Control Flags IF and TF

The control flags IF and TF play an important role in the interrupt process. When TF is set, the 8086 generates a processor exception, interrupt type 1. This interrupt is used by DEBUG in executing the T (trace) command. To trace an instruction, DEBUG first sets the TF, and then transfers control to the instruction to be traced. After the instruction is executed, the processor generates an interrupt type 1 because TF is set. DEBUG uses its own interrupt 1 routine to gain control of the processor.

The IF is used to control hardware interrupts. When IF is set, hardware devices may interrupt the 8086. External interrupts may be disabled (masked out) by clearing IF. Actually, there is a hardware interrupt, called **NMI (nonmaskable interrupt)** that cannot be masked out.

Both TF and IF are cleared by the processor before transferring to an interrupt routine so that the routine will not be interrupted. Of course, an interrupt routine can change the flags to enable interrupts to occur during its execution.

15.2
BIOS Interrupts

As indicated in Table 15.1, interrupt types 0 to 1Fh are known as BIOS interrupts. This is because most of these service routines are BIOS routines residing in the ROM segment F000h.

Interrupt Types 0–7

Interrupt types 0–7 are reserved by Intel, with types 0–4 being predefined. IBM uses type 5 for print screen. Types 6 and 7 are not used.

Interrupt 0—Divide Overflow A type 0 interrupt is generated when a DIV or IDIV operation produces an overflow. The interrupt 0 routine displays the message "DIVIDE OVERFLOW" and returns control to DOS.

Interrupt 1—Single Step As discussed in the last section, a type 1 interrupt is generated when the TF is set.

Interrupt 2—Nonmaskable Interrupt Interrupt 2 is the hardware interrupt that cannot be masked out by clearing the IF. The IBM PC uses this interrupt to signal memory and I/O parity errors that indicate bad chips.

Interrupt 3—Breakpoint The INT 3 instruction is the only single-byte interrupt instruction (opcode CCh); other interrupt instructions are two-byte instructions. It is possible to insert an INT 3 instruction anywhere in a program by replacing an existing opcode. The DEBUG program uses this feature to set up breakpoints for the G (go) command.

Interrupt 4—Overflow A type 4 interrupt is generated by the instruction INTO (interrupt if overflow) when OF is set. Programmers may write their own interrupt routine to handle unexpected overflows.

Interrupt 5—Print Screen The BIOS interrupt 5 routine sends the video screen information to the printer. An INT 5 instruction is generated by the keyboard interrupt routine (interrupt type 9) when the PrtSc (print screen) key is pressed.

Interrupt Types 8h—Fh

The 8086 has only one terminal for hardware interrupt signals. To allow more devices to interrupt the 8086, IBM uses an interrupt controller, the Intel 8259 chip, which can interface up to eight devices. Interrupt types 8–Fh are generated by hardware devices connected to the 8259. The original version of the PC uses only interrupts 8, 9, and Eh.

Interrupt 8—Timer The IBM PC contains a timer circuit that generates an interrupt once every 54.92 milliseconds (about 18.2 times per second). The BIOS interrupt 8 routine services the timer circuit. It uses the timer signals (ticks) to keep track of the time of day.

Interrupt 9—Keyboard This interrupt (9) is generated by the keyboard each time a key is pressed or released. The BIOS interrupt 9 routine reads a scan code and stores it in the keyboard buffer.

Interrupt E—Diskette Error The BIOS interrupt Eh routine handles diskette errors.

Interrupt Types 10h—1Fh

The interrupt routines 10h—1Fh can be called by application programs to perform various I/O operations and status checking.

Interrupt 10h—Video The BIOS interrupt 10h routine is the video driver. Details are covered in Chapters 12 and 16.

Interrupt 11h—Equipment Check The BIOS interrupt 11h routine returns the equipment configuration of the particular PC. The return code is placed in AX. Table 15.2 gives the interpretation of the bits returned in AX.

Interrupt 12h—Memory Size The BIOS interrupt 12h routine returns in AX the amount of **conventional memory** a computer has. Conventional memory refers to memory circuits with addresses below 640 K. The unit for the return value is in kilobytes.

Table 15.2 Equipment Check

Bits	Description
15–14	number of printers installed
13	= 1 if internal modem installed
12	= 1 if game adapter installed
11–9	number of RS-232 (serial) ports installed
8	not used
7–6	number of floppy disk drives (if bit 0 = 1)
	00 means 1
	01 means 2
	10 means 3
	11 means 4
5–4	initial video mode
	00 not used
	01 means 40 × 25 color text
	10 means 80 × 25 color text
	11 means 80 × 25 monochrome
3–2	system board RAM size (for original PC)
	00 = means 16 KB
	01 = means 32 KB
	10 = means 48 KB
	11 = means 64 KB
1	= 1 if math coprocessor installed
0	= 1 if floppy disk drive installed

Example 15.1 Suppose a computer has 512 KB conventional memory. What will be returned in AX if the instruction INT 12H is executed?

Solution: 512 = 200h, hence AX = 0200h.

Interrupt 13h—Disk I/O The BIOS interrupt 13h routine is the disk driver, it allows application programs to do disk I/O.

Interrupt 14h—Communications The BIOS interrupt 14h routine is the communications driver that interacts with the serial ports.

Interrupt 15h—Cassette This interrupt was used by the original PC for cassette interface and by the PC AT and PS/2 models for various system services.

Interrupt 16h—Keyboard I/O The BIOS interrupt 16h routine is the keyboard driver. Keyboard operations are found in Chapter 12.

Interrupt 17h—Printer I/O The BIOS interrupt 17h routine is the printer driver. The routine supports three functions: 0–2. Function 0 writes a character to the printer; input values are AH = 0, AL = character, DX = printer number. Function 1 initializes a printer port; input values are AH = 1, DX =

Table 15.3 Printer Status

Bits in AH	Meaning
7	= 1 printer not busy
6	= 1 print acknowledge
5	= 1 out of paper
4	= 1 printer selected
3	= 1 I/O error
2	not used
1	not used
0	= 1 printer timed-out

printer number. Function 2 gets printer status, input values are AH = 2, DX = printer number. For all functions, the status is returned in AH. Table 15.3 shows the meaning of the bits returned in AH.

Example 15.2 Write instructions to print a 0.

Solution: We use function 0 to do the printing. Because printers contain buffers for data, the 0 will not be printed until a carriage return or line feed character is sent. Thus,

```
MOV  AH,0         ;function 0, print char
MOV  AL,'0'       ;char 0
MOV  DX,0         ;printer 0
INT  17H          ;AH contains return code
MOV  AH,0         ;function 0, print char
MOV  AL,0AH       ;line feed
INT  17H
```

Interrupt 18h—BASIC The BIOS interrupt 18h routine transfers control to ROM BASIC.

Interrupt 19h—Bootstrap The BIOS interrupt 19h routine reboots the system.

Interrupt 1Ah—Time of Day The BIOS interrupt 1Ah routine allows a program to get and set the timer tick count, and in the case of PC AT and PS/2 models, it allows programs to get and set the time and date for the clock circuit chip.

Interrupt 1Bh—Ctrl-Break This interrupt is called by the INT 9 routine when the Ctrl-break key is pressed. The BIOS interrupt 1Bh routine contains only an IRET instruction. Users may write their own routine to handle the Ctrl-break key.

Interrupt 1Ch—Timer Tick INT 1Ch is called by the INT 8 routine each time the timer circuit interrupts. The BIOS interrupt 1Ch routine contains only an IRET instruction. Users may write their own service routine to perform timing operations. In section 15.5, we use it to update the displayed time.

Interrupts 1Dh—1Fh These interrupt vectors point to data instead of instructions. The interrupt 1Dh, 1Eh, and 1Fh vectors pointing to video initialization parameters, diskette parameters, and video graphics characters, respectively.

15.3 DOS Interrupts

The interrupt types 20h–3Fh are serviced by DOS routines that provide high-level service to hardware as well as system resources such as files and directories. The most useful is INT 21h, which provides many functions for doing keyboard, video, and file operations.

Interrupt 20h—Program Terminate Interrupt 20h can be used by a program to return control to DOS. But because CS must be set to the program segment prefix before using INT 20h, it is more convenient to exit a program with INT 21h, function 4Ch.

Interrupt 21h—Function Request The number of functions varies with the DOS version. DOS 1.x has functions 0–2Eh, DOS 2.x added new functions 2Fh–57h, and DOS 3.x added new functions 58h–5Fh. These functions may be classified as character I/O, file access, memory management, disk access, networking, and miscellaneous. More information is found in Appendix C.

Interrupts 22h—26h Interrupt routines 22h–26h handle Ctrl-Break, critical errors, and direct disk access.

Interrupt 27h—Terminate but Stay Resident Interrupt 27h allows programs to stay in memory after termination. We demonstrate this interrupt in section 15.6.

15.4 A Time Display Program

As an example of using interrupt routines, we now write a program that displays the current time. There are three versions, each getting more complex. In this section, we show the first version, which simply displays the current time in hours, minutes, and seconds. In section 15.5, we write the second version, which shows the time updated every second; and in section 15.6 we write the third version, which is a *memory resident program* that can display the time while other programs are running.

When the computer is powered up, the current time can be entered by the user or supplied by a real-time clock circuit that is battery powered. This time value is kept in memory and updated by a timer circuit using interrupt 8. A program can call the DOS interrupt 21h, function 2Ch, to access the time.

> **INT 21h, Function 2Ch:**
> **Time-of-Day**
>
> Input: AH = 2Ch
> Output: CH = hours (0-23),
>   CL = minutes (0-59),
>   DH = seconds (0-59),
>   DL = 1/100 seconds (0-99).

Our time display program has the following steps: (1) obtain the current time, (2) convert the hours, minutes, and seconds into ASCII digits, we ignore the fractions of a second, and (3) display the ASCII digits.

The program is organized into a MAIN procedure in program listing PGM15_1.ASM and two procedures GET_TIME and CONVERT in program listing PGM15_1A.ASM.

A time buffer, TIME_BUF, is initialized with the message of 00:00:00. The procedure MAIN first calls GET_TIME to store the current time in the time buffer. Then it uses INT 21h, function 9, to print out the string in the time buffer.

The procedure GET_TIME calls INT 21h function 2Ch to get the time, then calls CONVERT to convert the hours, minutes, and seconds into ASCII characters. The first step in procedure CONVERT is to divide the input number in AL by 10; this will put the ten's digit value in AL and unit's digit value in AH (note that the input value is less than 60). The second step is to convert the digits into ASCII.

Program Listing PGM15_1.ASM

```
TITLE PGM15_1: TIME_DISPLAY_VER_1
;program that displays the current time
;
        EXTRN   GET_TIME:NEAR
.MODEL  SMALL
.STACK  100H
.DATA
TIME_BUF    DB     '00:00:00$';time buffer hr:min:sec
;
.CODE
MAIN    PROC
        MOV     AX,@DATA
        MOV     DS,AX          ;initialize DS
;get and display time
        LEA     BX,TIME_BUF    ;BX points to TIME_BUF
        CALL    GET_TIME       ;put current time in TIME_BUF
        LEA     DX,TIME_BUF    ;DX points to TIME_BUF
        MOV     AH,09H         ;display time
        INT     21H
;exit
        MOV     AH,4CH         ;return
        INT     21H            ;to DOS
MAIN    ENDP
        END     MAIN
```

Program Listing PGM15_1A.ASM

```
TITLE PGM15_1A: GET AND CONVERT TIME TO ASCII
PUBLIC    GET_TIME
.MODEL    SMALL
.CODE
GET_TIME    PROC
;get time of day and store ASCII digits in time buffer
;input:   BX = address of time buffer
          MOV    AH,2CH        ;gettime
          INT    21H           ;CH = hr, CL = min, DH = sec
;convert hours into ASCII and store
          MOV    AL,CH         ;hour
          CALL   CONVERT       ;convert to ASCII
          MOV    [BX],AX       ;store
;convert minutes into ASCII and store
          MOV    AL,CL         ;minute
          CALL   CONVERT       ;convert to ASCII
          MOV    [BX+3],AX     ;store
;convert seconds into ASCII and store
          MOV    AL,DH         ;second
          CALL   CONVERT
          MOV    [BX+6],AX
          RET
GET_TIME    ENDP
;
CONVERT     PROC
;converts byte number (0-59) into ASCII digits
;input: AL = number
;output:AX = ASCII digits, AL = high digit,AH = low digit
          MOV    AH,0          ;clear AH
          MOV    DL,10         ;divide AX by 10
          DIV    DL            ;AH has remainder, AL has quotient
          OR     AX,3030H      ;convert to ASCII, AH has low digit
          RET                  ;AL has high digit
CONVERT     ENDP
;
          END
```

The program displays the time and terminates.

15.5 User Interrupt Procedures

To make the time display program more interesting, let us write a second version that displays the time and updates it every second.

One way to continuously update the time is to execute a loop that keeps obtaining the time via INT 21h, function 2Ch and displaying it. The problem here is to find a way to terminate the program.

Instead of pursuing this approach, we will write a routine for interrupt 1Ch. As mentioned earlier, this interrupt is generated by the INT 8 routine which is activated by a timer circuit about 18.2 times a second. When our interrupt routine is called, it will get the time and display it.

Our program will have a MAIN procedure that sets up the interrupt routine and when a key is pressed, it will deactivate the interrupt routine and terminate.

Set Interrupt Vector

To set up an interrupt routine, we need to (1) save the current interrupt vector, (2) place the vector of the user procedure in the interrupt vector table, and (3) restore the previous vector before terminating the program.

We use the INT 21h, function 35h, to get the old vector and function 25h to set up the new interrupt vector.

INT 21h, Function 25h:
Set Interrupt Vector

;store interrupt vector into vector table
Input: AH = 25h
           AL = Interrupt number
           DS:DX = interrupt vector
Output: none

INT 21h, Function 35h:
Get Interrupt Vector

;obtain interrupt vector from vector table
Input: AH = 35h
           AL = Interrupt number
Output: ES:BX = interrupt vector

The procedure SETUP_INT in program listing PGM15_2A.ASM saves an old interrupt vector and sets up a new vector. It gets the interrupt number in AL, a buffer to save the old vector at DS:DI, and a buffer containing the new interrupt vector at DS:SI. By reversing the two buffers, SETUP_INT can also be used to restore the old vector.

Program Listing PGM15_2A.ASM

```
TITLE PGM15_2A: SET INTERRUPT VECTOR
PUBLIC SETUP_INT
.MODEL SMALL
.CODE
SETUP_INT   PROC
;saves old vector and sets up new vector
;input: AL = interrupt number
;       DI = address of buffer for old vector
;       SI = address of buffer containing new vector
;save old interrupt vector
        MOV     AH,35H      ;function 35h, get vector
        INT     21H         ;ES:BX = vector
        MOV     [DI],BX     ;save offset
        MOV     [DI+2],ES   ;save segment
```

```
            ;setup new vector
                    MOV     DX,[SI]         ;DX has offset
                    PUSH    DS              ;save DS
                    MOV     DS,[SI+2]       ;DS has segment number
                    MOV     AH,25H          ;function 25h, set vector
                    INT     21H             ;
                    POP     DS              ;restore DS
                    RET
SETUP_INT           ENDP
            END
```

Cursor Control

Each display of the current time by INT 21h, function 9, will advance the cursor. If a new time is then displayed, it appears at a different screen position. So, to view the time updated at the same screen position we must restore the cursor to its original position before we display the time. This is achieved by first determining the current cursor position; then, after each print string operation, we move the cursor back.

We use the INT 10h, functions 3 and 2, to save the original cursor position and to move the cursor to its original position after each print string operation.

INT 10h, Function 2:
Move Cursor

Input: AH = 2
         BH = page number
         DH = row number
         DL = column number
Output: none

INT 10h, Function 3:
Get Cursor Position

Input: AH = 3
         BH = page number
Output: DH = row number
         DL = column number
         CH = starting scan line for cursor
         CL = ending scan line for cursor

Interrupt Procedure

When an interrupt procedure is activated, it cannot assume that the DS register contains the program's data segment address. Thus, if it uses any variables it must first reset the DS register. The DS register should be restored before ending the interrupt routine with IRET.

Program listing PGM15_2.ASM contains the MAIN procedure and the interrupt procedure TIME_INT. The steps in the MAIN procedure are (1) save the current cursor position, (2) set up the interrupt vector for TIME_INT, (3) wait for a key input, and (4) restore the old interrupt vector and terminate.

To do step 2, we use the pseudo-ops **OFFSET** and **SEG** to obtain the offset and segment of procedure TIME_INT; the vector is then stored in the buffer NEW_VEC. The procedure SETUP_INT, is called to set up the vector for interrupt type 1Ch, timer tick. The interrupt 16h, function 0 is used for step 3, key input. Procedure SETUP_INT is again used in step 4; this time SI points to the old vector and DI points to the vector for TIME_INT.

The steps in the procedure TIME_INT are (1) set DS, (2) get new time, (3) display time, (4) restore cursor position, and (5) restore DS.

The program operates like this: After setting up the cursor and interrupt vectors, the MAIN procedure just waits for a keystroke. In the meantime, the interrupt procedure, TIME_INT, keeps updating the time whenever the timer circuit ticks. After a key is hit, the old interrupt vector is restored and the program terminates.

Program Listing PGM15_2.ASM

```
TITLE PGM15_2: DISPLAY_TIME_VER_2
;program that displays the current time
;and updates the time 18.2 times a second
        EXTRN   GET_TIME:NEAR,SETUP_INT:NEAR
.MODEL SMALL
.STACK 100H
.DATA
TIME_BUF    DB   '00:00:00$'      ;time buffer hr:min:sec
CURSOR_POS  DW   ?                ;cursor position (row:col)
NEW_VEC     DW   ?,?              ;new interrupt vector
OLD_VEC     DW   ?,?              ;old interrupt vector
;
.CODE
MAIN    PROC
        MOV     AX,@DATA
        MOV     DS,AX            ;initialize DS
;
;save cursor position
        MOV     AH,3             ;function 3, get cursor
        MOV     BH,0             ;page 0
        INT     10H              ;DH = row, DL = col
        MOV     CURSOR_POS,DX    ;save it
;set up interrupt procedure by
;placing segment:offset of TIME_INT in NEW_VEC
        MOV     NEW_VEC,OFFSET TIME_INT    ;offset
        MOV     NEW_VEC+2,SEG TIME_INT     ;segment
        LEA     DI,OLD_VEC       ;DI points to vector buffer
        LEA     SI,NEW_VEC       ;SI points to new vector
        MOV     AL,1CH           ;timer interrupt
        CALL    SETUP_INT        ;setup new interrupt vector
;read keyboard
        MOV     AH,0
        INT     16H
;restore old interrupt vector
        LEA     DI,NEW_VEC       ;DI points to vector buffer
        LEA     SI,OLD_VEC       ;SI points to old vector
```

```
              MOV     AL,1CH              ;timer interrupt
              CALL    SETUP_INT           ;restore old vector
      ;
              MOV     AH,4CH              ;return
              INT     21H                 ;to DOS
      MAIN    ENDP
      ;
      TIME_INT        PROC
      ;interrupt procedure
      ;activated by the timer
              PUSH    DS                  ;save current DS
              MOV     AX,@DATA            ;set it to data segment
              MOV     DS,AX
      ;get new time
              LEA     BX,TIME_BUF         ;BX points to time buffer
              CALL    GET_TIME            ;store time in buffer
      ;display time
              LEA     DX,TIME_BUF         ;DX points to TIME_BUF
              MOV     AH,09H               ;display string
              INT     21H
      ;restore cursor position
              MOV     AH,2                ;function 2, move cursor
              MOV     BH,0                ;page 0
              MOV     DX,CURSOR_POS       ;cursor position,DH=row,DL=col
              INT     10H                 ;
              POP     DS                  ;restore DS
              IRET
      TIME_INT        ENDP                ;end of interrupt procedure
      ;
              END     MAIN
```

The LINK command should include the modules PGM15_2, PGM15_1A, and PGM15_2A.

15.6 Memory Resident Program

We will write the third version of DISPLAY_TIME as a **TSR (terminate and stay resident) program**. Normally, when a program terminates, the memory occupied by the program is used by DOS to load other programs. However, when a TSR program terminates, the memory occupied is not released. Thus, a TSR program is also called a **memory resident program**.

To return to DOS, a TSR program is terminated by using either INT 27h or INT 21h, function 31h. Our program uses INT 27h.

INT 27h:
Terminate and Stay Resident

Input: DS:DX = address of byte beyond the part that is
                to remain resident
Output: none

We write our program as a .COM program because to use interrupt 27h, we need to determine how many bytes are to remain memory resident. The structure of a .COM program makes this easy because there is only one program segment. Another reason for using a .COM program is the size consideration. As we saw in Chapter 14, a .COM program is smaller in size than its .EXE counterpart. So, to save space, TSR programs are often written as .COM programs.

Once terminated, a TSR program is not active. It must be activated by some external activity, such as a certain key combination or by the timer. The advantage of a TSR program is that it may be activated while some other program is running. Our program will become active when the Ctrl and right shift keys are pressed.

To keep the program small, it will not update the time. We leave it as an exercise for the reader to write a TSR program that updates the time every second.

The program has two parts, an initialization part that sets up the interrupt vector, and the interrupt routine itself. The procedure INITIALIZE initializes the interrupt vector 9 (keyboard interrupt) with the address of the interrupt procedure MAIN and then calls INT 27h to terminate. The address passed to INT 27h is the beginning address of the INITIALIZE procedure; this is possible because the instructions are no longer needed. The procedure INITIALIZE is shown in program listing PGM15_3A.ASM.

Program Listing PGM15_3A.ASM

```
        TITLE   PGM15_3A:SET UP TSR PROGRAM
        EXTRN   MAIN:NEAR,SETUP_INT:NEAR
        EXTRN   NEW_VEC:WORD,OLD_VEC:DWORD
PUBLIC INITIALIZE
C_SEG   SEGMENT                 PUBLIC
        ASSUME CS:C_SEG
INITIALIZE      PROC
;set up interrupt vector
        MOV     NEW_VEC,OFFSET MAIN     ;store address
        MOV     NEW_VEC+2,CS            ;segment
        LEA     DI,OLD_VEC              ;DI points to vector buffer
        LEA     SI,NEW_VEC              ;SI points to new vector
        MOV     AL,09H                  ;keyboard interrupt
        CALL    SETUP_INT               ;set interrupt vector
;exit to DOS
        LEA     DX,INITIALIZE
        INT     27H                     ;terminate and stay resident
INITIALIZE      ENDP
C_SEG   ENDS
        END
```

There are a number of ways for the interrupt routine to detect a particular key combination. The simplest way is to detect the control and shift keys by checking the keyboard flags. When activated by a keystroke, the interrupt routine calls the old keyboard interrupt routine to handle the key input. To detect the control and shift keys, a program can examine the keyboard flags at the BIOS data area 0000:0417h or use INT 16h, function 2.

15.6 Memory Resident Program

> **INT 16h, Function 2:**
> **Get Keyboard Flags**
>
> Input: AH = 2
> Output: AL = key flags
> bit   *meaning*
> 7 = 1   insert on
> 6 = 1   Caps Lock on
> 5 = 1   Num Lock on
> 4 = 1   Scroll Lock on
> 3 = 1   Alt key down
> 2 = 1   Ctrl key down
> 1 = 1   left shift key down
> 0 = 1   right shift key down

We will use the Ctrl and right shift key combination to activate and deactivate the clock display. When activated, the current time will be displayed on the upper right-hand corner. We must first save the screen data so that when the clock display is deactivated the screen can be restored.

The procedure SET_CURSOR sets the cursor at row 0 and the column given in DL. The procedure SAVE_SCREEN copies the screen data into a buffer called SS_BUF, and the procedure RESTORE_SCREEN moves the data back to the screen buffer. All three procedures are shown in program listing PGM15_3B.

Program Listing PGM15_3B.ASM

```
TITLE PGM15_3B: SAVE SCREEN AND CURSOR
      EXTRN SS_BUF:BYTE
      PUBLIC SAVE_SCREEN,RESTORE_SCREEN,SET_CURSOR
C_SEG SEGMENT              PUBLIC
      ASSUME CS:C_SEG
;
SAVE_SCREEN  PROC
;saves 8 characters from upper right hand corner of
;screen
      LEA    DI,SS_BUF     ;screen buffer
      MOV    CX,8          ;repeat 8 times
      MOV    DL,72         ;column 72
      CLD                  ;clear DF for string operation
SS_LOOP:
      CALL   SET_CURSOR    ;setup cursor at row 0,col DL
      MOV    AH,08H        ;read char on screen
      INT    10H           ;AH = attribute, AL = character
      STOSW                ;stores char and attribute
      INC    DL            ;next col
      LOOP   SS_LOOP
      RET
SAVE_SCREEN  ENDP
;
RESTORE_SCREEN             PROC
;restores saved screen
      LEA    SI,SS_BUF     ;SI points to buffer
      MOV    DI,8          ;repeat 8 times
      MOV    DL,72         ;column 72
```

```
            MOV     CX,1            ;1 char at a time
RS_LOOP:
            CALL    SET_CURSOR      ;move cursor
            LODSW                   ;AL = char, AH = attribute
            MOV     BL,AH           ;attribute to BL
            MOV     AH,09H          ;function 9, write char and attribute
            MOV     BH,0            ;page 0
            INT     10H
            INC     DL              ;next char position
            DEC     DI              ;move characters?
            JG      RS_LOOP         ;yes, repeat
            RET
RESTORE_SCREEN          ENDP
;
SET_CURSOR  PROC
;sets cursor at row 0, column DL
;input DL = column number
            MOV     AH,02           ;function 2, set cursor
            MOV     BH,0            ;page 0
            MOV     DH,0            ;row 0
            INT     10H
            RET
SET_CURSOR      ENDP
;
C_SEG ENDS
        END
```

We are now ready to write the interrupt routine. To determine whether to activate or deactivate the time display, we use the variable ON_FLAG, which is set to 1 when the time is being displayed. Procedure MAIN is the interrupt procedure.

The steps in procedure MAIN are (1) save all registers used and set up the DS and ES registers, (2) call the old keyboard interrupt routine to handle the key input, (3) check to see if both Ctrl and right shift keys are down; if not, then exit, (4) test ON_FLAG to determine status, and if ON_FLAG is 1 then restore screen and exit, (5) save current cursor position and also the display screen info, and (6) get time, display time, then exit.

In step 1, to set up the registers DS and ES we use CS. It might be tempting to use the value C_SEG instead; however, segment values cannot be used in a .COM program. In step 2, we need to push the FLAGS register so that the procedure call simulates an interrupt call. In step 6, we used the BIOS interrupt 10h instead of the DOS interrupt 21h, function 9, to display the time, because from experience, the INT 21h, function 9, tends to be unreliable in a TSR program.

Program Listing PGM15_3.ASM

```
TITLE PGM15_3: TIME_DISPLAY_VER_3
;memory resident program that shows current time of day
;called by Ctrl-rt shift key combination
;
        EXTRN   INITIALIZE:NEAR,SAVE_SCREEN:NEAR
        EXTRN   RESTORE_SCREEN:NEAR,SET_CURSOR:NEAR
        EXTRN   GET_TIME:NEAR
```

15.6 Memory Resident Program

```
                PUBLIC  MAIN
                PUBLIC  NEW_VEC,OLD_VEC,SS_BUF
C_SEG   SEGMENT                 PUBLIC
        ASSUME  CS:C_SEG, DS:C_SEG, SS:C_SEG
        ORG     100H
START:  JMP     INITIALIZE
;
SS_BUF          DB      16  DUP(?)     ;save screen buffer
TIME_BUF        DB      '00:00:00$'    ;time buffer hr:min:sec
CURSOR_POS      DW      ?              ;cursor position
ON_FLAG         DB      0              ;1 = interrupt procedure running
NEW_VEC         DW      ?,?            ;contains new vector
OLD_VEC         DD      ?              ;contains old vector
;
MAIN    PROC
;interrupt procedure
;save registers
        PUSH    DS
        PUSH    ES
        PUSH    AX
        PUSH    BX
        PUSH    CX
        PUSH    DX
        PUSH    SI
        PUSH    DI
;
        MOV     AX,CS           ;set DS
        MOV     DS,AX
        MOV     ES,AX           ;and ES to current segment
;call old keyboard interrupt procedure
        PUSHF                   ;save FLAGS
        CALL    OLD_VEC
;get keyboard flags
        MOV     AX,CS           ;reset DS
        MOV     DS,AX
        MOV     ES,AX           ;and ES to current segment
        MOV     AH,02           ;function 2, keyboard flags
        INT     16H             ;AL has flag bits
        TEST    AL,1            ;right shift?
        JE      I_DONE          ;no, exit
        TEST    AL,100B         ;Ctrl?
        JE      I_DONE          ;no, exit
;yes, process
        CMP     ON_FLAG,1       ;procedure active?
        JE      RESTORE         ;yes, deactivate
        MOV     ON_FLAG,1       ;no, activate
;—save cursor position and screen info
        MOV     AH,03           ;get cursor position
        MOV     BH,0            ;page 0
        INT     10H             ;DH = row, DL = col
        MOV     CURSOR_POS,DX   ;save it
        CALL    SAVE_SCREEN     ;save time display screen
;—position cursor to upper right corner
        MOV     DL,72           ;column 72
        CALL    SET_CURSOR      ;position cursor in row 0,col 72
```

```
                LEA     BX,TIME_BUF
                CALL    GET_TIME            ;get current time
        ;--display time
                LEA     SI,TIME_BUF
                MOV     CX,8                ;8 chars
                MOV     BH,0                ;page 0
        M1:     MOV     AH,0EH              ;write char
                LODSB                       ;char in AL
                INT     10H                 ;cursor is moved to next col
                LOOP    M1                  ;loop back if more chars
                JMP     RES_CURSOR          ;
        RESTORE:
        ;restore screen
                MOV     ON_FLAG,0           ;clears flag
                CALL    RESTORE_SCREEN
        ;restore saved cursor position
        RES_CURSOR:
                MOV     AH,02               ;set cursor
                MOV     BH,0
                MOV     DX,CURSOR_POS
                INT     10H
        ;restore registers
        I_DONE:
                POP     DI
                POP     SI
                POP     DX
                POP     CX
                POP     BX
                POP     AX
                POP     ES
                POP     DS
                IRET                        ;interrupt return
        MAIN    ENDP
        ;
        C_SEG   ENDS
                END     START               ;starting instruction
```

Because the program has been written as a .COM program, we need to rewrite the file containing the GET_TIME procedure with full segment directives. The file PGM15_3C.ASM contains GET_TIME, CONVERT, and SETUP_INT.

Program Listing PGM15_3C.ASM

```
TITLE   PGM15_3C: GET AND CONVERT TIME TO ASCII
        PUBLIC  GET_TIME,SETUP_INT
C_SEG   SEGMENT                 PUBLIC
        ASSUME  CS:C_SEG
;
GET_TIME        PROC
;get time of day and store ASCII digits in time buffer
;input:  BX = address of time buffer
```

```
                MOV     AH,2CH          ;get time
                INT     21H             ;CH = hr, CL =  min, DH = sec
        ;convert hours into ASCII and store
                MOV     AL,CH           ;hour
                CALL    CONVERT         ;convert to ASCII
                MOV     [BX],AX         ;store
        ;convert minutes into ASCII and store
                MOV     AL,CL           ;minute
                CALL    CONVERT         ;convert to ASCII
                MOV     [BX+3],AX       ;store
        ;convert seconds into ASCII and store
                MOV     AL,DH           ;second
                CALL    CONVERT         ;convert to ASCII
                MOV     [BX+6],AX       ;store
                RET
        GET_TIME        ENDP
        ;
        CONVERT         PROC
        ;converts byte number (0-59) into ASCII digits
        ;input: AL = number
        ;output: AX = ASCII digits, AL = high digit, AH = low
        ;digit
                MOV     AH,0            ;clear AH
                MOV     DL,10           ;divide AX by 10
                DIV     DL              ;AH has remainder, AL has quotient
                OR      AX,3030H        ;convert to ASCII, AH has low digit
                RET                     ;AL has high digit
        CONVERT         ENDP
        ;
        SETUP_INT       PROC
        ;input:  AL = interrupt type
        ;        DI = address of buffer for old vector
        ;        SI = address of buffer containing new vector
        ;save old interrupt vector
                MOV     AH,35H          ;function 35h, get vector
                INT     21H             ;ES:BX = vector
                MOV     [DI],BX         ;save offset
                MOV     [DI+2],ES       ;save segment
        ;setup new vector
                MOV     DX,[SI]         ;DX has offset
                PUSH    DS              ;save it
                MOV     DS,[SI+2]       ;DS has segment number
                MOV     AH,25H          ;function 25h, set vector
                INT     21H             ;
                POP     DS              ;restore DS
                RET
        SETUP_INT       ENDP
        ;
        C_SEG ENDS
                END
```

The LINK command should be LINK PGM15_3 + PGM15_3B + PGM15_3C + PGM15_3A. Notice that PGM15_3A is linked last so that the procedure INITIALIZE is placed at the end of the program. Writing TSR programs is tricky; if there are other TSR programs on your system, your program may not function properly.

Summary

- An interrupt may be requested by a hardware device or by a program using the INT instruction or generated internally by the processor.
- The INT instruction calls an interrupt routine by using an interrupt number.
- The 8086 supports 256 interrupt types and the interrupt vectors (addresses of the procedures) are stored in the first 1 KB of memory.
- The interrupts 0–1FH call BIOS interrupt routines and the interrupt vectors are set up by BIOS when the computer is powered up.
- The interrupts 20H–3Fh call DOS interrupt routines.
- Users can write their own interrupt routines to perform various tasks.
- A memory resident program may be activated by a combination of keystrokes.

Glossary

conventional memory	The first 640 KB of memory
hand-shaking	A protocol for devices to communicate with each other
hardware interrupt	A hardware device interrupting the processor
interrupt acknowledge signal	A signal generated by the processor accepting an interrupt request signal
interrupt number	A number identifying the type of interrupt
interrupt request signal	A signal sent by a hardware device to the processor requesting service
interrupt routine	A procedure invoked by an interrupt
interrupt vector	The address of an interrupt routine
interrupt vector table	The set of all interrupt vectors
memory resident program	A TSR program
NMI (nonmaskable interrupt)	A hardware interrupt that cannot be masked out by clearing the IF
processor exception	A condition of the processor that requires special handling
TSR (terminate and stay resident) program	A program that remains in memory after termination
software interrupt	An INT instruction

New Instructions

IRET

New Pseudo-Ops

OFFSET   SEG

Exercises

1. Compute the location of the interrupt vector for interrupt 20h.
2. Use DEBUG to find the value of the interrupt vector for interrupt 0.
3. Write instructions that use the BIOS interrupt 17h to print the message "Hello".
4. Write instructions that use the INT 21h, function 2Ah, to display the current date.

Programming Exercises

5. Write a program that will output the message "Hello" once every half second to the screen.
6. Modify PGM15_2.ASM so that INT 21h, function 9, is called to display the time only when the seconds change.
7. Write a memory resident program similar to PGM15_3.ASM using INT 21h, function 31h.

16

Color Graphics

Overview

In Chapter 12, we showed how the screen can be manipulated in text mode. In this chapter, we discuss the graphics modes of the PC. There are three common color graphics adapters for the PC: CGA (Color Graphics Adapter), EGA (Enhanced Graphics Adapter), and VGA (Video Graphics Array). We describe their operations and programming, and also show how to write an interactive video game program.

16.1 Graphics Modes

As noted in Chapter 12, the screen display is composed of lines traced by an electron beam; these lines are called **scan lines**. A dot pattern is created by turning the beam on and off during the scan; the dot patterns generate characters as well as pictures on the screen. The video signal controlling the scan is generated by a video adapter circuit in the computer.

A video adapter can vary the number of dots per line by changing the size of a dot. Some adapters can also change the number of scan lines.

Pixels

In graphics mode operation, the screen display is divided into columns and rows; and each screen position, given by a column number and row number, is called a **pixel** (picture element). The number of columns and rows give the *resolution* of the graphics mode; for example, a resolution of 320 × 200 means 320 columns and 200 rows. The columns are numbered from left to right starting with 0, and the rows are numbered from top to bottom starting with 0. For example, in a 320 × 200 mode, the upper-right corner pixel has column 319 and row 0, and the lower-right corner pixel has column 319 and row 199. See Figure 16.1.

16.1 Graphics Modes

Figure 16.1 Pixel Coordinates in 320 × 200 Mode

Depending on the mapping of rows and columns into the scan lines and dot positions, a pixel may contain one or more dots. For example, in the low-resolution mode of the CGA, there are 160 columns by 100 rows, but the CGA generates 320 dots and 200 lines; so a pixel is formed by a 2 × 2 set of dots. A graphics mode is called **APA (all points addressable)** if it maps a pixel into a single dot.

Table 16.1 shows the APA graphics modes of the CGA, EGA, and VGA. To maintain compatibility, the EGA is designed to display all CGA modes and the VGA can display all the EGA modes.

Mode Selection

The screen mode is normally set to text mode, hence the first operation to begin a graphics display is to set the display mode. We showed in Chapter 12 that the BIOS interrupt 10h handles all video functions; function 0 sets the screen mode.

Table 16.1 Video Adapter Graphics Display Modes

Mode Number (hex)	CGA Graphics
4	320 x 200 4 Color
5	320 x 200 4 Color (color burst off)
6	640 x 200 2 Color
	EGA Graphics
D	320 x 200 16 Color
E	640 x 200 16 Color
F	640 x 350 Monochrome
10	640 x 350 16 Color
	VGA Graphics
11	640 x 480 2 Color
12	640 x 480 16 Color
13	320 x 200 256 Color

> **INT 10h Function 0:**
> **Set Screen Mode**
>
> Input: AH = 0
>   AL = mode number
> Output: none

Example 16.1 Set the display mode to 640 × 200 two-color mode.

Solution: From Table 16.1, the mode number is 06h; thus, the instructions are

```
MOV   AH,0        ;function 0
MOV   AL,06H      ;mode 6
INT   10H         ;select mode
```

16.2 CGA Graphics

The CGA has three graphics resolutions: a *low resolution* of 160 × 100, a *medium resolution* of 320 × 200, and a *high resolution* of 640 × 200. Only the medium-resolution and high-resolution modes are supported by the BIOS INT 10h routine. Programs that use the low-resolution mode must access the video controller chip directly.

The CGA adapter has a display memory of 16 KB located in segment B800h; the memory addresses are from B800:0000 to B800:3FFF. Each pixel is represented by one or more bits, depending on the mode. For example,

Table 16.2 Sixteen Standard CGA Colors

I R G B	Color
0 0 0 0	Black
0 0 0 1	Blue
0 0 1 0	Green
0 0 1 1	Cyan
0 1 0 0	Red
0 1 0 1	Magenta (purple)
0 1 1 0	Brown
0 1 1 1	White
1 0 0 0	Gray
1 0 0 1	Light Blue
1 0 1 0	Light Green
1 0 1 1	Light Cyan
1 1 0 0	Light Red
1 1 0 1	Light Magenta
1 1 1 0	Yellow
1 1 1 1	Intense White

high resolution uses one bit per pixel and medium uses two bits per pixel. The pixel value identifies the color of the pixel.

Medium-Resolution Mode

The CGA can display 16 colors; Table 16.2 shows the 16 colors of the CGA. In medium resolution, four colors can be displayed at one time. This is due to the limited size of the display memory. Because the resolution is 320×200, there are $320 \times 200 = 64{,}000$ pixels. To display four colors, each pixel is coded by two bits, and the memory requirement is $64000 \times 2 = 128000$ bits or 16000 bytes. Thus, the 16-KB CGA display memory can only support four colors in this mode.

To allow different four-color combinations, the CGA in medium-resolution mode uses two **palettes**; a palette is a set of colors that can be displayed at the same time. Each palette contains three fixed colors plus a **background color** that can be chosen from any of the standard 16 colors. The background color is the default color of all pixels. Thus, a screen with the background color would show up if no data have been written. Table 16.3 shows the two palettes.

The default palette is palette 0, but a program can select either palette for display. A pixel value (0–3) identifies the color in the current selected palette; if we change the display palette, all the pixels change color. INT 10h, function 0Bh, can be used to select a palette or a background color.

INT 10h, Function 0Bh:
Select Palette or Background Color

Subfunction 0: Select Background
Input: AH = 0Bh
         BH = 0
         BL = color number (0–15)
Output: none

Subfunction 1: Select Palette
Input: AH = 0Bh
         BH = 1
         BL = palette number (0 or 1)
Output: none

Table 16.3 CGA Mode, Four-Color Palettes

Palette	Pixel Value	Color
0	0	Background
	1	Green
	2	Red
	3	Brown
1	0	Background
	1	Cyan
	2	Magenta
	3	White

Example 16.2 Write instructions that select palette 1 and a background color of light blue.

Solution: Light blue has color number 9. Thus,

```
MOV     AH,0BH          ;function 0Bh
MOV     BH,00H          ;select background color
MOV     BL,9            ;light blue
INT     10H
MOV     BH,1            ;select palette
MOV     BL,1            ;palette 1
INT     10H
```

Reading and Writing Pixels

To read or write a pixel, we must identify the pixel by its column and row numbers. The functions 0Dh and 0Ch are for read and write, respectively.

INT 10h, Function 0Ch:
Write Graphics Pixel

Input: AH = 0Ch
             AL = pixel value
             BH = page (for the CGA, this value is ignored)
             CX = column number
             DX = row number
Output: none

INT 10h, Function 0Dh:
Read Graphics Pixel

Input: AH = 0Dh
             BH = page (for the CGA, this value is ignored)
             CX = column number
             DX = row number
Output: AL = pixel value

Example 16.3 Copy the pixel at column 50, row 199, to the pixel at column 20, and row 40.

Solution: We first read the pixel at column 50, row 199, and then write to the pixel at column 20, row 40.

```
MOV     AH,0DH          ;read pixel
MOV     CX,50           ;column 50
MOV     DX,199          ;row 199
INT     10H             ;AL gets pixel value
MOV     AH,0CH          ;write pixel, AL is already set
MOV     CX,20           ;column 20
MOV     DX,40           ;row 40
INT     10H
```

High-Resolution Mode

In high-resolution mode, the CGA can display two colors, each pixel value is either 0 or 1; 0 for black and 1 for white. It is also possible to select a background color using INT 10h, function 0Bh. When a background color is selected, a 0 pixel value is the background color, and a pixel value of 1 is white.

We now show a complete graphics program.

Example 16.4 Write a program that draws a line in row 100 from column 301 to column 600 in high resolution.

Solution: The organization of the program is as follows: (1) set the display mode to 6 (CGA high resolution), (2) draw the line, (3) read a key input, and (4) set the mode back to 3 (text mode). Step 3 is included so that we can control when to return to text mode; otherwise, the line would disappear before we can take a good look.

Program Listing PGM16_1.ASM

```
TITLE PGM16_1: CGA LINE DRAWING
;draws horizontal line in high res
;in row 100 from col 301 to col 600
.MODEL    SMALL
.STACK    100H
;
.CODE
MAIN  PROC
;set graphics mode
      MOV     AX,6           ;select mode 6, hi res
      INT     10H
;draw line
      MOV     AH,0CH         ;write pixel
      MOV     AL,1           ;white
      MOV     CX,301         ;beginning col
      MOV     DX,100         ;row
L1:   INT     10H
      INC     CX             ;next col
      CMP     CX,600         ;more columns?
      JLE     L1             ;yes, repeat
;read keyboard
      MOV     AH,0
      INT     16H
;set to text mode
      MOV     AX,3           ;select mode 3, text mode
      INT     10H
;return to DOS
      MOV     AH,4CH         ;return
      INT     21H            ;to DOS
MAIN  ENDP
      END     MAIN
```

Writing Directly to Memory

When we wish to do fast screen updates, as in video game playing, we can bypass the BIOS routines and write directly to the CGA video display memory. To do so, we need to understand the organization of the CGA display memory. The CGA's 16-KB display memory is divided into two halves. Pixels in even-numbered rows are stored in the first 8 KB (B800:0000 to B800:1FFF), and pixels in odd-numbered rows are stored in the second 8 KB (B800:2000 to B800:3FFF). Each row is represented by 50h bytes. Figure 16.2 shows the relationship between the display memory address and the screen display.

To locate the bit positions for a particular pixel in a display mode, we first determine the starting byte of that row and then the offset in the row for that pixel. We now show an example.

Example 16.5 Let the graphics mode be mode 4. Determine the byte address and bit positions for the pixel in row 5, column 10.

Solution: Row 5 is the third odd-numbered row, so the starting byte for row 5 has an offset address of 2000h + 2 × 50h = 20A0h. In mode 4, each pixel is two bits, so each byte can store four pixels. Column 10 is the eleventh column in the row, so the pixel must be the third pixel in the third byte. The byte address is 20A0h + 2 = 20A2h. Pixels are stored starting from the left in a byte, so the third pixel has bit positions 3 and 2.

Example 16.6 Suppose the current display mode is mode 4. Write a pixel value of 10b at row 5, column 10.

Solution: We use the address computed in the last example. To write a pixel, we first read the byte containing the pixel, change the appropriate bits, and then write back. The reason for read before write is to preserve other pixel values contained in the same byte. To change the bits, we first clear them using an AND operation, and then write the data using an OR operation.

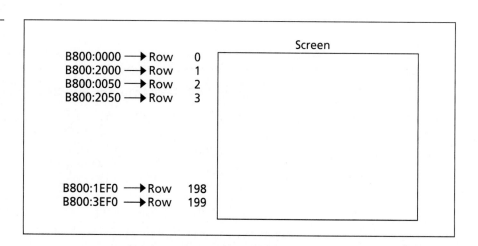

Figure 16.2 CGA Display Address

```
MOV     AX,0B800H       ;video memory segment number
MOV     ES,AX           ;place in ES
MOV     DI,20A2H        ;offset of byte
MOV     AL,ES:[DI]      ;move byte into AL
AND     AL,11110011B    ;clear the data bit positions
OR      AL,1000B        ;write 10b into bit positions 3,2
STOSB                   ;store back to memory
```

Displaying Text

It is possible to display text in graphics mode. Text characters in graphics mode are not generated from a character generator circuit as in text mode. Instead, the characters are selected from the character fonts stored in memory. Another difference between text mode and graphics mode is that the cursor is not being displayed in graphics mode. However, the cursor position can still be set by INT 10h, function 2.

Example 16.7 Display the letter "A" in red at the upper right corner of the screen. Use mode 4 and a background color of blue.

Solution: When we display characters in graphics mode, we use text coordinates. With the 320 × 200 resolution, there are only 40 text columns, see Table 16.4. Thus, the row and column numbers of the upper-right corner are 0 and 39, respectively. To display a red letter and blue background, we use palette 0 with blue background color.

The steps are as follows: (1) set to mode 4, default palette is 0, (2) set background color to blue, (3) position cursor, and (4) display letter "A" in red.

```
MOV     AH,0            ;set mode
MOV     AL,04H          ;mode 4
INT     10H
MOV     AH,0BH          ;function 0Bh
MOV     BH,00H          ;select background color
MOV     BL,3            ;blue
INT     10H
MOV     AH,02           ;set cursor
MOV     BH,0            ;page 0
MOV     DH,0            ;row 0
MOV     DL,39           ;col 39
INT     10H
MOV     AH,9            ;write char function
```

Table 16.4 Text Columns and Rows in Graphics Mode

Graphics Resolution	Text Columns	Text Rows
320 x 200	40	25
640 x 200	80	25
640 x 350	80	25
640 x 480	80	29

```
        MOV     AL,'A'          ;'A'
        MOV     BL,2            ;red color
        MOV     CX,1            ;write 1 char
        INT     10H
```

16.3 EGA Graphics

The EGA adapter can generate either 200 or 350 scan lines. To display the higher resolution, an **ECD (enhanced color display) monitor** is required. The EGA has sixteen *palette registers*; these registers store the current display colors. There are six color bits in each palette register; two for each primary color. This means that each palette register is capable of storing any one of 64 colors and thus, the EGA can display 16 colors out of 64 at one time. In the 16-color EGA modes, each pixel value selects a palette register. Initially, the 16 palette registers are loaded with the standard 16 CGA colors. To display other colors on the screen, a program can modify these registers using INT 10h, function 10h, subfunction 0h (see Appendix C).

The EGA adapter can emulate the CGA graphics modes, so that a program written for the CGA can run in EGA with the same colors. Its display memory can be configured by software. Depending on the display mode, the display memory may have a starting address of A0000h, B0000h, or B8000h. In displaying CGA modes, the EGA memory starts at B8000h so as to remain compatible with the CGA display memory.

In displaying EGA modes, the display memory has the following structure. It is located in segment A000h and uses up to 256 KB. To accommodate 256 KB in one segment, the EGA uses four modules of up to 64 KB each. The four modules, called **bit planes**, share the same 64 K memory addresses; each address refers to four bytes, one in each bit plane. The 8086 cannot access the bit planes directly; instead, all data transfer must go through EGA registers.

With this much storage, we can see that the display memory may hold more than one screen of graphics data. In EGA modes, the display memory is divided into *pages*, with each page being the size of one screen of data. The number of pages allowed depends on the graphics mode and the display memory size. For example, for the display mode D (320 × 200 with 16 colors) there are 64000 pixels and 4 bits for each pixel. Thus, the memory requirement for one screen is 32000 bytes. If the display memory is 256 KB, then it is possible to have eight display pages (0 to 7). There will be fewer pages if the memory is less.

When we use functions 0Ch and 0Dh to read or write pixels, the page number is specified in BH. These functions can be used on any page regardless of which page is being displayed.

Example 16.8 Assume that we are using a 16-color palette, write a green pixel to page 2 at column 0, row 0.

Solution: We use function 0Ch and a color value of 2.

```
        MOV     AH,0CH          ;write pixel function
        MOV     AL,2            ;green
        MOV     BH,2            ;page 2
        MOV     CX,0            ;column 0
        MOV     DX,0            ;row 0
        INT     10H
```

When a graphics mode is first selected, the active display page is automatically set to page 0. We can select a different active display page by using function 05h.

INT 10h, Function 5:
Select Active Display Page

Input: AH = 5
         AL = page number
Output: none

Example 16.9 Select page 1 to be displayed.

Solution:

```
MOV   AH,05H          ;select active display page
MOV   AL,1            ;page 1
INT   10H
```

Page switching can be used to do simple animation. Suppose we draw a figure in page 0, then draw the same figure at a slightly different position in page 1, and so on. Then, by quickly switching the active display page, we can see the figure move across the screen. This movement is limited by the total number of pages available. We show a more practical animation technique in section 16.5.

16.4 VGA Graphics

The VGA adapter has higher resolution than the EGA; it can display 640 × 480 in mode 12h. There are also more colors: the VGA can generate 64 levels of red, green, and blue. The combinations of the red, blue, and green colors produce 64^3 equals 256 K different colors. A maximum of 256 colors can be displayed at one time. The color values being displayed are stored in 256 video *DAC (digital to analog circuit) color registers*. There are 18 color bits in a color register; six for each primary color. To display all these colors, we need to have an **analog monitor**.

The VGA adapter can emulate the CGA and EGA graphics modes. In VGA mode, the display memory is organized into bit planes just like the EGA

Let's look at the VGA mode 13h, which supports 256 colors. In this mode, each pixel value is one byte, and it selects a color register. The color registers are loaded initially with a set of default values. It is possible to change the value in a color register; but let us first display the default colors.

Example 16.10 Give the instructions that will display the 256 default colors as 256 pixels in row 100.

Solution: We begin by selecting mode 13h, then we set up a loop to write the value of AL, which goes from 0 to 255 in columns 0 to 255.

```
        ;set mode
                MOV     AH,0            ;set mode
                MOV     AL,13H          ;to 13h
                INT     10H             ;
        ;display 256 pixels in row 100
                MOV     AH,0CH          ;write pixel function
                MOV     AL,0            ;start with pixel color 0
                MOV     BH,0            ;page 0
                MOV     CX,0            ;column 0
                MOV     DX,100          ;row 100
        L1:     INT     10H             ;write pixel
                INC     AL              ;next color
                INC     CX              ;next col
                CMP     CX,256          ;finished?
                JL      L1              ;no, repeat
```

We can set the color in a color register with function 10h.

INT 10h, Function 10h, Subfunction 10h:
Set Color Register

Input: AH = 10h
        AL = 10h
        BX = color register
        CH = green value
        CL = blue value
        DH = red value
Output: none

Example 16.11 Put the color values of 30 red, 20 green, and 10 blue into color register 5.

Solution:

```
        MOV     AH,10H          ;set color register
        MOV     AL,10H          ;
        MOV     BX,5            ;register 5
        MOV     DH,30           ;red value
        MOV     CH,20           ;green value
        MOV     CL,10           ;blue value
        INT     10H
```

It is also possible to set a block of color registers in one call; see Appendix C.

16.5 Animation

The movement of an object on the screen is simulated by erasing the existing object and then displaying it at a new location. We will use a small ball to illustrate the techniques in animation.

For the display, we need to pick a graphics mode, the ball color, and the background color. Because all adapters support CGA modes, let's choose mode 4. If we select palette 1 with a green background color, we can show a white ball moving on a green background. The ball will be represented by a square matrix of four pixels; its position is given by the upper left-hand pixel.

Ball Display

We will confine the ball to an area bounded by columns 10 and 300 and the rows 10 and 189. The boundary is shown in cyan. Initially, let us set the ball to the middle of the right-hand margin; that is, ball position is column 298, row 100.

The procedure SET_DISPLAY_MODE sets the display mode to 4, selects palette 1 and a green background color, and then draws a cyan border. The border is drawn by two macros DRAW_ROW and DRAW_COLUMN. The procedure DISPLAY_BALL displays the ball at column CX row DX with the color given in AL. Both procedures are in program listing PGM16_2A.ASM.

Program Listing PGM16_2A.ASM

```
TITLE PGM16_2A:
      PUBLIC  SET_DISPLAY_MODE, DISPLAY_BALL
.MODEL    SMALL
DRAW_ROW       MACRO          X
      LOCAL L1
;draws a line in row X from column 10 to column 300
      MOV     AH,0CH          ;draw pixel
      MOV     AL,1            ;cyan
      MOV     CX,10           ;column 10
      MOV     DX,X            ;row X
L1:   INT     10H
      INC     CX              ;next column
      CMP     CX,301          ;beyond column 300?
      JL      L1              ;no, repeat
      ENDM
;
DRAW_COLUMN    MACRO          Y
      LOCAL L2
;draws a line in column Y from row 10 to row 189
      MOV     AH,0CH          ;draw pixel
      MOV     AL,1            ;cyan
      MOV     CX,Y            ;column Y
      MOV     DX,10           ;row 10
L2:   INT     10H
      INC     DX              ;next row
      CMP     DX,190          ;beyond row 189?
      JL      L2              ;no, repeat
      ENDM
;
.CODE
SET_DISPLAY_MODE           PROC
;sets display mode and draws boundary
      MOV     AH,0            ;set mode
      MOV     AL,04H          ;mode 4, 320 x 200 4 color
      INT     10H
      MOV     AH,0BH          ;select palette
      MOV     BH,1
      MOV     BL,1            ;palette 1
      INT     10H             ;
```

```
        MOV     BH,0            ;set background color
        MOV     BL,2            ;green
        INT     10H
;draw boundary
        DRAW_ROW       10       ;draw row 10
        DRAW_ROW      189       ;draw row 189
        DRAW_COLUMN    10       ;draw column 10
        DRAW_COLUMN   300       ;draw column 300
        RET
SET_DISPLAY_MODE    ENDP
;
DISPLAY_BALL PROC
;displays ball at column CX and row DX with color given
;in AL
;input: AL = color of ball
;       CX = column
;       DX = row
        MOV     AH,0CH          ;write pixel
        INT     10H
        INC     CX              ;pixel on next column
        INT     10H
        INC     DX              ;down 1 row
        INT     10H
        DEC     CX              ;previous column
        INT     10H
        DEC     DX              ;restore DX
        RET
DISPLAY_BALL ENDP
        END
```

Notice that, to erase the ball, all we have to do is display a ball with the background color at the ball position. Thus we can use the DISPLAY_BALL procedure for both displaying and erasing.

To simulate ball movement, we define a ball velocity with two components, VEL_X and VEL_Y; each is a word variable. When VEL_X is positive, the ball is moving to the right, and when VEL_Y is positive, the ball is moving down. The position of the ball is given by CX (column) and DX (row). After displaying the ball at one position, we erase it and compute the new position by adding VEL_X to CX and VEL_Y to DX. The ball is then displayed at the new column and row position, and the process is repeated.

The following instructions display a ball at column CX, row DX; erase it; and display it in a new position determined by the velocity.

```
MOV     AL,3            ;color 3 in palette = white
CALL    DISPLAY_BALL    ;display white ball
MOV     AL,0            ;color 0 is background color
CALL    DISPLAY_BALL    ;erase ball
ADD     CX,VEL_X        ;new column
ADD     DX,VEL_Y        ;new row
MOV     AL,3            ;white color
CALL    DISPLAY_BALL    ;display ball at new position
```

Because the computer can execute instructions at such a high speed, the ball will be moving too fast on the screen for us to see. One way to solve the problem is to use a counter-controlled delay loop after each display of the ball. But due to different operation speeds of the various PC models, such a delay loop cannot give a consistent delay time. A better method is to use the timer. We noted in Chapter 15 that the timer ticks 18.2 times every second.

A timer interrupt procedure is needed for the timing, it will do the following: each time it is activated, it will set the variable TIMER_FLAG to 1. A ball-moving procedure will check this variable to determine if the timer has ticked; if so, it moves the ball and clears TIMER_FLAG to 0. The timer interrupt procedure TIMER_TICK is given in the program listing PGM16_2B.ASM.

Program Listing PGM16_2B.ASM

```
TITLE PGM16_2B: TIMER_TICK
;timer interrupt procedure
      EXTRN  TIMER_FLAG:BYTE
      PUBLIC TIMER_TICK
.MODEL SMALL
.CODE
;timer routine
TIMER_TICK   PROC
;save registers
      PUSH   DS                      ;save DS
      PUSH   AX
;
      MOV    AX,SEG TIMER_FLAG       ;get segment of flag
      MOV    DS,AX                   ;put in DS
      MOV    TIMER_FLAG,1            ;set flag
;restore registers
      POP    AX
      POP    DS                      ;restore DS
      IRET
TIMER_TICK   ENDP                    ;end timer routine
      END
```

Ball Bounce

If we continue to move the ball in the same direction, eventually, the ball will go beyond the boundary. To confine the ball to the given area, we show it bouncing off the boundary. First we test each new position before displaying the ball. If a position is beyond the boundary, we simply set the ball at the boundary; at the same time, we reverse the velocity component that caused the ball to move outside. This will move the ball back as if it bounced off the boundary. The procedure CHECK_BOUNDARY in program listing PGM16_2C.ASM checks for the boundary condition and modifies the velocity accordingly.

With the boundary check procedure written, we can write a MOVE_BALL procedure that waits for the timer and moves the ball. The MOVE_BALL procedure first erases the ball at the current position given by CX,DX; then it computes the new position by adding the velocity and calls CHECK_BOUNDARY to check the new position; finally, it checks the TIMER_FLAG to see if the timer has ticked; if so, it displays the ball at the new position. The MOVE_BALL procedure is in program listing PGM16_2C.ASM.

Program Listing PGM16_2C.ASM
```
TITLE PGM16_2C:
;contains MOVE_BALL and CHECK_BOUNDARY procedures
        EXTRN   DISPLAY_BALL:NEAR
        EXTRN   TIMER_FLAG:BYTE, VEL_X:WORD, VEL_Y:WORD
        PUBLIC  MOVE_BALL
.MODEL SMALL
.CODE
MOVE_BALL       PROC
;erase ball at current position and display ball at new
;position
;input:  CX = column of ball position
;        DX = row of ball position
;erase ball
        MOV     AL,0            ;color 0 is background color
        CALL    DISPLAY_BALL    ;erase ball
;get new position
        ADD     CX,VEL_X
        ADD     DX,VEL_Y
;check boundary
        CALL    CHECK_BOUNDARY
;wait for 1 timer tick to display ball
TEST_TIMER:
        CMP     TIMER_FLAG,1    ;timer ticked?
        JNE     TEST_TIMER      ;no, keep testing
        MOV     TIMER_FLAG,0    ;yes, reset flag
        MOV     AL,3            ;white color
        CALL    DISPLAY_BALL    ;show ball
        RET
MOVE_BALL       ENDP
;
CHECK_BOUNDARY          PROC
;determine if ball is outside screen, if so move it
;back in and change the ball direction
;input:  CX = column of ball position
;        DX = row of ball position
;output: CX = column of ball position
;        DX = row of ball position
;check column value
        CMP     CX,11           ;left of 11?
        JG      L1              ;no, go check right margin
        MOV     CX,11           ;yes, set to 11
        NEG     VEL_X           ;change direction
        JMP     L2              ;go test row boundary
L1:     CMP     CX,298          ;beyond right margin?
        JL      L2              ;no, go test row boundary
        MOV     CX,298          ;set column to 298
        NEG     VEL_X           ;change direction
;check row value
L2:     CMP     DX,11           ;above top margin?
        JG      L3              ;no, check bottom margin
        MOV     DX,11           ;set to 11
        NEG     VEL_Y           ;change direction
        JMP     DONE            ;done
L3:     CMP     DX,187          ;below bottom margin?
```

```
                JL      DONE                    ;no, done
                MOV     DX,187                  ;yes, set to 187
                NEG     VEL_Y                   ;change direction
DONE:
        RET
CHECK_BOUNDARY          ENDP
        END
```

We are now ready to write the main procedure. Our program will use the SETUP_INT procedure in program listing PGM15_2A in Chapter 15 to set up the interrupt vector. The steps in the main procedure are: (1) set up the graphics display and the TIMER_TICK interrupt procedure, (2) display the ball at the right margin with a velocity going up and to the left, (3) wait for the timer to tick, (4) call MOVE_BALL to move the ball, (5) wait for the timer to tick again to allow more time for the ball to stay on the screen, and (6) go to step 3. The main procedure is shown in program listing PGM16_2.ASM.

Program Listing PGM16_2.ASM

```
TITLE PGM16_2: BOUNCING BALL
        EXTRN   SET_DISPLAY_MODE:NEAR, DISPLAY_BALL:NEAR
        EXTRN   MOVE_BALL:NEAR
        EXTRN   SETUP_INT:NEAR, TIMER_TICK:NEAR
        PUBLIC  TIMER_FLAG, VEL_X, VEL_Y
.MODEL  SMALL
.STACK  100H
;
.DATA
NEW_TIMER_VEC   DW      ?,?
OLD_TIMER_VEC   DW      ?,?
TIMER_FLAG      DB      0
VEL_X           DW      -6
VEL_Y           DW      -1
;
.CODE
MAIN    PROC
        MOV     AX,@DATA
        MOV     DS,AX           ;initialize DS
;
;set graphics mode and draw border
        CALL    SET_DISPLAY_MODE
;set up timer interrupt vector
        MOV     NEW_TIMER_VEC, OFFSET TIMER_TICK ;offset
        MOV     NEW_TIMER_VEC+2,CS              ;segment
        MOV     AL,1CH                          ;interrupt type
        LEA     DI,OLD_TIMER_VEC        ;DI points to vector buffer
        LEA     SI,NEW_TIMER_VEC        ;SI points to new vector
        CALL    SETUP_INT
;start ball at column = 298, row = 100
;for the rest of the program CX will be column position
;of ball and DX will be row position
        MOV     CX,298
        MOV     DX,100
```

```
                MOV     AL,3                    ;white ball
                CALL    DISPLAY_BALL
;wait for timer tick before moving the ball
TEST_TIMER:
                CMP     TIMER_FLAG,1            ;timer ticked?
                JNE     TEST_TIMER              ;no, keep testing
                MOV     TIMER_FLAG,0            ;yes, clear flag
                CALL    MOVE_BALL               ;move to new position
;delay 1 timer tick
TEST_TIMER_2:
                CMP     TIMER_FLAG,1            ;timer ticked?
                JNE     TEST_TIMER_2            ;no, keep testing
                MOV     TIMER_FLAG,0            ;yes, clear flag
                JMP     TEST_TIMER              ;go get next ball position
MAIN    ENDP
        END     MAIN
```

To run the program, we need to link the object files PGM16_2 + PGM15_2A + PGM16_2A + PGM16_2B + PGM16_2C. One word of caution, however: this program has no way to terminate. So it may be necessary to reboot the system. In section 16.6.2 we discuss a way to terminate the program.

16.6
An Interactive Video Game

In the following sections, we'll develop the bouncing ball program into an interactive video game program. First, in section 16.6.1, we add sound to the program; when the ball hits the boundary a tone is generated. Second, in section 16.6.2, we add a paddle to allow the player to hit the ball. To keep things simple, the paddle only slides up and down along the left boundary and is controlled by the up and down arrow keys. If the paddle misses the ball when it arrives at the left margin, the game is terminated. The game can also be terminated by pressing the Esc key.

16.6.1
Adding Sound

The PC has a tone generator that can be set to generate particular tones for specified durations. The frequency of the tone generation can be specified by a timer circuit.

The timer circuit is driven by a clock circuit that has a rate of 1.193 MHz. This is beyond the range of human hearing, but the timer can generate output signals with lower frequencies. It does this by generating one pulse for every N incoming pulses, where N can be specified by a program. The number N is first loaded into a counter, then, after counting N incoming pulses, the circuit produces one pulse. The process is repeated until a different value is placed in the counter. For example, by placing a value of 1193 in the counter, the output is 1000 pulses every second, or 1000 Hz.

The next thing in tone generation is to determine the duration. To start the tone, we turn on the timer circuit; after a specific amount of time, we must turn it off. To keep time, we can use the TIMER_TICK interrupt routine. Because the TIMER_TICK procedure is activated once every 55 ms, we get half a second of delay in 9 ticks.

16.6 An Interactive Video Game

To access the timer circuit, we have to use the I/O instructions **IN** and **OUT**. They allow data to be moved between an I/O port and AL or AX. To read an 8-bit I/O port we use

```
IN    AL,port
```

where port is an I/O port number. Similarly, to write to a 8-bit I/O port we use

```
OUT   port,AL
```

There are three I/O ports involved here: port 42h for loading the counter, port 43h that specifies the timer operation, and port 61h that enables the timer circuit.

Before loading port 42h with the count, we load port 43h with the command code B6h; this specifies that the timer will generate square waves and that the port 42h will be loaded one byte at a time with the low byte first. The bit positions 0 and 1 in port 61h control the timer and its output. By setting them to 1, the timer circuit will be enabled.

The sound-generating procedure, BEEP, produces a tone of 1000 Hz for half a second. The steps are (1) load the counter (I/O port 42h) with 1193, (2) activate the timer, (3) allow the beep to last for about 500 ms, and (4) deactivate the timer. Procedure BEEP is shown in program listing PGM16_3A.ASM.

Program Listing PGM16_3A.ASM

```
TITLE   PGM16_3A: BEEP
;sound generating procedure
        EXTRN   TIMER_FLAG:BYTE
        PUBLIC  BEEP
.MODEL          SMALL
.CODE
BEEP    PROC
;generate beeping sound
        PUSH    CX              ;save CX
;initialize timer
        MOV     AL,0B6H         ;specify mode of operation
        OUT     43H,AL          ;write to port 43h
;load count
        MOV     AX,1193         ;count for 1000 Hz
        OUT     42H,AL          ;low byte
        MOV     AL,AH           ;high byte
        OUT     42H,AL
;activate speaker
        IN      AL,61H          ;read control port
        MOV     AH,AL           ;save value in AH
        OR      AL,11B          ;set control bits
        OUT     61H,AL          ;activate speaker
;500 ms delay loop
        MOV     CX,9            ;do 9 times
B_1:    CMP     TIMER_FLAG,1    ;check timer flag
        JNE     B_1             ;not set, loop back
        MOV     TIMER_FLAG,0    ;flag set, clear it
        LOOP    B_1             ;repeat for next tick
;turn off tone
        MOV     AL,AH           ;return old control value to AL
        OUT     61H,AL          ;restore control value
        POP     CX              ;restore CX
        RET
BEEP    ENDP
        END
```

We now write a new ball movement procedure that uses the sound-generating procedure BEEP. Whenever the ball hits the boundary, procedure BEEP is called to sound the tone. The new procedures are called MOVE_BALL_A and CHECK_BOUNDARY_A; both are contained in the program listing PGM16_3B.ASM.

Program Listing PGM16_3B.ASM

```
TITLE PGM16_3B: Ball Movement
;contains MOVE_BALL_A and  CHECK_BOUNDARY_A
      EXTRN    DISPLAY_BALL:NEAR, BEEP:NEAR
      EXTRN    TIMER_FLAG:BYTE, VEL_X:WORD, VEL_Y:WORD
      PUBLIC   MOVE_BALL_A
.MODEL SMALL
.CODE
MOVE_BALL_A PROC
;erase ball at current position and display ball at new
;position
;input:  CX = column
;        DX = row
;output: CX = column
;        DX = row
      MOV    AL,0           ;color 0 is background color
      CALL   DISPLAY_BALL   ;erase ball
;get new position
      ADD    CX,VEL_X
      ADD    DX,VEL_Y
;check boundary
      CALL   CHECK_BOUNDARY_A
;wait for 1 timer tick
TEST_TIMER_1:
      CMP    TIMER_FLAG,1   ;timer ticked?
      JNE    TEST_TIMER_1   ;no, keep testing
      MOV    TIMER_FLAG,0   ;yes, clarify
      MOV    AL,3           ;white color
      CALL   DISPLAY_BALL   ;show ball
      RET
MOVE_BALL_A ENDP
;
CHECK_BOUNDARY_A PROC
;determine if ball is outside screen, if so move it
;back in and change the ball direction
;input:  CX = column
;        DX = row
;output: CX = column
;        DX = row
;check column value
      CMP    CX,11          ;left of 11?
      JG     L1             ;no, go check right margin
      MOV    CX,11          ;yes, set to 11
      NEG    VEL_X          ;change direction
      CALL   BEEP           ;sound beep
      JMP    L2             ;go test row boundary
L1:   CMP    CX,299         ;beyond right margin?
      JL     L2             ;no, go test row boundary
      MOV    CX,298         ;set column to 298
      NEG    VEL_X          ;change direction
```

```
                    CALL    BEEP              ;sound beep
        ;check row value
        L2:         CMP     DX,11             ;above top margin?
                    JG      L3                ;no, check bottom margin
                    MOV     DX,11             ;set to 11
                    NEG     VEL_Y             ;change direction
                    CALL    BEEP
                    JMP     DONE              ;done
        L3:         CMP     DX,188            ;below bottom margin?
                    JL      DONE              ;no, done
                    MOV     DX,187            ;yes, set to 187
                    NEG     VEL_Y             ;change direction
                    CALL    BEEP              ;sound beep
        DONE:
                    RET
        CHECK_BOUNDARY_A    ENDP
        ;
                    END
```

16.6.2 Adding a Paddle

Next, let us add a paddle to the program. The paddle will move up and down along the left boundary as the player presses the up and down arrow keys.

Since the program does not know when a key may be pressed, we need to write an interrupt procedure for interrupt 9, the keyboard interrupt. This interrupt procedure differs from the one in Chapter 15 in that it will access the keyboard I/O port directly and obtain the scan code.

There are three I/O ports to be accessed. When the keyboard generates an interrupt, bit 5 of the I/O port 20h is set, and the scan code comes into port 60h. Port 61h, bit 7, is used to enable the keyboard. Therefore, the interrupt routine should read the data from port 60h, enable the keyboard by setting bit 7 in port 61h, and clear bit 5 of port 20h.

The interrupt procedure is called KEYBOARD_INT. When it obtains a scan code, it first checks to see if the scan code is a make or break code. If it finds a make code, it sets the variable KEY_FLAG and puts the make code in the variable SCAN_CODE. If it finds a break code, the variables are not changed. Procedure KEYBOARD_INT is in program listing PGM16_3C.ASM.

Program Listing PGM16_3C.ASM
```
        TITLE   PGM16_3C:Keyboard Interrupt
                EXTRN   SCAN_CODE:BYTE, KEY_FLAG:BYTE
                PUBLIC  KEYBOARD_INT
        .MODEL  SMALL
        .CODE
        KEYBOARD_INT PROC
        ;keyboard interrupt routine
        ;save registers
                PUSH    DS
```

```
        PUSH    AX
;set up DS
        MOV     AX,SEG SCAN_CODE
        MOV     DS,AX
;input scan code
        IN      AL,60H          ;read scan code
        PUSH    AX              ;save it
        IN      AL,61H          ;control port value
        MOV     AH,AL           ;save in AH
        OR      AL,80H          ;set bit for keyboard
        OUT     61H,AL          ;write back
        XCHG    AH,AL           ;get back control value
        OUT     61H,AL          ;reset control port
        POP     AX              ;recover scan code
        MOV     AH,AL           ;save scan code in AH
        TEST    AL,80H          ;test for break code
        JNE     KEY_0           ;yes, clear flags, goto KEY_0
;make code
        MOV     SCAN_CODE,AL    ;save in variable
        MOV     KEY_FLAG,1      ;set key flag
KEY_0:  MOV     AL,20H          ;reset interrupt
        OUT     20H,AL
;restore registers
        POP     AX
        POP     DS
        IRET
KEYBOARD_INT ENDP               ;end KEYBOARD routine
;
        END
```

We now add a paddle in column 11, and use the up and down arrow keys to move it. If the ball gets to column 11 and the paddle is not in position to hit the ball, the program terminates. The paddle is made up of 10 pixels; the initial position is from row 45 to row 54. We use two variables, PADDLE_TOP and PADDLE_BOTTOM, to keep track of its current position.

We need two procedures: DRAW_PADDLE, to display and erase the paddle; and MOVE_PADDLE, to move the paddle up and down. Both procedures are in program listing PGM16_3D.ASM.

Program Listing PGM16_3D.ASM

```
TITLE PGM16_3D: PADDLE CONTROL
;contains MOVE_PADDLE and DRAW_PADDLE
        EXTRN   PADDLE_TOP:WORD, PADDLE_BOTTOM:WORD
        PUBLIC  DRAW_PADDLE, MOVE_PADDLE
.MODEL  SMALL
.CODE
DRAW_PADDLE PROC
;draw paddle in column 11
;input: AL contains pixel value
;       2 (red) for display and 0 (green) to erase
;save registers
        PUSH    CX
        PUSH    DX
```

```
;
        MOV     AH,0CH              ;write pixel function
        MOV     CX,11               ;column 11
        MOV     DX,PADDLE_TOP       ;top row
DP1:    INT     10H
        INC     DX                  ;next row
        CMP     DX,PADDLE_BOTTOM    ;done?
        JLE     DP1                 ;no, repeat
;restore registers
        POP     DX
        POP     CX
        RET
DRAW_PADDLE ENDP
;
MOVE_PADDLE PROC
;move paddle up or down
;input: AX = 2 (to move paddle down 2 pixels)
;          = -2 (to move paddle up 2 pixels)
        MOV     BX,AX               ;copy to BX
;check direction
        CMP     AX,0
        JL      UP                  ;neg, move up
;move down, check paddle position
        CMP     PADDLE_BOTTOM,188   ;at bottom?
        JGE     DONE                ;yes, cannot move
        JMP     UPDATE              ;no, update paddle
;move up, check if at top
UP:     CMP     PADDLE_TOP,11       ;at top?
        JLE     DONE                ;yes, cannot move
;move paddle
UPDATE:
;—erase paddle
        MOV     AL,0                ;green color
        CALL    DRAW_PADDLE
;—change paddle position
        ADD     PADDLE_TOP,BX
        ADD     PADDLE_BOTTOM,BX
;—display paddle at new position
        MOV     AL,2                ;red
        CALL    DRAW_PADDLE
DONE:   RET
MOVE_PADDLE ENDP
        END
```

MOVE_PADDLE will either move the paddle up two pixels or down two pixels, depending on whether AX is positive or negative. However, if the paddle is already at the top, it will not move up; and if it is already at the bottom, it will not move down.

We are now ready to write the main procedure.

Program Listing PGM16_3.ASM

```asm
TITLE PGM16_3: PADDLE_BALL
        EXTRN   SET_DISPLAY_MODE:NEAR, DISPLAY_BALL:NEAR
        EXTRN   MOVE_BALL_A:NEAR, DRAW_PADDLE:NEAR
        EXTRN   MOVE_PADDLE:NEAR
        EXTRN   KEYBOARD_INT:NEAR, TIMER_TICK:NEAR
        EXTRN   SETUP_INT:NEAR, KEYBOARD_INT:NEAR
        PUBLIC  TIMER_FLAG, KEY_FLAG, SCAN_CODE
        PUBLIC  PADDLE_TOP, PADDLE_BOTTOM, VEL_X, VEL_Y
;
.MODEL   SMALL
.STACK   100H
.DATA
;
NEW_TIMER_VEC   DW      ?,?
OLD_TIMER_VEC   DW      ?,?
NEW_KEY_VEC     DW      ?,?
OLD_KEY_VEC     DW      ?,?
SCAN_CODE       DB      0
KEY_FLAG        DB      0
TIMER_FLAG      DB      0
PADDLE_TOP      DW      45
PADDLE_BOTTOM   DW      54
VEL_X           DW      -6
VEL_Y           DW      -1
;scan codes
UP_ARROW = 72
DOWN_ARROW = 80
ESC_KEY = 1
;
.CODE
MAIN    PROC
        MOV     AX,@DATA
        MOV     DS,AX                   ;initialize DS
;
;set graphics mode
        CALL    SET_DISPLAY_MODE
;draw paddle
        MOV     AL,2                    ;display red paddle
        CALL    DRAW_PADDLE
;set up timer interrupt vector
        MOV     NEW_TIMER_VEC,OFFSET TIMER_TICK  ;offset
        MOV     NEW_TIMER_VEC+2,CS               ;segment
        MOV     AL,1CH                  ;interrupt number
        LEA     DI,OLD_TIMER_VEC
        LEA     SI,NEW_TIMER_VEC
        CALL    SETUP_INT
;set up keyboard interrupt vector
        MOV     NEW_KEY_VEC,OFFSET KEYBOARD_INT  ;offset
        MOV     NEW_KEY_VEC+2,CS                 ;segment
        MOV     AL,9H                   ;interrupt number
        LEA     DI,OLD_KEY_VEC
        LEA     SI,NEW_KEY_VEC
        CALL    SETUP_INT
;start ball at column = 298, row = 100
```

```
                MOV     CX,298          ;column
                MOV     DX,100          ;row
                MOV     AL,3            ;white
                CALL    DISPLAY_BALL
;check key flag
TEST_KEY:
                CMP     KEY_FLAG,1      ;check key flag
                JNE     TEST_TIMER      ;not set, go check timer flag
                MOV     KEY_FLAG,0      ;flag set, clear it and check
                CMP     SCAN_CODE,ESC_KEY       ;Esc key?
                JNE     TK_1            ;no, check arrow keys
                JMP     DONE            ;Esc, terminate
TK_1:   CMP     SCAN_CODE,UP_ARROW      ;up arrow?
                JNE     TK_2            ;no, check down arrow
                MOV     AX,-2           ;yes, move up 2 pixels
                CALL    MOVE_PADDLE     ;
                JMP     TEST_TIMER      ;go check timer flag
TK_2:   CMP     SCAN_CODE,DOWN_ARROW    ;down arrow?
                JNE     TEST_TIMER      ;no, check timer flag
                MOV     AX,2            ;yes, move down 2 pixels
                CALL    MOVE_PADDLE     ;
;check timer flag
TEST_TIMER:
                CMP     TIMER_FLAG,1    ;flag set?
                JNE     TEST_KEY        ;no, check key flag
                MOV     TIMER_FLAG,0    ;yes, clear it
                CALL    MOVE_BALL_A     ;move ball to new position
;check if paddle missed ball
                CMP     CX,11           ;at column 11?
                JNE     TEST_KEY        ;no, check key flag
                CMP     DX,PADDLE_TOP   ;yes, check paddle
                JL      CP_1            ;missed, ball above
                CMP     DX,PADDLE_BOTTOM
                JG      CP_1            ;missed, ball below
;paddle hit the ball, delay one tick then
;move the ball and redraw paddle
DELAY:  CMP     TIMER_FLAG,1    ;timer ticked?
                JNE     DELAY           ;no, keep checking
                MOV     TIMER_FLAG,0    ;yes, reset flag
                CALL    MOVE_BALL_A
                MOV     AL,2            ;display red paddle
                CALL    DRAW_PADDLE
                JMP     TEST_KEY        ;check key flag
;paddle missed the ball, erase the ball and terminate
CP_1:   MOV     AL,0            ;erase ball
                CALL    DISPLAY_BALL
;-reset timer interrupt vector
DONE:   LEA     DI,NEW_TIMER_VEC
                LEA     SI,OLD_TIMER_VEC
                MOV     AL,1CH
                CALL    SETUP_INT
;-reset keyboard interrupt vector
                LEA     DI,NEW_KEY_VEC
                LEA     SI,OLD_KEY_VEC
                MOV     AL,9H
```

```
        CALL    SETUP_INT
;read key
        MOV     AH,0
        INT     16H
;reset to text mode
        MOV     AH,0            ;wait for input
        MOV     AL,3
        INT     10H
;return to DOS
        MOV     AH,4CH
        INT     21H
MAIN    ENDP
        END     MAIN
```

In the main procedure, we alternate between checking the key flag and the timer flag. If the key flag is set, we check the scan code: (1) Esc key will terminate the program, (2) Up arrow key will move the paddle up, (3) Down arrow key will move the paddle down, and (4) all other keys are ignored. If the timer flag is set, we call MOVE_BALL_A to move the ball to a new position, and if the ball is at column 11 but missed the paddle, we terminate the program.

To terminate the program, we first reset the interrupt vectors and wait for a key input. When a key is pressed, we reset the screen to text mode and return to DOS.

Summary

- Screen elements in graphics mode are called pixels.
- The common IBM graphics adapters are CGA, EGA, and VGA.
- The INT 10h routine handles all graphics operations.
- The CGA has a medium-resolution mode of 320×200 and a high-resolution mode of 640×200.
- The EGA has all the CGA modes plus a resolution of 640×350.
- The VGA has all the EGA modes plus a resolution of 640×480. It can also display 256 colors in the 320×200 mode.
- Animation involves erasing an object and displaying it at a new location.
- Sound generation can be achieved by writing to the I/O ports.
- Interactive video game programming requires trapping the keyboard interrupt.

Glossary

analog monitor	A monitor that can accept multilevel color signals
APA (all points addressable)	Graphics mode that maps a pixel into a single dot
background color	Default color of pixels
bit planes	Memory modules that share the same memory address
ECD (enhanced color display) monitor	A monitor that can display all EGA modes
palette	A collection of colors that can be displayed at the same time
pixel	Picture element
scan lines	Lines on the screen traced by a beam of electrons

New Instructions

IN   OUT

Exercises

1. Write instructions that will select graphics mode 320 × 200 with 16 colors.
2. Write instructions that will select palette 0 with white background for the CGA medium resolution mode.
3. Write instructions that will display a 10 × 10 green rectangle with the upper left-hand corner at column 150 and row 100 on a white background using CGA medium resolution.
4. Write instructions that will change a 10 × 10 green rectangle on white background into a cyan rectangle on a white background.

Programming Exercises

5. Modify the video game program in the chapter to add a second paddle in column 299 so that it becomes a 2-player game.
6. Modify the video game program in the chapter so that the ball speed decreases when it hits the boundary, but increases when it is hit by a paddle.

17

Recursion

Overview

A recursive procedure is a procedure that calls itself. Recursive procedures are important in high-level languages, but the way the system uses the stack to implement these procedures is hidden from the programmer. In assembly language, the programmer must actually program the stack operations, so this provides an opportunity to see how recursion really works.

Because you may have had only limited experience with recursion, sections 17.1–17.2 discuss the underlying ideas. Section 17.3 shows how that stack can be used to pass data to a procedure; this topic was also covered in Chapter 14. In sections 17.4–17.5, we apply this method to implement recursive procedures that call themselves once. The chapter ends with a discussion of procedures that make multiple recursive calls.

17.1 The Idea of Recursion

A process is said to be **recursive** if it is defined in terms of itself. For example, consider the following definition of a binary tree:

> A binary tree is either empty, or consists of a single element called the *root*, and whose remaining elements are partitioned into two disjoint subsets (the left and right subtrees), each of which is a binary tree.

Let us apply the definition to show that the following tree T is a binary tree:

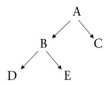

Choose A as the root of T. The tree T1, consisting of B, D, and E, is the left subtree of A and the tree T2, consisting of C, is the right subtree. We must show that T1 and T2 are binary trees.

Choose B as the root of T1. The trees T1$_a$ consisting of D and T1$_b$ consisting of E are the left and right subtrees. We must show that T1$_a$ and T1$_b$ are binary trees.

Choose D as the root of T1$_a$. The left and right subtrees of D are empty, and since an empty tree is a binary tree, T1$_a$ is a binary tree. For the same reason, T1$_b$ is a binary tree. Because T1$_a$ and T1$_b$ are binary trees, T1 must be a binary tree.

Now look at T2. It has a root C whose left and right subtrees are empty, so it is a binary tree.

Since T1 and T2 have been shown to be binary trees, tree T must also be a binary tree.

This simple example illustrates the main characteristics of recursive processes:

1. The main problem (showing that T is a binary tree) breaks down to simpler problems (showing that T1 and T2 are binary trees), and each of these problems is solved in exactly the same way as the main problem.

2. There must be an escape case (empty trees are binary trees) that lets the recursion terminate.

3. Once a subproblem has been solved (T1 is shown to be a binary tree), work proceeds on the next step of the original problem (showing that T2 is a binary tree).

17.2 Recursive Procedures

A recursive procedure calls itself. As a first example, consider the factorial of a positive integer. It may be defined nonrecursively as

$$\text{FACTORIAL}(1) = 1$$
$$\text{FACTORIAL}(N) = N \times (N-1) \times (N-2) \times \ldots 2 \times 1 \quad \text{if } N > 1$$

or, since

$$\text{FACTORIAL}(N-1) = (N-1) \times (N-2) \times \ldots 2 \times 1$$

we may write the following recursive definition:

$$\text{FACTORIAL}(1) = 1$$
$$\text{FACTORIAL}(N) = N \times \text{FACTORIAL}(N-1) \quad \text{if } N > 1$$

Let's rewrite this as an algorithm for a recursive procedure FACTORIAL:

```
1:  PROCEDURE FACTORIAL (input: N, output: RESULT)
2:  IF N = 1
3:     THEN
4:        RESULT = 1
5:     ELSE
```

```
6:    call FACTORIAL (input: N - 1, output: RESULT)
7:    RESULT = N x RESULT
8: END_IF
9: RETURN
```

In line 7, the value of RESULT on the right side is the value returned by the call to FACTORIAL at line 6.

For $N = 4$, we can trace the actions of the procedure as follows:

```
call FACTORIAL (4,RESULT)   /* begin first call */
call FACTORIAL (3,RESULT)   /* begin second call */
call FACTORIAL (2,RESULT)   /* begin third call */
call FACTORIAL (1,RESULT)   /* begin fourth call */
RESULT = 1
RETURN                      /* end fourth call */
```

The fourth call is the escape case. When it is finished, the third call is resumed at line 7:

```
RESULT = N x RESULT
```

On the right side, $N = 2$ and RESULT is 1, the value computed in the fourth call. We compute

```
RESULT = 2 x 1 = 2
```

and this call ends. The procedure then resumes the second call at line 7. In this call $N = 3$, so we compute

```
RESULT = 3 x RESULT = 3 x 2 = 6
```

which ends this call. Finally the procedure resumes the first call at line 7. In this call $N = 4$, so the result is

```
RESULT = 4 x RESULT = 4 x 6 = 24
```

and this is the value returned by the procedure.

This procedure has the properties of a recursive process that we noticed in the binary tree example. Each call to procedure FACTORIAL works on a simpler version of the original problem (finding the factorial of a smaller number), there is an escape case (the factorial of 1) and once a call has been completed, work continues on the previous call.

As a second example, consider the problem of finding the largest entry in an array A of N integers. If $N = 1$, then the largest entry is the only entry, A[1]. If $N > 1$, the largest entry is either A[N] or the biggest of the entries A[1] ... A[N − 1]. Here is an algorithm for a procedure.

```
1: PROCEDURE FIND_MAX(input: N, output: MAX)
2: IF N = 1
3:   THEN
4:     MAX = A[1]
5:   ELSE
6:     call FIND_MAX(N-1,MAX)
7:     IF A[N] > MAX
8:       THEN
9:         MAX = A[N]
10:      ELSE
11:        MAX = MAX
12:    END_IF
13: RETURN
```

In lines 7 and 11, the value MAX on the right side is the value returned by the call at line 6.

Let's trace the procedure for an array A of four entries: 10, 50, 20, 4.

```
call FIND_MAX(4,MAX)      /* first call */
call FIND_MAX(3,MAX)      /* second call */
call FIND_MAX(2,MAX)      /* third call */
call FIND_MAX(1,MAX)      /* fourth call */
```

As in the factorial example, the fourth call is the escape case. It returns MAX = A[1] = 10 and exits.

Now the third call resumes at line 7. Because A[2] (= 50) > MAX (= 10), the value returned from this call is MAX = 50.

Next the second call resumes at line 7. Because A[3] (= 20) < MAX (= 50), this call also returns MAX = 50.

Finally, we are back in the first call at line 7. Because A[4] (= 4) < MAX (= 50), this call returns MAX = 50, and this is the value returned to the calling program by the procedure.

17.3 Passing Parameters on the Stack

As we will see later, recursive procedures are implemented in assembly language by passing parameters on the stack (section 14.5.3). To see how this may be accomplished, consider the following simple program. It places the content of two memory words on the stack, and calls a procedure ADD_WORDS that returns their sum in AX.

Program Listing PGM17_1.ASM

```
 0:    TITLE  PGM17_1: ADD WORDS
 1:    .MODEL   SMALL
 2:    .STACK   100H
 3:    .DATA
 4:    WORD1    DW       2
 5:    WORD2    DW       5
 6:    .CODE
 7:    MAIN     PROC
 8:             MOV      AX,@DATA
 9:             MOV      DS,AX
10:             PUSH     WORD1
11:             PUSH     WORD2
12:             CALL     ADD_WORDS
13:             MOV      AH,4CH
14:             INT      21H
15:    MAIN     ENDP
16:    ADD_WORDS         PROC            NEAR
17:    ;adds two memory words
18:    ;stack on entry:   return addr.(top), word2, word1
19:    ;output: AX = sum
20:             PUSH     BP              ;save BP
21:             MOV      BP,SP
22:             MOV      AX,[BP+6]       ;AX gets WORD1
23:             ADD      AX,[BP+4]       ;AX has sum
24:             POP      BP              ;restore BP
25:             RET      4               ;exit
26:    ADD_WORDS         ENDP
27:             END      MAIN
```

After initializing DS, the program pushes the contents of WORD1 and WORD2 on the stack, and calls ADD_WORDS. On entry to the procedure, the stack looks like this:

```
SP──▶ | return_address (line 13)
      | 5   (WORD2 content)
      | 2   (WORD1 content)
```

At lines 20–21, the procedure first saves the original content of BP on the stack, and sets BP to point to the stack top. The result is

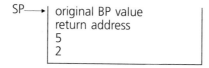

Now the data can be accessed by indirect addressing. BP is used for two reasons: (1) when BP is used in indirect addressing, SS is the assumed segment register, and (2) SP itself may not be used in indirect addressing. At line 22, the effective address of the source in the instruction

```
MOV AX, [BP+6]
```

is the stack top offset plus 6, which is the location of WORD1 content (2). Similarly, at line 23 the source in

```
ADD AX, [BP+4]
```

is the location of WORD2 content (5).

After restoring BP to its original value at line 24, the stack becomes

```
SP──▶ | return address
      | 5
      | 2
```

To exit the procedure and restore the stack to its original condition, we use

```
RET 4
```

This causes the return address to be popped into IP, and four additional bytes to be removed from the stack.

17.4 The Activation Record

Before attempting to code a recursive procedure, one issue must be resolved. The parameters (and local variables, if any) of the procedure are reinitialized each time the procedure is called. In both examples of section 17.2, the procedure is first called with parameter $N = 4$, then with $N = 3$, then with $N = 2$, then with $N = 1$. When a call has been completed, the procedure resumes the previous call at the point it left off. In order to do so, it must somehow "remember" that point, as well as the values of the parameters and local variables in that call. These values are known as the **activation record** of the call.

To illustrate, suppose we have a procedure that is called once from the main procedure, and then calls itself twice more. Before initiating the first call, the main procedure places the initial activation record on the stack and calls the procedure. The procedure saves BP and sets BP to point to the stack top, as was done in the example of the last section. The stack looks like this:

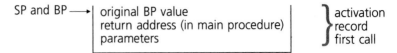

Using BP to access the parameters and local variables, the procedure executes its instructions. Before calling itself, it places the activation record for the next call on the stack. The return address that the recursive call places on the stack is that of the next instruction to be done in the procedure. As the second call begins, the procedure once again saves BP and sets BP to point to the stack top. The result is

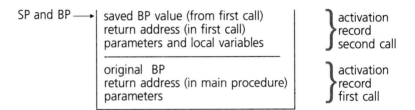

Now, as in the first call, the procedure uses BP to access the data for the second call. Before initiating the third call, its activation record is placed on the stack. The third call saves BP and sets it to point to the stack top. The stack becomes

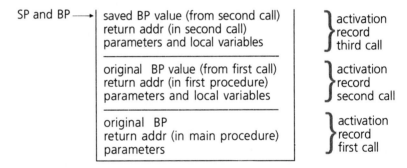

Let's suppose that the third call is the escape case. The result it computes may be placed in a register or memory location so that it is available to the second call when the second call resumes. After the third call is completed, the second call may be resumed by first popping BP to restore its previous value, and executing a return. The return places in IP the address of the next instruction to be done in the second call. As part of the return, the third call's parameters and local variables are popped off the stack and discarded, as was done in the example in the last section. The stack becomes

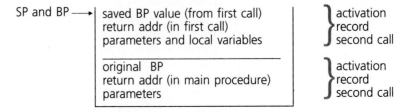

Now the second call resumes. It picks up the result of the third call and executes to completion. When it has finished and stored the result, the

Chapter 17 Recursion 363

stack is once again popped into BP, and control returns to the first call. As before, the second call's data are discarded. Now the stack looks like this:

SP and BP ⟶ | original BP value
return address (in main procedure)
parameters | } activation record first call

When the first call is done, the procedure restores BP to its original value, and control passes to the main procedure. As before, the parameters are discarded. The procedure stores the final result in a place where the main procedure can pick it up.

17.5 Implementation of Recursive Procedures

In this section, we show how recursive procedures may be implemented in assembly language.

Example 17.1 Code the FACTORIAL procedure of section 17.2. Call it in a program to compute the factorial of 3.

Solution: To make the code easier to follow, the algorithm is repeated here:

```
1: PROCEDURE FACTORIAL (input: N, output: RESULT)
2: IF N = 1
3:   THEN
4:     RESULT = 1
5:   ELSE
6:     call FACTORIAL (input: N - 1, output: RESULT)
7:     RESULT = N x RESULT
8: END_IF
9: RETURN
```

Program Listing PGM17_2.ASM
```
 0:    TITLE PGM17_2: FACTORIAL PROGRAM
 1:    .MODEL   SMALL
 2:    .STACK   100H
 3:    .CODE
 4:    MAIN     PROC
 5:        MOV    AX,3              ;N = 3
 6:        PUSH   AX                ;N on stack
 7:        CALL   FACTORIAL         ;AX has 3 factorial
 8:        MOV    AH,4CH
 9:        INT    21H               ;dos return
10:    MAIN     ENDP
11:    FACTORIAL    PROC      NEAR
12:    ; computes N factorial
13:    ; input:stack on entry - ret. addr.(top), N
14:    ; output AX
15:        PUSH   BP                ;save BP
16:        MOV    BP,SP             ;BP pts to stacktop
17:    ;if
18:        CMP    WORD PTR[BP+4],1  ;N = 1?
```

17.5 Implementation of Recursive Procedures

```
19:         JG      END_IF          ;no, N1
20: ;then
21:         MOV     AX,1            ;result = 1
22:         JMP     RETURN          ;go to return
23: END_IF:
24:         MOV     CX,[BP+4]       ;get N
25:         DEC     CX              ;N-1
26:         PUSH    CX              ;save on stack
27:         CALL    FACTORIAL       ;recursive call
28:         MUL     WORD PTR[BP+4]  ;RESULT = N*RESULT
29: RETURN:
30:         POP     BP              ;restore BP
31:         RET     2               ;return and discard N
32: FACTORIAL ENDP
33:         END     MAIN
```

The testing program puts 3 on the stack and calls FACTORIAL. At lines 15 and 16 the procedure saves BP and sets BP to point to the stack top. The stack looks like this:

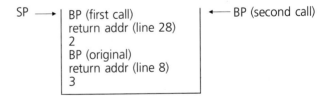

Now, at line 18 the current value of N is examined. We must use CMP WORD PTR [BP+4],1 rather than CMP [BP+4],1 because the assembler cannot tell from the source operand 1 whether to code this as a byte or word instruction.

Because $N \neq 1$, in lines 24–26 the data for the next call are prepared by retrieving the current value of N, decrementing it, and saving it on the stack.

At line 27, the second call ($N = 2$) is made. Once again, at lines 15 and 16, BP is saved and BP is set to point to the stack top. The stack becomes

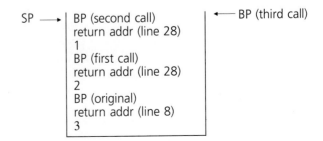

Since N is still not 1, the procedure calls itself one more time, and the stack looks like this:

Since N is now 1, the recursion can terminate. At line 21, the procedure places RESULT = 1 in AX, restores BP to its value in the second call and returns. The RET 2 at line 31 causes the return address in the second call (line 28 in the listing) to be placed in IP. RET 2 also causes parameter 1 to be popped off the stack. The stack becomes

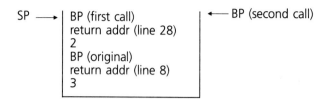

Now execution of the second call continues at line 28. Because the result of the third call is in AX, the procedure can multiply it by the current value of N, yielding RESULT = 2 × 1 = 2. The new result remains in AX. With this call complete, BP is restored and the first call resumed at line 28. The stack is now

```
SP ──▶ | BP (original)       | ◀── BP (first call)
       | return addr (line 8)|
       | 3 (value of N)      |
```

As before, the latest result is multiplied by N, yielding RESULT = 3 × 2 = 6. Control passes to line 8 in the main program, with the value of the factorial in AX.

Example 17.2 Code procedure FINDMAX of section 17.2, and test it in a program.

Solution: The algorithm for the procedure is reproduced here:

```
1:  PROCEDURE FIND_MAX (input: N, output: MAX)
2:  IF N = 1
3:    THEN
4:      MAX = 1
5:    ELSE
6:      call FIND_MAX(N - 1,MAX)
7:      IF A[N] > MAX
8:        THEN
9:          MAX = A[N]
10:       ELSE
11:         MAX = MAX /* value returned by call at line 6 */
12:     ENDIF
13: RETURN
```

Program Listing PGM17_3.ASM

```
0:      TITLE PGM17_3: FIND_MAX
1:      .MODEL   SMALL
2:      .STACK   100H
3:      .DATA
4:      A        DW      10,50,20,4
5:      .CODE
6:      MAIN     PROC
7:               MOV     AX,@DATA
8:               MOV     DS,AX           ;initialize DS
9:               MOV     AX,4            ;no. of elts in array
10:              PUSH    AX              ;parameter on stack
11:              CALL    FIND_MAX        ;returns MAX in AX
12:              MOV     AH,4CH
13:              INT     21H             ;dos exit
14:     MAIN     ENDP
15:     FIND_MAX PROC    NEAR
16:     ; finds the largest element in array A of N elements
17:     ; input: stack on entry - ret. addr. (top), N
18:     ; output: AX largest element
19:              PUSH    BP              ;save BP
20:              MOV     BP,SP           ;BP pts to stacktop
21:     ;if
22:              CMP     WORD PTR [BP+4],1  ;N=1?
23:              JG      ELSE_           ;no, go to set up next call
24:     ;then
25:              MOV     AX,A            ;MAX = A[1]
26:              JMP     END_IF1
27:     ELSE_:
28:              MOV     CX,[BP+4]       ;get N
29:              DEC     CX              ;N-1
30:              PUSH    CX              ;save on stack
31:              CALL    FIND_MAX        ;returns MAX in AX
32:     ;if
33:              MOV     BX,[BP+4]       ;get N
34:              SHL     BX,1            ;2N
35:              SUB     BX,2            ;2(N-1)
36:              CMP     A[BX],AX        ;A[N] > MAX?
37:              JLE     END_IF1         ;no, go to return
38:     ;then
39:              MOV     AX,A[BX]        ;yes, set MAX = A[N]
40:     END_IF1:
41:              POP     BP              ;restore BP
42:              RET     2               ;return and discard N
43:     FIND_MAX ENDP
44:              END     MAIN
```

The stacking of the activation records during the recursive calls in this example is similar to that of example 17.1, and is not shown here (see exercises).

At line 32, the procedure begins preparation for comparison of A[N] with the current value of MAX in AX. Recall from chapter 10 that the offset location of the Nth element of a word array A is A + 2 × (N − 1). Lines 33-35 put 2 × (N − 1) in BX, so that based mode may be used in the comparison at line 36. If MAX > A[N], we can leave it in AX, which means that the ELSE statement at line 11 of the algorithm need not be coded.

17.6
More Complex Recursion

In the preceding examples, the code for recursive procedures has involved only one recursive call; for example, the only call that procedure FACTORIAL (N) makes is to FACTORIAL (N − 1). However, it is possible that the code for a recursive procedure may involve multiple recursive calls.

As an example, suppose we would like to write a procedure to compute the binomial coefficients $C(n, k)$. These are the coefficients that appear in the expansion of $(x + y)^n$. The expansion takes the form

$$(x + y)^n = C(n, 0)x^n y^0 + C(n, 1)x^{n-1}y^1 + C(n, 2)x^{n-2}y^2 + \ldots + C(n, n-1)x^1 y^{n-1} + C(n, n)x^0 y^n$$

These coefficients also are used in the construction of Pascal's Triangle. For $n = 4$, the triangle is

$$
\begin{array}{c}
C(0, 0) \\
C(1, 0) \quad C(1, 1) \\
C(2, 0) \quad C(2, 1) \quad C(2, 2) \\
C(3, 0) \quad C(3, 1) \quad C(3, 2) \quad C(3, 3) \\
C(4, 0) \quad C(4, 1) \quad C(4, 2) \quad C(4, 3) \quad C(4, 4)
\end{array}
$$

The coefficients satisfy the following relation:

$$C(n, n) = C(n, 0) = 1$$
$$C(n, k) = C(n-1, k) + C(n-1, k-1) \quad \text{if} \quad n > k > 0$$

This means that in the triangle, the entries along the edges are all 1's, and an interior entry is the sum of the entries in the row above immediately to the left and right. So the triangle computes to

$$
\begin{array}{c}
1 \\
1 \quad 1 \\
1 \quad 2 \quad 1 \\
1 \quad 3 \quad 3 \quad 1 \\
1 \quad 4 \quad 6 \quad 4 \quad 1
\end{array}
$$

Let's apply the preceding definition to compute $C(3, 2)$:

$$C(3, 2) = C(2, 2) + C(2, 1)$$
$$C(2, 2) = 1$$
$$C(2, 1) = C(1, 1) + C(1, 0)$$
$$C(1, 1) = 1$$
$$C(1, 0) = 1$$
$$\text{So} \quad C(2, 1) = 1 + 1 = 2$$
$$\text{and } C(3, 2) = 1 + 2 = 3$$

Here is an algorithm for a procedure to compute C(n, k):

```
PROCEDURE BINOMIAL (input: N, K; output: RESULT)
IF (K = N) OR (K = 0)
 THEN
  RESULT = 1
 ELSE
  CALL BINOMIAL(N-1,K,RESULT1)
  CALL BINOMIAL(N-1,K-1,RESULT2)
  RESULT = RESULT1 + RESULT2
RETURN
```

17.6 More Complex Recursion

Example 17.3 Code the BINOMIAL procedure and call it in a program to compute C(3, 2).

Solution:

Program Listing PGM17_4.ASM

```
0:      TITLE   PGM17_4: BINOMIAL COEFFICIENTS
1:      .MODEL  SMALL
2:      .STACK  100H
3:      .CODE
4:  MAIN    PROC
5:          MOV     AX,2            ;K=2
6:          PUSH    AX
7:          MOV     AX,3            ;N=3
8:          PUSH    AX
9:          CALL    BINOMIAL        ;AX = RESULT
10:         MOV     AH,4CH
11:         INT     21H             ;DOS EXIT
12: MAIN    ENDP
13: BINOMIAL    PROC    NEAR
14:         PUSH    BP
15:         MOV     BP,SP
16:         MOV     AX,[BP+6]       ;get K
17: ;if
18:         CMP     AX,[BP+4]       ;K=N?
19:         JE      THEN            ;yes, nonrecursive case
20:         CMP     AX,0            ;K=0?
21:         JNE     ELSE_           ;no, recursive case
22: THEN:
23:         MOV     AX,1            ;RESULT = 1
24:         JMP     RETURN
25: ELSE_:
26: ;compute C(N-1,K)
27:         PUSH    [BP+6]          ;save K
28:         MOV     CX,[BP+4]       ;get N
29:         DEC     CX              ;N-1
30:         PUSH    CX              ;save N-1
31:         CALL    BINOMIAL        ;RESULT1 in AX
32:         PUSH    AX              ;save RESULT1
33: ;compute C(N-1,K-1)
34:         MOV     CX,[BP+6]       ;get K
35:         DEC     CX              ;K-1
36:         PUSH    CX              ;save K-1
37:         MOV     CX,[BP+4]       ;get N
38:         DEC     CX              ;N-1
39:         PUSH    CX              ;save N-1
40:         CALL    BINOMIAL        ;RESULT2 in AX
41: ;compute C(N,K)
42:         POP     BX              ;get RESULT1
43:         ADD     AX,BX           ;RESULT = RESULT1 + RESULT2
44: RETURN:
45:         POP     BP              ;restore BP
46:         RET     4               ;return and discard N and K
47: BINOMIAL    ENDP
48:         END     MAIN
```

Procedure BINOMIAL differs from the procedures of examples 17.1 and 17.2 in the following ways:

1. There are two escape cases, k = n or k = 0; in both cases, the call returns 1 in AX (line 23).
2. In the general case, computation of C(n, k) involves two recursive calls, to compute C(n − 1, k) and C(n − 1, k − 1).

All calls to BINOMIAL return the result in AX. After C(n − 1, k) is computed (line 31), the result (RESULT1 in the algorithm) is pushed onto the stack (line 32). At line 40, C(n − 1, k − 1) is computed and the result (RESULT2 in the algorithm) will be in AX. At lines 42–43, RESULT1 is popped into BX and added to RESULT2, so that AX will contain C(n, k) = C(n − 1, k) + C(n − 1, k − 1).

To completely understand how procedure BINOMIAL works, you are encouraged to trace the effect of the procedure on the stack, as was done in example 17.1.

Summary

- Recursive problem solving has the following characteristics: (1) The main problem breaks down to simpler problems, each of which is solved in the same way as the main problem; (2) there is a nonrecursive escape case; and (3) once a subproblem has been solved, work proceeds to the next step of the original problem.

- In assembly language, recursive procedures are implemented as follows: The calling program places the activation record for the first call on the stack and calls the procedure. The procedure uses BP to access the data it needs from the stack. Before initiating a recursive call, a procedure places the activation record for the call on the stack and calls itself. When a call is completed, BP is restored, the return address popped into IP, and the data for the completed call popped off the stack.

- The code for a procedure may involve more than one recursive call. Intermediate results may be saved on the stack, and retrieved when the original call resumes.

Glossary

activation record   Values of the parameters, local variables, and return address of a procedure call

recursive process   A process that is defined in terms of itself

Exercises

1. Write a recursive definition of a^n, where n is a nonnegative integer.
2. Ackermann's function is defined as follows for nonnegative integers m and n:

$$A(0, n) = n + 1$$

$$A(m, 0) = A(m - 1, 1)$$

$$A(m, n) = A(m - 1, A(m, n - 1)) \quad \text{if } m, n \neq 0$$

   Use the definition to show that $A(2,2) = 7$.

3. Trace the steps in example 17.2 (PGM17_3.ASM) and show the stack
   a. At line 20 in the initial (first) call to FIND_MAX.
   b. At line 20 in the second call to FIND_MAX.
   c. At line 20 in the third call to FIND_MAX.
   d. At line 20 in the fourth call to FIND_MAX. This is the escape case.
   e. At line 42 in the completion of the third call to FIND_MAX (after RET 2 has been executed). Also give the contents of AX.
   f. At line 42 in the completion of the second call to FIND_MAX (after RET 2 has been executed). Also give the contents of AX.
   g. At line 42 in the completion of the first call to FIND_MAX (after RET 2 has been executed). Also give the contents of AX. This is the value returned by the procedure.

Programming Exercises

4. Write a recursive assembly language procedure to compute the sum of the elements of a word array. Write a program to test your procedure on a four-element array.
5. The Fibonacci sequence 1, 1, 2, 3, 5, 8, 13, 21, 34, 55, ... may be defined recursively as follows:

$$F(0) = F(1) = 1$$

$$F(n) = F(n - 1) + F(n - 2) \quad \text{if } n > 1$$

   Write a recursive assembly language procedure to compute $F(n)$, and call it in a testing program to compute $F(7)$.

18

Advanced Arithmetic

Overview

Programs often must deal with data that are bigger than 16 bits, or contain fractions, or have special encoding. In the first three sections of this chapter, we discuss arithmetic operations on *double-precision numbers, BCD (binary-coded decimal) numbers*, and *floating-point numbers*. In section 18.4, we discuss the operation of the 8087 numeric coprocessor.

18.1 Double-Precision Numbers

We have shown that numbers stored in the 8086-based computer can be 8 or 16 bits. But even for 16-bit numbers, the range is limited to 0 to 65535 for unsigned numbers and −32768 to +32767 for signed numbers. To extend this range, a common technique is to use 2 words for each number. Such numbers are called **double-precision numbers**, and the range here is 0 to $2^{32}-1$ or 4,294,967,295 for unsigned and −2,147,483,648 to +2,147,483,647 for signed numbers.

A double-precision number may occupy two registers or two memory words. For example, if a 32-bit number is stored in the two memory words A and A+2, written A+2:A, then the upper 16 bits are in A+2 and the lower 16 bits are in A. If the number is signed, then the msb of A+2 is the sign bit. Negative numbers are represented in two's complement form.

Since the 8086/8088 can only operate on 8- or 16-bit numbers, operations on double-precision numbers must be emulated by software. In section 18.4, we show how the 8087 coprocessor can be used to do double-precision arithmetic.

18.1.1 Double-Precision Addition, Subtraction, and Negation

To add or subtract two 32-bit numbers, we first add or subtract the lower 16 bits and then add or subtract the higher 16 bits. However, the answer would be incorrect if the first addition or subtraction generates a carry or borrow.

One way to handle this problem is to use instructions to test the flags and adjust the result. A better method is to use two new instructions provided by the 8086. The instruction **ADC** (add with carry) adds the source operand and CF to the destination, and the instruction **SBB** (subtract with borrow) subtracts the source operand and CF from the destination. The syntax is

```
ADC    destination,source
SBB    destination,source
```

For our first example we'll add two 32-bit numbers.

Example 18.1 Write instructions to add the 32-bit number in A+2:A to the number in B+2:B.

Solution: We have to move the first number to registers before the addition.

```
MOV    AX,A        ;AX gets lower 16 bits of A
MOV    DX,A+2      ;DX gets upper 16 bits of A
ADD    B,AX        ;add the lower 16 bits to B
ADC    B+2,DX      ;add DX and CF to B+2
```

While the 32-bit sum is stored in B+2:B, the flags may not be set correctly. Specifically, the ZF and the PF, which depend on both values of B+2 and B, are set by the value in B+2 only. When it is important to set the flags correctly, we can use additional instructions.

The procedure DADD in program listing PGM18_1.ASM performs a double-precision add and leaves the flags in the same state as if the processor had a 32-bit add instruction. We assume the two numbers are in DX:AX and CX:BX, and the result is returned in DX:AX.

Program Listing PGM18_1.ASM
```
;Procedure for double precision addition with ZF and PF
;adjust
DADD    PROC
;input :  CX:BX = source operand
;         DX:AX = destination operand
;output:  DX:AX = sum
;save register SI
        PUSH  SI            ;SI is needed in the procedure
                            ;to store flags
        ADD   AX,BX         ;add lower 16 bits
        ADC   DX,CX         ;add upper 16 bits with carry
        PUSHF               ;save the flags on the stack
        POP   SI            ;put flags in SI
;test for zero
        JNE   CHECK_PF      ;if DX is not zero then ZF
                            ;is OK, go check PF
        TEST  AX,0FFFFH     ;DX = 0, check if AX = 0?
```

```
              JE       CHECK_PF          ;yes, ZF is OK
              AND      SI,0FFBFH         ;AX not zero, clear ZF bit in SI
;check PF
CHECK_PF:
              OR       SI,100B           ;set SI for even parity
              TEST     AX,0FFH           ;test AL for parity
              JP       RESTORE           ;AL has even parity, PF bit in
                                         ;SI is OK
              XOR      SI,100B           ;AL has odd parity, negate PF
                                         ;bit in SI
RESTORE:
              PUSH     SI                ;place new flags on stack
              POPF                       ;update FLAGS register
;restore SI
              POP      SI
              RET
DADD   ENDP
```

The SI register is used to manipulate the flag bits. We copy the flags into SI by pushing the FLAGS register and then popping to SI because the contents of the FLAGS register cannot be moved to SI directly. To adjust ZF, we examine both DX and AX, and for PF we examine AL; then we copy SI to the FLAGS register, again using the stack. Use the INCLUDE directive to include the file PGM18_1.ASM in your program if you want to use procedure DADD.

To obtain the negation of a double-precision number, we recall that the two's complement of a number is formed by adding a 1 to its one's complement.

Example 18.2 Write instructions to form the negation of A+2:A.

Solution: We first form the one's complement by using the NOT instruction, and then add a 1.

```
NOT    A+2               ;one's complement
NOT    A                 ;one's complement
INC    A                 ;add 1
ADC    A+2,0             ;take care of possible carry
```

For subtraction, again we subtract the low 16 bits first, then subtract the high-order words together with any borrow that might be generated.

Example 18.3 Write instructions to subtract the 32-bit number in A+2:A from B+2:B.

Solution:

```
MOV    AX,A              ;AX gets lower 16 bits of A
MOV    DX,A+2            ;DX gets upper 16 bits of A
SUB    B,AX              ;subtract the lower 16 bits
SBB    B+2,DX            ;subtract DX and CF from B+2
```

To set the flags correctly, we can use the same technique as in the case for addition; we will leave it as an exercise.

18.1.2 Double-Precision Multiplication and Division

Double-precision multiplication and division by powers of 2 can be achieved by using the shift operations, as was done in Chapter 7. To multiply by 2, we perform a left shift. To divide by 2 we perform a right shift.

Example 18.4 Write instructions to perform a left shift operation on A+2:A.

Solution: We start with a left shift on the low-order word, resulting in the msb being shifted into CF. Next, an RCL shifts the CF into the high-order word. The instructions are

```
SHL   A,1           ;low-order word shifted
RCL   A+2,1         ;shift CF into high-order word
```

Again, the OF, ZF, and the PF may be set incorrectly.
The next example shows multiplication by 2^{10}.

Example 18.5 Write instructions to perform 10 left shifts on A+2:A.

Solution: One may be tempted to place 10 in CL and use CL as the count in the shift operation. However, this causes 9 bits in the number to be lost. In multiple-precision shifts, we must do one shift at a time. The CX register may be used as a counter in a loop.

```
        MOV   CX,10       ;initialize counter
L1:     SAL   A,1         ;shift low-order word
        RCL   A+2,1       ;shift CF into high-order word
        LOOP  L1          ;repeat if count is not 0
```

The other shift and rotate operations are left as exercises.
When the multiplier is not a power of 2, we can simulate a multiplication operation with a series of additions. For example, to multiply two double-precision numbers *M* and *N*, we can form the product by adding the number *M N* times. A more efficient way to do multiplication and division of multiple precision numbers is to use the 8087 numeric processor instructions covered in section 18.4.

18.2 Binary-Coded Decimal Numbers

The **BCD (binary-coded decimal) number** system uses four bits to code each decimal digit, from 0000 to 1001. The combinations 1010 to 1111 are illegal in BCD. For example, the BCD representation of the decimal number 913 is 1001 0001 0011. The reason for using BCD numbers is that the conversion between decimal and BCD is relatively simple. In section 18.4, we give a procedure for conversion between decimal and BCD.
As we saw in Chapter 9, multiplication and division are needed to do decimal I/O. These are notoriously slow operations. For some business programs that perform a lot of I/O and only do simple calculations, much time can be saved if numbers are stored internally in BCD format. Needless

to say, the processor must make it easy for programs to do BCD arithmetic if the savings are to be realized.

We first look at the two ways of storing BCD numbers in memory.

18.2.1 Packed and Unpacked BCD

Because only four bits are needed to represent a BCD digit, two digits can be placed in a byte. This is known as **packed BCD form**. In **unpacked BCD form**, only one digit is contained in a byte. The 8086 has addition and subtraction instructions to perform with both forms, but for multiplication and division, the digits must be unpacked.

Example 18.6 Give the binary, packed BCD, and unpacked BCD representations of the decimal number 59.

Solution: 59 = 3Bh = 00111011, which is the binary representation. Because 5 = 0101 and 9 = 1001, the packed BCD representation is 01011001. The unpacked BCD representation is 00000101 00001001.

In the following sections, we cover the instructions needed to do arithmetic on unpacked BCD numbers.

18.2.2 BCD Addition and the AAA Instruction

In BCD operations, we do one digit at a time. It is possible to add two BCD digits and generate a non-BCD result. For example, suppose we add BL, which has 7, to AL, which has 6. The sum of 13 in AL is no longer a valid BCD digit. To adjust, we subtract 10 from AL and place a 1 in AH; then AX will contain the correct sum.

```
AH    00000000     AL    00000110
                   BL  + 00000111
                   AL    00001101    ;not a BCD digit
    +        1       - 00001010    ;adjust by subtracting a 10d
                                     ;from AL and adding a 1 to AH
AH    00000001     AL    00000011    ;result is 1 in AH and 3 in AL
```

We can get the same result by adding 6 to AL and then clearing the high nibble (bits 4–7) of AL. Because the value 13 in AL is greater than the correct result by 10, adding a 6 will make it too large by 16; clearing the high nibble has the effect of subtracting 16.

```
AH    00000000     AL    00001101    ;not a BCD digit
    +        1       + 00000110    ;adjust by adding 6 to AL
                                     ;and 1 to AH
AH    00000001     AL    00010011    ;and clearing the high nibble
AH    00000001     AL    00000011    ;of AL
```

The AAA Instruction

The 8086 does not have a BCD addition instruction, but it does have an instruction that performs the preceding adjustments: **AAA** (ASCII adjust for addition) instruction.

AAA has no operand (AL is assumed to be the operand). It is used after an add operation to adjust the BCD value in AL. It checks the low nibble of AL and the AF (auxiliary flag). If the low nibble of AL is greater than 9 or the AF is set, then a 6 is added to AL, the high nibble of AL is cleared, and a 1 is added to AH.

Both AF and CF are set if the adjustment is made. Other flags are undefined.

It is also possible to add two ASCII digits and use AAA to adjust the result to obtain BCD digits. This allows a program to input ASCII digits, add them, and store the result in BCD format. For example, suppose AL contains 36h (ASCII 6) and BL contains 37h (ASCII 7). We add BL to AL and then use AAA to adjust the result.

```
AH      00000000    AL      00110110
                    BL    + 00110111
AH      00000000    AL      01101101    ;low nibble not a BCD digit

      +        1        + 00000110      ;adjust by adding 6 to AL
                                        ;and adding 1 to AH
AH      00000001    AL      01110011    ;and clearing the high nibble
AH      00000001    AL      00000011    ;of AL
```

As another example, suppose AL is 39h (ASCII 9) and BL is 37h (ASCII 7).

```
AH      00000000    AL      00111001
                    BL    + 00110111
AH      00000000    AL      01110000    ;low nibble is a BCD digit
                                        ;but AF is set
      +        1        + 00000110      ;adjust by adding 6 to AL
                                        ;and 1 to AH
AH      00000001    AL      01110110    ;and clearing the high nibble
AH      00000001    AL      00000110    ;of AL
```

Example 18.7 Write instructions to perform decimal addition on the unpacked BCD numbers in BL and AL.

Solution: The first operation is to clear AH, then we add and adjust the result.

```
MOV     AH,0        ;prepare for possible carry
ADD     AL,BL       ;binary addition
AAA                 ;BCD adjust, AX contains sum
```

Example 18.8 Write instructions to add the two-digit BCD number in bytes B+1:B to the one contained in A+1:A. Assume the result is only two digits.

Solution: We add the low digit before the high digit.

```
MOV   AH,0           ;prepare for possible carry
MOV   AL,A           ;load BCD digit
ADD   AL,B           ;binary addition
AAA                  ;BCD adjust, AX contains sum
MOV   A,AL           ;store digit
MOV   AL,AH          ;put carry in AL
ADD   AL,A+1         ;add high digit of A, assume no
                     ;adjustment is needed
ADD   AL,B+1         ;add high digit of B, assume no
                     ;adjustment is needed
MOV   A+1,AL         ;store high digit
```

Multiple-digit addition is given as an exercise.

18.2.3
BCD Subtraction and the AAS Instruction

BCD subtraction is again performed one digit at a time. When one BCD digit is subtracted from another, a borrow may result. For example, suppose we subtract 7 from 26; we place 7 in BL, 2 in AH, and 6 in AL. After subtracting BL from AL, the result in AL is incorrect. The adjustment is to subtract 6 from AL, clear the high nibble, and subtract 1 from AH. This has the same effect as borrowing from AH and adding 10 to AL.

```
AH    00000010     AL    00000110
                   BL  - 00000111
AH    00000010     AL    11111111    ;not a BCD digit

    -        1       -  00000110    ;adjust by subtracting 6
AH    00000001     AL    11111001    ;from AL and 1 from AH
AH    00000001     AL    00001001    ;clear high nibble of AL and
                                     ;result in AH:AL is 19
```

The AAS Instruction

The **AAS** (ASCII adjust for subtraction) instruction performs BCD subtraction adjustment on the AL register. If the low nibble of AL is greater than 9 (low nibble of AL contains an invalid BCD number) or if the AF is set, AAS will subtract 6 from AL, clear the high nibble of AL, and subtract 1 from AH.

Example 18.9 Write instructions to subtract the two-digit BCD number in bytes B+1:B from the one contained in A+1:A. Assume the number in A+1:A is larger.

Solution: We subtract the low digit before the high digit.

```
MOV   AH,A+1         ;load high BCD digit of A
MOV   AL,A           ;load low digit of A
SUB   AL,B           ;subtract low digit of B
AAS                  ;adjust for borrow
```

```
        SUB   AH,B+1           ;subtract high digit of B
        MOV   A+1,AH           ;store high digit
        MOV   A,AL             ;store low digit
```

In subtracting the high digits, we were able to use the AH register because we assumed that no adjustment was needed; otherwise AL should be used as the result adjusted with AAS. For subtraction of three-digit numbers, and again start from the lowest digit to the highest. Three AAS adjustments are needed. The details are left as an exercise.

18.2.4
BCD Multiplication and the AAM Instruction

In this section, we show only single digit BCD multiplication. In section 18.4, we show how the 8087 can be used to perform multiple-digit BCD multiplication. Two BCD digits can be multiplied to produce a one- or two-digit product. We put the multiplicand in AL and the multiplier in a register or memory byte. After BCD multiplication, AX contains the BCD product.

To multiply 8 by 9, for example, we could put 8 in AL and 9 in BL. After doing the steps in BCD multiplication, the registers AH:AL contain the product 07 02.

The first step in BCD multiplication is to multiply the digits by ordinary binary multiplication. The binary product will be in AL. The second step is to convert the binary product to its BCD equivalent in AX.

With 8 in AL and 9 in BL, to do the first step we execute MUL BL. It puts 0048h = 72 in AX. This needs to be adjusted so that AH contains 07 and AL contains 02.

The AAM Instruction

The **AAM** (ASCII adjust for multiply) instruction performs the second step. It divides the contents of AL by 10. The quotient, corresponding to the ten's digit (7, in this example), is placed in AH; the remainder, corresponding to the unit's (2, in the example), is placed in AL.

In summary, to multiply the BCD digits in AL and BL, and put the BCD product in AX, execute

```
        MUL   BL               ;8-bit multiplication
        AAM                    ;BCD adjust, result in AX
```

18.2.5
BCD Division and the AAD Instruction

In this section, we show the division of a two digit BCD number by a single digit BCD number. The quotient is stored as a two digit BCD number (the leading digit may be 0). We put the dividend in AX and the divisor in a register or memory byte. After the BCD division AX will contain the BCD digits of the quotient.

For example, suppose we want to divide 97 by 5. Before division, AH:AL contains 09 07. The divisor 5 could be put in BL. Since the quotient is 19, after BCD division, AH:AL = 01 09.

There are three steps in BCD division:

1. Convert the dividend in AX from two BCD digits to their binary equivalent.
2. Do ordinary binary division. This puts the (binary) quotient in AL and the remainder in AH.
3. Convert the binary quotient in AL to its two-digit BCD equivalent in AX.

The AAD Instruction

The instruction **AAD** (ASCII adjust for division) does step 1. It multiplies AH by 10, adds the product to AL, then clears AH. For AH:AL = 09 07, multiplication of AH by 10 yields 90 = 5Ah, and adding this to the 7 in AL puts 61h = 01100001 in AL.

If the divisor is in BL, step 2 is done by executing DIV BL. AL gets the quotient, 13h = 19, and AH gets the remainder 02h.

Step 3 is done by executing AAM. It converts the 13h in AL to 01 09 in AH:AL.

In summary, to divide the two BCD digits in AX by the BCD digit in BL, execute

```
AAD             ;convert BCD dividend in AX to binary
DIV   BL        ;do binary division
AAM             ;AX has BCD quotient
```

18.3 Floating-Point Numbers

By using floating-point numbers, we can represent values that are very large and fractions that are very small in a uniform fashion. Before we look at the floating-point representation, we have to see how decimal fractions can be converted into binary.

18.3.1 Converting Decimal Fractions into Binary

Suppose the decimal fraction $0.D_1D_2\ldots D_n$ has a binary representation $0.B_1B_2\ldots B_m$. The bit B_1 is equal to the integer part of the product $0.D_1D_2\ldots D_n \times 2$. This is because if we multiply the binary representation by 2 we obtain $B_1.B_2\ldots B_m$; as the two products must be equal, so must their integer parts. If we multiply the fractional part of the previous product by 2, the integer part of the result will be B_2. We can repeat this process until B_m is obtained. Here is the algorithm:

Algorithm to convert a decimal fraction to an M digit binary fraction

```
Let X contain the decimal fraction
For i = 1 step 1 until m do
  Y = X × 2
  X = fractional part of Y
  Bᵢ = integer part of Y
end
```

Now let's look at some examples.

Example 18.10 Convert the decimal fraction 0.75 to binary.

Solution: *Step 1*, $X = 0.75$, $Y = 0.75 \times 2 = 1.5$, so B_1 is 0. *Step 2*, the new value of X is 0.5, so $Y = 0.5 \times 2 = 1.0$, and B_2 is 1. Since the new fractional part is 0, we are done. Thus, the binary representation of 0.75 is 0.11.

Example 18.11 Convert the decimal number 4.9 into binary.

Solution: We do this in two parts. First we convert the integer part into binary and get 100b. Next we convert the fractional part: *Step 1*, $X = 0.9$, $Y = 0.9 \times 2 = 1.8$, so B_1 is 1. *Step 2*, $X = 0.8$, $Y = 0.8 \times 2 = 1.6$, so B_2 is 1. *Step 3*, $X = 0.6$, $Y = 0.6 \times 2 = 1.2$, so B_3 is 1. *Step 4*, $X = 0.2$, $Y = 0.2 \times 2 = 0.4$, so B_4 is 0. *Step 5*, $X = 0.4$, $Y = 0.4 \times 2 = 0.8$, so B_5 is 0. At this point the new value for X is again 0.8, we can expect the computation to cycle. So the binary representation for 4.9 is 100.1110011001100. . . .

18.3.2 Floating-Point Representation

In the floating-point representation, each number is represented in two parts: a **mantissa**, which contains the leading significant bits in a number, and an **exponent**, which is used to adjust the position of the binary point. For example, the number 2.5 in binary is 10.1b, and its floating-point representation has a mantissa of 1.01 and an exponent of 1. This is because 10.1b can be written as 1.01×2^1. For numbers different from zero, the mantissa is stored as a value that is greater than or equal to 1 and less than 2. Such a mantissa is said to be *normalized*. Some floating-point representations do not store the integer part. Negative numbers are not complemented; they are stored in signed-magnitude format.

For numbers smaller than 1, if we normalize the mantissa the exponent will be negative. For example, the number 0.0001b is 1×2^{-4}. Negative exponents are not represented as signed numbers. Instead, a number called the **bias** is added to the exponent to create a positive number. For example, if we use eight bits for the exponent, then the number $(2^7 - 1)$ or 127 is chosen as the bias. To represent the number 0.0001b, we have a mantissa of 1.0 and an exponent of –4. After adding the bias of 127, we get 123 or 01111101b. Figure 18.1 shows the layout of a 32-bit floating-point representation. It starts with a sign bit, followed by an 8-bit exponent, and a 23-bit mantissa. We'll give examples in section 18.4.1.

18.3.3 Floating-Point Operations

To perform most arithmetic operations on floating-point numbers, the exponent and the mantissa must be first extracted, and then different operations are performed on them. For example, to multiply two real numbers

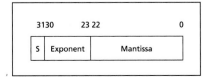

Figure 18.1 Floating-Point Representation

we have to add the exponents and multiply the mantissa; then the result is normalized and stored. However, if two real numbers are to be added, the number with the smaller exponent is shifted to the right so as to adjust the exponent to that of the other number; then the two mantissas are added and the result normalized.

Needless to say, all these operations are time consuming if emulated by software. The floating-point operations can be carried out much faster by using a specially designed circuit chip.

18.4 The 8087 Numeric Processor

The 8087 chip is designed to perform fast numeric operations for an 8088- or 8086-based system. It can operate on multiple-precision, BCD, and floating-point data.

18.4.1 Data Types

The 8087 supports three signed integer formats: word integer (16 bits), short integer (32 bits), and long integer (64 bits).

The 8087 supports a 10-byte packed BCD format which consists of a sign byte, followed by 9 bytes which contain 18 packed BCD digits; a positive sign is represented by 0h and a negative sign by 80h.

There are three floating-point formats:

Short real—Four data bytes with an 8-bit exponent and a 24-bit mantissa. The integer part is not stored.

Long real—Eight data bytes, with an 11-bit exponent and a 53-bit mantissa. Again, the integer part is not stored.

Temporary real—Ten data bytes, with a 15-bit exponent and a 64-bit mantissa. All mantissa bits, including the integer part, are stored.

Figure 18.2 shows the data types of the 8087. We give some examples.

Example 18.12 Represent the number −12345 as an 8087 packed BCD number.

Solution: For negative BCD numbers, the sign byte is 80h. There are a total of 18 BCD digits. Thus the number is 800000000000000012345h.

Example 18.13 Represent the number 4.9 as an 8087 short real.

Solution: From example 18.11, the binary representation for 4.9 is 100.1110011001100.... After normalization, the 24-bit mantissa is 1.00111001100110011001100110, and the exponent is 2. Adding the bias 127 to 2, we get 129 or 10000001b. The integer part is not stored, so the number is 0 10000001 00111001100110011001100 or 409CCCCCh.

Example 18.14 Represent the number −0.75 as an 8087 short real.

Data Formats	Range	Precision	Most Significant Byte								
Word integer	10^4	16 Bits	I_{15} ... I_0 Two's Complement								
Short integer	10^9	32 Bits	I_{31} ... I_0 Two's Complement								
Long integer	10^{18}	64 Bits	I_{63} ... I_0 Two's Complement								
Packed BCD	10^{18}	18 Digits	S $D_{17}D_{16}$ ... D_1D_0								
Short Real	$10^{\pm 38}$	24 Bits	S E_7 E_0 F_1 F_{23} F_0 Implicit								
Long Real	$10^{\pm 308}$	53 Bits	S E_{10} E_0 F_1 F_{62} F_0 Implicit								
Temporary Real	$10^{\pm 4932}$	64 Bits	S E_{14} E_0 F_0 F_{63}								

Integer: I
Packed BCD: $(-1)^S(D_{17}...D_0)$
Real: $(-1)^S(2^{E-Bias})(F_0.F_1...)$
bias = 127 for Short Real
      1023 for Long Real
      16383 for Temp Real

Figure 18.2 *8087 Data Types*

Solution: From example 18.12, the binary representation for 0.75 is 0.11b, so −7.5 is −0.11b. The normalized mantissa is 1.1, and the exponent is −1. Adding the bias 127 to −1, we get 126 or 01111110b. The integer part is not stored, so the number is
1 01111110 10000000000000000000000 or BF400000h.

18.4.2
8087 Registers

The 8087 has eight 80-bit data registers, and they function as a stack. Data may be pushed or popped from the stack. The top of the stack is addressed as ST or ST(0). The register directly beneath the top is addressed as ST(1). In general, the *i*th register in the stack is addressed as ST(i), where i must be a constant.

The data stored in these registers are in temporary real format. Memory data in other formats may be loaded onto the stack. When that happens, the data are converted into temporary real. Similarly, when storing data into memory, the temporary real data are converted to other data formats specified in the store instructions.

18.4.3
Instructions

The instructions for the 8087 include add, subtract, multiply, divide, compare, load, store, square root, tangent, and exponentiation. In doing a complex floating-point operation, the 8087 can be 100 times faster than an 8086 using an emulation program.

The coordination between the 8087 and the 8086 is like this. The 8086 is responsible for fetching instructions from memory. The 8087 monitors this instruction stream but does not execute any instructions until it finds an 8087 instruction. An 8087 instruction is ignored by the 8086, except when it contains a memory operand. In that case, the 8086 would access the operand and place it on the data bus; this is how the 8087 gains access to memory locations.

In this section, we'll show simple examples on the operations of load, store, add, subtract, multiply, and divide. Appendix F contains more information on these instructions and in the following sections we'll give some program examples.

Load and Store

The load instructions load a source operand onto the top of the 8087 stack. There are three load instructions: **FLD** (load real), **FILD** (integer load), and **FBLD** (packed BCD load). The syntax is

```
FLD     source
FILD    source
FBLD    source
```

where source is a memory location.

The type of the memory data is taken from the declared data type. For example, to load a word integer stored in the memory word NUMBER, we write the instruction FILD NUMBER. If the variable DNUM is defined by DD (Define Doubleword), then the instruction FILD DNUM loads a short integer. The instruction FLD can also be used to load an 8087 register to the top of the stack. For example, FLD ST(3).

Once a number is loaded onto the 8087 stack, we can convert it into any data type by simply storing it back into memory. This is a simple way of using the 8087 to perform type conversion. Let's look at the store instructions.

When storing the top of the stack to memory, the stack may or may not be popped. The instructions **FST** (store real) and **FIST** (integer store) do not pop the stack, while the instructions **FSTP** (store real and pop), **FISTP** (integer store and pop), and **FBSTP** (packed BCD store and pop) will pop the stack after the store operation. The syntax is

```
FST     destination
FIST    destination
FSTP    destination
FISTP   destination
FBSTP   destination
```

where destination is a memory location. The stored data type depends on the declared size of the memory operand.

Example 18.15 Write instructions to convert the short integer stored in the doubleword variable DNUM into a long real and store it in the quadword variable QNUM.

Solution: We use the load integer and store real instructions.

```
FILD    DNUM            ;load short integer
FSTP    QNUM            ;store long real and pop stack
```

Add, Subtract, Multiply, and Divide

We can add, subtract, multiply, and divide a memory operand or an 8087 register with the top of the 8087 stack. The instructions for real operands are **FADD** (add real), **FSUB** (subtract real), **FMUL** (multiply real), and **FDIV** (divide real). Each opcode can take zero, one, or two operands. An instruction with no operands assumes ST(0) as the source and ST(1) as the destination; the instruction also pops the stack. For example, FADD (with no operands) adds ST(0) to ST(1) and pops the stack.

In an instruction with one operand, the operand specifies a memory location as the source; the destination is assumed to be ST(0). For example, to subtract a short real in the double word variable DWORD from ST(0) we write FSUB DWORD.

A two operand instruction specifies ST(0) as one operand and ST(1) as the other operand. The stack is not popped. For example, the instruction FMUL ST(1), ST(0) multiplies ST(0) into ST(1); and FDIV ST(0),ST(2) divides ST(2) into ST(0). The syntax is

```
FADD    [[destination,]source]
FSUB    [[destination,]source]
FMUL    [[destination,]source]
FMUL    [[destination,]source]
FDIV    [[destination,]source]
```

where items in square brackets are optional.

There are also instructions for integer operands. They are **FIADD** (integer add), **FISUB** (integer subtract), **FIMUL** (integer multiply), and **FIDIV** (integer divide). The syntax is

```
FIADD   source
FISUB   source
FIMUL   source
FIDIV   source
```

Example 18.16 Write instructions to add the short reals stored in the variables NUM1 and NUM2, and store the sum in NUM3.

Solution: We load the first number, add the second, and store into the third location.

```
FLD     NUM1            ;load first number
FADD    NUM2            ;add second number
FSTP    NUM3            ;store result and pop
```

18.4.4 Multiple-Precision Integer I/O

A **multiple-precision** number is a number stored in multiple words. In section 18.4.1, you have already seen the special case of a double-precision number. Normally, conversions of multiple-precision numbers between their decimal and binary representations are very time consuming. We can use the 8087 to speed up the conversion process. To input a multiple-precision decimal number and convert it into binary, we first store it in BCD format. Then the 8087 can be used to convert the BCD into binary. To output a binary multiple-precision number in decimal, we first use the 8087 to convert it into BCD and then output the BCD digits.

The algorithm for reading digits and converting to packed BCD format is as follows:

Algorithm for Converting ASCII Digits to Packed BCD

```
read first char
case '-'         : set sign bit of BCD buffer
    '0' ... '9'  : convert to binary and push on stack
while char   <> CR
 read char
 case '0' ... '9'  : convert to binary and push on stack
end_while
repeat:
 pop stack
 assemble 2 digits to one byte
until all digits are popped
```

The algorithm is coded in procedure READ_INTEGER, which also converts the BCD number into temporary real format. We can convert the number into other binary formats by using different store instructions. The READ_INTEGER procedure is given in program listing PGM18_2.ASM. The input buffer is 10 bytes and contains 0's initially. We also assume the input number is at most 18 digits.

Program Listing PGM18_2.ASM

```
READ_INTEGER    PROC
;read multiple precision integer number and store as
;real number
;input:     BX = address of 10-byte buffer of 0's
        XOR    BP,BP       ;BP counts number of digits read
        MOV    SI,BX       ;copy of pointer
;read number and push digits on stack
        MOV    AH,01
        INT    21H         ;read
;check for negative
        CMP    AL,'-'
        JNE    RI_LOOP1    ;not negative
;negative, set sign byte to 80h
        MOV    BYTE PTR [BX+9],80H
        INT    21H         ;read next char
;check for CR
RI_LOOP1:
        CMP    AL,0DH      ;CR?
        JE     RI_1        ;CR, goto RI_1
;digit, convert to binary and save on stack
        AND    AL,0FH      ;convert ASCII to binary value
        INC    BP          ;increment count
        PUSH   AX          ;push on stack
        MOV    AH,01       ;read next char
        INT    21H
        JMP    RI_LOOP1    ;repeat
;pop number from stack and store as packed BCD
RI_1:
        MOV    CL,4        ;counter for left shifts
RI_LOOP2:
```

```
                POP     AX              ;low digit
                MOV     [BX],AL         ;store
                DEC     BP              ;more digits?
                JE      RI_4            ;no, exit loop
                POP     AX              ;yes, pop high digit
                SHL     AL,CL           ;shift to high nibble
                OR      [BX],AL         ;store
                INC     BX              ;next byte
                DEC     BP              ;more digits?
                JG      RI_LOOP2        ;yes, repeat
;convert to real
RI_4:           FBLD    TBYTE PTR[SI]   ;load BCD to 8087 stack
                FSTP    TBYTE PTR[SI]   ;store real to memory
                RET
READ_INTEGER ENDP
```

Once the numbers are converted to binary format, we may add, subtract, multiply, and divide them. As long as the results do not cause overflow, we can store the results as BCD numbers and print out the results in decimal using the following algorithm.

Algorithm for Printing Packed BCD Numbers

```
if sign bit is set, then print '-'
get high order byte
for 9 times do
  convert high BCD digit to ASCII and output
  convert low BCD digit to ASCII and output
  get next byte
end
```

The algorithm is coded as procedure PRINT_BCD given in program listing PGM18_3.ASM.

Program Listing PGM18_3.ASM

```
PRINT_BCD       PROC
;print BCD number in buffer
;input: BX = addresses of 10-byte
                TEST    BYTE PTR[BX+9],80H  ;check sign bit
                JE      PB_1                ;positive, skip
                MOV     DL,'-'              ;negative, output '-'
                MOV     AH,2
                INT     21H
PB_1:           ADD     BX,8            ;start with most significant digit
                MOV     CH,9            ;9 bytes
                MOV     CL,4            ;shift 4 times
PB_LOOP:
                MOV     DL,[BX]         ;get byte
                SHR     DL,CL           ;high digit to low nibble
                OR      DL,30H          ;convert to ASCII
                MOV     AH,2            ;output
                INT     21H
                MOV     DL,[BX]         ;get byte again
                AND     DL,0FH          ;mask out high nibble
```

```
                OR      DL,30H          ;convert low digit to ASCII
                MOV     AH,2            ;output
                INT     21H
                DEC     BX              ;next byte
                DEC     CH              ;more digits?
                JG      PB_LOOP         ;yes, repeat
                RET
PRINT_BCD       ENDP
```

When we combine 8086 and 8087 instructions in a program, we need to make sure the 8086 does not access a memory location for an 8087 result before the 8087 can finish an operation and store the result. To synchronize the 8086 with the 8087 we use the instruction **FWAIT**, which suspends the 8086 until the 8087 is finished executing.

Program listing PGM18_4 gives a program that reads in two multiple-precision numbers, and outputs the sum, difference, product, and quotient.

Program Listing PGM18_4.ASM

```
TITLE PGM18_4: MULTIPLE PRECISION ARITHMETIC
;inputs 2 multiple precision numbers
;outputs the sum, difference, product, and quotient
.MODEL     SMALL
.8087
.STACK
.DATA
NUM1       DT       0
NUM2       DT       0
SUM        DT       ?
DIFFERENCE DT                ?
PRODUCT    DT                ?
QUOTIENT   DT                ?
           CR       EQU      0DH
           LF       EQU      0AH
;
NEW_LINE   MACRO                        ;output CR and LF
           MOV      DL,CR
           MOV      AH,2
           INT      21H
           MOV      DL,LF
           INT      21H
           ENDM
;
DISPLAY    MACRO    X        ;output X on screen
           MOV      DL,X
           MOV      AH,2
           INT      21H
           ENDM
;
.CODE
;include I/O procedures
           INCLUDE  PGM18_2.ASM
           INCLUDE  PGM18_3.ASM
MAIN       PROC
```

```
                MOV     AX,@DATA
                MOV     DS,AX                   ;initialize DS
                MOV     ES,AX                   ;initialize ES

                DISPLAY '?'                     ;display prompt
                LEA     BX,NUM1                 ;BX points to buffer
                CALL    READ_INTEGER            ;input first number
                NEW_LINE
                DISPLAY '?'
                LEA     BX,NUM2                 ;BX points to buffer
                CALL    READ_INTEGER            ;input second number
                NEW_LINE
        ;compute sum
                FLD     NUM1                    ;load first number
                FLD     NUM2                    ;load second number
                FADD                            ;add
                FBSTP   SUM                     ;store and pop
                FWAIT                           ;synchronize 8086 and 8087
                LEA     BX,SUM                  ;BX points to SUM
                CALL    PRINT_BCD               ;output SUM
                NEW_LINE
        ;compute difference
                FLD     NUM1                    ;load first number
                FLD     NUM2                    ;load second number
                FSUB                            ;subtract second from first
                FBSTP   DIFFERENCE              ;store difference and pop
                FWAIT                           ;synchronize 8086 and 8087
                LEA     BX,DIFFERENCE           ;set pointer
                CALL    PRINT_BCD               ;output DIFFERENCE
                NEW_LINE
        ;compute product
                FLD     NUM1                    ;load first number
                FLD     NUM2                    ;load second number
                FMUL                            ;multiply
                FBSTP   PRODUCT                 ;store product and pop
                FWAIT                           ;synchronize 8086 and 8087
                LEA     BX,PRODUCT              ;BX points to PRODUCT
                CALL    PRINT_BCD               ;output PRODUCT
                NEW_LINE
        ;compute quotient
                FLD     NUM1                    ;load first number
                FLD     NUM2                    ;load second number
                FDIV                            ;divide first by second
                FBSTP   QUOTIENT                ;store quotient and POP
                FWAIT                           ;synchronize 8086 and 8087
                LEA     BX,QUOTIENT             ;set pointer
                CALL    PRINT_BCD               ;output QUOTIENT
                NEW_LINE
                MOV     AH,4CH                  ;return
                INT     21H                     ;to DOS
        MAIN    ENDP
                END     MAIN
```

18.4.5
Real-Number I/O

Numbers with fractions are called real numbers. The algorithm for reading real numbers is similar to that for integers. The digits are read in as BCD, then converted to floating point and scaled. To do the scaling, a counter is set to the number of digits after the decimal point.

Algorithm for Reading Real Numbers

```
repeat: read char
 case '-': set sign bit of BCD buffer
      '.': set flag
      '0' ... '9': convert to binary and push on stack
                   and if flag is set, increment counter
until CR
repeat:
 pop stack
 assemble 2 digits to one byte
until all digits are popped
load BCD onto 8087 stack
divide by nonzero count value
store back as real
```

The algorithm is coded as procedure READ_FLOAT given in program listing PGM18_5.ASM.

Program Listing PGM18_5.ASM

```
READ_FLOAT   PROC
;read and store real number
;input:    BX = address of 10-byte buffer of 0's
      XOR    DX,DX          ;DH = 1 for decimal point,
                            ;DL = no. of digits after decimal point
      XOR    BP,BP          ;BP counts number of digits read
      MOV    SI,BX          ;copy of pointer
;read number and push digits on stack
RF_LOOP1:
      MOV    AH,01          ;read char
      INT    21H
;check for negative
      CMP    AL,'-'
      JNE    RF_1           ;not negative, check '.'
;negative, set sign byte
      MOV    BYTE PTR [BX+9],80H
      JMP    RF_LOOP1       ;read next char
RF_1: CMP    AL,'.'         ;decimal point?
      JNE    RF_2           ;no, check CR
;decimal point, set DH to 1
      INC    DH
      JMP    RF_LOOP1       ;read next char
;check for CR
RF_2: CMP    AL,0DH
      JE     RF_3           ;CR, goto RF_3
;digit, convert to binary and save on stack
      AND    AL,0FH         ;convert ASCII to binary value
      INC    BP             ;increment count
      PUSH   AX             ;push on stack
```

```
                CMP     DH,0                    ;seen decimal point?
                JE      RF_LOOP1                ;no, read next char
                INC     DL                      ;yes, increment count
                JMP     RF_LOOP1                ;read next char
;pop number from stack and store as packed BCD
RF_3:
                MOV     CL,4                    ;counter for left shifts
RF_LOOP2:
                POP     AX                      ;get low digit
                MOV     [BX],AL                 ;store in buffer
                DEC     BP                      ;decrement count
                JE      RF_4                    ;done if 0
                POP     AX                      ;get high digit
                SHL     AL,CL                   ;move to high nibble
                OR      [BX],AL                 ;move to buffer
                INC     BX                      ;next byte
                DEC     BP                      ;more digits?
                JG      RF_LOOP2                ;yes, repeat
;convert to real
RF_4:   FBLD    TBYTE PTR[SI]                   ;load BCD to 8087 stack
        FWAIT                                   ;synchronize 8086 and 8087
        CMP     DL,0                            ;digits after decimal?
        JE      RF_5                            ;no scaling, goto RF_5
        XOR     CX,CX
        MOV     CL,DL                           ;digit count in CX
        MOV     AX,1                            ;prepare to form
        MOV     BX,10                           ;powers of 10
RF_LOOP3:
        IMUL    BX                              ;multiply 1 by 10
        LOOP    RF_LOOP3                        ;CX times
        MOV     [SI],AX                         ;save scaling factor
        FIDIV   WORD PTR[SI]                    ;divide by scaling factor
RF_5:   FSTP    TBYTE PTR[SI]                   ;store real to memory
        FWAIT                                   ;synchronize 8086 and 8087
        RET
READ_FLOAT      ENDP
```

Here, we assume that the number of digits after the decimal point is less than 5, which allows the scaling factor to be stored as a one-word signed integer.

To output real numbers, we first multiply the number by a scaling factor. Then we store the real number in BCD format, and output the digits with an appropriate decimal point. We print only four digits after the decimal point. So the scaling factor is 10000.

Algorithm for Printing Real Numbers with a Four-Digit Fraction

```
multiply real number by 10000
store as BCD
output BCD number with '.' inserted before last 4 digits
```

The algorithm is coded as procedure PRINT_FLOAT given in program listing PGM18_6.ASM.

Program Listing PGM18_6.ASM

```
PRINT_FLOAT PROC
;print top of 8087 stack
;input:  BX = address of buffer
;
        MOV     WORD    PTR[BX],10000       ;ten thousand
        FIMUL   WORD    PTR[BX]             ;scale up by 10000
        FBSTP   TBYTE   PTR[BX]             ;store as BCD
        FWAIT                               ;synchronize 8086 and 8087
        TEST    BYTE    PTR[BX+9],80H       ;check sign bit
        JE      PF_1                        ;0, goto PF_1
        MOV     DL,'-'          ;output '-'
        MOV     AH,2
        INT     21H
PF_1:   ADD     BX,8            ;point to high byte
        MOV     CH,7            ;14 digits before decimal point
        MOV     CL,4            ;4 shifts
        MOV     DH,2            ;2 times
PF_LOOP:
        MOV     DL,[BX]         ;get BCD digits
        SHR     DL,CL           ;move high digit to low nibble
        OR      DL,30H          ;convert to ASCII
        INT     21H             ;output
        MOV     DL,[BX]         ;get byte again
        AND     DL,0FH          ;mask out high digit
        OR      DL,30H          ;convert to ASCII
        INT     21H             ;output
        DEC     BX              ;next byte
        DEC     CH              ;decrement count
        JG      PF_LOOP         ;repeat if more bytes
        DEC     DH              ;second time?
        JE      PF_DONE         ;yes, done
        DISPLAY '.'             ;no, output decimal point
        MOV     CH,2            ;4 more digits after decimal point
        JMP     PF_LOOP         ;go print digits
PF_DONE:
        RET
PRINT_FLOAT ENDP
```

The program to combine these procedures is left as an exercise.

Summary

- Double-precision numbers increase the range of integers represented.

- The ADC and SBB instructions are used in performing double-precision addition and subtraction.

- Multiplication and division of double-precision numbers by powers of 2 can be implemented by shift and rotate instructions.

- In the BCD system, the decimal digits of a number are expressed in four bits. A number is stored in packed form if two BCD digits are contained in a byte; in unpacked form, one BCD digit is contained in a byte.
- The advantage of the BCD representation is that it is easy to convert decimal character input to BCD and back. The disadvantage is that decimal arithmetic is more complicated for the computer than ordinary binary arithmetic.
- The AAA instruction adjusts the sum in AL after addition.
- The AAS instruction adjusts the difference in AL after a subtraction.
- The AAM instruction takes the binary product of two BCD digits in AL, and produces a two-digit BCD product in AH:AL.
- The AAD instruction converts a two-digit BCD dividend in AH:AL into its binary equivalent in AL.
- Floating-point format consists of a sign bit, an exponent, and a mantissa.
- The 8087 numeric processor can perform a variety of numeric operations on integer, BCD, and real numbers.

Glossary

BCD (binary-coded decimal) system	A system of coding each decimal digit as four binary digits
bias	A number that is added to the exponents to make them positive
double-precision number	Number stored in two computer words
exponent	The part of a floating-point number consisting of the power
floating-point number	Number represented in memory in the form of exponent and mantissa
mantissa	The part of a floating-point number consisting of the significant digits
multiple-precision number	Number stored in multiple words
packed BCD form	Two BCD digits stored in a byte
unpacked BCD form	One BCD digit stored in a byte

New Instructions

AAA	FDIV	FLD
AAD	FIADD	FMUL
AAM	FIDIV	FST
AAS	FILD	FSTP
ADC	FIMUL	FSUB
FADD	FIST	FWAIT
FBLD	FISTP	SBB
FBSTP	FISUB	

New Pseudo-Ops

.8087

Exercises

For exercises 1 to 6, use only the 8086 instructions.

1. Write a procedure DSUB that will perform a double-precision subtraction of CX:BX from DX:AX and return the difference in DX:AX. DSUB should set the flags correctly.

2. Write a procedure DCMP that will perform a double-precision compare of CX:BX from DX:AX. The registers should not be changed, and the flags should be set correctly.

3. Write the instructions that will perform the following double-precision operations. Assume that the number is in DX:AX. Do single shifts and rotates.

    a. SHR
    b. SAR
    c. ROR
    d. ROL
    e. RCR
    f. RCL

4. A triple-precision number is a three-word (48-bit) number. Write instructions that will perform the following operations on the two triple-precision numbers stored in A+4:A+2:A and B+4:B+2:B.

    a. Add the second number to the first.
    b. Subtract the second number from the first.

5. Write instructions that will perform an arithmetic right shift on a triple-precision number stored in BX:DX:AX.

6. Suppose two unpacked 3-digit BCD numbers are stored in A+2:A+1:A and B+2:B+1:B. Write instructions that will

    a. add the second number to the first; assume the result is only three digits.
    b. subtract the second number from the first; assume that the first number is larger.

7. Represent the number –0.0014 as an 8087 short real.

8. Represent the number –2954683 as an 8087 packed BCD.

9. Write the floating-point instructions that will

    a. add an integer variable X to the top of the stack.
    b. divide a short real number Y into the top of the stack.
    c. store and pop the stack to a BCD number Z.

Programming Exercises

10. Write a program to read in two decimal numbers from the keyboard and output their sum. The numbers may be negative and have up to 20 digits. Do not use the 8087 instructions.

11. Write a program to read in two real numbers, with up to four decimal digits after the decimal point, and output their sum, difference, product, and quotient.

19

Disk and File Operations

Overview

Up till now, we have used disk storage exclusively as a repository for system and user program files. Disk files can also be used to store input and output data of a program. Common examples are databases and spreadsheets. In this chapter, we study disk organization, disk operations, and file handling.

19.1 Kinds of Disks

There are two kinds of disks, *floppy disks* and *hard disks*. Floppy disks are made of mylar and are flexible, hence the name. Hard disks are made of metal and are rigid. The surface of a disk is coated with a metallic oxide, and information is stored as magnetized spots.

Floppy and hard disk operations are similar. A disk drive unit reads and writes data on the disk with a *read/write head*, which moves radially in and out over the disk surface while the disk spins. Each head position traces a circular path called a **track** on the disk surface. The movement of the read/write head allows it to access different tracks.

Floppy Disks

A floppy disk is contained in a protective jacket and comes in 3½-inch or 5¼-inch diameter sizes. The jacket for a 5¼-inch disk is made of flexible plastic and has four cutouts (see Figure 19.1): (1) a center cutout so that the disk drive can clamp down on the disk and spin it; (2) an oval-shaped cutout that allows the read/write head to access the disk surface; (3) a small circular hole that aligns with an index hole on the disk used by the disk drive to identify the beginning of a track; and (4) a

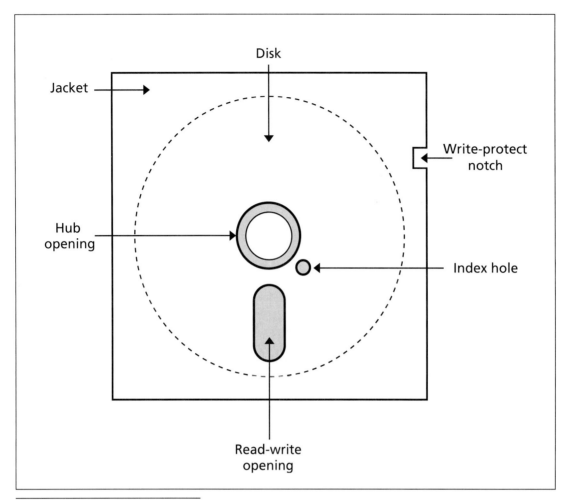

Figure 19.1 A 5¼-inch Floppy Disk

write-protect notch—if open, the disk can be read or written; if taped over, the disk can only be read.

The 3½-inch disk has a more sturdy construction. Its jacket is made of hard plastic, which makes it more rigid; it has a metal-reinforced hub for longer use and a metal sliding cover that protects the read/write head access opening. The write-protection hole operates differently from that of the 5¼-inch disk; the disk is write-protected when the hole is open. There is no index hole. Figure 19.2 shows a 3½-inch disk.

Hard Disks

A hard disk consists of one or more platters mounted on a common spindle. Both sides of a platter are used for recording, and there is one read/write head for each side of a platter. All the heads are connected to a common moving unit. See Figure 19.3.

The read/write head hovers just above the disk surface, never actually touching it during operations (unlike a floppy disk). The space between the head and the disk surface is so small that any dust particle would cause the head to crash onto the disk surface, so hard disks and their disk drives come in hermetically sealed cases.

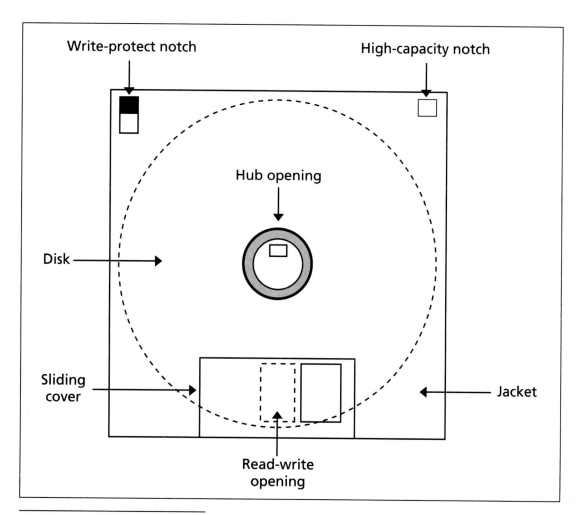

Figure 19.2 A 3½-inch Floppy Disk

Hard disk access is much faster than for a floppy disk for several reasons: (1) a hard disk is always rotating, so no time is lost in starting up the disk, (2) hard disks rotate at a much faster rate (usually about 3600 rpm, or revolutions per minute, versus 300 rpm for a floppy disk), and (3) because of its rigid surface and dust-free environment, the recording density is much greater.

19.2 Disk Structure

Information on a disk is stored in the tracks. When a disk is formatted, tracks are partitioned into 512-byte areas called **sectors**. DOS numbers tracks, starting with 0. Within a track, sectors are also numbered, starting with 1. The number of tracks and sectors per track depends on the kind of disk.

A **cylinder** is the collection of tracks that have the same number. For example, cylinder 0 for a floppy disk consists of track 0 on each side of the disk; for a hard disk, cylinder 0 consists of the tracks numbered 0 on both sides of each platter. Cylinders are so named because the tracks that make up a cylinder line up vertically and seem to form a physical cylinder

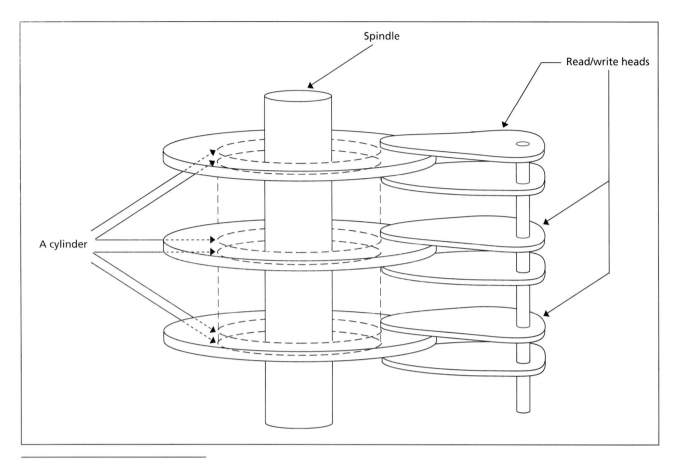

Figure 19.3 A Hard Disk

(see Figure 19.3). The number of cylinders a disk has is equal to the number of tracks on each surface.

DOS also numbers the surfaces that make up a disk, beginning with 0. A floppy disk has surfaces 0 and 1. A hard disk can have more surface numbers, because it may consist of several platters.

19.2.1 Disk Capacity

The capacity in bytes that can be stored on a disk can be calculated as follows:

capacity in bytes = surfaces × tracks/surface × sectors/track × 512 bytes/sector

For example, a 5¼-inch floppy disk has this capacity:

capacity in bytes = 2 surfaces × 40 tracks/surface × 9 sectors/track × 512 bytes/sector = 368,640 bytes

Tables 19.1A and 19.1B give the number of cylinders, sectors/track, surfaces, and capacity for some of the floppy and hard disks in use today.

The density of information on a floppy disk depends on the recording technique. Two common recording techniques are *double density* and *high density*. A high-density drive uses a narrow head and it can read double-density disks; however, a double-density drive cannot read a high-density disk.

Table 19.1A Floppy Disk Capacity

Kind of Disk	Cylinders	Sectors/Track	Capacity
5¼ in. double density	40	9	368,640 bytes
5¼ in. high density	80	15	1,228,800 bytes
3½ in. double density	80	9	737,280 bytes
3½ in. high density	80	18	1,474,560 bytes

Table 19.1B Hard Disk Capacity

Kind of Disk	Cylinders	Sectors/Track	Sides	Capacity
10 MB	306	17	4	10,653,696 bytes
20 MB	615	17	4	21,411,840 bytes
30 MB	615	17	6	32,117,760 bytes
60 MB	940	17	8	65,454,080 bytes

19.2.2 Disk Access

The method of accessing information for both floppy and hard disks is similar. The disk drive is under the control of the disk controller circuit, which is responsible for moving the heads and reading and writing data. Data are always accessed one sector at a time.

The first step in accessing data is to position the head at the right track. This may involve moving the head assembly—a slow operation. Once the head is positioned on the right track, it waits for the desired sector to come by; this takes additional time. Because all the tracks in a cylinder can be accessed without moving the head assembly, when DOS is writing data to a disk it fills a cylinder before going on to the next cylinder.

19.2.3 File Allocation

To keep track of the data stored on a disk, DOS uses a directory structure. The first tracks and sectors of a disk contain information about the disk's file structure. We'll concentrate on the structure of the 5¼-inch double-density floppy disk, which is organized as follows:

Surface	Track	Sectors	Information
0	0	1	boot record (used in start-up)
0	0	2–5	file allocation table (FAT)
0	0	6–9	file directory
1	0	1–3	file directory
1	0	4–9	data (as needed)
0	1	1–9	data (as needed)

The File Directory

DOS creates a 32-byte directory entry for each file. The format of an entry is as follows:

Byte	Function
0–7	filename (byte 0 is also used as a *status byte*)
8–10	extension
11	attribute (see below)
12–21	reserved by DOS
22–23	creation hour:minute:second
24–25	creation year:month:day
26–27	starting cluster number (see discussion of the FAT)
28–31	file size in bytes

There are seven sectors in the directory area, each with 512 bytes. Each file entry contains 32 bytes, so there is room for 7 × 512/32 = 112 entries. However, file entries also may be contained in subdirectories.

The directory is organized as a tree, with the main directory (a.k.a. *root directory*) as root, and the subdirectories as branches.

In a file directory entry, byte 0 is the file **status byte**. The FORMAT program assigns 0 to this byte; it means the entry has never been used. E5h means the file has been deleted. 2Eh indicates a subdirectory. Otherwise, byte 0 contains the first character of the filename.

When a new file is created, DOS uses the first available directory field to store information about the file.

Byte 11 is the **attribute byte**. Each bit specifies a file attribute (see Figure 19.4).

A **hidden file** is a file whose name doesn't appear in the directory search; that is, the DIR command. Hiding a file provides a measure of security in situations where several people use the same machine. A hidden file may not be run under DOS version 2 (it may be run under DOS version 3). However, the attribute may be changed (see section 19.2.8) and then it can be run.

The **archive bit** (bit 5) is set when a file is created. It is used by the BACKUP command that saves files. When a file is saved by BACKUP, this bit is cleared but changing the file will cause the archive bit to be set again. This way the BACKUP program knows which file has been saved.

The attribute byte is specified when the file is created, but as mentioned earlier, it may be changed. Normally when a file is created it has attribute 20h (all bits 0 except the archive bit).

An example of a file directory entry is given in section 19.3.

Clusters

DOS sets aside space for a file in **clusters.** For a particular kind of disk, a cluster is a fixed number of sectors (2 for a 5¼ in. double-density disk); in any case, the number of sectors in a cluster is always a power of 2.

Clusters are numbered, with cluster 0 being the last two sectors of the directory. Bytes 26 and 27 of the file's directory entry contain the starting cluster number of the file. The first data file on the disk begins at cluster 2.

Even if a file is smaller than a cluster (1024 bytes for a 5¼ in. double-density disk), DOS still sets aside a whole cluster for it. This means the disk is likely to have space that is not being used, even if DOS says it is full.

Figure 19.4 Attribute Byte

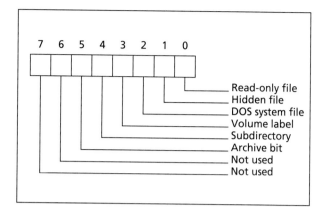

The FAT

The purpose of the **file allocation table (FAT)** is to provide a map of how files are stored on a disk. For floppy disks and 10-MB hard disks, FAT entries are 12 bits in length; for larger hard disks, FAT entries are 16 bits long. The first byte of the FAT is used to indicate the kind of disk (Table 19.2). For 12-bit FAT entries, the next two bytes contain FFh.

How DOS Reads a File

To see how the FAT is organized, let's take an example of how DOS uses the FAT to read a file (refer to Figure 19.5):

1. DOS gets the starting cluster number from the directory; let's suppose it is 2.
2. DOS reads cluster 2 from the disk and stores it in an area of memory called the **data transfer area (DTA)**. The program that initiated the read retrieves data from the DTA as needed.
3. Since entry 2 contains 4, the next cluster in the file is cluster 4. If the program needs more data, DOS reads cluster 4 into the DTA.
4. Entry 4 in the FAT contains FFFh, which indicates the last cluster in the file. In general, the process of obtaining cluster numbers from the FAT and reading data into the DTA continues until a FAT entry contains FFFh.

Table 19.2 The First Byte of the FAT for Some Disks

Kind of Disk	First Byte (hex)
5¼-in. double density	FD
5¼-in. high density	F9
3½-in. double density	F9
3½-in. high density	F0
Hard disk	F8

Figure 19.5 Example of a FAT

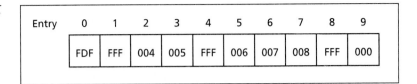

As another example, the FAT in Figure 19.5 shows a file that occupies clusters 3, 5, 6, 7, and 8.

How DOS Stores a File

To store a disk file, DOS does the following:

1. DOS locates an unused directory entry and stores the filename, attribute, creation time, and date.
2. DOS searches the FAT for the first entry indicating an unused cluster (000 means unused) and stores the starting cluster number in the directory. Let's suppose it finds 000 in entry 9.
3. If the data will fit in a cluster, DOS stores them in cluster 9 and places FFFh in FAT entry 9. If there are more data, DOS looks for the next available entry in the FAT; for example, Ah. DOS stores more data in cluster Ah, and places 00Ah in FAT entry 9. This process of finding unused clusters from the FAT, storing data in those clusters, making each FAT entry point to the next cluster continues until all the data have been stored. The last FAT entry for the file contains FFFh.

19.3 File Processing

In this section, we discuss a group of INT 21h functions called the *file handle functions*. These functions were introduced with DOS version 2.0 and make file operations much easier than the previous file control block (FCB) method. In the latter, the programmer was responsible for setting up a table that contained information about open files. With the file handle functions, DOS keeps track of open file data in its own internal tables, thus relieving the programmer of this responsibility. Another advantage of the file handle functions is that a user may specify file path names; this was not possible with the FCB functions.

In the following discussion, **reading** a file means copying all or part of an existing file into memory; **writing** a file means copying data from memory to a file; **rewriting** a file means replacing a file's content with other data.

19.3.1 File Handle

When a file is opened or created in a program, DOS assigns it a unique number called the **file handle**. This number is used to identify the file, so the program must save it.

There are five predefined file handles. They are

0	keyboard
1	screen
2	error output—screen
3	auxiliary device
4	printer

In addition to these files, DOS allows three additional user-defined files to be open (it is possible to raise the limit of open user files. See the DOS manual).

19.3.2 File Errors

There are many opportunities for errors in INT 21h file handling; DOS identifies each error by a code number. In the functions we describe here, if an error occurs then CF is set and the code number appears in AX. The following list contains the more common file-handling errors.

Hex Error Code	Meaning
1	invalid function number
2	file not found
3	path not found
4	all available handles in use
5	access denied
6	invalid file handle
C	invalid access code
F	invalid drive specified
10	attempt to remove current directory
11	not the same device
12	no more files to be found

In the following sections, we describe the DOS file handle functions. As with the DOS I/O functions we have been using, put a function number in AH and execute INT 21h.

19.3.3 Opening and Closing a File

Before a file can be used, it must be opened. To create a new file or rewrite an existing file, the user provides a filename and an attribute; DOS returns a file handle.

INT 21h, Function 3CH:
Open a New File/Rewrite a File

Input: AH = 3Ch
        DS:DX = address of filename, which is an ASCIIZ string
            (a string ending with a 0 byte)
        CL = attribute
Output: If successful, AX = file handle
        Error if CF = 1, error code in AX (3, 4, or 5)

The filename may include a path; for example, A:\PROGS\PROG1.ASM. Possible errors for this function are 3 (path doesn't exist), 4 (all file handles in use), or 5 (access denied, which means either that the directory is full or the file is a read-only file).

Example 19.1 Write instructions to open a new read-only file called FILE1.

Solution: Suppose the filename is stored as follows

```
FNAME    DB         'FILE1',0
HANDLE   DW         ?
```

The string FNAME containing the filename must end with a 0 byte. HANDLE will contain the file handle.

```
MOV   AX,@DATA
MOV   DS,AX           ;initialize DS
MOV   AH,3CH          ;open file function
LEA   DX,FNAME        ;DX has filename address
MOV   CL,1            ;read_only attribute
INT   21H             ;open file
MOV   HANDLE,AX       ;save handle or error code
JC    OPEN_ERROR      ;jump if error
```

If there were an error, the program would jump to OPEN_ERROR where we could print an error message.

To open an existing file, there is another function:

INT 21h, Function 3Dh:
Open an Existing File

Input: AH = 3Dh
          DS:DX = address of filename which is an ASCIIZ string
          AL = access code: 0 means open for reading
                              1 means open for writing
                              2 means open for both
Output: If successful, AX = file handle
          Error if CF = 1, error code in AX (2,4,5,12)

After a file has been processed, it should be closed. This frees the file handle for use with another file. If the file is being written, closing causes any data remaining in memory to be written to the file, and the file's time, date, and size to be updated in the directory.

INT 21H, Function 3Eh:
Close a File

Input: BX = file handle

Output: If CF = 1, error code in AX (6)

Example 19.2 Write some code to close a file. Suppose variable HANDLE contains the file handle.

Solution:

```
MOV    AH,3EH           ;close file function
MOV    BX,HANDLE        ;get handle
INT    21H              ;close file
JC     CLOSE_ERROR      ;jump if error
```

The only thing that could go wrong is that there might be no file corresponding to the file handle (error 6).

19.3.4 Reading a File

The following function reads a specified number of bytes from a file and stores them in memory.

> **INT 21H, Function 3Fh:**
> **Read a File**
>
> Input: AH = 3Fh
>   BX = file handle
>   CX = number of bytes to read
>   DS:DX = memory buffer address
> Output: AX = number of bytes actually read.
>   If AX = 0 or AX < CX, end of file encountered.
>   If CF = 1, error code in AX (5,6)

Example 19.3 Write some code to read a 512-byte sector from a file.

Solution: First we must set up a memory block (buffer) to receive the data:

```
.DATA
HANDLE   DW    ?
BUFFER   DB    512 DUP (0)
```

The instructions are

```
MOV    AX,@DATA
MOV    DS,AX            ;initialize DS
MOV    AH,3FH           ;read file function
MOV    BX,HANDLE        ;get handle
MOV    CX,512           ;read 512 bytes
INT    21H              ;read file. AX = bytes read
JC     READ_ERROR       ;jump if error
```

In some applications, we may want to read and process sectors until end of file (EOF) is encountered. The program can check for EOF by comparing AX and CX:

```
CMP    AX,CX            ;EOF?
JL     EXIT             ;yes, terminate program
JMP    READ_LOOP        ;no, keep reading
```

19.3.5
Writing a File

Function 40h writes a specified number of bytes to a file or device.

> **INT 21H, Function 40h:**
> **Write File**
>
> Input: AH = 40h
>   BX = file handle
>   CX = number of bytes to write
>   DS:DX = data address
> Output: AX = bytes written. If AX < CX, error (full disk)
>   If CF = 1, error code in AX (5,6)

It is possible that there is not enough room on the disk to accept the data; DOS doesn't regard this as an error, so the program has to check for it by comparing AX and CX.

Function 40h writes data to a file, but it can also be used to send data to the screen or printer (handles 1 and 4, respectively).

Example 19.4 Use function 40h to display a message on the screen.

Solution: Let's suppose the message is stored as follows:

```
.DATA
MSG    DB             'DISPLAY THIS MESSAGE'
```

The instructions are

```
MOV    AX,@DATA
MOV    DS,AX          ;initialize DS
MOV    AH,40H         ;write file function
MOV    BX,1           ;screen file handle
MOV    CX,20          ;length of message
LEA    DX,MSG         ;get address of MSG
INT    21H            ;display MSG
```

19.3.6
A Program to Read and Display a File

To show how the file handle functions work, we will write a program that lets the user enter a filename, then reads and displays the file on the screen.

Algorithm for displaying a file

```
Get filename from user
Open file
IF open error
  THEN
    display error code and exit
  ELSE
    REPEAT
      Read a sector into buffer
```

```
    Display buffer
  UNTIL end of file
  Close file
ENDIF
```

Program Listing PGM19_1.ASM

```
 0:     TITLE PGM19_1: DISPLAY FILE
 1:     .MODEL SMALL
 2:
 3:     .STACK 100H
 4:
 5:     .DATA
 6:     PROMPT   DB      'FILENAME:$'
 7:     FILENAME DB      30 DUP (0)
 8:     BUFFER   DB      512 DUP (0)
 9:     HANDLE   DW      ?
10:     OPENERR  DB      0DH,0AH,'OPEN ERROR - CODE'
11:     ERRCODE  DB      30H,'$'
12:
13:     .CODE
14:     MAIN    PROC
15:             MOV     AX,@DATA
16:             MOV     DS,AX           ;initialize DS
17:             MOV     ES,AX           ;and ES
18:             CALL    GET_NAME        ;read filename
19:             LEA     DX,FILENAME     ;DX has filename offset
20:             MOV     AL,0            ;access code 0 for reading
21:             CALL    OPEN            ;open file
22:             JC      OPEN_ERROR      ;exit if error
23:             MOV     HANDLE,AX       ;save handle
24:     READ_LOOP:
25:             LEA     DX,BUFFER       ;DX pts to buffer
26:             MOV     BX,HANDLE       ;get handle
27:             CALL    READ            ;read file. AX = bytes read
28:             OR      AX,AX           ;end of file?
29:             JE      EXIT            ;yes, exit
30:             MOV     CX,AX           ;CX gets no. of bytes read
31:             CALL    DISPLAY         ;display file
32:             JMP     READ_LOOP       ;exit
33:     OPEN_ERROR:
34:             LEA     DX,OPENERR      ;get error message
35:             ADD     ERRCODE,AL      ;convert error code to ASCII
36:             MOV     AH,9
37:             INT     21H             ;display error message
38:     EXIT:
39:             MOV     BX,HANDLE       ;get handle
40:             CALL    CLOSE           ;close file
41:             MOV     AH,4CH
42:             INT     21H             ;dos exit
43:     MAIN    ENDP
44:
45:     GET_NAME        PROC    NEAR
46:     ;reads and stores filename
47:     ;input: none
48:     ;output: filename stored as ASCIIZ string
```

```
49:            PUSH    AX              ;save registers used
50:            PUSH    DX
51:            PUSH    DI
52:            MOV     AH,9            ;display string fcn
53:            LEA     DX,PROMPT
54:            INT     21H             ;display data prompt
55:            CLD
56:            LEA     DI,FILENAME     ;DI pts to filename
57:            MOV     AH,1            ;read char fcn
58: READ_NAME:
59:            INT     21H             ;get a char
60:            CMP     AL,0DH          ;CR?
61:            JE      DONE            ;yes, exit
62:            STOSB                   ;no, store in string
63:            JMP     READ_NAME       ;keep reading
64: DONE:
65:            MOV     AL,0
66:            STOSB                   ;store 0 byte
67:            POP     DI              ;restore registers
68:            POP     DX
69:            POP     AX
70:            RET
71: GET_NAME   ENDP
72:
73: OPEN       PROC    NEAR
74: ;opens file
75: ;input: DS:DX filename
76: ;       AL access code
77: ;output: if successful, AX handle
78: ;        if unsuccessful, CF = 1, AX = error code
79:            MOV     AH,3DH          ;open file fcn
80:            MOV     AL,0            ;input only
81:            INT     21H             ;open file
82:            RET
83: OPEN       ENDP
84:
85: READ       PROC    NEAR
86: ;reads a file sector
87: ;input: BX file handle
88: ;       CX bytes to read (512)
89: ;       DS:DX buffer
90: ;output: if successful, sector in buffer
91: ;        AX number of bytes read
92: ;        if unsuccessful, CF= 1
93:            PUSH    CX
94:            MOV     AH,3FH          ;read file fcn
95:            MOV     CX,512          ;512 bytes
96:            INT     21H             ;read file into buffer
97:            POP     CX
98:            RET
99: READ       ENDP
100:
101:DISPLAY PROC   NEAR
102:;displays memory on screen
103:;input: BX = handle (1)
104:;       CX = bytes to display
```

```
105:;            DS:DX = data address
106:;output: AX = bytes displayed
107:         PUSH    BX
108:         MOV     AH,40H          ;write file fcn
109:         MOV     BX,1            ;handle for screen
110:         INT     21H             ;display file
111:         POP     BX
112:         RET
113:DISPLAY  ENDP
114:
115:CLOSE    PROC    NEAR
116:;closes a file
117:;input:  BX = handle
118:;output: if CF = 1, error code in AX
119:         MOV     AH,3EH          ;close file fcn
120:         INT     21H             ;close file
121:         RET
122:CLOSE    ENDP
123:
124:         END     MAIN
```

At line 18, procedure GET_NAME is called to receive the filename from the user and store it in array FILENAME as an ASCIIZ string. After FILENAME's offset is moved to DX, procedure OPEN is called at line 21 to open the file. The most likely errors are nonexistent file or path. If either happens, OPEN returns with CF set and the error code 2 or 3 in AL. The program converts the code to an ASCII character by adding it to the 30h in variable ERRCODE (line 35), and prints an error message with the appropriate code number. *Note:* typing mistakes will be treated as errors.

If the file opens successfully, AX will contain 5, the first available handle after the predefined handles.

At line 24, the program enters the main processing loop. First, procedure READ is called to read a sector into array BUFFER. CF is set if an error occurred, but the conceivable errors (access denied, illegal file handle) are not possible in this program, so AX will have the actual number of bytes read. If this is zero, EOF was encountered on the previous call to READ, and the program calls procedure CLOSE to close the file.

If AX is not 0, the number of bytes read is moved to CX (line 30) and procedure DISPLAY is called to display the bytes on the screen.

Sample Executions:

```
C>PGM19_1
FILENAME: A:A.TXT
THIS IS A SMALL TEST FILE

C>PGM19_1
FILENAME: A:B.TXT
OPEN ERROR - CODE 2 (nonexistent file)

C>PGM19_1
FILENAME: A:\PROGS\A.TXT
OPEN ERROR - CODE 3 (illegal path)
```

19.3.7
The File Pointer

The **file pointer** is used to locate a position in a file. When the file is opened, the file pointer is positioned at the beginning of the file. After a read operation, the file pointer indicates the next byte to be read; after writing a new file, the file pointer is at EOF (end of file).

The following function can be used to move the file pointer.

INT 21H, Function 42h:
Move File Pointer

Input: AH = 42h
          AL = movement code: 0 means move relative to
                                  beginning of file
                              1 means move relative to
                                  the current file pointer location
                              2 means move relative to
                                  the end of the file
          BX = file handle
          CX:DX = number of bytes to move (signed)
Output: DX:AX = new pointer location in bytes from the
                  beginning of the file
          If CF = 1, error code in AX (1,6)

CX:DX contains the number of bytes to move the pointer, expressed as a signed number (positive means forward, negative means backward). If AL = 0, movement is from the beginning of the file; if AL = 1, movement is from the current pointer position. If AL = 2, movement is from the end of the file.

If CX:DX is too large, the pointer could be moved past the beginning or end of the file. This is not an error in itself, but it will cause an error when the next file read or write is executed.

The following code moves the pointer to the end of the file and determines the file size:

```
MOV   AH,42H         ;move file ptr function
MOV   BX,HANDLE      ;get handle
XOR   CX,CX
XOR   DX,DX          ;0 bytes to move
MOV   AL,2           ;relative to end of file
INT   21H            ;move pointer to end.
                     ;DX:AX = file size
JC    MOVE_ERROR     ;error IF CF = 1
```

Application: Appending Records to a File

The following program creates a file of names. It prompts the user to enter names of up to 20 characters, one name per line. After each name is entered, the program appends it to the file and blanks the input line on the screen. The user indicates end of data by typing a CRTL-Z.

Algorithm for Main Program

```
Open NAMES file
Move file pointer to EOF
Print data prompt
```

```
WHILE a <CTRL-Z> has not been typed DO
 Get a name from the user and store in byte
 array NAMEFLD
 Write name to NAMES file
ENDWHILE
Close NAMES file
```

The program calls procedure GET_NAME to get a name from the user.

Algorithm for GET_NAME Procedure

```
Put blanks in first 20 bytes of NAMEFLD (last
         2 bytes are <CR><LF>)
REPEAT
 Read a character
 IF character is <CTRL-Z> (1Ah)
  THEN
    set CF and exit
  ELSE IF character is not <CR>
       THEN
          store character in NAMEFLD
 ENDIF
UNTIL character is <CR>
Blank input line on screen
```

Program Listing PGM19_2.ASM

```
 0:    TITLE PGM19_2: APPEND RECORDS
 1:    .MODEL  SMALL
 2:
 3:    .STACK  100H
 4:
 5:    .DATA
 6: PROMPT    DB    'NAMES:',0DH,0AH,'$'
 7: NAMEFLD   DB    20 DUP ('0'),0DH,0AH
 8: FILE      DB    'NAMES',0
 9: HANDLE    DW    ?
10: OPENERR   DB    0DH,0AH,'OPEN ERROR $'
11: WRITERR   DB    0DH,0AH,'WRITE ERROR $'
12:
13:    .CODE
14: MAIN      PROC
15:           MOV   AX,@DATA
16:           MOV   DS,AX          ;initialize DS
17:           MOV   ES,AX          ;and ES
18: ;open NAMES file
19:           LEA   DX,FILE        ;get addr of filename
20:           CALL  OPEN           ;open file
21:           JC    OPEN_ERROR     ;exit if error
22:           MOV   HANDLE,AX      ;save handle
23: ;move file pointer to eof
24:           MOV   BX,HANDLE      ;get handle
25:           CALL  MOVE_PTR       ;move pointer
26: ;print prompt
27:           MOV   AH,9           ;display string fcn
28:           LEA   DX,PROMPT      ;"NAMES:"
29:           INT   21H            ;display prompt
```

```
30: READ_LOOP:                          ;read names
31:         LEA     DI,NAMEFLD          ;DI pts to name
32:         CALL    GET_NAME            ;read name
33:         JC      EXIT                ;CF = 1 if end of data
34: ;append name to NAMES file
35:         MOV     BX,HANDLE           ;get handle
36:         MOV     CX,22               ;22 bytes for name, CR, LF
37:         LEA     DX,NAMEFLD          ;get addr of name
38:         CALL    WRITE               ;write to file
39:         JC      WRITE_ERROR         ;exit if error
40:         JMP     READ_LOOP           ;get next name
41: OPEN_ERROR:
42:         LEA     DX,OPENERR          ;get error message
43:         MOV     AH,9
44:         INT     21H                 ;display error message
45:         JMP     EXIT
46: WRITE_ERROR:
47:         LEA     DX,WRITERR          ;get error message
48:         MOV     AH,9
49:         INT     21H                 ;display error message
50: EXIT:
51:         MOV     BX,HANDLE           ;get handle
52:         CALL    CLOSE               ;close NAMES file
53:         MOV     AH,4CH
54:         INT     21H                 ;dos exit
55: MAIN    ENDP
56:
57: GET_NAME        PROC    NEAR
58: ;reads and stores a name
59: ;input: DI = offset address of NAMEFLD
60: ;output: name stored at NAMEFLD
61:         CLD
62:         MOV     AH,1                ;read char function
63: ;clear NAMEFLD
64:         PUSH    DI                  save ptr to NAMEFLD
65:         MOV     CX,20               ;name can have up to 20 chars
66:         MOV     AL,' '
67:         REP     STOSB               ;store blanks
68:         POP     DI                  ;restore ptr
69: READ_NAME:
70:         INT     21H                 ;read a char
71:         CMP     AL,1AH              ;end of data?
72:         JNE     NO                  ;no, continue
73:         STC                         ;yes, set CF
74:         RET                         ;and return
75: NO:
76:         CMP     AL,0DH              ;end of name?
77:         JE      DONE                ;yes, exit
78:         STOSB                       ;no, store in string
79:         JMP     READ_NAME           ;keep reading
80: ;clear input line
81: DONE:
82:         MOV     AH,2                ;print char fcn
83:         MOV     DL,0DH
84:         INT     21H                 ;execute CR
85:         MOV     DL,' '              ;get blank
```

```
 86:             MOV     CX,20
 87: CLEAR:
 88:             INT     21H
 89:             LOOP    CLEAR           ;clear input line
 90:             MOV     DL,0DH
 91:             INT     21H             ;reset cursor to start of line
 92:             RET
 93: GET_NAME ENDP
 94:
 95: OPEN        PROC NEAR
 96: ;opens file
 97: ;input: DS:DX    filename
 98: ;       AL access code
 99: ;output:if successful, AX handle
100:;        if unsuccessful, CF = 1, AX = error code
101:            MOV     AH,3DH          ;open file fcn
102:            MOV     AL,1            ;write only
103:            INT     21H             ;open file
104:            RET
105:OPEN        ENDP
106:
107:WRITE       PROC    NEAR
108:;writes a file
109:;input:  BX = handle
110:;        CX = bytes to write
111:;        DS:DX = data address
112:;output: AX = bytes written.
113:;        If unsuccessful, CF = 1, AX = error code
114:            MOV     AH,40H          ;write file fcn
115:            INT     21H             ;write file
116:            RET
117:WRITE       ENDP
118:
119:CLOSE       PROC    NEAR
120:;closes a file
121:;input:  BX = handle
122:;output: if CF = 1, error code in AX
123:            MOV     AH,3EH          ;close file fcn
124:            INT     21H             ;close file
125:            RET
126:CLOSE       ENDP
127:
128:MOVE_PTR        PROC    NEAR
129:;moves file pointer to eof
130:;input:  BX = file handle
131:;output: DX:AX = pointer position from beginning
132:            MOV     AH,42H          ;move ptr function
133:            XOR     CX,CX           ;0 bytes
134:            XOR     DX,DX           ;from end of file
135:            MOV     AL,2            ;movement code
136:            INT     21H             ;move ptr
137:            RET
138:MOVE_PTR        ENDP
139:
140:            END     MAIN
```

The program begins by using INT 21h, function 3Dh, to open the NAMES file. Since this function may only be used to open a file that already exists, a blank file NAMES must be created before the program is run the first time. To create such a file, enter DEBUG and follow these steps:

1. Use the N command to name the file (type N NAMES).
2. Put 0 in BX and CX (specify 0 file length).
3. Write file to disk (type W).

After the program has been run, the DOS TYPE command may be used to view it.

Sample execution: (The input names are actually entered on the same line, but will be shown on separate lines.)

```
C>PGM19_2
NAMES:
GEORGE WASHINGTON
JOHN ADAMS
<CTRL-Z>

C>TYPE NAMES
GEORGE WASHINGTON
JOHN ADAMS

C>PGM19_2
NAMES:
THOMAS JEFFERSON
HARRY TRUMAN
SUSAN B. ANTHONY
<CTRL-Z>

C>TYPE NAMES
GEORGE WASHINGTON
JOHN ADAMS
THOMAS JEFFERSON
HARRY TRUMAN
SUSAN B. ANTHONY
```

19.3.8 Changing a File's Attribute

In section 19.1.2, we saw that a file's attribute is specified when it is created (function 3Ch). The following function provides a way to get or change the attribute.

> **INT 21H, Function 43h:**
> **Get/Change File Attribute**
>
> Input: AH = 43h
> DS:DX = address of file pathname as ASCIIZ string
> AL = 0 to get attribute
> = 1 to change attribute
> CX = new file attribute (if AL = 1)
> Output: If successful, CX = current file attribute (if AL = 0)
> Error if CF = 1, error code in AX (2,3, or 5)

This function may not be used to change the volume label or subdirectory bits of the file attribute (bits 3 and 4).

Example 19.5 Change a file's attribute to hidden.

Solution:

```
MOV   AH,43H           ;get/change attribute fcn
MOV   AL,1             ;change attribute option
LEA   DX,FLNAME        ;get path
MOV   CX,1             ;hidden attribute
INT   21H              ;change attribute
JC    ATTR_ERROR       ;exit if error. AX = error code
```

19.4 Direct Disk Operations

Up to now, we have been talking about operations on files using the DOS INT 21h file handle functions. There are two other DOS interrupts for reading and writing disk sectors directly.

19.4.1 INT 25h and INT 26h

The DOS interrupts for reading and writing sectors are INT 25h and INT 26h, respectively. Before invoking these interrupts, the following registers must be initialized:

AL   = drive number (0 = drive A, 1 = drive B, etc.)
DS:BX = segment:offset of memory buffer
CX   = number of sectors to read or write
DX   = starting logical sector number (see following section)

Unlike INT 21h, there is no function number to put in AH. The interrupt routines place the contents of the FLAGS register on the stack, and it should be popped before the program continues. If CF = 1, an error has occurred and AX gets the error code.

Table 19.3 Logical Sectors

Surface	Track	Sectors	Logical Sectors	Information
0	0	1	0	Boot record
0	0	2–5	1–4	FAT
0	0	6–9	5–8	File directory
1	0	1–3	9–11 (9h–Bh)	File directory
1	0	4–9	12–17 (Ch–11h)	Data (as needed)
0	1	1–9	18–26 (12h–1Ah)	Data (as needed)

Logical Sector Numbers

In section 19.1.2, we identified positions on a disk by surface, track, and sector. DOS assigns a logical sector number to each sector, starting with 0. Logical sector numbers proceed along a track on surface 0, then continue on the same track on surface 1. Table 19.3 gives the correspondence between surface-track-sector and logical sector for the first part of a 5¼-inch floppy disk.

Reading a Sector

As an example of a direct disk operation, the following program reads the first sector of the directory (logical sector 5) of the disk in drive A.

Program Listing PGM19_3.ASM

```
 0:    TITLE PGM19_3: READ SECTOR
 1:    .MODEL   SMALL
 2:
 3:    .STACK   100H
 4:
 5:    .DATA
 6:    BUFF              DB    512 DUP (0)
 7:    ERROR_MSG         DB              'ERROR$'
 8:
 9:    .CODE
10:    MAIN     PROC
11:             MOV      AX,@DATA
12:             MOV      DS,AX          ;initialize DS
13:             MOV      AL,0           ;drive A
14:             LEA      BX,BUFF        ;BX has buffer offset
15:             MOV      CX,1           ;read 1 sector
16:             MOV      DX,5           ;start at sector 5
17:             INT      25H            ;read sector
18:             POP      DX             ;restore stack
19:             JNC      EXIT           ;jump if no error
20:    ;here if error
21:             MOV      AH,9
22:             LEA      DX,ERROR_MSG
23:             INT      21H            ;display error message
24:    EXIT:
25:             MOV      AH,4CH         ;dos exit
26:             INT      21H
27:    MAIN     ENDP
28:
29:             END      MAIN
```

To demonstrate the program, a disk containing two files A.TXT and B.TXT is placed in drive A, and the program is executed inside DEBUG. In this environment, the program performs the same function as DEBUG's L (load) command.

```
C>DEBUG PGM19_3.EXE

-G13  (execute through line 18 above)
AX=0100  BX=0000  CX=0000  DX=0005  SP=0062  BP=7420  SI=01B6  DI=0001
DS=0F12  ES=0EFB  SS=0F0B  CS=0F33  IP=0013  NV UP EI PL ZR NA PE NC
0F33:0013 5A        POP     DX

-D0   (dump buffer)
0F12:0000  41 20 20 20 20 20 20 20-54 58 54 20 00 00 00 00   A       TXT ....
0F12:0010  00 00 00 00 00 00 BD 19-22 16 02 00 80 00 00 00   .......=."......
0F12:0020  42 20 20 20 20 20 20 20-54 58 54 20 00 00 00 00   B       TXT ....
0F12:0030  00 00 00 00 00 00 23 24-8A 16 03 00 80 00 00 00   ......#$........
0F12:0040  00 F6 F6 F6 F6 F6 F6 F6-F6 F6 F6 F6 F6 F6 F6 F6   .vvvvvvvvvvvvvvv
0F12:0050  F6 F6 F6 F6 F6 F6 F6 F6-F6 F6 F6 F6 F6 F6 F6 F6   vvvvvvvvvvvvvvvv
0F12:0060  00 F6 F6 F6 F6 F6 F6 F6-F6 F6 F6 F6 F6 F6 F6 F6   .vvvvvvvvvvvvvvv
0F12:0070  F6 F6 F6 F6 F6 F6 F6 F6-F6 F6 F6 F6 F6 F6 F6 F6   vvvvvvvvvvvvvvvv
```

From the display, we can pick out the relative fields of the directory entries. For file A,

Offset (hex)	*Information*	*Bytes*
0–7	filename	41 20 20 20 20 20 20 20 A
8–A	extension	54 58 54 TXT
B	attribute	20
C–15	reserved by DOS	
16–17	creation time	BD 19
18–19	creation date	22 16
1A–1B	starting cluster	02
1C–1D	file size	80

The format of the creation hour:minute:second is hhhhhmmmmmmsssss. For this file,

$$19BDh = 00011\ 001101\ 11101$$
$$= 3{:}13{:}29$$

The year:month:day has form yyyyyyymmmmddddd where the year is relative to 1980 for this DOS version. We get

$$1622h = 0001011\ 0001\ 00010$$
$$= 11{:}1{:}2 \text{ (actually 91:1:2)}$$

Examining a File Allocation Table

As another example, we can put a disk that contains several files in drive A and use the preceding program to display the first part of the FAT, which begins at logical sector 1. If we change line 17 in the program to read MOV DX,1 and run the program inside DEBUG, the result is

```
-d0
0F12:0000  FD FF FF FF 4F 00 05 60-00 07 F0 FF 09 A0 00 0B
0F12:0010  C0 00 0D E0 00 0F 00 01-11 20 01 13 40 01 15 60
0F12:0020  01 17 80 01 19 A0 01 1B-C0 01 1D E0 01 1F 00 02
0F12:0030  21 20 02 23 40 02 25 60-02 27 80 02 29 A0 02 2B
0F12:0040  C0 02 2D E0 02 2F 00 03-31 20 03 33 40 03 35 60
0F12:0050  03 37 80 03 39 A0 03 3B-C0 03 3D E0 03 3F 00 04
0F12:0060  41 20 04 43 40 04 45 60-04 47 80 04 49 A0 04 4B
0F12:0070  C0 04 4D E0 04 4F 00 05-51 20 05 53 40 05 55 60
```

The FAT is hard to read in this form because FAT entries are 12 bits = 3 hex digits. To decipher the display, we need to form 3-digit numbers by alternately (1) taking two hex digits from a byte and the rightmost digit from the next byte, and (2) taking the remaining (leftmost) digit from that byte and the two digits from the next byte. Performing this operation on the preceding display, we get

```
CLUSTER    0   1   2   3   4   5   6   7   8   9   A   ...
CONTENTS  FFD FFF FFF 004 005 006 007 FFF 009 00A 00B ...
```

The first data file begins in cluster 2. The entry there is FFFh, so the file also ends in this cluster. The next file begins in cluster 3 and ends in cluster 7. The next one starts in cluster 8, and so on.

Summary

- The FORMAT program partitions each side of a disk into concentric circular areas called *tracks*. Each track is further subdivided into 512-byte sectors. The number of tracks and sectors depends on the kind of disk. A 5¼-inch double-density floppy disk has 40 tracks per surface and 9 sectors per track.

- In storing data, DOS fills a track on one side, then proceeds to a track on the other side.

- Data about files are contained in the file directory. A file entry includes name, extension, attribute, time, date, starting cluster, and file size.

- A file's attribute byte is assigned when it is opened. The attribute specifies whether a file is read-only, hidden, DOS system file, volume label, subdirectory, or has been modified. The usual file attribute is 20h.

- DOS sets aside space for a file in clusters. A cluster is a fixed number of sectors (2 for a double-density floppy disk). The first data file on the disk begins in cluster 2.

- The FAT (file allocation table) provides a map of how files are stored on the disk. Each FAT entry is 12 bytes. A file's directory entry contains the first cluster number $N1$ of the file. FAT entry $N1$ contains the cluster number $N2$ of the next cluster of the file if there is one; the last FAT entry for a file contains FFFh.

- The DOS INT 21h file handle functions provide a convenient way to do file operations. With them, a file is assigned a number called a *file handle* when it is opened, and a program may identify a file by this number.

- File handle functions are specified by putting a function number in AH and invoking INT 21h. The main functions are 3Ch for opening a new file, 3Dh for opening an existing file, 3Eh for closing a file, 3Fh for reading a file, 40h for writing a file, 42h for moving the file pointer, and 43h for changing the file attribute.

- DOS interrupts INT 25h and INT 26h may be used to read and write disk sectors.

Glossary

archive bit	Used to indicate the most recently modified version of a file
attribute byte	Specifies a file's attribute
cluster	A fixed number of sectors—depends on the kind of disk
cylinder	The collection of tracks on different surfaces that share a track number
data transfer area (DTA)	Area of memory that DOS uses to store data from a file
file allocation table (FAT)	Provides a map of file storage on a disk
file handle	A number used by INT 21h functions to identify a file
file pointer	Used to locate a position in a file
hidden file	A file whose name doesn't appear in a disk's directory search
read a file	Copy all or part of the file to memory
rewrite a file	Replace a file's contents by other data
sector	A 512-byte section of a track
status byte	Byte 0 in a file directory entry
track	A circular area on a disk
write a file	Copy data from memory to the file

Exercises

1. Verify that 1,228,800 bytes can be stored on a 5¼-inch floppy disk that has 80 cylinders and 15 sectors per track.

2. Suppose FAT entries for a disk are 12 bits = 3 hex digits in length. Suppose also that the disk contains three files: FILE1, FILE2, and FILE3, and the FAT begins like this:

ENTRY	2	3	4	5	6	7	8	9	A	B	C	D	E	F
CLUSTER	004	009	00B	FFF	00A	FFF	FFF	000	000	000	000	000	000	000

   a. If FILE1, FILE2, and FILE3 begin in clusters 2, 3, and 7, respectively, tell which clusters each of the files are in.

   b. When a file is erased, all its FAT entries are set to 000. Show the contents of the FAT after each the following operations are performed (assume the operations occur in the following order):
   - FILE1 is erased.
   - A 1500-byte file FILE4 is created.
   - FILE2 is erased.
   - A 500-byte file FILE5 is created.
   - A 1500-byte file FILE6 is created.

3. Write instructions to do the following operations. Assume that the file handle is contained in the word variable HANDLE.

   a. Move the file pointer 100 bytes from the beginning of a file.

   b. Move the file pointer backward 1 byte from the current location.

   c. Put the file pointer location in DX:AX.

4. From the DEBUG display of the file directory in section 19.4.1, determine the creation time, date, and size for file B.TXT.

Programming Exercises

5. Write a program that will copy a source text file into a destination file, and replace each lowercase letter by a capital letter. Use the DOS TYPE command to display the source and destination files.

6. Write a program that will take two text files, and display them side by side on the screen. You may suppose that the length of lines in each file is less than half the screen width.

7. Modify PGM19_2.ASM in section 19.3.7 so that it prompts the user to enter a name, and determines whether or not the name appears in the NAMES file. If so, it outputs its position in hex.

8. Modify PGM19_2.ASM in section 19.3.7 so that it prompts the user to enter a name. If the name is present in the NAMES file, the program makes a copy of the file with the name removed. Use the DOS TYPE command to display the original file and the changed file.

20

Intel's Advanced Microprocessors

Overview

We have so far been concentrating on the 8086/8088 processors. In this chapter, we take a look at Intel's advanced microprocessors, which have become very popular. We'll show that they are compatible with the 8086 and can execute 8086 programs. In addition, they have features that support memory protection and multitasking.

In section 20.1 we discuss the 80286. The operating system software needed to use the protected mode of the 80286 is discussed in section 20.2. In section 20.3 we discuss the 80386 and 80486 processors.

20.1 The 80286 Microprocessor

Like the 8086, the 80286 is also a 16-bit processor. It has all the 8086 registers and it can execute all the 8086 instructions. It was designed to be compatible with the 8086 and also support multitasking. This is achieved by having two modes of operation: **real address mode** (also called **real mode**), and **protected virtual address mode** (**protected mode**, for short).

In real address mode, the 80286 behaves like an 8086 and can execute programs written for the 8086 without modification. In addition to the 8086 instructions, it can execute some new instructions called the **extended instruction set**.

In protected mode, the 80286 supports multitasking and it can execute additional instructions needed for this purpose. There are also additional registers being used in this mode.

Let us start with the extended instruction set.

20.1.1
Extended Instruction Set

The extended instruction set contains some 8086 instructions with additional operand types as well as new instructions. They are push and pop, multiply, rotate and shift, string I/O, and high-level instructions.

PUSH and POP

The 80286 allows constants to be used in the PUSH instruction. The format is

```
PUSH    immediate
```

With this instruction, we no longer have to put a constant into a register and then push the register. For example, we can use PUSH 25 instead of MOV AX,25 and PUSH AX.

There are also instructions for pushing and popping all general registers. The instruction **PUSHA** (push all) pushes all the general registers in the following order: AX, CX, DX, BX, SP, BP, SI, and DI. The instruction **POPA** (pop all) pops all the general registers in the reverse order: DI, SI, BP, SP, BX, DX, CX, and AX. These two instructions are useful in procedures that need to save and restore all the registers. The formats are

```
PUSHA
POPA
```

Multiply

The 80286 has three new formats for IMUL that permit multiple operands:

```
IMUL    reg16,immed
IMUL    reg16,reg16,immed
IMUL    reg16,mem16,immed
```

where immed is a constant, reg16 is a 16-bit register, and mem16 is a memory word. The first format specifies an immediate operand as source and a general 16-bit register as destination. The second and third formats contain three operands: the first operand is a 16-bit register that stores the product, the multiplier and multiplicand are found in the second and third operands.

Here are some examples:

1. `IMUL BX,20`   ;BX and 20 are multipled and the
                  ;product is in BX
2. `IMUL AX,BX,20`   ;BX and 20 are multiplied and the
                     ;result is stored in AX
3. `IMUL AX,WDATA,20`   ;WDATA and 20 are multiplied and
                        ;the result is stored in AX

Note that only the low 16 bits of the product are stored. The CF and OF are cleared if the product can be stored as a 16-bit signed number; otherwise, they are set. The other flags are undefined.

Shifts and Rotates

The 80286 allows multiple shifts and rotates using a byte constant. There is no need to use the CL register. For example, we may use SHR AX,4 instead of the two instructions MOV CL,4 and SHR AX,CL.

String I/O

The 80286 allows multiple bytes for input and output operations. The input instructions are **INSB** (input string byte), and **INSW** (input string word). The instruction INSB (or INSW) transfers a byte (or a word) from the port addressed by DX into the memory location addressed by ES:DI. DI is then incremented or decremented according to the DF just like other string instructions. The REP prefix can be used to input multiple bytes or words.

The output instructions are **OUTSB** (output string byte), and **OUTSW** (output string word). The instruction OUTSB (or OUTSW) transfers a byte (or a word) from the memory location addressed by ES:SI to the port addressed by DX. SI is then incremented or decremented according to the DF just like other string instructions. The REP prefix can again be used to output multiple bytes or words.

High-Level Instructions

The high-level instructions allow block-structured high-level languages to check array limits and to create memory space on the stack for local variables. The instructions are **BOUND**, **LEAVE**, and **ENTER**. Because they are primarily used by compilers, we shall not discuss them further.

20.1.2 Real Address Mode

Address Generation

One of the major drawbacks of the 8086 lies in its use of a 20-bit address, which gives a memory space of only 1 megabyte. This 1-MB memory is further restricted by the structure of the PC, which reserves the addresses above 640 KB for video and other purposes. The 80286 uses a 24-bit address, so it has a memory address space of 2^{24} or 16 MB.

On first glance, it appears that the 80286 may solve a lot of the memory limitation problems. On closer examination, however, we see that programs running under DOS cannot use the extra memory. DOS is designed for the 8086/8088, which corresponds to the real mode of the 80286. In order to be compatible with the 8086, the 80286 real address mode generates a physical address the same way as the 8086; that is, the 16-bit segment number is shifted left four bits and then the offset is added. The 20-bit number formed becomes the low 20 bits of the 24-bit physical address; the high four bits are cleared. This gives us a limit of 1 MB.

Actually, the 80286 can access slightly more than 1 MB in real mode. To illustrate, let us use a segment number of FFFFh and an offset of FFFFh, the computed address is FFFF0h + FFFFh = 10FFEFh. In the 8086, the extra bit is dropped, resulting in a physical address of 0FFEFh. For the 80286, because there are 24 address lines, the memory location 10FFEFh is addressed. It is simple to see that for the FFFFh segment, bytes with offset addresses 10h to FFFFh have 21-bit addresses. Thus, in the real address mode, the 80286 can access almost 64 KB more than the 8086. This address space above 1 MB is used by DOS version 5.0 to load some of its routines, resulting in more memory for application programs. Note that on many PCs the twenty-first address bit must be activated by software before the higher memory can be accessed.

Programs Running Under DOS

Under DOS, the 80286 must operate in real mode. Any program written for the 8086 will run on an 80286 machine under DOS. A program for the 80286 may also contain extended instructions. To assemble a program with extended instructions, we must use the .286 assembly directive to avoid assembly errors.

As an example of extended instructions, let's write a procedure to output the contents of BX in hex. The algorithm is given in Chapter 7.

```
        .286
HEX_OUT   PROC
;output contents of BX in hex
        PUSHA                   ;save all registers
        MOV    CX,4             ;CX counts # of hex digits
;repeat loop 4 times
REPEAT:
        MOV    DL,BH            ;get the high byte
        SHR    DL,4             ;shift out low hex digit
        CMP    DL,9             ;see if output digit or letter
        JG     LETTER           ;go to LETTER if > 9
        OR     DL,30H           ;<=9, change to ASCII
        JMP    PRINT            ;output
LETTER:
        ADD    DL,37H            ;>9, convert to letter
PRINT:
        MOV    AH,2             ;output function
        INT    21H              ;output hex digit
        SHL    BX,4             ;shift next digit into first
                                ;position
        LOOP   REPEAT
        POPA                    ;restore registers
        RET
HEX_OUT   ENDP
```

20.1.3 Protected Mode

To fully utilize the power of the 80286, we need to operate it in protected mode. When executing in protected mode, the 80286 supports **virtual addressing**, which allows programs to be much bigger than the machine's physical memory size. Another protected mode feature is the support for **multitasking**, which allows several programs to be running at the same time. The 80286 is designed to execute in real mode when it is powered up. Switching it into protected mode is normally the job of the operating system. In section 20.2 we look at some software that executes in protected mode.

Virtual Addresses

Application programs running in protected mode still use segment and offset to refer to memory locations. However, the segment number no longer corresponds to a specific memory segment. Instead, it is now called a **segment selector** and is used by the system to locate a physical segment that may be anywhere in memory. Figure 20.1 shows a segment selector.

To keep track of the physical segments used by each program, the operating system maintains a set of **segment descriptor tables**. Each application program is given a **local descriptor table**, which contains

Figure 20.1 Segment Selector

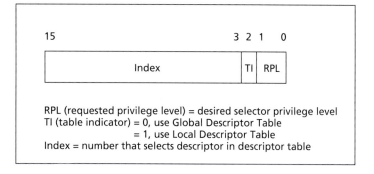

information about the program's segments. In addition, there is a **global descriptor table**, which contains information on segments that can be accessed by all programs.

The segment selector is used to access a **segment descriptor** contained in a segment descriptor table. As we see in Figure 20.2, a segment descriptor describes the type and size of the segment, whether the segment is present, and a 24-bit base address of the segment in memory.

The process of translating the segment and offset used in an application program into a 24-bit physical address goes like this. First, the TI bit in the selector is used to select the descriptor table; TI = 1 means the local descriptor table and TI = 0 means the global descriptor table. The location of the global table is stored in the register GDTR (global descriptor table register) while another register, the LDTR (local descriptor table register), stores the local table of the current running program. Next, a segment descriptor specified by the 13-bit index is accessed from the selected table to obtain the 24-bit segment address. The offset is then added to the segment address to obtain the physical address of the memory location.

A descriptor table may have up to 64 KB. Since a descriptor is 8 bytes each descriptor table can have up to 8 K (2^{13}) descriptors; each descriptor specifies one program segment. A program can choose either its local table or the global table, so it can specify up to 16 K segments. Since the maximum size of a segment is 64 KB, a program can use up to 16 K × 64 KB equals 2^{30}

Figure 20.2 Segment Descriptor

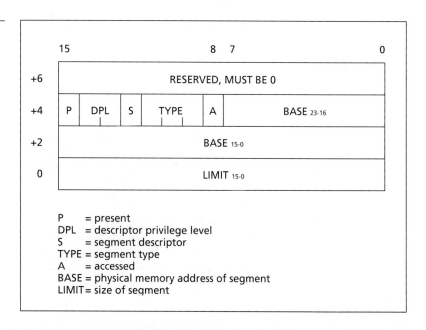

or 1 GB (gigabyte) of memory. This memory is known as **virtual memory**, because the 80286 only has 16 MB of physical memory.

The virtual segments of a program are maintained on the disk drive. The operating system may load the segments into memory as they are needed. It uses the P bit in a descriptor to keep track of whether the corresponding segment has been loaded into memory. If a virtual segment is not loaded, the P bit in the corresponding descriptor is cleared.

An example is a program that is bigger than the physical memory size. It must be loaded incrementally. When an instruction addresses a segment that is not loaded, the operating system is notified by the hardware in the form of an interrupt. The operating system then loads the segment and restarts the instruction. It may be necessary to save a memory segment to disk to make room for this new segment.

Tasks

The basic unit of execution in protected mode is a **task**, which is similar to a program execution in real mode. Each task has its own local descriptor table. At any one time, only one task can be executing, but the operating system can switch between tasks using an interrupt. Also, one task may call another task.

Because one task cannot access another task's local descriptor table, the memory segments of one task are protected from other tasks. To provide further protection, each task is assigned a **privilege level**. There are four privilege levels, 0–3. Level 0 is the most priviledged, and level 3 is the least. The operating system operates at level 0, and application programs operate at level 3. There are privileged instructions such as loading descriptor table registers that can be executed only by a task at level 0. A task operating at one level cannot access data at a more privileged level, and it cannot call a procedure at a less privileged level.

20.1.4 Extended Memory

As we have seen, the 80286 cannot access all its potential memory when operating in real mode; this is also true for the 80386 and 80486. The memory above 1 MB, called **extended memory**, is normally not available for DOS application programs. However, a program could access extended memory by using INT 15h. The two functions for dealing with extended memory are 87h and 88h. A program uses function 88h to determine the size of the extended memory available, and then uses function 87h to transfer data to and from the extended memory. A word of caution in using INT 15h to manipulate extended memory: parts of the extended memory may be used by other programs such as VDISK, and the memory may be corrupted by your program. A better method is for the program to call an extended-memory manager program for extended-memory access.

> **INT 15h Function 87h:**
> **Move Extended Memory Block**
>
> Input: AH = 87h
>   CX = number of words to move
>   ES:SI = address of Global Descriptor Table
> Output: AH = 0 if successful

When function 87h is called, the interrupt routine temporarily switches the processor to protected mode. After the data transfer, the processor is switched back to real mode. This is why a Global Descriptor Table is needed.

**INT 15h Function 88h:
Get Extended Memory Size**

Input: AH = 88h

Output: AX = amount of extended memory (in KB)

Program PGM20_1 copies the data from the array SOURCE to extended memory at 110000h and then copies back the information from extended memory at 110000h to the array DESTINATION. Since the program does not do any I/O, the memory can be examined in DEBUG.

Program Listing PGM20_1.ASM

```
TITLE PGM20_1: COPY EXTENDED MEMORY
.MODEL     SMALL
.286
.STACK
.DATA
SOURCE          DB              'HI, THERE!'
DESTINATION     DB              10 DUP(0)
        GDT     DB              48 DUP(?)       ;global table
SRC_ADDR        DB              ?,?,?           ;24-bit source address
DST_ADDR        DB              ?,?,?           ;24-bit dest. address
.CODE
MAIN    PROC
        MOV     AX,@DATA
        MOV     DS,AX
        MOV     ES,AX
;put 24-bit source address in SRC_ADDR
        MOV     WORD PTR SRC_ADDR,DS    ;get segment address
        SHL     WORD PTR SRC_ADDR,4     ;shift seg no. 4 places
        MOV     AX,DS                   ;get highest 4 bits
        SHR     AH,4
        MOV     SRC_ADDR+2,AH
        LEA     SI,SOURCE               ;source offset address
        ADD     WORD PTR SRC_ADDR,SI    ;add offset to segment
        ADC     SRC_ADDR+2,0            ;take care of carry
;put 24-bit destination address in DST_ADDR
        MOV     DST_ADDR,0              ;destination address is
        MOV     DST_ADDR+1,0            ;110000h
        MOV     DST_ADDR+2,11H
;set up registers
        LEA     SI,SRC_ADDR             ;source address
        LEA     DX,DST_ADDR             ;destination address
        MOV     CX,5                    ;number of words
        LEA     DI,GDT                  ;global table
;transfer data
        CALL    COPY_EMEM               ;copy to extended memory
;set up source address
        MOV     SRC_ADDR,0              ;source address is
        MOV     SRC_ADDR+1,0            ;110000h
```

20.1 The 80286 Microprocessor

```
                MOV     SRC_ADDR+2,11H
;set up destination address
        MOV     WORD PTR DST_ADDR,DS    ;get segment address
        SHL     WORD PTR DST_ADDR,4     ;shift seg no. 4 places
        MOV     AX,DS                   ;get highest 4 bits
        SHR     AH,4
        MOV     DST_ADDR+2,AH
        LEA     SI,DESTINATION          ;destination offset addr
        ADD     WORD PTR DST_ADDR,SI    ;add offset to segment
        ADC     DST_ADDR+2,0            ;take care of carry
;set up registers
        LEA     SI,SRC_ADDR             ;source address
        LEA     DX,DST_ADDR             ;destination address
        MOV     CX,5                    ;number of words
        LEA     DI,GDT                  ;global table
        CALL    COPY_EMEM               ;copy to DESTINATION
        MOV     AH,4CH                  ;DOS exit
        INT     21H
MAIN    ENDP
;
COPY_EMEM       PROC
;move block to and from extended memory
;input: ES:DI = address of 48 byte buffer to be used as GDT
;       CX = number of words to transfer
;       SI = source address (24 bits)
;       DX = destination address (24 bits)
;
;initilize global descriptor table by setting up six
;descriptors
        PUSHA                           ;save registers
;—first descriptor is null, i.e. 8 bytes of 0
        MOV     AX,0                    ;
        STOSW                           ;
        STOSW
        STOSW                           ;
        STOSW
;—second descriptor is set to 0, i.e. 8 bytes of 0
        STOSW                           ;
        STOSW
        STOSW                           ;
        STOSW
;—third descriptor is source segment
        SHL     CX,1            ;convert to number of bytes
        DEC     CX
        MOV     AX,CX           ;size of segment, in bytes
        STOSW                   ;
        MOVSB                   ;source address, 3 bytes
        MOVSB
        MOVSB
        MOV     AL,93H          ;access rights byte
        STOSB
        MOV     AX,0            ;
        STOSW
;—fourth descriptor is destination segment
        MOV     AX,CX           ;size of segment, in bytes
        STOSW                   ;
        MOV     SI,DX           ;destination address, 3 bytes
```

```
                MOVSB
                MOVSB
                MOVSB
                MOV     AL,93H          ;access rights byte
                STOSB
                MOV     AX,0            ;
                STOSW
;-fifth descriptor is set to 0
                STOSW                   ;
                STOSW
                STOSW                   ;
                STOSW
;-sixth descriptor is set to 0
                STOSW                   ;
                STOSW
                STOSW                   ;
                STOSW
;restore registers
                POPA
;transfer data
                MOV     SI,DI           ;ES:SI points to GDT
                MOV     AH,87H
                INT     15H
                RET
COPY_EMEM       ENDP
;
                END     MAIN
```

The copying is done by procedure COPY_EMEM. It receives in CX the number of words to transfer, in SI the location of a 24-bit source address, and in DI the location of a 24-bit destination address. The source and destination buffers can be anywhere in the 16-MB physical address space of the 80286. COPY_EMEM first sets up the global descriptor table which contains the source and destination buffers as program segments. It then uses INT 15h, function 87h to perform the transfer.

20.2 Protected-Mode Systems

Now that we have some idea of how the hardware functions in protected mode, let's turn to the software. At present, there is no standard multitasking operating system for the PC. We'll look at Windows 3 and OS/2. First, let's consider the process of multitasking.

Multitasking

In a single-task environment like DOS, one program controls the CPU and releases control only when it chooses to. An exception to this scenario is that of an interrupt. In a multitasking environment, however, such as Windows and OS/2, the operating system determines which program has control and several programs can be running at the same time. Actually, a program is given a small amount of time to execute, and when the time is up, another program is allowed to execute. By rotating quickly among several programs, the computer gives the impression that all the programs are executing at the same time.

20.2.1
Windows and OS/2

Windows 3

Windows 3 is the most popular **graphical user interface** (**gui**) on the PC. Each executing task is shown in a box on the screen, called a **window**. A window may be enlarged to occupy the entire screen or shrunk to a single graphics element called an **icon**. A Windows 3 application program may provide services, identified by a **menu**, to the user. To select an item in the menu, a user simply positions a screen pointer with a **mouse** at the item and clicks it.

Windows 3 can operate in one of three modes: *real mode, standard mode,* and *386 enhanced mode*. When Windows 3 runs on an 8086 machine or in the real address modes of the advanced processors, it operates in real mode. An application program must end before another one can be executed.

The standard mode of Windows 3 corresponds to the protected mode of the 80286. Windows 3 uses the multitasking features of the 80286 to support multiple Windows 3 applications. It can also execute a program written for DOS. However, to run such a program it must switch the processor back to real address mode. In this case, other applications cannot execute in the background. Windows 3 requires at least 192 KB of extended memory to run in this mode; otherwise it can only run in real mode.

The 386 enhanced mode of Windows corresponds to the protected mode of the 386. In the next section, we'll see that the 386 can execute multiple 8086 applications in protected mode. So, in 386 enhanced mode Windows 3 can perform multitasking on Windows 3 applications as well as DOS applications. A machine must have a 386 or 486 processor chip and at least 1 MB of extended memory to run Windows 3 in this mode.

Windows 3 is not a complete operating system, because it still needs DOS for many file operations. To run Windows 3, we must start in DOS and then execute the Windows 3 program.

OS/2

Unlike Windows 3, OS/2 is a complete operating system. OS/2 version 1 was designed for the protected mode of the 80286. It requires at least 2 MB of extended memory. OS/2 version 2 supports the 80386 protected mode.

Threads and Processes

Under OS/2, it is possible for a program to be doing several things simultaneously. For example, a program may display one file on the screen while at the same time it is copying another file to disk. The program itself is called a **process**, and each of the two tasks here is known as a **thread**. A thread is the basic unit of execution in OS/2, and we can see that it corresponds to a task supported by the hardware. A thread can create another thread by calling a system service routine.

To summarize, a process consists of one or more threads together with a number of system resources, such as open files and devices, that are shared by all the threads in the process. The concept of a process is similar to the notion of a program execution in DOS.

20.2.2 Programming

We only show some simple OS/2 programs as an illustration. More complex OS/2 programs and Windows 3 application programs are beyond the scope of this book.

One noticeable difference between DOS and OS/2 for the programmer is that, to do I/O and system calls in OS/2, a program must do a far call to a system procedure, instead of using the INT instruction. Parameters are to be pushed onto the stack before the call is made. This is done to optimize high-level language interface. The system procedures can be linked to the application program by including the appropriate system library. Actually, the library only contains a reference to the procedure and not the code. The system procedure is contained in a .DLL file and is linked when the program is loaded. Linking modules at loading time is called *dynamic linking* and is used by OS/2. OS/2 function calls are known as *application program interface (API)*.

"Hello" Program

As a first example, we show a program that prints out 'Hello!'. The program is shown in program listing PGM20_2.ASM.

Program Listing PGM20_2.ASM
```
TITLE PGM20_2: PRINT HELLO
.286
.MODEL   SMALL
.STACK
;
.DATA
MSG    DB     'HELLO!'
NUM_BYTES DW    0
;
.CODE
       EXTRN DOSWRITE:FAR, DOSEXIT:FAR
MAIN PROC
;put arguments for DosWrite on stack
       PUSH   1            ;file handle for screen
       PUSH   DS           ;address of message: segment
       PUSH   OFFSET MSG   ;offset
       PUSH   5            ;length of message
       PUSH   DS           ;addr of number of bytes written: seg
       PUSH   OFFSET NUM_BYTES  ;offset
       CALL   DOSWRITE     ;write to screen
;put arguments for DosExit on stack
       PUSH   1            ;action code 1 = end all threads
       PUSH   0            ;return code 0
       CALL   DOSEXIT      ;exit
MAIN ENDP
       END    MAIN
```

Notice that we do not have to initialize DS. When a program is loaded, OS/2 sets DS to the data segment and it does not create a PSP for the program; furthermore, OS/2 supports only .EXE files.

We have used two API functions, DosWrite to write to the screen, and DosExit to terminate the program. DosWrite writes to a file; the arguments are file handle, address of buffer, length of buffer, and address of bytes-out variable. The file handle for the screen is 1. The bytes-out variable receives the number of bytes written to the file; the value can be used to check for errors. The arguments must be pushed on the stack in the order given before calling DosWrite.

DosExit can be used to terminate a thread or all threads in a process. The arguments are (1) an action code to terminate a thread or all threads, and (2) a return code that is passed back to the system that created the process. The arguments for normal exit consist of an action code 1 to end all threads and a return code 0.

In OS/2, the called procedures are responsible for clearing the stack of arguments sent to them when they return. Thus there are no POP instructions in our program.

The API functions DosWrite and DosExit are defined in the library file called DOSCALLS.LIB. As a matter of fact, all API functions used in this book are contained there. To link the program, we use the following command:

```
LINK PGM20_2,,,DOSCALLS.
```

Echo Program

As a second program, we write a program to echo a string typed at the keyboard.

Program Listing PGM20_3.ASM

```
TITLE   PGM20_3: ECHO PROGRAM
.286
.MODEL  SMALL
.STACK
;
.DATA
BUFFER      DB          20 DUP(0)
NUM_CHARS   DW          0
NUM_BYTES   DW          0
;
.CODE
        EXTRN   DOSREAD:FAR, DOSWRITE:FAR, DOSEXIT:FAR
MAIN    PROC
;put arguments for DosRead on stack
        PUSH    0               ;file handle for keyboard
        PUSH    DS              ;address of buffer: segment
        PUSH    OFFSET BUFFER   ;offset
        PUSH    20              ;length of buffer
        PUSH    DS              ;addr of no. of chars read: segment
        PUSH    OFFSET NUM_CHARS    ;offset
        CALL    DOSREAD         ;read from keyboard
;put arguments for DosWrite on stack
        PUSH    1               ;file handle for screen
        PUSH    DS              ;address of message: segment
        PUSH    OFFSET BUFFER   ;offset
        PUSH    NUM_CHARS       ;length of message
        PUSH    DS              ;addr of no. of bytes written: segment
        PUSH    OFFSET NUM_BYTES ;offset
        CALL    DOSWRITE        ;write to screen
;put arguments for DosExit on stack
        PUSH    1               ;action code 1=end all threads
        PUSH    0               ;return code 0
        CALL    DOSEXIT         ;exit
MAIN    ENDP
        END     MAIN
```

We use the API function DosRead to read from the keyboard. DosRead inputs from a file and it takes the arguments: file handle, buffer address, buffer length, and address of chars_read variable. The file handle for the keyboard is 0. DosRead reads in the keys until the buffer is filled or a carriage return is typed. The number of characters read is returned in the chars-read variable.

We have treated the screen and keyboard as files for DosWrite and DosRead. There are also Vio (video) and Kbd (keyboard) API functions that can perform more I/O operations.

The preceding two programs are only meant as an introduction to OS/2 programming. A full treatment requires a separate book.

20.3 80386 and 80486 Microprocessors

The 80386 and 80486 are both 32-bit microprocessors. As noted in Chapter 3, they are very similar, with the exception that the 80486 contains the floating-point processor circuits. In the following treatment, we'll concentrate on the 80386, because the 80486 can be treated like a fast 80386 with a floating-point processor.

The 80386 has both a real address mode and a protected mode of operation, just like the 80286.

20.3.1 Real Address Mode

The 80386 has eight 32-bit general registers: EAX, EBX, ECX, EDX, ESI, EDI, EBP, ESP. Each register contains a 16-bit 8086 counterpart; for example, AX is the lower 16 bits of EAX. There are six 16-bit segment registers: CS, SS, DS, ES, FS, and GS, with DS, ES, FS, and GS being data segment registers. The 32-bit EFLAGS register contains in it the 16-bit FLAGS register, and the 32-bit EIP register contains the 16-bit IP register. There are also debug registers, control registers, and test registers. In addition, there are registers for protected mode memory management and protection.

In real address mode, the 80386 can execute all of the 80286 real address mode instructions. Hence, to the programmer the 80386 real address mode is similar to the 8086 with extensions to the instruction set and registers.

The 80386 uses 32-bit addresses, but in real address mode it generates an address like an 8086, so it can address at most 1 MB plus 64 KB just like an 80286.

20.3.2 Protected Mode

The 80386 in protected mode can execute all 80286 instructions. When an 80286 protected mode operating system is used on an 80386, a segment descriptor contains a 24-bit base address so only 16 MB of physical memory are available. Actually, because there is no wraparound it can access 16 MB plus 64 KB.

The 80386 in protected mode allows a segment descriptor to contain a 32-bit address and the offset can also have 32 bits, giving a segment size of 2^{32} or 4 gigabytes; this is also the size of the physical memory address space. A program can still use 2^{14} segments, so the virtual memory space is $2^{32} \times 2^{14}$, which is 2^{46} or 64 terabytes. This should be sufficient for any application program in the foreseeable future.

Page-Oriented Virtual Memory

It is possible to organize the virtual memory into pages. The operating system can set a bit in a control register to indicate the use of page tables. When this happens, the 32-bit address in the segment descriptor is treated as a page selector that selects one of the 1-K page tables from a page directory, and a page number in the selected page table and an offset in the page. The page directory contains 1 K tables, and each table contains 1 K pages, and each page is 4 KB. Hence, the total address possible is 2^{32} or the entire 4 gigabytes of physical space. Each page is 4 KB of contiguous addresses of physical memory.

Virtual 8086 Mode

The 80386 supports execution of one or more 8086 programs in an 80386 protected mode environment. The processor executes in virtual 8086 (V86) mode when the VM (virtual machine) bit in the EFLAGS register is set. In V86 mode, the segment registers are used in the same fashion as in real address mode; that is, an address is computed by adding the offset to the segment number shifted four bits. This linear address can be mapped to any physical address by the use of paging.

20.3.3 Programming the 80386

Sixteen-Bit Programming

The real mode 80386 instructions with only 16-bit operands are essentially 80286 instructions. There are some new instructions, and they are given in Appendix F.

Thirty-Two-Bit Programming

In 32-bit programming, both operand size and offset address are 32 bits. The machine opcodes for 32-bit 386 instructions are actually the same as those for 16-bit instructions. It turns out that the 80386 has two modes of operations, 16-bit mode and 32-bit mode. Since the instruction opcodes for 32-bit and 16-bit are the same, the operand type must depend on the current mode of the 386. Byte-size operands are not affected by the operating mode.

When the 80386 is in protected mode, it can operate in either 16-bit or 32-bit mode; the operating mode is identified in the segment descriptor in each task. However, it can only operate in 16-bit mode when it is in real address mode.

Mixing 16- and 32-Bit Instructions

It is possible to mix 16-bit and 32-bit instructions in the same program. An operand-size override prefix (66h) can be placed before an instruction to override the default operand size. In 16-bit mode, the prefix switches the operand size to 32 bits, and in 32-bit mode the same prefix switches the operand size to 16 bits. One prefix must be used for each instruction.

There is also an address size override prefix (67h), which overrides the offset address size. It is used in a similar manner as the operand size prefix, and they both can be used in the same instruction.

We demonstrate by writing a program for DOS (16-bit real mode) using 32-bit operands. The program given in program listing PGM20_4.ASM reads in two unsigned double-precision numbers and outputs their sum. The addition is performed by 32-bit registers.

Program Listing PGM20_4.ASM

```
TITLE PGM20_4: 32-BIT OPERATIONS
;input two 32-bit numbers and output their sum
;uses 386 32-bit operations
.386
.MODEL      SMALL
S_SEG SEGMENT             USE16 STACK
      DB     256 DUP (?)
S_SEG ENDS
;
D_SEG SEGMENT             USE16
FIRST DD     0            ;stores first 32-bit number
D_SEG ENDS
;
NEW_LINE    MACRO
;go to next line
      MOV    AH,2
      MOV    DL,0AH
      INT    21H
      MOV    DL,0DH
      INT    21H
      ENDM
;
PROMPT MACRO
;output prompt
      MOV    DL,'?'
      MOV    AH,2
      INT    21H
      ENDM
;
C_SEG SEGMENT             USE16
      ASSUME              CS:C_SEG,DS:D_SEG,SS:S_SEG
MAIN  PROC
      MOV    AX,D_SEG
      MOV    DS,AX        ;initialize DS
;output prompt
      PROMPT
;clear EBX
      MOV    EBX,0
;read character
L1:   MOV    AH,1
      INT    21H
;check for CR
      CMP    AL,0DH
      JE     NEXT         ;CR, get next number
;place digit in EBX
      AND    AL,0FH       ;convert to binary
      IMUL   EBX,10       ;multiply EBX by 10
      MOVZX  ECX,AL       ;move AL to ECX and extend with 0's
      ADD    EBX,ECX      ;add digit
;repeat
      JMP    L1
;save first number
NEXT: MOV    FIRST,EBX
;next line
```

```
                NEW_LINE
;output prompt
                PROMPT
;clear EBX
                MOV     EBX,0
;read character
L2:             MOV     AH,1
                INT     21H
;check for CR
                CMP     AL,0DH
                JE      SUMUP           ;CR, sum up
;place digit in EBX
                AND     AL,0FH          ;convert to binary
                IMUL    EBX,10          ;multiply EBX by 10
                MOVZX   ECX,AL          ;move AL to EBX and extend with 0's
                ADD     EBX,ECX         ;add digit
;repeat
                JMP     L2
;sum up
SUMUP:          ADD     EBX,FIRST       ;EBX has sum
;convert to decimal
                MOV     EAX,EBX         ;move sum to EAX
                MOV     EBX,10          ;divisor is 10
                MOV     CX,0            ;initialize counter
L3:             MOV     EDX,0
                DIV     EBX             ;divide EBX into EDX:EAX
                PUSH    DX              ;DX is reminder, EAX is quotient
                INC     CX              ;increment count
                CMP     EAX,0           ;done?
                JG      L3              ;no, repeat
;next line
                NEW_LINE
                MOV     AH,2            ;output function
;output
L4:             POP     DX              ;get digit
                OR      DL,30H          ;convert to ASCII
                INT     21H             ;output
                LOOP    L4
;
                MOV     AH,4CH          ;return
                INT     21H             ;to DOS
MAIN            ENDP
C_SEG           ENDS
                END     MAIN
```

We have used an 80386 instruction **MOVZX** which moves a source operand into a bigger size register and zero extends the leading bits. To assemble 386 instructions, we need to use the **.386** directive. However, when the .386 directive is used, the assembler assumes that the operating mode is 32-bit mode. When we are running programs under the real address mode of the 386, we have to specify a default mode of 16 bits. This can only be done with the full segment directives. A segment can be specified with a *use* type. For example, to specify a 16-bit use type we wrote D_SEG SEGMENT USE16 in the program. The use type, USE16 specifies both operand size and offset address size are 16 bits; and all our segments have the use type USE16.

Summary

- The 80286 can operate in either real address mode or protected mode.
- In real address mode, the 80286 operates like an 8086.
- The 80286 uses 24-bit addresses, allowing it a total memory space of 16 MB. However, in real address mode, it can only access 1 MB.
- In protected mode, the 80286 can use 1 gigabytes (GB) of virtual memory.
- Windows 3 has three modes of operations: real mode, standard mode, and 386 enhanced mode.
- OS/2 version 1 supports the 80286 protected mode and version 2 supports the 80386 protected mode.
- System services in OS/2 are coded as far calls.
- The 80486 is like an 80386 with a floating-point unit.
- The 80386/80486 operates as an 80286 in real address mode.
- In protected mode, the 80386/80486 supports paging and a virtual 8086 mode. It can also execute all 80286 instructions.

Glossary

dynamic linking	Linking modules at the time of loading
extended instruction set	Set of new instructions first used by the 80186 and 80188 processors, can also be executed by the 80286, 80386, and 80486 processors
extended memory	Memory above 1 MB
global descriptor table	A segment descriptor table that contains information about the segments that can be accessed by all tasks
graphical user interface, gui	A user interface that uses pointers to commands, and special graphics symbols
icon	A graphical element representing a command or program
local descriptor table register (LDTR)	A register that holds the address of a local descriptor table
menu	A set of command selections displayed in a window
mouse	A pointing device used to control cursor position on a display screen
multitasking	A technique that allows more than one program (task) to run concurrently
privilege level	A measure of a program's ability to execute special commands
process	A program execution
protected (address) mode	A mode of operation by the advanced processors that protects the memory used by

	one program from other concurrent programs
real (address) mode	The mode of operation in which an address contained in an instruction corresponds to a physical address
segment descriptor	An entry in a descriptor table that describes a program segment
segment descriptor table	A table that contains segment descriptors, there are two kinds of segment descriptor tables, global descriptor table and local descriptor table
segment selector	The value of a segment register when the processor is running under protected mode, it identifies a segment in a descriptor table
task	A program unit with its own segments
thread	A subtask of a process
virtual address	An address contained in an instruction that does not correspond to any particular physical address
virtual memory	Disk memory used by the operating system to store segments of a task that are not needed currently
window	A rectangular area on the screen

New Instructions

```
BOUND           INSW            OUTSB
ENTER           LEAVE           OUTSW
INS             MOVZX           POPA
INSB            OUTS            PUSHA
```

New Pseudo-ops

```
.286            .386
```

Exercises

1. Write a procedure for OS/2 that will input a string, and then echoes the string ten times on 10 different lines.
2. Use 80386 instructions to multiply two 32-bit numbers.
3. Use the 386 instructions given in Appendix F to write a procedure that outputs the position of the leftmost set bit in the register BX.

Programming Exercises

4. Modify program PGM20_4.ASM so that it will output the sum of two signed double-precision numbers.

Part Three

Appendices

Appendix A

IBM Display Codes

The IBM PC uses an extended set of ASCII characters for its screen display. Table A.1 shows the ASCII characters. The control characters BS (backspace), HT (tab), CR (carriage return), ESC (escape), SP (space) correspond to the keys Backspace, Tab, Enter, Esc, and space bar; LF (line feed) advances the cursor to the next line, BEL (bell) sounds the beeper, and FF (form feed) advances the printer to the next page.

Table A.2 shows the extended set of 256 display characters. When a display code is written to the active page of the display memory, the corresponding character shows up on the screen. To write to the display memory, we can use INT 10h functions 9h, 0Ah, 0Eh, and 13h. The functions 9h and 0Ah write all values to the display memory. The functions 0Eh and 13h recognize the control character codes 07h (bell), 08h (backspace), 0Ah (line feed), and 0Dh (carriage return) and perform the control functions instead of writing these codes to the display memory.

Table A.1
ASCII Code

DEC	HEX	CHAR	DEC	HEX	CHAR	DEC	HEX	CHAR	DEC	HEX	CHAR
0	00		32	20	(SP)	64	40	@	96	60	`
1	01		33	21	!	65	41	A	97	61	a
2	02		34	22	"	66	42	B	98	62	b
3	03		35	23	#	67	43	C	99	63	c
4	04		36	24	$	68	44	D	100	64	d
5	05		37	25	%	69	45	E	101	65	e
6	06		38	26	&	70	46	F	102	66	f
7	07	(BEL)	39	27	'	71	47	G	103	67	g
8	08	(BS)	40	28	(	72	48	H	104	68	h
9	09	(HT)	41	29	)	73	49	I	105	69	i
10	0A	(LF)	42	2A	*	74	4A	J	106	6A	j
11	0B		43	2B	+	75	4B	K	107	6B	k
12	0C	(FF)	44	2C	,	76	4C	L	108	6C	l
13	0D	(CR)	45	2D	-	77	4D	M	109	6D	m
14	0E		46	2E	.	78	4E	N	110	6E	n
15	0F		47	2F	/	79	4F	O	111	6F	o
16	10		48	30	0	80	50	P	112	70	p
17	11		49	31	1	81	51	Q	113	71	q
18	12		50	32	2	82	52	R	114	72	r
19	13		51	33	3	83	53	S	115	73	s
20	14		52	34	4	84	54	T	116	74	t
21	15		53	35	5	85	55	U	117	75	u
22	16		54	36	6	86	56	V	118	76	v
23	17		55	37	7	87	57	W	119	77	w
24	18		56	38	8	88	58	X	120	78	x
25	19		57	39	9	89	59	Y	121	79	y
26	1A		58	3A	:	90	5A	Z	122	7A	z
27	1B	(ESC)	59	3B	;	91	5B	[	123	7B	{
28	1C		60	3C	<	92	5C	\	124	7C		
29	1D		61	3D	=	93	5D	]	125	7D	}
30	1E		62	3E	>	94	5E	^	126	7E	~
31	1F		63	3F	?	95	5F	_	127	7F	

Blank spaces indicate control characters that are not used on the IBM PC.

**Table A.2
IBM Extended
Character Set**

DEC	HEX	CHAR	DEC	HEX	CHAR	DEC	HEX	CHAR	DEC	HEX	CHAR	DEC	HEX	CHAR
000	00	BLANK	026	1A	→	052	34	4	078	4E	N	104	68	h
001	01	☺	027	1B	←	053	35	5	079	4F	O	105	69	i
002	02	☻	028	1C	∟	054	36	6	080	50	P	106	6A	j
003	03	♥	029	1D	↔	055	37	7	081	51	Q	107	6B	k
004	04	♦	030	1E	▲	056	38	8	082	52	R	108	6C	l
005	05	♣	031	1F	▼	057	39	9	083	53	S	109	6D	m
006	06	♠	032	20	(SPACE) (SP)	058	3A	:	084	54	T	110	6E	n
007	07	•	033	21	!	059	3B	;	085	55	U	111	6F	o
008	08	◘	034	22	"	060	3C	<	086	56	V	112	70	p
009	09	○	035	23	#	061	3D	=	087	57	W	113	71	q
010	0A	◙	036	24	$	062	3E	>	088	58	X	114	72	r
011	0B	♂	037	25	%	063	3F	?	089	59	Y	115	73	s
012	0C	♀	038	26	&	064	40	@	090	5A	Z	116	74	t
013	0D	♪	039	27	'	065	41	A	091	5B	[	117	75	u
014	0E	♫	040	28	(	066	42	B	092	5C	\	118	76	v
015	0F	☼	041	29	)	067	43	C	093	5D	]	119	77	w
016	10	►	042	2A	*	068	44	D	094	5E	^	120	78	x
017	11	◄	043	2B	+	069	45	E	095	5F	_	121	79	y
018	12	↕	044	2C	,	070	46	F	096	60	`	122	7A	z
019	13	‼	045	2D	—	071	47	G	097	61	a	123	7B	{
020	14	¶	046	2E	.	072	48	H	098	62	b	124	7C	|
021	15	§	047	2F	/	073	49	I	099	63	c	125	7D	}
022	16	▬	048	30	0	074	4A	J	100	64	d	126	7E	~
023	17	↨	049	31	1	075	4B	K	101	65	e	127	7F	⌂
024	18	↑	050	32	2	076	4C	L	102	66	f	128	80	Ç
025	19	↓	051	33	3	077	4D	M	103	67	g	129	81	ü

Appendix A IBM Display Codes

Table A.2 IBM Extended Character Set

DEC	HEX	CHAR	DEC	HEX	CHAR	DEC	HEX	CHAR	DEC	HEX	CHAR	DEC	HEX	CHAR
130	82	é	156	9C	£	182	B6	┤	208	D0	╨	234	EA	Ω
131	83	â	157	9D	¥	183	B7	╕	209	D1	╤	235	EB	δ
132	84	ä	158	9E	Pt	184	B8	╖	210	D2	╥	236	EC	∞
133	85	à	159	9F	ƒ	185	B9	╣	211	D3	╙	237	ED	ø
134	86	å	160	A0	á	186	BA	║	212	D4	╘	238	EE	∈
135	87	ç	161	A1	í	187	BB	╗	213	D5	╒	239	EF	∩
136	88	ê	162	A2	ó	188	BC	╝	214	D6	╓	240	F0	≡
137	89	ë	163	A3	ú	189	BD	╜	215	D7	╫	241	F1	±
138	8A	è	164	A4	ñ	190	BE	╛	216	D8	╪	242	F2	≥
139	8B	ï	165	A5	Ñ	191	BF	┐	217	D9	┘	243	F3	≤
140	8C	î	166	A6	ª	192	C0	└	218	DA	┌	244	F4	⌠
141	8D	ì	167	A7	º	193	C1	┴	219	DB	█	245	F5	⌡
142	8E	Ä	168	A8	¿	194	C2	┬	220	DC	▄	246	F6	÷
143	8F	Å	169	A9	⌐	195	C3	├	221	DD	▌	247	F7	≈
144	90	É	170	AA	¬	196	C4	─	222	DE	▐	248	F8	°
145	91	æ	171	AB	½	197	C5	┼	223	DF	▀	249	F9	∙
146	92	Æ	172	AC	¼	198	C6	╞	224	E0	α	250	FA	·
147	93	ô	173	AD	¡	199	C7	╟	225	E1	β	251	FB	√
148	94	ö	174	AE	«	200	C8	╚	226	E2	Γ	252	FC	ⁿ
149	95	ò	175	AF	»	201	C9	╔	227	E3	π	253	FD	²
150	96	û	176	B0	░	202	CA	╩	228	E4	Σ	254	FE	■
151	97	ù	177	B1	▒	203	CB	╦	229	E5	σ	255	FF	(SPACE) (SP)
152	98	ÿ	178	B2	▓	204	CC	╠	230	E6	µ			
153	99	Ö	179	B3	│	205	CD	═	231	E7	τ			
154	9A	Ü	180	B4	┤	206	CE	╬	232	E8	φ			
155	9B	¢	181	B5	╡	207	CF	╧	233	E9	⊖			

SP means space.

Appendix B

DOS Commands

In this appendix, we give some common DOS commands.

Note: in the following, two special characters can be used within a file name or extension. The ? character used in any position indicates that any character can occupy that position in the file name or extension; The * character used in any position indicates that any character can occupy that position and *all remaining positions* in the file name or extension.

BACKUP

Creates a backup of disk files.

Example: `BACKUP C: A:`

Copies the files in the current C directory to a backup in disk A.

CLS (Clear Screen)

Clears the display screen and moves the cursor to the upper left corner.

Example: `CLS`

COPY

Copies files from one disk and directory to another.

Example 1: `COPY A:FILE1.TXT B:`

Copies the file FILE1.TXT from drive A to drive B. The current drive need not be specified in the command. It is also possible to give the copy a different name.

Example 2: `COPY FILE1.TXT B:FILE2.TXT`

Copies FILE1.TXT from the disk in the current drive to FILE2.TXT on the disk in drive B.

Example 3: `COPY A:*.* B:`

Copies all files from drive A to drive B.

DATE

Changes the date known to the system. The date is recorded as a directory entry on any files you create. The format is *mm-dd-yy*.

Example: `DATE 07-14-90`

DIR (Directory)

Lists the directory entries.

Example 1:   `DIR`

Lists all directory entries in the current drive. Each entry has a file name, size, and date. The entries in a different directory or different drive can also be listed by specifying the name of the drive or directory.

Example 2:   `DIR C*.*`

Lists all directory entries of files that begin with C and have any extension.

ERASE (or DEL)

Erases a file.

Example 1:   `ERASE FILE1.TXT`

Erases the file called FILE1.TXT from the current drive and directory.

Example 2:   `ERASE *.OBJ`

Erases all files with an .OBJ extension in the current drive.

FORMAT

Initializes a disk.

Example: `FORMAT A:`

Formats the disk in drive A. *Caution:* formatting a disk destroys any previous contents of the disk. A new disk must be formatted before it can be used.

PRINT

Prints files on the printer.

Example: `PRINT A:MYFILE.TXT`

Prints the file called MYFILE.TXT in drive A.

RENAME (or REN)

Changes the name of a file.

Example: `REN FILE1.TXT MYFILE.TXT`

Renames the file FILE1.TXT to MYFILE.TXT.

RESTORE

Restores files from a backup disk.

Example: `RESTORE A: C:`

Copies the backup files from disk A to disk C.

TIME

Changes the time known to the system. The time is recorded as a directory entry on any files you create. The format is *hh:mm:ss*. The range of hours is 0–23.

Example: `TIME 16:47:00`

TYPE

Displays the contents of a file on the display screen.

Example: `TYPE MYFILE.TXT`

Displays the file called MYFILE.TXT.

B.1 Tree-Structured Directories

DOS versions 2.1 and later provide the capability of placing related disk files in their own directories.

When a disk is formatted, a single directory called the *root directory* is created. It can hold up to 112 files for a double-sided, double-density 5¼ inch floppy disk.

The root directory can contain the names of other directories called *subdirectories*. These subdirectories are treated just like ordinary files; they have names of 1–8 characters and an optional one- to three-character extension.

To illustrate the following commands, we'll use the following tree-structured directory as an example.

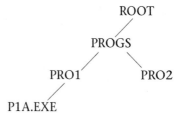

Here, PROGS is a subdirectory of the root directory. PRO1 and PRO2 are subdirectories of PROGS. P1A.EXE is a file in PRO1.

A *path* to a file consists of a sequence of subdirectory names separated by backslashes (\), and ending with the file name. If the sequence begins with a \, then the path begins at the ROOT DIRECTORY. If not, it begins with the current directory.

CHDIR (or CD)

Changes the current directory.

Example 1: `CD\`

Makes the root directory the current directory of the logged drive.

Example 2: `CD\PROGS`
Makes PROGS the current directory of the logged drive.

Example 3: `CD PRO1`

After example 2, makes PRO1 the current directory.

Example 4: `CD\PRO1`

DOS would reply "invalid directory" because PRO1 is not a subdirectory of the root directory.

Example 5: `CD`

This command causes the path to the current directory to be display so after example 3, if C is the logged drive, DOS would respond with C:\PROGS\PRO1.

MKDIR (or MD)

Creates a subdirectory on the specified disk.
As examples, we'll create the preceding tree structure on the disk in drive C:

```
C>CD\
C>MD\PROGS
C>MD\PROGS\PRO1
C>MD\PROGS\PRO2
```

RMDIR (or RD)

Removes a subdirectory from a disk. The subdirectory must be empty. The last directory in a specified path is the one removed.
As examples, we'll erase file P1A.EXE and remove all the preceding directories from the disk in drive C:

```
C>ERASE\PROGS\PRO1\P1A.EXE
C>RD\PROGS\PRO1
C>RD\PROGS\PRO2
C>RD\PROGS
```

Appendix C

BIOS and DOS Interrupts

C.1 Introduction

In this appendix, we show some of the common BIOS and DOS interrupt calls. We begin with interrupt 10h; interrupts 0 to Fh are not normally used by application programs, their names are given in Table C.1.

C.2 BIOS Interrupts

Interrupt 10: Video

Function 0h:
Select Display Mode
Selects video display mode.
Input: AH = 0h
              AL = video mode
Output: none

Function 1h:
Change Cursor Size
Selects the start and ending lines for the cursor.
Input: AH = 1h
              CH (bits 0–4) = starting line for cursor
              CL (bits 0–4) = ending line for cursor
Output: none

Table C.1 Interrupts 0 to 0Fh

Interrupt Type	Usage
0h	Divide by zero
1h	Single step
2h	NMI
3h	Breakpoint
4h	Overflow
5h	PrintScreen
6h	Reserved
7h	Reserved
8h	Timer tick
9h	Keyboard
0Ah	Reserved
0Bh	Serial communications (COM2)
0Ch	Serial communications (COM1)
0Dh	Fixed disk
0Eh	Floppy disk
0Fh	Parallel printer

Function 2h:
Move Cursor
Positions the cursor.
Input:　　AH = 2h
　　　　　BH = page
　　　　　DH = row
　　　　　DL = column
Output:　none

Function 3h:
Get Cursor Position and Size
Obtains the current position and size of the cursor.
Input:　　AH = 3h
　　　　　BH = page
Output:　CH = starting line for cursor
　　　　　CL = ending line for cursor
　　　　　DH = row
　　　　　DL = column

Function 5h:
Select Active Display Page
Input:　　AH = 5h
　　　　　AL = page
　　　　　DH = row
　　　　　DL = column
Output:　none

Function 6h:
Scroll Window Up
Scrolls the entire screen or a window up by a specified number of lines.
Input:　　AH = 6h
　　　　　AL = number of lines to scroll
　　　　　　　　(if zero, entire window is blanked)
　　　　　BH = attribute for blanked lines

CH,CL = row, column of upper left corner of windows
DH,DL = row, column of lower right corner of windows
Output: none

Function 7h:
Scroll Window Down
Scrolls the entire screen or a window down by a specified number of lines
Input: AH = 7h
          AL = number of lines to scroll
              (if zero, entire window is blanked)
          BH = attribute for blanked lines
          CH,CL = row, column of upper left corner of window
          DH,DL = row, column of lower right corner of window
Output: none

Function 8h:
Read Character and Attribute at Cursor
Obtains the ASCII character and its attribute at the cursor position.
Input: AH = 8h
          BH = page
Output: AH = attribute
          AL = character

Function 9h:
Write Character and Attribute at Cursor
Writes an ASCII character and its attribute at the cursor position.
Input: AH = 9h
          AL = character
          BH = page
          BL = attribute (text mode) or color (graphics mode)
          CX = count of characters to write
Output: none

Function 0Ah:
Write Character at Cursor
Writes an ASCII character at the cursor position. The character receives the attribute of the previous character at that position.
Input: AH = 0Ah
          AL = character
          BH = page
          CX = count of characters to write
Output: none

Function 0Bh:
Set Palette, Background, or Border
Selects a palette, background color, or border color.
Input: To select the background color and border color
              AH = 0Bh
              BH = 0
              BL = color
              To select palette (320 × 200 four-color mode)
              AH = 0Bh
              BH = 1
              BL = palette
Output: none

Function 0Ch:
Write Graphics Pixel
Input: AH = 0Ch
           AL = pixel value
           BH = page
           CX = column
           DX = row
Output: none

Function 0Dh:
Read Graphics Pixel
Obtains a pixel value.
Input: AH = 0Dh
           BH = page
           CX = column
           DX = row
Output: AL = pixel value

Function 0Eh:
Write Character in Teletype Mode
Writes an ASCII character at the cursor position, then increments cursor position.
Input: AH = 0Eh
           AL = character
           BH = page
           BL = color (graphics mode)
Output: none
Note: the attribute of the character cannot be specified.

Function 0Fh:
Get Video Mode
Obtains current display mode.
Input: AH = 0Fh
Output: AH = number of character columns
           AL = display mode
           BH = active display page

Function 10h, Subfunction 10h:
Set Color Register
Sets individual VGA color register.
Input: AH = 10h
           AL = 10h
           BX = color register
           CH = green value
           CL = blue value
           DH = red value
Output: none

Function 10h, Subfunction 12h:
Set Block of Color Registers
Sets a group of VGA color registers.
Input: AH = 10h
           AL = 12h
           BX = firstcolor register
           CX = number of color registers
           ES:DX = segment:offset of color table
Output: none

Note: the table consists of a group of three-byte entries corresponding to red, green, and blue values for each color register.

Function 10h, Subfunction 15h:
Get Color Register
Obtains the red, green, and blue values of a VGA color register.
Input: AH = 10h
           AL = 15h
           BX = color register
Output: CH = green value
           CL = blue value
           DH = red value

Function 10h, Subfunction 17h:
Get Block of Color Registers
Obtains the red, green, and blue values of a group of VGA color registers.
Input: AH = 10h
           AL = 17h
           BX = first color register
           CX = number of color registers
           ES:DX = segment:offset of buffer to receive color list
Output: ES:DX = segment:offset of buffer

Note: the color list consists of a group of three-byte entries corresponding to red, green, and blue values for each color register.

Interrupt 11h: Get Equipment Configuration

Obtains the equipment list code word.
Input: none
Output: AX = equipment list code word
           (bits 14–15 = number of printers installed,
           13 = internal modem,
           12 = game adapter,
           9–11 = number of serial ports,
           8 is reserved,
           6–7 = number of floppy disk drives,
           4–5 = initial video mode,
           2–3 = system board RAM size, original PC
           2 used by PS/2,
           1 = math coprocessor,
           0 = floppy disk installed)

Interrupt 12h: Get Conventional Memory Size

Returns the amount of conventional memory.
Input: none
Output: AX = memory size (in KB)

Interrupt 13h: Disk I/O

Function 2h:
Read Sector
Reads one or more sectors.
Input: AH = 2h
           AL = number of sectors

CH = cylinder
CL = sector
DH = head
DL = drive (0–7Fh = floppy disk, 80h–FFh = fixed disk)
ES:BX = segment:offset of buffer

Output:
If function successful
CF = clear
AH = 0
AL = number of sectors transferred
If function unsuccessful
CF = set
AH = error status

Function 3h:
Write Sector
Writes one or more sectors.
Input: AH = 3h
AL = number of sectors
BX = firstcolor register
CH = cylinder
CL = sector
DH = head
DL = drive (0–7Fh = floppy disk, 80h–FFh = fixed disk)
ES:BX = segment:offset of buffer
Output: If function successful
CF = clear
AH = 0
AL = number of sectors transferred
If function unsuccessful
CF = set
AH = error status

Interrupt 15h; Cassette I/O and Advanced Features for AT, PS/2

Function 87h:
Move Extended Memory Block
Transfers data between conventional memory and extended memory.
Input: AH = 87h
CX = number of words to move
ES:SI = segment:offset of Global Descriptor Table
Output: If function successful
CF = clear
AH = 0
AL = number of sectors transferred
If function unsuccessful
CF = set
AH = error status

Function 88h:
Get Extended Memory Size
Obtains amount of extended memory
Input: AH = 88h
Output: AX = extended memory size (in KB)

Interrupt 16h: Keyboard

Function 0h:
Read Character from Keyboard
Input: AH = 0h
Output: AH = keyboard scan code
         AL = ASCII character

Function 2h:
Get Keyboard Flags
Obtains key flags that describe the status of the function keys.
Input: AH = 2h
Output: AL = flags

Bit	If Set
7	Insert on
6	Caps Lock on
5	Num Lock on
4	Scroll Lock on
3	Alt key is down
2	Ctrl key is down
1	left shift key is down
0	right shift key is down

Function 10h:
Read Character from Enhanced Keyboard
Input: AH = 0h
Output: AH = keyboard scan code
         AL = ASCII character

Note: this function can be used to return scan codes for control keys such as F11 and F12.

Interrupt 17h: Printer

Function 0h:
Write Character to Printer
Input: AH = 0
         AL = character
         DX = printer number
Output: AH = status

Bit	If Set
7	printer not busy
6	printer acknowledge
5	out of paper
4	printer selected
3	I/O error
2	unused
1	unused
0	printer timed out

C.3
DOS Interrupts

Interrupt 21h

Function 0h:
Program Terminate
Terminates the execution of a program.
Input: AH = 0h
              CS = segment of PSP
Output: none

Function 1h:
Keyboard Input
Waits for a character to be read at the standard input device (unless one is ready), then echoes the character to the standard output device and returns the ASCII code in AL.
Input: AH = 01h
Output: AL = character from the standard input device

Function 2h:
Display Output
Outputs the character in DL to the standard output device.
Input: AH = 02h
              DL = character
Output: none

Function 5h:
Printer Output
Outputs the character in DL to the standard printer device.
Input: AH = 05h
              DL = character
Output: none

Function 09h:
Print String
Outputs the characters in the print string to the standard output device.
Input: AH = 09h
              DS:DX = pointer to the character string ending with '$'
Output: none

Function 2Ah:
Get Date
Returns the day of the week, year, month and date.
Input: AH = 2ah
Output: AL = Day of the week (0=SUN, 6=SAT)
              CX = Year (1980–2099)
              DH = Month (1–12)
              DL = Day (1–31)

Function 2Bh:
Set Date
Sets the date.
Input: AH = 2Bh
              CX = year (1980–2099)
              DH = month (1–12)
              DL = day (1–31)

Output: AL = 00h, if the date is valid
FFh, if the date is not valid

Function 2Ch:
Get Time
Returns the time: hours, minutes, seconds and hundredths of seconds.
Input: AH = 2Ch
Output: CH = hours (0–23)
CL = minutes (0–59)
DH = seconds (0–59)
DL = hundredths (0–99)

Function 2Dh:
Set Time
Sets the time.
Input: AH = 2Dh
CH = Hours (0–23)
DH = Seconds (0–59)
CL = Minutes (0–59)
DL = Hundredths (0–99)
Output: AL = 00h if the time is valid
FFh if the time is not valid

Function 30h:
Get DOS Version Number
Returns the DOS version number.
Input: AH = 30h
Output: BX = 0000H
CX = 0000H
AL = major version number
AH = minor version number

Function 31h:
Terminate Process and Remain Resident
Terminates the current process and attempts to set the initial allocation block to the memory size in paragraphs.
Input: AH = 31h
AL = return code
DX = memory size in paragraphs
Output: none

Function 33h:
Ctrl-break Check
Set or get the state of BREAK (Ctrl-break checking).
Input: AH = 33h
AL = 00h, to request current state
01h, to set the current state
DL = 00h, to set current state OFF
01h, to set current state ON
Output: DL = The current state (00h=OFF, 01h=ON)

Function 35h:
Get Vector
Obtains the address in an interrupt vector.
Input: AH = 35h

AL = interrupt number
Output: ES:BX = pointer to the interrupt handling routine.

Function 36h:
Get Disk Free Space
Returns the disk free space (available clusters, clusters/drive, bytes/sector).
Input: AH = 36h
DL = drive (0=default, 1=A)
Output: BX = Available clusters
DX = clusters/drive
CX = bytes/sector
AX = FFFFh if the drive in DL is invalid, otherwise the number of sectors per cluster

Function 39h:
Create Subdirectory (MKDIR)
Creates the specified directory.
Input: AH = 39h
DS:DX = pointer to an ASCIIZ string
Output: AX = error codes if carry flag is set

Function 3Ah:
Remove Subdirectory (RMDIR)
Removes the specified directory.
Input: AH = 3Ah
DS:DX = pointer to an ASCIIZ string
Output: AX = error codes if carry flag is set

Function 3Bh:
Change the Current Directory(CHDIR)
Changes the current directory to the specified directory.
Input: AH = 3Bh
DS:DX = pointer to an ASCIIZ string
Output: AX = error codes if carry flag is set

Function 3Ch:
Create a File (CREAT)
Creates a new file or truncates an old file to zero length in preparation for writing.
Input: AH = 3Ch
DS:DX = pointer to an ASCIIZ string
CX = attribute of the file
Output: AX = error codes if carry flag is set
16-bit handle if carry flag not set

Function 3Dh:
Open a File
Opens the specified file.
Input: AH = 3Dh
DS:DX = pointer to an ASCIIZ path name
AL = access Code
Output: AX = error codes if carry flag is set
16-bit handle if carry flag not set

Function 3Eh:
Close a File Handle
Closes the specified file handle.
Input: AH = 3Eh
         BX = file handle returned by open or create
Output: AX = error codes if carry flag is set
         none if carry flag not set

Function 3Fh:
Read from a File or Device
Transfers the specified number of bytes from a file into a buffer location.
Input: AH = 3Fh
         BX = file handle
         DS:DX = buffer address
         CX = number of bytes to be read
Output: AX = number of bytes read
         error codes if carry flag set

Function 40h:
Write to a File or Device
Transfers the specified number of bytes from a buffer into a specified file.
Input: AH = 40h
         BX = file handle
         DS:DX = address of the data to write
         CX = number of bytes to be write
Output: AX = number of bytes written
         error codes if carry flag set

Function 41h:
Delete a File from a Specified Directory (UNLINK)
Removes a directory entry associated with a file name.
Input: AH = 41h
         DS:DX = address of an ASCIIZ string
Output: AX = error codes if carry flag set
         none if carry flag not set

Function 42h:
Move File Read Write Pointer (LSEEK)
Moves the read/write pointer according to the method specified.
Input: AH = 42h
         CS:DX = distance (offset) to move in bytes
         AL = method of moving (0,1,2)
         BX = file handle
Output: AX = error codes if carry flag set
         DX:AX = new pointer location if carry flag not set

Function 47h:
Get Current Directory
Places the full path name (starting from the root directory) of the current directory for the specified drive in the area pointed to by DS:SI.
Input: AH = 47h
         DS:SI = pointer to a 64-byte user memory area
         DL = drive number (0=default, 1=A, etc.)
         error codes if carry flag set

Output: DS:SI = filled out with full path name from the root if carry is not set
AX = error codes if carry flag is set

Function 48h:
Allocate Memory
Allocates the requested number of paragraphs of memory.
Input: AH = 48h
BX = number of paragraphs of memory requested
Output: AX:0 = points to the allocated memory block
AX = error codes if carry flag set
BX = size of the largest block of memory available (in paragraphs) if the allocation fails

Function 49h:
Free Allocated Memory
Frees the specified allocated memory.
Input: AH = 49h
ES = segment of the block to be returned
Output: AX = error codes if carry flag set
none if carry flag not set

Function 4Ch:
Terminate a Process (EXIT)
Terminates the current process and transfers control to the invoking process.
Input: AH = 4Ch
AL = return code
Output: none

Interrupt 25h: Absolute Disk Read

Input: AL = drive number
CX = number of sectors to read
DX = beginning logical sector number
DS:BX = transfer address
Output: If successful CF = 0
If unsuccessful CF = 1 and AX contains error code

Interrupt 26h: Absolute Disk Write

Input: AL = drive number
CX = number of sectors to read
DX = beginning logical sector number
DS:BX = transfer address
Output: If successful CF = 0
If unsuccessful CF = 1 and AX contains error code

Interrupt 27h: Terminate but Stay Resident

Input: DX = offset of beginning of free space, segment is with respect to PSP.
Output: none

Appendix D

MASM and LINK Options

D.1 MASM

The MASM assembler translates an assembly language source file into a machine language object file. It generates three files, as shown:

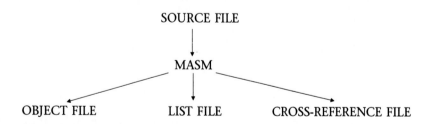

The *object file* contains the machine language translation of the assembly language source code, plus other information needed to produce an executable file.

The *list file* is a text file that gives assembly language code and the corresponding machine code, a list of names used in the program, error messages, and other statistics. It is helpful in debugging.

The *cross-reference file* lists names used in the program and line numbers where they appear. It makes large programs easier to follow. As generated, it is not readable; the CREF utility program may be used to convert it to a legible form.

MASM Command Line

For MASM version 5.0, the most general command line is

```
MASM options source_file,object_file,list_file,cross-ref_file
```

MASM 4.0 has the same command line, except that the options appear last.

The default extension for the object file is .OBJ, for the listing file it is .LST, and for the cross-reference file it is .CRF.

For example, suppose MASM is on a disk in drive C, source file FIRST.ASM is on a disk in drive A, and C is the logged drive. To create object file FIRST.OBJ, listing file FIRST.LST, and cross-reference file FIRST.CRF on drive A, we could type

```
C>MASM A:FIRST.ASM,A:FIRST.OBJ,A:FIRST.LST,A:FIRST.CRF
```

A simpler way to get the same result is

```
C>MASM A:FIRST,A:,A:,A:
```

A semicolon instead of a comma on the MASM command line tells the assembler not to generate any more files. For example, if we type

```
C>MASM A:FIRST,A:;
```

Then MASM will generate only FIRST.OBJ. If we type

```
C>MASM A:FIRST,A:,A:;
```

Then we get FIRST.OBJ, FIRST.LST, but not FIRST.CRF.

It's also possible to let MASM prompt you for the files you want. For example, suppose we want .OBJ and .CRF files only.

```
C>MASM A:FIRST
Microsoft (R) Macro Assembler Version 5.10
Copyright (C) Microsoft Corp 1981, 1988. All rights reserved.

Object filename [FIRST.OBJ]:    A:<Enter>
Source listing  [NUL.LST]:      <Enter>
Cross-reference [NUL.CRF]:      A:FIRST <Enter>

50140 + 234323 Bytes symbol space free
                              0 Warning Errors
                              0 Severe  Errors
```

The first response just given means that we accept the name FIRST.OBJ for the object file. The second one means that we don't want a listing file (NUL means no file). The third one means we want a cross-reference file called FIRST.CRF.

Options

The MASM options control the operations of the assembler and the format of the output files. Table D.1 gives a list of some commonly used ones. For a complete list, see the Microsoft Programmer's Guide.

Several options may be specified on a command line. For example,

```
C>MASM /D /W2 /Z /ZI FIRST;
```

Table D.1 Some MASM Options

Option	Action
/A	Arrange source segments in alphabetical order.
/C	Create a cross-reference file.
/D	Create pass 1 listing (see below).
/ML	Make names case sensitive.
/R	Accept 8087 floating-point instructions.
/S	Leave source segments in original order.
/W{0|1|2}	Set error level display: (default = 1): 0 = illegal statements 1 = ambiguous or questionable statements 2 = statements that may produce inefficient code
/Z	Display the lines containing errors.
/ZI	Write symbolic information to the object file (use with CODEVIEW).

A MASM Demonstration

To show what the MASM output files look like, the following program SWAP.ASM will be assembled. It swaps the content of two memory words.

Program Listing PGMD_1.ASM
```
TITLE PGMD_1: SWAP WORDS
.MODEL SMALL
.STACK 100H
.DATA
WORD1   DW      10
WORD2   DW      20
.CODE
MAIN    PROC
        MOV     AX,@DATA
        MOV     DS,AX
        MOV     AX,WORD1
        XCHG    AX,WORD2
        MOV     WORD1,AX
        MOV     AH,4CH
        INT     21H
ENDP
        END     MAIN
```

```
C>MASM A:PGMD_1,A:,A:,A:

Microsoft (R) Macro Assembler Version 5.10
Copyright (C) Microsoft Corp 1981, 1988. All rights reserved.

  47358 + 390893 Bytes symbol space free
                        0 Warning Errors
                        0 Severe  Errors
```

The listing file is shown in Figure D.1.

```
C>TYPE A:PGMD_1.LST
```

Down the left side of the listing are the line numbers. Next we have a column of offset addresses (in hex), relative to stack, data, and code segments. After that comes the machine code translation (in hex) of the instructions.

Two-Pass Assembly and the SYMBOL TABLE

MASM makes two passes through the source file. On the first pass, MASM checks for syntax errors and creates a *symbol table* of names and their relative locations within a segment. To keep track of locations, it uses a *location counter*. The location counter is reset to 0 at the beginning of a

```
Microsoft (R) Macro Assembler Version 5.10    9/6/91 00:43:35
PGMD_1: SWAP WORDS                                                Page-1
     1                              TITLE    PGMD_1:SWAP WORDS
     2                              .MODEL   SMALL
     3                              .STACK   100H
     4                              .DATA
     5 0000  000A                   WORD1    DW     10
     6 0002  0014                   WORD2    DW     20
     7                              .CODE
     8 0000                         MAIN     PROC
     9 0000  B8 ---- R                       MOV    AX,@DATA
    10 0003  8E D8                           MOV    DS,AX
    11 0005  A1 000O R                       MOV    AX,WORD1
    12 0008  87 06 0002 R                    XCHG   AX,WORD2
    13 000C  A3 0000 R                       MOV    WORD1,AX
    14 000F  B4 4C                           MOV    AH,4CH
    15 0011  CD 21                           INT    21H
    16 0013                         MAIN     ENDP
    17                              END      MAIN
Microsoft (R) Macro Assembler Version 5.10    9/6/91 00:43:35
PGMD_1: SWAP WORDS                          Symbols-1
Segments and Groups:

         N a m e                    Length   Align   CombineClass
DGROUP . . . . . . . . . .          GROUP
     _DATA . . . . . . .            0004     WORD    PUBLIC 'DATA'
         STACK . . . . . .          0100     PARA    STACK  'STACK'
_TEXT . . . . . . . . .             0013     WORD    PUBLIC 'CODE'

Symbols:

         N a m e                    Type     Value   Attr
MAIN. . . . . . . . . . .           N PROC   0000    _TEXT   Length = 0013
WORD1 . . . . . . . . .             L WORD   0000    _DATA
WORD2 . . . . . . . . .             L WORD   0002    _DATA

@CODE . . . . . . . . .             TEXT     _TEXT
@CODESIZE . . . . . .               TEXT     0
@CPU. . . . . . . . . .             TEXT     0101h
@DATASIZE . . . . . .               TEXT     0
@FILENAME . . . . . .               TEXT     PGMD_1
@VERSION. . . . . . .               TEXT     510
        17 Source Lines
        17 Total Lines
        20 Symbols
 47358 + 390893 Bytes symbol space free
         0 Warning Errors
         0 Severe Errors
```

Figure D.1 PGMD_1.LST

segment. When an instruction is encountered, the location counter is increased by the number of bytes needed for the machine code of the instruction. When a name is encountered, it is entered in the symbol table along with the location counter's value. The symbol table appears near the bottom of the .LST file; in the preceding example, the symbols are MAIN, WORD1, and WORD2. The MASM /D option causes the .LST file to include pass 1 error messages. Whether these are actually errors is determined in pass 2.

On the second pass, MASM completes error checking and machine codes the instructions, except for those instructions that refer to names in other object modules. The .LST file is also created.

The reason MASM needs two passes to assemble a program is that some instructions may refer to names that appear later on in the source file. These instructions can be machine-coded only after their relative locations have been determined from the symbol table.

The object file (PGMD_1.OBJ) that MASM creates is not executable. The final addresses of the variables need to be determined by the LINK program (see later description). In the .LST file, these addresses are marked by a "R" (relocatable) symbol (lines 9, 10, 11, 12, 13).

The Cross-Reference File

The *cross-reference file* (here PGMD_1.CRF) contains information on names—where they are defined and the line numbers where they appear in the .LST file. The .CRF file is not printable; the CREF program, on the DOS disk, converts it to a .REF file that has an ASCII format:

```
Microsoft Cross-Reference   Version 5.10   Fri Sep 06 01:33:52 1991
PGMD_1: SWAP WORDS
  Symbol Cross Reference        (# definition, + modification)   Cref-1

@CPU . . . . . . . . . . .     1#
@VERSION . . . . . . . .       1#

CODE . . . . . . . . . . .     7

DATA . . . . . . . . . . .     4
DGROUP . . . . . . . . .       9

MAIN . . . . . . . . . . .     8#           16           17

STACK. . . . . . . . . .       3           #3

WORD1. . . . . . . . . .       5#           11           13+
WORD2. . . . . . . . . .       6#           12+

_DATA. . . . . . . . . .       4#
_TEXT. . . . . . . . . .       7#

11 Symbols
```

Figure D.2 PGMD_1.REF

Appendix D MASM and LINK Options   467

```
C>CREF A:PGMD_1;

Microsoft (R) Cross-Reference Utility Version 5.10
Copyright (C) Microsoft Corp 1981-1985, 1987. All rights reserved.

11 Symbols
```

The output is the file PGMD_1.REF, which can be printed by using the TYPE command (Figure D.2).

```
C>TYPE PGMD_1.REF
```

D.2 LINK

The job of the LINK program is to link object files (and possibly library files) into a single executable file. To do this, it must resolve reference to names used in one module but defined in another. The mechanism for doing this is explained in Chapter 14. LINK must be used even if there is only one object file.

The input to LINK is one or more object and library files, and the output is a run file and an optional loadmap file, as shown:

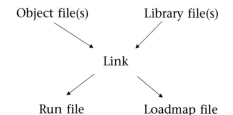

The run file is an executable machine language program. The loadmap file gives the size and relative location of the program segments.

LINK Command Line

For LINK version 5.0, the most general command line is

LINK options object_file_list,run_file,loadmap_file,library_list

The only option you will be likely to use is /CO, which causes extra information for CODEVIEW to be included.

The *object_file_list* is a list of object files to be linked. It begins with the name of the object file containing the main program; the other object files usually contain procedures that are called by the main program and by each other. The file names are separated by blanks or "+".

The *run_file* has an .EXE extension. It is an executable file unless the program is a .COM format program, in which case one more step is needed to produce an executable file. .COM programs are discussed in Chapter 14.

The *library_list* consists of library files, if any, separated by blanks or "+". Library files usually have a .LIB extension, and they often contain standard routines used by many programs, such as I/O routines. An example appears in Chapter 14.

For example, suppose LINK is on a disk in drive C and the files to be linked are in drive A. The main object file is FIRST.OBJ, other object files are SECOND.OBJ and THIRD.OBJ. To create a run file FIRST.EXE and a loadmap file FIRST.MAP, we could type

```
C>LINK A:FIRST+SECOND+THIRD,A:FIRST,A:FIRST;
```

or just

```
C>LINK A:FIRST+SECOND+THIRD,A:,A:;
```

The semicolon at the end means that there are no library files. As with MASM, it's possible to run LINK interactively:

```
C>LINK FIRST+SECOND+THIRD

Microsoft (R) Overlay Linker Version 3.64
Copyright (C) Microsoft Corp 1983-1988. All rights
reserved.

Run File [FIRST.EXE]:     <Enter>
List File [NUL.MAP]       A:FIRST <Enter>
Libraries: [.LIB]         <Enter>
```

The first response means that we accept the name FIRST.EXE for the run file. The second response means we want to call the loadmap file FIRST.MAP. The third response means that there are no library files.

A LINK Demonstration

Let's link PGMD_1 above:

```
C>LINK A:PGMD_1,A:,A:;

Microsoft (R) Overlay Linker Version 3.64
Copyright (C) Microsoft Corp 1983-1988. All rights
reserved.

C>
```

Here is the loadmap file:

```
C>TYPE A:PGMD_1.MAP

 Start  Stop                Length Name           Class
 00000H 00012H 00013H _TEXT        CODE
 00014H 00017H 00004H _DATA        DATA
 00020H 0011FH 00100H STACK        STACK

 Origin                            Group
 0001:0                            DGROUP

Program entry point at 0000:0000
```

The file gives the relative size and location of the program segments.

Appendix E

DEBUG and CODEVIEW

E.1 Introduction

This appendix covers the DEBUG and CODEVIEW debuggers. DEBUG is available on the DOS disk, and CODEVIEW comes with the Microsoft Macro Assembler, version 5.0 or later. DEBUG is a primitive but utilitarian program with a small, easy-to-learn command set. CODEVIEW is a much more sophisticated program that may be used to debug Pascal, BASIC, FORTRAN, C, or assembly language code. The user can simultaneously view source code, registers, flags, and selected variables.

E.2 DEBUG

Since most of the DEBUG commands will work in CODEVIEW, you should read the sections on DEBUG even if you will ultimately be using CODEVIEW. Table E.1 summarizes the most useful DEBUG commands. For a complete list, see the DOS user's manual.

A Debug Demonstration

To demonstrate the DEBUG commands, we'll use PGM4_2.ASM, which displays "HELLO!" on the screen.

Program Listing PGM4_2.ASM
```
TITLE PGM4_2: PRINT STRING PROGRAM
.MODEL   SMALL
.STACK   100H
```

472 Appendix E DEBUG and CODEVIEW

```
        .DATA
MSG     DB      'HELLO!$'
        .CODE
MAIN    PROC
;initialize DS
        MOV AX,@DATA
        MOV DS,AX           ;initialize DS
;display message
        LEA DX,MSG          ;get message
        MOV AH,9            ;display string function
        INT 21h             ;display message
;return to DOS
        MOV AH,4CH
        INT 21h             ;DOS exit
MAIN    ENDP
        END     MAIN
```

After assembling and linking the program, we take it into DEBUG (the user's response appears in boldface).

```
C>DEBUG PGM4_2.EXE
-
```

DEBUG comes back with its "-" command prompt. To view the registers, type "R"

```
-R
AX=0000  BX=0000  CX=0121  DX=0000  SP=0100  BP=0000  SI=0000  DI=0000
DS=0EFB  ES=0EFB  SS=0F0B  CS=0F1C  IP=0000  NV UP DI PL NZ NA PO NC
0F1C:0000 B81B0F         MOV     AX,0F1B
```

The display shows the contents of the registers in hex. The third line of the display gives the segment:offset address of the first instruction in the program, along with its machine code and assembly code. The letter pairs at the end of the second line are the current settings of some of the status and control flags. The flags displayed and the symbols DEBUG uses are the following:

Flag	Clear (0) Symbol	Set (1) Symbol
Overflow Flag	NV	OV
Direction flag	UP	DN
Interrupt flag	DI	EI
Sign flag	PL	NG
Zero flag	NZ	ZR
Auxiliary carry flag	NA	AC
Parity flag	PO	PE
Carry flag	NC	CY

Table E.1 DEBUG Commands

Optional parameters are enclosed in curly brackets. All constants are hexadecimal.

Command	Action
D {start {end}} {range}	Dump bytes in hex format
Examples:	
D 100	Dump 80h bytes starting at DS:100h
D CS:100 120	Dump bytes from CS:100h to CS:120h
D	Dump 80h bytes starting at DS:last+1 where last is the last byte displayed
E start {list}	Enter data in list beginning at start
Examples:	
E DS:0 A B C	Enter Ah,Bh,Ch in bytes DS:0,DS:1,DS:2
E ES:100 1 2 'ABC'	Enter 1 in ES:100h, 2 in ES:101h, 41h in ES:102, 42h in ES:103, 43h in ES:104h
E 25	Enter bytes interactively starting at DS:25. Space bar moves to next byte, Return terminates
G {=start} {addr1 addr2 . . addrn}	Go (execute) at start, with breakpoints at addr1, addr2, . . addrn
Examples:	
G	Execute at CS:IP to completion
G =100	Execute at CS:100h to completion
G 100 300 200	Execute at CS:IP, stop of first of breakpoints CS:100h, CS:300h, or CS:200h encountered
G =100 150	Execute at CS:100h, breakpoint at CS:150h
L address {drive start_sector end_sector}	Load absolute disk sectors or named program (see N command) Drive specified by number (0 = A, 1 = B, 2 = C, etc.)
Examples:	
L DS:100 0 C 1B	Load sectors Ch to 1Bh from the disk in drive A at DS:100h
L 8FD0:0 1 2A 3B	Load sectors 2Ah to 3Bh from the disk in drive B at address 8FD0h
L DS:100	Load named file at DS:100h
N filename	Set current filename for L and W commands
Example:	
N myfile	Set load/write name to myfile
Q	Quit DEBUG and return to DOS
R {register}	Display/Change contents of register
Examples:	
R	Display registers and flags
RAX	Display AX and change contents if desired

T {=start} {value}	Trace "value" instructions from start
Examples:	
T	Trace the instruction at CS:IP
T =100	Trace the instruction at CS:100h
T =100 5	Trace 5 instructions starting at CS:100h
T 4	Trace 4 instructions starting at CS:IP
U {start {end}} {range}	Unassemble data in instruction format
Examples:	
U 100	Unassemble about 32 bytes starting at CS:100h
U CS:100 110	Unassemble from CS:100h to CS:110h
U 200 L 20	Unassemble 20h instructions starting at CS:200h
U	Unassemble about 32 bytes starting at last+1, where last is the last byte unassembled
W {start}	Write the BX:CS bytes to file (see N command)
Example:	
W 100	Write the BX:CX bytes stored at CS:100h

To change the contents of a register—for example, DX—to 1ABCh, type

```
-RDX
DX 0000
:1ABC
```

DEBUG responds by displaying the current content of DX, then displays a colon and waits for the us to enter the new content. We enter 1ABC and press the Enter key (DEBUG assumes that all numbers the user types are expressed in hex, so no "h" is needed). To retain the current content of DX, we would just hit the Enter key after the colon.

To verify the change, we can display the registers again.

```
-R
AX=0000  BX=0000  CX=0121  DX=1ABC  SP=0100  BP=0000  SI=0000 DI=0000
DS=0EFB  ES=0EFB  SS=0F0B  CS=0F1C  IP=0000  NV UP DI PL NZ NA PO NC
0F1C:0000 B81B0F      MOV   AX,0F1B
```

Now let's trace down to the INT 21h.

```
-T
AX=0F1B  BX=0000  CX=0121  DX=1ABC  SP=0100  BP=0000  SI=0000  DI=0000
DS=0EFB  ES=0EFB  SS=0F0B  CS=0F1C  IP=0003  NV UP DI PL NZ NA PO NC
0F1C:0003 8ED8          MOV     DS,AX

-T
AX=0F1B  BX=0000  CX=0121  DX=0002  SP=0100  BP=0000  SI=0000  DI=0000
DS=0F1B  ES=0EFB  SS=0F0B  CS=0F1C  IP=0009  NV UP DI PL NZ NA PO NC
0F1C:0009 B409          MOV     AH,09
```

Note that DEBUG seemingly "skipped" the instruction LEA DX,MSG. Actually, that instruction was executed (we can tell because DX has new contents). DEBUG occasionally executes an instruction without pausing to display the registers.

```
-T
AX=091B  BX=0000  CX=0121  DX=0002  SP=0100  BP=0000  SI=0000  DI=0000
DS=0F1B  ES=0EFB  SS=0F0B  CS=0F1C  IP=000B  NV UP DI PL NZ NA PO NC
0F1C:000B CD21          INT     21
```

If we were to hit "T" again, DEBUG would start to trace INT 21h, which is not what we want.

From the last register display, we see that INT 21h is a two-byte instruction. Since IP is currently 000Bh, the next instruction must be at 000Dh, and we can set up a breakpoint there:

```
-GD
HELLO!
AX=0924  BX=0000  CX=0121  DX=0002  SP=0100  BP=0000  SI=0000  DI=0000
DS=0F1B  ES=0EFB  SS=0F0B  CS=0F1C  IP=000D  NV UP DI PL NZ NA PO NC
0F1C:000D B44C          MOV     AH,4C
```

The INT 21h, function 9, displays "HELLO!" and execution stops at the breakpoint 000Dh. To finish execution, just type "G":

```
-G
Program terminated normally.
```

This message indicates the program has run to completion. The program must be reloaded to be executed again. So let's leave DEBUG.

To demonstrate the U command, let's reenter DEBUG and use it to list our program:

```
C>DEBUG PGM4_2.EXE

-U
0F1C:0000 B81B0F          MOV     AX,0F1B
0F1C:0003 8ED8            MOV     DS,AX
0F1C:0005 8D160200        LEA     DX,[0002]
0F1C:0009 B409            MOV     AH,09
0F1C:000B CD21            INT     21
0F1C:000D B44C            MOV     AH,4C
0F1C:000F CD21            INT     21
0F1C:0011 015BE8          ADD     [BP+DI-18],BX
0F1C:0014 3BEE            CMP     BP,SI
0F1C:0016 E88AF3          CALL    F3A3
0F1C:0019 E97E08          JMP     089A
0F1C:001C 8D1E8E09        LEA     BX,[098E]
```

DEBUG has unassembled about 32 bytes; that is, interpreted the contents of these bytes as instructions. The program ends at 000Fh, and the rest is DEBUG's interpretation of the garbage that follows as assembly code. To list just our program, we type

```
-U 0 F

0F1C:0000 B81B0F          MOV     AX,0F1B
0F1C:0003 8ED8            MOV     DS,AX
0F1C:0005 8D160200        LEA     DX,[0002]
0F1C:0009 B409            MOV     AH,09
0F1C:000B CD21            INT     21
0F1C:000D B44C            MOV     AH,4C
0F1C:000F CD21            INT     21
```

In the unassembly listing, DEBUG replaces names by the segments or offsets assigned to those names. For example, instead of MOV AX,@DATA we have MOV AX,01FB. LEA DX,MSG becomes LEA DX,[0002] because 0002h is the offset in segment .DATA assigned to MSG.

To demonstrate the D command, let's dump that part of memory that contains the message "HELLO!". First, we execute the two statements that initialize DS:

```
-G5
AX=0F1B  BX=0000  CX=0121  DX=0000  SP=0100  BP=0000  SI=0000  DI=0000
DS=0F1B  ES=0EFB  SS=0F0B  CS=0F1C  IP=0005  NV UP DI PL NZ NA PO NC
0F1C:0005 8D160000     LEA    DX,[0000]   DS:0000=4548
```

Now we dump memory starting at DS:0

```
-D0
0F1B:0000  21 00 48 45 4C 4C 4F 21-24 C4 02 8B 1E 46 43 D1  !.HELLO!$....FC.
0F1B:0010  E3 D1 E3 8B 87 BC 3D 8B-97 BE 3D 89 86 7C FF 89  ......=...=..|..
0F1B:0020  96 7E FF 05 0C 00 52 50-E8 7D 6A 83 C4 04 50 E8  .~....RP.}j...P.
0F1B:0030  6C FB 83 C4 02 0A C0 75-03 E9 F6 FE C6 06 D9 37  l......u.......7
0F1B:0040  FF 8B 1E 46 43 D1 E3 8B-87 A0 3C A3 60 3E 8B 1E  ...FC.....<.`>..
0F1B:0050  46 43 8A 87 E6 3C 2A E4-A3 5A 3C D1 E3 D1 E3 8B  FC...<*..Z<.....
0F1B:0060  87 FC 31 0B 87 FE 31 75-03 E8 9E FD B8 FF FF 8B  ..1...1u........
0F1B:0070  E5 5D C3 90 55 8B EC 83-EC 08 56 C6 06 0C 42 FF  .]..U.....V...B.
```

DEBUG has displayed 80h bytes of memory. The contents of each byte is shown as two hex digits. For example, the current content of byte 0000h is seen to be 48h. Across the first row, we have the contents of bytes 0–7h, then a dash, then bytes 8–Fh. The contents of bytes 10h through 1Fh are shown in the second row, and so on. To the right of the display, the content of memory is interpreted as characters (unprintable characters are indicated by a dot).

To display just the message "HELLO!$", we type

```
-D2 8
0F1B:0000           48 45 4C 4C 4F 21 24      HELLO!$
```

Before moving on, let us take note of one peculiarity of memory dumps. We usually write the contents of a word in the order high byte, low byte. However, a DEBUG memory dump displays a word contents in the order low byte, high byte. For example, the word whose address is 0h contains 4548h, but DEBUG displays it as 48 45. This can be confusing when we are interpreting memory as words.

Now let's use the E command to change the message from "HELLO!" to "GOODBYE!"

```
-E2 'GOODBYE!$'
```

To verify the change, we will dump memory

```
-D0 F
0F1B:0000  21 00 47 4F 4F 44 42 59-45 21 24 8B 1E 46 42 D1    !.GOODBYE!$..FC.
```

Now let's execute to completion.

```
-G
GOODBYE!
Program terminated normally
```

The E command can also be used to enter data interactively. Suppose, for example, we would like to change the contents of bytes 200h–204h. Before doing so, let's have a look at the current content:

```
-D 200 204
0F1B:0200  0C FF 5A E9 48              ..Z.H
```

Now let's put 1,2,3,4,5 in these bytes.

```
-E 200
0F1B:0200   0C.1    FF.2    5A.3    E9.4    48.5    F3.
```

DEBUG begins by displaying the current content of byte 0200h, namely 0Ch, and waits for us to enter the new content. We type 1 and hit the space bar. Next DEBUG displays the content of byte 0201, which is FFh, and again waits for us to enter the new content. We type 2 and hit the space bar to go on to the next byte. After 5 has been entered in byte 204h, DEBUG displays the content of byte 205h, which is F3. Since we don't want to enter any more data, just hit the Enter key to get back to the command prompt.

Now let's have a look at memory:

```
-D 200 204
0F1B:0200  01 02 03 04 05              .....
```

In the process of entering data, if we had wanted to leave the contents of a byte unchanged, we would just hit the space bar to go on to the next byte, or hit return to get back to the command prompt.

E.3 CODEVIEW

CODEVIEW is a powerful debugger that enables the user to view both high-level and assembly language source code during the debugging process. There are two operating modes: *window* and *sequential*. In sequential mode, CODEVIEW behaves more or less like DEBUG; sequential mode must be used if your machine is not an IBM compatible or the program is assembled and linked without options. In window mode, all the capabilities of CODEVIEW are available, and for that reason it is the only mode we will discuss. Because CODEVIEW is a large program with many features, we do not attempt to be comprehensive in the following discussion.

Program Preparation

To debug in window mode, the code segment of the program must have class 'CODE', for example,

```
C_SEG    SEGMENT 'CODE'
```

Note: the simplified segment directive .CODE generates a code segment with default class 'CODE'.

When the program is assembled and linked, the /ZI and /CO options should be specified; for example,

```
MASM /ZI MYPROG;
LINK /CO MYPROG;
```

These options cause symbolic information for CODEVIEW to be included in the .EXE file. Because this makes the file a lot bigger, the program should be assembled and linked in the ordinary way after it has been debugged.

Entering CODEVIEW

The command line for entering CODEVIEW is

```
CV {options} filename
```

File name is the name of an executable file. The options control CODEVIEW'S start-up behavior. Here is a partial list (see the Microsoft manual for the complete set):

Option	Action
/D	You are using an IBM compatible that does not support certain IBM-specific trapping functions.
/I	You are using a non-IBM-compatible computer and want to be able to use CTRL-C and CTRL-break to stop a program.
/M	You have a mouse but don't want to use it.
/P	You have a non-IBM EGA and have problems running CODEVIEW.
/S	You have a non-IBM compatible and want to be able to see the output screen.
/W	You have an IBM compatible and want to use window mode.

More than one option may be specified. For example,

```
CV /D /M /W Myprog
```

Note that with CODEVIEW, unlike DEBUG, it is not necessary to use a file extension.

Window Mode

To demonstrate some of CODEVIEW's features, we will assemble and link the program we used to demonstrate DEBUG (PGM4_2.ASM) and take it into CODEVIEW.

```
C>MASM /ZI A:PGM4_2;
Microsoft (R) Macro Assembler Version 5.10
Copyright (C) Microsoft Corp 1981, 1988. All rights reserved.

  50094 + 289327 Bytes symbol space free

      0 Warning Errors
      0 Severe  Errors

C>LINK /CO A:PGM4_2;

Microsoft (R) Overlay Linker Version 3.64
Copyright (C) Microsoft Corp 1983-1988. All rights reserved.

C>CV A:PGM4_2
```

Figure E.1 shows window mode display. We see three windows: a *display window* at the top, a *dialog window* at the bottom, and a *register window* at the right side.

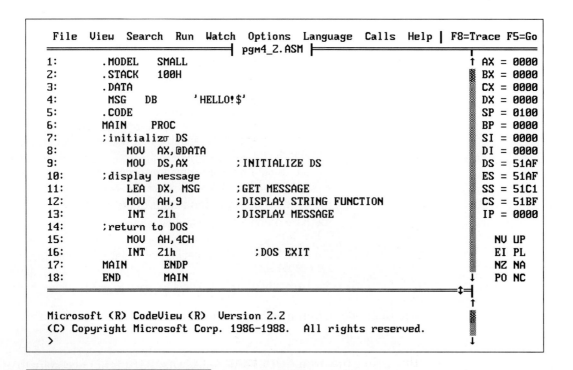

Figure E.1 CODEVIEW Window Mode Display

The display window shows the source code, with the current instruction in reverse video or in a different color. Lines with previously set breakpoints are highlighted.

The dialog window is where you can enter commands, but as we will see, the function keys can be used for many commands.

The register window shows the contents of the registers and the flags. The flag symbols are the same as DEBUG's.

It is also possible to activate a *watch window*, which will display selected variables and conditions.

Controlling the Display

The appearance of the display may be controlled with the keyboard or a mouse. Table E.2 shows the keys and key combinations. For mouse operations, see the Microsoft manual.

Controlling Program Execution

Table E.3 shows the function keys that may be used to set and clear breakpoints, trace through a program, or execute to a breakpoint.

Selecting from the Menus

The menu bar at the top of the screen has nine titles. The two commands at the end (TRACE and GO) are provided for mouse users.

1. To open a menu, press Alt and the first letter of the title. For example, Alt-F to open the File menu. This causes a menu box to be displayed.

Table E.2 Display Commands

Key	Function
F1	Displays initial on-line help screen.
F2	Toggles the register window.
F3	Switches between source, mixed, or assembly modes. Source mode shows source code in the display window, assembly mode shows assembly language instructions, and mixed mode shows both.
F4	Switches to the output screen. The output screen shows output from the program. Press any key to return to the display screen.
F6	Moves cursor between display and dialog windows.
CTRL-G	Increases size of the window the cursor is in.
CTRL-T	Decreases size of the window the cursor is in.
Up arrow	Moves cursor up one line.
Down arrow	Moves cursor down one line.
PgUp	Scrolls up one page.
PgDn	Scrolls down one page. Stops at bottom of file if in source mode, behaves like DEBUG's U command in other modes.
Home	Scrolls to top of file if cursor is in display window, or to top of command buffer if in dialog window.

Table E.3 Function Key Commands

Key	Function
F5	Executes to the next breakpoint or to the end of the program if no breakpoint encountered.
F7	Sets a temporary breakpoint on the line with the cursor and executes to that line, unless another breakpoint or end of program is encountered.
F8	Traces the next source line, if in source mode, or the next instruction if in assembly mode. If the source line is a call, it enters the called routine. *Note:* it will execute through DOS function calls.
F9	Sets or clears a breakpoint on the line with the cursor. If the line does not have a breakpoint, it sets one on the line. If it already has a breakpoint, the breakpoint is cleared.
F10	Executes the next program step. Like F8 except that calls are executed rather than traced.

2. Use the up and down arrow keys to make a selection. When the item you want is highlighted, press Enter.
3. For most menu selections, the choice is executed immediately, however, some selections require a response.
4. If a response is needed, a dialog box opens up and you type the needed information.

The escape key can be pressed to cancel a menu. When a menu is open, the left and right arrow keys may be used to move from one menu to another.

The RUN Menu

This menu contains selections for running the program. Table E.4 gives the choices.

Watch Commands

One of the most useful of CODEVIEW's features is the ability to monitor variables and expressions. The watch commands described hereafter specify the variables and expressions to be watched.

Table E.4 RUN Menu Selections

Selection	Action
Start	Runs the program from the beginning. Program will run to completion unless a breakpoint or watch statement (see below) is encountered.
Restart	Restarts the program but doesn't begin to execute it. Any previously set breakpoints or watch statements will still be in effect.
Execute	Executes in slow motion from the current instruction. To stop execution, press a key or mouse button.
Clear breakpoints	Clears all breakpoints. Doesn't affect watch statements.

The watch commands can be entered from the watch menu, but it's easier to enter them as dialog commands; also, with dialog watch commands a range of variables can be specified.

Watching Memory

The watch command to monitor memory is

```
W{type} range
```

where range is either

```
start_address end_address
```

or

```
L count
```

and count is the number of values to be displayed.

Type is one of the following:

Type	Meaning
None	default
B	hex byte
A	ASCII
I	signed decimal word
U	unsigned decimal word
W	hex word
D	hex doubleword
S	short real
L	long real
T	10-byte real

The default type is the last type specified by a DUMP, ENTER, WATCH, or TRACEPOINT command; otherwise it is B.

For example, suppose that array A has been declared as

```
A       DW      37,12,18,96,45,3
```

and DS has been initialized to 4A7Dh, the segment number of the .DATA segment.

The dialog commands

```
>W A
>WI A
>WI A L6
>WW A L6
>WI A 4
>W 100 104
```

Create the following watch window:

```
0)  A    :    4A7D:0000    25   %
1)  A    :    4A7D:0000         37
2)  A L6 :    4A7D:0000         37    12    18    96    45    3
3)  A L6 :    471D:0000     0025  000C  0012  0060  002D  0003
4)  A 4  :    47AD:0000         37    12    18
5)  100 104 : 47AD:0100       6400  8448  6912
```

In (0), CODEVIEW displays both hex and ASCII values of variable A. In (1), we ask for A to be displayed as a signed integer. In (2), we want to see the array A of six words, displayed as integers. In (3), we ask for array A to be displayed in hex. In (4), we ask for the following range to be displayed in decimal: start_address = A = 0000h, end_address = 0004h. In (5), we specify range DS:0100h to DS:0104h. The display is in decimal, because that was the type used in (4).

Now as the program is traced or executed, the values in the watch window will change as the program changes memory.

Watching the Stack

We can monitor the stack as a special case of a memory range. For example, suppose SS:SP = 4A6C:000Ah and BP = 000Ch. To monitor six stack words as decimal integers, type

```
>WI  SP  L6
```

and the watch window shows

```
0)  sp 1 6 :  4A6C:000A    1813  5404  2009  5404  2741  5404
```

also BP may be used as a stack pointer; for example,

```
>WI  BP  L6
```

and the watch window shows

```
1)  bp 1 6 :  4A6C:000C    5404  2009  5404  2741  5404  3085
```

Watching Expressions

The watch window may also be used to monitor the value of a symbolic expression. The syntax is

```
W?    expression {,format}
```

where expression can be a single variable or a complex expression involving several variables and constants. The optional format is a single letter that specifies how the expression will be displayed. Some possibilities are

Format	Output Format
d	signed decimal integer
i	signed decimal integer
u	unsigned decimal integer
x	hexadecimal integer
c	single character

Here are some examples, using the array A defined earlier. Suppose that AX = 1 and BX = 4.

```
>W?  A
>W?  A,d
>W?  AX + BX
>W?  A + 2*AX
```

and the watch window is

```
0)      A        :   0x0025
1)      A,d:         37
2)      AX + BX  :   0x0005
3)      A + 2*AX :   0X0027
```

In (0), the expression to be displayed is just the variable A. It appears as 0x0025 (the notation 0xdigits is the C language notation for hexadecimal digits). In (1), we ask for A to be displayed with a decimal format. In (2), we get the sum of the contents of registers AX and BX. In (3), we ask for the the sum of A and 2 times the contents of AX.

Register Indirection

Sometimes we would like to keep track of a byte or word that is being pointed to by a register; for example, [BX] or [BP + 4]. CODEVIEW does not allow the square bracket pointer notation, but uses the following symbols instead:

Assembly Language Symbol	Codeview Symbol
BYTE PTR [register]	BY register
WORD PTR [register]	WO register
DWORD PTR [register]	DW register

For example, suppose that BX contain 0100h, and memory looks like this:

Offset	Contents
0100h	ABh
0101h	CDh
0102h	EFh
0103h	00h

The following watch commands

```
>W? BY BX
>W? WO BX
>W? WO BX+2
```

produce this watch window:

```
0)   BY BX    :  0x00ab
1)   WO BX    :  0xcdab
2)   WO BX+2  :  0x00ef
```

Removing Lines from the WATCH WINDOW

To remove a line from the watch window, the Y (yank) command can be used. Its syntax is

```
Y number
```

where number is the number of the line to be removed. The command Y * causes all the lines to be removed.

Tracepoints

You can specify a variable or range of variables as a trace point. When the variable(s) change, the program will break execution. The syntax is

```
TP? expression {,format}
```

or

```
TP{type} range
```

where format, type, and range are the same as for the W command. CODEVIEW displays the expression, variable, or range of variables in the same format as the W command, except that the display is intense. For example, we could type

```
TPI A L6
```

and CODEVIEW would display

```
0)    A L6  :   4A7D:0000    37  12  18  96  45  3
```

in the watch window. If any element of the array A changes, execution would break.

Watchpoints

A watchpoint breaks execution when a specified expression becomes nonzero (true). The command line for setting a watchpoint is

```
WP?   expression {,format}
```

where expression is a relational expression involving variables and possibly constants.

For example, suppose that A is defined as

```
A     DW .  25h
```

and the current values of AX and BX are 5 and 2, respectively. The dialog commands

```
>WP? AX>BX
>WP? AX - BX - 3
>WP? A > 25
>WP? A = 25
```

will create the following watch window

```
0)    AX>BX     : 0x0001
1)    AX - BX - 3 : 0x0000
2)    A > 25 : 0x0000
3)    A = 25: 0x0025
```

The display following (0) indicates that execution will break if AX > BX is true. Because AX has 5 and BX has 2, this is currently true and execution would break immediately. CODEVIEW indicates true by the notation 0x0001.

In (1), execution will break if AX − BX − 3 is nonzero. Currently, AX − BX − 3 = 5 − 2 − 3 = 0, so this condition is false. CODEVIEW indicates false by the notation 0x0000.

In (2), execution will break if A > 25, which is currently false.

In (3), execution will break if A = 25. This is currently true, so execution would break immediately. CODEVIEW shows the current value of A as 0x0025.

DEBUG Commands in CODEVIEW

Most of the DEBUG commands can be used as dialog commands in CODEVIEW. When working in source mode, symbolic labels may be used in commands. For example, if BELOW is a label in a program, then

```
G BELOW
```

causes execution to break at this label if encountered. In the D and E commands, a type can be specified. The syntax for E is

```
E {type} address {list}
```

D has the same syntax. Type comes from the same list of one-letter specifiers that are used for the W command. For example,

```
EI A   17 -1 456 8900 -29
```

will let the user enter the preceding five decimal integers in array A.

Appendix F

Assembly Instruction Set

In this appendix, we show the binary encoding of a typical 8086 instruction and give a summary of the common 8086, 8087, 80286, and 80386 instructions.

F.1 Typical 8086 Instruction Format

A machine instruction for the 8086 occupies from one to six bytes. For most instructions, the first byte contains the opcode, the second byte contains the addressing modes of the operands, and the other bytes contain either address information or immediate data. A typical two-operand instruction has the format given in Figure F.1

In the first byte, we see a six-bit opcode that identifies the operation. The same opcode is used for both 8- and 16-bit operations. The size of the operands is given by the W bit: W = 0 means 8-bit data and W = 1 means 16-bit data.

For register-to-register, register-to-memory, and memory-to-register operations, the REG field in the second byte contains a register number and the D bit specifies whether the register in the REG field is a source or destination operand, D = 0 means source and D = 1 means destination. For other types of operations, the REG field contains a three-bit extension of the opcode.

Byte 1			Byte 2			Byte 3	Byte 4	Byte 5	Byte 6
7 6 5 4 3 2	1	0	7 6	5 4 3	2 1 0	low disp or data	high disp or data	low data	high data
OPCODE	D	W	MOD	REG	R/M				

Figure F.1 Opcode Format

MOD=11			Effective Address Calculation			
R/M	W = 0	W = 1	R/M	MOD = 00	MOD = 01	MOD = 10
000	AL	AX	000	(BX) + (SI)	(BX) + (SI) + D8	(BX) + (SI) + D16
001	CL	CX	001	(BX) + (DI)	(BX) + (DI) + D8	(BX) + (DI) + D16
010	DL	DX	010	(BP) + (SI)	(BP) + (SI) + D8	(BP) + (SI) + D16
011	BL	BX	011	(BP) + (DI)	(BP) + (DI) + D8	(BP) + (DI) + D16
100	AH	SP	100	(SI)	(SI) + D8	(SI) + D16
101	CH	BP	101	(DI)	(DI) + D8	(DI) + D16
110	DH	SI	110	DIRECT ADDRESS	(BP) + D8	(BP) + D16
111	BH	DI	111	(BX)	(BX) + D8	(BX) + D16

MOD = 11 means register mode.

MOD = 00 means memory mode with no displacement, except when R/M = 110, then a 16-bit displacement follows.

MOD = 01 means memory, with 8-bit displacement following (D8).

MOD = 10 means memory mode with 16-bit displacement following (D16).

Figure F.2 MOD and R/M Fields

The combination of the W bit and the REG field can specify a total of 16 registers, see Table F.1

The second operand is specified by the MOD and R/M fields. Figure F.2 shows the various modes.

For segment registers, the field is indicated by SEG. Table F.2 shows the segment register encodings.

F.2 8086 Instructions

The following set of 8086 instructions appears in alphabetical order. In the set

- (register) stands for the contents of the register
- (EA) stands for the contents of the memory location given by the effective address EA
- flags affected means those flags that are modified by the instruction according to the result
- flags undefined means the values of those flags are unreliable
- disp means 8-bit displacement
- disp-low disp-hi means 16-bit displacement

Table F.1 Register Encoding

REG	W = 0	W = 1
000	AL	AX
001	CL	CX
010	DL	DX
011	BL	BX
100	AH	SP
101	CH	BP
110	DH	SI
111	BH	DI

Table F.2 Segment Register Encoding

SEG	Register
00	ES
01	CS
10	SS
11	DS

AAA: ASCII Adjust for Addition

Corrects the result in AL of adding two unpacked BCD digits or two ASCII digits.
Format: AAA
Operation: If the lower nibble of AL is greater than 9 or if AF is set to 1, then AL is incremented by 6, AH is incremented by 1, and AF is set to 1. This instruction always clears the upper nibble of AL and copies AF to CF.
Flags: Affected—AF, CF
Undefined—OF, PF, SF, ZF
Encoding: 00110111
37

AAD: ASCII Adjust for Division

Adjusts the unpacked BCD dividend in AX in preparation for division.
Format: AAD
Operation: The unpacked BCD operand in AX is converted into binary and stored in AL. This is achieved by multiplying AH by 10 and adding the result to AL. AH is then cleared.
Flags: Affected—PF, SF, ZF
Undefined—AF, CF, OF
Encoding: 11010101 00001010
D5   0A

AAM: ASCII Adjust for Multiplication

Converts the result of multiplying two BCD digits into unpacked BCD format. Can be used in converting numbers lower than 100 into unpacked BCD format.
Format: AAM
Operation: The contents of AL are converted into two unpacked BCD digits and placed in AX. AL is divided by 10 and the quotient is placed in AH and the remainder in AL.

Flags: Affected—PF, SF, ZF
Undefined—AF, CF, OF
Encoding: 11010100 00001010
          D4   0A

AAS: ASCII Adjust for Subtraction

Corrects the result in AL of subtracting two unpacked BCD numbers.

Format: AAS
Operation: If the lower nibble of AL is greater than 9 or if AF is set to 1, then AL is decremented by 6, AH is decremented by 1, and AF is set to 1. This instruction always clears the upper nibble of AL and copies AF to CF.
Flags: Affected—AF, CF
Undefined—OF, PF, SF, ZF
Encoding: 00111111
          3F

ADC: Add with Carry

The carry flag is added to the sum of the source and destination.

Format: ADC destination,source
Operation: If CF = 1, then (dest) = (source) + (dest) + 1
If CF = 0, then (dest) = (source) + (dest)
Flags: Affected—AF, CF, OF, PF, SF, ZF
Encoding: Memory or register with register
000100dw mod reg r/m
Immediate to accumulator
0001010w data
Immediate to memory or register
100000sw mod 010 r/m data
(s is set if a byte of data is added to 16-bit memory or register.)

ADD: Addition

Format: ADD destination,source
Operation: (dest) = (source) + (dest)
Flags: Affected—AF, CF, OF, PF, SF, ZF
Encoding: Memory or register with register
000000dw mod reg r/m
Immediate to accumulator
0000010w data
Immediate to memory or register
100000sw mod 000 r/m data
(s is set if a byte data is added to 16-bit memory or register.)

AND: Logical AND

Format: AND destination,source
Operation: Each bit of the source is ANDed with the corresponding bit in the destination, with the result stored in the destination. CF and OF are cleared.
Flags: Affected—CF, OF, PF, SF, ZF
Undefined: AF
Encoding: Memory or register with register
001000dw mod reg r/m
Immediate to accumulator
0010010w data

Immediate to memory or register
```
1000000w mod 100 r/m data
```

CALL: Procedure Call

Format: CALL target
Operation: The offset address of the next sequential instruction is pushed onto the stack, and control is transferred to the target operand. The target address is computed as follows: (1) intrasegment direct, offset = IP + displacement, (2) intrasegment indirect, offset = (EA), (3) intersegment direct, segment:offset given in instruction, and (4) intersegment indirect, segment = (EA +2), offset = (EA).
Flags: Affected—none
Encoding: Intrasegment Direct
```
11101000 disp-low disp-high
```
Intra-segment Indirect
```
11111111 mod 010 r/m
```
Intersegment Direct
```
10011010 offset-low offset-high seg-low seg-high
```
Intersegment Indirect
```
11111111 mod 011 r/m
```

CBW: Convert Byte to Word

Converts the signed 8-bit number in AL into a signed 16-bit number in AX.
Format: CBW
Operation: If bit 7 of AL is set, then AH gets FFh.
           If bit 7 of AL is clear, then AH is cleared.
Flags: Affected—none
Encoding: 10011000
           98

CLC: Clear Carry Flag

Format: CLC
Operation: Clears CF
Flags: Affected—CF
Encoding: 11111000
           F8

CLD: Clear Direction Flag

Format: CLD
Operation: Clears DF
Flags: Affected—DF
Encoding: 11111100
           FC

CLI: Clear Interrupt Flag

Disables maskable external interrupts.
Format: CLI
Operation: Clears IF
Flags: Affected—IF
Encoding: 11111010
           FA

CMC: Complement Carry Flag

Format: CMC
Operation: Complements CF
Flags: Affected—CF
Encoding: `11110100`
            `F5`

CMP: Compare

Compares two operands by subtraction. The flags are affected, but the result is not stored.

Format: `CMP destination,source`
Operation: The source operand is subtracted from the destination and the flags are set according to the result. The operands are not affected.
Flags: Affected—AF, CF, OF, PF, SF, ZF
Encoding: Memory or register with register
            `001110dw mod reg r/m`
            Immediate with accumulator
            `0011110w data`
            Immediate with memory or register
            `100000sw mod 111 r/m data`

CMPS/CMPSB/CMPSW: Compare Byte or Word String

Compares two memory operands. If preceded by a REP prefix, strings of arbitrary size can be compared.

Format: `CMPS source-string, dest-string`
            or
            `CMPSB`
            or
            `CMPSW`
Operation: The dest-string indexed by ES:DI is subtracted from the source-string indexed by SI. The status flags are affected. If the control flag DF is 0, then SI and DI are incremented; otherwise, they are decremented. The increments are 1 for byte strings and 2 for word strings.
Flags: Affected—AF, CF, OF, PF, SF, ZF
Encoding: `1010011w`

CWD: Convert Word to Double Word

Converts the signed 16-bit number in AX into a signed 32-bit number in DX:AX.

Format: CWD
Operation: If bit 15 of AX is set, then DX gets FFFF.
            If bit 15 of AX is clear, then DX is cleared.
Flags: Affected—none
Encoding: `10011001`
            `99`

DAA: Decimal Adjust for Addition

Corrects the result in AL of adding two packed BCD operands.

Format: DAA
Operation: If the lower nibble of AL is greater than 9 or if AF is set to 1, then AL is incremented by 6, and AF is set to 1. If AL is

greater than 9Fh or if the CF is set, then 60h is added to AL and CF is set to 1.

Flags: Affected—AF, CF, PF, SF, ZF
Undefined—OF

Encoding:
```
00100111
27
```

DAS: Decimal Adjust for Subtraction

Corrects the result in AL of subtracting two packed BCD operands.

Format: `DAS`
Operation: If the lower nibble of AL is greater than 9 or if AF is set to 1, then 60h is subtracted from AL and CF is set to 1.
Flags: Affected—AF, CF, PF, SF, ZF
Encoding:
```
00101111
2F
```

DEC: Decrement

Format: `DEC destination`
Operation: Decrements the destination operand by 1.
Flags: Affected—AF, OF, PF, SF, ZF
Encoding:
Register (word)
```
01001 reg
```
Memory or register
```
1111111w mod 001 r/m
```

DIV: Divide

Performs unsigned division.

Format: `DIV source`
Operation: The divisor is the source operand, which is either memory or register. For byte division (8-bit source) the dividend is AX, and for word division (16-bit source) the dividend is DX:AX. The quotient is returned to AL (AX for word division), and the remainder is returned to AH (DX for word division). If the quotient is greater than 8 bits (16 bits for word division), then an INT 0 is generated.
Flags: Undefined—AF, CF, OF, PF, SF, ZF
Encoding:
```
1111011w mod 110 r/m
```

ESC: Escape

Allows other processors, such as the 8087 coprocessor, to access instructions. The 8086 processor performs no operation except to fetch a memory operand for the other processor.

Format: `ESC external-opcode,source`
Flags: none
Encoding:
```
11011xxx mod xxx r/m
```
(The xxx sequence indicates an opcode for the coprocessor.)

HLT: Halt

Causes the processor to enter its halt state to wait for an external interrupt.

Format: `HLT`
Flags: none
Encoding:
```
11110100
F4
```

IDIV: Integer Divide

Performs signed division.

Format: `IDIV source`

Operation: The divisor is the source operand, which is either memory or register. For byte division (8-bit source) the dividend is AX, and for word division (16-bit source) the dividend is DX:AX. The quotient is returned to AL (AX for word division), and the remainder is returned to AH (DX for word division). If the quotient is greater than 8 bits (16 bits for word division), then an INT 0 is generated.

Flags: Undefined—AF, CF, OF, PF, SF, ZF

Encoding: `1111011w mod 111 r/m`

IMUL: Integer Multiply

Performs signed multiplication.

Format: `IMUL source`

Operation: The multiplier is the source operand, which is either memory or register. For byte multiplication (8-bit source) the multiplicand is AL, and for word multiplication (16-bit source) the multiplicand is AX. The product is returned to AX (DX:AX for word multiplication). The flags CF and OF are set if the upper half of the product is not the sign-extension of the lower half.

Flags: Affected—CF, OF
    Undefined—AF, PF, SF, ZF

Encoding: `1111011w mod 101 r/m`

IN: Input Byte or Word

Format: `IN accumulator,port`

Operation: The contents of the accumulator are replaced by the contents of the designated I/O port. The port operand is either a constant (for fixed port), or DX (for variable port).

Flags: Affected —none

Encoding:
```
Fixed port
1110010w port
Variable port
1110110w
```

INC: Increment

Format: `INC destination`

Operation: Increments the destination operand by 1.

Flags: Affected—AF, OF, PF, SF, ZF

Encoding:
```
Register (word)
01000 reg
Memory or register
1111111w mod 000 r/m
```

INT: Interrupt

Transfers control to one of 256 interrupt routines.

Format: `INT interrupt-type`

Operation: The FLAGS register is pushed onto the stack, then TF and IF are cleared, CS is pushed onto the stack and then filled by the high-order word of the interrupt vector, IP is pushed onto the stack and then filled by the low-order word of the interrupt vector.

Flags: Affected—IF, TF
Encoding: Type 3
```
11001100
```
Other types
```
11001101 type
```

INTO: Interrupt if Overflow

Generates an INT 4 if OF is set.

Format: `INTO`
Operation: If OF = 1, then same operation as INT 4. If OF = 0, then no operation takes place.
Flags: If OF=1 then OF and TF are cleared.
If OF=0 then no flags are affected.
Encoding:
```
11001110
CE
```

IRET: Interrupt Return

Provides a return from an interrupt routine.

Format: `IRET`
Operation: Pops the stack into the registers IP, CS, and FLAGS.
Flags: Affected—all
Encoding:
```
11001111
CF
```

J(condition): Jump Short, If Condition Is Met

Format: `J(condition) short-label`
Operation: If the condition is true, then a short jump is made to the label. The label must be within –128 to +127 bytes of the next instruction.
Flags: Affected—none

Instruction	Jump If	Condition	Encoding
JA	above	CF = 0 and ZF = 0	77 disp
JAE	above or equal	CF = 0	73 disp
JB	below	CF = 1	72 disp
JBE	below or equal	CF = 1 or ZF = 1	76 disp
JC	carry	CF = 0	72 disp
JCXZ	CX is 0	(CF or ZF) = 0	E3 disp
JE	equal	ZF = 1	74 disp
JG	greater	ZF = 0 and SF = OF	7F disp
JGE	greater or equal	ZF = OF	7D disp
JL	less	(SF xor OF) = 1	7C disp
JLE	less or equal	(SF xor OF) or ZF = 1	7E disp
JNA	not above	CF = 1 or ZF = 1	76 disp
JNAE	not above or equal	CF = 1	72 disp
JNB	not below	CF = 0	73 disp
JNBE	not below or equal	CF = 0 and ZF = 0	77 disp
JNC	not carry	CF = 0	73 disp
JNE	not equal	ZF = 0	75 disp

JNG	not greater	(SF xor OF) or ZF = 1	7E disp
JNGE	not greater nor equal (SF xor OF) = 1	7C disp	
JNL	not less	SF = OF	7D disp
JNLE	not less nor equal	ZF = 0 and SF = OF	7F disp
JNO	not overflow	OF = 0	71 disp
JNP	not parity	PF = 0	7B disp
JNS	not sign	SF = 0	79 disp
JNZ	not zero	ZF = 0	75 disp
JO	overflow	OF = 1	70 disp
JP	parity	PF = 1	7A disp
JPE	parity even	PF = 1	7A disp
JPO	parity odd	PF = 0	7B disp
JS	sign	SF = 1	78 disp
JZ	zero	ZF = 1	74 disp

JMP: Jump

Format: `JMP target`
Operation: Control is transferred to target label.
Flags: Affected—none
Encoding: Intrasegment direct
      `11101001 disp-low disp-hi`
      Intrasegment direct short
      `11101011 disp`
      Intersegment direct
      `11101010`
      Intersegment indirect
      `11111111 mod 101 r/m`
      Intrasegment indirect
      `11111111 mod 100 r/m`

LAHF: Load AH from Flags

Format: `LAHF`
Operation: The low eight bits of the FLAGS register are transferred to AH.
Flags: Affected—none
Encoding: `10011111`
      `9F`

LDS: Load Data Segment Register

Loads the DS register with a segment address and a general register with an offset so that data at the segment:offset may be accessed.

Format: `LDS destination,source`
Operation: The source is a doubleword memory operand. The lower word is placed in the destination register, and the upperword is placed in DS.
Flags: Affected—none
Encoding: `11000101 mod reg r/m`

LEA: Load Effective Address

Loads an offset memory address to a register.

Format: `LEA destination,source`
Operation: The offset address of the source memory operand is placed in the destination, which is a general register.
Flags: Affected—none
Encoding: `10001101 mod reg r/m`

LES: Load Extra Segment Register

Loads the ES register with a segment address and a general register with an offset so that data at the segment:offset may be accessed.

Format: `LES destination,source`
Operation: The source is a doubleword memory operand. The lower word is placed in the destination register, and the upperword is placed in ES.
Flags: none
Encoding: `11000100 mod reg r/m`

LOCK: Lock Bus

In a multiprocessor environment, locks the bus.

Format: `LOCK`
Operation: LOCK is used as a prefix that can precede any instruction. The bus is locked for the duration of the execution of the instruction to prevent other processors from accessing memory.
Flags: none
Encoding: `11110000`
`F0`

LODS/LODSB/LODSW: Load Byte or Word String

Transfers a memory byte or word indexed by SI to the accumulator.

Format: `LODS source-string`
or
`LODSB`
or
`LODSW`
Operation: The source byte (word) is loaded into AL (or AX). SI is incremented by 1 (or 2) if DF is clear; otherwise SI is decremented by 1 (or 2).
Flags: Affected—none
Encoding: `1010110w`

LOOP

Loop until count is complete.

Format: `LOOP short-label`
Operation: CX is decremented by 1, and if the result is not zero then control is transferred to the labeled instruction; otherwise control flows to the next instruction.
Flags: Affected—none
Encoding: `11100010 disp`
`E2`

LOOPE/LOOPZ: Loop if Equal/Loop If zero

A loop is controlled by the counter and the ZF.

Format: `LOOPE short-label`
or

```
                        LOOPZ short-label
Operation:              CX is decremented by 1, if the result is not zero and ZF = 1,
                        then control is transferred to the labeled instruction; other-
                        wise, control flows to the next instruction.
Flags:                  Affected—none
Encoding:               11100001 disp
                        E1
```

LOOPNE/LOOPNZ: Loop If Not Equal/Loop If Not Zero

A loop is controlled by the counter and the ZF.
```
Format:                 LOOPNE short-label
                        or
                        LOOPNZ short-label
Operation:              CX is decremented by 1, if the result is not zero and ZF = 0,
                        then control is transferred to the labeled instruction; other-
                        wise, control flows to the next instruction.
Flags:                  Affected—none
Encoding:               11100000 disp
                        E0
```

MOV: Move

Move data.
```
Format:                 MOV destination,source
Operation:              Copies the source operand to the destination operand.
Flags:                  Affected—none
Encoding:               To memory from accumulator
                        1010001w addr-low addr-high
                        To accumulator from memory
                        1010000w addr-low addr-high
                        To segment register from memory or register
                        10001110 mod 0 seg r/m
                        To memory or register from segment register
                        10001100 mod 0 seg r/m
                        To register from memory or register/ To memory from reg
                        100010d1 mod reg r/m (addr-low addr-high)
                        To register from immediate-data
                        1011w reg data (data-high)
                        To memory or register from immediate-data
                        1100011w mod 000 r/m data (data-high)
```

MOVS/MOVSB/MOVSW: Move Byte or Word String

Transfers memory data addressed by SI to memory location addressed by ES:DI. Multiple bytes (or words) can be transferred if the prefix REP is used.
```
Format:                 MOVS dest-string,source-string
                        or
                        MOVSB
                        or
                        MOVSW
Operation:              The source string byte (or word) is transferred to the destina-
                        tion operand. Both SI and DI are then incremented by 1 (or
                        2 for word strings) if DF = 0; otherwise, both are
                        decremented by 1 (or 2 for word strings).
Flags:                  Affected—none
Encoding:               1010010w
```

MUL: Multiply

Unsigned multiplication.
Format: `MUL source`
Operation: The multiplier is the source operand which is either memory or register. For byte multiplication (8-bit source) the multiplicand is AL and for word multiplication (16-bit source) the multiplicand is AX. The product is returned to AX (DX:AX for word multiplication). The flags CF and OF are set if the upper half of the product is not zero.
Flags: Affected—CF, OF
    Undefined—AF, PF, SF, ZF
Encoding: `1111011w mod 100 r/m`

NEG: Negate

Forms two's complement.
Format: `NEG destination`
Operation: The destination operand is subtracted from all 1's (0FFh for bytes and 0FFFFh for words). Then a 1 is added and the result placed in the destination.
Flags: Affected—AF, CF, OF, PF, SF, ZF
Encoding: `1111011w mod 011 r/m`

NOP: No Operation

Format: `NOP`
Operation: No operation is performed.
Flags: Affected—none
Encoding: `10010000`
    `90`

NOT: Logical Not

Format: `NOT destination`
Operation: Forms the one's complement of the destination.
Flags: Affected—none
Encoding: `1111011w mod 010 r/m`

OR: Logical Inclusive Or

Format: `OR destination,source`
Operation: Performs logical OR operation on each bit position of the operands and places the result in the destination.
Flags: Affected—CF, OF, PF, SF, ZF
    Undefined—AF
Encoding: Memory or register with register
    `000010dw mod reg r/m`
    Immediate to accumulator
    `0000110w data`
    Immediate to memory or register
    `1000000w mod 001 r/m`

OUT: Output Byte or Word

Format: `OUT accumulator,port`
Operation: The contents of the designated I/O port are replaced by the contents of the accumulator. The port is either a constant (for fixed port) or DX (for variable port).

Flags: Affected—none
Encoding: Fixed Port
1110011w port
Variable port
1110111w

POP: Pop Word Off Stack to Destination

Format: `POP destination`
Operation: The contents of the destination are replaced by the word at the top of the stack. The stack pointer is incremented by 2.
Flags: Affected—none
Encoding: General register
`01011 reg`
Segment register
`000 seg 111`
Memory or register
`10001111 mod 000 r/m`

POPF: Pop Flags Off Stack

Format: `POPF`
Operation: Transfers flag bits from the top of the stack to the FLAGS register and then increments SP by 2.
Flags: Affected—all
Encoding: `10011101`
9D

PUSH: Push Word onto Stack

Format: `PUSH source`
Operation: Decrements the SP register by 2 and then transfers a word from the source operand to the new top of stack.
Flags: none
Encoding: General register
`01010reg`
Segment register
`000 seg 110`
Memory or register
`11111111 mod 110 r/m`

PUSHF: Push Flags onto Stack

Format: `PUSHF`
Operation: Decrements SP by 2 and transfers flag bits to the top of the stack.
Flags: Affected—none
Encoding: `10011100`
9C

RCL: Rotate Left Through Carry

Rotates destination left through the CF flag one or more times.
Format: `RCL destination,1`
or
`RCL destination,CL`
Operation: The first format rotates the destination once through CF resulting in the msb being placed in CF and the old CF ended in the lsb. To rotate more than once, the count must be

placed in CL. When the count is 1 and the leftmost two bits of the old destination are equal, then OF is cleared; if they are unequal, OF is set to 1. When the count is not 1, then OF is undefined. CL is not changed.

Flags: Affected—CF,OF
Encoding:
```
110100vw mod 010 r/m
If v=0, count=1
If v=1, count=(CL)
```

RCR: Rotate Right Through Carry

Rotates destination right through the CF flag one or more times.

Format:
```
RCR destination,1
```
or
```
RCR destination,CL
```

Operation: The first format rotates the destination once through CF resulting in the lsb being placed in CF and the old CF ended in the msb. To rotate more than once, the count must be placed in CL. When the count is 1 and the leftmost two bits of the new destination are equal, then OF is cleared; if they are unequal, OF is set to 1. When the count is not 1, then OF is undefined. CL is not changed.

Flags: Affected—CF, OF
Encoding:
```
110100vw mod 011 r/m
If v = 0, count = 1
If v = 1, count = (CL)
```

REP/REPZ/REPE/REPNE/REPNZ: Repeat String Operation

The string operation that follows is repeated while (CX) is not zero.

Format: `REP/REPZ/REPE/REPNE/REPNZ string-instruction`

Operation: The string operation is carried out until (CX) is decremented to 0. For CMPS and SCAS operations, the ZF is also used in terminating the iteration. For REP/REPZ/REPE the CMPS and SCAS operations are repeated if (CX) is not zero and ZF is 1. For REPNE/REPNZ, the CMPS and SCAS operations are repeated if (CX) is not zero and ZF is 0.

Flags: See the associated string instruction.
Encoding:
```
REP/REPZ/REPE    11110011
REPNE/REPNZ      11110010
```

RET: Return from Procedure

Returns control after a called procedure has been executed.

Format: `RET [pop-value]`

Operation: If RET is within a NEAR procedure, it is translated into an intrasegment return, which updates the IP by popping one word from the stack. If RET is within a FAR procedure, it is translated into an intersegment return that updates both the IP and CS. The optional pop value specifies a number of bytes in the stack to be discarded. These are parameters passed to the procedure.

Flags: Affected—none
Encoding: Intrasegment
```
11000011
```
Intrasegment with pop value
```
11000010
```

Intersegment
```
11001011
```
Intersegment with pop value
```
11001010
```

ROL: Rotate Left

Rotates destination left one or more times.
Format: `ROL destination,1`
           or
           `ROL destination,CL`
Operation: The first format rotates the destination once; CF also gets the msb. To rotate more than once, the count must be placed in CL. When the count is 1 and the new CF is not the same as the msb, then the OF is set, otherwise, OF is cleared. When the count is not 1, then OF is undefined. CL is not changed.
Flags: Affected—CF, OF
Encoding:
```
110100vw mod 000 r/m
If v = 0, count = 1
If v = 1, count = (CL)
```

ROR: Rotate Right

Rotates destination right one or more times.
Format: `ROR destination,1`
           or
           `ROR destination,CL`
Operation: The first format rotates the destination once; CF also gets the lsb. To rotate more than once, the count must be placed in CL. When the count is 1 and the leftmost two bits of the new destination are equal, then OF is cleared; if they are unequal, OF is set to 1. When the count is not 1, then OF is undefined. CL is not changed.
Flags: Affected—CF, OF
Encoding:
```
110100vw mod 001 r/m
If v = 0, count = 1
If v = 1, count = (CL)
```

SAHF: Store AH in FLAGS Register

Format: `SAHF`
Operation: Stores five bits of AH into the lower byte of the FLAGS register. Only the bits corresponding to the flags are transferred. The flags in the lower byte of FLAGS register are SF = bit 7, ZF = bit 6, AF = bit 4, PF = bit 2, and CF = bit 0.
Flags: Affected—AF, CF, PF, SF, ZF
Encoding:
```
10011110
9E
```

SAL/SHL: Shift Arithmetic Left/Shift Logical Left

Format: `SAL/SHL destination,1`
           or
           `SAL/SHL destination,CL`
Operation: The first format shifts the destination once; CF gets the msb and a 0 is shifted into the lsb. To shift more than once, the count must be placed in CL. When the count is 1 and the

new CF is not the same as the msb, then the OF is set; otherwise, OF is cleared. When the count is not 1, then OF is undefined. CL is not changed.

Flags: Affected—CF, OF, PF, SF, ZF
Undefined—AF

Encoding:
```
110100vw mod 100 r/m
If v = 0, count = 1
If v = 1, count = (CL)
```

SAR: Shift Arithmetic Right

Format:
```
SAR destination,1
```
or
```
SAR destination,CL
```

Operation: The first format shifts the destination once; CF gets the lsb and the msb is repeated (sign is retained). To shift more than once, the count must be placed in CL. When the count is 1 OF is cleared. When the count is not 1, then OF is undefined. CL is not changed.

Flags: Affected—CF, OF, PF, SF, ZF
Undefined—AF

Encoding:
```
110100vw mod 111 r/m
If v = 0, count = 1
If v = 1, count = (CL)
```

SBB: Subtract with Borrow

Format:
```
SBB destination,source
```

Operation: Subtracts source from destination; and if CF is 1 then subtract 1 from the result. The result is placed in the destination.

Flags: Affected—AF, CF, OF, PF, SF, ZF

Encoding: Memory or register with register
```
000110dw mod reg r/m
```
Immediate from accumulator
```
0001110w data
```
Immediate from memory or register
```
100000sw mod 011 r/m data
```
(s is set if an immediate-data-byte is subtracted from 16-bit memory or register.)

SCAS/SCASB/SCASW: Scan Byte or Word String

Compares memory against the accumulator. Used with REP, it can scan multiple memory locations for a particular value.

Format:
```
SCAS dest-string
```
or
```
SCASB
```
or
```
SCASW
```

Operation: Subtracts the destination byte (or word) addressed by DI from AL (or AX). The flags are affected but the result is not saved. DI is incremented (if DF = 1), or decremented (if DF = 0) by 1 (byte strings) or 2 (word strings).

Flags: Affected—AF, CF, OF, PF, SF, ZF

Encoding:
```
1010111w
```

SHR: Shift Logical Right

Format:	`SHR destination,1`
	or
	`SHR destination,CL`
Operation:	The first format shifts the destination once; CF gets the lsb and a 0 is shifted into the msb. To shift more than once, the count must be placed in CL. When the count is 1 and the leftmost two bits are equal, then OF is cleared; otherwise, OF is set to 1. When the count is not 1, then OF is undefined. CL is not changed.
Flags:	Affected—CF, OF, PF, SF, ZF
	Undefined—AF
Encoding:	`110100vw mod 101 r/m`
	`If v = 0, count = 1`
	`If v = 1, count = (CL)`

STC: Set Carry Flag

Format:	`STC`
Operation:	CF is set to 1.
Flags:	Affected—CF
Encoding:	`11111001`
	`F9`

STD: Set Direction Flag

Format:	`STD`
Operation:	DF is set to 1.
Flags:	Affected—DF
Encoding:	`11111101`
	`FD`

STI: Set Interrupt Flag

Format:	`STI`
Operation:	IF is set to 1, thus enabling external interrupts.
Flags:	Affected—IF
Encoding:	`11111011`
	`FB`

STOS/STOSB/STOSW: Store Byte or Word String

Stores the accumulator into memory. When used with REP, it can store multiple memory locations with the same value.

Format:	`STOS dest-string`
	or
	`STOSB`
	or
	`STOSW`
Operation:	Stores AL (or AX) into the destination byte (or word) addressed by DI. DI is incremented (DF = 1), or decremented (DF = 0) by 1 (byte strings) or 2 (word strings).
Flags:	Affected—none
Encoding:	`1010101w`

SUB: Subtract

Format: `SUB destination,source`
Operation: Subtracts source from destination. The result is placed in the destination.
Flags: Affected—AF, CF, OF, PF, SF, ZF
Encoding: Memory or register with register
`001010dw mod reg r/m`
Immediate from accumulator
`0010110w data`
Immediate from memory or register
`100000sw mod 101 r/m data`
(s is set if an immediate-data-byte is subtracted from 16-bit memory or register.)

TEST: Test (Logical Compare)

Format: `TEST destination,source`
Operation: The two operands are ANDed to affect the flags. The operands are not affected.
Flags: Affected—CF, OF, PF, SF, ZF
Undefined—AF
Encoding: Memory or register with register
`1000010w mod reg r/m`
Immediate with accumulator
`1010100w data`
Immediate with memory or register
`1111011w mod 000 r/m data`

WAIT

Format: `WAIT`
Operation: The processor is placed in a wait state until activated by an external interrupt.
Flags: Affected—none
Encoding: `10011011`
`9B`

XCHG: Exchange

Format: `XCHG destination,source`
Operation: The source operand and the destination operand are interchanged.
Flags: Affected—none
Encoding: Register with accumulator
`10010reg`
Memory or register with register
`1000011w mod reg r/m`

XLAT: Translate

Performs a table lookup translation.
Format: `XLAT source-table`
Operation: BX must contain the offset address of the source table, which is at most 256 bytes. AL should contain the index of the table element. The operation replaces AL by the contents of the table element addressed by BX and AL.
Flags: Affected—none
Encoding: `11010111`
`D7`

XOR: Exclusive OR

Format: `XOR destination,source`
Operation: The exclusive OR operation is performed bit-wise with the source and destination operands; the result is stored in the destination. CF and OF are cleared.
Flags: Affected—CF, OF, PF, SF, ZF
Undefined: AF
Encoding: Memory or register with register
`001100dw mod reg r/m`
Immediate to accumulator
`0011010w data`
Immediate to memory or register
`1000000w mod 110 r/m data`

F.3 8087 Instructions

The 8087 uses several data types, when transferring data to or from memory, the memory data definition determines the data type format. Table F.3 shows the association between the 8087 data types and the memory data definitions. In this section we only give 8087 instructions for simple arithmetic operations. Check the 8087 manual for other instructions.

FADD: Add Real

Format: `FADD`
or
`FADD source`
or
`FADD destination,source`
Operation: Adds a source operand to the destination. For the first form, the source operand is the top of the stack and the destination is ST(1). The top of the stack is popped, and its value is added to the new top. For the second form, the source is either short real or long real in memory; the destination is the top of the stack. For the third form, one of the operands is the top of the stack and the other is another stack register; the stack is not popped.

Table F.3 8087 Data Types

Data Type	Size (bits)	Memory Definition	Pointer Type
Word integer	16	DW	WORD PTR
Short integer	32	DD	DWORD PTR
Long integer	64	DQ	QWORD PTR
Packed decimal	80	DT	TBYTE PTR
Short real	32	DD	DWORD PTR
Long real	64	DQ	QWORD PTR
Temporary real	80	DT	TBYTE PTR

FBLD: Packed Decimal Load

Format: `FBLD source`
Operation: Loads a packed decimal number to the top of the stack. The source operand is of type DT (10 bytes).

FBSTP: Packed BCD Store and Pop

Format: `FBSTP destination`
Operation: Converts the top of the stack to a packed BCD format and stores the result in the memory destination. Then the stack is popped.

FDIV: Divide Real

Format: `FDIV`
or
`FDIV source`
or
`FDIV destination,source`
Operation: Divides the destination by the source. For the first form, the source operand is the top of the stack and the destination is ST(1). The top of the stack is popped and its value is used to divide into the new top. For the second form, the source is either short real or long real in memory; the destination is the top of the stack. For the third form, one of the operands is the top of the stack and the other is another stack register; the stack is not popped.

FIADD: Integer Add

Format: `FIADD source`
Operation: Adds the source operand to the top of the stack. The source operand can be either a short integer or a word integer.

FIDIV: Integer Divide

Format: `FIDIV source`
Operation: Divides the top of the stack by the source. The source operand can be either a short integer or a word integer.

FILD: Integer Load

Format: `FILD source`
Operation: Loads a memory integer operand onto the top of the stack. The source operand is either word integer, short integer, or long integer.

FIMUL: Integer Multiply

Format: `FIMUL source`
Operation: Multiplies the source operand to the top of the stack. The source operand can be either a short integer or a word integer.

FIST: Integer Store

Format: `FIST destination`
Operation: Rounds the top of the stack to an integer value and stores to a memory location. The destination may be word integer or short integer. The stack is not popped.

FISTP: Integer Store and Pop

Format: `FISTP destination`
Operation: Rounds the top of the stack to an integer value and stores to a memory location. Then the stack is popped. The destination may be word integer, short integer, or long integer.

FISUB: Integer Subtract

Format: `FISUB source`
Operation: Subtracts the source operand from the top of the stack. The source operand can be either a short integer or a word integer.

FLD: Load Real

Format: `FLD source`
Operation: Loads a real operand onto the top of the stack. The source may be a stack register ST(i), or a memory location. For a memory operand, the data type may be any of the real formats.

FMUL: Multiply Real

Format: `FMUL`
            or
            `FMUL source`
            or
            `FMUL destination,source`
Operation: Multiplies a source operand to the destination. For the first form, the source operand is the top of the stack and the destination is ST(1). The top of the stack is popped and its value is multiplied to the new top. For the second form, the source is either short real or long real in memory; the destination is the top of the stack. For the third form, one of the operands is the top of the stack and the other is another stack register; the stack is not popped.

FST: Store Real

Format: `FST destination`
Operation: Stores the top of the stack to a memory location or another stack register. The memory destination may be short real (doubleword) or long real (quadword). The stack is not popped.

FSTP: Store Real and Pop

Format: `FSTP destination`
Operation: Stores the top of the stack to a memory location or another stack register. Then the stack is popped. The memory destination may be short real (doubleword), long real (quadword), or temporary real (10 bytes).

FSUB: Subtract Real

Format: `FSUB`
            or
            `FSUB source`
            or
            `FSUB destination,source`

Operation: Subtracts a source operand from the destination. For the first form, the source operand is the top of the stack and the destination is ST(1). The top of the stack is popped and its value is subtracted from the new top. For the second form, the source is either short real or long real in memory; the destination is the top of the stack. For the third form, one of the operands is the top of the stack and the other is another stack register; the stack is not popped.

F.4 80286 Instructions

The real-mode 80286 instruction set includes all 8086 instructions plus the extended instruction set. The extended instruction set contains five groups of instructions, (1) multiply with immediate values (IMUL), (2) input and output strings (INS and OUTS), (3) stack operations (POPA, PUSH immediate, PUSHA), and (4) shifts and rotates with immediate count values, and (5) instructions for translating high-level language constructs (BOUND and ENTER). We only give the instructions in groups 1–4.

IMUL: Integer Immediate Multiply

Format: `IMUL destination,immediate`
or
`IMUL destination,source,immediate`

Operation: For the first format, the immediate operand, which must be a byte, is multiplied with the destination, which must be a 16-bit register. The lower 16-bit of the result is stored in the register. For the second format, the 8- or 16-bit immediate operand is multiplied with the source operand, which may be a 16-bit register or a memory word. The lower 16-bit of the result is stored in the destination, which must be a 16-bit register. The flags CF and OF are set if the upper half of the product is not the sign-extension of the lower half.

Flags: Affected—CF, OF
Undefined—AF, PF, SF, ZF

Encoding: `011010s1 mod reg r/m data [data if s=0]`

INS/INSB/INSW: Input from Port to String

Transfers a byte or word string element from a port to memory. Multiple bytes or words can be transferred if the prefix REP is used.

Format: `INS destination-string,port`
or
`INSB`
or
`INSW`

Operation: A byte or word is transferred from the port designated by DX to the location ES:DI. DI is then incremented by 1 (or 2 for word strings) if DF = 0; otherwise, DI is decremented by 1 (or 2 for word strings).

Flags: Affected—none
Encoding: `0110110w`

OUTS/OUTSB/OUTSW: Output String to Port

Transfers a byte or word string element from memory to a port. Multiple bytes or words can be transferred if the prefix REP is used.

Format: `OUTS destination-string,port`
              or
              `OUTSB`
              or
              `OUTSW`

Operation: A byte or word is transferred from memory located at DS:SI to the port designated by DX. SI is then incremented by 1 (or 2 for word strings) if DF = 0; otherwise, SI is decremented by 1 (or 2 for word strings).

Flags: Affected—none
Encoding: `0110111w`

POPA: Pop All General Registers

Format: `POPA`
Operation: The registers are popped in the order DI, SI, BP, SP, BX, DX, CX, and AX.
Encoding: `01100001`
              `61`

PUSH: Push Immediate

Format: `PUSH data`
Operation: The data may be 8 or 16 bits. A data byte is signed extended into 16 bits before pushing onto the stack.
Flags: Affected—none
Encoding: `011010s0 data [data if s = 0]`

PUSHA: Push All General Registers

Format: `PUSHA`
Operation: The registers are pushed in the order AX, CX, DX, BX, original SP, BP, SI, and DI.
Flags: Affected—none
Encoding: `01100000`
              `60`

The general format of shifts and rotates with immediate count values is:

`Opcode destination,immediate`

where opcode is any one of RCL, RCR, ROL, ROR, SAL, SHL, SAR, and SHR. If the immediate value is 1, then the instruction is the same as an 8086 instruction. For an immediate value of 2–31, the instruction operates like an 8086 instruction in which CL contains the value. The 80286 does not allow a constant count value to be greater than 31.

The encodings for immediate values of 2–31 are

      RCL
`1100000w mod 010 r/m`
      RCR
`1100000w mod 011 r/m`
      ROL
`1100000w mod 000 r/m`
      ROR
`1100000w mod 001 r/m`

```
        SAL/SHL
1100000w mod 100 r/m
        SAR
1100000w mod 111 r/m
        SHR
1100000w mod 101 r/m
```

F.5 80386 Instructions

The real-mode 80386 instruction set includes all real-mode 80286 instructions plus their 32-bit extensions, together with six groups of new instructions, (1) bit scans, (2) bit tests, (3) move with extensions, (4) set byte on condition, (5) double-precision shifts, and (6) move to or from special registers. We only give instructions in groups 1–5.

Bit Scan Instructions

The bit scan instructions are BSF (bit scan forward) and BSR (bit scan reverse). They are used to scan an operand to find the first set bit, and they differ only in the direction of the scan.

Formats: `BSF destination,source`
or
`BSR destination,source`

Operation: The destination must be a register, the source is either a register or a memory location. They must be both words or both doublewords. The source is scanned for the first set bit. If the bits are all 0, then ZF is cleared; otherwise, ZF is set and the destination register is loaded with the bit position of the first set bit. For BSF the scanning is from bit 0 to the msb, and for BSR the scanning is from the msb to bit 0.

Flags: Affected—ZF

Encoding: BSF
`00001111 10111101 mod reg r/m`
BSR
`00001111 10111101 mod reg r/m`

Bit Test Instructions

The bit test instructions are BT (bit test), BTC (bit test and complement), BTR (bit test and reset), and BTS (bit test and set). They are used to copy a bit from the destination operand to the CF so that the bit can be tested by a JC or JNC instruction.

Format: `BT destination,source`
or
`BTC destination,source`
or
`BTR destination,source`
or
`BTS destination,source`

Operation: The source specifies a bit position in the destination to be copied to the CF. BT simply copies the bit to CF, BTC copies the bit and complements it in the destination, BTR copies the bit and resets it in the destination, and BTS copies the bit and sets it in the destination. The source is either a 16-bit register, 32-bit register, or an 8-bit constant. The destination may be a 16-bit or 32-bit register or memory. If the source is a register, then the source and destination must have the same size.

Flags: Affected—CF

Encoding: Source is 8-bit immediate data:
```
BT
00001111 10111010 mod 100 r/m
BTC
00001111 10111010 mod 111 r/m
BTR
00001111 10111010 mod 110 r/m
BTS
00001111 10111010 mod 101 r/m
```
Source is register:
```
BT
00001111 10100011 mod reg r/m
BTC
00001111 10111011 mod reg r/m
BTR
00001111 10110011 mod reg r/m
BTS
00001111 10101011 mod reg r/m
```

Move with Extension Instructions

The move with extension instructions are MOVSX (move with sign-extend) and MOVZX (move with zero-extend). These instructions move a small source into a bigger destination and extend to the upper half with the sign or a zero.

Format: `MOVSX destination,source`
            or
            `MOVZX destination,source`

Operation: The destination must be a register, the source is either a register or memory. If the source is a byte (or word) the destination is a word (or doubleword). MOVSX copies and sign extends the source into the destination. MOVZX copies and zero extends the source into the destination.

Flags: Affected—none

Encoding: `MOVSX`
```
00001111 1011111w mod reg r/m
```
`MOVZX`
```
00001111 1011011W mod reg r/m
```

Set Byte on Condition Instructions

The set byte on condition instructions set the destination byte to 1 if the condition is true and clear it if the condition is false.

Format: `SET(condition) destination`

Operation: The destination is either an 8-bit register or memory. It is set to 1 if condition is true and to 0 if condition is false.

Flags: Affected—none

Encoding: `00001111 opcode mod 000 r/m`
            (the opcode byte is given in the following in hex)

Instruction	Set If	Condition	Opcode
SETA	above	CF = 0 and ZF = 0	97
SETAE	above or equal	CF = 0	93
SETB	below	CF = 1	92
SETBE	below or equal	CF = 1 or ZF = 1	96
SETC	carry	CF = 0	92
SETE	equal	ZF = 1	94
SETGG	greater	ZF = 0 and SF = OF	9F
SETGE	greater or equal	ZF = OF	9D
SETL	less	(SF xor OF) = 1	9C
SETLE	less or equal	(SF xor OF) or ZF = 1	9E
SETNA	not above	CF = 1 or ZF = 1	96
SETNAE	not above or equal	CF = 1	92
SETNB	not below	CF = 0	93
SETNBE	not below or equal	CF = 0 and ZF = 0	97
SETNC	not carry	CF = 0	93
SETNE	not equal	ZF = 0	95
SETNG	not greater	(SF xor OF) or ZF = 1	9E
SETNGE	not greater nor equal	(SF xor OF) = 1	9C
SETNL	not less	SF = OF	9D
SETNLE	not less nor equal	ZF = 0 and SF = OF	9F
SETNO	not overflow	OF = 0	91
SETNP	not parity	PF = 0	9B
SETNS	not sign	SF = 0	99
SETNZ	not zero	ZF = 0	95
SETO	overflow	OF = 1	90
SETP	parity	PF = 1	9A
SETPE	parity even	PF = 1	9A
SETPO	parity odd	PF = 0	9B
SETS	sign	SF = 1	98
SETZ	zero	ZF = 1	94

Double-Precision Shift Instructions

The double-precision shift instructions are SHLD (double-precision shift left) and SHRD (double-precision shift right).

Format: `SHLD destination,source,count`
or
`SHRD destination,source,count`

Operation: The destination is either register or memory, the source is a register, and both must be of the same size (either 16 or 32 bits). Count is either an 8-bit constant or CL. The count specifies the number of shifts for the destination. Instead of shifting in zeros as in the case of the single-precision shifts, the bits shifted into the destination are from the source. However, the source is not altered. The SF, ZF, and PF flags are set according to the result; CF is set to the last bit shifted out; OF and AF are undefined.

Flags: Affected—SF, ZF, PF, CF
Undefined—OF, AF

Encoding: Count is immediate data:
SHLD
00001111 10100100 mod reg r/m [disp] data
SHRD
00001111 10101100 mod reg r/m [disp] data
Count is CL:
SHLD
00001111 10100101 mod reg r/m [disp]
SHRD
00001111 10101101 mod reg r/m [disp]

Appendix G

Assembler Directives

This appendix describes the most important assembler directives. To explain the syntax, we will use the following notation:

| | separates choices
{ } enclosed items are optional
[ ] repeat the enclosed items 0 or more times

If syntax is not given, the directive has no required or optional arguments.

.ALPHA

Tells the assembler to arrange segments in alphabetical order. Placed before segment definitions.

ASSUME

Syntax: `ASSUME segment_register:name [,segment_register: name]`

Tells the assembler to associate a segment register with a segment name.

Example: `ASSUME CS:C_SEG, DS:D_SEG, SS:S_SEG, ES:D_SEG`

Note: the name NOTHING cancels the current segment register association. In particular, ASSUME NOTHING cancels segment register associations made by previous ASSUME statements.

.CODE

Syntax: `.CODE {name}`

A simplified segment directive (MASM 5.0) for defining a code segment.

.COMM

Syntax: `.COMM definition [,definition]`

where definition has the syntax NEAR|FAR label:size{:count}
label is a variable name
size is BYTE, WORD, DWORD, QWORD, or TBYTE
count is the number of elements contained in the variable
(default = 1)

Defines a communal variable; such a variable has both PUBLIC and EXTRN attributes, so it can be used in different assembly modules.

Examples: `COMM    NEAR WORD1:WORD`
                `COMM    FAR  ARR1:BYTE:10, ARR2:BYTE:20`

COMMENT

Syntax: `COMMENT delimiter {text}`
            `{text}`
            `delimiter {text}`

where delimiter is the first nonblank character after the COMMENT directive. Used to define a comment. Causes the assembler to ignore all text between the first and second delimiters. Any text on the same line as the second delimiter is ignored as well.

Examples:

```
COMMENT * Uses an asterisk as the delimiter. All this
text is ignored *
COMMENT + This text and the following instruction is ig-
nored too +    MOV    AX,BX
```

.CONST

A simplified segment directive for defining a segment containing data that will not be changed by the program. Used mostly in assembly language routines to be called by a high-level language.

.CREF and .XCREF

Syntax: `.CREF {name [,name]}`
            `.XCREF {name [,name]}`

In the generation of the cross-reference (.CRF) file, .CREF directs the generation of cross-referencing of names in a program. .CREF with no arguments causes cross-referencing of all names. This is the default directive.
.XCREF turns off cross-referencing in general, or just for the specified names.

Example:

```
.XCREF                      ;turns off cross-referencing
.
.
.CREF                       ;turns cross-referencing back on
.
.
.XCREF   NAME1,NAME2        ;turns off cross-referencing
                            ;of NAME1 and NAME2
```

.DATA and .DATA?

Simplified segment directives for defining data segments. .DATA defines an initialized data segment and .DATA? defines an uninitialized data segment. Uninitialized data consist of variables defined with "?". .DATA? is used mostly with assembly language routines to be called from a high-level language. For stand-alone assembly language programs, the .DATA segment may contain uninitialized data.

Data-Defining Directives

Directive	Meaning
DB	define byte
DD	define doubleword (4 bytes)
DF	define farword (6 bytes); used only with 80386 processor
DQ	define quadword (8 bytes)
DT	define tenbyte (10 bytes)
DW	define word (2 bytes)

Syntax: `{name} directive initializer [,initializer]`

where name is a variable name. If name is missing, memory is allocated but no name is associated with it. Initializer is a constant, constant expression, or ?. Multiple values may be defined by using the DUP operator. See Chapter 10.

DOSSEG

Tells the assembler to adopt the DOS segment-ordering convention. For a SMALL model program, the order is code, data, stack. This directive should appear before any segment definitions.

ELSE

Used in a conditional block. The syntax is

```
Condition
    statements1
ELSE
    statements2
ENDIF
```

If Condition is true, statements1 are assembled; if Condition is false, statements2 are assembled. See Chapter 13 for the form of Condition.

END

Syntax: `END {start_address}`

Ends a source program. Start_address is a name where execution is to begin when the program is loaded. For a program with only one source module, start_address would ordinarily be the name of the main procedure or a label indicating the first instruction. For a program with several modules, each module must have an END but only one of them can specify a start_address.

ENDIF

Ends a conditional block. See Chapter 13.

ENDM

Ends a macro or repeat block. See MACRO and REPT.

ENDP

Ends a procedure. See PROC.

ENDS

Ends a segment or structure. See SEGMENT and STRUC.

EQU

Syntax: There are two forms, numeric equates and string equates. A numeric equate has the form

```
name   EQU   numeric_expression
```

A string equate has the form

```
name   EQU   <string>
```

The EQU directive assigns the expression following EQU to the constant symbol name. Numeric_expression must evaluate to a number. The assembler replaces each occurrence of name in a program by numeric_expression or string. No memory is allocated for name. Name may not be redefined.

Examples:

```
MAX                        EQU 32767
MIN                        EQU MAX - 10
PROMPT                     EQU <'type a line of text:$'>
ARG                        EQU <[DI + 2]>
```

Use in a program:

```
.DATA
         MSG  DB    PROMPT
.CODE
MAIN PROC
         MOV  AX,MIN    ;equivalent to MOV AX,32757
         MOV  BX,ARG    ;equivalent to MOV BX,[DI+2]
```

= (equal)

Syntax: `name = expression`

where expression is an integer, constant expression, or a one or two-character string constant.
The directive = works like EQU, except that names defined with = can be redefined later in a program.

Examples:

```
CTR = 1
         MOV  AX,CTR    ;translates to MOV AX,1
CTR = CTR + 5
         MOV  BX,CTR    ;translates to MOV BX,6
```

The = directive is often used in macros. See Chapter 13.

.ERR Directives

These are conditional error directives that can be used to force the assembler to display an error message during assembly, for debugging purposes. The assembler displays the message "Forced error", with an identifying number. See Chapter 13.

Directive	Number	Forced error if
.ERR1	87	encountered during assembly pass 1
.ERR2	88	encountered during assembly pass 2
.ERR	89	encountered
.ERRE expression	90	expression is false (0)

.ERRNZ expression	91	expression is true (nonzero)
.ERRNDEF name	92	name has not been defined.
.ERRDEF name	93	name has been defined.
.ERRB <argument>	94	argument is blank
.ERRNB <argument>	95	argument is not blank
.ERRIDN <arg1>,<arg2>	96	arg1 and arg2 are identical
.ERRDIF <arg1>,<arg2>	97	arg1 and arg2 are different

EVEN

Advances the location counter to the next even address.

EXITM

Used in a macro or repeat block. Tells the assembler to terminate the macro or repeat block expansion.

EXTRN

Syntax: `EXTRN name:type [,name:type]`

Informs the assembler of an external name; that is, a name defined in another module. Type must match the type declared for the name in the other module. Type can be NEAR, FAR, PROC, BYTE, WORD, DWORD, FWORD, QWORD, TBYTE, or ABS. See Chapter 14.

.FARADATA and .FARDATA?

Syntax: `.FARDATA {name}`
              `.FARDATA? {name}`

Used primarily with compilers for defining extra data segments.

GROUP

Syntax: `name GROUP segment [,segment]`

A group is a collection of segments that are associated with the same starting address. Variables and labels defined in the segments of the group are assigned addresses relative to the start of the group, rather than relative to the beginning of the segments in which they are defined. This makes it possible to refer to all the data in the group by initializing a single segment register. *Note:* the same result can be obtained by giving the same name and a PUBLIC attribute to all the segments.

IF directives

These directives are used to grant the assembler permission to assemble the statements following the directives, depending on conditions. A list may be found in Chapter 13.

INCLUDE

Syntax: `INCLUDE filespec`

where filespec specifies a file containing valid assembly language statements. In addition to a file name, filespec may include a drive and path.
The directive causes the assembler to insert the contents of the file at the position of the INCLUDE in the source file, and to begin processing the file's statements.

Examples: `INCLUDE MACLIB`
`INCLUDE C:\BIN\PROG1.ASM`

LABEL

Syntax: `name LABEL type`

where type is BYTE, WORD, DWORD, FWORD, QWORD, TBYTE, or the name of a previously-defined structure.
This directive provides a way to define or redefine the type associated with a name.

Example:

```
WORD_ARR      LABEL   WORD
BYTE_ARR      DB  100 DUP (0)
```

Here WORD_ARR defines a 50-word array, and BYTE_ARR defines a 100-byte array. The same address is assigned to both variables.

.LALL

Causes the assembler to list all statements in a macro expansion, except those preceded by a double semicolon.

.LIST and .XLIST

.LIST causes the assembler to include the statements following the .LIST directive in the source program listing. .XLIST causes the listing of the statements following the .XLIST directive to be suppressed.

LOCAL

Syntax: `LOCAL name [,name]`

Used inside a macro. Each time the assembler encounters a LOCAL name during macro expansion, it replaces it by a unique name of form ??number. In this way duplicate names are avoided if the macro is called several times in a program. See Chapter 13.

MACRO and ENDM

Syntax: `name MACRO {parameter [,parameter]}`

These directives are used to define a macro.

Example:

```
EXCHANGE      MACRO          WORD1,WORD2
              PUSH  WORD1
              PUSH  WORD2
              POP   WORD1
              POP   WORD2
              ENDM
```

See Chapter 13.

.MODEL

Syntax: `.MODEL memory_model`

A simplified segment directive for defining a memory model. Memory model can be any of the following:

Model	Description
TINY	code and data in one segment
SMALL	code in one segment data in one segment
MEDIUM	code in more than one segment data in one segment
COMPACT	code in one segment data in more than one segment
LARGE	code in more than one segment data in more than one segment no array larger than 64 KB
HUGE	code in more than one segment data in more than one segment arrays may be larger than 64 KB

ORG

Syntax: `ORG expression`

where expression must resolve to a 2-byte number.
Sets the location counter to the value of expression. For example, in a .COM program, the directive ORG 100h sets the location counter to 100h, so that variables will be assigned addresses relative to the start of the program, rather than in the 100h-byte program segment prefix, which precedes the program in memory. Another use of ORG is to define a data area that can be shared by several variables. For example,

```
.DATA
WORD1_ARR   DW    100 DUP (?)
ORG  0
WORD2_ARR   DW    50 DUP (?)
WORD3_ARR   DW    50 DUP (?)
```

This definition causes WORD2_ARR and the first 50 words in WORD1_ARR to occupy the same memory space. Similarly, WORD3_ARR and the last 50 words of WORD1_ARR occupy the same space.

%OUT

Syntax: `%OUT text`

where text is a line of ASCII characters.
Used to display a message at a specified place in an assembly listing. Often used during conditional assembly.

Example:

```
IFNDEF       SUM
             SUM  DW          ?
             %OUT   SUM is defined here
ENDIF
```

If SUM had not been previously defined, it would be defined here and the message would be displayed.

PAGE

Syntax: `PAGE {{length},width}`

where length is 10-255 and width is 60-132. Default values are length = 50 and width = 80.

Used to create a page break or to specify the maximum number of lines per page and the maximum number of characters per line in a program listing.

Examples:

```
PAGE                            ;creates a page break
PAGE 50,70                      ;sets maximum page length to 50
                                ;and maximum page width to 70
PAGE ,132                       ;sets maximum page width to 132
```

PROC and ENDP

Syntax: `name PROC distance`
              `name ENDP`

where distance is NEAR or FAR. Default is NEAR.
Used to begin and end a procedure definition. See Chapter 8.

Processor and Coprocessor Directives

The following directives define the instruction set recognized by MASM. These directives must be placed outside segment declarations. In the following, 8086 includes 8088. 8087, 80287, and 80387 are coprocessors.

Directive	Enables assembly of instructions for processors and coprocessors
.8086	8086, 8087
.186	8086, 8087, and 80186 additional instructions
.286	8086, 80287, and additional 80286 nonprivileged instructions
.286P	same as .286 plus 80286 privileged instructions
.386	8086, 80387 and 80286 and 80386 nonprivileged instructions
.386P	same as .386 plus 80386 privileged instructions
.8087	8087; disables instructions unique to the 80287 and 80387
.287	8087, and 80287 additional instructions
.387	8087, 80287, and 80387 additional instructions

PUBLIC

Syntax: `PUBLIC name [,name]`

where name is a variable, label, or numeric equate defined in the module containing the directive.

Used to make names in this module available for use in other modules. Not to be confused with the PUBLIC combine-type, which is used to combine segments. See Chapter 14.

PURGE

Syntax: `PURGE macroname [,macroname]`

where macroname is the name of a macro.

Used to delete macros from memory during assembly. This might be necessary if the system does not have enough memory to keep all the macros a program needs in memory at the same time.

Example:

```
MAC1                         ;expand macro MAC1
PURGE MAC1                   ;don't need it anymore
```

.RADIX

Syntax: `.RADIX base`

where base is a decimal number in the range 2–16.
Specifies the default radix for representation of integer constants. This means that in the absence of a "b", "d", or "h" as the last character in the representation of an integer, the assembler will assume the number is represented in the base specified by the directive. The default is 10 (decimal).

Examples:

```
.DATA
.RADIX  16                   ;hexadecimal
A   DW  1101                 ;interpreted as 1101h
.RADIX  2
B   DW  1101                 ;interpreted as 1101b
```

RECORD

Used to define a record variable. This is a byte or word variable in which specific bit fields can be accessed symbolically. See the Microsoft Macro Assembler Programmer's Guide.

REPT and ENDM

Syntax:
```
REPT expression
    statements
ENDM
```

where expression must evaluate to a 16-bit unsigned number.
Defines a repeat block. REPT causes the statements in the block to be assembled the number of times equal to the value of expression. A repeat block can be placed at the position where the statements are to be repeated, or it can be put inside a macro. See Chapter 13.

.SALL

Causes the assembler to suppress the listing of macro expansions.

SEGMENT and ENDS

Syntax:
```
name SEGMENT {align} {combine} {'class'}
     statements
name ENDS
```

where   align is PARA, BYTE, WORD, or PAGE
          combine is PUBLIC, COMMON, STACK, or AT
          class is a name enclosed in single quotes

These directive define a program segment. Align, combine, and class specify how the segment will be aligned in memory, combined with other segments, and ordered with respect to other segments. See Chapter 14.

.SEQ

Directs the assembler to leave the segments in their original order. Has the same effect as .ALPHA.

.STACK

Syntax: `.STACK {size}`

where size is a positive integer.
A simplified segment directive which defines a stack segment of size bytes. Default size is 1 kilobyte.

STRUC and ENDS

Used to declare a structure. This is a collection of data objects that can be accessed symbolically as a single data object. See the *Microsoft Macro Assembler Programmer's Guide*.

SUBTTL

Syntax: `SUBTTL {text}`

Causes a subtitle of up to 60 characters to be placed on the third line of each page in an assembly listing. May be used more than once.

TITLE

Syntax: `TITLE {text}`

Causes a title to be placed on each page of an assembly listing. May be used only once.

.XALL

Causes the assembler to list all statements in a macro expansion that produce code. Comments are suppressed.

.XCREF

See .CREF.

.XLIST

See .LIST.

Appendix H

Keyboard Scan Codes

The keyboard communicates with the processor by scan codes assigned to the keys. When a key is pressed, the keyboard sends a make code to the computer, and when a key is released a break code is sent. Table H.1 shows the make codes of the original 83-key IBM keyboard; a break code can be obtained from the make codes by ORing it with 80h.

The INT 9 routine is responsible for getting the scan codes from the I/O port and placing an ASCII code and the scan code in the keyboard buffer. We can classify the keys into ASCII keys, function keys, and shift keys. The ASCII keys include the character keys, the space bar, and the control keys Esc, Enter, Backspace, and Tab; these keys have corresponding ASCII codes. The function keys include F1 to F10, the arrow keys, Pg Up, Pg Dn, Home, End, Ins, and Del. These keys do not have ASCII codes, and a 0 is used to indicate a function key in the keyboard buffer. The shift keys include left and right shifts, Caps Lock, Ctrl, Alt, Num Lock, and Scroll Lock. The scan codes of the shift keys are not placed in the keyboard buffer. Instead, the INT 9 routine uses the keyboard flags byte (address 0000:0417) to keep track of the shift keys. The keyboard flags can be retrieved by using INT 16h, function 2.

When certain shift keys are down, the INT 9 routine places different scan codes in the keyboard buffer to indicate key combinations. Table H.2 shows the scan codes for key combinations.

The 101-key enhanced keyboard uses a different set of make and break codes. However, except for the new keys F11 and F12, the INT 9 routine still generates the 83-key scan codes for the keyboard buffer to maintain compatibility. Table H.3 shows the new scan codes generated by the INT 9 routine for the enhanced keyboard. There are also some new combination scan codes. These new scan codes can only be retrieved by INT 16h functions 10h and 11h.

When the Ctrl key is down, INT 9 will generate different ASCII codes for letter keys. Table H.4 shows the scan code and ASCII for the key combinations.

Table H.1 83-Key Keyboard Scan Codes

Hex Scan Code	Key	Hex Scan Code	Key	Hex Scan Code	Key
01	Esc	1D	Ctrl	39	Space bar
02	1	1E	A	3A	Caps Lock
03	2	1F	S	3B	F1
04	3	20	D	3C	F2
05	4	21	F	3D	F3
06	5	22	G	3E	F4
07	6	23	H	3F	F5
08	7	24	J	40	F6
09	8	25	K	41	F7
0A	9	26	L	42	F8
0B	0	27	; :	43	F9
0C	- _	28	' "	44	F10
0D	= +	29	` ~	45	Num Lock
0E	Back Space	2A	Left Shift	46	Scroll Lock
0F	Tab	2B	\ |	47	7 Home
10	Q	2C	Z	48	8 Up Arrow
11	W	2D	X	49	9 Pg Up
12	E	2E	C	4A	- (num)
13	R	2F	V	4B	4 Left Arrow
14	T	30	B	4C	5 (num)
15	Y	31	N	4D	6 Right Arrow
16	U	32	M	4E	+ (num)
17	I	33	, <	4F	1 End
18	O	34	. >	50	2 Down Arrow
19	P	35	/ ?	51	3 Pg Dn
1A	[{	36	Right Shift	52	0 Ins
1B	] }	37	Prt Sc	53	Del .
1C	Enter	38	Alt		

Table H.2 Scan Codes for Combination Keys

Scan Code	Keys	Scan Code	Keys	Scan Code	Keys
54	Shift F1	65	Ctrl F8	75	Ctrl End
55	Shift F2	66	Ctrl F9	76	Ctrl PgDn
56	Shift F3	67	Alt F10	77	Ctrl Home
57	Shift F4	68	Alt F1	78	Alt 1
58	Shift F5	69	Alt F2	79	Alt 2
59	Shift F6	6A	Alt F3	7A	Alt 3
5A	Shift F7	6B	Alt F4	7B	Alt 4
5B	Shift F8	6C	Alt F5	7C	Alt 5
5C	Shift F9	6D	Alt F6	7D	Alt 6
5D	Shift F10	6E	Alt F7	7E	Alt 7
5E	Ctrl F1	6F	Alt F8	7F	Alt 8
5F	Ctrl F2	70	Alt F9	80	Alt 9
60	Ctrl F3	71	Alt F10	81	Alt 0
61	Ctrl F4	72	Ctrl PrtSc	82	Alt -
62	Ctrl F5	73	Ctrl Left Arrow	83	Alt =
63	Ctrl F6	74	Ctrl Right Arrow	84	Ctrl PgUp
64	Ctrl F7				

Table H.3 Scan Codes for Enhanced Keyboard

Scan Code	Keys	Scan Code	Keys	Scan Code	Keys
85	F11	90	Ctrl + (num)	9B	Alt Left Arrow
86	F12	91	Ctrl Dn Arrow	9D	Alt Right Arrow
87	Shift F11	92	Ctrl Ins	9F	Alt End
88	Shift F12	93	Ctrl Del	A0	Alt Down Arrow
89	Ctrl F11	94	Ctrl Tab	A1	Alt PgDn
8A	Ctrl F12	95	Ctrl / (num)	A2	Alt Ins
8B	Alt F11	96	Ctrl * (num)	A3	Alt Del
8C	Alt F12	97	Alt Home	A4	Alt / (num)
8D	Ctrl Up Arrow	98	Alt Up Arrow	A5	Alt Tab
8E	Ctrl - (num)	99	Alt PgUp	A6	Alt Enter (num)
8F	Ctrl 5 (num)				

(num) means numeric keypad keys.

Table H.4 ASCII Codes for Combination Keys

Keys	ASCII Code	Scan Code	Keys	ASCII Code	Scan Code
Ctrl A	1	1E	Ctrl N	E	31
Ctrl B	2	30	Ctrl O	F	18
Ctrl C	3	2E	Ctrl P	10	19
Ctrl D	4	20	Ctrl Q	11	10
Ctrl E	5	12	Ctrl R	12	13
Ctrl F	6	21	Ctrl S	13	1F
Ctrl G	7	22	Ctrl T	14	14
Ctrl H	8	23	Ctrl U	15	16
Ctrl I	9	17	Ctrl V	16	2F
Ctrl J	A	24	Ctrl W	17	11
Ctrl K	B	25	Ctrl X	18	2D
Ctrl L	C	26	Ctrl Y	19	15
Ctrl M	D	32	Ctrl Z	1A	2C

Index

$ (end of string), 73
%OUT assembler directive
* (asterisk), as DOS special character, 445
; (semicolon), in assembly language program, 14, 55
= (equal) pseudo-op, in REPT macro, 268
? (question mark), as DOS special character, 445

A

AAA instruction (ASCII adjust for addition), 376–377, 491
AAD instruction (ASCII adjust for division), 378–379, 491
AAM instruction (ASCII adjust for multiply), 378, 491–492
AAS instruction (ASCII adjust for subtraction), 377–378, 492
Absolute disk read/write, DOS interrupts for, 460
Accumulator register (AX), 40–41
Activation records, 361–363
Active display page, 235
   selecting, 240, 450
ADC instruction (add with carry), 372, 492
ADD instruction, 62–63, 492
   flags and, 85, 88–89
   overflow, 83–84, 85–86
Add-in boards or cards, 4
Addition
   BCD, 376–377, 494–495
   with carry flag, 372, 492
   with decimal adjust, 494–495
   double-precision, 372–373

   with 8087 processor, 384
   instructions, 62–63, 376–377, 491, 492, 494–495
   number systems and, 24–25
   overflow and, 83–85
Address, 4–5
   base address of an array, 180
   in call by reference, 302–303
   contents vs., 5–6
   display modes, CGA, 337
   in instruction pointer (IP), 9
   loading (LEA instruction), 74, 498–499
   logical, 42
   of memory word, 6
   physical, 41
Address bus, 7
   in fetch-execute cycle, 10
Address register, 39
   base register (BX) as, 41
Addressing modes, 181–189
   See also Real address mode
   arrays and, 179
   based, 184–186
   based indexed, 194–196
   indexed, 185–186
   register indirect, 182–183
   string instructions vs., 205
AF (auxiliary carry flag), 82, 83
Align type of segment declaration, 292–293
All points addressable (APA) graphics mode, 332
.ALPHA directive, 517
ALU (arithmetic and logic unit), 8
American Standard Code for Information Exchange. *See* ASCII character codes
Analog monitor, for VGA, 340

AND conditions, high-level vs. assembly languages, 103
AND instructions, 119–121, 492–493
   TEST instruction and, 122
AND truth table, 118
Animation, 340, 341–347
APA (all points addressable) graphics mode, 332
Appending records to file, 410–414
Application program interface (API), in OS/2, 431, 433
Application programs, memory segments for, 47
Archive bit, 400
Arithmetic and logic unit (ALU), 8
Arithmetic operations
   See also specific operations
   accumulator register (AX) for, 40–41
   advanced, 371–394
      binary-coded decimal numbers, 374–379
      double-precision numbers, 371–374
      8087 instructions, 384
      floating-point numbers, 379–381
      multiple-precision number I/O, 384–388
      with real numbers, 389–391
   in arithmetic and logic unit (ALU), 8
   overflow and, 83–85
   pointer and index registers for, 44
   shift instructions for, 117, 122–127, 504–505
Array elements
   See also Arrays
   adding, 183
   reversing order of, 183–184
   specifying addresses for, 181
Arrays, 58–59

531

See also Array elements
addressing modes for, 181–189
application example, averaging test scores, 195–197
one-dimensional, 179–181
processing, string instructions for, 205–228
role of, 179
sorting, *selectsort* method, 189–192
two-dimensional, 179, 192–194
    based indexed addressing mode for, 194–195
    locating elements in, 193–194
    storage order for, 192–193
Arrow keys, programming, 247–252
ASCII adjust instructions
for addition (AAA), 376–377, 491
for division (AAD), 378–379, 491
for multiply (AAM), 378, 491–492
for subtraction (AAS), 377–378, 492
ASCII character codes, 30–31, 441–444
in arrays, 58–59
for combination keys, 530
converting case of, 120–121
converting to numbers, AND instructions for, 120
display characters and, 234
extended character set, 443–444
in INT 21h instructions, 68
jump instructions and, 97
translating to EBCDIC code, 197–200
ASCII digits, converting to packed BCD, 385–386
ASCII keys, 244
.ASM files, assembly modules, 285
Assembler
See also Microsoft Macro Assembler
assembly language syntax for, 54
creating object file with, 70, 71–72
object modules produced by, 285
role of, 13
Assembler directives, 54, 517–526
See also specific directives
arrays, 58–59
byte variables, 56
operand fields in, 55
pseudo-ops, 55
word variables, 56–57
Assembly language
See also Assembly language programs
advantages of, 13–14
described, 12–13
high-level language translation to, 64–65
sample, stack use, 144–145
Assembly language programs, 53–80
appending records to a file, 410–414
averaging test scores, 195–197
ball bounce, 344–347
ball display, 342–344
basic instructions, 60–64

case conversion, 120–121, 287–289
coding and decoding secret message, 198–200
combined 8087/8086 instructions, 387–388
converting ASCII digits to packed BCD, 385–386
counting vowels and consonants, 215–217
creating and running, 70–73
designing, top-down method, 108–112
echo, 432–433
extended memory management, 427–429
"Hello" messages, 431–432
    .EXE vs. .COM format, 283–284
INT 10h example, 243–244
jump instruction example, 93–94
macro expansions in .LST file, 259–261
macro library use in, 266–267
named constants, 59
OS/2, 431–433
printing packed BCD integers, 386–387
printing real numbers, 390–391
procedures in, 146–147
program data, 56–57
reading and displaying a file, 406–409
reading real numbers, 389–390
reading and storing a character string, 209–211
recursive procedures in, 363–369
sample, 14–15, 69–70, 75–76
    with high-level structures, 108–112
    multiplication procedure, 150–157
stacks in, 139–145
structure of, 65–67
substring search, 220–222
syntax, 54–56
terminating, 70
for time display, 316–318
top-down design of, 108–112
variables, 57–59
Assembly modules, 285
linking, 287–291
Assembly time, macros vs. procedures and, 276
ASSUME pseudo-op, 295, 517
Asterisk (*), as DOS special character, 445
Attribute byte (display character), 235–237
Attribute byte (file attribute), 400, 401
Attributes of characters, 234
current, for character at cursor, 242
Auxiliary carry flag (AF), 82, 83
Averaging test scores, 195–197
AX (accumulator register), 40–41

B

Background color, 334, 451
BACKUP (DOS program), 445
archive bit and, 400
Ball display, 342–344
Ball manipulation
for animation, 344–347
in interactive video game, 347, 349–350
Base, in number systems, 20
Base address of an array, 180
Base pointer (BP) register, 45
Base register (BX), 41
Based addressing mode, 184–185
segment overrides in, 189
Based indexed addressing mode, 194–196
Basic Input/Output System routines. *See* BIOS routines
BASIC interrupt (Interrupt 18h), 315
BCD. *See* Binary-coded decimal number system
BEEP procedure, 348–349
Bias, 380
Binary digits (bits), 3
Binary fractions, converting decimal fractions to, 379–380
Binary number system, 19, 20
addition and subtraction in, 25
ASCII codes in, 31–32
decimal and hex conversions, 22–23
decimal and hex equivalents, 20, 21
in program data, 56
two's complements, 26–28
Binary-coded decimal number system (BCD), 374–379
addition (AAA instruction), 376–377
division (AAD instruction), 378–379
8087 numeric processor and, 381–382, 384–388
multiplication (AAM instruction), 378
packed vs. unpacked BCD form, 375
subtraction (AAS instruction), 377–378
BIOS (Basic Input/Output System) routines, 46–47
interrupt routines, 67–69, 310–316, 449–455
    ASCII code display and, 246
    keyboard functions, 246–247
    text mode display functions, 238–244
in start-up operation, 49
Bit patterns
masks, 119
modifying
    applications for, 130–134

logic instructions for, 117, 118–122, 492–493, 501, 508
rotate instructions for, 117, 122, 127–130, 502–503, 504
shift instructions for. See Shift instructions
Bit planes
  in EGA display memory, 339
  in VGA display memory, 340
Bit positions, 6
Bit scan instructions (80386), 513
Bit strings, 3
  machine language, 7, 12
Bit test instructions, 513–514
Bits (binary digits), 3
  See also Bit patterns; Bit strings
  flags, 45
  least significant (lsb), 26
  manipulating, high-level vs. assembly language and, 117
  mask, 119
  most significant (msb), 26
BIU. *See* Bus interface unit
Blinking bit, 235, 236
Boot program, 49
Bootstrap interrupt (Interrupt 19h), 315
Border, setting color for, 451
Bouncing ball program, 342–347
  interactive video game from, 347–355
BOUND instruction, in 80286, 423
BP (base pointer) register, 45
Branching structures, high-level vs. assembly languages, 98–104
BREAK, checking status of, 457
Break code, 245
Breakpoint interrupt (Interrupt 3), 313
Buffer, keyboard, 246
Bus interface unit (BIU), 8, 9
  connection to EU, 9
  in fetch-execute cycle, 10
Buses, 7
  locking, 499
BX (base register), 41
Byte arrays. *See* Character strings; Memory strings
Byte variables, 57
Bytes, 4
  bit positions in, 6
  changing bit patterns in, 117
  converting to words, 167, 493
  disk capacity, 398–399
  dividing, 165, 167
  hex digits and, 20
  integer storage in, 26–28
  multiplying, 162

C

CALL instructions, 146, 147–149, 493
  activation records of, 361–363
  direct vs. indirect, 147
  NEAR vs. FAR procedures and, 286
  in OS/2, 431
  in program example, 151, 152, 153, 154
  in recursive procedures, 357–369
  using stack with, 303–305, 360–361
Call by reference, 302–303
Call by value, 302
Carriage return-line feed, macro for, 265
Carry flag (CF), 82
  clearing, (CLC instruction), 493
  complementing (CMC instruction), 494
  setting (STC instruction), 506
Case, for assembly language code, 54
Case conversion program, 75–76
CASE structure, high-level vs. assembly languages, 101–103
Cassette interrupt (Interrupt 15h), 314, 454
CBW instruction (convert byte to word), 167, 493
Central processing unit (CPU), 4, 7–9
  bus interface unit (BIU), 8, 9
  execution unit (EU), 8
  jump instructions and, 95, 97
CF (carry flag), 82
CGA. *See* Color graphics adapter
Character cell, 233
Character representation, 30–33
Character strings
  in arrays, 58–59
  counting vowels and consonants in, 215–217
  displaying, 73–75
  DISP_STR *procedure for,* 212–214
  macro for, 265–266
  reading and storing, 209–211
Characters
  attribute bytes and, 235–237
  attributes of, 234
  at cursor
    displaying and advancing cursor, 243
    displaying with any attribute, 242
    displaying with current attribute, 242
  in program data, 56
  reading, 241
  reading from keyboard, 455
  writing to printer, 455
CHDIR (CD), 447–448, 458
CLC instruction (clear carry flag), 493
CLD instruction (clear direction flag), 206, 493
Clear (destination bit), AND instruction for, 119, 121
Clear Screen (CLS), 445
Clearing flags, instructions for, 493
CLI (clear interrupt flag), 493
Clock circuit
  Interrupt 1Ah and, 315
  tone generation and, 347
Clock period, 11
Clock pulses, 10–11
Clock rate (clock speed), 11
Closing a file, 404–405, 459
CLS (clear screen), 445
Clusters, 400
CMC instruction (complement carry flag), 494
CMP instruction (compare), 494
  jump conditions and, 95, 97
  OR instruction vs., 121
CMPS instruction, 223, 494
CMPSB instruction (compare string byte), 217–222, 223, 494
CMPSW instruction (compare string word), 217, 494
.CODE assembler directive, 66, 299, 517
  in sample program, 76
Code segment, 15, 44
  .COM programs and, 281
  declaration syntax, 65
CODEVIEW program, 479–488
  DEBUG commands in, 488
Coding and decoding a secret message, 198–200
Color display, 235, 236
  BIOS interrupt routines, 451, 452–453
Color graphics, 331–356
  display modes, 331–332
    CGA, 332, 333–339
    EGA, 332, 339–340
    selecting, 332–333
    VGA, 332, 340–341
Color graphics adapter (CGA), 232, 233
  changing cursor size for, 238
  graphics display modes, 332, 333–339
  number of display pages for, 234
  pixel size and, 332
  port address, 48
  selecting active display page for, 240
  selecting display mode for, 238
  writing directly to memory in, 337–338
Color graphics adapter types, 331. *See also specific types*
Color monitor, 232. *See also* Color display
Color registers
  getting, 453
  setting (VGA), 340, 341, 452–453
Column-major order, array storage in, 192, 193
COM 1/COM 2. *See* Serial ports
.COM programs, 281–285
  .EXE programs vs., 281, 282–285
Combine type of segment declaration, 293–294
.COMM assembler directive, 517–518
COMMAND.COM, 46
Command line
  CODEVIEW, 479

LINK program, 467–448
Microsoft Macro Assembler (MAIM), 462–463
Commands
   DEBUG, 473–474
   DOS, 445–448
   internal vs. external, 46
Comments
   in assembly language programs, 14, 518
   comment field syntax, 54, 55–56
   for documenting procedures, 147
   using, 55–56
Communications interrupt (Interrupt 14h), 314
COMPACT memory model, 299
Compare instruction. *See* CMP instruction
Comparing memory strings, 217–222
Compiler, role of, 13
Complement (destination bit), XOR instruction for, 119, 120
Complement carry flag (CMC instruction), 494
Composite monitor, 232
Computers. *See* IBM personal computers
Conditional jump instructions, 94–97, 497–498
   high-level vs. assembly language structures, 98–104
Conditional loop instructions
   REPEAT loop, 107–108
   WHILE loop, 106–107
   WHILE vs. REPEAT, 108
Conditional macros, 272–275
Conditional pseudo-ops, 272–273
   for macro library, 264–265
Consonants, counting, 215–217
.CONST pseudo-op, 299, 300, 518
Constants, named, 59
Contents, address vs., 5–6
Control bus, 7
   in fetch-execute cycle, 10
Control characters, 31, 32
   in INT 21h instructions, 68–69
Control flags, 45, 81, 82, 205
   DEBUG example, 88, 89
   direction flag (DF), 205–206
   in interrupt routine, 312
Control keys, 244
Conventional memory, Interrupt 12h and, 313–314, 453
COPY (DOS command), 445
Count register (CX), 41
CPU. *See* Central processing unit
CREF utility program, 461, 466–467
Cross-reference (.CRF) file, 72, 461, 466–467, 518
CS (instruction register), 45
Ctrl-Break (Interrupt 1Bh), 315
CTRL-BREAK check (Interrupt 21h), 457
CTRL-Z (end of data), 410

Cursor
   advancing to next position, 243
   changing size of, 238–239, 449
   displaying character with attribute at, 241, 242, 451
   getting position and size of, 239–240, 450
   moving on screen, 239, 450
   programming arrow keys for, 247–252
   reading character at, 241
   restoring position of, 320
   writing character and attribute at, 451
CWD instruction (convert word to doubleword), 166–167, 494
CX (count register), 41
Cylinder, 397–398

D

DAA instruction, 494–495
Daisy wheel printers, 12
DAS instruction, 494
Data calls, by value and reference, 302–303. *See also* CALL instructions
Data bus, 7
   in fetch-execute cycle, 10
   microprocessors and, 38, 39
.DATA directive, 66, 299, 518–519
   assembler and, 74–75
   in sample program, 76
.DATA? pseudo-op, 299, 300, 518–519
Data register (DX), in 8086, 39, 40–41
Data registers, in 8087, 382
Data segment, 15, 44
   .COM programs and, 281
   .DATA directive for, 66
   declaration syntax, 66
Data segment register, loading, 498
Data storage, in registers, 8
Data transfer area (DTA), 401
Data transfer instructions
   accumulator register (AX), 40–41
   MOV instruction, 60, 61
Data types, 8087 numeric processor, 381–382, 508
Data-defining pseudo-ops, variables and, 57–59
DATE (DOS command), 446
Date, INT 21h functions and, 456–457
DEBUG program, 87–90, 471–478
   CODEVIEW and, 488
   commands, 473–474
   exiting, 90
   flags shown in, 87–90, 472
   interrupt routine and, 312
   memory dumps, 477
Debuggers. *See* CODEVIEW program; DEBUG program
Debugging, source listing (.LST) file for, 72
DEC instruction (decrement), 62, 495

jump instruction and, 97
overflow and, 85
Decimal adjust for addition/subtraction, 494–495
Decimal fractions, converting to binary, 379–380
Decimal input, INDEC procedure for, 170–175
Decimal number system, 19–20
   addition and subtraction in, 24, 25
   ASCII codes in, 31–32
   binary and hex conversions, 22–23
   binary and hexadecimal equivalents, 21
   binary-coded, 374–379
      8087 numeric processor and, 381–382, 384–388
   in program data, 56
   signed and unsigned integer representation, 28–30
Decimal output, OUTDEC procedure for, 167–170
Decision making, flags and, 81
Decoder circuit, in fetch-execute cycle, 10
Decoding program, 198–200
Decrement instruction. *See* DEC instruction
DEL (DOS command), 446
Deleting a file, DOS interrupt for, 459
Destination index (DI) register), 45
Destination operand, 55
Devices
   I/O, 3, 11–12
   peripheral, 3
   serial vs. parallel port, 9
DF. *See* Direction flag
DI (destination index) register, 45
Digital circuits, 3
DIR (directory list), 446
Direct mode, 181, 182
Direct procedure call, 147
Direction flag (DF), 205–206
   clearing and setting, 206, 493, 506
Directives. *See* Pseudo-operation code; *specific directives*
Directory, getting, 459–460
Directory structure, 399–402, 447–448
Disjoint memory segments, 47
Disk controller circuit, access controlled by, 399
Disk drives, 11, 398
Disk I/O interrupt (Interrupt 13h), 314, 453–454
Disk operating system. *See* DOS
Disk operations, 395
   DOS interrupts and, 415–418
Disk space, checking, 458
Diskette error (Interrupt E), 313
Disks
   See also Floppy disks; Hard disks
   accessing information on, 399
   capacity of, 398–399
   clusters on, 400

FAT location on, 401
file allocation on, 399–402
structure of, 397–398
types of, 395–397
DISP_STR procedure, 212–214
Displacement, 184
Display
    INT 10h functions and, 238–244,
        449–455
    INT 21h functions and, 456
    screen positions, 234
    scrolling screen or window
        up/down, 240–241, 450–451
Display memory (video buffer), 232
Display modes, 232–233
    getting, 243, 452
    selecting, 238, 449
Display monitor. See Monitor
Display pages, 234
    active, 235
    selecting, 240, 450
    attribute bytes in, 235–237
    sample program, 237–238
Displaying a file, program for, 406–409
DIV instruction (divide), 165–167, 495
Divide overflow, 165–166
    BIOS interrupt routine (Interrupt 0),
        312
    processor exception for, 310
Division
    ASCII adjust for (AAD) instruction,
        378–379, 491
    BCD, 378–379
    data register (DX) for, 41
    DIV/IDIV instructions for, 161, 165–
        167, 495, 496
    double-precision, 374
    with 8087 processor, 384
    methods for, 127
    shift instructions for, 117, 122,
        125–127
Do_FUNCTION procedure, for pro-
        gramming arrow keys, 247–252
Dollar sign ($), for string display, 73
DOS (disk operating system), 46
    commands, listed, 445–448
    directory structure, 400–402,
        447–448
    disk structure and, 397, 398
    file processing, 402–415
    INT (interrupt) instructions for. See
        DOS interrupts
    programs for 80286, 424
    returning to, 265, 316
    versions, 46, 457
DOS interrupts, 67–69, 316, 456–460
    See also specific interrupts
    file handle functions, 402–415
    for reading and writing sectors,
        415–418
DOS prompt (C), COMMAND.COM
        and, 46
DOSSEG directive, 519
Dot matrix printers, 12

Double-density drives and disks, 398
Double-precision numbers, 371–374
    adding, subtracting, or negating,
        372–373
    multiplying and dividing, 374
    shift instructions, 515–516
Doublewords, converting words to,
        166–167, 494
DTA (data transfer area), 401
DUP pseudo-op (duplicate), 180–181
DX (data register), 41
Dynamic linking, in OS/2, 431

E

EBCDIC code, translating ASCII code
        to, 197–200
ECD (enhanced color display) monitor,
        339
EGA. See Enhanced graphics adapter
8086 microprocessor
    clock rate of, 11
    coordination with 8087 processor,
        382–383, 387–388
    fetch-execute cycle in, 10
    flags and, 81
    hardware interrupts, 309–310
    IBM PC family and, 37, 38
    instruction format, 489–490
    instructions, listed, 490–508
    organization of, 7, 8–9, 39–45
    virtual 8086 mode, 434
8088 microprocessor, 38
80186 microprocessor, 38
80188 microprocessor, 38
80286 microprocessor, 38, 421–429
    instructions, 511–513
    OS/2 and, 430
    Windows 3 and, 430
80386/80386SX microprocessors, 38–
        39, 433–436
    instructions, 513–516
    OS/2 and, 430
    programming, 434–436
    Windows 3 and, 430
80486/80486SX microprocessors, 39,
        433
    Windows 3 and, 430
80387 numeric processor, 39
8087 numeric processor, 381–391
    coordination with 8086 micropro-
        cessor, 382–383, 387–388
    data types, 381–382, 508
    instructions for, 382–384, 508–511
    registers, 382
.8087 pseudo-op, 387
8259 chip (interrupt controller), 313
ELSE pseudo-op, in macros, 272, 273,
        274, 275, 519
Empty stack, 140
Encoding and decoding a message,
        198–200
END directive, 67, 519

in sample program, 76
ENDIF pseudo-op, macro file and, 265,
        520
ENDM pseudo-op (end macro defini-
        tion), 257, 258, 520, 522, 525
ENDP pseudo-op (end procedure), 519,
        524
ENDS directive (declare structure), 526
ENDS pseudo-op (end segment or struc-
        ture), 519, 525
Enhanced color display (ECD) moni-
        tor, 339
Enhanced graphics adapter (EGA), 232,
        233,
        339–340
    changing cursor size for, 238
    graphics display modes, 332, 339–
        340
    number of display pages for, 234
    port address, 48
    selecting active display page for, 240
Enhanced keyboard, scan codes for,
        529
ENTER instruction, in 80286, 423
EQU (equates) pseudo-op, 59, 75, 520
Equal (=) pseudo-op, in REPT macro,
        268
Equipment check interrupt (Interrupt
        11h), 313, 314, 453
ERASE (DOS command), 446
.ERR directives, 520–521
    for incorrect macro, 275
Errors, in macro expansion, 262
ESC instruction (escape), 495
EU. See Execution unit
EVEN directive, 521
Exchange instruction. See XCHG in-
        struction
EXE2BIN (DOS utility), .EXE programs
        vs. .COM programs and, 284–285
.EXE program
    .COM program vs., 281, 282–285
    creating, 73
    from library file, 289–291
    from object modules, 287–289
    with full segment definitions,
        295–298
Execution of instructions, 9–11
Execution time, macros vs. procedures
        and, 276
Execution unit (EU), 8
    connection to BIU, 9
EXIT (terminate process), Interrupt
        21h for, 460
Exiting DEBUG program, 90
EXITM assembler directive, 521
Expanding a macro, 258
Expansion slots, 4
Exponent, 380
Extended Binary Coded Decimal Inter-
        change Code. See EBCDIC code
Extended character set, 31, 443–444
Extended instruction set
    in 80286, 421, 422–423

536 Index

microprocessors and, 38
Extended memory, 426–429
    BIOS interrupts, 454
Extended-memory manager programs, 426
Extension instructions, 514
External commands, 46
EXTRN pseudo-op, 286, 521

F

FADD instruction (add real), 384, 508
FAR procedures, 146, 285–286
.FARDATA/FARDATA? directives, 521
FAT. *See* File allocation table
FBLD instruction (packed BCD load), 383, 509
FBSTP instruction (packed BCD store and pop), 383, 509
FDIV instruction (divide real), 384, 509
Fetch-execute cycle, 9–10
    machine language for, 12
    timing of, 10–11
FIADD instruction (integer add), 384, 509
FIDIV instruction (integer divide), 384, 509
Fields, in assembly language syntax, 54–56
FILD instruction (integer load), 383, 509
File allocation table (FAT), 401–402
    displaying, 417–418
File attribute, 400, 401, 403
    changing, 414–415
    specifying, 403
File errors, 403
File extension, 46
    .ASM (assembly language source file), 70
File handles, 402–403
    closing, 459
File name, 46
    special characters with, 445
File pointer, 410
    appending records to file with, 410–414
    moving, 459
File size, cluster size and, 400
Files, 46
    allocation of on disk, 399–402
    appending records to, 410–414
    changing attributes of, 414–415
    creating, 457
    directory structure, 400
    opening and closing, 403–405, 458–459
    processing of, file handle functions, 402–415. *See also specific functions*
    program module, 285–291
    reading, 402, 405
    reading and displaying, 406–409
    rewriting, 402, 403–404
    writing, 402, 406
FIMUL instruction (integer multiply), 384, 509
Firmware, 7
FIST instruction (integer store), 383, 509
FISTP instruction (integer store and pop), 383, 510
FISUB instruction (integer subtract), 384, 510
Fixed disk. *See* Hard disk
Flags, 81
    clearing, instructions for, 493
    instructions and, 85–87
        AND, OR, XOR, 119, 492–493, 501, 508
        CMP example, 95, 97
        DEBUG, 87–90, 472
        jumps, 95
        rotates, 129
        shifts, 123, 125
    in interrupt routine, 312
    loading AH from (LAHF instruction), 498
    overflow and, 83–85
FLAGS register, 39, 40, 45, 81–83
    in interrupt routine, 310, 312
    jump instructions and, 95
    storing AH in (SAHF instruction), 504
FLD instruction (load real), 383, 510
Floating-point numbers, 379–381
    8087 processor and, 381–391
    80486 processor and, 39, 433
    representation of, 380
Floppy disks, 11, 395–396, 397
    See also Disks
    capacity of, 398, 399
    file allocation on, 399–402
Flow control instructions, 93–116
    jump instructions, 93–98
FMUL instruction (multiply real), 384, 510
FOR loop, high-level vs. assembly language, 104–106
"Forced error" message, for incorrect macro, 275
FORMAT (DOS command), 446
    status byte and, 400
Fractions. *See* Real numbers
FST instruction (store real), 383, 510
FSTP instruction (store real and pop), 383, 510
FSUB instruction (subtract real), 384, 510–511
Function key commands, CODEVIEW, 481–482
Function keys, 245
    programming, for screen editor, 247–252
    scan codes for, 245
Function requests. *See specific interrupts*
FWAIT instruction (suspend 8086 processor), 387

G

Game, interactive video, 347–355
Game controller, port address, 48
Global descriptor table, 425, 426, 427
Global descriptor table register (GDTR), 425
Global variables, 300–302
Graphical user interface (GUI), 46, 430
Graphics modes, 232–233, 331–333
    animation techniques, 341–347
    CGA, 332, 333–339
    displaying text in, 338–339
    EGA, 339–340
    selecting, 332–333
    VGA, 332, 340–341
Graphics pixels, reading or writing, 335, 452
Gray scale, 232
GROUP assembler directive, 521
GUI (graphical user interface), 46, 430

H

Halt instruction (HLT), 495
Hand-shaking, 310
Hard disks, 11, 395, 396–397, 398
    See also Disks
    capacity of, 398, 399
    file allocation table (FAT) on, 401
    port address, 48
    structure of, 397–398
Hardcopy, 12
Hardware components
    BIOS routines and, 46
    microcomputers, 3–9
    software vs., 45
Hardware interrupts, 309–310
    IF (interrupt flag) and, 312
    nonmaskable (NMI), 312
Hex error codes, file handling errors, 403
Hex numbers. *See* Hexadecimal number system
Hexadecimal number system, 19, 20–22
    addition and subtraction in, 24–25
    ASCII codes in, 31–32
    decimal and binary conversions, 22–23
    digital and binary equivalents, 19, 21
    in program data, 56
HEX_OUT macro, 270–272
Hidden, changing file attribute to, 415
Hidden files, 400
High resolution mode, CGA, 336
High-density drives and disks, 398
High-level instructions, in 80286, 423
High-level languages, 13
    advantages of, 13

Index **537**

bit pattern changes and, 117
jump instructions and, 98–104
loop structures and, 104–108
program design with, 108–112
translated to assembly language, 64–65
HLT instruction (halt), 495
Holding register, in fetch-execute cycle, 10
HUGE memory model, 299

I
IBM character set, 441–444
   displaying, sample program for, 93–94
IBM mainframes, EBCDIC code used by, 197
IBM personal computers
   extended character set for, 31
   keyboard, 244–247
      scan codes, 33, 245–246, 527–529
   monitor for, 231–232
   organization of, 37–52, 45–49
      I/O port addresses, 49
      memory, 47–48
      operating system, 46–47
   start-up operation, 49
   text mode programming for, 234–244
   video adapters and display modes, 232–233
Icons, in Windows program, 430
IDIV instruction (integer divide), 165–167, 496
IF assembler directives, 521
IF (constant exp is nonzero), 273
IF (interrupt flag), 45
   in interrupt routine, 312
IF1 (assembler making first pass), 273
   macro file and, 264–265
IF2 (assembler making second pass), 273
IFB (arg is missing), 273
IFDEF (symbol is defined or EXTRN), 273
IFDIF (strings are not identical), 273
IFE (exp is zero), 273
IFIDN (strings are identical), 273
IFNB (arg is not missing), 273
   macro using, 274
IFNDEF (symbol is not defined or EXTRN), 273
IF-THEN structure, 98–99
IF-THEN-ELSE structure, 100–101
Immediate mode, 181, 182
IMUL instruction (integer multiply), 161–164, 496
   in 80286, 422, 511
IN instruction (input byte or word), 496
   for accessing timer circuit, 348
INC (increment) instruction, 63, 496

flags and overflow with, 85, 86, 89–90
INCLUDE pseudo-op, 169–170, 521–522
   macro library and, 264
INDEC procedure, 170–175
Indefinite repeat (IRP) macro, 269–270
Index registers, 39, 40
   direction flags and, 205–206
Indexed addressing mode, 185
   segment overrides in, 189
Indirect procedure call, 147, 304
Input overflow, 174
Input/output addresses, 9
Input/output (I/O) devices, 3, 11–12.
   See also Interrupt routines
Input/output operations
   accumulator register (AX) for, 41
   data register (DX) for, 41
   with 8087 processor, 384–391
   with 80286 processor, 511–512
   instruction syntax, 67–69
   multiple-precision integer, 384–388
   in OS/2, 431–433
   real number, 389–391
   shift and rotate instructions in, 130–134
Input/output ports, 9
   port addresses, 48–49
Ins (Insert) key, 245–246
INS instruction (input from port to string), 511
INSB instruction (input string byte), 423, 511
Instruction pointer (IP), 9, 45
   jump instructions and, 95
Instruction prefetch, 9
Instruction queue, 9
Instruction set, 8
Instructions, 54
   See also specific instructions; specific types
   assembly language, 12–13, 14, 15
   basic, 60–64
   syntax, 54
   creating, macros for, 258
   8086, 490–508
   8087 numeric processor, 382–384, 508–511
      combining with 8086 instructions, 387–388
   80286, 511–513
   80386, 513–516
   execution of, 9–11
   flags and, 85–87
      DEBUG example, 87–90
   flow control, 93–116. *See also* Jump instructions
   format for, 489–490
   logic, 117, 118–122
   machine language, 7, 12
   rotate, 117, 127–130
      in binary I/O, 130–131
      in hex I/O, 131–134

shift, 117, 122–127
   in binary I/O, 130–131
   in hex I/O, 131–134
   string, 205–228
INSW instruction (input string word), 423, 511
INT instruction (interrupt), 67–69, 310, 312, 496–497
Integer operands, 8087 instructions, 384
Integers, representation of, 26–28
Integrated-circuit (IC) chips, 3
Intel 8259 chip (interrupt controller), 313
Intel microprocessors, 37–39, 421–438.
   See also specific microprocessors
Intensity bit, 235, 236
Interactive video game, 347–355
Internal commands, 46
Interrupt 0 (divide overflow), 312
Interrupt 1 (single step), 312, 450
Interrupt 1Ah (time of day), 315
Interrupt 1Bh (Ctrl-Break), 315
Interrupt 1Ch (timer tick), 316
   time updating program with, 318–322
Interrupt 1Dh-Interrupt 1Fh, 316
Interrupt 2 (nonmaskable interrupt), 312
Interrupt 3 (breakpoint), 313
Interrupt 4 (overflow), 313
Interrupt 5 (print screen), 313
Interrupt 8 (timer), 313
   timer tick interrupt and, 316
Interrupt 9 (keyboard), 313
   Ctrl-Break interrupt and, 315
Interrupt 10h (video), 313, 332, 449–453
   listed, 238–243
   programming examples, 243–244
   for palette or background color (CGA), 334
   for reading/writing graphics pixels (CGA), 335
   for selecting display page (EGA), 340
   for setting color register (VGA), 341
   in text mode, 238–244
   for time display, 325, 326
Interrupt 11h (equipment check), 313, 314, 453
Interrupt 12h (memory size), 313, 453
Interrupt 13h (disk I/O), 314, 453–454
Interrupt 14h (communications), 314
Interrupt 15h (cassette), 314, 454
Interrupt 15h (extended memory), 426–429
Interrupt 16h (keyboard I/O), 314, 455
   keyboard services with, 246–247
Interrupt 17h (printer I/O), 314–315, 455
Interrupt 18h (BASIC), 315
Interrupt 19h (bootstrap), 315
Interrupt 20h (program terminate), 316

538 Index

Interrupt 21H functions, 67–69, 316
   ASCII Code display and, 246
   for displaying a string, 73–75
   file errors with, 403
   file handle functions, 402–415
      Changing a file's attribute, 414–415
      moving file pointer, 410–414
      opening and closing files, 403–405
      reading a file, 405
      writing a file, 406
   in sample program, 75, 76
   for time-of-day display, 316–318
Interrupt 22h - Interrupt 26h (DOS interrupts), 316
Interrupt 25h (read sector), 415, 416
Interrupt 26h (write sector), 415
Interrupt 27h (terminate but stay resident), 316
   time display program with, 322–329
Interrupt acknowledge signal, 310
Interrupt controller, 313
   port address, 48
Interrupt E (diskette error), 313
Interrupt flag (IF), 45
   clearing, 493
   in interrupt routine, 312
   setting (STI instruction), 506
Interrupt instruction (INT), 67–69, 310, 312, 496–497
Interrupt number, 310
Interrupt request signal, 309
Interrupt routines, 309
   address calculation for, 310–311
   returning from (IRET instruction), 312, 497
   in time display programs, 316–329
Interrupt vector table, 311
Interrupt vectors, 47, 310–311
   getting addresses of, 457–458
   setting up, 319
Interrupts
   BIOS, 310, 312–316. *See also specific interrupts*
   DOS, 316
   hardware, 309–310
   nonmaskable (NMI), 312
   processor exception, 310
   software, 310
INTO instruction (interrupt if overflow), 497
Invoking a macro, 258
I/O. *See entries beginning with "Input/output"*
IP (instruction pointer), 9, 45
   jump instructions and, 95
IRET instruction (interrupt return), 312, 497
IRP macro (indefinite repeat), 269–270

J

Jump instructions, 93–98, 497–498
   CMP instruction and, 95, 97
   conditional, 94–97, 497–498
   high-level vs. assembly language structures, 98–104
   example, 93–94
   high-level languages and, 98–104
JMP (unconditional jump), 98, 498
JNZ (jump if not zero), 94, 95
   role of, 93

K

KB (kilobyte), 11
Keyboard, 11, 244–247
   ASCII code and, 21, 22
   hardware interrupts and, 309
   INT 16h functions, 246–247, 455
   INT 21h functions, 456, 457
   operation of, 246
   scan codes, 33, 245–246, 527–529
Keyboard buffer, 246
Keyboard controller, port address, 48
Keyboard flags, 245–246, 323–324
Keyboard interrupt (Interrupt 9), 313
Keyboard I/O interrupt (Interrupt 16h), 314
Kilobyte (KB), 11

L

LABEL pseudo-op (declare operand type), 187–188, 522
Labels
   cross-reference file and, 72
   of macros, 262–263
LAHF instruction (load AH from flags), 498
.LALL (list all), 522
   for macro expansions, 261, 262
LARGE memory model, 299
Laser printers, 12
LDS instruction (load data segment register), 498
LDTR (local descriptor table register), 425
LEA instruction (load effective address), 74, 498–499
   in sample program, 75, 76
Least significant bit (lsb), 26
LEAVE instruction, in 80286, 423
LES instruction (load extra segment register), 499
LIB utility, 289–291
Library files
   for macros, 264–266
   for object modules, 289–291
   in OS/2, 431
Line feed/carriage return, macro for, 265
LINK program, 73, 467–469
   command line, 467–468
   example, 468–469
   .EXE programs vs. .COM programs and, 284–285
   library files and, 289–291
   object modules combined by, 285, 286–287, 467
Linking, in OS/2, 431
List file, as MASM output, 461
.LIST assembler directives, 522
Lists. *See* Arrays
Load Effective Address. *See* LEA instruction
Load instructions, for 8087, 383
Loading memory strings, 211–214
Local descriptor table, 424–425
   multitasking and, 426
Local descriptor table register (LDTR), 425
Local labels, in macros, 262–263
LOCAL pseudo-op, 262–263, 513
Location counter (MASM), 464, 466
   ORG lOOh and, 282
LOCK instruction (lock bus), 499
LODS instruction, 223, 499
LODSB instruction (load string byte), 211–214, 223, 499
LODSW instruction (load string word), 211, 223, 499
Logic instructions, 117, 118–122
   accumulator register (AX) for, 40–41
   AND, OR, XOR, 119–121, 492–493, 501, 508
   role of, 117
Logic operations, in arithmetic and logic unit (ALU), 8.
See also Logic instructions
Logical address, 42
Logical sector numbers, 416
Long real floating-point format, 381
Loop, defined, 104
Loop counter, count register (CX) as, 41
LOOP instructions, 93, 94, 499–500
   high-level vs. assembly languages, 104–108
Lowercase letters, converting to uppercase, 120–121, 287–289
LSEEK, 459
.LST file (source listing file), 72, 259
   macro expansion in, 259–261
   options for, 261–262
   macro library files and, 264

M

Machine code, in source listing (.LST) file, 72
Machine language, 12
   defined, 7
   instruction sets, 8
MACRO pseudo-op, 258, 522
Macros, 257–280
   conditional, 272–275
   conditional pseudo-ops in, 272–273
   defined, 257
   expanding, 258

    in .LST file, 259–262
    assembly errors, 262
  IF pseudo op in, 273
  IFNB pseudo-op in, 274
  illegal invocations, 259
  incorrect, .ERR directive for, 275
  invoking, 258
  invoking other macros with, 263–264, 270–272
  library file for, 264–266
    sample program using, 266–267
  local labels in, 262–263
  optimum use of, 276
  output, 270–272
  procedures vs., 257, 276
  recursive, 264
  repetition, 268–270
  role of, 257
  syntax for, 257–258
  useful examples, 265–266
Magnetic disks, 11
Make code, 245
Mantissa, 380
Masks
  for AND, OR, XOR instructions, 119, 120
  for TEST instruction, 122
MASM. *See* Microsoft Macro Assembler
MB (megbyte), 6
MCGA. *See* Multi-color graphics array
MDA. *See* Monochrome display adapter
MEDIUM memory model, 299
Medium resolution mode, CGA, 333, 334–335
Mega, defined, 6
Megabyte (MB), 6
Megahertz (MHz), 11
Memory
  allocating, 460
  extended, 426–429
  freeing, 460
  physical, in 80386, 434, 435
  virtual, 38, 426
    in 80386, 38, 433
Memory (hardware), 4–7
  access to, 80286 microprocessor and, 38
  operations on, 6–7
Memory byte circuits, 4
  addresses of, 4–6
  contents of, 5
  RAM vs. ROM, 7
Memory dumps, DEBUG, 477
Memory errors, nonmaskable interrupts and, 312
Memory location, 6
  adding or subtracting contents of, 62–63
  clearing, 121
  exchanging contents of, 60, 61
  IBM PC, 47–48
  instruction pointer (IP), 45
  for interrupt vectors, 311
  logical addresses, 42

  negating contents of, 64
  physical addresses, 41
  registers and, 8
    FLAGS register, 45
    pointer and index registers, 44–45
    segment register, 41–44
  reserved, 47
  transferring data to and from, 60, 61
  virtual addresses, 424–426
Memory management, 281–308
  .COM vs. .EXE programs and, 281, 282–285
  in 80286, 423–424
  program modules and, 285–291
Memory manager programs, 426
Memory map, 48
Memory models, 65, 299
  choosing, 299–300
  declaration syntax, 65, 299
  .MODEL directive for, 65
Memory protection, protected mode and, 38
Memory-resident programs. *See* Terminate-and-stay-resident programs
Memory segments, 41–42
  disjoint, 47
Memory size interrupt (Interrupt 12h), 313, 453
Memory strings
  comparing, 217–222
  defined, 205
  finding substrings of, 219–222
  loading, 211–214
  moving, 206–209
  scanning, 214–217
  storing, 209–211
Memory word, 6. *See also* Words
Menus, in Windows program, 430
Messages, inserting in programs, 75
Microcomputer system, components of, 3–9
Microprocessors, 37–39, 421–438
  See also specific microprocessors
  address size and, 5–6
  data registers in, 39
  defined, 4
  fetch-execute cycle in, 9–10
  organization of (8086), 7, 8–9, 39–45
  shift or rotate instructions and, 122
  speed of, 10–11
Microsoft Library Manager, 289–291
Microsoft Macro Assembler (MASM), 461–467
  command line, 462–463
  creating machine language file with, 70, 71–73
  example, 464–467
  full segment definitions and, 291
  LINK program and, 286–289
  macros and, 257, 258
    "forced error" message, 275
    invoking other macros, 264

    library files, 264
    local labels, 263
  options, 463
  segment definitions, 65
  syntax for, 54
MKDIR (MD), 448, 458
Mode numbers, for video adapters, 233
  selecting, 238
.MODEL directive, 65, 299, 522–523
Monitor, 12, 231–232
  analog, for VGA, 340
  display pages, 234
  port addresses for, 48
  video adapter and, 232, 233
Monochrome display adapter (MDA), 232, 233
  attribute bytes for, 235–236, 237
  changing cursor size for, 238–239
  display memory capacity, 234
Monochrome monitor, 232. *See also* Monochrome display
Most significant bit (msb), 26
Motherboard, 4, 5
Mouse, for Windows, 430
MOV instruction, 60–61, 500
  for clearing a register, AND instruction vs., 121
  flags and, 85, 86
    DEBUG example, 88
  macro for, 258
  in sample program, 75, 76
Moving memory strings, 206–209
MOVS instruction, 223, 224, 500
MOVSB instruction (move string byte), 206–208, 223, 224, 500
MOVSW instruction (move string word), 208–209, 223, 500
MOVSX instruction (move with sign-extend), 514
MOVZX instruction (move with zero-extend), 435, 436, 514
MS DOS, 46. *See also* DOS
MUL instruction (multiply), 161–164, 501
Multi-color graphics array (MCGA), 232, 233
  selecting active display page for, 240
Multiple-precision numbers, with 8087 processor, 384–388
Multiplication
  ASCII adjust for (AAM) instruction, 378, 491–492
  BCD, 378
  data register (DX) for, 41
  double-precision, 374
  with 8087 processor, 384
  in 80286, 422, 511
  methods for, 127
  MUL/IMUL instructions for, 161–164, 496, 501
  procedure for, 150–157
  shift instructions for, 117, 122
    overflow and, 124
    SAL (shift arithmetic left), 124

SHL (shift left), 123–124
signed vs. unsigned, 161–162
MULTIPLY procedure, 150–157
Multitasking, 429
    80286 and, 421
    protected (virtual address) mode and, 38, 421
    Windows and OS/2 for, 430

N

Name field, in assembly language syntax, 54–55
Named constants, 59
Natural language, high-level language and, 13
NEAR procedures, 146, 285–286
    RET instruction and, 149
NEG (negation) instruction, 64, 501
    flags and, 85, 86–87, 89
Negation, double-precision, 373
Negative integers, 26–28
    two's complement representation of, 27–28
Nibble, 18
Nonmaskable interrupt (NMI), 312
NOP instruction (no operation), 501
Normal video, 235
NOT instruction (logical not), 121, 501
NOT truth table, 118
Number systems, 19–22
    addition and subtraction in, 24–25
    in assembly language programs, 56
    converting between, 22–23
Numbers, converting ASCII digits to, 120

O

Object (.OBJ) files, 285
    creating, 70, 73
    LINK program for, 73
    as MASM output, 461, 466
Object modules, 285
    library files for, 289–291
OF (overflow flag), 82, 83
Offset address of operand
    in based indexing addressing mode, 194
    obtaining, 184–187
Offset (of memory location), 42
OFFSET pseudo-op, 321
One-dimensional arrays, 179–181
One's complement of binary number, 26
    NOT instruction and, 121
Opcode, 9, 55
    format for, 489–490
Opening a file, 403–404
Operand field, in assembly language syntax, 55
Operands, 9
    of ADD instructions, 62

addressing modes for, 181–189
declaring types of, 187–188
destination vs. source, 55
of 8087 instructions, 384
in instruction format, 489, 490
of MOV instruction, 61, 64
obtaining offset address for, 184–187
overriding type of, 187, 188
of segment declaration, 291–295
of string instructions, 223–224
of SUB instructions, 62
type agreement of, 64, 186–187
    overriding, 187–188
of XCHG instruction, 61
Operating system
    IBM PC, 46–47
    multitasking, 429–433
    role of, 46
    in start-up operation, 49
Operation code. *See* Opcode
Operation field, in assembly language syntax, 55
Operations, in assembly language syntax, 54
OR conditions, high-level vs. assembly languages, 103–104
OR instructions (logical inclusive or), 119–121, 501
OR truth table, 118
ORG 100h pseudo-op, in .COM program, 282, 523
OS/2 operating system, 429, 430
    programming in, 431–433
OUT instruction (output byte or word), for accessing timer circuit, 348, 501–502
OUT instruction (output string to port), 512
OUTDEC procedure, 167–170
Output macros, 270–272
OUTSB instruction (output string byte), 423, 512
OUTSW instruction (output string word), 423, 512
Overflow, 83–85
    divide, 165–166, 310, 312
    input, 174
    interrupt instruction for (INTO), 497
    shift instructions and, 124
Overflow flag (OF), 82, 83
Overflow interrupt (Interrupt 4), 313

P

Packed BCD form, 375
    converting ASCII digits to, 385–386
    decimal adjust for addition/subtraction, 494–495
    8087 numeric processor and, 381–382, 385–386, 508, 509
    printing numbers in, 386–387

Paddle, adding to video game, 350–352
PAGE assembler directive, 524
Page-oriented virtual memory, in 80386, 434
Pages, in EGA mode, 339
Palette registers, EGA, 339
Palettes, 334
    setting, 451
Paragraph, 42
Paragraph boundary, 42
Parallel port, 9
    port address, 48
Parity errors, nonmaskable interrupts and, 312
Parity flag (PF), 82
PC DOS, 46. *See also* DOS
%OUT assembler directive, 523
Peripheral devices (peripherals), 3
Personal computers. *See* IBM personal computers
PF (parity flag), 82
Physical address, 41
Physical memory, in 80386, 434, 435
Pixels, 233, 331–332
    default color of (background color), 334
    reading or writing, 335, 452
Pointer registers, 39, 40
    register indirect mode and, 182
POP instructions, 142–143, 502
    in 80286, 422
    in program example, 151, 152, 156
POPA instruction, in 80286, 422, 512
POPF instructions, 142, 153, 502
Ports, I/O, 9
    port addresses, 48–49
Positional number system, 19–20
Power loss, RAM vs. ROM and, 7
Prefixes, string instruction, REP (repeat), 207–208
PRINT (DOS command), 446
Print Screen interrupt (Interrupt 5), 313
Printer, INT 21h functions and, 456
Printer I/O interrupt (Interrupt 17h), 314–315, 455
Printers, 12
Printing packed BCD numbers, 386–387
Printing real numbers, with four-digit fractions, 390–391
Privilege level, 426
PROC pseudo-op (begin procedure), 524
Procedures, 15, 146
    beginning and ending, 524
    calling, 493. *See also* CALL instructions
    communication between, 147, 300–305
    for decimal I/O, 167–175
    documenting, 147
    macros vs., 257, 276
    NEAR vs. FAR, 285–286
    recursive, 357, 358–360

activation records and, 361–363
implementation of, 363–366
with multiple calls, 367–369
    returning from, 146, 147, 148, 149, 503–504
    separate files for (program modules), 285–291
    syntax of, 146–147, 285–286
    using stack with, 303–305, 360–361
Process, in OS/2, 430
Processor exception, 310
Program data, 56–57
Program execution, tasks vs., 426
Program loop constructions, count register (CX) in, 41
Program modules, 285–291
Program segment prefix (PSP), 74
Program segments, 44, 65–67
    .COM programs and, 281–282
    full definitions for, 291–298
    in protected mode, 424–426
    simplified definitions for, 299–300
Program size, macros vs. procedures and, 276
Program structure, 65–67, 281
    .COM programs, 281–285
Program terminate interrupt (Interrupt 20h), 316
Programs
    See also Assembly language programs; Software
    .COM, 281–285
    CPU and, 7
    designing, top-down method, 108–112
    DOS
        for 80286, 424
        for 80386, 434–436
    firmware (ROM-based), 7
    jump example, 93–94
    stack segments of, 139
    terminating, 456
    testing. *See* CODEVIEW program; DEBUG program
Protected (virtual address) mode, 38
    in 80286, 421, 424–426
    in 80386, 433–434
    multitasking and, 429
    OS/2 and, 430
    Windows 3 and, 430
Pseudo-operation code (pseudo-ops), 55
    ASSUME, 295
    conditional, 272–273
        for macro library, 264–265
    data-defining, 57
    DUP (duplicate), 180–181
    .8087, 387
    ELSE, in macros, 272, 273, 274, 275
    ENDM (end macro definition), 258
    EQU (equates), 59, 75
    = (equal), in REPT macro, 268
    EXTRN, 286
    IF1...ENDIF, for macro file, 264–265
    INCLUDE, 169–170

LABEL (declare operand type), 187–188
LOCAL, for macros, 262–263
MACRO, 258
    for named constants, 59
OFFSET, 321
ORG 100h, 282
PTR (override operand type), 187, 188
PUBLIC, 286
SEG, 321
SEGMENT, 291–298
.286, 424
.386, 435
PSP (Program segment prefix), 74
    ORG 100h and, 282
PTR pseudo-op (override operand type), 187, 188
PUBLIC pseudo-op, 286, 524
PURGE directive, 524–525
PUSH instructions, 140, 141, 502
    in 80286, 422, 512
    in program example, 151, 152, 153
PUSHA instruction, in 80286, 422, 512–513
PUSHF instruction, 140, 141, 502

Q
Question mark (?), as DOS special character, 445
Quitting a program, Interrupt 20h for, 316

R
.RADIX assembler directive, 525
RAM (random access memory), 7
RCL instruction, 128, 502–503
RCR instruction, 129, 503
    application example, 130
READ_STR procedure, 209–211, 213–214
Read operations, 6–7
    in fetch-execute cycle, 10
Read sector
    INT 13h for, 453–454
    INT 25h for, 415, 416
Read-only memory. *See* ROM
Read/write head, 395
Reading from disk, DOS interrupt for, 460
Reading a file, 405
    defined, 402
    DOS interrupt for, 459
    program for, 406–409
Reading graphics pixels, 335, 452
Reading and storing a character string, 209–211
Real address mode (real mode), 38
    in 80286, 421, 423–424
    in 80386, 433
Real mode, Windows 3 in, 430

Real numbers, 389
    8087 operations with, 389–391
Rebooting the system, Interrupt 19h for, 315
RECORD assembler directive, 525
Records, appending to file, 410–414
Recursion, 357–370
Recursive macros, 264
Recursive procedures, 357, 358–360
    activation records and, 361–363
    implementation of, 363–366
    with multiple calls, 367–369
    passing parameters on stack for, 360–361
Recursive process, defined, 357–358
Register indirect mode, 182–183
    segment register override in, 188–189
    string instructions vs., 205
Register mode, 181, 182
Registers, 8, 39
    adding or subtracting contents of, 62–63
    adding to, 63
    clearing, 121
    color, 340, 341
    double-precision numbers and, 371
    in 8086 microprocessor, 39–45. *See also specific types*
    in 8087 numeric processor, 382
    in 80286, 422, 425
    in 80386, 433
    exchanging contents of, 60, 61
    in instruction format, 489–490, 491
    in interrupt routine, 310
    negating contents of, 64
    restoring after macro, 259
    stack use vs., 303–304
    in start-up operation, 49
    subtracting from, 63
    testing for zero, 121
    transferring data between, 60, 61
RENAME (REN), 446
REP instruction (repeat), count register (CX) for, 41, 50, 503
REP prefix (repeat), 207–208
    in 80286, 423
REPE prefix (repeat while equal), in string comparisons, 218, 219
REPEAT loop
    high-level vs. assembly language, 107–108
    WHILE loop vs., 108
Repetition macros, 268–270
REPNE instruction (repeat while not equal), in string scanning, 215, 216, 217, 503
REPNZ prefix (repeat while not zero), 215, 503
REPT macro (repeat block of statements), 268–269, 525
REPZ prefix (repeat while zero), in string comparisons, 218
Resolution, 233, 331

CGA, 333
EGA, 339
VGA, 340
RESTORE (DOS command), 446
RET instruction (return), 146, 147, 148, 149, 503–504
 in program example, 151, 152, 156–157
Return address, in interrupt routine, 310
Reverse video, 235
Rewriting a file, 402, 403–404
RGB monitor, 232
RMDIR (RD), 448, 458
ROL instruction (rotate left), 126, 127, 128, 504
ROM (read-only memory), 7
 BIOS interrupt routines in, 310, 312–316
ROM-based programs (firmware), 7
 memory segment for, 48
ROM BASIC, transferring control to, 315
Root directory, 400
ROR instruction (rotate right), 127–128, 504
Rotate instructions, 117, 122, 127–130, 502–503, 504
 application examples, 130–134
 applying, reversing bit pattern, 130
 in 80286, 422
 role of, 117
Row-major order, array storage in, 192–193
Run file, creating and executing, 70, 73

S

SAHF instruction (store AH in FLAGS register), 505
SAL instruction (shift arithmetic left), 124, 504–505
.SALL (suppress all), for macro expansions, 261, 262, 525
SAR instruction (shift arithmetic right), 125, 126, 505
SBB instruction (subtract with borrow), 372, 373, 505
Scan codes
 keyboard and, 33, 245–246, 527–529
 keyboard buffer and, 246
Scan lines, 331
Scanning memory strings, 214–217
SCAS instruction, 223, 505
SCASB instruction (scan string byte), 214–217, 223, 505
SCASW instruction (scan string word), 214, 505
Screen display. See Display; Monitor
Screen editor, sample program, 247–252

Scrolling screen or window up/down, 240–241, 450–451
Searching, for substrings of strings, 219–222
Secret message, coding and decoding, 198–200
Sectors, 397
 logical, 416
 reading, program for, 416–417
SEG pseudo-op, 321
Segment:offset form of address (logical address), 42–43
Segment definitions
 full form of, 291–298
 simplified, 299–300
Segment descriptor, 425, 426
 in 80386, 433
Segment descriptor tables, 424–425
Segment directive, 291–292
Segment number, 42
Segment overrides, 188–189
SEGMENT pseudo-op, 291–298, 525
Segment registers, 39, 41–44, 499. See also Program segments
Segment selector, in protected mode, 424, 425
Segments. See Program segments
SELECT procedure, for sorting an array, 190–191
Selectsort method, 189–192
Semicolons
 in assembly language programs, 14, 55
 is assembler instructions, 72
.SEQ assembler directive, 526
Serial ports, 9
 port addresses, 48
Set (destination bit), OR instruction for, 119, 120
Set byte on condition instructions, 514–515
SF (sign flag), 82, 83
Shift instructions, 117, 122–127
 application examples, 130–134
 applying, reversing bit pattern, 130
 division by, 117, 122, 125–127, 374
 double-precision, 374, 515–516
 in 80286, 422
 multiplication by, 117, 122, 123–124, 374
 overflow and, 124
 role of, 117, 122
 SAL (shift arithemtic right), 124, 504–505
 SAR (shift arithmetic right), 125, 126, 505
 SHL (shift logical left), 123–124, 504–505
 SHR (shift logical right), 125, 126, 506
Shift keys, 245
 information stored on, 245–246
 scan codes for, 245

SHL instruction (shift left), 123–124, 504–505
 application example, 130
Short real floating-point format, 381
SHR instruction (shift right), 125, 126, 506
SI (source index) register, 45
Sign flag (SF), 82, 83
Signed integers, 26–28
 decimal interpretation, 28–30
 division by IDIV instruction, 165–167, 496
 division by right shifts, 126
 8087 support, 381
 multiplication by IMUL instruction, 161–162, 496
Signed jumps, 95, 96, 97
Signed overflow, 83, 84, 85
Single step interrupt (Interrupt 1), 312
Single-flag jumps, 95, 96
16-bit programming, 434
16-color display, attribute byte for, 235
.SMALL model, 67, 299–300
Software, 45
 programming languages, 12–14
Software interrupts, 310
Sorting arrays, selectsort method, 189–192
Sound, adding, 347–350
Source index (SI) register, 45
Source listing file. See .LST file
Source operand, 55
Source program file, creating, 70–71
SP (stack pointer) register, 44
Special characters, with DOS commands, 445
Stack, 44, 139
 accessing or placing items on, 189, 303–305, 360–361
 adding to (PUSH/PUSHF instructions), 140–141
 application example, 144–145
 in .COM vs. .EXE programs, 282–283
 8087 data registers as, 382
 empty, 140
 removing items from (POP/POPF instructions), 142–143
 top of, 139
.STACK directive, 66, 299, 526
 in sample program, 76
Stack pointer (SP) register, 44
Stack segment, 15, 44
 .COM programs and, 281
 declaring, 140
 syntax for, 66
Standard mode, Windows 3 in, 430
Start-up operation, IBM PC, 49
Statements
 in assembly language programs, 14
 assembly language syntax, 54
Status byte, in file directory, 420
Status flags, 45, 81, 82–83, 205
 DEBUG example, 88, 89

DIV/IDIV instructions and, 165
jump instructions and, 95
MUL/IMUL instructions and, 162
Status registers, 39
STC instruction (set carry flag), 506
STD instruction (set direction flag), 206, 506
STI instruction (set interrupt flag), 506
Storage, magnetic disks, 11
Storing memory strings, 209–211
STOS instruction, 223, 506
STOSB instruction (store string byte), 209–211, 223, 506
STOSW instruction (store string word), 209, 223, 506
String, defined, 205. *See also* Character strings; Memory strings
String instructions, 205–228
    CMPS, 223, 494
    CMPSB (compare string byte), 217–222, 494
    CMPSW (compare string word), 217, 494
    direction flags and, 205–206
    in 80286, 423
    general form of, 223–224
    INSB (input string byte), 423
    INSW (input string word), 423
    LODS, 499
    LODSB (load string byte), 211–214, 499
    LODSW (load string word), 211, 499
    MOVSB (move string byte), 206–208, 500
        REP prefix and, 207–208
    MOVSW (move string word), 208–209, 500
    OUTSB (output string byte), 423
    OUTSW (output string word), 423
    register indirect addressing mode vs., 205
    REP prefix (repeat), 207–208
    SCAS, 505
    SCASB (scan string byte), 214–217, 505
    SCASW (scan string word), 214, 505
    STOS, 223, 506
    STOSB (store string byte), 209–211, 506
    STOSW (store string word), 209, 506
String operations
    count register (CX) for, 41
    DI (destination index) and, 45
Strings, 205. *See* Character strings; Memory strings
STRUC assembler directive, 526
Structure, declaring (STRUC directive), 526
SUB instruction, 62–63, 507
    for clearing a register, AND instruction vs., 121
    flags and
        DEBUG example, 89

    overflow, 84, 85, 86
    in sample program, 75, 76
Subdirectories, 400
    managing, 448, 458
Substrings, searching for, 219–222
Subtraction
    ASCII adjust for (AAS) instruction, 377–378, 492
    BCD, 377–378, 495
    by bit complementation and addition, 28
    decimal adjust for (DAS instruction), 495
    double-precision, 372, 373
    with 8087 processor, 384
    instructions, 62–63, 377–378, 492, 505, 507
    number systems and, 24–25
    overflow and, 84–85
    real (FSUB instruction), 384, 510–511
SUBTTL instruction (subtitle display), 526
SWAP procedure, for sorting an array, 190–191
Symbol table (MASM), 464
Syntax
    assembly language, 54–56
    based and indexed addressing modes, 184
    input/output instructions, 67–69
    procedure declaration, 146–147
System board, 4
System reboot, Interrupt 19h for, 315

T

Tasks, in protected mode, 426
Teletype mode, writing character in, 452
Temporary real floating-point format, 381
Terminate-and-stay-resident (TSR) programs, 322
    for time display, 322–329
Terminate-but-stay-resident interrupt (Interrupt 27h), 316, 460
Terminating a process (EXIT), Interrupt 21h for, 460
Terminating a program, Interrupt 20h for, 316
TEST instruction, 122, 507
Test scores, averaging, 195–197
Text, displaying in graphics mode, CGA, 338–339
Text mode, 232
    character generation in, 233
    display pages in, 234
    graphics mode vs., 338
    mode numbers, 233
    programming, 234–244
        INT 10h functions, 238–244
    video adapter and, 233

TF (trap flag), in interrupt routine, 312
32-bit programming, 434
Thread, in OS/2, 430
386 enhanced mode, Windows 3 in, 430. *See also* 80386 microprocessor
.386 pseudo-op, 435
Time, INT 21h functions and, 457
TIME (DOS command), 447
Time of day interrupt (Interrupt 1Ah), 315
Time display
    program for, 316–318
    program for updating, 318–322
    TSR program for, 322–329
Timer circuit, for tone generation, 347–348
Timer interrupt (Interrupt 8), 313
Timer tick count, Interrupt 1Ah and, 315
Timer tick interrupt (Interrupt 1Ch), 316
    time updating program with, 318–322
TITLE assembler directive, 526
Tone generation, 347–350
Top of the stack, 139
Top-down program design, 108–112
    procedures in, 146
Tracepoints, in CODEVIEW, 486–487
Tracks, 395, 397
Translating character codes. *See* XLAT instruction
Trap flag (TF), in interrupt routine, 312
Truth tables, for logic operators, 118
TSR programs. *See* Terminate-and-stay-resident programs
.286 pseudo-op, 424
Two-dimensional arrays, 179, 192–194
    based indexed addressing mode for, 194–195
    locating elements in, 193–194
    storage order for, 192–193
    in test score averaging program, 196
Two's complement of a binary number, 27–28
    double-precision negation and, 373
TYPE (DOS command), 447
Typeahead buffer. *See* Keyboard buffer

U

Unconditonal (JMP) jump instructions, 98
Underline characters, 236, 237
UNLINK, DOS interrupt for, 459
Unpacked BCD form, 375
Unsigned integers, 26
    decimal interpretation, 28–30
    division by DIV instruction, 165–166, 495
    division by right shifts, 126

multiplication by MUL instruction, 161–162, 501
Unsigned jumps, 95, 96, 97
Unsigned overflow, 83, 84
Uppercase letters, converting to lowercase, 120–121, 287–289
User commands (DOS), 46
User interrupt procedures, 318–329

V

Variables, 57–59
   arrays, 58–59
      base address of, 180
      one-dimensional, 179–181
   byte, 57
   cross-reference file and, 72
   global, 300–302
   word, 57–58
VGA. *See* Video graphics array
Video adapters, 12, 232, 233
   graphics display modes, 332
   scan lines and, 331
Video buffer. *See* Display memory
Video controller, 232
   display modes and, 232–233
Video display. *See* Display; *specific types*
Video display memory, 47
   segments for, 48
Video game, interactive, 347–355
Video graphics array (VGA), 232, 233
   graphics display modes, 332, 340–341
   number of display pages for, 234
   selecting active display page for, 240
Video interrupt (Interrupt 10h), 313, 332, 449–453
   for palette or background color, CGA, 334
   for reading/writing graphics pixels, CGA, 335

for selecting display page (EGA), 340
for setting color register, 341
Video modes. *See* Display modes
Virtual address mode. *See* Protected mode
Virtual addresses, 424–426
Virtual 8086 mode, 38, 434
Virtual memory, 426
   access to, 38
   in 80386, 38, 433
Virtual program segments, 426
Vowels, counting, 215–217

W

WAIT instruction, 507
Watch commands, in CODEVIEW, 482–487
Watchpoints, in CODEVIEW, 487
WHILE loop
   high-level vs. assembly language, 106–107
   REPEAT loop vs., 108
Wildcard characters, with DOS commands, 445
Window
   defined, 430
   scrolling up or down, 240–241, 450–451
Window mode display, in CODEVIEW, 480–481
Windows 3 environment, 429, 430
Word arrays. *See* Strings
Word variables, 57–58
   high and low bytes of, 58
   moving word into word, invoking macro for, 258
Words
   bit positions in, 6
   changing bit patterns in, 117

converting bytes to, 167, 493
converting to doublewords, 166–167, 494
defined, 6
dividing, 165, 166–167
double-precision numbers and, 371
integer storage in, 26–28
moving into words, macro for, 258
multiplying, 162
Write operations, 6, 7
   in fetch-execute cycle, 10
Write sector
   INT 13h for, 454
   INT 26h for, 415
Write-protect notch, 396, 397
Writing to disk, DOS interrupt for, 460
Writing a file, 406
   defined, 402
   DOS interrupt for, 459
Writing graphics pixels, 335, 452

X

.XALL, for macro expansions, 261, 262, 526
XCHG instruction (exchange), 60, 61, 507
   flags and, 85
.XCREF (cross-reference file), 518, 526
XLAT instruction (translate), 179, 197–200, 507
.XLIST assembler directives, 522, 526
XOR instruction, 119–121, 508
XOR truth table, 118

Z

Zero, testing register for, 121
Zero flag (ZF), 45, 82, 83